AA

THE
CARAVAN
& CAMPING
GUIDE
2020

Published by AA Publishing, a trading name of AA Media Limited, whose registered office is Grove House, Lutyens Close, Lychpit Basingstoke, Hampshire RG24 8AG. Registered number 06112600

52nd edition 2019

The contents of this publication are believed correct at the time of printing. Nevertheless, the publishers cannot be held responsible for any errors or omissions or for any changes in the details given in this guide or for the consequences of any reliance on the information provided by the same. This does not affect your statutory rights.

Assessments of the AA campsites are based on the experience of the AA Caravan & Camping Inspectors on the occasion(s) of their visit(s) and therefore descriptions given in this guide necessarily contain an element of subjective opinion which may not reflect or dictate a reader's own opinion on another occasion. See pages 10–11 for a clear explanation of how, based on our Inspectors' inspection experiences, campsites are graded.

AA Media Limited strives to ensure accuracy of the information in this guide at the time of printing. Due to the constantly evolving nature of the subject matter the information is subject to change. AA Media Limited will gratefully receive any advice from our readers of any necessary updated information.

For any enquiries relating to this guide, please contact lifestyleguides@aamediagroup.co.uk

Website addresses are included in some entries as specified by the respective establishment. Such websites are not under the control of AA Media Limited and as such AA Media Limited has no control over them and will not accept any responsibility or liability in respect of any and all matters whatsoever relating to such websites including access, content, material and functionality. By including the addresses of third party websites the AA does not intend to solicit business or offer any security to any person in any country, directly or indirectly.

This guide was compiled by the AA Lifestyle Guides team and Servis Filmsetting Ltd, Stockport.

Country and county opening page descriptions: Nick Channer.

Cover design: Austin Taylor and Tracey Freestone

Special thanks to the following people for their work in creating this guide: Jackie Bates, Carly Bristow, Geoff Chapman, David Hancock, Liz Haynes, Lin Hutton, David Popey and Jacqui Savage.

Photographs in the preliminary pages and gazetteer are provided by the establishments. Credits for other images used are as follows (l = left, r = right):

3 courtesy of The Old Brick Kilns (Barney, Norfolk); 4 courtesy of York Meadows Caravan Park (Sheriff Hutton, York); 5 courtesy of Polmanter Touring Park (St Ives, Cornwall); 20–25 site images courtesy of Concierge Camping; 28 AA/J Tims; 29 courtesy of Tristram Caravan & Camping Park; 31 AA/J Tims; 33 courtesy of Treloy Touring Park; 35 courtesy of Bron Derw Touring Caravan Park; 37 courtesy of River Valley Holiday Park; 42 Vincent Lowe/Alamy Stock; 47 courtesy of Woodhall Country Park; 50–51 AA/J Tims; 60 AA/A Burton; 106 AA/S Day; 125 AA/J Tims; 126 AA/A Burton; 156 AA/A Newey; 190 AA/A Newey; 217l AA/J Tims; 217r AA/S Day; 218 AA/A Baker; 242 AA/A Burton; 260 AA/T Mackie; 288 AA/L Noble; 282 AA/J Tims; 311 AA/J Tims; 312 AA/W Voysey; 316-317 AA/J Henderson; 319 AA/D Henderson; 350 AA/J Henderson; 350-351 AA/M Bauer; 352 AA/C Warren; 382–383 AA/ C Hill; 387 AA/C Hill.

Every effort has been made to trace the copyright holders, and we apologise in advance for any unintentional omissions or errors. We would be pleased to apply any corrections in a following edition of this publication.

Maps prepared by the Mapping Services Department of AA Publishing.

Maps © AA Media Limited 2019.

Contains Ordnance Survey data © Crown copyright and database right 2019.

Ireland map contains data available from openstreetmap.org © under the Open Database License found at opendatacommons.org

A CIP catalogue record for this book is available from the British Library.

Printed in Italy by Printer Trento.

ISBN: 978-0-7495-8200-5

A05712

Contents

Welcome to the
AA Caravan & Camping Guide 2020

More and more people are spending their holidays in the UK and a trip outdoors – in a tent, caravan, glamping site or motorhome – is how they're choosing to go about it. The sheer variety of different types of outdoor accommodation continues to amaze us as we compile the guide.

Under the stars

Glamping options are now a common feature at many sites and you can expect to see wooden pods, tipis, yurts, bell tents, safari tents, shepherd's huts, vintage caravans and the like across the UK. This guide lists more than 200 places where you can choose to camp in luxury – check out our list of sites with glamping options on pages 44–47.

And it's not just about new forms of camping. More sites than ever before are expanding and upgrading their offering and facilities. Last year's Overall Campsite of the Year, Concierge Camping in West Sussex, talks about the levels of investment needed to keep a top-class site up and running – see pages 20–26 for details.

Award-winning sites

Following nominations by our inspectors, we award an overall Campsite of the Year winner (page 14) from four national finalists; five regional winners, a Glamping winner and a Holiday Centre winner. All are selected for their outstanding overall quality and high levels of customer care and all of them have not stopped in their pursuit of the perfect park. Two special awards recognise the best small campsite, and the most improved campsite.

Platinum parks

To recognise this push for ever higher standards, we are showcasing the Platinum award. This is given to parks with a quality score of 95% with a 5-Pennant grading. See page 32 for the full list of 'Platinum Parks' in this year's guide.

The best sites for...

There are so many ways to recognise a quality site. In addition to the Pennant ratings and quality scores, we also provide quick reference lists (pages 28–32) that detail the AA inspectors' favourite campsites. For example, it might be because the park has stunning views or a good restaurant on site.

There are so many different ways to choose a place to stay and we hope you find this guide invaluable in helping you plan your next expedition into the great outdoors.

How to use the
AA Caravan & Camping Guide

1.

STANHOE   Map 13 TF83

3.

Places to visit

Norfolk Lavender, HEACHAM, PE31 7JE, 01485 570384
www.norfolk-lavender.co.uk

Walsingham Abbey Grounds & Shirehall Museum, LITTLE WALSINGHAM,
NR22 6BP, 01328 820510
www.walsinghamabbey.com

4.

The Rickels Caravan & Camping Park
▶▶▶ 85%

5.

tel: 01485 518671 **Bircham Road PE31 8PU**
email: therickelscaravanandcampingpark@hotmail.co.uk

6.

dir: *Take A149 (south of King's Lynn) signed Cromer (and A148). Right at roundabout onto A148 signed Fakenham and Cromer. Left on B1153 signed Flitcham and Great Bircham. In Great Bircham right onto B115 signed Stanhoe. At crossroads (junction with B1454) straight across (Stanhoe). Site on left.*

12.

Set in three acres of grassland, with sweeping country views this adults-only park has a pleasant, relaxing atmosphere. The meticulously maintained grounds and facilities are part of the attraction, and the slightly sloping land has some level areas and sheltering for tents. A field is available to hire for rallies.

7.

8.

Open: All year **Last arrival:** 21.00 **Last departure:** 11.00

Pitches: * 🚐 from £16; 🚙 from £16; ▲ from £12

9.

Leisure: 🖵

Facilities: 🖨 ☺ ✳ WiFi

Services: 🚰 🔅 🚽 🛢 🖉

10.

Within 3 miles: 🖉 ⓢ

11.

Additional site information: 3 acre site. Adults only. 🐕 🔇 Cars can be parked by caravans and tents. Awnings permitted. No groundsheets.

2.

15.
14.
13.

1. Location
Place names are listed alphabetically within each county.

2. Map reference
Each site is given a map reference for use in conjunction with the atlas section at the back of the guide. The map reference comprises the guide map page number, the National Grid location square and a two-figure map location reference.
For example: **Map 19 NZ90**.
19 refers to the page number of the map section at the back of the guide.
NZ is the National Grid lettered square (representing 100,000sq metres) in which the location will be found.
9 is the figure reading across the top or bottom of the map page.
0 is the figure reading down each side of the map page.

3. Places to visit
Suggestions of nearby places to visit for adults and children.

4. Site name and rating
▶ Campsites are listed in descending order of their Pennant rating. Sites are rated from 1 to 5 Pennants and are also awarded a score ranging from 50–100% according to how they compare with other parks within the same Pennant rating. For further explanation see pages 10–11.

5. Contact details

6. Directions

Brief directions from a recognisable point, such as a main road, are included in each entry. Please contact the individual site for more detailed directions or use the AA Route Planner at **theAA.com**, and enter the site's postcode.

7. Description

Descriptions are based on information supplied by the AA inspector at the time of the last visit.

Please note: The AA Pennant classification is based on the touring pitches and the facilities only.

AA inspectors do not visit or report on statics or chalets for hire under the AA Caravan & Camping quality standards scheme. However, the AA has a category of **HOLIDAY HOME PARK** and these static caravan, chalet or lodge-only parks are inspected.

8. Opening, arrival and departure times

Parks are not necessarily open all year and while most sites permit arrivals at any time, checking beforehand is advised (see page 12).

9. Pitches

Rates given after each appropriate symbol ⊞ (caravan), ⊟ (motorhome), ⊼ (tent) are the minimum overnight cost for one unit. The prices can vary according to the number of people in the party, but some parks have a fixed fee per pitch regardless of the number of people. Please note that some sites charge separately for certain facilities, including showers; and some sites charge a different rate for pitches with or without electricity. Prices are supplied to us in good faith by the site operators and are as accurate as possible. They are, however, only a guide and are subject to change during the currency of this publication. ⋔ indicates that the campsite offers one or more types of glamping accommodation (see point 13, below)

* If this symbol appears before the prices, it indicates that the prices are for 2019.

10. Symbols

These are divided into Pitches, Leisure, Facilities, Services and Within 3 miles sections. A guide to the symbols can be found on page 9 and on pages throughout the guide.

11. Additional site information

This includes information about the size of the site, whether dogs are accepted or not, whether cars can be parked by a caravan or tent, and whether awnings are permitted. We also include any restrictions and any additional facilities the site would like their visitors to be made aware of. If the site offers glamping, further information is shown at the end of the entry. As most sites now accept credit and debit cards, we only indicate those that don't accept cards ⊜.

12. Photograph

Optional photograph(s) supplied by the campsite.

13. Glamping

⋔ The campsite offers one or more types of 'glamorous camping' accommodation, i.e. wooden pods, tipis, yurts, bell tents, safari tents, shepherd's huts, vintage caravans etc. Details are shown at the bottom of the entry.

14. Best of British

Best of British A group of around 50 parks, both large and small, which focus on high quality facilities and amenities. **www.bob.org.uk**

15. David Bellamy Awards

Many AA recognised sites are also recipients of a David Bellamy Award for Conservation. The awards are graded Gold, Silver and Bronze.

The symbols we show indicate the 2018/19 winners as this was the most up-to-date information at the time of going to press. For the 2019/20 winners please see **www.bellamyparks.co.uk**

Facilities for disabled guests

The Equality Act 2010 provides legal rights for disabled people including access to goods, services and facilities, and means that service providers may have to consider making adjustments to their premises. For more information about the Act see: www.gov.uk/definition-of-disability-under-equality-act-2010

If a site has told us that they provide facilities for disabled visitors their entry in the guide will include the following symbol: ♿

The sites in this guide should be aware of their responsibilities under the Act. However, we recommend that you always phone in advance to ensure the site you have chosen has facilities to suit your needs.

Guide to symbols

Pitches
🚐 Caravan
🚍 Motorhome
⛺ Tent
⛺ Glamping accommodation

Leisure
🏊 Indoor swimming pool
🏊 Outdoor swimming pool
🎾 Tennis court
🎱 Games room
🛝 Children's playground
✋ Kids' club
🐎 Stables & horse riding
⛳ Golf course
🚣 Boat hire
🚲 Cycle hire
🎬 Cinema
🎵 Entertainment
🎣 Fishing

Ⓤ Mini golf
🏊 Watersports
🤸 Gym
⚽ Sports field
⛳ Pitch n putt

Facilities
🛁 Baths/showers
⊙ Electric shaver sockets
💈 Hairdryer
❄ Ice packs facility
🍼 Baby facilities
♿ Disabled facilities
Ⓢ Shop or supermarket on site or within 200 yards
🍳 BBQ area
🪑 Picnic area
WiFi WiFi available
🚗 Car hire can be arranged

Services
🍽 Café or restaurant
🍔 Fast food/Takeaway
🔌 Electric hook-up
🚐 Motorhome service point
🧺 Launderette
🍷 Licensed bar
🛍 Calor Gas
🍃 Campingaz
🔋 Battery charging
Ⓣ Toilet fluid

Other
🐕 Dogs accepted
🚫 No dogs permitted
🚫 No credit or debit cards
* 2019 prices
Ⓤ rating not confirmed

The AA classification scheme

AA parks are classified on a 5-point scale according to their style and the range of facilities they offer. As the number of Pennants increases, so the quality and variety of facilities is generally greater.

What can you expect at an AA-rated park?

All AA parks must meet a minimum standard: they should be clean, well maintained and welcoming. In addition they must have a local authority site licence (unless specially exempt), and satisfy local authority fire regulations.

The AA inspection

Each campsite that applies for AA recognition receives an unannounced visit each year by one of the AA's highly qualified team of inspectors. They make a thorough check of the site's touring pitches, facilities and hospitality. The sites pay an annual fee for the inspection, recognition and rating, and receive a text entry in the *AA Caravan & Camping Guide*.

AA inspectors pay when they stay overnight on a site. The criteria used by the inspectors in awarding the AA Pennant rating is shown on this and the opposite page.

AA Quality percentage score

AA rated Campsites, Caravan Parks, Holiday Centres, Holiday Home Parks and Glamping-only sites are awarded a percentage score alongside their Pennant rating. This is a qualitative assessment of various factors including customer care and hospitality, toilet facilities and park landscaping. The % score runs from 50% to 100% and indicates the relative quality of parks with the same number of Pennants. For example, one 3-Pennant park may score 70%, while another 3-Pennant park may achieve 90%. Like the Pennant rating, the percentage is reassessed annually.

The Pennant criteria

One Pennant parks

These parks offer a fairly simple standard of facilities including:

- No more than 30 pitches per acre
- At least 5% of the total pitches allocated to touring caravans
- An adequate drinking water supply and reasonable drainage
- Washroom with flush toilets and toilet paper provided, unless no sanitary facilities are provided in which case this should be clearly stated
- Chemical disposal arrangements, ideally with running water, unless tents only
- Adequate refuse disposal that is clearly signed
- Well-drained ground and some level pitches
- Entrance and access roads of adequate width and surface
- Location of emergency phone clearly signed
- Emergency phone numbers fully displayed

Two Pennant parks

Parks in this category should meet all of the above requirements, but offer an increased level of facilities, services, customer care, security and ground maintenance. They should include the following:

- Separate washrooms, including at least two male and two female toilets and washbasins per 30 pitches
- Hot and cold water direct to each basin
- Externally lit toilet blocks
- Warden available during day, times to be indicated
- Whereabouts of shop/chemist is clearly signed
- Dish-washing facilities, covered and lit
- Basic security (i.e. lockable gate and/or CCTV)
- Reception area

Three Pennant parks

Many parks come within this rating and the range of facilities is wide. All parks will be of a very good standard and will meet the following minimum criteria:

- Facilities, services and park grounds are clean and well maintained, with buildings in good repair and attention paid to customer care and park security

- Evenly surfaced roads and paths
- Clean modern toilet blocks with all-night lighting and containing toilet seats in good condition, soap and hand dryers or paper towels, mirrors, shelves and hooks, shaver and hairdryer points, and lidded waste bins in female toilets
- Modern shower cubicles with sufficient hot water and attached, private changing space
- Electric hook-ups
- Some hardstanding/wheel runs/firm, level ground
- Laundry with automatic washing and drying facilities, separate from toilets
- Children's playground with safe equipment
- 24-hour public phone on site or nearby where mobile reception is poor
- Warden availability and 24-hour contact number clearly signed

 ### Four Pennant parks
These parks have achieved an excellent standard in all areas, including landscaping of grounds, natural screening and attractive park buildings, and customer care and park security. Toilets are smart, modern and immaculately maintained, and generally offer the following facilities:
- Spacious vanity unit-style washbasins, at least two male and two female per 25 pitches
- Fully-tiled shower cubicles with doors, dry areas, shelves and hooks, at least one male and one female per 30 pitches
- Availability of washbasins in lockable cubicles, or combined toilet/washing cubicles, or a private/family room with shower/toilet/washbasin

Other requirements are:
- Baby changing facilities
- A shop on site, or within reasonable distance
- Warden available 24 hours
- Reception area open during the day, with tourist information available
- Internal roads, paths and toilet blocks lit at night
- Maximum 25 pitches per campable acre
- Toilet blocks heated October to Easter
- Approximately 50% of pitches with electric hook-ups
- Approximately 10% of pitches have hardstandings
- Late arrivals enclosure
- Security barrier and/or CCTV

 ### Five Pennant Premier parks
Premier parks are of an extremely high standard, set in attractive surroundings with superb mature landscaping. Facilities, security and customer care are of an exceptional quality. As well as the above they will also offer:

- First-class toilet facilities including several designated self-contained cubicles, ideally with toilet, washbasin and shower
- Toilet block(s) should be heated
- Ideally electric hook-ups to 75% of pitches
- Approximately 20% of pitches have hardstandings
- Some fully-serviced 'super' pitches: of larger size, with water and electricity supplies connected
- A motorhome service point
- Excellent security

Many Premier Parks will also provide:
- Heated swimming pool
- Well-equipped shop
- Café or restaurant and bar
- A designated walking area for dogs (if accepted)

HOLIDAY CENTRES
In this category we distinguish parks that cater for all holiday needs including cooked meals and entertainment. They provide:
- A wide range of on-site sports, leisure and recreational facilities
- Supervision and security at a very high level
- A choice of eating outlets
- Facilities for touring caravans that equal those available to rented holiday accommodation
- A maximum density of 25 pitches per acre
- Clubhouse with entertainment
- Laundry with automatic washing machines

HOLIDAY HOME PARKS
These are static-only parks offering holiday caravans, chalets or lodges for hire and catering for all holiday needs. They provide:
- Quality holiday hire caravans and chalets or luxurious lodges
- A wide range of on-site sports, leisure and recreational facilities
- Supervision and security at a very high level
- A choice of eating outlets
- Clubhouse with entertainment

GLAMPING-ONLY SITES
These sites, offering a different camping experience from touring with caravans, motorhomes and tents, are also inspected and rated from 1 to 5 Pennants. This is an assessment of the quality and variety of facilities a site offers.

Platinum Pennants ▶▶▶▶▶
Platinum Pennants are awarded to camping sites scoring 95% and above with a 5-Pennant rating.

Gold Pennants ▶▶▶▶▶
AA Gold Pennants are awarded to camping sites scoring 90% and above within the 1–5 Pennant ratings.

Useful information

Booking information

It is advisable to book in advance during peak holiday seasons and in school or public holidays. It is also wise to check whether or not a reservation entitles you to a particular pitch. It does not necessarily follow that an early booking will secure the best pitch; you may simply have the choice of what is available at the time you check in.

Some parks may require a deposit on booking which may be non-returnable if you have to cancel your holiday. If you do have to cancel, notify the proprietor at once because you may be held legally responsible for partial or full payment unless the pitch can be re-let. Consider taking out insurance such as AA Travel Insurance: visit theAA.com/travel-insurance or call 0808 169 1195 for details to cover a lost deposit or compensation. Some parks will not accept overnight bookings unless payment for the full minimum period (e.g. two or three days) is made.

Last arrival Unless otherwise stated, parks will usually accept arrivals at any time of the day or night, but some have a special 'late arrivals' enclosure where you have to make temporary camp to avoid disturbing other people on the park. Please note that on some parks access to the toilet block is by key or pass card only, so if you know you will be late, do check what arrangements can be made.

Last departure Most parks will specify their latest departure time. Do check with the park if this is not given. If you overstay the departure time you could be charged for an extra day.

Chemical closet disposal point

You will usually find one on every park, except those catering only for tents. It must be a specially constructed unit, or a toilet permanently set aside for the purpose of chemical disposal and with adjacent rinsing and soak-away facilities. However, some local authorities are concerned about the effect of chemicals on bacteria in cesspools etc, and may prohibit or restrict provision of chemical closet disposal points in their areas.

Complaints

If you have any complaints speak to the park proprietor or supervisor immediately, so that the matter can be sorted out on the spot. If this personal approach fails you may decide, if the matter is serious, to approach the local authority or tourist board. AA guide users may also write to:

The Caravan & Camping Scheme Co-ordinator,
AA Media, Grove House, Lutyens Close,
Lychpit, Basingstoke RG24 8AG

AA Media may at its sole discretion investigate any complaints received from guide users for the purpose of making any necessary amendments to the guide. AA Media will not in any circumstances act as representative or negotiator or undertake to obtain compensation or enter into further correspondence or deal with the matter in any other way whatsoever. The AA will not guarantee to take any specific action.

Dogs

Dogs may or may not be accepted at parks; this is entirely at the owner's or warden's discretion (assistance dogs should be accepted). Even when the park states that they accept dogs, it is still discretionary, and certain breeds may not be considered as suitable, so we strongly advise that you check when you book. Some sites have told us they do not accept dangerous breeds. (The following breeds are included in the Dangerous Dogs Act 1991 – Pit Bull Terrier, Japanese Tosa, Dogo Argentino and Fila Brasileiro). Dogs should always be kept on a lead and under control, and letting them sleep in cars is not encouraged.

Electric hook-up

Many parks have electric hook-ups on some, or all, of their pitches; if you need an electric connection you should request it when making your booking. Generally the voltage is 240v AC, 50 cycles, although this can vary slightly according to the location. The supply can vary considerably from 5 amps to 16 amps although 16 amps is becoming the norm – again you should check with the campsite if this is important to you. Remember, if your consumption is greater than the supply the electricity will trip out and need resetting.

Electric hook-up connections are now standardised in the UK with the blue coloured safety connectors. However, it is good practice to always connect your cable to your caravan, motorhome or tent electric distribution unit **before** connecting to the hook-up supply.

It is also important that tents or trailer tents have a Residual Circuit Device (RCD) for safety reasons and to avoid overloading the circuit. Caravans and motorhomes have RCDs built in. You should remember that if your RCD trips out at 16 amps and the campsite supply is say 10 amps you can easily overload the supply and cause the hook-up to trip out.

It is quite easy to check what demands your appliances can place on the supply at any one time. Details are normally available in the caravan or motorhome handbooks which show the wattage of appliances fitted.

The amperage used is based on the wattage of appliance divided by the supply voltage.

The following table is a quick check of electrical consumption, depending what is switched on.

Average amperage (based on a 240v supply)

Caravan fridge (125 watts)	0.5 amps
Caravan heater set at (500 watts)	2.1 amps
Caravan heater set at (1000 watts)	4.2 amps
Caravan heater set at (2000 watts)	8.4 amps
Caravan water heater (850 watts)	3.5 amps
Kettle (domestic type) (1500 watts)	6.3 amps
Kettle (low wattage type) (750 watts)	3.1 amps
Hairdryer (2100 watts)	8.8 amps
Microwave (750 watts)	3.1 amps
TV (flat-screen LED type) (30 watts)	0.13 amps
Battery charger (built-in type) (200 watts)	0.8 amps

Motorhomes

At some parks motorhomes are only accepted if they remain static throughout the stay. Also check that there are suitable level pitches at the parks where you plan to stay.

Overflow pitches

Campsites are legally entitled to use an overflow field which is not a normal part of their camping area for up to 28 days in any one year as an emergency method of coping with additional numbers at busy periods. When this 28-day rule is being invoked site owners should increase the numbers of sanitary facilities accordingly. In these circumstances the extra facilities are sometimes no more than temporary portacabins.

Parking

Some park operators insist that cars are left in a parking area separate from the pitches; others will not allow more than one car to be parked beside each caravan, tent or glamping unit.

Park restrictions

Many parks in our guide are selective about the categories of people they will accept on their parks. In the caravan and camping world there are many restrictions and some categories of visitor are banned altogether. Where a park has told us of a restriction/s this is included in the notes in their entry.

On many parks in this guide, unaccompanied young people, single-sex groups, single adults, and motorcycle groups will not be accepted. AA Media takes no stance in this matter, basing its Pennant classification on facilities, quality and maintenance. On the other hand, some parks cater well for teenagers and offer magnificent sporting and leisure facilities as well as lively entertainment events; others have only very simple amenities. A small number of parks in our guide exclude all children in order to create an environment aimed at holiday makers in search of total peace and quiet (see page 43).

Pets

The importation of animals into the UK is subject to strict controls. Penalties for trying to avoid these controls are severe. For the most up-to-date information on travelling with pets as well as updates on changes to the controls when the UK leaves the European Union, visit www.gov.uk/take-pet-abroad/overview or try the PETS Helpline on 0370 241 1710.

Seasonal touring pitches

Some park operators allocate a number of their hardstanding pitches for long-term seasonal caravans. These pitches can be reserved for the whole period the campsite is open, generally between Easter and September, and a fixed fee is charged for keeping the caravan on the park for the season. These pitches are in great demand, especially in popular tourist areas, so enquire well in advance if you wish to book one.

Shops

The range of provisions in shops is usually in proportion to the park's size. As far as AA Pennant requirements are concerned, a mobile shop calling several times a week, or a general store within easy walking distance of the park is acceptable.

AA Campsites of the Year

PLASSEY LEISURE PARK ▶▶▶▶▶
EYTON, WREXHAM, page 381

More than fifty years ago the Brookshaw family started developing their farmyard and buildings into a must-do leisure destination. The result of year-on-year planning and investment is a lovely park set in several hundred acres of quiet farm and meadowland in the Dee Valley. The superb toilet facilities include individual cubicles for total privacy and security, while the Edwardian farm buildings have been converted into the notable Shippon Restaurant, a coffee shop and over 20 independent retail outlets, including hair and beauty salons and chic gift shops. There is plenty here to entertain all age groups, from a swimming pool to free fishing and use of the 9-hole golf course. A Welsh castle-themed children's play park is a unique feature and for families there are two miles of nature trails through 247 acres of woods and farmland. Holiday homes are located within The Pines area and a choice of standard or fully serviced touring pitches for caravans or motorhomes are very well spaced to create optimum privacy. For that memorable glamping experience, luxury lodges, with spacious decked areas that include a hot tub, are also a feature. Grounds presentation is excellent with neat grassed surfaces, indigenous and cultivated planting and pretty seasonal flowers.

EYE KETTLEBY LAKES ▶▶▶▶▶
MELTON MOWBRAY, LEICESTERSHIRE, page 208

A haven for lovers of coarse fishing and walking, this long-established leisure destination, located in the hamlet of Eye Kettleby, provides very high standards. The outdoor areas are exceptional; guests can expect to find water features, nature areas, winding paths through beautiful designated walking areas, well-maintained roads and good clear signage throughout the park. The setting and landscaping of the nine fishing lakes is stunning and the considered and colourful planting really enhances the whole park. Accommodation is located in lodges, smart wooden pods in a glamping forest and well laid-out touring fields. Pitches are well-spaced, immaculately maintained and very private with mature hedging between them; the majority are fully serviced. All facilities, including toilets, showers, washrooms and waste disposal areas, are of a very high standard and kept spotlessly clean. A fine Scandinavian log building houses the stylish reception area, a well-stocked shop, a café with an inviting alfresco seating area, and a refurbished clubhouse where regular entertainment is provided. Impressive ongoing investment and refurbishment since the park joined the AA Pennant Scheme in 2018 has seen the well-deserved achievement of coveted Platinum status for 2020.

Following nominations by our inspectors, we award an overall winner from three national finalists, five regional winners, a holiday centre winner and a glamping-only site winner – all are selected for their outstanding overall quality and high levels of customer care. Our two special awards recognise the best small campsite and the most improved campsite.

SCOTLAND

HUNTLY CASTLE CARAVAN PARK ▷▷▷▷▷ 90%
HUNTLY, ABERDEENSHIRE, page 321

Huntly Castle Caravan Park is a quality parkland site set in 15 acres of beautifully landscaped grounds within striking distance of the Speyside Malt Whisky Trail, the beautiful Moray coast and the Cairngorm Mountains. It is a well-established and particularly well-maintained park, and owners Hugh and Debbie Ballantyne have very high standards, which results in exceptional toilet facilities, attractive landscaping and the provision of some fully serviced pitches. Hugh and Debbie are to be commended for their continuing investment, resulting in regular improvements to enhance the customer experience. The site is surrounded by mature trees, shrubs and floral displays to create a peaceful and relaxing atmosphere, and pitch density is excellent, providing optimum privacy. The park is located close to the River Deveron, with easy access to the peaceful riverside path, and the attractive town of Huntly, with its ruined castle plus a wide variety of restaurants and shops, is only a five-minute walk away. The park is the ideal base for a main holiday destination, weekend break or an overnight stop due to the close proximity of the main A96 trunk road from Inverness to Aberdeen. A worthy winner of the Scotland Campsite of the Year Award.

SOUTH WEST ENGLAND

EAST FLEET FARM TOURING PARK ▶▶▶▶▶
WEYMOUTH, DORSET, page 177

Set on a working organic farm and in a unique location on the shores of the Fleet Lagoon, this top-notch park overlooks Chesil Beach and the sea, with direct access to the South West Coast Path. There is a wide variety of pitches, including hardstandings and fully serviced pitches, and the largest family tents can be accommodated. It offers excellent new toilet and shower facilities with family rooms – added for the 2019 season – and there are good play facilities for children, including an excellent new fenced play area for younger ones and a separate play barn with table tennis and other activities. The Old Barn has a tasteful bar and lovely patio area, where customers are welcome to take their own food, or order locally and have the food delivered to the bar. In addition, there is 'Festival Food', an area for pizzas and fish and chips, which is very popular with guests. The park is well positioned for visiting Weymouth and Portland, as well as other local attractions, such as the Abbotsbury Swannery and the Abbotsbury Subtropical Gardens. There is a fine drive along the coast road from East Fleet to Bridport with spectacular views of Chesil Beach. Upgraded to Platinum Pennants for 2020, East Fleet Farm Touring Park fully deserves the South West Campsite of the Year Award.

AA Campsites of the Year *continued*

SOUTH EAST ENGLAND

LINCOLN FARM PARK ►►►►►
STANDLAKE, OXFORDSHIRE, page 237–

Tucked away in sleepy Oxfordshire village close to the River Thames, Lincoln Farm is a long-established and beautifully landscaped family-run park, offering a truly excellent camping or caravanning experience. There are top class facilities throughout and the combination of sound investment by the owner along with passionate and caring new managers, has seen significant improvements over the past two years. There are excellent leisure facilities, with two pools plus a gym and sauna, and there's also a spa/massage facility. Big changes were made to the reception area for 2019, with beautiful planters and hanging baskets adding colour and a welcoming first impression. Inside, the newly presented shop area has a real wow factor, with bespoke shelving stocked with goodies, new flooring and paintwork; the gym and games room both have new equipment. On the park, the hardstanding pitches are generously sized and immaculately maintained, and the spotlessly clean toilet facilities offer good levels of privacy, including fully serviced bathrooms. There's an impressive new children's play area and there are plans to add beauty salon/hairdressers in the former information centre, and a pétanque pitch. This is the perfect base for visiting the many attractions.

HEART OF ENGLAND

CLIPPESBY HALL ►►►►►
CLIPPESBY, NORFOLK, page 222

A lovely country house estate with camping and touring facilities spread over eight distinctive areas, with a choice of secluded pitches hidden among the trees or in family-orientated pitches set in sheltered sunny glades. Guests can expect spacious pitches and good privacy. The general landscaping and well-maintained grounds are impressive and there's still very much a natural feel and level of exclusivity across the park. The 'Quiet Gardens' are very pleasant and are worth exploring and kids will enjoy the bug hotel and aviary. New for 2019, the fabulous 'Basecamp' amenity area has a new-look reception, a stylish bar and café area serving breakfasts, light lunches and evening pizzas and gourmet burgers, and a well-stocked mini-market. Decor, fixtures and fittings are very smart, and teamed with plenty of natural light it makes for a very strong first impression on arrival at the park. Excellent hardstanding pitches are available as the park is open all year. The toilet facilities, appointed to a very good standard with high levels of cleanliness, provide a wide choice of privacy cubicles. There are pine lodges with private hot tubs, cottages and four new shepherd's huts for holiday lets. A worthy winner of the Heart of England award.

NORTH WEST ENGLAND

THE QUIET SITE ▷▷▷▷▷ 93%
WATERMILLOCK, CUMBRIA, page 119

A meandering narrow road gently climbs up from the banks of Ullswater, creating a warm feeling of anticipation and on arrival at The Quiet Site, one is immediately aware of the care and thought involved in the restoration of the original stone buildings, which have been sympathetically converted into a bar and entertainment facility with original character enhanced by the decor and furnishings. The new Zero Waste Shop, amenities blocks, offering excellent privacy options and reception are other notable buildings and on arrival the accommodation and touring areas, one is greeting by stunning views of the lake and surrounding undulating beautiful countryside. Just 20 minutes away by car you'll find some of the best fell walking in the Lake District; maps of walks closer by are provided, including the 20-mile circular Ullswater Way that passes the impressive 20-metre high Aira Force waterfall. Caravans, motorhomes and tents enjoy very good, level terraced pitches and at the top of the site there are camping pods and comfortable Hobbit Holes for hire. This is a site justifiably proud of its green credentials, with a bio-mass boiler that heats all the water for the toilet and shower facilities. Free WiFi is available across the whole site and a warm welcome is assured.

NORTH EAST ENGLAND

KNIGHT STAINFORTH HALL ▷▷▷▷▷ 92%
STAINFORTH, NORTH YORKSHIRE, page 306

Located near Settle and the River Ribble in the Yorkshire Dales National Park with stunning views of the surrounding countryside, this constantly improving family site is sheltered by mature woodland and the peaceful location ensures the only distractions are the welcome sounds of bleating new-born lambs and birdsong. Holiday home exteriors are uniformly decorated and equipped with stylish decking and 'skirting' to conceal service connections. Generously spaced touring caravan and motorhome pitches have high hedges to enhance privacy, and a large family camping field is located close to the excellent adventure playground. The centrally located modern amenities block is stylishly decorated, equipped with modern fixtures and fittings and provides good privacy options. The landscaped grounds are immaculately maintained and an annual planting programme ensures both maturity and freshness, balanced by pretty colourful seasonal floral displays. At the entrance to the park, a large and impressive stone building contains a good reception, shop area selling essentials and The Knights Table Bar & Bistro, providing everything from homemade cakes and pastries to more substantial freshly prepared meals. Sunday lunch is popular with both on-site families and locals.

AA Campsites of the Year *continued*

HOLIDAY CENTRE OF THE YEAR

HENDRA HOLIDAY PARK ▶▶▶▶▶
NEWQUAY, CORNWALL, page 76

Hendra Holiday Park is a much-loved and long-established leisure park located on the edge of Newquay, Cornwall's busiest holiday destination, with fabulous beaches, lively entertainment and a host of family-orientated attractions. Among the few AA Platinum-rated Holiday Centres, it remains independently owned and is superbly managed by a loyal, hard-working team. The vast complex offers holiday statics, smart lodges, glamping, an excellent touring area and top quality facilities, with something for everyone, from the stunning Oasis Pool (indoor fun pool and outdoor pool), the children's club for the over 6s and activities like skateboarding, archery, Segway tours and zorbing for older children, to evening entertainment for adults during high season, a fish and chip shop and a fantastic coffee shop. The touring pitches, occupying 12 fields, are set amid mature trees and shrubs, and some have fully serviced facilities, while the five toilet and showers blocks are spotlessly maintained. All amenities are open to the public. This site generates most of its own electricity from a 1.5-megawatt solar farm. The Hendra Pod Village area has 10 smart wooden pods for hire. This park offers the complete holiday package for all close to the north Cornwall coast.

GLAMPING SITE OF THE YEAR

LLANFAIR HALL ▶▶▶▶ 91%
DWYRAN, ISLE OF ANGLESEY, page 355

Located on a small, peaceful rural estate and convenient for Newborough Beach and many of Anglesey's attractions, this must-do holiday destination is perfect for that 'away from it all' experience, whether for an active weekend away or a relaxing break. Five large pods, created from seasoned wood and lined with sheep's wool for extra insulation, are carefully equipped with specially designed furnishings, including sumptuous 100% cotton bedlinen and towels, Freeview TV/DVD, free WiFi, and all benefit from quality en suite wet rooms with shower, washbasin and toilet. In addition to some cooking and food storage facilities, a communal, well-equipped campers' kitchen, drying room and outdoor covered barbecue are also provided. Outdoor pizza ovens are also a very popular feature. The larger log cabin is ideal for families and a light-limiting policy ensures breath-taking views of the night sky. New for 2019 is Peibio, a large 18th-century barn which has been cleverly renovated and converted into a multi-purpose base complete with private garden with hot tub for couples or larger groups. With a background in enterprise education and army recruitment, John and Lucy Miller only started this new innovative holiday destination in 2013 and are justifiable winners of many tourism awards for their enthusiasm and flair.

SMALL CAMPSITE OF THE YEAR

CHAROLAND FARM ►►►► 81%
GREENHALGH, LANCASHIRE, page 203

A peacefully located, adults-only touring park based on an award-winning beef cattle and sheep farm, in the hamlet of Greenhalgh in rural Lancashire, ideal for touring the many Fylde Coast attractions, with arguably Britain's most famous resort, Blackpool, as well as Lytham St Annes and Fleetwood all within a twelve-mile distance. The site is surrounded by meadows and farmland making this an ideal spot for walks and cycle trails. All pitches are firm, with reinforcing mesh installed, and benefit from 16amp electric hook up. Central all-level areas are surfaced with very attractive sunken bricks, which complement the colour of the lush grassed areas. Touring and camping areas are surrounded by high neat hedges to eliminate external noises and new trees and shrubs have been planted between pitches, to assist in the creation of optimum privacy. Level, surfaced access to amenities benefits the less mobile and smart modern showers and toilet facilities are located in a sympathetic barn conversion. A small chalet contains a good range of tourist information and a small supermarket is just a 15-minute walk away. The park also benefits from a good gated security system, to ensure peace of mind.

MOST IMPROVED CAMPSITE

BEECH CROFT FARM ►►►►► 94%
BUXTON, DERBYSHIRE, page 121

Peacefully located, yet close to many attractions and facilities, this constantly improving farm caravan and camping park is an increasingly popular destination for both couples and families. The undulating fields have been terraced to provided level, well-spaced touring and motorhome pitches with the benefit of optimum privacy and superb rural views. A large lush camping field provides generously sized pitches, all with electric hook-up via a prepayment card system, and a community campers' cabin is also available. The centrally located rural stone amenities block provides under-floor heating, smart decor, quality modern fixtures and good privacy options for both individuals and families. Four-legged customers are also pampered with a superb dog wash. A signed reception building contains a good registration area, excellent tourist information displays and a very well stocked shop selling camping essentials. A wide range of foodstuffs, including local produce, and a daily bakery delivery, are additional features. Gaining planning permission for improvements is challenging within National Park authority areas and John, Julie and Jodie Gregory's hard work, year-on-year investment and the resulting excellent standards are clear to see at this fine site.

CONCIERGE CAMPING
A TRULY REMARKABLE SITE

This campsite in West Sussex – winner of last year's overall site of the year – is so popular it's hard to get in. Our camping co-ordinator, **David Hancock**, visited Concierge Camping to find out why they are so successful.

Having acquired the historic Ratham Estate in West Ashling, near Chichester in 2011, a working farm until the 1990s, Guy and Tracey Hodgkin set about bringing it back to its former glory. After three years of letting sheep graze and just cutting hay in a field close to their 15th-century farmhouse, Guy decided he needed to do something different with it as it was costing him money. The field has since been transformed into one of best campsites in Britain, and in 2019 Concierge Camping won the AA England and Overall Campsite of the Year Award.

Developing the park has been a labour of love for the Hodgkins, and since opening in 2015 with just 15 touring pitches, they have added four magnificent safari lodges in their own paddock, and in 2018 they extended the park to accommodate caravans and motorhomes on 27 huge, fully-serviced pitches.

Guy admits that 'it was a very selfish project really as I couldn't find anyone in England who did camping the way I wanted to or had all the elements I like in one place. It stems back to when we travelled across Europe in a campervan. We stayed on some great sites and they just do camping so much better, with nicer sized pitches and quality facilities.' He adds, 'Many sites in England are very traditional or they just haven't moved with the times, failing to reinvest money to improve them in line with the expectations of the modern-day camper, caravanner or motorhome owner.'

RAISING THE QUALITY BAR
It's true to say that Guy and Tracey are camping's new trailblazers, they have raised the quality bar to which all campsites should aspire – Concierge Camping is a small, luxury park and the attention to detail throughout is truly

Brazier on reception terrace

remarkable. Money has been lavished on developing the park, everything is top spec and the couple are very hands-on as concierges of the park.

In the swish reception there's a local produce shop selling fresh pastries, croissants and breads from an artisan bakery, great coffee, local meats and barbecue essentials, and an informal continental-style café serving local wines and beers – you can order a bottle of local fizz and then sit and relax alfresco on smart rattan chairs beneath a sail canopy on the decked terrace.

The state-of-the-art amenity block is top-hotel standard and certainly has the wow factor – Ratham Estate toiletries (note the branded orange loo rolls), air-blade hand-driers, eight stunning waterfall shower rooms, an excellent family/disabled room, piped Smooth Radio, stylish Concierge Camping branding on glass doors, and an ice machine ideal for your gin and tonic. The heating/boiler system is the best – warming the block in winter and providing air conditioning in summer.

EMPEROR PITCHES – BREAKING NEW GROUND
The park offers 27 spacious hardstanding pitches in a beautifully landscaped area, with thick laurel hedging between pitches to offer plenty of seclusion. All pitches are fully serviced, with 16- or 32-amp electrical supply, free WiFi, TV and satellite connection, and some are spacious enough (14mtrs x 6mtrs) to accommodate large American RVs.

In 2018, the Hodgkins introduced their unique Emperor pitches to the park. Each of the huge (15mtrs x 8mtrs) pitches has a day-living, mini safari tent beside the gravel

Stylish shower room

23

Inside a safari lodge

hardstanding, so there's no need to pack or erect your awning. Where else would you find a pitch offering you a self-contained tent replete with Smart TV, dishwasher, fridge-freezer, coffee machine, wood-fired oven and burner, and a decked area for unwinding and relaxing? They're not on the cheap side though – fees range from £60 to £125 a night depending on the season and day of the week, but they are very popular with people who enjoy the freedom of touring with a caravan or motorhome but desire the comfort and luxury touches to be found at a swish hotel.

LUXURY LODGES – SAFARI STYLE
The quirky, luxury styling and meticulous attention to detail extend to the four fabulous safari-style lodges, idyllically situated beside a babbling chalk stream in a separate, adjoining meadow. Resembling lodges found in Africa, with exposed timber frames supporting a hardy canvas exterior and a spacious deck with smart rattan outdoor furnishings, they are hugely impressive.

Naturally, they ooze style and comfort and make even a winter stay very cosy as there's underfloor heating throughout. Along with a state-of-the-art, Aga-style range in the fully fitted kitchen, you'll find a dishwasher, fridge-freezer and Nespresso coffee machine.

There's a 40" satellite TV, remote-controlled blinds, a Bluetooth speaker system, and a super bathroom with a hi-tech rainforest shower, fully plumbed toilet and Ratham Estate toiletries – all very much creating a home-from-home experience. Two of the lodges are 2 storeys and accommodate up to 6 people and two are single storey for up to 4 people each.

SUCCESS AND FUTURE DEVELOPMENTS

Building a quality and attractive website with a bespoke booking system and spending up to £45K a year on marketing the park has certainly contributed to the success of Concierge Camping. 'Our repeat business is fantastic with 95% returning time and again because they love what we do here and they are recommending us to friends and family, which is great', says Guy. 'New people are finding us but they can't get in so they are booking up well in advance and outdoing (and frustrating) our existing customers. One customer who came when we first opened in 2015 has only just managed to get in again as we're always fully booked when he wants to stay.'

Guy adds, 'We're very lucky, fitting people in our biggest problem due our size and offering only 27 pitches. Yes, we could be bigger, but we don't want to be as it will distract from what we're doing and what we are about. Other than a few tweaks to some of the pitches and extending the reception, we are planning few changes at the park.'

BUT THE GOOD NEWS IS...

Having trademarked the Concierge Camping name in Britain and Europe, Guy and Tracey plan to develop the brand and a create a niche group of five parks of similar quality over the next 15 years, perhaps Scotland, the Midlands, Devon, and one or two in France. 'The idea is to develop existing sites, make them smaller in the Concierge Camping model with bigger pitches and state-of-the-art facilities', says Guy. 'It won't be yet as we still have much to learn and we need another two years here to get the details right. If you think about it, we have the branding, the systems and the website are all set up, the advertising is in place and the concept works, so developing the brand in a few select locations in Britain and in France is very exciting indeed.'

Safari tent interior

Innovation with technology

Guy believes owners need to embrace and invest in modern technology to set themselves apart and be successful. 'Campsites need to evolve to keep up with the demands and expectations of today's caravanner or motorhome owner – just look at the quality and size of the units that are on the road. I looked at modern innovations in technology to improve how things should work and be more efficient on a campsite. For example, with the showers, I installed sensors to save water and they are far easier to use.'

'The heat pump technology in our toilet block is far more efficient than traditional brick-built toilet blocks. Our block is ultra-insulated, meaning we only have to turn the heating on for three months of the year, the rest of the time they keep warm through the heat of the showers. In winter, the block costs just 12p a day to run, which is great. Our costs to stay open all year are very low compared to a park with traditional toilet blocks, which are too expensive to run, hence why many close at the end of October.'

'The roof solar panel runs the toilet block and most of the time we can run it on 16-amp with a maximum of 24-amp, that's heating, hot water, air conditioning in summer, everything - it's super-efficient. Also, unlike most parks, our electric infrastructure to the pitches comes out of a central hub, with each pitch being on a spur, so if the electric trips they are only affecting themselves, just that pitch.'

Guy concludes by saying that 'It's all about looking at things differently to how they have been done in the past and investing in modern, innovative technology.'

First-time campers: a checklist of Dos, and a couple of Don'ts

Key. O – caravano M – motorhomes T = tents

Before you leave home or the site (hitching)

▶ Before you go away for the first time practise putting up your tent; hitching and unhitching your caravan; reversing your motorhome or towed van into an enclosed space. **(CMT)**

▶ Make a list of all the essentials you need to take with you. Mains lead, gas cylinder, levelling ramps and/or chocks... all the way through to small essentials like a box of matches, spare fuses, and a torch (check batteries). **(CMT)**

▶ Check all interior items are safely stored, cupboards closed, all interior electrics are set correctly, turn off gas bottles, make sure roof lights and windows are closed and the external door is locked. **(CM)**

▶ Empty fresh and waste water containers and toilet cassettes. **(CM)**

▶ Check that corner steadies are raised tightly, and chocks and steps stowed. **(C)**

▶ Connect tow bracket electric plugs, check that the breakaway safety cable is connected and, if used, that the anti-snake device is fitted correctly. **(C)**

▶ Check the caravan's noseweight. **(C)**

▶ Adjust the hitch height – i.e. above the car's towball. **(C)**

▶ Secure the hitch on the towball. **(C)**

▶ Use the jockey wheel to raise the car about 2.5cm to ensure the caravan and car are properly coupled. If fitted, also check the tow hitch indicator (green = correctly coupled). **(C)**

▶ Raise the jockey wheel and lock in position. **(C)**

▶ Check that the caravan number plate is secure (and that it replicates the towing vehicle's number plate). **(C)**

▶ Ask another person to stand behind the caravan or motorhome to check all the lights and indicators work. **(CM)**

▶ On leaving a site disconnect the hook-ups and make that final check of the empty pitch. **(CM)**

Arriving at your destination (unhitching)

▶ Tell the site this is your first time. They're more likely to go out of their way to help. **(CMT)**

▶ Listen to what the site staff tell you when you arrive (if you're a family, it's a good idea for you all to step into reception – that way you all understand the same message). **(CMT)**

▶ Check caravan handbrake is on, chocks are in place and corner steadies are lowered. **(C)**

▶ Lower jockey wheel and level the caravan and then lock in place. **(C)**

▶ Give everyone in the family designated tasks when you arrive on site (finding the way to the toilet block, locating the nearest fresh water point etc). **(CMT)**

▶ Get to know your surroundings. An early-evening stroll around any campsite is a great opportunity to check out the facilities. **(CMT)**

▶ Say hello to your neighbours. They might just come in handy, and who knows you might a make a lot of new friends. **(CMT)**

DON'T churn up the grass. You're only ruining things for subsequent visitors. If you have a bit of a mishap, let the staff know so they can rectify things as soon as possible.

And finally **DON'T** be afraid to ask. All the campsites in this guide are adept at helping first-timers – most will happily guide you to your pitch if you ask. Although you'll soon find your fellow campers are happy to chip in and help out, too.

There's even more useful information on how to safely tow a caravan or trailer at:
www.theaa.com/motoring_advice/general-advice/towing-advice-what-you-need-to-know.html

The best sites for...

If you're looking for a site with a specific quality or recommended facilities, the following lists will help.

WATERSIDE PITCHES

ENGLAND

South End Caravan Park,
 Barrow-in-Furness, Cumbria
Hill of Oaks & Blakeholme,
 Windermere, Cumbria
River Dart Country Park,
 Ashburton, Devon
Riverside C&C Park,
 South Molton, Devon
Sleningford Watermill Caravan Camping Park,
 North Stainley, North Yorkshire

SCOTLAND

Banff Links Caravan Park,
 Banff, Aberdeenshire
Inver Mill Farm Caravan Park,
 Dunkeld, Perth & Kinross
Skye C&C Club Site,
 Edinbane, Isle of Skye

WALES

Riverside Camping,
 Caernarfon, Gwynedd

NORTHERN IRELAND

Rushin House Caravan Park,
 Belcoo, County Fermanagh

STUNNING VIEWS

ENGLAND

Tristram C&C Park,
 Polzeath, Cornwall
Sykeside Camping Park,
 Patterdale, Cumbria
Warcombe Farm C&C Park,
 Woolacombe, Devon
Highlands End Holiday Park,
 Bridport, Dorset

East Fleet Farm Touring Park,
 Weymouth, Dorset
Sea Barn Farm,
 Weymouth, Dorset
New Hall Farm Touring Park,
 Southwell, Nottinghamshire
Wimbleball Lake,
 Dulverton, Somerset
Howgill Lodge,
 Bolton Abbey, North Yorkshire
Wolds Way Caravan and Camping,
 West Knapton, North Yorkshire

CHANNEL ISLANDS

Rozel Camping Park,
 St Martin, Jersey

SCOTLAND

Carradale Bay Caravan Park,
 Carradale, Argyll & Bute
Oban C&C Park,
 Oban, Argyll & Bute
Resipole Farm Holiday Park,
 Acharacle, Highland
Invercoe C&C Park,
 Glencoe, Highland
John O'Groats Caravan Site,
 John O'Groats, Highland
Strathfillan Wigwam Village,
 Tyndrum, Stirling

WALES

Bron-Y-Wendon Caravan Park,
 Llanddulas, Conwy
Bodnant Caravan Park,
 Llanwrst, Conwy
Beach View Caravan Park,
 Abersoch, Gwynedd
Tyn-y-Mur Touring & Camping,
 Abersoch, Gwynedd
Trawsdir Touring C&C Park,
 Barmouth, Gwynedd

Eisteddfa,
 Criccieth, Gwynedd
Fishguard Bay Resort,
 Fishguard, Pembrokeshire
Skysea C&C Park,
 Port Eynon, Swansea

GOOD ON-SITE RESTAURANTS

ENGLAND

Stroud Hill Park,
 St Ives, Cambridgeshire
Tristram C&C Park,
 Polzeath, Cornwall
Park Cliffe Camping & Caravan Estate,
 Windermere, Cumbria
Hidden Valley Park,
 Braunton, Devon
Cofton Holidays,
 Dawlish, Devon
Highlands End Holiday Park,
 Bridport, Dorset
Bay View Holiday Park,
 Bolton le Sands, Lancashire
The Old Brick Kilns,
 Barney, Norfolk
Beaconsfield Farm Caravan Park,
 Shrewsbury, Shropshire

CHANNEL ISLANDS

Durrell Wildlife Camp,
 Trinity, Jersey

SCOTLAND

Sands of Luce Holiday Park,
 Sandhead, Dumfries & Galloway
Glen Nevis C&C Park,
 Fort William, Highland

Tristram Caravan & Camping Park, Cornwall

TOP TOILETS

ENGLAND

Carnon Downs C&C Park,
  Truro, Cornwall
Skelwith Fold Caravan Park,
  Ambleside, Cumbria
Beech Croft Farm,
  Buxton, Derbyshire
Crealy Theme Park & Resort,
  Clyst St Mary, Devon
Riverside C&C Park,
  South Molton, Devon
Meadowbank Holidays,
  Christchurch, Dorset
Shamba Holidays,
  St Leonards, Dorset
Ord House Country Park,
  Berwick-upon-Tweed, Northumberland
Teversal C&C Club Site,
  Teversal, Nottinghamshire
The Old Oaks Touring & Glamping Park,
  Glastonbury, Somerset
Moon & Sixpence,
  Woodbridge, Suffolk
Riverside Caravan Park,
  High Bentham, North Yorkshire
Wayside Holiday Park,
  Pickering, North Yorkshire

SCOTLAND

Beecraigs C&C Site,
  Linlithgow, West Lothian
Skye C&C Club Site,
  Edinbane, Isle of Skye

ON-SITE FISHING

ENGLAND

Fields End Water Caravan Park & Fishery,
  Doddington, Cambridgeshire
Upper Tamar Lake,
  Kilkhampton, Cornwall
Back of Beyond Touring Park,
  St Leonards, Dorset
Woodland Waters,
  Ancaster, Lincolnshire
Lakeside Caravan Park & Fisheries,
  Downham Market, Norfolk

Northam Farm Caravan & Touring Park,
  Brean, Somerset
Marsh Farm Caravan Site,
  Saxmundham, Suffolk
Sumners Ponds Fishery & Campsite,
  Barns Green, West Sussex

SCOTLAND

Hoddom Castle Caravan Park,
  Ecclefechan, Dumfries & Galloway
Resipole Farm Holiday Park,
  Acharacle, Highland
Milton of Fonab Caravan Park,
  Pitlochry, Perth & Kinross

WALES

Afon Teifi C&C Park,
  Newcastle Emlyn, Carmarthenshire
Ynysymaengwyn Caravan Park,
  Tywyn, Gwynedd

THE KIDS

ENGLAND

Trevornick,
  Holywell Bay, Cornwall
Eden Valley Holiday Park,
  Lostwithiel, Cornwall
Golden Valley C&C Park,
  Ripley, Derbyshire
Freshwater Beach Holiday Park,
  Bridport, Dorset
Brokerswood Country Park,
  Westbury, Wiltshire
Golden Square C&C Park,
  Helmsley, North Yorkshire
Goosewood Holiday Park,
  Sutton-on-the-Forest, North Yorkshire

SCOTLAND

Beecraigs C&C Site,
  Linlithgow, West Lothian
Blair Castle Caravan Park,
  Blair Atholl, Perth & Kinross

WALES

Home Farm Caravan Park,
  Marian-Glas, Isle of Anglesey
Trawsdir Touring C&C Park,
  Barmouth, Gwynedd
Kiln Park Holiday Centre,
  Tenby, Pembrokeshire

BEING ECO-FRIENDLY

ENGLAND

South Penquite Farm,
  Blisland, Cornwall
Camping Caradon Touring Park,
  Looe, Cornwall
River Dart Country Park,
  Ashburton, Devon
Brook Lodge Farm C&C Park,
  Cowslip Green, Somerset

SCOTLAND

Carradale Bay Caravan Park,
  Carradale, Argyll & Bute
Shieling Holidays Mull,
  Craignure, Isle of Mull

WALES

Caerfai Bay Caravan & Tent Park,
  St Davids, Pembrokeshire

▶▶▶▶▶ Platinum Parks

Platinum Parks are the very best sites in the UK, having achieved a 5-Pennant rating with a quality score of 95% and over.

ENGLAND

CORNWALL

BUDE
Wooda Farm Holiday Park

CARLYON BAY
Carlyon Bay Caravan & Camping Park

CRANTOCK
Trevella Park

HOLYWELL BAY
Trevornick

MEVAGISSEY
Seaview Gorran Haven Holiday Park

NEWQUAY
Hendra Holiday Park

PADSTOW
Padstow Touring Park

POLZEATH
Gunvenna Holiday Park

REDRUTH
Globe Vale Holiday Park

ST IVES
Polmanter Touring Park
Trevalgan Touring Park

ST JUST-IN-ROSELAND
Trethem Mill Touring Park

TRURO
Carnon Downs Caravan & Camping Park

WHITE CROSS
Piran Meadows Resort and Spa

CUMBRIA

AMBLESIDE
Skelwith Fold Caravan Park

DEVON

AXMINSTER
Hawkchurch Resort & Spa

NEWTON ABBOT
Dornafield
Ross Park

SIDMOUTH
Oakdown Country Holiday Park

DORSET

BRIDPORT
Highlands End Holiday Park

POOLE
South Lytchett Manor Caravan & Camping Park

WAREHAM
Wareham Forest Tourist Park

WEYMOUTH
East Fleet Farm Touring Park

ISLE OF WIGHT

NEWBRIDGE
The Orchards Holiday Caravan Park

RYDE
Whitefield Forest Touring Park

WOOTTON BRIDGE
Woodside Bay Lodge Retreat

LANCASHIRE

SILVERDALE
Silverdale Caravan Park

LEICESTERSHIRE

MELTON MOWBRAY
Eye Kettleby Lakes

LINCOLNSHIRE

CAISTOR
Caistor Lakes Leisure Park

NORFOLK

BARNEY
The Old Brick Kilns

CLIPPESBY
Clippesby Hall

NORTHUMBERLAND

BELFORD
South Meadows Caravan Park

OXFORDSHIRE

HENLEY-ON-THAMES
Swiss Farm Touring & Camping

STANDLAKE
Lincoln Farm Park Oxfordshire

SOMERSET

BISHOP SUTTON
Bath Chew Valley Caravan Park

BREAN
Warren Farm Holiday Centre

CHEDDAR
Cheddar Woods Resort & Spa

GLASTONBURY
Old Oaks Touring & Glamping

WEST SUSSEX

CHICHESTER
Concierge Camping

CHANNEL ISLANDS

JERSEY

TRINITY
Durrell Wildlife Camp

SCOTLAND

FIFE

ST ANDREWS
Cairnsmill Holiday Park
Craigtoun Meadows Holiday Park

WALES

ISLE OF ANGLESEY

MARIAN-GLAS
Home Farm Caravan Park

WREXHAM

EYTON
Plassey Holiday Park

▶▶▶▶▶▶ Premier Parks

Premier Parks are among the top sites in the UK, having achieved either a 5 gold (pages 31–32) or 5 black (pages 33–35) Pennant rating.

ENGLAND

CAMBRIDGESHIRE

DODDINGTON
Fields End Water Caravan Park & Fishery

ST IVES
Stroud Hill Park

CHESHIRE

CODDINGTON
Manor Wood Country Caravan Park

WHITEGATE
Lamb Cottage Caravan Park

CORNWALL

HAYLE
St Ives Bay Holiday Park

NEWQUAY
Monkey Tree Holiday Park
Treloy Touring Park

PERRANPORTH
Perran Sands Holiday Park

PORTHTOWAN
Porthtowan Tourist Park

ST IVES
Ayr Holiday Park

ST MERRYN
Atlantic Bays Holiday Park

WATERGATE BAY
Watergate Bay Touring Park

CUMBRIA

BEWALDETH
Keswick Reach Lodge Retreat

KESWICK
Castlerigg Hall Caravan & Camping Park

POOLEY BRIDGE
Park Foot Caravan & Camping Park

SILLOTH
Stanwix Park Holiday Centre

WATERMILLOCK
The Quiet Site

WINDERMERE
Park Cliffe Camping & Caravan Estate

DEVON

BRAUNTON
Hidden Valley Park

CLYST ST MARY
Crealy Theme Park & Resort

COMBE MARTIN
Stowford Farm Meadows

DARTMOUTH
Woodlands Grove Caravan &
    Camping Park

DAWLISH
Cofton Holidays

DREWSTEIGNTON
Woodland Springs Adult Touring Park

SAMPFORD PEVERELL
Minnows Touring Park

SIDMOUTH
Salcombe Regis Caravan & Camping
    Park

SOUTH MOLTON
Riverside Caravan & Camping Park

TAVISTOCK
Woodovis Park

WOOLACOMBE
Twitchen House Holiday Village
Warcombe Farm Caravan &
    Camping Park

DORSET

BRIDPORT
Freshwater Beach Holiday Park

CHARMOUTH
Wood Farm Caravan & Camping Park

Treloy Touring Park, Cornwall

POOLE
Rockley Park

WEYMOUTH
Weymouth Bay Holiday Park

KENT

ASHFORD
Broadhembury Caravan & Camping Park

MARDEN
Tanner Farm Touring Caravan &
Camping Park

LANCASHIRE

CAPERNWRAY
Old Hall Caravan Park

LINCOLNSHIRE

WOODHALL SPA
Woodhall Country Park

NORFOLK

HOPTON ON SEA
Hopton Holiday Village

HUNSTANTON
Searles Leisure Resort

NORTHUMBERLAND

BELLINGHAM
Bellingham Camping & Caravanning
Club Site

BERWICK-UPON-TWEED
Ord House Country Park

HALTWHISTLE
Herding Hill Farm Touring &
Camping Site

NOTTINGHAMSHIRE

TEVERSAL
Teversal Camping & Caravanning
Club Site

SHROPSHIRE

SHREWSBURY
Beaconsfield Farm Caravan Park
Oxon Hall Touring Park

WHEATHILL
Wheathill Touring Park

SOMERSET

BATH
Bath Mill Lodge Retreat

BREAN
Holiday Resort Unity

BRIDGETOWN
Exe Valley Caravan Site

BURNHAM-ON-SEA
Burnham-on-Sea Holiday Village

WATCHET
Doniford Bay Holiday Park

WELLS
Wells Touring Park

WIVELISCOMBE
Waterrow Touring Park

STAFFORDSHIRE

LONGNOR
Longnor Wood Holiday Park

SUFFOLK

DUNWICH
Haw Wood Farm Caravan Park

LEISTON
Cakes & Ale

WOODBRIDGE
Moon & Sixpence

WEST SUSSEX

CHICHESTER
Concierge Glamping

PAGHAM
Church Farm Holiday Park

WORCESTERSHIRE

HONEYBOURNE
Ranch Caravan Park

NORTH YORKSHIRE

ALLERSTON
Vale of Pickering Caravan Park

FILEY
Flower of May Holiday Park

HIGH BENTHAM
Riverside Caravan Park

WYKEHAM
St Helens in the Park

SOUTH YORKSHIRE

Waleswood Caravan and Camping Park

SCOTLAND

ABERDEENSHIRE

HUNTLY
Huntly Castle Caravan Park

DUMFRIES & GALLOWAY

BRIGHOUSE BAY
Brighouse Bay Holiday Park

GATEHOUSE OF FLEET
Auchenlarie Holiday Park

EAST LOTHIAN

DUNBAR
Thurston Manor Leisure Park

PERTH & KINROSS

BLAIR ATHOLL
Blair Castle Caravan Park

STIRLING

ABERFOYLE
Trossachs Holiday Park

SCOTTISH ISLANDS

ISLE OF ARRAN

KILMORY
Runach Arainn

WALES

ISLE OF ANGLESEY

DULAS
Tyddyn Isaf Caravan Park

DWYRAN
LLanfair Hall

CARMARTHENSHIRE

NEWCASTLE EMLYN
Cenarth Falls Holiday Park

GWYNEDD

BARMOUTH
Trawsdir Touring Caravans &
Camping Park

PWLLHELI
Hafan y Môr Holiday Park

GWYNEDD

TAL-Y-BONT
Islawrffordd Caravan Park

MONMOUTHSHIRE

LLANVAIR DISCOED
Penhein Glamping

PEMBROKESHIRE

ST DAVIDS
Caerfai Bay Caravan & Tent Park

POWYS

BRECON
Pencelli Castle Caravan & Camping Park

NORTHERN IRELAND

COUNTY ANTRIM

BUSHMILLS
Ballyness Caravan Park

▶▶▶▶▶ Premier Parks

ENGLAND

CORNWALL

HAYLE
Riviere Sands Holiday Park

LEEDSTOWN
Calloose Caravan & Camping Park

LOOE
Camping Caradon Touring Park
Tencreek Holiday Park

LOSTWITHIEL
Eden Valley Holiday Park

PADSTOW
The Retreats @ Padstow Holiday Park

ST AGNES
Beacon Cottage Farm Touring Park

ST AUSTELL
River Valley Holiday Park

TRURO
Cosawes Park
Truro Caravan and Camping Park

CUMBRIA

APPLEBY-IN-WESTMORLAND
Wild Rose Park

FLOOKBURGH
Lakeland Leisure Park

KIRKBY LONSDALE
Woodclose Caravan Park

PENRITH
Lowther Holiday Park

ULVERSTON
Bardsea Leisure Park

WINDERMERE
Hill of Oaks & Blakeholme

DEVON

COMBE MARTIN
Newberry Valley Park

DAWLISH
Lady's Mile Holiday Park

ILFRACOMBE
Hele Valley Holiday Park

KENNFORD
Kennford International Holiday Park

KINGSBRIDGE
Island Lodge Caravan & Camping Site
Parkland Caravan and Camping Site

PAIGNTON
Beverley Park Caravan & Camping Park

TAVISTOCK
Harford Bridge Holiday Park
Langstone Manor Camping &
   Caravan Park

WOOLACOMBE
Golden Coast Holiday Village
Woolacombe Bay Holiday Village & Spa

DORSET

CHARMOUTH
Newlands Holidays

CHIDEOCK
Golden Cap Holiday Park

CHRISTCHURCH
Meadowbank Holidays

HOLDITCH
Crafty Camping

ST LEONARDS
Shamba Holidays

SHAFTESBURY
Dorset Country Holidays

SWANAGE
Ulwell Cottage Caravan Park

WEYMOUTH
Littlesea Holiday Park
Seaview Holiday Park

ESSEX

MERSEA ISLAND
Waldegraves Holiday Park

ISLE OF WIGHT

WHITECLIFF BAY
Whitecliff Bay Holiday Park

KENT

AYLESFORD
Kits Coty Glamping

LANCASHIRE

BLACKPOOL
Marton Mere Holiday Village

BOLTON LE SANDS
Bay View Holiday Park

FAR ARNSIDE
Hollins Farm Camping & Caravanning

Bron Derw Touring Caravan Park, Conwy

▶▶▶▶▶ **Premier Parks** *continued*

FLEETWOOD
Cala Gran Holiday Park

THORNTON
Kneps Farm Holiday Caravan Park

LINCOLNSHIRE
CLEETHORPES
Thorpe Park Holiday Centre

MABLETHORPE
Golden Sands Holiday Park

MERSEYSIDE
SOUTHPORT
Riverside Holiday Park

NORFOLK
BELTON
Rose Farm Touring & Camping Park

CAISTER-ON-SEA
Caister-on-Sea Holiday Park

GREAT YARMOUTH
Seashore Holiday Park

KING'S LYNN
King's Lynn Caravan and Camping Park

NORTH WALSHAM
Two Mills Touring Park

NORTHAMPTONSHIRE
BULWICK
New Lodge Farm Caravan &
   Camping Site

NORTHUMBERLAND
BERWICK-UPON-TWEED
Berwick Holiday Park
Haggerston Castle Holiday Park

HALTWHISTLE
Herding Hill Farm, Glamping site

RUTLAND
GREETHAM
Rutland Caravan & Camping

SHROPSHIRE
BRIDGNORTH
Stanmore Hall Touring Park

TELFORD
Severn Gorge Park

SOMERSET
CROWCOMBE
Quantock Orchard Caravan Park

EAST SUSSEX
BEXHILL
Kloofs Caravan Park

ST LEONARDS
Combe Haven Holiday Park

WARWICKSHIRE
HARBURY
Harbury Fields

WILTSHIRE
LANDFORD
Greenhill Farm Caravan & Camping Park

EAST RIDING OF YORKSHIRE
FLAMBOROUGH
Thornwick Bay Holiday Village

SKIPSEA
Skirlington Leisure Park

SPROATLEY
Burton Constable Holiday Park &
   Arboretum

TUNSTALL
Sand le Mere Holiday Village

NORTH YORKSHIRE
ALNE
Alders Caravan Park

HARROGATE
Ripley Caravan Park
Rudding Holiday Park

HELMSLEY
Golden Square Caravan & Camping Park

OSMOTHERLEY
Cote Ghyll Caravan & Camping Park

RIPON
Riverside Meadows Country Caravan Park

SNAINTON
Jasmine Caravan Park

SUTTON-ON-THE-FOREST
Goosewood Holiday Park

THIRSK
Hillside Caravan Park

CHANNEL ISLANDS
GUERNSEY
CASTEL
Fauxquets Valley Campsite

JERSEY
ST MARTIN
Rozel Camping Park

SCOTLAND
SOUTH AYRSHIRE
AYR
Craig Tara Holiday Park

WEST DUNBARTONSHIRE
BALLOCH
Lomond Woods Holiday Park

DUMFRIES & GALLOWAY
ECCLEFECHAN
Hoddom Castle Caravan Park

KIRKCUDBRIGHT
Seaward Holiday Park

EAST LOTHIAN
LONGNIDDRY
Seton Sands Holiday Village

MORAY
LOSSIEMOUTH
Silver Sands Holiday Park

STIRLING
TYNDRUM
Strathfillan Wigwam Village

WALES
CEREDIGION
NEW QUAY
Quay West Holiday Park

CONWY
LLANDDULAS
Bron-Y-Wendon Caravan Park

LLANRWST
Bron Derw Touring Caravan Park

DENBIGHSHIRE
PRESTATYN
Presthaven Beach Holiday Park

GWYNEDD
BARMOUTH
Hendre Mynach Touring Caravan &
   Camping Park

BETWS GARMON
Bryn Gloch Caravan & Camping Park

DINAS DINLLE
Dinlle Caravan Park

PORTHMADOG
Greenacres Holiday Park

MONMOUTHSHIRE
USK
Pont Kemys Caravan & Camping Park

PEMBROKESHIRE
TENBY
Kiln Park Holiday Centre

POWYS
BUILTH WELLS
Fforest Fields Caravan & Camping Park

CHURCHSTOKE
Daisy Bank Caravan Park

LLANIDLOES
Red Kite Touring Park

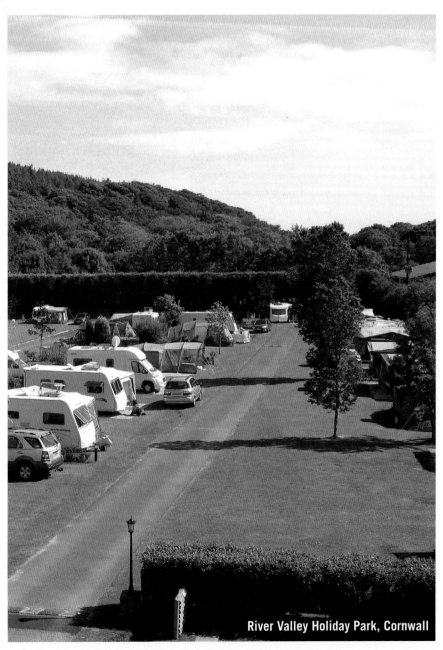

River Valley Holiday Park, Cornwall

Gold Pennant parks

Gold Pennants are awarded to sites with a quality score of 90% and above within the 1–5 Pennant ratings.

ENGLAND

CAMBRIDGESHIRE
COMBERTON
▷▷▷▷▷ Highfield Farm Touring Park

DODDINGTON
▷▷▷▷▷ Fields End Water Caravan Park & Fishery

ST IVES
▷▷▷▷▷ Stroud Hill Park

CHESHIRE
CODDINGTON
▷▷▷▷▷ Manor Wood Country Caravan Park

WHITEGATE
▷▷▷▷▷ Lamb Cottage Caravan Park

CORNWALL
HAYLE
▷▷▷▷ St Ives Bay Holiday Park

HELSTON
▷▷▷▷ Lower Polladras Touring Park

MARAZION
▷▷▷▷ Wayfarers Caravan & Camping Park

NEWQUAY
▷▷▷▷ Monkey Tree Holiday Park
▷▷▷▷ Treloy Touring Park
▷▷▷▷ Trencreek Holiday Park

PERRANPORTH
▷▷▷▷ Perran Sands Holiday Park

POLZEATH
▷▷▷ Southwinds Caravan & Camping Park
▷▷▷ Tristram Caravan & Camping Park

PORTHTOWAN
▷▷▷▷ Porthtowan Tourist Park

PORTREATH
▷▷▷▷ Tehidy Holiday Park

REDRUTH
▷▷▷▷ Lanyon Holiday Park

ROSUDGEON
▷▷▷▷ Kenneggy Cove Holiday Park

ST IVES
▷▷▷▷ Ayr Holiday Park

ST JUST [NEAR LAND'S END]
▷▷▷ Roselands Caravan and Camping Park

ST MERRYN
▷▷▷▷ Atlantic Bays Holiday Park

SENNEN
▷▷▷▷ Trevedra Farm Caravan & Camping Site

SUMMERCOURT
▷▷▷▷ Carvynick Holiday Park

TRURO
▷▷▷▷ Summer Valley Touring Park

WADEBRIDGE
▷▷▷▷ The Laurels Holiday Park

WATERGATE BAY
▷▷▷▷ Watergate Bay Touring Park

CUMBRIA
BEWALDETH
▷▷▷▷ Keswick Reach Lodge Retreat

CARLISLE
▷▷▷▷ Green Acres Caravan Park

KESWICK
▷▷▷▷ Castlerigg Hall Caravan & Camping Park

POOLEY BRIDGE
▷▷▷▷ Park Foot Caravan & Camping Park

SILLOTH
▷▷▷▷ Stanwix Park Holiday Centre

WATERMILLOCK
▷▷▷▷ The Quiet Site

WINDERMERE
▷▷▷▷ Park Cliffe Camping & Caravan Estate

DERBYSHIRE
BUXTON
▷▷▷▷ Beech Croft Farm
▷▷▷▷ Lime Tree Park

MATLOCK
▷▷▷▷ Lickpenny Caravan Site

DEVON
AXMINSTER
▷▷▷▷ Andrewshayes Holiday Park

BERRYNARBOR
▷▷▷▷ Mill Park Touring Caravan & Camping Park

BRAUNTON
▷▷▷▷ Hidden Valley Park

BUCKFASTLEIGH
▷▷ Churchill Farm Campsite

CLYST ST MARY
▷▷▷▷ Crealy Theme Park & Resort

COMBE MARTIN
▷▷▷▷ Stowford Farm Meadows

DARTMOUTH
▷▷▷▷ Woodlands Grove Caravan & Camping Park

DAWLISH
▷▷▷▷ Cofton Holidays

DREWSTEIGNTON
▷▷▷▷ Woodland Springs Adult Touring Park

MORTEHOE
▷▷▷▷ North Morte Farm Caravan & Camping Park

SAMPFORD PEVERELL
▷▷▷▷ Minnows Touring Park

SIDMOUTH
▷▷▷▷ Salcombe Regis Caravan & Camping Park

SOUTH MOLTON
▷▷▷▷ Riverside Caravan & Camping Park

TAVISTOCK
▷▷▷▷ Woodovis Park

TORQUAY
▷▷▷ Widdicombe Farm Touring Park

WOOLACOMBE
▷▷▷▷ Twitchen House Holiday Village
▷▷▷▷ Warcombe Farm Caravan & Camping Park

DORSET
BRIDPORT
▷▷▷▷ Freshwater Beach Holiday Park
▷▷▷ Graston Copse Holiday Park

CHARMOUTH
►►►► Wood Farm Caravan & Camping Park

CORFE CASTLE
►►►► Corfe Castle Camping & Caravanning Club Site

LYME REGIS
►►►► Shrubbery Touring Park

POOLE
►►►► Rockley Park

ST LEONARDS
►►►► Back of Beyond Touring Park

WEYMOUTH
►►► Pebble Bank Caravan Park
►►► Rosewall Camping
►►► West Fleet Holiday Farm
►►►► Weymouth Bay Holiday Park

WIMBORNE MINSTER
►►►► Charris Camping & Caravan Park

GLOUCESTERSHIRE
CHELTENHAM
►►►► Briarfields Motel & Touring Park

CIRENCESTER
►►►► Mayfield Park

HAMPSHIRE
LINWOOD
►►► Red Shoot Camping Park

ISLE OF WIGHT
SHANKLIN
►►►► Ninham Country Holidays

KENT
ASHFORD
►►►► Broadhembury Caravan & Camping Park

MARDEN
►►►►► Tanner Farm Touring Caravan & Camping Park

LANCASHIRE
CAPERNWRAY
►►►►► Old Hall Caravan Park

LINCOLNSHIRE
BOSTON
►►►► Long Acres Touring Park

TATTERSHALL
►►►► Tattershall Lakes Country Park

WOODHALL SPA
►►►► Petwood Caravan Park
►►►► Woodhall Country Park

NORFOLK
HOPTON ON SEA
►►►►► Hopton Holiday Village

HUNSTANTON
►►►►► Searles Leisure Resort

NORTHUMBERLAND
BAMBURGH
►►►► Glororum Caravan Park
►►►► Waren Caravan & Camping Park

BELLINGHAM
►►►►► Bellingham Camping & Caravanning Club Site

BERWICK-UPON-TWEED
►►►►► Ord House Country Park

HALTWHISTLE
►►►►► Herding Hill Farm Touring & Camping Site

NOTTINGHAMSHIRE
TEVERSAL
►►►►► Teversal Camping & Caravanning Club Site

OXFORDSHIRE
BLETCHINGDON
►►►► Greenhill Leisure Park

SHROPSHIRE
SHREWSBURY
►►►► Beaconsfield Farm Caravan Park
►►►► Cartref Caravan & Camping
►►►► Oxon Hall Touring Park

WHEATHILL
►►►► Wheathill Touring Park

SOMERSET
BATH
►►►►► Bath Mill Lodge Retreat

BREAN
►►►► Holiday Resort Unity
►►►► Northam Farm Caravan & Touring Park

BRIDGETOWN
►►►►► Exe Valley Caravan Site

BURNHAM-ON-SEA
►►►►► Burnham-on-Sea Holiday Village

COWSLIP GREEN
►►► Brook Lodge Farm Camping & Caravan Park

PORLOCK
►►►► Burrowhayes Farm Caravan & Camping Site & Riding Stables

SHEPTON MALLET
►► Greenacres Camping

TAUNTON
►►►► Cornish Farm Touring Park

WATCHET
►►►► Doniford Bay Holiday Park

WELLS
►►►► Wells Touring Park

WIVELISCOMBE
►►►► Waterrow Touring Park

STAFFORDSHIRE
LONGNOR
►►►►► Longnor Wood Holiday Park

SUFFOLK
DUNWICH
►►►► Haw Wood Farm Caravan Park

KESSINGLAND
►►►► Heathland Beach Holiday Park

LEISTON
►►►► Cakes & Ale

SAXMUNDHAM
►►► Marsh Farm Caravan Site

WOODBRIDGE
►►►► Moon & Sixpence

WEST SUSSEX
BARNS GREEN
►►►► Sumners Ponds Fishery & Campsite

CHICHESTER
►►►►► Concierge Glamping

PAGHAM
►►►► Church Farm Holiday Park

WEST MIDLANDS
MERIDEN
►►►► Somers Wood Caravan Park

WILTSHIRE
AMESBURY
►►► Stonehenge Touring Park

SALISBURY
►►►► Coombe Touring Park

WORCESTERSHIRE
HONEYBOURNE
►►►►► Ranch Caravan Park

►Gold Pennant parks *continued*

EAST RIDING OF YORKSHIRE
BRANDESBURTON
▶▶▶ Blue Rose Caravan Country Park

NORTH YORKSHIRE
ALLERSTON
▶▶▶▶ Vale of Pickering Caravan Park

FILEY
▶▶▶ Crows Nest Caravan Park
▶▶▶▶ Flower of May Holiday Park

HIGH BENTHAM
▶▶▶▶ Riverside Caravan Park

ROBIN HOOD'S BAY
▶▶▶ Grouse Hill Caravan Park
▶▶▶▶ Middlewood Farm Holiday Park

SCARBOROUGH
▶▶▶ Arosa Caravan & Camping Park

STAINFORTH
▶▶▶ Knight Stainforth Hall Caravan & Campsite

WHITBY
▶▶▶ Ladycross Plantation Caravan Park

WYKEHAM
▶▶▶▶ St Helens in the Park

SOUTH YORKSHIRE
WALES
▶▶▶▶ Waleswood Caravan and Camping Park

CHANNEL ISLANDS

GUERNSEY
ST SAMPSON
▶▶▶ Le Vaugrat Camp Site

SCOTLAND

ABERDEENSHIRE
HUNTLY
▶▶▶▶ Huntly Castle Caravan Park

ARGYLL & BUTE
CARRADALE
▶▶ Carradale Bay Caravan Park

DUMFRIES & GALLOWAY
BRIGHOUSE BAY
▶▶▶▶ Brighouse Bay Holiday Park

GATEHOUSE OF FLEET
▶▶▶▶ Auchenlarie Holiday Park

SANDHEAD
▶▶▶ Sands of Luce Holiday Park

WIGTOWN
▶▶ Drumroamin Farm Camping & Touring Site

EAST LOTHIAN
DUNBAR
▶▶▶ Belhaven Bay Caravan & Camping Park
▶▶▶▶ Thurston Manor Leisure Park

HIGHLAND
AVIEMORE
▶▶▶ Aviemore Glamping

FORT WILLIAM
▶▶▶ Glen Nevis Caravan & Camping Park

WEST LOTHIAN
EAST CALDER
▶▶▶▶ Linwater Caravan Park

LINLITHGOW
▶▶▶▶ Beecraigs Caravan & Camping Site

PERTH & KINROSS
BLAIR ATHOLL
▶▶▶▶ Blair Castle Caravan Park

PITLOCHRY
▶▶▶ Milton of Fonab Caravan Park

SCOTTISH BORDERS
LAUDER
▶▶▶ Thirlestane Castle Caravan & Camping Site

STIRLING
ABERFOYLE
▶▶▶▶ Trossachs Holiday Park

BLAIRLOGIE
▶▶▶ Witches Craig Caravan & Camping Park

SCOTTISH ISLANDS

ISLE OF ARRAN
KILMORY
▶▶▶▶ Runach Arainn

ISLE OF SKYE
EDINBANE
▶▶▶ Skye Camping & Caravanning Club Site

WALES

ISLE OF ANGLESEY
DULAS
▶▶▶▶ Tyddyn Isaf Caravan Park

DWYRAN
▶▶▶▶▶ LLanfair Hall

CARMARTHENSHIRE
NEWCASTLE EMLYN
▶▶▶▶▶ Cenarth Falls Holiday Park

CEREDIGION
ABERAERON
▶▶▶ Aeron Coast Caravan Park

DENBIGHSHIRE
RHUALLT
▶▶▶▶ Penisar Mynydd Caravan Park

GWYNEDD
BARMOUTH
▶▶▶▶ Trawsdir Touring Caravans & Camping Park

CRICCIETH
▶▶▶▶ Eisteddfa

LLANDWROG
▶▶▶▶ White Tower Caravan Park

PWLLHELI
▶▶▶▶ Hafan y Môr Holiday Park

TAL-Y-BONT
▶▶▶▶▶ Islawrffordd Caravan Park

MONMOUTHSHIRE
LLANVAIR DISCOED
▶▶▶▶ Penhein Glamping

PEMBROKESHIRE
FISHGUARD
▶▶▶▶ Fishguard Bay Resort

ST DAVIDS
▶▶▶▶ Caerfai Bay Caravan & Tent Park

POWYS
BRECON
▶▶▶▶ Pencelli Castle Caravan & Camping Park

SWANSEA
RHOSSILI
▶▶▶ Pitton Cross Caravan & Camping Park

NORTHERN IRELAND

COUNTY ANTRIM
BUSHMILLS
▶▶▶▶ Ballyness Caravan Park

AA

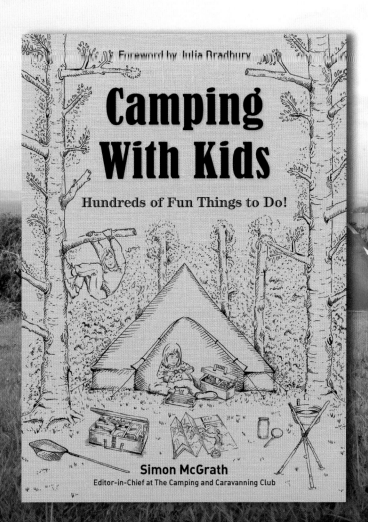

Foreword by Julia Bradbury

Camping With Kids

Hundreds of Fun Things to Do!

Simon McGrath

Editor-in-Chief at The Camping and Caravanning Club

With 400 cool campsite-based ideas on getting back
to nature, learning survival skills, weather watching,
cooking, bushcraft – and just having fun – *Camping
With Kids* takes the stress out of camping, even
when it's raining.

AVAILABLE FROM ALL GOOD BOOK STORES

AA Holiday Centres

These parks cater for all holiday needs. See page 11 for further information.

ENGLAND

CORNWALL
HAYLE
►►►►► St Ives Bay Holiday Park

LOOE
►►►►► Tencreek Holiday Park

NEWQUAY
►►►►► Hendra Holiday Park

PERRANPORTH
►►►►► Perran Sands Holiday Park

WATERGATE BAY
►►►►► Watergate Bay Touring Park

CUMBRIA
FLOOKBURGH
►►►►► Lakeland Leisure Park

POOLEY BRIDGE
►►►►► Park Foot Caravan & Camping Park

SILLOTH
►►►► Solway Holiday Village
►►►►► Stanwix Park Holiday Centre

DEVON
WOOLACOMBE
►►►►► Golden Coast Holiday Village
►►►►► Twitchen House Holiday Village

DORSET
BRIDPORT
►►►►► Freshwater Beach Holiday Park

WEYMOUTH
►►►►► Littlesea Holiday Park
►►►►► Seaview Holiday Park

ESSEX
MERSEA ISLAND
►►►►► Waldegraves Holiday Park

ST OSYTH
►►►► The Orchards Holiday Park

ISLE OF WIGHT
WHITECLIFF BAY
►►►►► Whitecliff Bay Holiday Park

LANCASHIRE
BLACKPOOL
►►►►► Marton Mere Holiday Village

LONGRIDGE
►►►► Beacon Fell View Holiday Park

LINCOLNSHIRE
CLEETHORPES
►►►►► Thorpe Park Holiday Centre

MABLETHORPE
►►►►► Golden Sands Holiday Park

MERSEYSIDE
SOUTHPORT
►►►►► Riverside Holiday Park

NORFOLK
BELTON
►►►► Wild Duck Holiday Park

CAISTER-ON-SEA
►►►►► Caister-on-Sea Holiday Park

HUNSTANTON
►►►►► Searles Leisure Resort

NORTHUMBERLAND
BERWICK-UPON-TWEED
►►►►► Haggerston Castle Holiday Park

SOMERSET
BREAN
►►►►► Holiday Resort Unity
►►►►► Warren Farm Holiday Centre

BURNHAM-ON-SEA
►►►►► Burnham-on-Sea Holiday Village

WEST SUSSEX
SELSEY
►►►► Warner Farm

EAST RIDING OF YORKSHIRE
FLAMBOROUGH
►►►►► Thornwick Bay Holiday Village

SKIPSEA
►►►►► Skirlington Leisure Park

TUNSTALL
►►►►► Sand le Mere Holiday Village

NORTH YORKSHIRE
FILEY
►►►► Blue Dolphin Holiday Park
►►►►► Flower of May Holiday Park
►►►► Primrose Valley Holiday Park
►►►► Reighton Sands Holiday Park

SCOTLAND

SOUTH AYRSHIRE
AYR
►►►►► Craig Tara Holiday Park

DUMFRIES & GALLOWAY
GATEHOUSE OF FLEET
►►►►► Auchenlarie Holiday Park

EAST LOTHIAN
LONGNIDDRY
►►►►► Seton Sands Holiday Village

WALES

DENBIGHSHIRE
PRESTATYN
►►►►► Presthaven Beach Holiday Park

GWYNEDD
PORTHMADOG
►►►►► Greenacres Holiday Park

PWLLHELI
►►►►► Hafan y Môr Holiday Park

PEMBROKESHIRE
TENBY
►►►►► Kiln Park Holiday Centre

SWANSEA
SWANSEA
►►►► Riverside Caravan Park

NORTHERN IRELAND

COUNTY ANTRIM
BALLYCASTLE
►►►► Causeway Coast Holiday Park

Adults only – no children parks

The following parks are children-free sites with facilities just for adults.

ENGLAND

CAMBRIDGESHIRE
DODDINGTON
Fields End Water Caravan Park & Fishery

GUYHIRN
Tall Trees Leisure Park

ST IVES
Stroud Hill Park

CHESHIRE
LOWER WITHINGTON
Welltrough Hall Farm Caravan Site

WETTENHALL
New Farm Caravan Park

WHITEGATE
Lamb Cottage Caravan Park

CORNWALL
CHACEWATER
Killiwerris Touring Park

MARAZION
Wayfarers Caravan & Camping Park

ROSE
Higher Hendra Park

CUMBRIA
CARLISLE
Green Acres Caravan Park

MEALSGATE
Larches Caravan Park

DEVON
BARNSTAPLE
Hallsdown Farm Touring Site

DREWSTEIGNTON
Woodland Springs Adult Touring Park

TORQUAY
Widdicombe Farm Touring Park

DORSET
HOLDITCH
Crafty Camping

SHAFTESBURY
Lower Liston Farm Touring Park

ST LEONARDS
Back of Beyond Touring Park

GLOUCESTERSHIRE
CHELTENHAM
Briarfields Motel & Touring Park

LANCASHIRE
BLACKPOOL
Manor House Caravan Park

ESPRICK
Charoland Farm

LEICESTERSHIRE
MELTON MOWBRAY
Eye Kettleby Lakes

LINCOLNSHIRE
BOSTON
Long Acres Touring Park
Orchard Park

CAISTOR
Caistor Lakes Leisure Park
Wolds View Touring Park

NORFOLK
NORTH WALSHAM
Two Mills Touring Park

STANHOE
The Rickels Caravan & Camping Park

SWAFFHAM
Breckland Meadows Touring Park

NORTHAMPTONSHIRE
BULWICK
New Lodge Farm Caravan &
   Camping Site

NOTTINGHAMSHIRE
SOUTHWELL
New Hall Farm Touring Park

OXFORDSHIRE
BURFORD
Wysdom Touring Park

SHROPSHIRE
SHREWSBURY
Beaconsfield Farm Caravan Park

TELFORD
Severn Gorge Park

WHEATHILL
Wheathill Touring Park

SOMERSET
BISHOP SUTTON
Bath Chew Valley Caravan Park

BRIDGETOWN
Exe Valley Caravan Site

GLASTONBURY
Old Oaks Touring & Glamping

HIGHBRIDGE
Greenacre Place Touring Caravan Park

SPARKFORD
Long Hazel Park

WELLS
Wells Touring Park

WIVELISCOMBE
Waterrow Touring Park

STAFFORDSHIRE
LONGNOR
Longnor Wood Holiday Park

SUFFOLK
HOLLESLEY
Run Cottage Touring Park

THEBERTON
Sycamore Park

WOODBRIDGE
Moat Barn Touring Caravan Park

WEST MIDLANDS
MERIDEN
Somers Wood Caravan Park

EAST RIDING OF YORKSHIRE
BRANDESBURTON
Blue Rose Caravan Country Park

NORTH YORKSHIRE
HARROGATE
Shaws Trailer Park

HELMSLEY
Foxholme Caravan Park

YORK
Rawcliffe Manor Caravan Park

WEST YORKSHIRE
BARDSEY
Glenfield Caravan Park

WALES

MONMOUTHSHIRE
ABERGAVENNY
Wernddu Caravan Park

POWYS
CHURCHSTOKE
Daisy Bank Caravan Park

CRICKHOWELL
Riverside Caravan & Camping Park

LLANIDLOES
Red Kite Touring Park

WREXHAM
OVERTON
The Trotting Mare Caravan Park

Glamping sites

These campsites offer one or more types of glamping accommodation, i.e. wooden pods, tipis, yurts, bell tents, safari tents, shepherd's huts, geo domes and vintage caravans.

ENGLAND

BERKSHIRE

FINCHAMPSTEAD
California Chalet & Touring Park

CHESHIRE

DELAMERE
Fishpool Farm Caravan Park

LOWER WITHINGTON
Welltrough Hall Farm Caravan Site

CORNWALL & ISLES OF SCILLY

BLISLAND
South Penquite Farm

BODMIN
Mena Farm

BRYHER (ISLES OF SCILLY)
Bryher Camp Site

BUDE
Willow Valley Holiday Park
Wooda Farm Holiday Park

CRANTOCK
Trevella Park

HAYLE
Atlantic Coast Holiday Park
St Ives Bay Holiday Park

HOLYWELL BAY
Trevornick

KILKHAMPTON
Upper Tamar Lake

NEWQUAY
Hendra Holiday Park
Porth Beach Holiday Park
Trenance Holiday Park

PERRANPORTH
Perran Sands Holiday Park
Tollgate Farm Caravan & Camping Park

POLZEATH
Gunvenna Holiday Park

PORTREATH
Tehidy Holiday Park

PORTSCATHO
Trewince Farm Touring Park

RUTHERNBRIDGE
Ruthern Valley Holidays

ST AUSTELL
Meadow Lakes Holiday Park

ST MARY'S (ISLES OF SCILLY)
Garrison Campsite

ST MERRYN
Tregavone Touring Park

TRURO
Summer Valley Touring Park

WADEBRIDGE
Lowarth Glamping

CUMBRIA

APPLEBY-IN-WESTMORLAND
Wild Rose Park

KESWICK
Castlerigg Hall Caravan & Camping Park

KIRKBY LONSDALE
Woodclose Caravan Park

MILNTHORPE
Hall More Caravan Park

NETHER WASDALE
Church Stile Farm & Holiday Park

PATTERDALE
Sykeside Camping & Caravan Park

PENRITH
Lowther Holiday Park

PENTON
Twin Willows

POOLEY BRIDGE
Waterfoot Caravan Park

SILLOTH
Stanwix Park Holiday Centre

WATERMILLOCK
The Quiet Site
Ullswater Holiday Park

WINDERMERE
Hill of Oaks & Blakeholme
Park Cliffe Camping & Caravan Estate

DERBYSHIRE

RIPLEY
Golden Valley Caravan & Camping Park

ROSLISTON
Beehive Woodland Lakes

DEVON

ASHILL
Leafy Fields Glamping

AXMINSTER
Andrewshayes Holiday Park

BERRYNARBOR
Mill Park Touring Caravan & Camping Park

CLAYHIDON
Kingsmead Centre Camping

CLYST ST MARY
Crealy Theme Park & Resort

COMBE MARTIN
Newberry Valley Park

CROYDE
Bay View Farm Caravan & Camping Park

DAWLISH
Lady's Mile Holiday Park

DREWSTEIGNTON
Woodland Springs Adult Touring Park

ILFRACOMBE
Hele Valley Holiday Park

KENTISBEARE
Forest Glade Holiday Park

KINGSBRIDGE
Parkland Caravan and Camping Site

PAIGNTON
Whitehill Country Park

SIDMOUTH
Oakdown Country Holiday Park

SOURTON CROSS
Bundu Camping & Caravan Park

TAVISTOCK
Harford Bridge Holiday Park
Langstone Manor Camping & Caravan Park
Woodovis Park

WOOLACOMBE
Woolacombe Bay Holiday Village & Spa

DORSET

BERE REGIS
Rowlands Wait Touring Park

BRIDPORT
Graston Copse Holiday Park
Highlands End Holiday Park

CHARMOUTH
Newlands Holidays

CHIDEOCK
Golden Cap Holiday Park

CORFE CASTLE
Woodyhyde Camp Site

FERNDOWN
St Leonards Farm Caravan &
    Camping Park

HOLDITCH
Crafty Camping

LYME REGIS
Shrubbery Touring Park

OWERMOIGNE
Sandyholme Holiday Park

POOLE
South Lytchett Manor Caravan &
    Camping Park

SHAFTESBURY
Dorset Country Holidays

ST LEONARDS
Back of Beyond Touring Park

SWANAGE
Herston Caravan & Camping Park
Ulwell Cottage Caravan Park

WAREHAM
East Creech Farm Campsite

WEYMOUTH
Seaview Holiday Park

WIMBORNE MINSTER
Charris Camping & Caravan Park

GLOUCESTERSHIRE

CHELTENHAM
Briarfields Motel & Touring Park

HAMPSHIRE

LINWOOD
Red Shoot Camping Park

HERTFORDSHIRE

HODDESDON
Lee Valley Caravan Park Dobbs Weir

ISLE OF WIGHT

BRIGHSTONE
Grange Farm

WHITECLIFF BAY
Whitecliff Bay Holiday Park

KENT

ASHFORD
Broadhembury Caravan & Camping Park

AYLESFORD
Kits Coty Glamping

MARDEN
Tanner Farm Touring Caravan &
    Camping Park

WHITSTABLE
Homing Park

LANCASHIRE

BOLTON LE SANDS
Bay View Holiday Park

CROSTON
Royal Umpire Caravan Park

FAR ARNSIDE
Hollins Farm Camping & Caravanning

SILVERDALE
Silverdale Caravan Park

THORNTON
Kneps Farm Holiday Caravan Park

LEICESTERSHIRE

MELTON MOWBRAY
Eye Kettleby Lakes

LINCOLNSHIRE

CAISTOR
Wolds View Touring Park

LANGWORTH
Barlings Country Holiday Park

TATTERSHALL
Tattershall Lakes Country Park

WOODHALL SPA
Woodhall Country Park

LONDON

LONDON E4
Lee Valley Campsite

LONDON N9
Lee Valley Camping & Caravan Park

MERSEYSIDE

SOUTHPORT
Riverside Holiday Park

NORFOLK

BELTON
Rose Farm Touring & Camping Park
Wild Duck Holiday Park

CROMER
Forest Park

HUNSTANTON
Searles Leisure Resort

KING'S LYNN
King's Lynn Caravan and Camping Park

NORTHAMPTONSHIRE

BULWICK
New Lodge Farm Caravan &
    Camping Site

NORTHUMBERLAND

BAMBURGH
Waren Caravan & Camping Park

BELFORD
South Meadows Caravan Park

BELLINGHAM
Bellingham Camping & Caravanning
    Club Site

BERWICK-UPON-TWEED
Ord House Country Park

HALTWHISTLE
Herding Hill Farm, Glamping site

NOTTINGHAMSHIRE

TEVERSAL
Teversal Camping & Caravanning
    Club Site

OXFORDSHIRE

FRINGFORD
Glebe Leisure

HENLEY-ON-THAMES
Swiss Farm Touring & Camping

SHROPSHIRE

MINSTERLEY
Old School Campsite

SHREWSBURY
Cartref Caravan & Camping

WEM
Lower Lacon Caravan Park

SOMERSET

BISHOP SUTTON
Bath Chew Valley Caravan Park

BREAN
Holiday Resort Unity

BURNHAM-ON-SEA
Burnham-on-Sea Holiday Village

COWSLIP GREEN
Brook Lodge Farm Camping &
    Caravan Park

DULVERTON
Wimbleball Lake

GLASTONBURY
Old Oaks Touring & Glamping

MARTOCK
Southfork Caravan Park

STAFFORDSHIRE

LONGNOR
Longnor Wood Holiday Park

Glamping sites *continued*

SUFFOLK

HOLLESLEY
Run Cottage Touring Park

WEST SUSSEX

BARNS GREEN
Sumners Ponds Fishery & Campsite

CHICHESTER
Concierge Glamping

WILTSHIRE

BERWICK ST JAMES
Stonehenge Campsite & Glamping Pods

LANDFORD
Greenhill Farm Caravan & Camping Park

EAST RIDING OF YORKSHIRE

BRANDESBURTON
Dacre Lakeside Park

SPROATLEY
Burton Constable Holiday Park &
    Arboretum

NORTH YORKSHIRE

ALLERSTON
Vale of Pickering Caravan Park

ALNE
Alders Caravan Park

CHOP GATE
Lordstones Country Park

FILEY
Flower of May Holiday Park

KIRKLINGTON
Camp Kátur

MASHAM
Old Station Holiday Park

NORTHALLERTON
Otterington Park

ROBIN HOOD'S BAY
Grouse Hill Caravan Park
Middlewood Farm Holiday Park

ROSEDALE ABBEY
Rosedale Abbey Caravan Park

THIRSK
Hillside Caravan Park

WYKEHAM
St Helens in the Park

CHANNEL ISLANDS

GUERNSEY

CASTEL
Fauxquets Valley Campsite

ST SAMPSON
Le Vaugrat Camp Site

VALE
La Bailloterie Camping

JERSEY

ST MARTIN
Rozel Camping Park

TRINITY
Durrell Wildlife Camp

ISLE OF MAN

KIRK MICHAEL
Glen Wyllin Campsite

SCOTLAND

ABERDEENSHIRE

MINTLAW
Aden Caravan and Camping Park

ARGYLL & BUTE

OBAN
Oban Caravan & Camping Park

SOUTH AYRSHIRE

BARRHILL
Barrhill Holiday Park

DUMFRIES & GALLOWAY

BRIGHOUSE BAY
Brighouse Bay Holiday Park

ECCLEFECHAN
Hoddom Castle Caravan Park

GATEHOUSE OF FLEET
Auchenlarie Holiday Park

KIRKCUDBRIGHT
Seaward Holiday Park

PALNACKIE
Barlochan Caravan Park

SANDYHILLS
Sandyhills Bay Holiday Park

WEST DUNBARTONSHIRE

BALLOCH
Lomond Woods Holiday Park

FIFE

ST ANDREWS
Cairnsmill Holiday Park
Craigtoun Meadows Holiday Park

HIGHLAND

ACHARACLE
Resipole Farm Holiday Park

AVIEMORE
Aviemore Glamping

DUROR
Achindarroch Touring Park

EVANTON
Black Rock Caravan Park

FORT WILLIAM
Glen Nevis Caravan & Camping Park

GLENCOE
Invercoe Caravan & Camping Park

EAST LOTHIAN

DUNBAR
Belhaven Bay Caravan & Camping Park

WEST LOTHIAN

EAST CALDER
Linwater Caravan Park

LINLITHGOW
Beecraigs Caravan & Camping Site

PERTH & KINROSS

BLAIR ATHOLL
Blair Castle Caravan Park

SCOTTISH BORDERS

PAXTON
Paxton House Caravan Park

PEEBLES
Crossburn Caravan Park

STIRLING

TYNDRUM
Strathfillan Wigwam Village

SCOTTISH ISLANDS

ISLE OF ARRAN

KILDONAN
Seal Shore Camping and Touring Site

KILMORY
Runach Arainn

ISLE OF SKYE

EDINBANE
Skye Camping & Caravanning Club Site

WALES

ISLE OF ANGLESEY

DWYRAN
LLanfair Hall

CARMARTHENSHIRE

LLANDDAROG
Carmarthen Caravan Park

GWYNEDD

ABERSOCH
Bryn Bach Caravan & Camping Site

BARMOUTH
Hendre Mynach Touring Caravan &
    Camping Park
Trawsdir Touring Caravans &
    Camping Park

CAERNARFON
Plas Gwyn Caravan & Camping Park
Riverside Camping

CRICCIETH
Eisteddfa

DINAS DINLLE
Dinlle Caravan Park

MONMOUTHSHIRE

LLANVAIR DISCOED
Penhein Glamping

PEMBROKESHIRE

FISHGUARD
Fishguard Bay Resort

HAVERFORDWEST
Nolton Cross Caravan Park

TENBY
Kiln Park Holiday Centre

POWYS

BUILTH WELLS
Fforest Fields Caravan & Camping Park

CHURCHSTOKE
Daisy Bank Caravan Park

LLANDRINDOD WELLS
Disserth Caravan & Camping Park

SWANSEA

PONTARDDULAIS
River View Touring Park

WREXHAM

BRONINGTON
The Little Yurt Meadow

EYTON
Plassey Holiday Park

Woodhall Country Spa, Lincolnshire

Island camping

The island locations listed in this guide may have different rules and regulations for caravanning and camping. If unsure, always call ahead of your trip to check.

CHANNEL ISLANDS

Tight controls are operated because of the narrow width of the mainly rural roads. On all of the islands tents can be hired on recognised campsites and some sites offer luxury glamping units. Early booking is strongly recommended during July and August.

Alderney

Neither caravans nor motorhomes are allowed, and campers must have a confirmed booking on the one official campsite before they arrive on the island.

Guernsey

Only islanders may own and use towed caravans, but a limited number of motorhomes are permitted on the island. The motorhome, used for overnight accommodation, must be not more than 9.45 metres long and 2.3 metres wide, must be booked into an authorised site (Fauxquets Valley Campsite, La Bailloterie or Le Vaugrat Camp Site) and a permit must be obtained from the site operator before embarking on a ferry for Guernsey – Condor Ferries will not accept motorhomes without this permit.

The permit must be displayed in the window at all times, motorhomes must return to the site each night, and permits are valid for a maximum of one month. Permission is not required to bring a trailer tent to the island. (See www.gov.gg).

Herm and Sark

These two small islands are traffic free. Herm has a small campsite for tents, and these can also be hired. Sark has two campsites. New arrivals are met from the boat by a tractor which carries people and luggage up the steep hill from the harbour. All travel is on foot, by bike, or by horse and cart.

Jersey

Visiting caravans and motorhomes (size restrictions apply) require a permit (maximum one month) that must be displayed at all times and they are restricted to one journey to, and one journey from, the campsite and the port. Bookings should be made through the chosen campsite and they will also arrange a permit. Caravans must remain on the designated campsites for the period of the permit. Motorhomes can travel around the island on a daily basis but must return to the designated campsite each night. For more details: www.gov.je/travel/informationadvice/travellers/pages/caravan.aspx

ISLE OF MAN

A permit may be required, and obtained in advance. For details see www.gov.im/categories/leisure-and-entertainment/camping/

ISLES OF SCILLY

Caravans and motorhomes are not allowed on the islands, and campers must stay at official sites. Booking is advisable on all sites, especially during school holidays.

SCOTLAND

For advice on wild camping in Scotland see the Scottish Outdoor Access Code website (www.outdooraccess-scotland.scot)

Arran, Coll, Islay and Mull

All have official campsites and welcome caravans, motorhomes and tents; wild camping is also permitted but access rights apply (check each island's website for details).

Skye

Caravans, motorhomes and tents are permitted and there are official campsites.

England

BERKSHIRE

FINCHAMPSTEAD
Map 5 SU76

Places to visit

West Green House Gardens, HARTLEY WINTNEY, RG27 8JB, 01252 844611
www.westgreenhouse.co.uk

Museum of English Rural Life, READING, RG1 5EX, 0118 378 8660
www.merl.org.uk

Great for kids: The Look Out Discovery Centre, BRACKNELL, RG12 7QW,
01344 354400, www.bracknell-forest.gov.uk/be

California Chalet & Touring Park

▶▶▶ 84%

tel: 0118 973 3928 & 07917 055444 **Nine Mile Ride RG40 4HU**
email: enquiries@californiapark.co.uk **web:** www.californiapark.co.uk
dir: *From A321 (south of Wokingham), right onto B3016 to Finchampstead. Follow Country Park signs on Nine Mile Ride.*

A simple, peaceful and well located woodland site with secluded pitches among the trees, adjacent to the country park. Several pitches occupy a prime position beside the lake with their own fishing area. The site has large hardstandings and the toilet block has quality vanity units and fully tiled showers. The sparsely planted trees allow sunshine onto pitches. Future investment plans remain very positive for this well located park.

Open: All year **Last arrival:** flexible **Last departure:** noon

Pitches: * 🚐 from £25; 🚐 from £25; ▲ from £20 🏠; 44 hardstanding pitches

Leisure: ⚠ 🎣

Facilities: 🛁 ☉ 🦱 ⛐ ⑤ ➿ WiFi

Services: 🔌 🗑 🧺 🛒 🔒 T

Within 3 miles: 🎣 ∪ ◎ 🎬

Additional site information: 5.5 acre site. 🐕 Cars can be parked by caravans and tents. Awnings permitted. No ground fires, no washing of caravans.

Glamping available: Wooden pods. **Changeover days:** Any day

Additional glamping information: Cars can be parked by pods

NEWBURY
Map 5 SU46

Places to visit

Highclere Castle & Gardens, HIGHCLERE, RG20 9RN, 01635 253210
www.highclerecastle.co.uk

Great for kids: The Living Rainforest, HAMPSTEAD NORREYS, RG18 0TN,
01635 202444, www.livingrainforest.org

Bishops Green Farm Camp Site
▶▶▶ 85%

tel: 01635 268365 **Bishops Green RG20 4JP**
web: www.bishopsgreenfarm.co.uk
dir: *Exit A339 (opposite New Greenham Park) towards Bishops Green and Ecchinswell. Site on left, approximately 0.5 mile by barn.*

A sheltered and secluded meadowland park close to the Hampshire–Berkshire border, offering very clean and well-maintained facilities, including a toilet block with a disabled/family room. There are woodland and riverside walks to be enjoyed around the farm, and coarse fishing is also available. The site is very convenient for visiting the nearby market town of Newbury with an attractive canal in the town centre.

Open: 1 April to 2nd week in October **Last arrival:** 20.00 **Last departure:** 11.30

Pitches: * 🚐 from £20; 🚐 from £20; ▲ from £20; 10 hardstanding pitches

Leisure: 🎣

Facilities: 🛁 ⚙ ⑤

Services: 🔌 🗑

Additional site information: 1.5 acre site. 🐕 2 dogs permitted per pitch. Cars can be parked by caravans and tents. Only 1 car can be parked by caravan. Awnings permitted. Quiet after 21.00. Visitors' charge applicable.

BRISTOL

See Cowslip Green (Somerset)

CAMBRIDGESHIRE

COMBERTON
Map 12 TL35

Places to visit

IWM Duxford, DUXFORD, CB22 4QR, 020 7416 5000
www.iwm.org.uk/visits/iwm-duxford

Chilford Hall Vineyard, LINTON, CB21 4LE, 01223 895600
www.chilfordhall.co.uk

Great for kids: Linton Zoo Conservation Park, LINTON, CB21 4NT, 01223 891308
www.lintonzoo.com

Highfield Farm Touring Park
▶▶▶▶ 92%

tel: 01223 262308 **Long Road CB23 7DG**
email: enquiries@highfieldfarmtouringpark.co.uk
web: www.highfieldfarmtouringpark.co.uk
dir: M11 junction 12, A603 (Sandy). 0.5 mile, right onto B1046 to Comberton.

Run by a very efficient and friendly family, the park is on a well-sheltered hilltop, with spacious pitches including a cosy backpackers' and cyclists' area, and separate sections for couples and families. Around the family farm there is a one and a half mile marked walk that has stunning views.

Open: April to October **Last arrival:** 20.00 **Last departure:** 14.00

Pitches: 🚐 🚌 ⋏; 52 hardstanding pitches

Facilities: 🖃 ☉ ℉ ⚒ ⑤

Services: 🔌 ⑤ ⇩ ⬥ ⊘ Ⓣ

Within 3 miles: ⅃ ℘ ↺

Additional site information: 8 acre site. 🖈 Maximum 2 dogs per pitch. Cars can be parked by caravans and tents. Awnings permitted. Postbox.

DODDINGTON

Places to visit

WWT Welney Wetland Centre, WELNEY, PE14 9TN, 01353 860711
www.wwt.org.uk/welney

Flag Fen Archaeology Park, PETERBOROUGH, PE6 7QJ, 01733 864468
www.vivacity-peterborough.com/museums-and-heritage/flag-fen

DODDINGTON
Map 12 TL49

Premier Park

Fields End Water Caravan Park & Fishery
▶▶▶▶▶ 92%

tel: 01354 740199 **Benwick Road PE15 0TY**
email: info@fieldsendfishing.co.uk **web:** www.fieldsendwater.co.uk
dir: Exit A141, follow signs to Doddington. At clock tower in Doddington turn right into Benwick Road. Site 1.5 miles on right after sharp bends.

This meticulously planned and executed park makes excellent use of its slightly elevated position in The Fens. The fully serviced pitches, all with very generous hardstandings, are on smart terraces with sweeping views of the countryside. The two toilet blocks contain several combined cubicle spaces, and there are shady walks through mature deciduous woodland adjacent to two large and appealingly landscaped fishing lakes. High quality pine lodges are available as holiday lets.

Open: All year (restricted service: seasonal café) **Last arrival:** 20.00 **Last departure:** noon

Pitches: 🚐 🚌 ⋏; 26 hardstanding pitches

Leisure: ℘ **Facilities:** 🖃 ☉ ℉ ⚒ ⅃ ⑤ ♨ WiFi

Services: 🔌 ⑤ ⥮ ⇩ Ⓣ

Within 3 miles: ⅃ ◎

Additional site information: 20 acre site. Adults only. 🖈 Cars can be parked by caravans and tents. Awnings permitted. No large groups.

GUYHIRN
Map 12 TF40

Places to visit

Peckover House & Garden, WISBECH, PE13 1JR, 01945 583463
www.nationaltrust.org.uk/peckover

WWT Welney Wetland Centre, WELNEY, PE14 9TN, 01353 860711
www.wwt.org.uk/welney

Tall Trees Leisure Park
▶▶▶▶ 77%

tel: 01945 450952 & 450131 **Gull Road PE13 4ER**
email: enquiries@talltreesleisurepark.co.uk **web:** www.talltreesleisurepark.co.uk
dir: A47 from Peterborough towards Wisbech. Left onto B1187 signed Guyhirn.

Tall Trees Leisure Park is a family-run caravan site set in 35 acres of a former commercial fruit farm. There are 59 electric pitches, each with its own water tap, set out in two perfectly level and maturely landscaped fields. There is also a separate, large rally field. Toilets are provided in well-maintained raised buildings and include a toilet and shower block; the reception also houses a small shop. Security is given high priority with an entrance barrier and CCTV. Please note, no tents are allowed on the park.

Open: All year **Last arrival:** 17.00 **Last departure:** noon

Pitches: * 🚐 from £16.50; 🚌 from £16.50; 6 seasonal pitches

Facilities: 🖃 ⚒ ⅃ ⑤ **Services:** 🔌 ⥮ ⬥ ⊘ Ⓣ

Within 3 miles: ℘ ⊟

Additional site information: 35 acre site. Adults only. 🖈 Cars can be parked by caravans. Awnings permitted.

HEMINGFORD ABBOTS Map 12 TL27

Places to visit

RSPB - Fen Drayton Lakes, SWAVESEY, CB24 4RB, 01954 233260
www.rspb.org.uk/reserves-and-events/reserves-a-z/fen-drayton-lakes

Houghton Mill, HOUGHTON, PE28 2AZ, 01480 301494
www.nationaltrust.org.uk/houghton-mill-and-waterclose-meadows

Great for kids: The Raptor Foundation, WOODHURST, PE28 3BT, 01487 741140
www.raptorfoundation.org.uk

Quiet Waters Caravan Park

►►► 83%

tel: 01480 463405 **PE28 9AJ**

email: quietwaters.park@btopenworld.com **web:** www.quietwaterscaravanpark.co.uk
dir: From A14 junction 25 (east of Huntingdon) follow Hemingford Abbots signs. Site in village centre.

This is an attractive little site on the banks of the Great Ouse that has been in the same family ownership for over 80 years. It is found in a really charming village just a mile from the A14, making an ideal centre from which to tour the Cambridgeshire area. There are fishing opportunities, rowing boats for hire and many walks and cycling routes directly from the park. There are holiday statics for hire.

Open: April to October **Last arrival:** 20.00 **Last departure:** noon

Pitches: 🚐 🚆 ▲; 18 hardstanding pitches

Leisure: ✎

Facilities: 🏠 ☺ 🗗 ✳ ⚴ WiFi

Services: 🖳 🗑 🔒 🖉

Within 3 miles: ⚲ ∪ 🛶 ⚲ 🖰 🖺

Additional site information: 1 acre site. 🐕 Dogs must be kept on leads at all times. Cars can be parked by caravans and tents. Awnings permitted. Boat mooring.

HUNTINGDON

Places to visit

Ramsey Abbey Gatehouse, RAMSEY, PE26 1DH, 01284 747500
www.nationaltrust.org.uk/ramsey-abbey-gatehouse

RSPB - Fen Drayton Lakes, SWAVESEY, CB24 4RB, 01954 233260
www.rspb.org.uk/reserves-and-events/reserves-a-z/fen-drayton-lakes

Great for kids: The Raptor Foundation, WOODHURST, PE28 3BT, 01487 741140
www.raptorfoundation.org.uk

HUNTINGDON   Map 12 TL27

Huntingdon Boathaven & Caravan Park
▶▶▶ 80%

tel: 01480 411977 **The Avenue, Godmanchester PE29 2AF**
email: info@huntingdonboathaven.co.uk **web:** www.huntingdonboathaven.co.uk
dir: *A14 junction 24, follow Godmanchester and Huntingdon signs onto B1044. Under A14, at mini-roundabout 2nd exit into Post Street. Just before A14 flyover bridge, left into site.*

A small, well laid out site overlooking a boat marina and the River Ouse, set close to the A14 and within walking distance of Huntingdon town centre. The toilets are clean and well kept. A pretty area beside the marina has been created for tents, with wide views across the Ouse Valley. Weekend family activities are organised throughout the season.

Open: All year (restricted service: Winter – open subject to weather conditions)
Last arrival: 21.00 **Last departure:** variable

Pitches: * 🚐 from £21; 🚌 from £21; 🛆 from £12; 18 hardstanding pitches; 12 seasonal pitches

Leisure: 🎣

Facilities: 🛒 ☉ 🅿 ⚒ ♿ 🎪 WiFi

Services: 🔌 🛒 🔒 🖉

Within 3 miles: 🏃 🚴 ⚡ 🎯 🛒

Additional site information: 2 acre site. 🐕 Dogs must be kept on leads at all times and owners must clear up after their dogs. Cars can be parked by caravans. Awnings permitted. Boat mooring and boat hire available.

ST IVES

Places to visit

The Farmland Museum and Denny Abbey, WATERBEACH, CB25 9PQ, 01223 860988
www.english-heritage.org.uk/visit/places/denny-abbey-and-the-farmland-museum

Oliver Cromwell's House, ELY, CB7 4HF, 01353 662062
www.olivercromwellshouse.co.uk

ST IVES   Map 12 TL37

Premier Park

Stroud Hill Park
▶▶▶▶▶ 93%

tel: 01487 741333 & 07831 119302 **Fen Road, Pidley PE28 3DE**
email: stroudhillpark@gmail.com **web:** www.stroudhillpark.co.uk
dir: *Exit B1040 in Pidley, follow signs for Lakeside Lodge Complex, into Fen Road, site on right in 0.75 mile.*

Stroud Hill Park is a superb, adults-only landscaped touring caravan site designed to a very high specification in Pidley. This premier site has been awarded many industry accolades in recognition of the high standard of the on-site facilities. At the heart of the site is a green oak-framed building which houses the reception, bar and restaurant (The Barn Restaurant) along with excellent toilets and showers. The facilities are built to be accessible to all. There are 60 pitches (44 hardstanding and 16 grass pitches), all with 16 amp electric hook-up, fresh water connection and grey water disposal, and large motorhomes can be accommodated. Coarse fishing, pay-as-you-go golf courses and ten-pin bowling are among the attractions nearby. Well-behaved dogs are welcome.

Open: All year **Last arrival:** 22.00 (arrival from 09.00) **Last departure:** 17.00

Pitches: * 🚐 from £25; 🚌 from £25; 🛆 from £19; 44 hardstanding pitches; 10 seasonal pitches

Leisure: 🏊 🎣   **Facilities:** 🛒 ☉ 🅿 ⚒ ♿ WiFi

Services: 🔌 🅾 🍴 🍽 🔒 🅃   **Within 3 miles:** 🏃 ⛳ ◎ 🚴 ⚡ 🎯 🛒

Additional site information: 6 acre site. Adults only. 🐕 Cars can be parked by caravans and tents. Awnings permitted. No late-stay fee. Car hire can be arranged.

See advert opposite

PITCHES: 🚐 Caravans 🚌 Motorhomes 🛆 Tents 🏠 Glamping accommodation **SERVICES:** 🔌 Electric hook-up 🅾 Launderette 🍸 Licensed bar 🔒 Calor Gas 🖉 Campingaz 🅃 Toilet fluid 🍽 Café/Restaurant 🍴 Fast Food/Takeaway ⚡ Battery charging ⚙ Motorhome service point
* 2019 prices 🚫 No credit or debit cards 🐕 Dogs permitted 🚫 No dogs

WISBECH | Map 12 TF40

Places to visit

Peckover House & Garden, WISBECH, PE13 1JR, 01945 583463
www.nationaltrust.org.uk/peckover

Great for kids: WWT Welney Wetland Centre, WELNEY, PE14 9TN, 01353 860711
www.wwt.org.uk/welney

Little Ranch Leisure

►►► 87%

tel: 01945 860066 **Begdale, Elm PE14 0AZ**
web: www.littleranchleisure.co.uk
dir: From roundabout on A47 (south-west of Wisbech), take Redmoor Lane to Begdale.

A friendly family site set in an apple orchard, with 25 fully serviced pitches and a beautifully designed, spacious toilet block. The site overlooks two fishing lakes and pitches are available by the water; the famous horticultural auctions at Wisbech are nearby.

Open: All year

Pitches: 🚐 🚃 ▲; 40 hardstanding pitches

Facilities: ☺ 🅿 ✳ ♿

Services: 🚮 🔲 ↯

Within 3 miles: 🎣 🛒 🛍

Additional site information: 10 acre site. 🐕 🐾 Cars can be parked by caravans and tents. Awnings permitted.

CHESHIRE

CODDINGTON | Map 15 SJ45

Places to visit

Cholmondeley Castle Gardens, CHOLMONDELEY, SY14 8AH, 01829 720383
www.cholmondeleycastle.com

Hack Green Secret Nuclear Bunker, NANTWICH, CW5 8AP, 01270 629219
www.hackgreen.co.uk

Great for kids: Dewa Roman Experience, CHESTER, CH1 1NL, 01244 343407
www.dewaromanexperience.co.uk

Chester Zoo, CHESTER, CH2 1EU, 01244 380280
www.chesterzoo.org

Premier Park

Manor Wood Country Caravan Park

►►►►► 92%

tel: 01829 782990 & 07762 817827 **Manor Wood CH3 9EN**
email: info@manorwoodcaravans.co.uk **web:** www.cheshire-caravan-sites.co.uk
dir: From A534 at Barton, turn opposite Cock O'Barton pub signed Coddington. Left in 100 yards. Site 0.5 mile on left.

A secluded landscaped park in a tranquil country setting with extensive views towards the Welsh Hills across the Cheshire Plain. The park offers fully serviced pitches, a heated outdoor swimming pool and all-weather tennis courts. The generous pitch density provides optimum privacy and the superb amenity block has excellent decor, underfloor heating and smart modern facilities with very good privacy options. Wildlife is encouraged and there is a fishing lake; country walks and nearby pubs are added attractions. A stylish, new combined reception, shop and café with patio overlooking the lake was opened for 2019 and an on-site hairdressing salon is an additional feature.

Open: All year (restricted service: October to March – swimming pool closed)
Last arrival: 19.00 **Last departure:** 11.00

Pitches: 🚐 🚃 ▲; 38 hardstanding pitches; 30 seasonal pitches

Leisure: 🏊 🅰 ♨ 🎱 🎣 ⊕

Facilities: 🛁 ☺ 🅿 ✳ ♿ 🎪 WiFi

Services: 🚮 🔲 ↯

Within 3 miles: 🛒 🛍

Additional site information: 8 acre site. 🐕 Awnings permitted. No noise after 23.00. Table tennis, pool table.

LEISURE: 🏊 Indoor swimming pool 🏊 Outdoor swimming pool 🅰 Children's playground 👶 Kids' club ♨ Tennis court 🎱 Games room 📺 Separate TV room 🏌 Golf course 🏌 Pitch n putt ⛵ Boats for hire 🚲 Bikes for hire 🎬 Cinema 🎵 Entertainment 🎣 Fishing ⊙ Mini golf 🏄 Watersports 🏋 Gym 🏐 Sports field ♘ Stables
FACILITIES: 🛁 Baths/Shower ☺ Electric shaver sockets 🅿 Hairdryer ✳ Ice Pack Facility 👶 Baby facilities ♿ Disabled facilities 🛍 Shop on site or within 200yds 🍖 BBQ area 🪑 Picnic area WiFi WiFi

Places to visit

Jodrell Bank Discovery Centre, JODRELL BANK, SK11 9DL, 01477 571766
www.jodrellbank.net

Little Moreton Hall, CONGLETON, CW12 4SD, 01260 272018
www.nationaltrust.org.uk/little-moreton-hall

Great for kids: Chester Zoo, CHESTER, CH2 1EU, 01244 380280
www.chesterzoo.org

Fishpool Farm Caravan Park
►►►► 86%

tel: 01606 883970 & 07501 506583 **Fishpool Road CW8 2HP**
email: enquiries@fishpoolfarmcaravanpark.co.uk
web: www.fishpoolfarmcaravanpark.co.uk
dir: *From A49 (Tarporley to Cuddington road), onto A54 signed Chester. At Fishpool Inn left onto B5152 (Fishpool Road). Site on right.*

Located within easy reach of many notable attractions and a short walk from The Fishpool Arms, this constantly improving park provides well spaced level pitches and a smart amenity block with good privacy options. A small clubhouse is open at busy times and there are many walking opportunities and children's activities include a good playground and woodland features for the little ones. A pod village offers seven well-equipped pods with en suite facilities and an adjacent private jacuzzi.

Open: 15 February to 15 January **Last arrival:** 19.00 **Last departure:** noon
Pitches: * 🚐 from £25; 🚐 from £26; ▲ from £25; 🏠 see price below;
14 hardstanding pitches
Leisure: 🎣 ▢ ⚽
Facilities: 🏠 ☺ 🅿 ❄ ♿ 🔥 🗂 WiFi
Services: 🔌 🔟 🔋
Within 3 miles: ⚓ 🎣 ∪ ◎ 🎿
Additional site information: 5.5 acre site. 🐕 Cars can be parked by caravans and tents. Awnings permitted. No noise after 23.00. Dog walks, play area.
Glamping available: Wooden pods from £80.
Additional glamping information: Jacuzzi available.

Places to visit

Capesthorne Hall, CAPESTHORNE, SK11 9JY, 01625 861221
www.capesthorne.com

Welltrough Hall Farm Caravan Site
►►► 83%

tel: 07734 605965 **SK11 9EF**
email: welltroughnick@gmail.com **web:** www.welltroughcaravansite.co.uk
dir: *Entrance on junction with Trap Street.*

Located in a stunning elevated lush grassed area on an arable and beef cattle farm on the outskirts of the peaceful hamlet of Lower Withington, this park offers lovely views of the countryside and nearby Jodrell Bank from the spacious fully serviced pitches. Shower and toilet facilities are housed in purpose built or portacabins and future plans include additional modern facilities. Although an adults-only site, a 3-acre dog walk and a hot and cold doggie wash are available, in addition to an on-site farm shop. For a unique glamping experience, there's a shepherd's hut with private hot tub and two pods, one with en suite facilities and a hot tub on decking, overlooking the surrounding countryside.

Open: All year **Last arrival:** 21.00 **Last departure:** noon
Pitches: 🚐 🚐; 🏠 see prices below; 17 hardstanding pitches
Facilities: 🏠 WiFi
Services: 🔌 🔟 🔋 🔧 🔒 ⌀
Within 3 miles: ⚓ 🎣 ∪ 🛒
Additional site information: 1.5 acre site. Adults only. 🐕 Cars can be parked by caravans. Awnings permitted. Inform site owner if friends or relatives are to visit. Own beef for sale.
Glamping available: Shepherd's hut with hot tub from £80; foxhole pod from £70; badger pod with hot tub from £90.
Additional glamping information: 2 night minimum stay. Wooden pod has en suite facility. Cars can be parked by units.

NORTHWICH — Map 15 SJ67

Places to visit

Arley Hall & Gardens, NORTHWICH, CW9 6NA, 01565 777353
www.arleyhallandgardens.com

Lion Salt Works, MARSTON, CW9 6ES, 01606 275066
www.lionsaltworks.westcheshiremuseums.co.uk

Belmont Camping
►►► 85%

tel: 01606 891235 & 07530 450019 **Belmont Hall, Great Budworth CW9 6HN**
email: belmontcamping@aol.com **web:** www.belmontcamping.co.uk
dir: *M56 junction 10, take A559 to Northwich. After 3 miles entrance at junction of A559 and Pole Lane (Note: for sat nav use post code CW9 6JA).*

Part of a former small country estate in Great Budworth, under five miles from Northwich, a long meandering drive with a fine display of mature trees and fishing lakes is the approach to the peaceful touring and camping areas. Pitch density is generous to enhance privacy, and all caravan and motorhomes have either hardstandings and electric hook-ups or full services to include waste water disposal. Well-equipped toilet and shower facilities are located within a former indoor horse training arena.

Open: All year **Last arrival:** by prior arrangement **Last departure:** by prior arrangement

Pitches: from £16; from £16; from £16; 15 hardstanding pitches

Leisure:

Facilities:

Services:

Within 3 miles:

Additional site information: 1 acre site. Cars can be parked by caravans and tents. Awnings permitted. No noise after 23.00, children must be supervised, no campfires. Nature walk.

SIDDINGTON — Map 15 SJ87

Places to visit

Capesthorne Hall, CAPESTHORNE, SK11 9JY, 01625 861221
www.capesthorne.com

Gawsworth Hall, GAWSWORTH, SK11 9RN, 01260 223456
www.gawsworthhall.com

Great for kids: Jodrell Bank Discovery Centre, JODRELL BANK, SK11 9DL, 01477 571766, www.jodrellbank.net

Capesthorne Hall
►►►► 88%

tel: 01625 861221 **Congleton Road SK11 9JY**
email: info@capesthorne.com **web:** www.capesthorne.com
dir: *Access to site from A34 between Congleton to Wilmslow. Phone site for detailed directions.*

Located within the grounds of the notable Jacobean Capesthorne Hall, this lush, all level site provides generously sized pitches, all with electricity and most with hardstandings. The Scandanavian-style amenity block has a smart, quality, modern interior and very good privacy levels. Guests also have the opportunity to visit the award-winning gardens on certain days and there are many extensive walking opportunities leading directly from the camping areas.

Open: March to October **Last arrival:** 22.00 **Last departure:** noon

Pitches: from £25; from £25; 30 hardstanding pitches

Facilities:

Services:

Within 3 miles:

Additional site information: 5 acre site. Cars can be parked by caravans. Awnings permitted. Minimum stay 3 nights on bank holiday weekends. No motorised scooters or skateboards. Gas BBQs only. Touring area may close if large events take place (contact site for details). Access to Capesthorne Hall and Gardens – additional cost for hall only.

WETTENHALL	Map 15 SJ66

Places to visit

Cholmondeley Castle Gardens, CHOLMONDELEY, SY14 8AH, 01829 720383
www.cholmondeleycastle.com

New Farm Caravan Park
▶▶▶ 88%

tel: 01270 528213 & 07970 221112 **Long Lane CW7 4DW**
email: info@newfarmcheshire.com **web:** www.newfarmcheshire.co.uk
dir: *M6 junction 16, A500 towards Nantwich, right onto Nantwich bypass (A51). At lights turn right, follow A51, Caster and Tarporely signs. After Calveley right into Long Lane, follow site sign. Site in 2 miles.*

Diversification at New Farm led to the development of four fishing lakes and the creation of a peaceful small touring park. The proprietors provide a very welcome touring destination within this peaceful part of Cheshire. Expect good landscaping, generous hardstanding pitches, a spotless toilet block, and good attention to detail throughout. Nearly all pitches are very spacious and fully serviced. Please note, there is no laundry.

Open: All year **Last arrival:** 20.00 (earliest arrival from 13.30) **Last departure:** 11.30

Pitches: 🚐 🚐; 23 hardstanding pitches; 10 seasonal pitches

Leisure: ✐

Facilities: 🚾 ☝ 🏓 WiFi

Services: ☺ 🛒 ↯

Within 3 miles: ↧ ∪ ≑ 🖫

Additional site information: 40 acre site. Adults only. 🐕 Maximum 2 dogs per pitch. Cars can be parked by caravans. Awnings permitted. No noise after 22.00.

WHITEGATE	Map 15 SJ66

Places to visit

Beeston Castle, BEESTON, CW6 9TX, 01829 260464
www.english-heritage.org.uk/visit/places/beeston-castle-and-woodland-park

Chester Cathedral, CHESTER, CH1 2HU, 01244 324756
www.chestercathedral.com

Premier Park

Lamb Cottage Caravan Park
▶▶▶▶▶ 93%

BestofBritish

tel: 01606 882302 **Dalefords Lane CW8 2BN**
email: info@lambcottage.co.uk **web:** www.lambcottage.co.uk
dir: *From A556 turn at Sandiway lights into Dalefords Lane, signed Winsford. Site 1 mile on right.*

A secluded and attractively landscaped adults-only park in a glorious location where the emphasis is on peace and relaxation. The serviced pitches are spacious with wide grass borders for sitting out and the high quality toilet block is spotlessly clean and immaculately maintained. A good central base for exploring this area, with access to nearby woodland walks and cycle trails.

Open: All year **Last arrival:** 20.00 **Last departure:** noon

Pitches: 🚐 🚐; 45 hardstanding pitches; 14 seasonal pitches

Facilities: 🚾 ☺ 🏓 ♿ WiFi

Services: ☺ 🛒 ↯

Within 3 miles: ↧ ✐ ∪ 🖫

Additional site information: 6 acre site. Adults only. 🐕 Cars can be parked by caravans. Awnings permitted. No tents (except trailer tents), no commercial vehicles.

PITCHES: 🚐 Caravans 🚐 Motorhomes 🛆 Tents 🏠 Glamping accommodation **SERVICES:** ☺ Electric hook-up 🖫 Launderette 🍷 Licensed bar
🔥 Calor Gas ⊘ Campingaz T Toilet fluid 🍽 Café/Restaurant 🍟 Fast Food/Takeaway 🔋 Battery charging ↯ Motorhome service point
* 2019 prices ⊘ No credit or debit cards 🐕 Dogs permitted ⊗ No dogs

Cornwall

It's not hard to see why thousands of tourists and holidaymakers flock to Cornwall every year. It has just about everything – wild moorland landscapes, glorious river valley scenery, picturesque villages and miles of breathtaking coastline. It has long been acknowledged as one of Britain's top holiday destinations.

Cornwall's southerly latitude and the influence of the Gulf Stream make the county the mildest and sunniest climate in Britain. It's not surprising therefore that one of its greatest and most popular pursuits is surfing. With more than 80 surfing spots, and plenty of sporting enthusiasts who make their way here to enjoy other similar coastal activities, such as wave-surfing, kite surfing and blokarting, the county is an internationally famous surfing hot spot. Blessed with wonderful surf beaches, Newquay is Cornwall's surfing capital. Nearby Watergate Bay is renowned for its glassy waves and Sennen, near Land's End, is where you might even get to surf with dolphins. Certainly the sea is strikingly blue here and the sands dazzlingly white.

A long-running TV series, filmed in a scenic location, is often a guaranteed way to boost tourism and that is certainly the case at Port Isaac on the north Cornwall coast. The village doubles as Portwenn in the drama *Doc Martin*, starring Martin Clunes as the irascible local GP. Much of Port Isaac has been used for location shooting over the years and it's quite common to bump into actors from the series at different points in the village when filming is taking place. Many films and TV series have been shot in Cornwall – including productions of Daphne du Maurier's *Jamaica Inn* and *Rebecca*, though the original version of the latter, made in 1940, was Alfred Hitchcock's first film in Hollywood and shot entirely in California.

In the book, the setting is a large house on the Cornish coast where the atmosphere is decidedly gothic. Daphne du Maurier modelled the house – which she called Manderley – and its location on the Menabilly estate, near Fowey. *Rebecca* was

published in 1938 and five years later the writer made Menabilly her home. The house is not open to the public, but it is possible to explore the setting for the story on foot, following a leafy path from the car park at Menabilly Barton Farm to Polridmouth Bay where there are two secluded and remote coves. A bird's eye view of the entire area is possible from the path to Gribben Head, though Menabilly, at the heart of the story, is hidden by trees, thus preserving the mystery of the book.

The Cornish coastline offers breathtakingly beautiful scenery. The north coast is open and exposed; the 735-ft High Cliff, between Boscastle and St Gennys, represents the highest sheer drop cliff in the county. The Lizard, at Cornwall's most southerly point, is a geological masterpiece of awesome cliffs, stacks and arches.

In recent years new or restored visitor attractions have helped to increase tourism in the region – Tim Smit has been the inspiration and driving force behind two of the county's most visited attractions. The Eden Project is famous for its giant geodesic domes housing exotic plants from different parts of the globe, while nearby the Lost Gardens of Heligan at Pentewan has impressive kitchen gardens and a wildlife hide.

Perhaps the last word on this magical corner of Britain should go to Daphne du Maurier. In her book *Vanishing Cornwall*, published in 1967, she wrote: 'A county known and loved in all its moods becomes woven into the pattern of life, something to be shared. As one who sought to know it long ago…in a quest for freedom, and later put down roots and found content, I have come a small way up the path. The beauty and the mystery beckon still.'

◁ Shipwreck near Land's End

CORNWALL & ISLES OF SCILLY

ASHTON   Map 2 SW62

Places to visit

Godolphin House, GODOLPHIN CROSS, TR13 9RE, 01736 763194
www.nationaltrust.org.uk/godolphin

Poldark Tin Mine and Gardens, TRENEAR, TR13 0ES, 01326 573173
www.poldarkmine.org.uk

Great for kids: Flambards, HELSTON, TR13 0QA, 01326 573404
www.flambards.co.uk

Boscrege Caravan & Camping Park
▶▶▶ 80%

tel: 01736 762231 **TR13 9TG**
email: enquiries@caravanparkcornwall.com web: www.caravanparkcornwall.com
dir: *A394 from Helston signed Penzance. In Ashton (Lion and Lamb pub on right) right
into Higher Lane, approximately 1.5 miles (thatched cottage on right) left at site sign.
(Note: for recommended towing route contact the park).*

A quiet and bright little touring park divided into small paddocks with hedges, that
offers plenty of open spaces for children to play in. This family-owned park has
clean, well-painted toilet facilities and neatly trimmed grass. By an Area of
Outstanding Natural Beauty at the foot of Tregonning Hill, this site makes an ideal
base for touring the southern tip of Cornwall; Penzance, Land's End, St Ives and the
beaches in between are all within easy reach.

Open: All year (restricted service: November to Easter – no caravans, motorhomes or
tents) **Last arrival:** 22.00 **Last departure:** 11.00

Pitches: 🚐 from £15; 🚐 from £15; ▲ from £15; 10 seasonal pitches

Leisure: 🛝 ⚽

Facilities: 🏠 ☺ 🗝 ☀ 🍴 🎴 WiFi

Services: 🔌 🗄 🚼 🔒 🗑 T

Within 3 miles: 🎣 🗝 ⛳ ◎ 🏄 🎯 🟊 $

Additional site information: 14 acre site. 🚗 Cars can be parked by caravans and tents.
Awnings permitted. No fires, no noise after 23.00, no groups. Microwave and freezer
available; fresh eggs available. Car hire can be arranged.

BLACKWATER

Places to visit

Royal Cornwall Museum, TRURO, TR1 2SJ, 01872 272205
www.royalcornwallmuseum.org.uk

East Pool Mine, POOL, TR15 3NP, 01209 315027
www.nationaltrust.org.uk/east-pool-mine

Great for kids: National Maritime Museum Cornwall, FALMOUTH, TR11 3QY,
01326 313388, www.nmmc.co.uk

BLACKWATER   Map 2 SW74

Trevarth Holiday Park
▶▶▶▶ 87%

tel: 01872 560266 **TR4 8HR**
email: trevarth@btconnect.com web: www.trevarth.co.uk
dir: *Exit A30 at Chiverton roundabout onto B3277 signed St Agnes. At next roundabout
follow Blackwater signs. Site on right in 200 metres.*

A neat and compact park with touring pitches laid out on attractive, well-screened
high ground adjacent to the A30 and A39 junction. This pleasant little park is
centrally located for touring, and is maintained to a very good standard. There is a
large grassed area for children to play on which is away from all tents.

Open: April to October **Last arrival:** 21.30 **Last departure:** 11.30

Pitches: * 🚐 from £15; 🚐 from £15; ▲ from £15; 16 hardstanding pitches;
8 seasonal pitches

Leisure: 🛝 🔍

Facilities: 🏠 ☺ 🗝 ☀ WiFi

Services: 🔌 🗄 🚼 ⬆ 🔒 🗑

Within 3 miles: 🗝 🏄 ⛳ $

Additional site information: 4 acre site. 🚗 Cars can be parked by caravans and tents.
Awnings permitted. No gazebos, no noise after 22.30.

BLISLAND   Map 2 SX17

Places to visit

Lanhydrock, LANHYDROCK, PL30 4AB, 01208 265950
www.nationaltrust.org.uk/lanhydrock

Tintagel Old Post Office, TINTAGEL, PL34 0DB, 01840 770024
www.nationaltrust.org.uk/tintagel-old-post-office

South Penquite Farm
▶▶▶ 87%

tel: 01208 850491 & 07494 864246 **South Penquite PL30 4LH**
email: camping@southpenquite.co.uk web: www.southpenquite.co.uk
dir: *From Exeter on A30 exit at 1st sign to St Breward on right, (from Bodmin 2nd sign on
left). Follow narrow road across Bodmin Moor. Ignore left and right turns until South
Penquite Farm Lane on right in 2 miles.*

This genuine 'back to nature' site is situated high on Bodmin Moor on a farm
committed to organic agriculture. As well as camping there are facilities for adults
and children to learn about conservation, organic farming and the local
environment, including a fascinating and informative farm trail (pick up a leaflet);
there is also a Geocaching trail. Toilet facilities are enhanced by a timber building
with quality showers and a good disabled facility. The site has designated areas
where fires may be lit. Organic home-reared lamb burgers and sausages are for
sale, and one field contains four Mongolian yurts, available for holiday let. In
addition, there is bunkhouse accommodation and one wooden pod adjoining.

Open: April to October **Last arrival:** dusk **Last departure:** 14.30

Pitches: 🚐 ▲ 🏠

Leisure: 🛝 🔍 🎣

Facilities: 🏠 ☺ ☀ 🎴

Services: 🗄

LEISURE: 🏊 Indoor swimming pool 🏊 Outdoor swimming pool 🛝 Children's playground 🖐 Kids' club 🎾 Tennis court 🔍 Games room ▭ Separate TV room
🏌 Golf course ⛳ Pitch n putt ⛵ Boats for hire 🚲 Bikes for hire 🎬 Cinema 🎵 Entertainment 🎣 Fishing ◎ Mini golf 🏄 Watersports 🏋 Gym 🏟 Sports field ⛺ Stables
FACILITIES: 🏠 Baths/Shower ☺ Electric shaver sockets 🗝 Hairdryer ☀ Ice Pack Facility 🚼 Baby facilities ♿ Disabled facilities $ Shop on site or within 200yds
🍴 BBQ area 🎴 Picnic area WiFi WiFi

Within 3 miles: ⚓ ↻ 🛒

Additional site information: 4 acre site. ⊗ Cars can be parked by tents. Awnings permitted. No caravans, no pets. Camp fires permitted.

Glamping available: Wooden pod, yurts. **Changeover days:** Any day

Additional glamping information: Yurts: 2 night minimum stay. Cars can be parked by units.

BODMIN	Map 2 SX06

Places to visit

Restormel Castle, RESTORMEL, PL22 0EE, 01208 872687
www.english-heritage.org.uk/visit/places/restormel-castle

Lanhydrock, LANHYDROCK, PL30 4AB, 01208 265950
www.nationaltrust.org.uk/lanhydrock

Great for kids: Eden Project, ST AUSTELL, PL24 2SG, 01726 811911
www.edenproject.com

Mena Farm

▶▶▶▶ 83%

tel: 01208 831845 **PL30 5HW**
email: enquiries@menafarm.co.uk **web:** www.menafarm.co.uk
dir: Exit A30 onto A389 (north) signed Lanivet and Wadebridge. In 0.5 mile 1st right, pass under A30. 1st left signed Lostwithiel and Fowey. In 0.25 mile right at top of hill. 0.5 mile, 1st right. Entrance 100 yards on right.

This grassy site is about four miles from the Eden Project and midway between the north and south Cornish coasts. Set in a secluded, elevated position with high hedges for shelter, it offers plenty of peace and quiet. There is a small coarse fishing lake on site, hardstanding pitches, a shop, and three bell tents are available for hire. The site is on the Saint's Way, and nearby is the neolithic hill fort of Helman Tor, the highest point on Bodmin Moor. Approximately one mile away is a fish and chip restaurant in Lanivet — and from this village, there is a bus service to Bodmin.

Open: All year **Last arrival:** 22.00 **Last departure:** noon

Pitches: 🚐 🚍 🅰 🏠; 3 hardstanding pitches

Leisure: 🎱 🎣 🏓 ⚽ 🎯
Facilities: 🏪 ☉ ℙ ✳ ♿ 🅂 🚿 🪑 📶
Services: 🔌 🅂 🏧 📦 ⚓ 🔋 🧺 🅃
Within 3 miles: ⚓ ↻ 🚴 🎿

Additional site information: 4 acre site. 🐕 No dangerous dogs. Cars can be parked by caravans and tents. Awnings permitted. No noise after 22.00. No generators. Nature trails, bike service. Car hire can be arranged.

Glamping available: 3 bell tents. **Changeover days:** Any day

Additional glamping information: Bell tents are fully equipped including bedding (sleeps 4). No dogs or pets. Cars can be parked by units.

BRYHER (ISLES OF SCILLY)	Map 2 SV81

Bryher Camp Site

▶▶▶ 87%

tel: 01720 422068 **TR23 0PR**
email: relax@bryhercampsite.co.uk **web:** www.bryhercampsite.co.uk
dir: Accessed from the mainland by ferry, plane or by boat from main island of St Mary's.

Set on the smallest inhabited Scilly Isle with spectacular scenery and white beaches, this tent-only site is in a sheltered valley surrounded by hedges. Pitches are located in paddocks at the northern end of the island which is only a short walk from the quay. There is a good, modern toilet block, and plenty of peace and quiet. Although located in a very quiet area, the Fraggle Rock Bar and a well-equipped shop are within easy reach. There is easy boat access to all the other islands.

Open: April to October

Pitches: 🅰 🏠

Facilities: 🏪 ☉ ℙ ✳ 🪑

Services: 🅂 📦 🔋 🧺

Within 3 miles: 🅂

Additional site information: 2.25 acre site. No pets.

Glamping available: Bell tents. **Changeover days:** Saturdays (July and August); any day April to June and September to October.

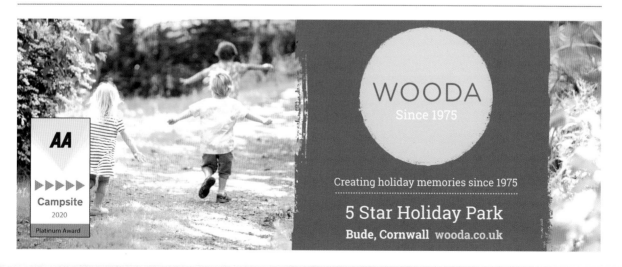

PITCHES: 🚐 Caravans 🚍 Motorhomes 🅰 Tents 🏠 Glamping accommodation **SERVICES:** 🔌 Electric hook-up 🅂 Launderette 🍺 Licensed bar 🔥 Calor Gas 🔥 Campingaz 🅃 Toilet fluid 🍽 Café/Restaurant 🍔 Fast Food/Takeaway 🔋 Battery charging ⚓ Motorhome service point * 2019 prices ⊘ No credit or debit cards 🐕 Dogs permitted ⊗ No dogs

BUDE — Map 2 SS20

See also Holsworthy (Devon)

Places to visit

Penhallam Manor, WEEK ST MARY, EX22 6XW,
www.english-heritage.org.uk/visit/places/penhallam-manor

Platinum Park

Wooda Farm Holiday Park

▶ ▶ ▶ ▶ ▶

tel: 01288 352069 **Poughill EX23 9HJ**
email: stay@wooda.co.uk web: www.wooda.co.uk
dir: *From A39 at Stratton follow Poughill and brown site signs into Stamford Hill. Approximately 1 mile to site on right. Avoid Stone Hill, which is unsuitable for towing vehicles/motorhomes.*

An attractive park set on raised ground overlooking Bude Bay, with lovely sea views. The park is divided into paddocks by hedges and mature trees, and offers high quality facilities in extensive colourful gardens. A variety of activities is provided by way of the large sports hall and hard tennis court, and there's a super children's playground. There are holiday static caravans for hire. An interactive information screen in the reception area is for customer use.

Open: April to early November (restricted service: April to May and mid September to early November — bar, takeaway and cocktail bar; shop reduced opening hours)
Last arrival: 20.00 **Last departure:** 10.30

Pitches: 🚐 from £23; 🚚 from £16; ⛺ from £16; 🏠 see prices below; 80 hardstanding pitches; 10 seasonal pitches
Leisure: 🎱 🏊 🎣 ▭ 🎿 ⛳ 🎯 ⚽
Facilities: 🚿 ☺ 🔥 ✳ ♿ 🅂 �ंडा 🚽 WiFi
Services: 🔌 🗑 🍴 🍱 🍺 🏧 ⚓ 🔥 🐕 Ⓣ
Within 3 miles: ∪ ◎ 🎿 🏕 🐴 🎠

Additional site information: 50 acre site. 🐕 Restrictions on certain dog breeds. Cars can be parked by caravans and tents. Awnings permitted. No skateboards, rollerblades or scooters. Woodland walks, nature trails, farmyard animals, beauty salon and art studio, cocktail bar, cycle trail, sports facilities.

Glamping available: Vintage caravan from £200 for 3 nights, eco lodges, cottages.
Changeover days: Friday and Monday

Additional glamping information: Vintage caravan: sleeps 2. Short breaks available (Friday to Monday; Monday to Friday; Friday to Friday). Cars can be parked by units.

See advert on page 63

Upper Lynstone Caravan Park

▶ ▶ ▶ ▶ 89%

tel: 01288 352017 **Lynstone EX23 0LP**
email: reception@upperlynstone.co.uk web: www.upperlynstone.co.uk
dir: *From Bude follow Widemouth Bay signs. Site 0.75 mile south of Bude on coastal road (Vicarage Road becomes Lynstone Road) on right.*

There are extensive views over Bude to be enjoyed from this quiet, sheltered family-run park, a terraced grass site suitable for all units. There's a spotlessly clean and top quality toilet block, plus a children's playground and a reception with a shop that sells basic food supplies and camping spares. Static caravans are available for holiday hire. A path leads directly to the coastal footpath with its stunning sea views, and the old Bude Canal is just a stroll away.

Open: April to October **Last arrival:** 21.00 **Last departure:** 10.00
Pitches: 🚐 🚚 ⛺; 8 hardstanding pitches
Leisure: 🎱
Facilities: 🚿 ☺ 🔥 ✳ ♿ 🅂 🚽 WiFi
Services: 🔌 🗑 🏧 🔥 🐕 Ⓣ
Within 3 miles: 🎣 ⛳ ∪ ◎ 🎿 🏕 🐴 🎠

Additional site information: 6 acre site. 🐕 Cars can be parked by caravans and tents. Awnings permitted. No groups. Family bathroom.

Willow Valley Holiday Park

▶ ▶ ▶ ▶ 87%

tel: 01288 353104 **Bush EX23 9LB**
email: willowvalley@talk21.com web: www.willowvalley.co.uk
dir: *On A39, 0.5 mile north of junction with A3072 at Stratton.*

A small sheltered park in the Strat Valley with level grassy pitches and a stream running through it. All areas of this attractive park have been improved, including a smart toilet block and an excellent reception and shop. The park has direct access from the A39, and is only two miles from the sandy beaches at Bude. There are four pine lodges for holiday hire.

Open: All year **Last arrival:** 21.00 **Last departure:** 11.00
Pitches: 🚐 🚚 ⛺ 🏠; 8 hardstanding pitches

Leisure: ⚒

Facilities: ⊙ ℙ ✳ ⚷ 🖫 ♨ ⊓ WiFi

Services: ⊕ 🗗 🕅 ⊞ ⚏ T

Within 3 miles: ⚓ ♪ ∪ ◎ ⚐ ✦

Additional site information: 11 acre site. 🐕 Cars can be parked by caravans and tents. Awnings permitted.

Glamping available: Bell tents

Additional glamping information: Bell tents have double beds, 2 air beds.

CAMELFORD Map 2 SX18

Places to visit

Tintagel Castle, TINTAGEL, PL34 0HE, 01840 770328
www.english-heritage.org.uk/visit/places/tintagel-castle

Tintagel Old Post Office, TINTAGEL, PL34 0DB, 01840 770024
www.nationaltrust.org.uk/tintagel-old-post-office

Lakefield Caravan Park
▶▶▶ 82%

tel: 01840 213279 **Lower Pendavey Farm PL32 9TX**
email: lakefieldequestriancentre@btconnect.com **web:** www.lakefieldcaravanpark.co.uk
dir: From A39 in Camelford onto B3266, right at T-junction, site 1.5 miles on left.

Set in a rural location, this friendly park is part of a specialist equestrian centre, and offers good quality services. All the facilities are immaculate and spotlessly clean. Riding lessons and hacks are always available, with a BHS qualified instructor. Newquay, Padstow and Bude are all easily accessed from this site.

Open: Easter or April to October **Last arrival:** 22.00 **Last departure:** 11.00

Pitches: ⊞ ⇋ Å

Leisure: ✪

Facilities: ⊙ ℙ ✳

Services: ⊕ 🕅 ⚏ 🔒 ⊘ T

Within 3 miles: ⚓ ♪ ∪ ⚐ 🖫

Additional site information: 5 acre site. 🐕 Cars can be parked by caravans and tents. Awnings permitted. On-site lake.

CARLYON BAY

Places to visit

The Shipwreck and Heritage Centre, ST AUSTELL, PL25 3NX, 01726 69897
www.shipwreckcharlestown.com

The Lost Gardens of Heligan, PENTEWAN, PL26 6EN, 01726 845100
www.heligan.com

Great for kids: Wheal Martyn, ST AUSTELL, PL26 8XG, 01726 850362
www.wheal-martyn.com

Eden Project, ST AUSTELL, PL24 2SG, 01726 811911
www.edenproject.com

CARLYON BAY Map 2 SX05

Platinum Park

Carlyon Bay Caravan & Camping Park
▶▶▶▶▶

tel: 01726 812735 **Bethesda, Cypress Avenue PL25 3RE**
email: holidays@carlyonbay.net **web:** www.carlyonbay.net
dir: Exit A390 west of St Blazey, left onto A3092 for Par, right in 0.5 mile. Cypress Avenue to Carlyon Bay.

An attractive, secluded site set amongst a belt of trees with background woodland. The spacious grassy park is beautifully landscaped and offers quality toilet and shower facilities and plenty of on-site attractions, including a well-equipped games room, TV room, an inviting swimming pool, and occasional family entertainment. It is less than half a mile from a sandy beach and the Eden Project is approximately two miles away.

Open: Easter to late September (restricted service: Easter to mid May and mid to end September – swimming pool, takeaway and shop closed) **Last arrival:** 21.00 **Last departure:** 11.00

Pitches: ⊞ ⇋ Å; 12 hardstanding pitches **Leisure:** ⬚ ⚒ ♣ ⬚ 🎵 ✪

Facilities: ⊙ ℙ ✳ ⚷ 🖫 ♨ WiFi **Services:** ⊕ 🗗 ⚏ ⚏ ⫯ 🔒 ⊘ T

Within 3 miles: ⚓ ♪ ∪ ◎ ⚐ ✦ 🐕

Additional site information: 35 acre site. 🐕 Cars can be parked by caravans and tents. Awnings permitted. No noise after 23.00, no hoverboards or motorised scooters (except invalid mobility scooters). Crazy golf. Children's entertainment July to August only.

See advert on page 66

CARNHELL GREEN
Map 2 SW63

Places to visit

Godolphin House, GODOLPHIN CROSS, TR13 9RE, 01736 763194
www.nationaltrust.org.uk/godolphin

St Michael's Mount, MARAZION, TR17 0HS, 01736 710265
www.stmichaelsmount.co.uk

Great for kids: RSPB Marazion Marsh, MARAZION, TR17 0AA, 01736 360624
www.rspb.org.uk/reserves-and-events/reserves-a-z/marazion-marsh

Lavender Fields Touring Park
►►►► 83%

tel: 01209 832188 & 07855 227773 **Penhale Road TR14 0LU**
email: info@lavenderfieldstouring.co.uk **web:** www.lavenderfieldstouring.co.uk
dir: *Exit A30 at Camborne West junction. At top of slip road left at roundabout, 2nd exit, through Roseworthy, left after Roseworthy signed Carnhell Green, over level crossing to T-junction, turn left. Site 750 yards on right.*

A family owned and run park in the heart of the Cornish countryside on the outskirts of the idyllic village of Carnhell Green, yet only a short car or bus ride to towns and glorious golden beaches. Developed on an old mine waste site, the park is maturing well, with lush grass and neat and tidy pitches, and has a smart toilet block and some good hardstandings for larger units. There are wonderful countryside views to the south which gives this site a pleasant open feel. A kettle in the dishwash area is provided for campers' use. Dogs are very welcome to accompany their owners and can stay free of charge.

Open: All year **Last arrival:** 20.00 **Last departure:** 10.00
Pitches: 🚐 from £12.50; 🚎 from £12.50; ▲ from £10; 21 hardstanding pitches; 5 seasonal pitches
Leisure: ⚠ **Facilities:** 🛁 ☉ ℱ ☀ ✦ ⑤ 🍴 ☖
Services: 🔌 🗑 ⬆ 🔒
Within 3 miles: ↨ ✎ ∪ ◎ ≋ ≟ 日

Additional site information: 6 acre site. ➤ Cars can be parked by caravans and tents. Awnings permitted.

CHACEWATER
Map 2 SW74

Places to visit

Royal Cornwall Museum, TRURO, TR1 2SJ, 01872 272205
www.royalcornwallmuseum.org.uk

Trelissick, TRELISSICK, TR3 6QL, 01872 862090
www.nationaltrust.org.uk/trelissick

Killiwerris Touring Park
►►►► 85%

tel: 01872 561356 & 07734 053593 **Penstraze TR4 8PF**
email: killiwerris@aol.com **web:** www.killiwerris.co.uk
dir: *Take A30 towards Penzance, at Chiverton Cross roundabout take 3rd exit signed St Agnes. At next mini-roundabout take Blackwater exit, in 500 yards left into Kea Downs Road, park 1 mile on right.*

A small, adults-only, family-run touring park, just five miles from Truro and four miles from the coastal village of St Agnes, making it an ideal base for exploring west Cornwall. The site has a sunny aspect yet is sheltered by mature trees giving it a very private feel. The facilities are of an exceptionally high standard and include a modern and smart amenity block. It is a peaceful spot in which to relax and get away from the crowds.

Open: All year **Last arrival:** 21.00 **Last departure:** 11.00
Pitches: 🚐 🚎; 17 hardstanding pitches
Facilities: 🛁 ☉ ℱ ☀ ✦ ⑤
Services: 🔌 🗑
Within 3 miles: ↨ ✎ ∪ 日

Additional site information: 2.2 acre site. Adults only. ➤ Cars can be parked by caravans. Awnings permitted. Car hire can be arranged.

LEISURE: 🏊 Indoor swimming pool 🏊 Outdoor swimming pool ⚠ Children's playground 👐 Kids' club 🎾 Tennis court 🎱 Games room 📺 Separate TV room
↨ Golf course ⛳ Pitch n putt ⛵ Boats for hire 🚲 Bikes for hire 🎬 Cinema 🎵 Entertainment ✎ Fishing ◎ Mini golf 🏄 Watersports 🏋 Gym 🏟 Sports field ∪ Stables
FACILITIES: 🛁 Baths/Shower ☉ Electric shaver sockets ℱ Hairdryer ☀ Ice Pack Facility 🍼 Baby facilities ✦ Disabled facilities ⑤ Shop on site or within 200yds
🍴 BBQ area 🪑 Picnic area 📶 WiFi

COVERACK   Map 2 SW71

Places to visit

Great for kids: Cornish Seal Sanctuary, GWEEK, TR12 6UG, 01326 221361
www.visitsealife.com/gweek

Flambards, HELSTON, TR13 0QA, 01326 573404
www.flambards.co.uk

Little Trevothan Caravan & Camping Park
►►►► 85%

tel: 01326 280260 **Trevothan TR12 6SD**
email: holidays@littletrevothan.co.uk **web:** www.littletrevothan.co.uk
dir: *A3083 onto B3293 signed Coverack, approximately 2 miles after Goonhilly Earth Station, right at petrol station onto unclassified road. Approximately 1 mile, turn 3rd left. Site 0.5 mile on left.*

A secluded site, with excellent facilities, near the unspoilt fishing village of Coverack, with a large recreation area and good play equipment for children. Ongoing investment includes an excellent refurbished amenity block and new roadways. The nearby sandy beach has lots of rock pools for children to play in, and the many walks starting from both the park and the village offer stunning scenery.

Open: March to October **Last arrival:** 21.00 **Last departure:** 11.00

Pitches: 🚐 from £14.50; 🚌 from £14.50; ▲ from £14.50; 14 hardstanding pitches; 18 seasonal pitches

Leisure: 🛝 🎣 🛏 ⚽

Facilities: 🖼 ☺ ℙ ⚒ ⚐ 🖻 🖬 WiFi

Services: 🔌 🔲 🎱 🛒 🧴 📭 T

Within 3 miles: ℘ ⛵

Additional site information: 10.5 acre site. 🐕 Cars can be parked by caravans and tents. Awnings permitted. Quiet time between 22.00–08.00. Large playing field with children's play area.

CRANTOCK (NEAR NEWQUAY)

Places to visit

Trerice, TRERICE, TR8 4PG, 01637 875404
www.nationaltrust.org.uk/trerice

CRANTOCK (NEAR NEWQUAY)   Map 2 SW76

Platinum Park

Trevella Park
►►►►►

tel: 01637 830308 **TR8 5EW**
email: holidays@trevella.co.uk **web:** www.trevella.co.uk
dir: *Between Crantock and A3075.*

A well established and very well-run family site, with outstanding floral displays. Set in a rural area close to Newquay, this stunning park boasts three teeming fishing lakes for both the experienced and novice angler, and a superb outdoor swimming pool and paddling area. The spotlessly clean toilet facilities include excellent en suite wet rooms. All areas are neat and clean and the whole park looks stunning. Canvas geodomes, fully equipped ready-erected tents and safari tents are available for hire.

Open: 27 March to 30 October (restricted service: Easter to mid May and mid September to October – pool closed) **Last arrival:** 21.00 **Last departure:** 10.00

Pitches: 🚐 from £23.40; 🚌 from £23.40; ▲ from £14.40; 🏠 see prices below; 60 hardstanding pitches; 12 seasonal pitches

Leisure: 🏊 🛝 🎣 ℘

Facilities: 🖼 ☺ ℙ ⚒ ⚐ 🖻 🖬 ⌐ 🛒 WiFi

Services: 🔌 🔲 🎱 🍺 🛒 🧴 📭 T

Within 3 miles: ⛳ ⛵ ↻ ◎ ⛵ ⛵ ⛳

Additional site information: 60 acre site. 🐕 Cars can be parked by caravans and tents. Awnings permitted. Families and couples only – under 21's conditions apply, (please check). Crazy golf, children's ranger activities, 3 children's play areas, games room, nature trail. Fresh croissants and pasties available.

Glamping available: Safari tents from £57; geo domes from £69; safari lodges from £88; safari en suite tents from £81. **Changeover days:** Monday, Friday and Saturday

Additional glamping information: Geo domes have hot tubs. Cars can be parked by units.

Treago Farm Caravan Site
►►►► 89%

tel: 01637 830277 **TR8 5QS**
email: info@treagofarm.co.uk **web:** www.treagofarm.co.uk
dir: *From A3075 (west of Newquay) follow Crantock signs. Site signed beyond village.*

A grass site in open farmland in a south-facing sheltered valley with a fishing lake. This friendly family park has spotless toilet facilities, which include three excellent heated family rooms, a good shop and bar with takeaway food, and it has direct access to Crantock and Polly Joke beaches, National Trust land and many natural beauty spots.

Open: April to early October (restricted service: mid May, mid September to October – reduced hours in shop and bar) **Last arrival:** 22.00 **Last departure:** 18.00

Pitches: 🚐 🚌 ▲   **Leisure:** 🎣 🛏

Facilities: 🖼 ☺ ℙ ⚒ 🖻 🖬 ⌐

Services: 🔌 🔲 🎱 🍺 🛒 🧴 📭 T

Within 3 miles: ⛳ ℘ ↻ ◎ ⛵ ⛳

Additional site information: 5 acre site. 🐕 Cars can be parked by caravans and tents. Awnings permitted.

PITCHES: 🚐 Caravans 🚌 Motorhomes ▲ Tents 🏠 Glamping accommodation **SERVICES:** 🔌 Electric hook-up 🔲 Launderette 🍺 Licensed bar 🖿 Calor Gas 🧴 Campingaz T Toilet fluid 🍴 Café/Restaurant 🍟 Fast Food/Takeaway 🛒 Battery charging 📭 Motorhome service point * 2019 prices 🚫 No credit or debit cards 🐕 Dogs permitted 🚫 No dogs

CRANTOCK (NEAR NEWQUAY) *continued*

Quarryfield Holiday Park
▶▶▶ 85%

tel: 01637 872792 & 830338 **TR8 5RJ**
email: info@quarryfield.co.uk **web:** www.quarryfield.co.uk
dir: *From A3075 (Newquay to Redruth road) follow Crantock signs. Site signed.*

This park has a private path down to the dunes and golden sands of Crantock Beach, about 10 minutes away, and it is within easy reach of all that Newquay has to offer, particularly for families. The park has very modern facilities, and provides plenty of amenities including a great swimming pool.

Open: Easter to October **Last arrival:** 23.00 **Last departure:** 10.00

Pitches: * 🚐 from £14; 🚌 from £14; ▲ from £14; 33 seasonal pitches

Leisure: ⚡ 🛝 🔍

Facilities: 🚿 ☉ 🖅 ✳ ♿ ⑤ 🚻 🍴 WiFi

Services: 🔌 ⑥ 🚽 🍴 ♨ ⏚ 🛒 🔌 ∅

Within 3 miles: ⚓ 🎣 ∪ ◎ 🦅 🍴 📅

Additional site information: 10 acre site. 🐕 Cars can be parked by caravans and tents. Awnings permitted. No campfires, quiet after 22.30.

CUBERT
Map 2 SW75

Places to visit
Trerice, TRERICE, TR8 4PG, 01637 875404
www.nationaltrust.org.uk/trerice

Great for kids: Dairy Land Farm World, NEWQUAY, TR8 5AA, 01872 510246
www.dairylandfarmworld.com

Cottage Farm Touring Park
▶▶▶▶ 84%

tel: 01637 831083 **Treworgans TR8 5HH**
email: contact@cottagefarmpark.co.uk **web:** www.cottagefarmpark.co.uk
dir: *From A392 towards Newquay, left onto A3075 towards Redruth. In 2 miles right signed Cubert, right again in 1.5 miles signed Crantock, left in 0.5 mile.*

A small grassy touring park situated in the tiny hamlet of Treworgans, in sheltered open countryside close to a lovely beach at Holywell Bay. This quiet family-run park boasts very good quality facilities including a fenced playground for children, with a climbing frame, swings, slides etc.

Open: April to September **Last arrival:** 22.30 **Last departure:** noon

Pitches: 🚐 🚌 ▲; 2 hardstanding pitches

Leisure: 🛝

Facilities: 🚿 ☉ 🖅 ✳ ♿

Services: 🔌 ⑥ 🛒

Within 3 miles: ⚓ 🎣 ∪ ◎ 🦅 🍴 📅 ⑤

Additional site information: 2 acre site. 🐕 Cars can be parked by caravans and tents. Awnings permitted. No noise after 23.00.

FALMOUTH
Map 2 SW83

Places to visit
Pendennis Castle, FALMOUTH, TR11 4LP, 01326 316594
www.english-heritage.org.uk/visit/places/pendennis-castle

Trebah Garden, MAWNAN SMITH, TR11 5JZ, 01326 252200
www.trebah-garden.co.uk

Great for kids: National Maritime Museum Cornwall, FALMOUTH, TR11 3QY, 01326 313388, www.nmmc.co.uk

---

Tregedna Farm Touring Caravan & Tent Park
▶▶▶ 82%

tel: 01326 250529 **Maenporth TR11 5HL**
email: enquiries@tregednafarmholidays.co.uk **web:** www.tregednafarmholidays.co.uk
dir: *Take A39 from Truro to Falmouth. Turn right at Hill Head roundabout. Site 2.5 miles on right.*

Set in the picturesque Maen Valley, this gently-sloping, south-facing park is part of a 100-acre farm. It is surrounded by beautiful wooded countryside just minutes from the beach, and has spacious pitches and well-kept facilities.

Open: April to September **Last arrival:** 22.00 **Last departure:** 13.00

Pitches: * 🚐 from £18; 🚌 from £18; ▲ from £18; 6 hardstanding pitches

Leisure: 🛝

Facilities: 🚿 ☉ ✳

Services: 🔌 ⑥

Within 3 miles: ⚓ 🎣 ◎ 🦅 🍴 📅 ⑤

Additional site information: 12 acre site. 🐕 🐾 1 dog only per pitch. Cars can be parked by caravans and tents. Awnings permitted. No open fires. Boat storage.

GORRAN

Places to visit
The Lost Gardens of Heligan, PENTEWAN, PL26 6EN, 01726 845100
www.heligan.com

Caerhays Castle Gardens, GORRAN, PL26 6LY, 01872 501310
www.caerhays.co.uk

Great for kids: Wheal Martyn, ST AUSTELL, PL26 8XG, 01726 850362
www.wheal-martyn.com

Eden Project, ST AUSTELL, PL24 2SG, 01726 811911
www.edenproject.com

LEISURE: 🏊 Indoor swimming pool ⚡ Outdoor swimming pool 🛝 Children's playground 🪁 Kids' club 🎾 Tennis court 🔍 Games room 📺 Separate TV room ⚓ Golf course 🏌 Pitch n putt 🚣 Boats for hire 🚲 Bikes for hire 🎬 Cinema 🎵 Entertainment 🎣 Fishing ◎ Mini golf 🏄 Watersports 🏋 Gym 🏟 Sports field ∪ Stables
FACILITIES: 🚿 Baths/Shower ☉ Electric shaver sockets 🖅 Hairdryer ✳ Ice Pack Facility 🍼 Baby facilities ♿ Disabled facilities ⑤ Shop on site or within 200yds 🍴 BBQ area 🍴 Picnic area WiFi WiFi

GORRAN
Map 2 SW94

Treveor Farm Campsite
▶▶▶ 86%

tel: 01726 842387 **PL26 6LW**

email: info@treveorfarm.co.uk **web:** www.treveorfarm.co.uk

dir: *From St Austell bypass left onto B3273 for Mevagissey. On hilltop before descent to village turn right onto unclassified road for Gorran. Right in 5 miles, site on right.*

A small family-run camping park set on a working farm, with grassy pitches backing onto mature hedging. This quiet site, with good facilities, is close to beaches and offers a large coarse fishing lake.

Open: April to October **Last arrival:** 21.00 **Last departure:** 11.00

Pitches: 🚐 🚐 🅰; 12 hardstanding pitches

Leisure: 🏴

Facilities: 🛁 ⊙ 🍳 ✳ 📶

Services: 🔌 🔲

Within 3 miles: 🛬 🏧

Additional site information: 4 acre site. 🐕 Cars can be parked by caravans and tents. Awnings permitted.

Treveague Farm Caravan & Camping Site
▶▶▶ 84%

tel: 01726 842295 **PL26 6NY**

email: treveaguefarmcampsite@outlook.com **web:** www.treveaguefarm.co.uk

dir: *B3273 from St Austell towards Mevagissey, pass Pentewan at top of hill, right signed Gorran. Past Heligan Gardens towards Gorran Churchtown. Follow brown tourist signs from fork in road. (Note: roads to site are single lane and very narrow. It is advisable to follow these directions and not sat nav).*

Spectacular panoramic coastal views can be enjoyed from this rural park, which is set on an organic farm and well equipped with modern facilities. A stone-faced toilet block with a Cornish slate roof is an attractive feature, as is the building that houses the smart reception, café and shop, which sells meat produced on the farm. There is an aviary with exotic birds, and also chinchillas are kept. A footpath leads to the fishing village of Gorran Haven in one direction, and the secluded sandy Vault Beach in the other. The site is close to a bus route.

Open: April to September **Last arrival:** 21.00 **Last departure:** 11.00

Pitches: 🚐 🚐 🅰

Leisure: 🏴 ⚽

Facilities: 🛁 ⊙ 🍳 ✳ ♿ 🏧 🏷

Services: 🔌 🔲 🍽 🍴 🚮 🔋

Within 3 miles: 🛬 🏊 🛬

Additional site information: 4 acre site. 🐕 Cars can be parked by caravans and tents. Awnings permitted. Fire pits available to hire. Bird and animal hide. Fresh croissants and baguettes available.

GORRAN HAVEN
Map 2 SX04

Places to visit

Caerhays Castle Gardens, GORRAN, PL26 6LY, 01872 501310
www.caerhays.co.uk

The Lost Gardens of Heligan, PENTEWAN, PL26 6EN, 01726 845100
www.heligan.com

Great for kids: Wheal Martyn, ST AUSTELL, PL26 8XG, 01726 850362
www.wheal-martyn.com

Eden Project, ST AUSTELL, PL24 2SG, 01726 811911
www.edenproject.com

Trelispen Caravan & Camping Park
▶ 75%

tel: 01726 843501 **PL26 6NT**

email: trelispen@care4free.net **web:** www.trelispen.co.uk

dir: *B3273 from St Austell towards Mevagissey, on hilltop at crossroads before descent into Mevagissey turn right onto unclassified road to Gorran. Through village, 2nd right towards Gorran Haven, site signed on left in 250 metres. (Note: it is advisable to follow these directions not sat nav).*

A quiet rural site set in three paddocks, and sheltered by mature trees and hedges. The simple toilets have plenty of hot water, and there is a small laundry. Sandy beaches, pubs and shops are nearby, and Mevagissey is two miles away. There is a bus stop 100 yards from the site with a regular service to Mevagissey and St Austell.

Open: Easter and April to October **Last arrival:** 22.00 **Last departure:** noon

Pitches: 🚐 🚐 🅰

Facilities: 🛁 ⊙ ✳

Services: 🔌 🔲

Within 3 miles: 🚲 🏊 🛬 🏧

Additional site information: 2 acre site. 🐕 🐕 Cars can be parked by caravans and tents. Awnings permitted. 30-acre nature reserve.

PITCHES: 🚐 Caravans 🚐 Motorhomes 🅰 Tents 🏠 Glamping accommodation **SERVICES:** 🔌 Electric hook-up 🔲 Launderette 🍽 Licensed bar 🔥 Calor Gas 🔥 Campingaz 🅃 Toilet fluid 🍴 Café/Restaurant 🚮 Fast Food/Takeaway 🔋 Battery charging 🔧 Motorhome service point * 2019 prices 🚫 No credit or debit cards 🐕 Dogs permitted 🚫 No dogs

HAYLE
Map 2 SW53

Places to visit
Tate St Ives, ST IVES, TR26 1TG, 01736 796226
www.tate.org.uk/stives

Barbara Hepworth Museum & Sculpture Garden, ST IVES, TR26 1AD, 01736 796226
www.tate.org.uk/visit/tate-st-ives/barbara-hepworth-museum-and-sculpture-garden

Premier Park

St Ives Bay Holiday Park
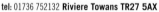 ▶▶▶▶▶ 93% HOLIDAY CENTRE

tel: 01736 752274 **73 Loggans Road, Upton Towns TR27 5BH**
email: enquiries@stivesbay.co.uk web: www.stivesbay.co.uk
dir: *Exit A30 at Hayle then immediately right onto B3301 at mini-roundabouts. Site entrance 0.5 mile on left.*

An extremely well-maintained holiday park with a relaxed atmosphere situated adjacent to a three mile beach. The various camping fields are set in hollows amongst the sand dunes and are very tastefully laid out, with the high camping fields enjoying stunning views over St Ives Bay. The touring sections are in a number of separate locations around the extensive site. The park is specially geared for families and couples, and as well as the large indoor swimming pool there are two pubs with seasonal entertainment. There are 17 wooden camping pods for hire.

Open: Easter to 30 October **Last arrival:** anytime **Last departure:** 09.00
Pitches: 🚐 🚎 ▲; 🏠 see price below; **Leisure:** 🏊 ⋀ 🏓 ♣ ⟋ 🎵 ✎
Facilities: 🛁 ☉ ☇ ☼ ⚸ 🛉 🚮 WiFi
Services: 🔌 🔋 🚽 🍴 🍺 🛒 🖾 🚮 ⚐ ⊤ **Within 3 miles:** 🛴 ∪ ◎ ≋
Additional site information: 90 acre site. No pets. Crazy golf.
Glamping available: Wooden pods from £165 per week. **Changeover days:** Saturday
Additional glamping information: Cars can be parked by units

Premier Park

Riviere Sands Holiday Park
▶▶▶▶▶ 88% HOLIDAY HOME PARK

tel: 01736 752132 **Riviere Towans TR27 5AX**
email: rivieresands@haven.com web: www.haven.com/rivieresands
dir: *A30 towards Redruth. Follow signs into Hayle, straight on at double mini-roundabout. Turn right opposite petrol station signed Towans and beaches. Park 1 mile on right.*

Close to St Ives and with direct access to a safe, white-sand beach, Riviere Sands is an exciting holiday park with much to offer families. Children can enjoy the crazy golf, amusements, swimming pool complex, and the beach, of course; the evening entertainment for adults is extensive and lively. There is a good range of holiday caravans and apartments.

Open: 24 March to 30 October
Holiday Homes: Sleep 8 Bedrooms 2 Bathrooms 1 Toilet 1 Microwave Freezer TV Sky/Freeview
Leisure: 🏊 ⋙ ⋀ 👐 ⚽ **Additional site information:** ⊗

Atlantic Coast Holiday Park
▶▶▶▶ 85%

tel: 01736 752071 **53 Upton Towans, Gwithian TR27 5BL**
email: enquiries@atlanticcoastpark.co.uk web: www.atlanticcoastpark.co.uk
dir: *From A30 into Hayle, right at double roundabout. Site 1.5 miles on left.*

Fringed by the sand dunes of St Ives Bay and close to the golden sands of Gwithian Beach, the small, friendly touring area continues to improve year on year and offers fully serviced pitches. There's freshly baked bread, a takeaway and a bar next door. This park is ideally situated for visitors to enjoy the natural coastal beauty and attractions of south-west Cornwall. There is superb landscaping and planting, and campers have the use of facilities such as a kettle and microwave. Static caravans are available for holiday hire.

Open: March to early January **Last arrival:** 20.00 **Last departure:** 11.00
Pitches: * 🚐 from £27; 🚎 from £27; ▲ from £27; 🏠 see prices below; 4 hardstanding pitches
Leisure: ⋀ ♣ ⟋
Facilities: 🛁 ☉ ☇ ☼ ⚸ 🛉 🚮 WiFi
Services: 🔌 🔋 🛒 ⊤
Within 3 miles: 🛴 ⟋ ∪ ◎ ≋ ✦
Additional site information: 4.5 acre site. 🐾 Cars can be parked by caravans and tents. Awnings permitted. No commercial vehicles, gazebos or day tents. Freshly baked bread, croissants, pasties, newspapers available.
Glamping available: Shepherd's hut from £100. **Changeover days:** Any day (Saturday only high season).
Additional glamping information: Own private hot tub and decking area. Cars can be parked by units.

Higher Trevaskis Caravan & Camping Park
▶▶▶ 88%

tel: 01209 831736 **Gwinear Road, Connor Downs TR27 5JQ**
email: info@highertrevaskiscaravanpark.co.uk
web: www.highertrevaskiscaravanpark.co.uk
dir: *On A30 at Hayle roundabout take exit signed Connor Downs, in 1 mile right signed Carnhell Green. Site 0.75 mile just after level crossing.*

An attractive paddocked and terraced park in a sheltered rural position on a valley side with views towards St Ives. The terrace areas are divided by hedges. This secluded park is personally run by welcoming owners who ensure it remains a peaceful location.

Open: mid April to September **Last arrival:** 20.00 **Last departure:** 10.30
Pitches: 🚐 from £16; 🚎 from £16; ▲ from £16; 11 hardstanding pitches; 1 seasonal pitch
Leisure: ⚽
Facilities: 🛁 ☉ ☇ ☼ 🛉 WiFi
Services: 🔌 🔋 🛒 🖾 ⚐ ⊤
Within 3 miles: 🛴 ⟋ ◎ ≋
Additional site information: 6.5 acre site. 🐾 Maximum 2 dogs per pitch, certain dog breeds not accepted (contact site for details). Dog and wet suit shower area. Cars can be parked by caravans and tents. Awnings permitted. 5mph speed limit on site, ball games permitted on designated field only.

Treglisson Touring Park
▶▶▶ 83%

tel: 01736 753141 **Wheal Alfred Road TR27 5JT**
email: treglisson@hotmail.co.uk **web:** www.treglisson.co.uk
dir: *From A30 (Camborne towards Penzance) take 4th exit at roundabout signed Hayle. Left at next mini-roundabout, follow site signs. Approximately 1.5 miles past golf course, site sign on left.*

A small secluded site in a peaceful wooded meadow and a former apple and pear orchard. This quiet rural site has level grass pitches and a well-planned modern toilet block, and is just two miles from the glorious beach at Hayle with its vast stretch of golden sand.

Open: Spring Bank Holiday to end September **Last arrival:** 20.00 **Last departure:** 11.00

Pitches: 🚐 🚑 ⛺; 6 hardstanding pitches

Leisure: ⚠

Facilities: 🏠 ☉ ☂ ☼ 🚿 ♨ WiFi

Services: 🔌 🗐 🔋

Within 3 miles: 🚶 ⛳ ⌣ ◎ ⛴ 🏧

Additional site information: 3 acre site. 🐕 Cars can be parked by caravans and tents. Awnings permitted. Maximum 6 people per pitch, maximum tent size of 7 metres.

HELSTON	Map 2 SW62

See also Ashton

Places to visit
Great for kids: Flambards, HELSTON, TR13 0QA, 01326 573404
www.flambards.co.uk

Cornish Seal Sanctuary, GWEEK, TR12 6UG, 01326 221361
www.visitsealife.com/gweek

Lower Polladras Touring Park
▶▶▶▶ 90%

tel: 01736 762220 **Carleen, Breage TR13 9NX**
email: lowerpolladras@btinternet.com **web:** www.lower-polladras.co.uk
dir: *From Helston take A394 then B3302 (Hayle Road) at Ward Garage, 2nd left to Carleen, site 2 miles on right.*

An attractive rural park with extensive views of surrounding fields, appealing to families who enjoy the countryside. The planted trees and shrubs are maturing, and help to divide the area into paddocks with spacious grassy pitches. The site has a dish-washing area, a games room, a dog and nature walk, two fully serviced family rooms and WiFi.

Open: April to January **Last arrival:** 21.00 **Last departure:** 11.00

Pitches: * 🚐 from £15; 🚑 from £15; ⛺ from £15; 28 hardstanding pitches; 17 seasonal pitches

Leisure: ⚠ 🎣 ⚽

Facilities: 🏠 ☉ ☂ ☼ 🚿 ♨ 🗐 🍴 ♨ WiFi

Services: 🔌 🗐 🔋 ⚓ 🎱 ⊘ T

Within 3 miles: 🚶 ⛳ ⌣ ◎ ⛴ 🏧 🎣 🏇

Additional site information: 4 acre site. 🐕 Cars can be parked by caravans and tents. Awnings permitted. No drones, hoverboards or camp fires. Caravan storage.

Skyburriowe Farm
▶▶▶ 83%

tel: 01326 221646 **Garras TR12 6LR**
email: bkbenney@hotmail.co.uk **web:** www.skyburriowefarm.co.uk
dir: *From Helston take A3083 to The Lizard. After Culdrose Naval Airbase continue straight on at roundabout, in 1 mile left at Skyburriowe Lane sign. In 0.5 mile right at Skyburriowe B&B/Campsite sign. Pass bungalow to farmhouse. Site on left.*

A leafy no-through road leads to this picturesque farm park in a rural location on the Lizard Peninsula. The toilet block offers excellent quality facilities, and most pitches have electric hook-ups. There are some beautiful coves and beaches nearby and for a great day out Flambards theme park is also close by. Under the supervision of the owner, children are permitted to watch his herd of Friesian cows being milked.

Open: April to October **Last arrival:** 22.00 **Last departure:** 11.00

Pitches: * 🚐 from £16; 🚑 from £16; ⛺ from £16; 4 hardstanding pitches

Facilities: 🏠 ☉ ☼ 🚿 WiFi

Services: 🔌 🔋 Within 3 miles: 🚶 ⛳ ⌣ ◎ 🏇 🎣 🏧

Additional site information: 4 acre site. 🐕 Cars can be parked by caravans and tents. Awnings permitted. Quiet after 23.00. Fresh seasonal vegetables available.

HOLYWELL BAY	Map 2 SW75

Places to visit
Trerice, TRERICE, TR8 4PG, 01637 875404
www.nationaltrust.org.uk/trerice

Platinum Park

Trevornick
▶▶▶▶▶

tel: 01637 830531 & 832905 **TR8 5PW**
email: bookings@trevornick.co.uk **web:** www.trevornick.co.uk
dir: *3 miles from Newquay exit A3075 towards Redruth. Follow Cubert and Holywell Bay signs.*

A large seaside holiday complex with excellent facilities and amenities. There is plenty of entertainment including a children's club and an evening cabaret, adding up to a full holiday experience for all the family. A sandy beach is just a 15-minute footpath walk away. The park has 36 Euro tents for hire, plus luxury static caravans.

Open: 5 April to 7 September and 19 October to 2 November **Last arrival:** 21.00 **Last departure:** 10.00

Pitches: 🚐 🚑 ⛺ 🏕 53 hardstanding pitches; 8 seasonal pitches

Leisure: 🏊 ⚠ 🎣 🎯 ▢ 🚶 ♟ ♫ ⛳ ☺

Facilities: 🏠 ☉ ☂ ☼ 🚿 ♨ 🗐 ♨ WiFi

Services: 🔌 🗐 🍴 🍽 ⚓ 🔋 ⊘ T

Within 3 miles: ⌣ ◎ ⛴ 🏇 🎣

Additional site information: 20 acre site. 🐕 Cars can be parked by caravans and tents. Awnings permitted. Families and couples only. Arcade, dog walking field.

Glamping available: Ready-erected tents. **Changeover days:** Saturday

Additional glamping information: Ready-erected tents are fully equipped; some are dog friendly. Cars can be parked by ready-erected tents.

PITCHES: 🚐 Caravans 🚑 Motorhomes ⛺ Tents 🏕 Glamping accommodation **SERVICES:** 🔌 Electric hook-up 🗐 Launderette ♨ Licensed bar 🔥 Calor Gas ⊘ Campingaz T Toilet fluid 🍴 Café/Restaurant 🍽 Fast Food/Takeaway 🔋 Battery charging ♨ Motorhome service point * 2019 prices 🚫 No credit or debit cards 🐕 Dogs permitted ⊗ No dogs

KENNACK SANDS   Map 2 SW71

Places to visit

Cornish Seal Sanctuary, GWEEK, TR12 6UG, 01326 221361
www.visitsealife.com/gweek

Great for kids: Flambards, HELSTON, TR13 0QA, 01326 573404
www.flambards.co.uk

Silver Sands Holiday Park
▶▶▶ 88%

tel: 01326 290631 **Gwendreath TR12 7LZ**
email: info@silversandsholidaypark.co.uk **web:** www.silversandsholidaypark.co.uk
dir: *From Helston follow signs to St Keverne. After Goonhilly Satellite Station turn right at
crossroads signed Kennack Sands, 1.5 miles, left at Gwendreath sign, site 1 mile.
(Note: it is advisable to follow these directions not sat nav).*

A small, family-owned park in a remote location, with individually screened pitches
providing sheltered suntraps. The owners continue to upgrade the park, improving
the landscaping, access roads and toilets; lovely floral displays greet you on arrival.
A footpath through the woods leads to the beach and the local pub. One of the
nearby beaches is the historic Mullion Cove, and for the children a short car ride
will ensure a great day out at Flambards theme park.

Open: 21 March to 2 November **Last arrival:** 18.00 **Last departure:** 11.00

Pitches: 🚐 🚌 ▲

Leisure: 🎢 ⚽

Facilities: 🛁 ☉ ☂ ✳ ⑤ 🚽 🎍 🏕 WiFi

Services: 🔌 🔟 🛢 🧴

Within 3 miles: ⚓ 🎣 ∪ 🚣

Additional site information: 9 acre site. 🐕 Cars can be parked by caravans and tents
(except when ground is saturated). Awnings permitted. No noise after 22.00. Woodland
walk to the beach. Car hire can be arranged.

KILKHAMPTON   Map 2 SS21

Upper Tamar Lake
▶▶ 75%

tel: 01288 321712 **Upper Tamar Lake EX23 9SB**
email: info@swlakestrust.org.uk **web:** www.southwestlakes.co.uk
dir: *From A39 at Kilkhampton onto B3254, left in 0.5 mile onto unclassified road, follow
signs for approximately 4 miles to site.*

A well-trimmed, slightly sloping site overlooking the lake and surrounding
countryside, with several signed walks. The site benefits from the excellent facilities
provided for the watersports centre and coarse anglers, with a rescue launch on the
lake when the flags are flying. A good family site, with Bude's beaches and the
surfing waves only eight miles away.

Open: April to October **Last arrival:** 17.00 **Last departure:** 11.00

Pitches: * 🚐 from £12; 🚌 from £12; ▲ from £12 🏠; 2 hardstanding pitches

Leisure: 🎢 🎣

Facilities: 🛁 ☂ ✳ ♿ 🎍

Services: 🔌 🔟 🎍

Within 3 miles: ⚓ ∪ 🚣 🚴 🚆 ⑤

Additional site information: 1 acre site. 🐕 Cars can be parked by caravans and tents.
Awnings permitted. No open fires, off-ground BBQs only. No swimming in lake. Canoeing,
sailing, windsurfing, kayaking hire and launch, stand up paddle boarding.

Glamping available: Wooden pods.

Additional glamping information: Cars can be parked by pods.

LEEDSTOWN (NEAR HAYLE)   Map 2 SW63

Places to visit

East Pool Mine, POOL, TR15 3NP, 01209 315027
www.nationaltrust.org.uk/east-pool-mine

Godolphin House, GODOLPHIN CROSS, TR13 9RE, 01736 763194
www.nationaltrust.org.uk/godolphin

Calloose Caravan & Camping Park
▶▶▶▶▶ 88%

tel: 01736 850431 & 0800 328 7589 **TR27 5ET**
email: sales@calloose.co.uk **web:** www.calloose.co.uk
dir: *From Hayle take B3302 to Leedstown, turn left opposite village hall before
entering village. Site 0.5 mile on left at bottom of hill.*

A comprehensively equipped leisure park in a remote rural setting in a small
river valley. This very good park is busy and bustling, and offers bright, clean
toilet facilities, an excellent games room, an inviting pool, a good children's play
area, and log cabins and static caravans for holiday hire.

Open: All year **Last arrival:** 22.00 **Last departure:** 11.00

Pitches: 🚐 🚌 ▲; 29 hardstanding pitches

Leisure: 🏊 🎢 🎱 🖵

Facilities: ☉ ☂ ✳ ♿ ⑤ 🎍

Services: 🔌 🛢 🔟 🔟 🎍 🛒 🛢 🧴 ⒯

Within 3 miles: 🎣

Additional site information: 12.5 acre site. 🐕 Cars can be parked by caravans and
tents. Awnings permitted. No noise after midnight, no pets in statics or log cabins.
Crazy golf, skittle alley.

LOOE

Places to visit

Antony House, TORPOINT, PL11 2QA, 01752 812191
www.nationaltrust.org.uk/antony

Mount Edgcumbe House & Country Park, TORPOINT, PL10 1HZ, 01752 822236
www.mountedgcumbe.gov.uk

Great for kids: Wild Futures' Monkey Sanctuary, LOOE, PL13 1NZ, 01503 262532
www.monkeysanctuary.org

LOOE
Map 2 SX25

Premier Park

Camping Caradon Touring Park
▶▶▶▶▶ 84%

tel: 01503 272388 **Trelawne PL13 2NA**
email: enquiries@campingcaradon.co.uk **web:** www.campingcaradon.co.uk
dir: *Site signed from junction of A387 and B3359, between Looe and Polperro. Take B3359 towards Pelynt then 1st right. Site 250 metres on left.*

Set in a quiet rural location between the popular coastal resorts of Looe and Polperro, this family-run and developing eco-friendly park is just one and half miles from the beach at Talland Bay. The site caters for both families and couples. The owners take great pride in the site and offer some quality facilities and service to their campers throughout their stay; their constant aim is to provide a carefree and relaxing holiday. The local bus stops just inside the park entrance.

Open: All year (restricted service: November to March – prior bookings only)
Last arrival: 20.00 **Last departure:** 11.00

Pitches: 🚐 🚐 ▲; 23 hardstanding pitches

Leisure: ⚴ 🔍

Facilities: 🏠 ☉ ℉ ☀ ⬅ ⑤ ☴ WiFi

Services: 🔌 🗑 🍺 🍽 ⬛ 🔋 ⬆ 🛢 ⌀ Ⓣ

Within 3 miles: 🕳 ◎ 🚴 ⚑

Additional site information: 3.5 acre site. 🐕 Cars can be parked by caravans and tents. Awnings permitted. Quiet from 23.00–07.00 and barrier not operational. Family room with TV, undercover washing-up area, RCD lead hire, rallies welcome. Shop open Easter to end September.

Premier Park

Tencreek Holiday Park
▶▶▶▶▶ 84% HOLIDAY CENTRE

tel: 01503 262447 **Polperro Road PL13 2JR**
email: reception@tencreek.co.uk **web:** www.dolphinholidays.co.uk
dir: *Take A387 1.25 miles from Looe. Site on left.*

Occupying a lovely position with extensive countryside and sea views, this holiday centre is in a rural spot but close to Looe and Polperro. There is a full family entertainment programme, with an indoor swimming pool, an adventure playground and an exciting children's club. The superb amenity blocks include several private family shower rooms with toilet and washbasin.

Open: All year **Last arrival:** 22.00 **Last departure:** 10.00

Pitches: * 🚐 from £16.25; 🚐 from £16.25; ▲ from £11; 12 hardstanding pitches; 120 seasonal pitches

Leisure: ⚴ ⚴ ✋ ♨ 🔍 ♫ ⚽

Facilities: 🏠 ☉ ℉ ☀ ⬅ ⑤ 🍺 WiFi

Services: 🔌 🗑 🍺 🍽 ⬛ 🔋 ⬆ 🛢 ⌀ Ⓣ

Within 3 miles: 🚴 🕳 ⛳ ◎ 🚴 ⚑ ▤

Additional site information: 24 acre site. 🐕 Families and couples only. Multi-sports pitch.

LOSTWITHIEL
Map 2 SX15

Places to visit

Restormel Castle, RESTORMEL, PL22 0EE, 01208 872687
www.english-heritage.org.uk/visit/places/restormel-castle

Lanhydrock, LANHYDROCK, PL30 4AB, 01208 265950
www.nationaltrust.org.uk/lanhydrock

Great for kids: Eden Project, ST AUSTELL, PL24 2SG, 01726 811911
www.edenproject.com

Premier Park

Eden Valley Holiday Park
▶▶▶▶▶ 87%

tel: 01208 872277 **PL30 5BU**
email: edenvalleyholidaypark@btconnect.com **web:** www.edenvalleyholidaypark.co.uk
dir: *1.5 miles south-west of Lostwithiel on A390 turn right at brown/white sign in 400 metres. (Note: it is advisable to follow these directions not sat nav).*

A grassy park set in attractive paddocks with mature trees. The gradual upgrading of facilities continues, and both buildings and grounds are carefully maintained and contain an impressive children's play area. This park is ideally located for visiting the Eden Project, the nearby golden beaches and sailing at Fowey. There are also two self-catering lodges.

Open: Easter or April to October **Last arrival:** 22.00 **Last departure:** 11.30

Pitches: 🚐 from £15.50; 🚐 from £15.50; ▲ from £15.50; 40 hardstanding pitches; 25 seasonal pitches

Leisure: ⚴ 🔍 ⊕

Facilities: 🏠 ☉ ℉ ☀ ⬅ ⑤ ☴ WiFi

Services: 🔌 🗑 🔋 ⬆ 🛢 ⌀

Within 3 miles: 🚴 🕳 ⛳ ◎ 🚴 ⚑

Additional site information: 12 acre site. 🐕 No large dogs. Cars can be parked by caravans and tents. Awnings permitted. Table football, pool, table tennis, football. Walks, wildlife conservation information room.

LUXULYAN
Map 2 SX05

Places to visit

Restormel Castle, RESTORMEL, PL22 0EE, 01208 872687
www.english-heritage.org.uk/visit/places/restormel-castle

Eden Project, ST AUSTELL, PL24 2SG, 01726 811911
www.edenproject.com

Great for kids: Wheal Martyn, ST AUSTELL, PL26 8XG, 01726 850362
www.wheal-martyn.com

Croft Farm Holiday Park
► ► ► 80%

tel: 01726 850228 **PL30 5EQ**
email: enquiries@croftfarm.co.uk **web:** www.croftfarm.co.uk
dir: *Exit A30 at Bodmin onto A391 towards St Austell. In 7 miles left at double roundabout onto unclassified road towards Luxulyan/Eden Project, continue to roundabout at Eden, left signed Luxulyan. Site 1 mile on left. (Note: do not approach any other way as roads are very narrow).*

A peaceful, picturesque setting at the edge of a wooded valley, and only one mile from The Eden Project. Facilities include a well-maintained toilet block, a well-equipped dishwashing area, replete with freezer and microwave, and a revamped children's play area reached via an attractive woodland trail. There is a good bus service to St Austell and Luxulyan (the bus stop is at the site's entrance) and trains run to Newquay.

Open: 21 March to 21 January **Last arrival:** 18.00 **Last departure:** 11.00
Pitches: 🚐 🚏 ▲; 18 hardstanding pitches; 10 seasonal pitches
Leisure: ◕
Facilities: 🛁 ☉ 🇫 ⚛ 🇸 🎋 WiFi
Services: 🔌 🗑 🚽 🔒 ⊘ T
Within 3 miles: ↧ ◢ ◔ ⚶ 日

Additional site information: 10.5 acre site. 🐾 Cars can be parked by caravans and tents. Awnings permitted. No skateboarding, ball games only in playing field, quiet between 23.00–07.00. Woodland walk, information room.

MARAZION

Places to visit

St Michael's Mount, MARAZION, TR17 0HS, 01736 710265
www.stmichaelsmount.co.uk

Trengwainton Garden, PENZANCE, TR20 8RZ, 01736 363148
www.nationaltrust.org.uk/trengwainton

MARAZION
Map 2 SW53

Wayfarers Caravan & Camping Park
► ► ► ► 93%

tel: 01736 763326 **Relubbus Lane, St Hilary TR20 9EF**
email: jean@wayfarerspark.co.uk **web:** www.wayfarerspark.co.uk
dir: *Exit A30 onto A394 signed Helston. 2 miles, left at roundabout onto B3280 signed Goldsithney. Through Goldsithney. Site 1 mile on left on bend (Note: slow down at 1st brown sign; it is advisable to ignore sat nav as directions are not suitable if towing a caravan).*

Located in the centre of St Hilary, two and half miles from St Michael's Mount, this is a quiet, sheltered park in a peaceful rural setting. It offers spacious, well-drained pitches and very well maintained facilities. The new bistro is an excellent addition and serves breakfast daily and evening meals three nights a week.

Open: March to October, Christmas and New Year **Last arrival:** 18.00
Last departure: 11.00
Pitches: * 🚐 from £22; 🚏 from £22; ▲ from £20; 21 hardstanding pitches; 6 seasonal pitches
Facilities: 🛁 ☉ 🇫 ⚛ ⚳ 🇸 🎋 🎋 WiFi
Services: 🔌 🗑 🚽 🍴 🛒 🔒 ⊘ T
Within 3 miles: ↧ ◢ ◔ ◉ ⚶

Additional site information: 4.8 acre site. Adults only. Awnings permitted. No pets, flag/light poles or flags. Quiet time 23.00–7.00. Car hire can be arranged.

Wheal Rodney Holiday Park
► ► ► 86%

tel: 01736 710605 **Gwallon Lane TR17 0HL**
email: reception@whealrodney.co.uk **web:** www.whealrodney.co.uk
dir: *Exit A30 at Crowlas, signed Rospeath. Site 1.5 miles on right. From Marazion centre turn opposite Fire Engine Inn, site 500 metres on left.*

Set in a quiet rural location surrounded by farmland, with level grass pitches, well-kept facilities, bell tents, holiday cottages and a good swimming pool. Within half a mile are the beach at Marazion and the causeway or ferry to St Michael's Mount. A cycle route is within 400 yards; Penzance is only a short car or cycle ride away.

Open: Easter to October **Last arrival:** 20.00 **Last departure:** 11.00
Pitches: 🚐 🚏 ▲
Leisure: 🏊
Facilities: 🛁 ☉ 🇫 ⚛ 🇸 WiFi
Services: 🔌 🗑 🛒
Within 3 miles: ↧ ◢ ◔ ◉ ⚶

Additional site information: 2.5 acre site. 🐾 Cars can be parked by caravans and tents. Awnings permitted. Quiet after 22.00. Car hire can be arranged.

MAWGAN PORTH

Places to visit

Prideaux Place, PADSTOW, PL28 8RP, 01841 532411
prideauxplace.co.uk

Goss Moor National Nature Reserve, CARNE, 01726 891096
www.gov.uk/government/publications/cornwalls-national-nature-reserves/
cornwalls-nature-reserves

LEISURE: 🏊 Indoor swimming pool 🏊 Outdoor swimming pool ⚠ Children's playground 🧒 Kids' club 🎾 Tennis court 🎱 Games room 📺 Separate TV room ⛳ Golf course 🏌 Pitch n putt 🚣 Boats for hire 🚲 Bikes for hire 🎬 Cinema 🎵 Entertainment 🎣 Fishing ⛳ Mini golf 🏄 Watersports 🏋 Gym ⚽ Sports field 🐴 Stables
FACILITIES: 🛁 Baths/Shower ☉ Electric shaver sockets 🇫 Hairdryer ⚛ Ice Pack Facility 👶 Baby facilities 🇸 Disabled facilities 🇸 Shop on site or within 200yds 🎋 BBQ area 🎋 Picnic area WiFi WiFi

MAWGAN PORTH   Map 2 SW86

Sun Haven Valley Country Holiday Park
▶▶▶▶ 86%

tel: 01637 860373 & 0800 634 6744 **TR8 4BQ**
email: sunhaven@sunhavenvalley.com **web:** www.sunhavenvalley.com
dir: Exit A30 at Highgate Hill junction for Newquay; follow signs for airport. At T-junction turn right. At beach level in Mawgan Porth take only road inland, then 0.25 mile. Site 0.5 mile beyond 'S' bend.

An attractive site with level pitches on the side of a river valley; being just off the B3276 this makes an ideal base for touring the Padstow and Newquay areas. The very high quality facilities include a TV lounge and a games room in a Swedish-style chalet, and a well-kept adventure playground. Trees and hedges fringe the park, and the ground is well drained.

Open: Easter to October **Last arrival:** 20.30 **Last departure:** 10.30

Pitches: * ⊟ from £14; ⊟ from £14; ⋀ from £14; 15 hardstanding pitches

Leisure: ⩍ ♦ ⊡

Facilities: ⌂ ℙ ✳ ⅃ ⑤ ♨ WiFi

Services: ⊟ ⑤ 🛢 ⌀ ⊤

Within 3 miles: ↨ ↗ ◎ ≋

Additional site information: 5 acre site. ⊀ Cars can be parked by caravans and tents. Awnings permitted. Families and couples only, no noise after 22.30. Microwave available, table tennis, woodland walk, dog exercise field.

Trevarrian Holiday Park
▶▶▶▶ 86%

tel: 01637 860381 & 0845 225 5910 (Calls cost 7p per minute plus your phone company's access charge) **TR8 4AQ**
email: holiday@trevarrian.co.uk **web:** www.trevarrian.co.uk
dir: From A39 at St Columb roundabout turn right onto A3059 towards Newquay. Fork right in approximately 2 miles for St Mawgan onto B3276. Turn right, site on left.

A well-established and well-run holiday park overlooking Mawgan Porth beach. This park has a wide range of attractions including a free entertainment programme in peak season and a 10-pin bowling alley with licensed bar. It is only a short drive to Newquay and approximately 20 minutes to Padstow.

Open: All year **Last arrival:** 22.00 **Last departure:** 11.00

Pitches: ⊟ ⊟ ⋀; 10 hardstanding pitches

Leisure: ≋ ♦ ⊡ ⅃ ☺

Facilities: ☺ ℙ ✳ ⅃ ⑤ WiFi

Services: ⊟ ⑤ ⌀ 🍴 🍺 🛢 ⅃ 🛢 ⌀ ⊤

Within 3 miles: ↨ ↗ ∪ ◎ ≋ ⊟

Additional site information: 7 acre site. ⊀ Cars can be parked by caravans and tents. Awnings permitted. No noise after midnight. Crazy golf.

MEVAGISSEY   Map 2 SX04

See also Gorran and Pentewan

Places to visit

The Lost Gardens of Heligan, PENTEWAN, PL26 6EN, 01726 845100
www.heligan.com

The Shipwreck and Heritage Centre, ST AUSTELL, PL25 3NX, 01726 69897
www.shipwreckcharlestown.com

Platinum Park

Seaview Gorran Haven Holiday Park
▶▶▶▶▶

tel: 01726 843425 & 01626 818350 **Boswinger PL26 6LL**
email: seaview@swholidayparks.co.uk web: www.seaviewinternational.com
dir: *From St Austell take B3273 signed Mevagissey. Turn right before entering village.*
Follow brown tourist signs to site. (Note: very narrow lanes to this site; it is advisable
to follow these directions not sat nav).

An attractive holiday park set in a beautiful environment overlooking Veryan Bay,
with colourful landscaping, including attractive flowers and shrubs. It continues
to offer an outstanding holiday experience. A seasonal area, along with non-
electric camping is provided with impressive toilet and shower facilities. The
beach is just half a mile away. There is also an 'off the lead' dog walk, and a
'ring and ride' bus service to Truro, St Austell and Plymouth stops at the park
gate. Static caravans and lodges are available for holiday hire.

Open: April to end September **Last arrival:** 22.00 **Last departure:** 10.00
Pitches: 🚐 🚎 ⛺; 27 hardstanding pitches; 31 seasonal pitches
Leisure: 🏊 ⛹ 🎣 ⚽
Facilities: 🛁 ☉ 🌡 ✳ ⛑ 🍴 🚻 🎎 🛒 WiFi
Services: 🔌 🚾 🍽 ⚙ 🚰 🛢 🧺 T
Within 3 miles: ⚓ 🚲 U ◎ 🎣 ⛵
Additional site information: 28 acre site. 🐕 Restrictions on certain dog breeds. Cars
can be parked by caravans and tents. Awnings permitted. Crazy golf, volleyball,
badminton, scuba diving, boules, tennis, football pitch, dog walking area.

NEWQUAY

Places to visit

Blue Reef Aquarium, NEWQUAY, TR7 1DU, 01637 878134
www.bluereefaquarium.co.uk/newquay

Trerice, TRERICE, TR8 4PG, 01637 875404
www.nationaltrust.org.uk/trerice

Great for kids: Dairy Land Farm World, NEWQUAY, TR8 5AA, 01872 510246
www.dairylandfarmworld.com

Newquay Zoo, NEWQUAY, TR7 2LZ, 01637 873342
www.newquayzoo.org.uk

NEWQUAY   Map 2 SW86

AA HOLIDAY CENTRE
OF THE YEAR 2020

Platinum Park

Hendra Holiday Park
▶▶▶▶▶ HOLIDAY CENTRE

tel: 01637 875778 **TR8 4NY**
email: enquiries@hendra-holidays.com web: www.hendra-holidays.com
dir: *A30 onto A392 signed Newquay. At Quintrell Downs over roundabout, signed Lane,*
site 0.5 mile on left.

A large complex with holiday statics and superb facilities including an indoor fun
pool and an outdoor pool. There is a children's club for the over 6s, evening
entertainment during high season, a skateboard park, fish and chip shop and a
fantastic coffee shop. The touring pitches, occupying 12 fields, are set amid mature
trees and shrubs, and some have fully serviced facilities. All amenities are open to
the public. This site generates most of its own electricity from a 1.5 megawatt solar
farm. The Hendra Pod Village area has 10 smart wooden pods for hire. This park
offers the complete holiday package for all, including children of all ages. As well
as the beaches at Newquay, there are plenty of attractions in the area.

Open: 29 March to 4 November (restricted service: April to Spring Bank Holiday and
September to October – outdoor pool closed) **Last arrival:** dusk **Last departure:** 10.00
Pitches: * 🚐 from £14.80; 🚎 from £14.80; ⛺ from £14.80; 🏠 see prices below;
35 hardstanding pitches
Leisure: 🏊 🏊 ⛹ 🖐 🔍 🎱 🎵 ⛳ ⚽ ☉

Facilities: 🏠 ☉ 🏳 ✳ ⚹ 🚿 🛁 ⛨ 🚻 🎤 🐕 WiFi
Services: 🔌 🔃 🍺 🍴 🚮 🔋 ⚡ 🔥 ⏚ ⌀ T
Within 3 miles: ⅃ ⌀ ∪ ◎ ⛴ ⅄ 🎏

Additional site information: 80 acre site. 🐕 Families and couples only. Land train rides, skate and scooter park, indoor play centre.

Glamping available: Wooden pods (unfurnished) from £40; premium pods (equipped) from £80. **Changeover days:** Any day

Additional glamping information: Wooden pods have heating, lighting, outside tables and chairs, outside storage chest and BBQ stand. Premium pods have in addition 1 double bed and 2 single beds, fridge, kettle, crockery and cutlery, washing-up bowl. Minimum stay 3 nights. Cars can be parked by pods.
See advert on page 75

Treloy Touring Park
▶ ▶ ▶ ▶ ▶ 93%

tel: 01637 872063 **TR8 4JN**
email: stay@treloy.co.uk **web:** www.treloy.co.uk
dir: On A3059 (St Columb Major to Newquay road).

An attractive site with fine countryside views, that is within easy reach of resorts and beaches. The pitches are set in four paddocks with mainly level but some slightly sloping grassy areas. Maintenance and cleanliness are very high. There is a heated swimming pool and separate paddling pool surrounded by a paved patio area with tables, an excellent reception, shop and first aid room. Three dedicated family shower rooms are available.

Open: 16 May to 12 September **Last arrival:** 20.00 **Last departure:** 10.00

Pitches: 🚐 from £19; 🚍 from £19; ⛺ from £19; 30 hardstanding pitches; 15 seasonal pitches

Leisure: 🏊 ⚂ 🎯 ♫ ⚽

Facilities: 🏠 ☉ 🏳 ✳ ⚹ 🚿 🛁 ⛨ 🚻 🐕 WiFi

Services: 🔌 🔃 🍺 🍴 🚮 🔋 ⏚ ⏚ 🔥 ⌀ T

Within 3 miles: ⅃ ⌀ ∪ ◎ ⛴ ⅄ 🎏

Additional site information: 23 acre site. 🐕 Cars can be parked by caravans and tents. Awnings permitted. No noise after 23.00. Concessionary green fees at Treloy Golf Club. Car hire can be arranged.
See advert on page 79

Monkey Tree Holiday Park
▶ ▶ ▶ ▶ ▶ 90%

tel: 01872 572032 **Hendra Croft, Scotland Road TR8 5QR**
email: enquiries@monkeytreeholidaypark.co.uk
web: www.monkeytreeholidaypark.co.uk
dir: From M5 at Exeter take A30 to Redruth (ignore all signs for Newquay). At Carland Cross roundabout (with windmills on right) continue to follow signs for Perranporth. After 1 mile turn right at Boxheater junction onto B3285 signposted Perranporth. After 0.5 mile turn right at crossroads into Scotland Road. After 1 mile, park on left.

A large, well-managed holiday park situated on Cornwall's north coast close to Newquay and just minutes from Fistral Beach and Perranporth Beach – perfectly placed for surfing and great family days out. There's something for everyone here and the whole park is impressive, very neat and tidy, and the 700 pitches include standard, serviced, premium, super, super-deluxe and ultra-deluxe pitches, the latter having en suite facilities on the pitch. There are also five dedicated pitches for RVs and motorhomes over 24ft long, and 64 holiday homes for hire. Facilities include eight well-maintained toilet blocks, an outdoor heated pool, a fishing lake, and a clubhouse with nightly entertainment in season.

Open: from 24 March **Last arrival:** 18.00 **Last departure:** 10.00

Pitches: * 🚐 from £4.25; 🚍 from £30.70; ⛺ from £4.25

Leisure: 🏊 ⚂ 👐 🎯 ▭ ♫ ⌀

Facilities: 🏠 ☉ ⚹ 🛁 🚻 🎤 🐕 WiFi

Services: 🔌 🔃 🍺 🍴 🚮 🔋 ⏚ 🔥 ⌀

Within 3 miles: ⅃ ∪

Additional site information: 56 acre site. 🐕 Cars can be parked by caravans and tents. Awnings permitted.

NEWQUAY *continued*

Trencreek Holiday Park
▶▶▶▶ 90%

tel: 01637 874210 **Hillcrest, Higher Trencreek TR8 4NS**
email: trencreek@btconnect.com **web:** www.trencreekholidaypark.co.uk
dir: *A392 to Quintrell Downs, right towards Newquay, left at 2 mini-roundabouts into Trevenson Road to site.*

An attractively landscaped park in the village of Trencreek, with modern toilet facilities of a very high standard. Two well-stocked fishing lakes, and evening entertainment in the licensed clubhouse, are extra draws. Located about two miles from Newquay with its beaches and surfing opportunities.

Open: Spring Bank Holiday to mid September (restricted service: Easter to Spring Bank Holiday – bar and swimming pool closed) **Last arrival:** 22.00 **Last departure:** noon

Pitches: * 🚐 from £12.70; 🚗 from £12.70; ▲ from £12.70; 8 hardstanding pitches

Leisure: 🏊 🎱 ▢ 🎣

Facilities: 🚿 ☉ 💈 ✳ 👍 🖪 🚻 🎪 WiFi

Services: 🔌 🔲 ➡ ▯ 🏧 🛒 🛁 🧺 🛆 Ⓣ

Within 3 miles: 🏌 ∪ ◎ 🛶 🥢 🎯 🎡

Additional site information: 10 acre site. ⊗ Cars can be parked by caravans and tents. Awnings permitted. Families and couples only.

Porth Beach Holiday Park
▶▶▶▶ 85%

tel: 01637 876531 **Porth TR7 3NH**
email: info@porthbeach.co.uk **web:** www.porthbeach.co.uk
dir: *From Newquay take A3058 towards St Columb Major. At roundabout left onto B3276 signed Padstow. Site on right.*

This attractive, popular park offers level, grassy pitches in neat and tidy surroundings. It is a well-run site set in meadowland in a glorious location adjacent to excellent sands of Porth Beach. The site offers two fully-equipped camping pods positioned on a raised terrace.

Porth Beach Holiday Park

Open: March to November **Last arrival:** 18.00 **Last departure:** 10.00

Pitches: 🚐 🚗 ▲ 🏠; 19 hardstanding pitches

Facilities: 🚿 ☉ 👍 WiFi

Services: 🔌 🔲 🏧 ▯ 🛁 🧺

Within 3 miles: 🏌 🎣 ∪ ◎ 🛶 🥢 🎯 🎡 🏪

Additional site information: 6 acre site. 🐾 Cars can be parked by caravans and tents. Awnings permitted. Families and couples only.

Glamping available: Wooden pods. **Changeover days:** Any day

Additional glamping information: Wooden pods: 2 sets of single bunk beds, electricity, lighting and heating. Cars can be parked by pods.

See advert on page 81

Trethiggey Holiday Park
▶▶▶▶ 84%

tel: 01637 877672 **Quintrell Downs TR8 4QR**
email: enquiries@trethiggey.co.uk **web:** www.trethiggey.co.uk
dir: *A30 onto A392 signed Newquay at Quintrell Downs roundabout, left onto A3058, pass Newquay Pearl centre. Site 0.5 mile on left.*

A family-owned park in a rural setting that is ideal for touring this part of Cornwall. It is pleasantly divided into paddocks with maturing trees and shrubs, and offers coarse fishing and tackle hire. This site has a car park for campers as the camping fields are set in a car-free zone for children's safety. New owners took over in March 2019, so expect some positive changes.

Open: March to December **Last arrival:** 18.00 **Last departure:** 10.30

Pitches: 🚐 from £10; 🚗 from £10; ▲ from £10; 20 hardstanding pitches; 8 seasonal pitches

Leisure: 🎪 🎱 🎣

Facilities: 🚿 ☉ 💈 ✳ 👍 🚻 🎪 🐕 WiFi

Services: 🔌 🔲 ▯ 🛁 🧺

Within 3 miles: 🏌 ∪ ◎ 🛶 🥢 🎯 🎡 🏪

Additional site information: 15 acre site. 🐾 Cars can be parked by caravans and tents. Awnings permitted. No noise after 22.00. Recreation field.

Trenance Holiday Park

▶▶▶▶ 82%

tel: 01637 873447 **Edgcumbe Avenue TR7 2JY**
email: enquiries@trenanceholidaypark.co.uk **web:** www.trenanceholidaypark.co.uk
dir: *From Rejerrah on A3075 towards Newquay take A395 signed A392 and Newquay. At next roundabout right onto A3058 signed St Columb Minor. At double mini-roundabouts, right into Treninnick Hill. Site 1st right.*

A mainly static park popular with tenters, close to Newquay's vibrant nightlife, and with a café serving excellent breakfasts and takeaways. Set on high ground in an urban area of town, with cheerful owners and clean facilities; the site offers a motorhome service point. The local bus stops at the site entrance.

Open: mid April to mid September (restricted service: mid April to mid May – shop closed)
Last arrival: 22.00 **Last departure:** 10.00

Pitches: * 🚐 from £17; 🚍 from £17; ▲ from £17 🏠

Leisure: 🎱

Facilities: 🏚 ☉ 🅿 ☀ & ⑤ WiFi

Services: 🔌 ⑤ 🍴 🛒 ⤴ 🔋 🧴 Ⓣ

Within 3 miles: ⚓ 🚴 ∪ ◎ ≋ ⚓ 🖽

Additional site information: 12 acre site. Cars can be parked by caravans and tents. Awnings permitted. No pets, no noise after midnight.

Glamping available: Wooden pods. **Changeover days:** Any day

Additional glamping information: Wooden pods: electricity supplied. No drainage or water. No en suite toilets. Cars can be parked by pods.

Trebellan Park

▶▶▶ 85%

tel: 01637 830522 **Cubert TR8 5PY**
email: enquiries@trebellan.co.uk **web:** www.trebellan.co.uk
dir: *South of Newquay from A392 onto A3075 towards Rejerrah. In approximately 4 miles, turn right signed Cubert. Left in 0.75 mile onto unclassified road.*

A terraced grassy rural park within a picturesque valley with views of Cubert Common, and adjacent to the Smuggler's Den, a 16th-century thatched inn. This park has a very inviting swimming pool and three well-stocked coarse fishing lakes.

Open: May to October **Last arrival:** 21.00 **Last departure:** 10.00

Pitches: * 🚐 from £22; 🚍 from £22; ▲ from £16

Leisure: 🎱 🏓 🎣

Facilities: 🏚 ☉ 🅿 ☀ & 🏓 WiFi

Services: 🔌 ⑤ 🛒

Within 3 miles: ⚓ ∪ ◎ ≋ ⑤

Additional site information: 8 acre site. Cars can be parked by caravans and tents. Awnings permitted. Families and couples only.

Riverside Holiday Park

▶▶▶ 83%

tel: 01637 873617 **Gwills Lane TR8 4PE**
email: info@riversideholidaypark.co.uk **web:** www.riversideholidaypark.co.uk
dir: *A30 onto A392 signed Newquay. At Quintrell Downs at roundabout follow Lane sign. 2nd left in 0.5 mile onto unclassified road signed Gwills. Site in 400 yards.*

A sheltered valley beside a river in a quiet location is the idyllic setting for this lightly wooded park that caters for families and couples only; the site is well placed for exploring Newquay and Padstow. There is a lovely swimming pool. The site is close to the wide variety of attractions offered by this major resort. Self-catering lodges, cabins and static vans are for hire.

Open: Easter to end October **Last arrival:** 22.00 **Last departure:** 10.00

Pitches: 🚐 🚍 ▲

Leisure: 🏊 ♨ 🎣 🖃

Facilities: 🏚 ☉ 🅿 ☀ & ⑤ WiFi

Services: 🔌 ⑤ 🍴 🏧 🛒 🔋 🧴 Ⓣ

Within 3 miles: ⚓ 🚴 ∪ ◎ ≋ ⚓ 🖽

Additional site information: 11 acre site. Cars can be parked by caravans and tents. Awnings permitted. Families and couples only.

PITCHES: 🚐 Caravans 🚍 Motorhomes ▲ Tents 🏠 Glamping accommodation **SERVICES:** 🔌 Electric hook-up ⑤ Launderette 🍴 Licensed bar 🔋 Calor Gas 🧴 Campingaz Ⓣ Toilet fluid 🍴 Café/Restaurant 🏧 Fast Food/Takeaway 🔋 Battery charging ⤴ Motorhome service point * 2019 prices ⊗ No credit or debit cards 🐕 Dogs permitted ⊗ No dogs

PADSTOW
Map 2 SW97

See also Rumford

Places to visit

Prideaux Place, PADSTOW, PL28 8RP, 01841 532411
prideauxplace.co.uk

The Shipwreck and Heritage Centre, ST AUSTELL, PL25 3NX, 01726 69897
www.shipwreckcharlestown.com

Great for kids: Eden Project, ST AUSTELL, PL24 2SG, 01726 811911
www.edenproject.com

Platinum Park

Padstow Touring Park
▶▶▶▶▶

tel: 01841 532061 **PL28 8LE**
email: bookings@padstowtouringpark.co.uk **web:** www.padstowtouringpark.co.uk
dir: 1 mile south of Padstow, on east side of A389 (Padstow to Wadebridge road).

Improvements continue at this top quality park set in open countryside above the quaint fishing town of Padstow, which can be approached via a footpath directly from the park. This site is divided into paddocks by maturing bushes and hedges that create a peaceful and relaxing holiday atmosphere. The main facility blocks have been designed and decorated to a very high standard, plus there is a good children's play area, a well-stocked shop and an excellent coffee lounge with a decked terrace offering country views.

Open: All year **Last arrival:** 21.00 **Last departure:** 11.00

Pitches: 🚐 from £24; 🚌 from £24; ▲ from £15; 77 hardstanding pitches

Leisure: ⚙

Facilities: 🛁 ☉ 🦮 ✳ 🚻 🖐 🎱 ♨ WiFi

Services: 🔌 🗑 ⚕ 🔒 🚰 T

Within 3 miles: 🚶 ⛳ ⛵ ◎ ⚽ ✈

Additional site information: 13.5 acre site. 🐕 Cars can be parked by caravans and tents. Awnings permitted. No groups, no noise after 22.00. Freshly baked bread, coffee lounge, camp kitchen, dog wash.

Premier Park

The Retreats @ Padstow Holiday Park
▶▶▶▶▶ 85% HOLIDAY HOME PARK

tel: 01841 532289 **Cliffdowne PL28 8LB**
email: mail@padstowholidaypark.co.uk **web:** www.padstowholidaypark.co.uk
dir: Exit A39 onto either A389 or B3274 to Padstow. Site signed 1.5 miles before Padstow.

In an Area of Outstanding Natural Beauty and within a mile of the historic fishing village of Padstow (which can be reached via a footpath), this static-only park with 12 well-equipped units for hire has seen huge investment in recent years and provides comfortable relaxing accommodation in a quiet and peaceful atmosphere. A superb building houses the reception, coffee lounge and an impressive 20-metre swimming pool. This is a quiet base that is convenient for the many attractions Cornwall has to offer.

Open: early February to early January

Holiday Homes: Sleep 4 Bedrooms 2 Bathrooms 1 Toilet 2 Two-ring burner Microwave Freezer TV Sky/Freeview DVD player WiFi

Leisure: ⚙

Within 3 miles: ⛳ ♨

Additional site information: 🐕

PENTEWAN
Map 2 SX04

Places to visit

The Lost Gardens of Heligan, PENTEWAN, PL26 6EN, 01726 845100
www.heligan.com

The Shipwreck and Heritage Centre, ST AUSTELL, PL25 3NX, 01726 69897
www.shipwreckcharlestown.com

Great for kids: Eden Project, ST AUSTELL, PL24 2SG, 01726 811911
www.edenproject.com

Little Winnick Touring Park
▶▶▶▶ 85%

tel: 01726 843687 **PL26 6DL**
email: mail@littlewinnick.co.uk **web:** www.littlewinnick.co.uk
dir: A390 to St Austell, then B3273 towards Mevagissey, site in 3 miles on left.

A small, well maintained rural site within walking distance of Pentewan and its beautiful beach. It has neat level pitches, including some hardstanding pitches, an excellent children's play area, and an ultra-modern toilet block. It borders the River Winnick and also the Pentewan cycle trail from St Austell to Pentewan, and The Lost Gardens of Heligan and Mevagissey are nearby. There is a bus stop outside the park to Mevagissey and Gorran Haven or St Austell (Asda), Charlestown and Fowey.

Open: Easter to early October **Last arrival:** 20.00 **Last departure:** 11.00

Pitches: 🚐 🚌 ▲; 38 hardstanding pitches; 10 seasonal pitches

Leisure: ⚙ ✪

Facilities: 🛁 ☉ 🦮 ✳ 🚻 🎱 🖐 🅿 WiFi

Services: 🔌 🗑 ⚕ ⚕

Within 3 miles: 🚶 ⛳ 🚣 ✈ 🎬

Additional site information: 14 acre site. 🐕 Cars can be parked by caravans and tents. Awnings permitted. No noise 22.00–07.00.

Heligan Caravan & Camping Park

▶▶▶▶ 84%

tel: 01726 842714 & 844414 **PL26 6BT**
email: info@heligancampsite.com **web:** www.heligancampsite.com
dir: From A390 take B3273 for Mevagissey at crossroads signed 'No caravans beyond this point'. Right onto unclassified road towards Gorran, site 0.75 mile on left.

A pleasant peaceful park adjacent to The Lost Gardens of Heligan, with views over St Austell Bay and well-maintained facilities, including a smart disabled/family room. Guests can also use the extensive amenities at the sister park, Pentewan Sands, and there's a footpath with direct access to The Lost Gardens of Heligan

Open: 4 January to 17 November (restricted service: reception opening times: 09.00–11.00 and 17.00–18.00) **Last arrival:** 22.00 **Last departure:** 10.30

Pitches: * ⊞ from £11.40; ⊞ from £11.40; ▲ from £8.10; 27 hardstanding pitches; 10 seasonal pitches

Leisure: ⚠

Facilities: 🏪 ☺ 🦮 ※ 🖐 💲 🐾 WiFi

Services: 🔌 🔄 🚽 🖐 🔋 🧴

Within 3 miles: 🚶 🌾 ∪ ⚓ 🎣 🏕

Additional site information: 12 acre site. 🐕 Cars can be parked by caravans and tents. Awnings permitted. Woodland walk and cycling trail.

PERRANPORTH

Places to visit

Royal Cornwall Museum, TRURO, TR1 2SJ, 01872 272205
www.royalcornwallmuseum.org.uk

Trerice, TRERICE, TR8 4PG, 01637 875404
www.nationaltrust.org.uk/trerice

Great for kids: Blue Reef Aquarium, NEWQUAY, TR7 1DU, 01637 878134
www.bluereefaquarium.co.uk/newquay

Premier Park

Perran Sands Holiday Park

▶▶▶▶▶ 91% HOLIDAY CENTRE

tel: 01872 573551 **TR6 OAQ**
email: perransands@haven.com **web:** www.haven.com/perransands
dir: A30 onto B3285 towards Perranporth. Site on right before descent on hill into Perranporth.

Situated amid 500 acres of protected dune grassland, and with a footpath through to the surf and three miles of golden sandy beach, this lively park is set in a large village-style complex. It offers a complete range of on-site facilities and entertainment for all the family, which makes it an extremely popular park. There are two top-of-the-range facility blocks. Safari tents, supertents, geo domes and yurts are available for hire.

Open: mid March to end October (restricted service: mid March to May and September to end October – some facilities may be reduced) **Last arrival:** 22.00 **Last departure:** 10.00

Pitches: ⊞ ⊞ ▲; 🏠 see prices below; 28 hardstanding pitches

Leisure: 🏊 🏖 ⚠ 🖐 🎵 🎯 ⚽

Facilities: 🏪 ☺ 🦮 ※ 🖐 💲 🚻 WiFi

Services: 🔌 🔄 🍺 🍽 🛒 🖐 🧴

Within 3 miles: 🚶 🌾 ∪ ◎ ⚓

Additional site information: 550 acre site. 🐕 Maximum 2 dogs per booking, certain dog breeds banned. No commercial vehicles, no bookings by persons under 21 years unless a family booking.

Glamping available: Safari tents from £129; super tents from £99; yurts from £198; geo domes from £239. **Changeover days:** Monday, Friday, Saturday

Additional glamping information: All glamping units: minimum stay 3 nights, kitchen, no sink.

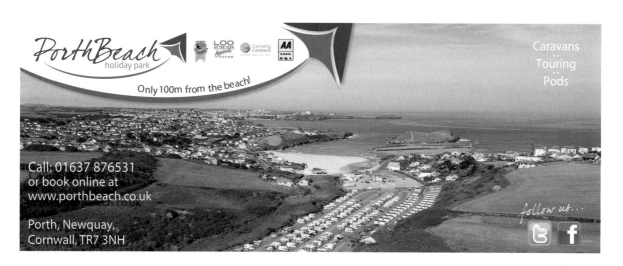

PITCHES: ⊞ Caravans ⊞ Motorhomes ▲ Tents 🏠 Glamping accommodation **SERVICES:** 🔌 Electric hook-up 🔄 Launderette 🍺 Licensed bar 🔵 Calor Gas 🧴 Campingaz 🅣 Toilet fluid 🍽 Café/Restaurant 🛒 Fast Food/Takeaway 🔋 Battery charging 🖐 Motorhome service point * 2019 prices 🚫 No credit or debit cards 🐕 Dogs permitted ⊗ No dogs

PERRANPORTH *continued*

Tollgate Farm Caravan & Camping Park
►►►► 85%

tel: 01872 572130 **Budnick Hill TR6 0AD**
email: enquiries@tollgatefarm.co.uk web: www.tollgatefarm.co.uk
dir: *Exit A30 onto B3285 to Perranporth. Site on right 1.5 miles after Goonhavern.*

A quiet site in a rural location with spectacular coastal views. Pitches are divided into four paddocks sheltered and screened by mature hedges, and there's a fully-equipped campers' kitchen. Children will enjoy the play equipment and pets' corner. The three miles of sand at Perran Bay are just a walk away through the sand dunes, or by car it is a three-quarter mile drive. There are five fully-serviced premium pitches (three grass- and two hard-standing) as well as five camping pods for hire. There are also wardens on site.

Open: Easter to September **Last arrival:** 20.00 **Last departure:** 10.30
Pitches: 🚐 🚍 ▲ 🏠; 10 hardstanding pitches; 12 seasonal pitches
Leisure: 🛝 ⚽
Facilities: 🛁 ☉ 🎽 ❄ 🔥 🔊 🚰 🛒 **WiFi**
Services: 🔌 🔲 🚰 ⬆️ 🔒 🗑 T
Within 3 miles: 🎣 🛶 ⛳ U ◎ 🛶 🏊 🎿 日

Additional site information: 10 acre site. 🚗 Cars can be parked by caravans and tents. Awnings permitted. No large groups. Car hire can be arranged.

Glamping available: Wooden pods

Additional glamping information: Wooden pods: minimum stay 2 nights (off-peak season), 3 nights (peak season). Sleep 4.

Higher Golla Touring & Caravan Park
►►► 87%

tel: 01872 573963 & 07800 558407 **Penhallow TR4 9LZ**
email: trevor.knibb@gmail.com web: www.caravanparkincornwall.com
dir: *A30 onto B3284 towards Perranporth (straight on at junction with A3075). Approximately 2 miles. Site signed on right.*

This peacefully located park is just two miles from Perranporth and its stunning beach, and extensive country views can be enjoyed from all the touring pitches. It has high quality and immaculate toilet facilities, and every pitch has electricity and a water tap.

Open: 4 May to 21 September (restricted service: low and mid season (excluding Spring Bank Holiday) – shop closed) **Last arrival:** 20.00 **Last departure:** 10.30
Pitches: 🚐 from £17; 🚍 from £17; ▲ from £17; 2 hardstanding pitches; 4 seasonal pitches
Facilities: 🛁 ☉ 🎽 ❄ 🔊 🚰 **WiFi**
Services: 🔌 🔲 ⬆️ 🔒 T
Within 3 miles: 🎣 🛶 U ◎ 🏊

Additional site information: 3 acre site. 🚗 Cars can be parked by caravans and tents. Awnings permitted. No kite flying, quiet between 21.00–08.00. Debit cards accepted (no credit cards). Large dog walk.

Perranporth Camping & Touring Park
►►► 77%

tel: 01872 572174 **Budnick Road TR6 0DB**
email: info@perranporth-camping.co.uk web: www.perranporth-camping.co.uk
dir: *At mini-roundabout in Perranporth take B3285 towards Newquay. 0.5 mile to site.*

A pleasant site, great for families and just a five-minute, easy walk to Perranporth's beautiful beach and less than 10 minutes to the shops and restaurants in the town centre. There is a clubhouse/bar and heated swimming pool for the sole use of those staying on the site. There is also a takeaway food outlet and small shop. Nine static caravans are available for holiday hire.

Open: Easter to September (restricted service: end September – shop, swimming pool and club facilities closed) **Last arrival:** 23.00 **Last departure:** noon
Pitches: 🚐 🚍 ▲; 4 hardstanding pitches
Leisure: 🏊 🛝 🎯 ▢
Facilities: 🛁 ☉ 🎽 ❄ ♿ 🔊 🚰 **WiFi**
Services: 🔌 🔲 🍽 🚰 🔒 🗑 T
Within 3 miles: 🎣 🛶 U ◎ 🏊 🎿

Additional site information: 6 acre site. 🚗 Cars can be parked by caravans and tents. Awnings permitted. No noise after 23.00.

POLPERRO   Map 2 SX25

Places to visit
Restormel Castle, RESTORMEL, PL22 0EE, 01208 872687
www.english-heritage.org.uk/visit/places/restormel-castle

Great for kids: Wild Futures' Monkey Sanctuary, LOOE, PL13 1NZ, 01503 262532
www.monkeysanctuary.org

Great Kellow Farm Caravan & Camping Site
►►► 79%

tel: 01503 272387 **Lansallos PL13 2QL**
email: enquiries@greatkellowfarm.co.uk web: www.greatkellowfarm.co.uk
dir: *From Looe to Pelynt. In Pelynt left at church follow Lansallos sign. Left at crossroads. 0.75 mile, at staggered crossroads left, follow site signs. (Note: access is via single track lanes. It is advisable to follow these directions not sat nav).*

Set on a high level grassy paddock with extensive views of Polperro Bay, this attractive site is on a working dairy and beef farm, and close to National Trust properties and gardens. It is situated in a very peaceful location close to the fishing village of Polperro. A new toilet and shower block, opened in 2019, offers excellent facilities, along with a dishwashing area.

Open: March to 3 January **Last arrival:** 22.00 **Last departure:** noon
Pitches: 🚐 from £14; 🚍 from £14; ▲ from £14; 20 seasonal pitches

Facilities: Services: 🔌
Within 3 miles: 🎣 ⛳ ⑤

Additional site information: 3 acre site. 🐕 Cars can be parked by caravans and tents. Awnings permitted. No noise after 23.00.

POLRUAN   Map 2 SX15

Places to visit
Restormel Castle, RESTORMEL, PL22 0EE, 01208 872687
www.english-heritage.org.uk/visit/places/restormel-castle

Great for kids: Wild Futures' Monkey Sanctuary, LOOE, PL13 1NZ, 01503 262532
www.monkeysanctuary.org

Polruan Holidays-Camping & Caravanning
▶▶▶▶ 85%

tel: 01726 870263 **Polruan-by-Fowey PL23 1QH**
email: polholiday@aol.com **web:** www.polruanholidays.co.uk
dir: *A38 to Dobwalls, left onto A390 to East Taphouse. Left onto B3359. Right in 4.5 miles signed Polruan.*

A very rural and quiet site in a lovely elevated position above the village, with immaculate pitches and stunning views of the sea. The River Fowey passenger ferry is close by, and the site has a good shop, a spacious reception area, and barbecues are available to borrow. The bus for Polperro and Looe stops outside the gate, and the foot ferry to Fowey, which runs until 11pm, is only a 10-minute walk away.

Open: Easter to October **Last arrival:** 21.00 **Last departure:** 11.00
Pitches: 🚐 🚍 ⛺; 7 hardstanding pitches
Leisure: ⚠
Facilities: 🏠 ☺ 🎣 ⚒ ⑤ 🚻 🚽 🛒 WiFi
Services: 🔌 ⑤ 🔋 🅃
Within 3 miles: 🎣 ⛳ ♨ 🏊

Additional site information: 3 acre site. 🐕 Cars can be parked by caravans and tents. Awnings permitted. No skateboards, rollerskates, bikes, water pistols or water bombs. Car hire can be arranged.

POLZEATH   Map 2 SW97

Places to visit
Tintagel Castle, TINTAGEL, PL34 0HE, 01840 770328
www.english-heritage.org.uk/visit/places/tintagel-castle

Platinum Park

Gunvenna Holiday Park
▶▶▶▶▶

tel: 01208 862405 **St Minver PL27 6QN**
email: gunvenna.bookings@gmail.com **web:** www.gunvenna.com
dir: *From A39 north of Wadebridge take B3314 (Port Isaac road), site 4 miles on right.*

An attractive park with extensive rural views in a quiet country location, yet within three miles of Polzeath. This popular park is family owned and run, and provides good facilities in an ideal position for touring north Cornwall. The park has excellent hardstanding pitches, maturing landscaping and a beautiful indoor swimming pool with a glass roof. A mini wooden glamping cabin, a railway carriage, a holiday cottage and static caravans are for hire. The beach at Polzeath is very popular with the surfers.

Open: Easter to October **Last arrival:** 20.30 **Last departure:** 11.00
Pitches: 🚐 🚍 ⛺ 🏠; 33 hardstanding pitches; 18 seasonal pitches
Leisure: 🏊 ⚠ ♣
Facilities: 🏠 ⊙ ☺ 🎣 ⚒ ⑤ 🚻 🚽 WiFi
Services: 🔌 ⑤ 🍺 🔋 🛠 🅃
Within 3 miles: ♨ 🎣 ♨ 🏊 🏇

Additional site information: 10 acre site. 🐕 Cars can be parked by caravans and tents. Awnings permitted. Children under 16 years must be accompanied by an adult in the pool. Owners must clear up after their dogs.

Glamping available: Cabin, railway carriage. **Changeover days:** Any day
Additional glamping information: Cars can be parked by units.

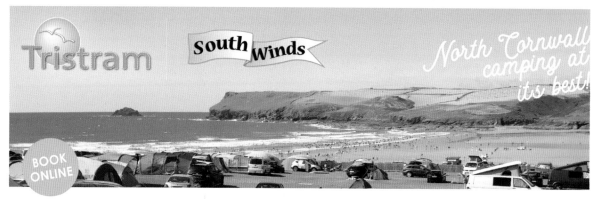
PITCHES: 🚐 Caravans 🚍 Motorhomes ⛺ Tents 🏠 Glamping accommodation **SERVICES:** 🔌 Electric hook-up ⑤ Launderette 🍺 Licensed bar 🔋 Calor Gas 🗲 Campingaz 🅃 Toilet fluid 🍽 Café/Restaurant 🚽 Fast Food/Takeaway 🔋 Battery charging 🛠 Motorhome service point
* 2019 prices 🚫 No credit or debit cards 🐕 Dogs permitted ⊗ No dogs

POLZEATH *continued*

Southwinds Caravan & Camping Park

▶ ▶ ▶ 90%

tel: 01208 863267 & 862215 **Polzeath Road PL27 6QU**
email: info@southwindscamping.co.uk **web:** www.polzeathcamping.co.uk
dir: *Exit B3314 onto unclassified road signed Polzeath, site on right just past turn to New Polzeath.*

A peaceful site with beautiful sea and panoramic rural views, within walking distance of a golf complex, and just three quarters of a mile from beach and village. There are three spacious fields that offer plenty of room for cars to be parked by tents or caravans. There's an impressive reception building, replete with tourist information, TV, settees and a range of camping spares. Dogs are welcome.

Open: May to mid September **Last arrival:** 21.00 **Last departure:** 10.30

Pitches: * 🚐 from £20; 🚎 from £20; ▲ from £20

Facilities: 🛁 ⊙ ☂ ✳ ♿ 📶

Services: 🔌 🔄 🍴 ⚙ 🛒 🎁 🗑 Ⓣ

Within 3 miles: ⚓ ╱ ∪ ◎ ≋ ⚐ 🎯 目 💲

Additional site information: 16 acre site. 🐾 Cars can be parked by caravans and tents. Awnings permitted. Families and couples only, no disposable BBQs, no noise 23.00–07.00. Restaurant and farm shop adjacent, Stepper Field open mid July to August.

See advert on page 83

Tristram Caravan & Camping Park

▶ ▶ ▶ 90%

tel: 01208 862215 **PL27 6TP**
email: info@tristramcampsite.co.uk **web:** www.polzeathcamping.co.uk
dir: *From B3314 onto unclassified road signed Polzeath. Through village, up hill, site 2nd right.*

An ideal family site, positioned on a gently sloping cliff with grassy pitches and glorious sea views, which are best enjoyed from the terraced premier pitches, or over lunch or dinner at Café India adjacent to the reception overlooking the beach. There is direct, gated access to the beach, where surfing is very popular, and the park has a holiday bungalow for rent. The local amenities of the village are only a few hundred yards away.

Open: March to October (restricted service: mid September – reseeding the site) **Last arrival:** 21.00 **Last departure:** 10.00

Pitches: * 🚐 from £26; 🚎 from £26; ▲ from £26

Facilities: 🛁 ⊙ ☂ ✳ ♿ 💲 📶

Services: 🔌 🔄 🍴 ⚙ 🛒 🎁 🗑 Ⓣ

Within 3 miles: ⚓ ╱ ∪ ◎ ≋ ⚐ 目

Additional site information: 10 acre site. 🐾 Cars can be parked by caravans and tents. Awnings permitted. No ball games, no disposable BBQs, no noise between 23.00–07.00. Surf equipment hire.

See advert on page 83

PORTHTOWAN   Map 2 SW64

Premier Park

Porthtowan Tourist Park

▷ ▷ ▷ ▷   93%

tel: 01209 890256 **Mile Hill TR4 8TY**
email: admin@porthtowantouristpark.co.uk **web:** www.porthtowantouristpark.co.uk
dir: *From A30 at Redruth follow Portreath, B3300 and brown camping signs. On B3300 in approximately 2 miles turn right at T-junction, follow site sign. Site on left at top of hill.*

A neat, level grassy site on high ground above Porthtowan, with plenty of shelter from mature trees and shrubs. The superb toilet facilities considerably enhance the appeal of this peaceful rural park, which is almost midway between the small seaside resorts of Portreath and Porthtowan, with their beaches and surfing. The site has a well-stocked shop and there is a purpose-built games and meeting room with a good library where tourist information leaflets are available. A tearoom adjacent to the campsite serves takeaway meals during the peak season (limited opening hours at other times of the year).

Porthtowan Tourist Park

Open: April to end September **Last arrival:** 19.00 **Last departure:** 11.00

Pitches: 🚐 from £20; 🚙 from £20; ▲ from £17; 14 hardstanding pitches

Leisure: ⚠ ◖ ✿

Facilities: 🛖 ☉ ℉ ✳ ♿ 🖪 🎍 WiFi

Services: 🔌 🔆 🛒 ⬇ 🔋 🖉 🅣

Within 3 miles: ↓ ✐ ∪ ⇲ 日

Additional site information: 5 acre site. 🐕 Cars can be parked by caravans and tents. Awnings permitted. No bikes or skateboards during school summer holidays. Table tennis and pool table.

See advert below

PITCHES: 🚐 Caravans 🚙 Motorhomes ▲ Tents 🏕 Glamping accommodation **SERVICES:** 🔌 Electric hook-up 🖪 Launderette 🍷 Licensed bar 🛢 Calor Gas 🍃 Campingaz 🅣 Toilet fluid 🍽 Café/Restaurant 🍔 Fast Food/Takeaway 🔋 Battery charging ⬇ Motorhome service point * 2019 prices 🚫 No credit or debit cards 🐕 Dogs permitted ⊗ No dogs

PORTHTOWAN *continued*

Wheal Rose Caravan & Camping Park

▶▶▶▶   76%

tel: 01209 891496 **Wheal Rose TR16 5DD**
email: whealrose@aol.com **web:** www.whealrosecaravanpark.co.uk
dir: *Exit A30 at Scorrier sign, follow signs to Wheal Rose, onto A3047 then into Westway, site 0.5 mile on left.*

A quiet, peaceful park in a secluded valley setting, which is well placed for visiting both the lovely countryside and the surfing beaches of Porthtowan (two miles away). The friendly owner works hard to keep this park in immaculate condition, with a bright toilet block and well-trimmed pitches. There is a swimming pool and a games room.

Open: March to December **Last arrival:** 21.00 **Last departure:** 11.00
Pitches: 🚐 🚍 ▲; 6 hardstanding pitches
Leisure: 🏊 ⚽ 🎯
Facilities: ⊙ 𝒫 ✳ ♿ 🚿 🚻 🎦 WiFi
Services: 🔌 🔲 🛒 🛢 🧺 T
Within 3 miles: 🛶 𝒫 U 🚲 🍴

Additional site information: 6 acre site. 🐾 Cars can be parked by caravans and tents. Awnings permitted. 5mph speed limit, minimum noise after 23.00, gates locked 23.00.

Places to visit

East Pool Mine, POOL, TR15 3NP, 01209 315027
www.nationaltrust.org.uk/east-pool-mine

Tehidy Holiday Park

▶▶▶▶   90%

tel: 01209 216489 **Harris Mill, Illogan TR16 4JQ**
email: holiday@tehidy.co.uk **web:** www.tehidy.co.uk
dir: *Exit A30 at Redruth/Portreath junction onto A3047 to 1st roundabout. Left onto B3300. At junction straight over signed Tehidy Holiday Park. Past Cornish Arms pub, site 800 yards at bottom of hill on left.*

An attractive wooded location in a quiet rural area only two and a half miles from popular beaches. Mostly level pitches on tiered ground offer good privacy and seating, and the toilet facilities are bright and modern. Holiday static caravans and wooden wigwams are available for hire.

Tehidy Holiday Park

Open: All year (restricted service: November to March — shop and part of shower block closed) **Last arrival:** 20.00 **Last departure:** 10.00

Pitches: ⌂ ⌂ Å 🛖; 11 hardstanding pitches; 4 seasonal pitches

Leisure: /🛝 🎣 ▭ ☺

Facilities: 🛁 ☉ ℗ ☼ ♿ 🛁 🎇 🎏 🚮 WiFi

Services: 🔌 🔘 🛒 ⌀ T

Within 3 miles: 🚲 ℘ ∪ ◎ 🏌 ✈ 🎡

Additional site information: 4.5 acre site. Cars can be parked by caravans and tents. Awnings permitted. No pets, no noise after 23.00. Pre-booking required for large motorhomes and caravans. Off licence, cooking shelter, trampoline.

Glamping available: Wooden wigwams. **Changeover days:** Any day

Additional glamping information: Wooden wigwams (sleep maximum of 5) offer cooking shelter, heating, fridge/freezer, microwave, kettle, TV and BBQ and picnic bench. Cars can be parked by wigwams.

See advert opposite

PORTSCATHO   Map 2 SW83

Places to visit

St Mawes Castle, ST MAWES, TR2 5DE, 01326 270526
www.english-heritage.org.uk/visit/places/st-mawes-castle

Trelissick, TRELISSICK, TR3 6QL, 01872 862090
www.nationaltrust.org.uk/trelissick

Trewince Farm Touring Park
►►► 🛖🛖%

tel: 01872 580430 **TR2 5ET**
email: info@trewincefarm.co.uk **web:** www.trewincefarm.co.uk
dir: *From St Austell take A390 towards Truro. Left on B3287 to Tregony, follow signs to St Mawes. At Trewithian, turn left to St Anthony. Site 0.75 mile past church.*

A site on a working farm with spectacular sea views from its elevated position. There are many quiet golden sandy beaches close by, and boat launching facilities and mooring can be arranged at the nearby Percuil River Boatyard. The village of Portscatho with shops, pubs and attractive harbour is approximately one mile away.

Open: April to September **Last arrival:** 21.00 **Last departure:** 10.30

Pitches: * ⌂ from £14; ⌂ from £14; Å from £14; 🛖 see price below

Facilities: 🛁 ☉ ℗ ☼ 🎏

Services: 🔌 🔘 🛒

Within 3 miles: ℘ 🏌 ✈ 🎡

Additional site information: 3 acre site. 🐕 ⊛ Cars can be parked by caravans and tents. Awnings permitted.

Glamping available: Wooden pods from £45.

Additional glamping information: No dogs in pods or surrounding area. Cars can be parked by pods.

REDRUTH

Map 2 SW64

Places to visit

East Pool Mine, POOL, TR15 3NP, 01209 315027
www.nationaltrust.org.uk/east-pool-mine

Pendennis Castle, FALMOUTH, TR11 4LP, 01326 316594
www.english-heritage.org.uk/visit/places/pendennis-castle

Great for kids: National Maritime Museum Cornwall, FALMOUTH, TR11 3QY,
01326 313388, www.nmmc.co.uk

Platinum Park

Globe Vale Holiday Park

▶▶▶▶▶

tel: 01209 891183 **Radnor TR16 4BH**
email: info@globevale.co.uk **web:** www.globevale.co.uk
dir: *From A30 at roundabout (north-east of Redruth) follow Portreath and B3300
signs. At next crossroads right into Radnor Road, follow brown site signs. In 0.5 mile
turn left at site sign. Site 0.5 mile on left.*

A family owned and run park set in a quiet rural location yet close to some
stunning beaches and coastline. The park's touring area has a number of full
facility hardstanding pitches, a high quality toilet block, a comfortable lounge
bar serving bar meals, and holiday static caravans.

Open: All year **Last arrival:** 20.00 **Last departure:** 10.00
Pitches: 🚐 from £20; 🚐 from £20; ▲ from £20; 57 hardstanding pitches;
10 seasonal pitches

Leisure: ⚫ ⚽ ☺
Facilities: 🚿 ☀ ⚫ ⓢ WiFi
Services: 🔌 ⓔ ⚫ ⓞ 🍴 ⚫ 🚮 ⚫ ⚫ ⚫ 🅣
Within 3 miles: ⚫ ⚫ ⚫

Additional site information: 18 acre site. 🐾 Cars can be parked by caravans and
tents. Awnings permitted. Shower block heated in winter.

See advert on page 87

Lanyon Holiday Park

▶▶▶▶ 90%

tel: 01209 313474 **Loscombe Lane, Four Lanes TR16 6LP**
email: info@lanyonholidaypark.co.uk **web:** www.lanyonholidaypark.co.uk
dir: *Exit A30 signed Camborne and Pool onto A3047. Straight on at next two lights. Pass
Tesco Extra on left. Right signed Four Lanes, over rail bridge. In Four Lanes right at
staggered crossroads onto B2397, 2nd right at Pencoys Hall into Loscombe Lane. Site on
left in approximately 400 metres.*

A small, friendly rural park in an elevated position with fine views to distant St Ives
Bay. This family owned and run park continues to be upgraded in all areas; there is
a smart toilet block and two family rooms. The park has a very inviting swimming
pool and a well-stocked bar and restaurant (open on Fridays and Saturdays from
late May until 1st September and each evening during summer school holiday
times). Stithians Reservoir for fishing, sailing and windsurfing is two miles away,
and the site is close to a cycling trail. Two holiday cottages are available for hire.

Open: March to October (restricted service: March to Spring Bank Holiday and 1st
weekend in September to October – bar and restaurant closed. March and October – pool
closed) **Last arrival:** 21.00 **Last departure:** 11.00

Pitches: 🚐 🚐 ▲; 5 seasonal pitches
Leisure: ⚫ ⚫ ⚫ 🖵 🎵
Facilities: 🚿 ☺ ⚫ ☀ 🛋 WiFi
Services: 🔌 ⓔ ⚫ 🍴 🚮 ⚫
Within 3 miles: ⚫ ⚫ ⚫ ◎ ⚫ ⚫ ⚫ ⓢ

Additional site information: 14 acre site. 🐾 Cars can be parked by caravans and tents.
Awnings permitted. Families only, no commercial vehicles. Breakfast catering van during
peak season school holidays.

St Day Tourist Park
► ► ► ► 81%

tel: 01209 820459 **Church Hill, St Day TR16 5LE**
email: holidays@stday.co.uk
dir: *On A30 from Bodmin towards Redruth. 2 miles after Chiverton roundabout, left onto A3047 to Scorrier. Site signed. 2 miles, left at Crossroads Motel onto B3298. Follow campsite signs, site on right.*

This rurally located park, run by keen, friendly owners, is situated in a quiet area between Falmouth and Newquay and within close walking distance of the attractive village of St Day. It provides a very good touring area with modern, centrally positioned toilet facilities. The touring pitches are divided by hedging plants to create some privacy. There is a separate small field for tents.

Open: Easter to October **Last arrival:** phone site if arriving after 18.00
Last departure: 10.30

Pitches: 🚐 🚎 Å

Facilities: 🏠 🅿 ⚒ 🔥 🅰 🛒 🍽 🎴 WiFi

Services: 🔌 🗑 🔋 **Within 3 miles:** ↻ ⊟

Additional site information: 6 acre site. 🐕 Cars can be parked by caravans and tents. Awnings permitted.

Cambrose Touring Park
► ► ► 80%

tel: 01209 890747 **Portreath Road TR16 4HT**
email: cambrosetouringpark@gmail.com **web:** www.cambrosetouringpark.co.uk
dir: *A30 onto B3300 towards Portreath. Approximately 0.75 mile at 1st roundabout right onto B3300. Take unclassified road on right signed Porthtowan. Site 200 yards on left.*

Situated in a rural setting surrounded by trees and shrubs, this park is divided into grassy paddocks. It is about two miles from the harbour village of Portreath. The site has an excellent swimming pool with a sunbathing area.

Open: April to October **Last arrival:** 22.00 **Last departure:** 11.30

Pitches: * 🚐 from £13; 🚎 from £13; Å from £13; 6 seasonal pitches

Leisure: ⚡ 🎱 ⚽

Facilities: 🏠 ☉ 🅿 ⚒ 🔥 🅰 WiFi

Services: 🔌 🗑 🍺 🔋 🛒 ⟁ T

Within 3 miles: ↧ ↻ ◎ ⊟

Additional site information: 6 acre site. 🐕 Cars can be parked by caravans and tents. Awnings permitted. No noise after 23.30. Mini football pitch.

Stithians Lake Country Park
► ► ► 75%

tel: 01209 860301 **Stithians Lake, Menherion TR16 6NW**
email: stithiansoa@swlakestrust.org.uk **web:** www.southwestlakes.co.uk
dir: *From Redruth take B3297 towards Helston. Follow brown tourist signs to Stithians Lake, entrance by Golden Lion Inn.*

This simple campsite is a two-acre field situated adjacent to the Watersports Centre, which forms part of a large activity complex beside Stithians Lake. The refurbished toilet and shower facilities at the centre include a family room, there is an excellent waterside café that also serves breakfasts. This is the perfect campsite for watersport enthusiasts.

Open: 3 April to 31 October **Last arrival:** anytime **Last departure:** 11.00

Pitches: * 🚐 from £14; 🚎 from £14; Å from £14

Leisure: ⚁ ✎

Facilities: ⚒ 🅰 WiFi

Services: 🔌 🗑 🍽

Within 3 miles: ↻ ↧ ↦ ⊟ 🔥

Additional site information: 2.1 acre site. 🐕 Cars can be parked by caravans and tents. Awnings permitted. No noise after midnight, no swimming in lake, charges apply to use equipment on lake.

| ROSE | Map 2 SW75 |

Places to visit

Trerice, TRERICE, TR8 4PG, 01637 875404
www.nationaltrust.org.uk/trerice

Newquay Zoo, NEWQUAY, TR7 2LZ, 01637 873342
www.newquayzoo.org.uk

Higher Hendra Park
► ► ► 80%

tel: 01872 571496 & 07932 572580 **Higher Hendra, Treamble TR4 9PS**
email: cowe43@btinternet.com **web:** www.higherhendraholidays.com
dir: *From A30 between Carland Cross and Zelah Hill take B3285 signed Goonhavern and Perranporth. 0.5 mile turn right into Scotland Road signed Rejerrah. At T-junction right on A3075 signed Newquay. In 300 yards left signed Rejerrah. In approximately 0.75 mile site on right.*

Situated down quiet lanes close to Perranporth, this small adults-only touring park comprises just 10 very spacious pitches (8 hardstandings; 2 grass) set in a neat and well-landscaped semi-circle surrounding a paddock, all with electricity and stunning views across rolling fields to St Agnes Beacon. Good quality toilet and shower facilities are housed in a smart cabin. This is a very peaceful base – perfect for walking and visiting the nearby beaches.

Open: All year **Last departure:** 10.00

Pitches: 🚐 from £20; 🚎 from £20; 8 hardstanding pitches

Facilities: 🏠 ⚒

Services: 🔌 🗑

Within 3 miles: ↧ ↻ 🔥

Additional site information: 2 acre site. Adults only. 🐕 Cars can be parked by caravans. Awnings permitted.

PITCHES: 🚐 Caravans 🚎 Motorhomes Å Tents 🏕 Glamping accommodation **SERVICES:** 🔌 Electric hook-up 🗑 Launderette 🍺 Licensed bar 🛢 Calor Gas ⟁ Campingaz T Toilet fluid 🍽 Café/Restaurant 🍟 Fast Food/Takeaway 🔋 Battery charging ⚡ Motorhome service point * 2019 prices 🚫 No credit or debit cards 🐕 Dogs permitted 🚫 No dogs

ROSUDGEON
Map 2 SW52

Places to visit

Trengwainton Garden, PENZANCE, TR20 8RZ, 01736 363148
www.nationaltrust.org.uk/trengwainton

Great for kids: Flambards, HELSTON, TR13 0QA, 01326 573404
www.flambards.co.uk

Kenneggy Cove Holiday Park
▶ ▶ ▶ ▶   92%

tel: 01736 763453 **Higher Kenneggy TR20 9AU**
email: enquiries@kenneggycove.co.uk **web:** www.kenneggycove.co.uk
dir: On A394 between Penzance and Helston, turn into unclassified lane opposite sign
for site.

Set in an Area of Outstanding Natural Beauty with spectacular sea views, this
family-owned park is quiet and well kept. There is a well-equipped children's play
area, superb toilets, and, in addition to a variety of meals available in the excellent
site café, takeaway pizzas are baked on site. A short walk along a country footpath
leads to the Cornish Coastal Path, and onto the golden sandy beach at Kenneggy
Cove. It's a half mile walk to the main road to pick up the local bus which goes to
Penzance or Helston, with many pretty Cornish coves en route. There is also a fish
and chip shop and Chinese restaurant with takeaway a short drive away.

Open: mid May to end September **Last arrival:** 21.00 **Last departure:** 11.00

Pitches: * 🚐 from £19; 🚍 from £19; ⛺ from £19

Leisure: 🎪 ⚽

Facilities: 🛁 ☉ 🅿 ✳ 🔥 🍴 **WiFi**

Services: 🔌 🔲 🚮 🧺 ⛽ 🔒 🐾

Within 3 miles: 🏌 🎣 ↻ 🚣 ⛵

Additional site information: 4 acre site. 🐕 🐕 Cars can be parked by caravans and
tents. Awnings permitted. No large groups, no noise after 22.00. Fresh bakery items,
breakfasts, home-made evening meals.

RUMFORD
Map 2 SW87

Places to visit

Prideaux Place, PADSTOW, PL28 8RP, 01841 532411
prideauxplace.co.uk

Great for kids: Crealy Theme Park & Resort, CLYST ST MARY, EX5 1DR,
01395 233200, www.crealy.co.uk

Music Water Touring Park
▶ ▶ ▶   81%

tel: 01841 540257 **PL27 7SJ**
email: info@musicwatertouringpark.co.uk **web:** www.musicwatertouringpark.co.uk
dir: From A39 at Winnards Perch roundabout take B3274 signed Padstow. Left in 2 miles
onto unclassified road signed Rumford and St Eval. Site 500 metres on right.

Set in a peaceful location yet only a short drive to the pretty fishing town of
Padstow, and many sandy beaches and coves. This family owned and run park has
grassy paddocks, and there is a quiet lounge bar and a separate children's games
room.

Open: April to October **Last arrival:** 23.00 **Last departure:** 10.30

Pitches: 🚐 🚍 ⛺

Leisure: 🏊 🎪 🎱

Facilities: ☉ 🅿 ✳ 🍴 🔥

Services: 🔌 🔲 🚮 🧺 🔒 🐾

Within 3 miles: 🏌 🎣 ↻ 🚣 ⛵ 🐎 🎣 🏪

Additional site information: 8 acre site. 🐕 🐾 Maximum 2 dogs per pitch (no Pit Bull
Terriers). Cars can be parked by caravans and tents. Awnings permitted. One tent per
pitch. Pets' corner (ponies, chickens).

RUTHERNBRIDGE
Map 2 SX06

Places to visit

Prideaux Place, PADSTOW, PL28 8RP, 01841 532411
prideauxplace.co.uk

Cornwall's Regimental Museum, BODMIN, PL31 1EG, 01208 72810
www.cornwalls-regimentalmuseum.org

Great for kids: Pencarrow, BODMIN, PL30 3AG, 01208 841369
www.pencarrow.co.uk

Crealy Theme Park & Resort, CLYST ST MARY, EX5 1DR, 01395 233200
www.crealy.co.uk

Ruthern Valley Holidays

▶ ▶ ▶   84%

tel: 01208 831395 **PL30 5LU**
email: camping@ruthernvalley.com **web:** www.ruthernvalley.com
dir: A389 through Bodmin, follow St Austell signs, then Lanivet signs. At top of hill right
onto unclassified road signed Ruthernbridge. Follow signs.

An attractive woodland site peacefully located in a small river valley west of
Bodmin Moor. This away-from-it-all park is ideal for those wanting a quiet holiday,
and the informal pitches are spread in four natural areas, with plenty of sheltered

LEISURE: 🏊 Indoor swimming pool 🏊 Outdoor swimming pool 🎪 Children's playground 🧒 Kids' club 🎾 Tennis court 🎱 Games room 📺 Separate TV room
🏌 Golf course 🏌 Pitch n putt 🚣 Boats for hire 🚲 Bikes for hire 🎬 Cinema 🎵 Entertainment 🎣 Fishing ⛳ Mini golf 🏄 Watersports 🏋 Gym 🏟 Sports field ⛺ Stables
FACILITIES: 🛁 Baths/Shower ☉ Electric shaver sockets 🅿 Hairdryer ✳ Ice Pack Facility 🍼 Baby facilities ♿ Disabled facilities 🏪 Shop on site or within 200yds
🔥 BBQ area 🍴 Picnic area **WiFi** WiFi

space. There are also 12 lodges, heated wooden wigwams, wooden pods, 'mega' pods and static holiday vans for hire.

Open: All year **Last arrival:** 20.30 **Last departure:** noon

Pitches: 🚐 🚌 Å 🏠; 2 hardstanding pitches

Leisure: ⛲

Facilities: ☉ ✳ ⑤ 🍴 🚻 **WiFi**

Services: 🔌 ⑥ 🎢 🔋 🔒 ⌀ Ⓣ

Within 3 miles: 🚶 🏕 ∪

Additional site information: 7.5 acre site. ⊗ Cars can be parked by caravans and tents. Awnings permitted. No noise 22.30–07.00, no fires. Farm animals. Freshly baked bread and croissants.

Glamping available: 4 wooden wigwams; 3 wooden pods.

Additional glamping information: Cars can be parked by units

ST AGNES	Map 2 SW75

Places to visit

Royal Cornwall Museum, TRURO, TR1 2SJ, 01872 272205
www.royalcornwallmuseum.org.uk

Trerice, TRERICE, TR8 4PG, 01637 875404
www.nationaltrust.org.uk/trerice

Premier Park

Beacon Cottage Farm Touring Park
►►►►► 84%

tel: 01872 552347 & 07879 413862 **Beacon Drive TR5 0NU**
email: jane@beaconcottagefarmholidays.co.uk
web: www.beaconcottagefarmholidays.co.uk
dir: *From A30 at Threeburrows roundabout take B3277 to St Agnes, left into Goonvrea Road, right into Beacon Drive, follow brown sign to site.*

A neat and compact site on a working farm, utilising a cottage and outhouses, an old orchard and adjoining walled paddock. The location on a headland looking north-east along the coast has stunning views towards St Ives, and the keen friendly family owners keep all areas of their site very well maintained.

Open: April to October **Last arrival:** 20.00 **Last departure:** noon

Pitches: * 🚐 from £20; 🚌 from £20; Å from £20; 6 hardstanding pitches; 6 seasonal pitches

Leisure: ⚏ ⚽

Facilities: 🛁 ☉ 🎣 ✳ 🚻 **WiFi**

Services: 🔌 ⑥ 🔋 ⌁ 🔒 ⌀

Within 3 miles: 🚶 🎣 ∪ ◎ 🏄 🎿 ⑤

Additional site information: 5 acre site. 🐕 Cars can be parked by caravans and tents. Awnings permitted. No large groups, no noise after 22.00. Secure year-round caravan storage, dog exercise field.

Presingoll Farm Caravan & Camping Park
►►►► 85%

tel: 01872 552333 **TR5 0PB**
email: pam@presingollfarm.co.uk **web:** www.presingollfarm.co.uk
dir: *From A30 at Chiverton roundabout take B3277 towards St Agnes. Site 3 miles on right.*

An attractive rural park adjoining farmland, with extensive views of the coast beyond. Family owned and run, with level grass pitches, and a modernised toilet block in smart converted farm buildings. There is also a campers' room with microwave, freezer, kettle and free coffee and tea, and a children's play area. This is an ideal base for touring the Newquay and St Ives areas.

Open: Easter and April to October **Last departure:** 10.00

Pitches: * 🚐 from £17; 🚌 from £17; Å from £17; 6 hardstanding pitches

Leisure: ⚏

Facilities: 🛁 ☉ 🎣 ✳ ♿ ⑤ 🚻 **WiFi**

Services: 🔌 ⑥ 🔋

Within 3 miles: 🚶 🎣 ∪

Additional site information: 5 acre site. 🐕 Cars can be parked by caravans and tents. Awnings permitted. No large groups. Car hire can be arranged.

ST AUSTELL
Map 2 SX05

See also Carlyon Bay

Places to visit

The Shipwreck and Heritage Centre, ST AUSTELL, PL25 3NX, 01726 69897
www.shipwreckcharlestown.com

Eden Project, ST AUSTELL, PL24 2SG, 01726 811911
www.edenproject.com

Great for kids: Wheal Martyn, ST AUSTELL, PL26 8XG, 01726 850362
www.wheal-martyn.com

Premier Park

River Valley Holiday Park
▶▶▶▶▶ 89%

tel: 01726 73533 **London Apprentice PL26 7AP**
email: mail@rivervalleyholidaypark.co.uk **web:** www.rivervalleyholidaypark.co.uk
dir: *Take B3273 from St Austell to London Apprentice. Site signed, direct access to site from B3273.*

A neat, well-maintained family-run park set in a pleasant river valley. The quality toilet block and attractively landscaped grounds make this a delightful base for a holiday. All pitches are hardstanding, mostly divided by low fencing and neatly trimmed hedges, and the park offers a good range of leisure facilities, including an inviting swimming pool, a games room, an internet room, and an excellent children's play area. There is direct access to river walks and an off-road cycle trail to the beach at Pentewan. The site is on the bus route to St Austell.

Open: April to end September **Last arrival:** 21.00 **Last departure:** 11.00
Pitches: * ⊞ from £18; ⊞ from £18; ▲ from £18; 45 hardstanding pitches

Leisure: ⌀ ⌂ ● ⚘
Facilities: ▭ ⊙ ⌱ ✳ ⅃ ⓢ WiFi
Services: ⌸ ⌥
Within 3 miles: ↧ ⌱ ∪ ⌇ ⌦ ⊟

Additional site information: 2 acre site. ⌖ Cars can be parked by caravans and tents. Awnings permitted.

Meadow Lakes Holiday Park
▶▶▶▶ 87%

tel: 01726 882540 & 01934 823288 **Hewas Water PL26 7JG**
email: info@meadow-lakes.co.uk **web:** www.meadow-lakes.co.uk
dir: *From A390 (4 miles south-west of St Austell) onto B3287 signed Tregony. 1 mile, site on left.*

Set in a quiet rural area, this extensive park is divided into paddocks with mature hedges and trees, and has its own coarse fishing lakes. This friendly, family park has enthusiastic and hands-on owners — all facilities are immaculate and spotlessly clean. The park offers organised indoor and outdoor activities for children in the summer holidays (there is a play barn for when the weather is unsuitable for using the two outdoor play areas), and at other times caters for adult breaks. There are animals in pens which children can enter. Self-catering lodges, static caravans, wooden pods and smaller cabins are available for hire. The bus to Truro and St Austell stops within half a mile of the site.

Open: mid March to mid January **Last arrival:** 20.00 **Last departure:** 11.00
Pitches: * ⊞ from £12; ⊞ from £12; ▲ from £12; ⌂ see price below;
11 hardstanding pitches; 30 seasonal pitches

Leisure: ⌀ ⌂ ⌇ ● ▢ ⌱ ⚽

Facilities: 🏠 ⚙ ✳ ♿ 🛁 🍴 🚻 WiFi

Services: 🔌 🔲 🍽 🚿 🔒

Within 3 miles: ⌕ ∪ ⚲ 🎱

Additional site information: 56 acre site. 🐕 Cars can be parked by caravans and tents. Awnings permitted. No commercial vehicles, no noise after 23.00. Table tennis, zip wire, hot tub hire, playbarn, air hockey.

Glamping available: Wooden pods from £45. **Changeover days:** Any day

Additional glamping information: Wooden pods: check in at 16.00; departure by 10.00. Cars can be parked by pods.

See advert on page 95

Court Farm Campsite
▶▶▶ 85%

tel: 01726 823684 & 07973 773681 **St Stephen PL26 7LE**
email: info@courtfarmcornwall.co.uk **web:** www.courtfarmcornwall.co.uk
dir: *Take A3058 towards St Austell, through St Stephen (pass Peugeot garage), right at St Stephen/Coombe Hay/Langreth/Industrial site sign. Site 400 yards on right.*

Set in a peaceful rural location, this large camping field offers plenty of space, and is handy for the Eden Project and the Lost Gardens of Heligan. An excellent new amenity block opened in 2019 and provides very high standards. Star-gazing facilities at the Roseland Observatory (including astronomy lectures) which are among the on-site attractions. It is a five-minute walk to a Co-op store, and also to the bus stop on the Newquay to St Austell route.

Open: May to September **Last arrival:** by dark **Last departure:** 11.00

Pitches: 🚐 🚙 🅰; 5 hardstanding pitches

Leisure: ⚽

Facilities: 🏠 ⊙ ✳ 🚿 🚻 WiFi

Services: 🔌 🔲 🚿

Within 3 miles: ⌕ ⚲ ∪ 🎱 🛁

Additional site information: 4 acre site. 🐕 Cars can be parked by caravans and tents. Awnings permitted. No noise after dark.

| ST BLAZEY GATE | Map 2 SX05 |

Places to visit

Eden Project, ST AUSTELL, PL24 2SG, 01726 811911
www.edenproject.com

St Catherine's Castle, FOWEY, PL23 1JH, 0370 333 1181
www.english-heritage.org.uk/visit/places/st-catherines-castle

Great for kids: Wheal Martyn, ST AUSTELL, PL26 8XG, 01726 850362
www.wheal-martyn.com

Doubletrees Farm
▶▶▶▶ 83%

tel: 01726 812266 **Luxulyan Road PL24 2EH**
email: doubletreesfarm@gmail.com **web:** www.doubletreesfarm.co.uk
dir: *On A390 at Blazey Gate. Turn by Leek Seed Chapel, almost opposite petrol station. After approximately 300 yards turn right by public bench into site.*

A popular park with terraced pitches that offers superb sea and coastal views. It is close to beaches, and the Eden Project is only a 20-minute walk away. This site is very well maintained by the friendly owners and the facilities are spotlessly clean. There is a Chinese restaurant and a fish and chip shop just 300 yards away.

Open: All year **Last arrival:** 20.00 **Last departure:** 11.30

Pitches: * 🚐 from £16; 🚙 from £16; 🅰 from £16; 10 hardstanding pitches

Facilities: 🏠 ⊙ ✳ ♿ 🚻 WiFi

Services: 🔌 🔲 🚿 🔧 🔒

Within 3 miles: ⌕ ⚙ ∪ ◎ 🎱 🛁

Additional site information: 1.57 acre site. 🐕 🚫 Cars can be parked by caravans and tents. Awnings permitted. No noise after 22.30hrs.

ST COLUMB MAJOR — Map 2 SW96

Places to visit

Prideaux Place, PADSTOW, PL28 8RP, 01841 532411
prideauxplace.co.uk

Cornwall's Regimental Museum, BODMIN, PL31 1EG, 01208 72810
www.cornwalls-regimental-museum.org

Great for kids: Pencarrow, BODMIN, PL30 3AG, 01208 841369
www.pencarrow.co.uk

Crealy Theme Park & Resort, CLYST ST MARY, EX5 1DR, 01395 233200
www.crealy.co.uk

Trewan Hall
▶▶▶▶ 86%

tel: 01637 880261 & 07900 677397 **TR9 6DB**
email: enquiries@trewan-hall.co.uk **web:** www.trewan-hall.co.uk
dir: *From A39 north of St Columb Major (do not enter town) turn left signed Talskiddy and St Eval. Site 1 mile on left.*

Trewan Hall lies at the centre of a Cornish estate amid 36 acres of wooded grounds. The site's extensive amenities include good toilet facilities, hook-ups and good security, plus a 25-metre swimming pool, and a free, live theatre in a stone barn throughout July and August. The campsite shop stocks everything from groceries to camping equipment. The site also has fine gardens, four acres of woodland for dog walking and a field available for ball games. St Columb is just a short walk away.

Open: 10 May to 9 September (restricted service: low season – shop opens for shorter hours) **Last arrival:** 20.00 **Last departure:** noon

Pitches: * 🚐 from £22.75; 🚐 from £22.75; ▲ from £16

Leisure: 🏊 🎣 🛝 🎱 🎵 ⚽

Facilities: 🛁 ⊙ 🧴 ✳ ♿ 🖺 ㎡ 📶

Services: 🔌 🔲 ♨ 🧺 📦 🌿 Ⓣ

Within 3 miles: ⛳ ∪ ◎ ⛸ 🎯

Additional site information: 14.27 acre site. 🐕 Cars can be parked by caravans and tents. Awnings permitted. Families and couples only, no cycling, no driving on fields from midnight to 08.00, no noise after 23.00. Library, billiard room, table tennis, pool table, woodland walk for dogs.

ST IVES

Places to visit

Barbara Hepworth Museum & Sculpture Garden, ST IVES, TR26 1AD, 01736 796226
www.tate.org.uk/visit/tate-st-ives/barbara-hepworth-museum-and-sculpture-garden

Tate St Ives, ST IVES, TR26 1TG, 01736 796226
www.tate.org.uk/stives

ST IVES — Map 2 SW54

Platinum Park

Polmanter Touring Park
▶▶▶▶▶

Best of British

tel: 01736 795640 **Halsetown TR26 3LX**
email: reception@polmanter.co.uk **web:** www.polmanter.co.uk
dir: *Signed from B3311 at Halsetown.*

A well-developed touring park on high ground, Polmanter is an excellent choice for family holidays – high quality is evident everywhere, from the immaculate, modern toilet blocks to the outdoor swimming pool and hard tennis courts. The pitches are individually marked and sited in meadows, and the tastefully landscaped park also offers a field with full-facility hardstanding pitches to accommodate larger caravans and motorhomes. The smart reception and shop is housed in a building that has two upstairs apartments available for hire. The fishing port of St Ives and the beaches are just a mile and a half away, and there is a convenient bus service in high season.

Open: 1 April to 28 October (restricted service: mid September to mid May – pool closed) **Last arrival:** 21.00 **Last departure:** 11.00

Pitches: 🚐 from £25; 🚐 from £25; ▲ from £19.50; 60 hardstanding pitches

Leisure: 🏊 🛝 ♿ 🎱 ⚽ **Facilities:** 🛁 ⊙ 🧴 ✳ ♿ 🖺 📶

Services: 🔌 🔲 🍽 🍴 ♨ 📦 ⛟ 🌿 Ⓣ

Within 3 miles: ⛳ 🎣 ∪ ◎ ⛸ 🎯 🎾 🏇

Additional site information: 20 acre site. 🐕 Cars can be parked by caravans and tents. Awnings permitted. Family camping only, no skateboards, rollerblades or heelys. Putting green, treatment rooms, indoor soft play, shop on site.

See advert opposite

PITCHES: 🚐 Caravans 🚚 Motorhomes ⛺ Tents 🏕 Glamping accommodation SERVICES: ⚡ Electric hook-up 🧺 Launderette 🍺 Licensed bar
🔥 Calor Gas ⛽ Campingaz 🚽 Toilet fluid 🍽 Café/Restaurant 🍔 Fast Food/Takeaway 🔋 Battery charging ⛽ Motorhome service point
* 2019 prices 🚫 No credit or debit cards 🐕 Dogs permitted 🚫 No dogs

ST IVES *continued*

Platinum Park

Trevalgan Touring Park

▶▶▶▶▶

Best of British

tel: 01736 791892 **Trevalgan TR26 3BJ**
email: reception@trevalgantouringpark.co.uk **web:** www.trevalgantouringpark.co.uk
dir: *From A30 follow holiday route to St Ives. B3311 through Halsetown to B3306. Left towards Land's End. Site signed 0.5 mile on right.*

Serious investment by the hands-on owners has taken place over the last few years at this welcoming park, which is set in a rural area on the coastal road from St Ives to Zennor. The park is surrounded by mature hedges but there are still extensive views over the sea. There is a smart wood-clad reception and shop (daily-baked bread and pastries are available), excellent upmarket toilet facilities which have family rooms and underfloor heating, and extensive landscaping across the park that has resulted in more spacious pitches which offer both privacy and shelter. A regular bus service connects the park with St Ives from late May to September. A good base for motorhomes.

Open: May to 29 September **Last arrival:** 20.00 **Last departure:** 11.00
Pitches: 🚐 from £18; 🚍 from £18; ▲ from £18; 13 hardstanding pitches
Leisure: ⚠ ◣ ⚽ **Facilities:** 🛁 ⊙ ℱ ✳ & ⑤ WiFi
Services: ⊕ 🗑 ⬆ 🛢 ⌀ Ⓣ
Within 3 miles: ↧ ℐ ∪ ◎ ⛵ ⚘ 🎏

Additional site information: 9 acre site. 🐾 Cars can be parked by caravans and tents. Awnings permitted. Fresh bread, pastries, coffee, local produce available.

See advert opposite

Premier Park

Ayr Holiday Park

▶▶▶▶ **90%**

tel: 01736 795855 **TR26 1EJ**
email: recept@ayrholidaypark.co.uk **web:** www.ayrholidaypark.co.uk
dir: *From A30 follow St Ives 'large vehicles' route via B3311 through Halsetown onto B3306. Site signed towards St Ives town centre.*

A well-established park on a cliff side overlooking St Ives Bay, with a heated toilet block that makes winter holidaying more attractive. There are stunning views from most pitches, and the town centre, harbour and beach are only half a mile away, with direct access to the coastal footpath. This makes an excellent base for surfing enthusiasts. Please note that it is advisable not to follow sat nav; use these directions and avoid the town centre.

Open: All year **Last arrival:** 22.00 **Last departure:** 11.00
Pitches: 🚐 🚍 ▲; 31 hardstanding pitches
Leisure: ◢ ⚠ ◣
Facilities: 🛁 ⊙ ℱ ✳ & ⑤ 🎏 WiFi
Services: ⊕ 🗑 🍴 🎰 ⬆ 🛢 ⌀ Ⓣ
Within 3 miles: ↧ ℐ ∪ ◎ ⛵ ⚘ 🎏

Additional site information: 6 acre site. 🐾 Cars can be parked by caravans and tents. Awnings permitted. No disposable BBQs.

LEISURE: 🏊 Indoor swimming pool 🏊 Outdoor swimming pool ⚠ Children's playground 👦 Kids' club 🎾 Tennis court 🎱 Games room 📺 Separate TV room
↧ Golf course 🎯 Pitch n putt ⛵ Boats for hire 🚲 Bikes for hire 🎬 Cinema 🎵 Entertainment 🎣 Fishing ◎ Mini golf 🏄 Watersports 💪 Gym 🏈 Sports field ∪ Stables
FACILITIES: 🛁 Baths/Shower ⊙ Electric shaver sockets ℱ Hairdryer ✳ Ice Pack Facility 👶 Baby facilities & Disabled facilities ⑤ Shop on site or within 200yds
🍴 BBQ area 🎏 Picnic area WiFi WiFi

Higher Penderleath Caravan & Camping Park
▶▶▶▶ 83%

tel: 01736 798403 & 07840 208542 **Towednack TR26 3AF**
email: holidays@penderleath.co.uk **web:** www.penderleath.co.uk
dir: *From A30 take A3074 towards St Ives. Left at 2nd mini-roundabout, approximately 3 miles to T-junction. Left, then immediately right. Next left.*

Set in a rugged rural location, this tranquil park has extensive views towards St Ives Bay and the north coast. Facilities are all housed in modernised granite barns, and include spotless toilets with fully serviced shower rooms, and there's a quiet licensed bar with beer garden, a food takeaway, breakfast room and bar meals. The owners are welcoming and helpful. There is a bus service to St Ives, available in high season.

Open: All year **Last arrival:** 21.30 **Last departure:** 10.30

Pitches: ⊞ ⊞ ⋏; 5 seasonal pitches

Leisure: ⋀ ⬟ **Facilities:** 🖬 ⊙ ℱ ☀ ⅚ ⑤ 🖢

Services: ⊕ ⑥ 🍴 🍴 🛒 🛒 ⚓ ⌀ 🅃

Within 3 miles: ⌿ ℘ ∪ ⊚ ⛵ ⛵ ⊞

Additional site information: 10 acre site. ⋔ Dogs must be well behaved and on a fixed short lead. Cars can be parked by caravans and tents. Awnings permitted. No campfires, no noise after 23.00.

Roselands Caravan and Camping Park
▶▶▶ 90%

tel: 01736 788571 & 07718 745065 **Dowran TR19 7RS**
email: info@roselands.co.uk **web:** www.roselands.co.uk
dir: *From A30 (Penzance bypass) onto A3071 for St Just. 5 miles, left at sign after tin mine chimney, follow signs to site.*

A small, friendly park in a sheltered rural setting, an ideal location for a quiet family holiday. The owners continue to upgrade the park, with new electrics to pitches and smart new signage added in 2019, and in addition to the attractive little bar there is an indoor games room, children's playground and good toilet facilities.

Open: March to October **Last arrival:** 21.00 **Last departure:** 11.00

Pitches: ⊞ ⊞ ⋏

Leisure: ⋀ ⬟

Facilities: 🖬 ⊙ ℱ ☀ ⑤ 🖢 🖵 📶

Services: ⊕ ⑥ 🍴 ⚓ ⌀ 🅃

Within 3 miles: ⌿ ℘ ∪ ⛵

Additional site information: 4 acre site. ⋔ Cars can be parked by caravans and tents. Awnings permitted. Dog walks on moor adjacent to park.

PITCHES: ⊞ Caravans ⊞ Motorhomes ⋏ Tents ⌂ Glamping accommodation **SERVICES:** ⊕ Electric hook-up ⑥ Launderette 🍴 Licensed bar
⚓ Calor Gas ⌀ Campingaz 🅃 Toilet fluid 🍴 Café/Restaurant 🛒 Fast Food/Takeaway 🛒 Battery charging ⛟ Motorhome service point
* 2019 prices ⊛ No credit or debit cards ⋔ Dogs permitted ⊗ No dogs

ST JUST (NEAR LAND'S END) *continued*

Trevaylor Caravan & Camping Park

►►► 86%

tel: 01736 787016 & 07816 992519 **Botallack TR19 7PU**
email: trevaylor@cornishcamping.co.uk **web:** www.cornishcamping.co.uk
dir: *On B3306 (St Just to St Ives road), site on right 0.75 mile from St Just.*

A sheltered grassy site located off the beaten track in a peaceful location at the western tip of Cornwall; it makes an ideal base for discovering Penzance and Land's End. The dramatic coastline and the pretty villages nearby are truly unspoilt. Clean, well-maintained facilities including a good shop are offered along with a bar serving meals. The enthusiastic owners offer pitches with electric hook-ups and a shower block with heating. An open-top bus stops at the entrance to the site.

Open: All year **Last arrival:** 21.00 **Last departure:** 11.00

Pitches: ⊕ ⊕ ▲; 11 hardstanding pitches

Leisure: ⚴ ◕ ▭

Facilities: ⌂ ℱ ✳ ⑤ WiFi

Services: ◉ ⑤ ▯ ◍ ⑩ ⚏ ⚒ ⚐ ⬧ 🄣

Within 3 miles: ⚲ ⚘ ⋃ ⚏

Additional site information: 6 acre site. ⌁ Cars can be parked by caravans and tents. Awnings permitted. Quiet after 22.00.

Secret Garden Caravan & Camping Park

►►► 81%

tel: 01736 788301 **Bosavern House TR19 7RD**
email: mail@bosavern.com **web:** www.secretbosavern.com
dir: *Exit A3071 near St Just onto B3306 (Land's End road). Site 0.5 mile on left.*

A neat little site in a walled garden behind a guest house, where visitors can enjoy breakfast, and snacks in the bar in the evening. This site is in a fairly sheltered location with all grassy pitches. Please note that there is no children's playground.

Open: March to October **Last arrival:** 22.00 **Last departure:** noon

Pitches: ⊕ ⊕ ▲

Facilities: ⌂ ⊙ ✳ WiFi

Services: ◉ ⑤ ▯ ⚏ ⚒

Within 3 miles: ⚲ ⚘ ⚏ ⑤

Additional site information: 1.5 acre site. ⌁ Cars can be parked by caravans and tents. Awnings permitted. No open fires or fire pits.

ST JUST-IN-ROSELAND

Places to visit

St Mawes Castle, ST MAWES, TR2 5DE, 01326 270526
www.english-heritage.org.uk/visit/places/st-mawes-castle

Trelissick, TRELISSICK, TR3 6QL, 01872 862090
www.nationaltrust.org.uk/trelissick

ST JUST-IN-ROSELAND Map 2 SW83

Platinum Park

Trethem Mill Touring Park

►►►►►

tel: 01872 580504 **TR2 5JF**
email: reception@trethem.com **web:** www.trethem.com
dir: *From Tregony on A3078 to St Mawes. 2 miles after Trewithian, follow signs to site.*

A quality park in all areas, immaculately maintained and with good amenities including a reception, shop, laundry and disabled/family room. This carefully-tended and sheltered park is in a lovely rural setting, with spacious pitches separated by young trees and shrubs. The very keen family who own the site are continually looking for ways to enhance its facilities. A pizza van, serving excellent wood-fired pizzas, visits the site once a week. Year on year improvements, high standards and great attention to detail across the park ensures Trethem Mill is one of Cornwall's top parks.

Open: April to mid October **Last arrival:** 19.00 **Last departure:** 11.00

Pitches: * ⊕ from £24; ⊕ from £24; ▲ from £24; 67 hardstanding pitches

Leisure: ⚴ ✿ **Facilities:** ⌂ ⊙ ℱ ✳ ⚅ ⑤ WiFi

Services: ◉ ⑤ ⚐ ⚐ ⬧ 🄣

Within 3 miles: ⚘ ⚏ ⚏

Additional site information: 11 acre site. ⌁ Cars can be parked by caravans and tents. Awnings permitted. No bikes, skateboards or rollerblades. Information centre. Car hire can be arranged.

See advert opposite

ST MARY'S (ISLES OF SCILLY)
Map 2 SV91

Places to visit

Isles of Scilly Museum, ST MARY'S, TR21 0JT, 01720 422337
www.iosmuseum.org

Bant's Carn Burial Chamber and Halangy Down Ancient Village, ST MARY'S, TR21 0NS, 0370 333 1181
www.english-heritage.org.uk/visit/places/bants-carn-burial-chamber-and-halangy-down-ancient-village

Garrison Campsite

►►► 86%

tel: 01720 422670 **Tower Cottage, The Garrison TR21 0LS**
email: info@garrisonholidays.com **web:** www.garrisonholidays.com
dir: *10 minutes' walk from quay to site.*

Set on the top of an old fort with superb views, this park offers tent-only pitches in a choice of well-sheltered paddocks, including eight fully-equipped, ready-erected tents which are available for hire. There are modern toilet facilities (with powerful showers), a superb children's play area and a good shop at this attractive site, which is only 10 minutes from the town, the quay and the nearest beaches. There is easy access to the other islands via the direct boat service from the Hugh Town quay; the campsite owners will transport all luggage, camping equipment etc to and from the quay. Good food is available in the many hostelries in the main town.

Open: Easter to October **Last arrival:** 20.00 **Last departure:** 19.00

Pitches: * ⚠ from £26; ⚑ see prices below

Facilities: 🏠 ☺ ☂ ✳ Ⓢ **Services:** 🔌 🗑 🔋 🛒 ⚒

Within 3 miles: ⚓ 🎣 ∪ ⛷ ≈

Additional site information: 9.5 acre site. ⚑ Dogs by prior arrangement only. No cars on site, no open fires.

Glamping available: Ready-erected tents from £165. **Changeover days:** Monday to Saturday

Additional glamping information: Ready-erected tents sleep 1-4 people (£275 for 4), minimum stay 3 nights. No dogs allowed.

ST MERRYN (NEAR PADSTOW)
Map 2 SW87

Places to visit

Prideaux Place, PADSTOW, PL28 8RP, 01841 532411
prideauxplace.co.uk

Great for kids: Crealy Theme Park & Resort, CLYST ST MARY, EX5 1DR, 01395 233200, www.crealy.co.uk

Premier Park

Atlantic Bays Holiday Park
►►►► 90%

tel: 01841 520855 **St Merryn PL28 8PY**
email: info@atlanticbaysholidaypark.co.uk **web:** www.atlanticbaysholidaypark.co.uk
dir: *From A30 south-west of Bodmin take exit signed Victoria and Roche, 1st exit at roundabout. At Trekenning roundabout 4th exit signed A39 and Wadebridge. At Winnards Perch roundabout left, B3274 signed Padstow. Left in 3 miles, follow signs.*

Atlantic Bays has a mix of hardstanding and grass pitches, a high quality toilet and shower block and a comfortable bar and restaurant. The park is set in a rural area yet only two miles from the coast and beautiful sandy beaches, and within easy reach of the quaint fishing village of Padstow, and Newquay for fantastic surfing.

Open: March to 2 January **Last arrival:** 21.00 **Last departure:** noon

Pitches: 🚐 🚍 ⚠; 50 hardstanding pitches; 6 seasonal pitches

Leisure: 🎱 🎣 ☼

Facilities: ☺ ☂ ✳ ♿ Ⓢ 🍴 🗂 🚻 WiFi

Services: 🔌 🗑 🍴 🍺 ⚒ Ⓣ

Within 3 miles: ⚓ 🎣 ∪ ◎ ⛷ ≈ 🎯

Additional site information: 27 acre site. ⚑ Cars can be parked by caravans and tents. Awnings permitted.

trethem mill ★★★★★ **touring park**

Bestof British

CAMPSITE OF THE YEAR SOUTH WEST WINNER
Caravan & Camping Awards 2018-2019

01872 580504   St Just-in-Roseland   Nr St Mawes   Cornwall   TR2 5JF   www.trethem.com

ST MERRYN (NEAR PADSTOW) *continued*

Carnevas Holiday Park
▶▶▶▶ 86%

tel: 01841 520230 **Carnevas Farm PL28 8PN**
email: carnevascampsite@aol.com web: www.carnevasholidaypark.com
dir: *From St Merryn on B3276 towards Porthcothan Bay. In approximately 2 miles turn right at site sign onto unclassified road opposite Tredrea Inn. Site 0.25 mile on right.*

A family-run park on a working farm, divided into four paddocks on slightly sloping grass. The toilets are central to all areas, and there is a small licensed bar serving bar meals. An ideal base for exploring the fishing town of Padstow or the surfing beach at Newquay.

Open: April to October (restricted service: April to end May and early September to end October – shop, bar and restaurant closed)

Pitches: * 🚐 from £13.50; 🚌 from £13.50; ⛺ from £13.50

Leisure: 🅐 🔍

Facilities: 🏠 ☉ 🌡 ✳ ᵬ 🖇 WiFi

Services: 🔌 🔋 📶 🍴 ♨ 🛒 🔱 🔒 🧼 T

Within 3 miles: ⅃ ℰ ∪ ⚓

Additional site information: 8 acre site. 🐾 Cars can be parked by caravans and tents. Awnings permitted. No skateboards, no supermarket deliveries.

Tregavone Touring Park
▶▶▶ 83% 🏛

tel: 01841 520148 & 07812 841024 **Tregavone Farm PL28 8JZ**
email: info@tregavonefarm.co.uk web: www.tregavonefarm.co.uk
dir: *From A389 towards Padstow, right after Little Petherick. In 1 mile just after Padstow Holiday Park turn left onto unclassified road signed Tregavone. Site on left in approximately 1 mile.*

Situated on a working farm with unspoilt country views, this spacious grassy park, run by friendly family owners, has seen investment in recent years which includes the addition of a quality shower block. Tregavone Touring Park makes the ideal base for exploring the north Cornish coast and the seven local golden beaches with surfing areas, or for enjoying quiet country walks that lead from the park.

Open: March to October **Last arrival:** 22.00 **Last departure:** 10.00

Pitches: * 🚐 from £18; 🚌 from £18; ⛺ from £18; 🏕 see price below; 24 seasonal pitches

Leisure: 🅐 ⚙

Facilities: 🏠 ☉ 🌡 ✳ 🖇 🎋 WiFi

Services: 🔌 🔋 🛒 🔱

Within 3 miles: ⅃ ℰ ∪ ◎ ⚓ ⚓

Additional site information: 3 acre site. 🐾 Cars can be parked by caravans and tents. Awnings permitted. Dogs must be kept on leads at all times, no noise after 23.00, BBQs and fire pits to be put on blocks. Fresh eggs and fresh bread available; forest school and yoga on site.

Glamping available: Bell tents from £30. **Changeover days:** Friday

Additional glamping information: Furnished with double beds, fridge, shared kitchen area with BBQ, gas stove, fire pit and picnic table. Under-shelter canvas for eating and drinking. Cars can be parked by bell tents.

Trevedra Farm Caravan & Camping Site
▶▶▶▶ 92%

tel: 01736 871818 & 871835 **TR19 7BE**
email: trevedra@btconnect.com web: www.trevedrafarm.co.uk
dir: *Take A30 towards Land's End. After junction with B3306 turn right into farm lane. (Note sat nav directs beyond site entrance to next lane which is unsuitable for caravans).*

A working farm, just a mile from Land's End, with sea views over Gwynver Beach to the Scilly Isles beyond. This popular campsite offers an excellent and well-appointed toilet block, a well-stocked shop plus cooked breakfasts, Sunday roasts and evening meals are available from the food bar; takeaway is also available. The heated amenity block includes four separate bathrooms. There is direct access to the coastal footpath, and two beautiful beaches are just a short walk away.

Open: Easter (or April) to October **Last arrival:** 19.00 (later arrivals by prior arrangement) **Last departure:** 10.30

Pitches: 🚐 🚌 ⛺

Facilities: 🏠 ☉ 🌡 ✳ ᵬ 🖇 WiFi

Services: 🔌 🔋 🍴 ♨ 🛒 🔱 🔒 🧼 T

Within 3 miles: ⅃ ℰ ⚓

Additional site information: 8 acre site. 🐾 Cars can be parked by caravans and tents. Awnings permitted. No open fires, no noise 22.00–08.00. Fresh produce, newspapers, bread, milk, local meat available. Car hire can be arranged.

Places to visit

Trerice, TRERICE, TR8 4PG, 01637 875404
www.nationaltrust.org.uk/trerice

Blue Reef Aquarium, NEWQUAY, TR7 1DU, 01637 878134
www.bluereefaquarium.co.uk/newquay

Great for kids: Dairy Land Farm World, NEWQUAY, TR8 5AA, 01872 510246
www.dairylandfarmworld.com

LEISURE: 🏊 Indoor swimming pool 🏊 Outdoor swimming pool 🅐 Children's playground 🪁 Kids' club 🎾 Tennis court 🔍 Games room 🖥 Separate TV room
⅃ Golf course 🏌 Pitch n putt 🚣 Boats for hire 🚲 Bikes for hire 🎬 Cinema 🎵 Entertainment 🎣 Fishing ◎ Mini golf 🏄 Watersports 🏋 Gym ⚙ Sports field ∪ Stables
FACILITIES: 🏠 Baths/Shower ☉ Electric shaver sockets 🌡 Hairdryer ✳ Ice Pack Facility 🍼 Baby facilities ᵬ Disabled facilities 🖇 Shop on site or within 200yds
🎋 BBQ area 🎋 Picnic area WiFi WiFi

SUMMERCOURT   Map 2 SW85

Carvynick Holiday Park
▶▶ ▶▶ ▶▶ ▶▶ 94%

tel: 01872 510716 **TR8 5AF**
email: info@carvynick.co.uk **web:** www.carvynick.co.uk
dir: *Accessed from A3058.*

Set within the gardens of an attractive country estate, this spacious, dedicated American RV Park provides full facility pitches on hardstanding. The extensive on-site amenities, shared by the high-quality time share village, include an indoor leisure area with swimming pool, fitness suite, badminton court and a bar and restaurant serving good food.

Open: All year **Last arrival:** 16.00 (late arrivals possible) **Last departure:** 11.00

Pitches: * ▭ from £26; ▭ from £26; ▲ from £16; 47 hardstanding pitches

Leisure: ⚲ **Facilities:** ▭ ☉ ❄ ⬥ ⑤ 🚿 ⊓ WiFi

Services: ⚡ ⑤ 🍴 🍴 ⌷ ↯

Additional site information: 13 acre site. 🐕 Dogs must be kept on leads. Cars can be parked by caravans. Awnings permitted.

TINTAGEL   Map 2 SX08

See also Camelford

Places to visit

Tintagel Castle, TINTAGEL, PL34 0HE, 01840 770328
www.english-heritage.org.uk/visit/places/tintagel-castle

Tintagel Old Post Office, TINTAGEL, PL34 0DB, 01840 770024
www.nationaltrust.org.uk/tintagel-old-post-office

Great for kids: Tamar Otter & Wildlife Centre, LAUNCESTON, PL15 8GW, 01566 785646, www.tamarotters.co.uk

Headland Caravan & Camping Park
▶▶▶ 77%

tel: 01840 770239 **Atlantic Road PL34 0DE**
email: headland.caravan@btconnect.com **web:** www.headlandcaravanpark.co.uk
dir: *From B3263 follow brown tourist signs through village to Headland.*

A peaceful family-run site in the mystical village of Tintagel, close to the ruins of King Arthur's Castle. There are two well-terraced camping areas with sea and countryside views, immaculately clean toilet facilities, and good, colourful planting across the park. The Cornish coastal path and the spectacular scenery are just two of the attractions here, and there are safe bathing beaches nearby. Holiday statics are for hire.

Open: Easter to October **Last arrival:** 21.00

Pitches: * ▭ from £16; ▭ from £15; ▲ from £16; 1 hardstanding pitches

Leisure: ⚲

Facilities: ▭ ☉ ❄ ❄ ⑤ WiFi

Services: ⚡ ⑤ ▭ ⌷ ⬛ ↯ ⊤

Within 3 miles: ✎ ∪ ≋ ⌇

Additional site information: 5 acre site. 🐕 Dogs must be exercised off site. Cars can be parked by caravans and tents. Awnings permitted. Quiet after 23.00. No camp fires.

TRURO   Map 2 SW84

See also Portscatho

Places to visit

Royal Cornwall Museum, TRURO, TR1 2SJ, 01872 272205
www.royalcornwallmuseum.org.uk

Trelissick, TRELISSICK, TR3 6QL, 01872 862090
www.nationaltrust.org.uk/trelissick

Platinum Park

Carnon Downs Caravan & Camping Park
▶▶▶▶▶

tel: 01872 862283 **Carnon Downs TR3 6JJ**
email: info@carnon-downs-caravanpark.co.uk
web: www.carnon-downs-caravanpark.co.uk
dir: *Take A39 from Truro towards Falmouth. 1st left at Carnon Downs roundabout, site signed.*

A beautifully mature park set in meadowland and woodland close to the village amenities of Carnon Downs. The four toilet blocks provide exceptional facilities in bright modern surroundings. An extensive landscaping programme has been carried out to give more spacious pitch sizes, and there is an exciting children's playground with modern equipment, plus a football pitch. A stylish new reception, shop and bar area has now opened.

Open: All year **Last arrival:** 22.00 **Last departure:** 11.00

Pitches: * ▭ from £27; ▭ from £27; ▲ from £24; 80 hardstanding pitches

Leisure: ⚲ ⌂

Facilities: ▭ ☉ ❄ ❄ ⬥ WiFi

Services: ⚡ ⑤ 🍴 ▭ ↯ ⬛ ⊘ ⊤

Within 3 miles: ⬥ ✎ ∪ ≋ ⌇ ⊟ ⑤

Additional site information: 33 acre site. 🐕 Cars can be parked by caravans and tents. Awnings permitted. No children's bikes in July and August. Babies' and children's bathroom. Freshly baked bread. Car hire can be arranged.

TRURO *continued*

Premier Park

Cosawes Park
▶▶▶▶▶ 85%

tel: 01872 863724 **Perranarworthal TR3 7QS**
email: info@cosawes.com web: www.cosawes.co.uk
dir: *Exit A39 midway between Truro and Falmouth. Direct access at site sign after Perranarworthal.*

A small touring park, close to Perranarworthal, in a peaceful wooded valley, midway between Truro and Falmouth, with a two-acre touring area. There are spotless toilet facilities (with underfloor heating) that include two smart family rooms. Its stunning location is ideal for visiting the many nearby hamlets and villages close to the Carrick Roads, a stretch of tidal water, which is a centre for sailing and other boats.

Open: All year **Last arrival:** 21.00 **Last departure:** 10.00

Pitches: 🚐 from £19; 🚐 from £19; ▲ from £17; 30 hardstanding pitches; 15 seasonal pitches

Facilities: 🛁 ☉ 🅟 ✳ 🔥 🎋 WiFi

Services: 🔌 🗑 🧺 ♨ 🔒

Within 3 miles: 🎣 🧲 ∪ ◎ 🛶 ⚑ 🏪

Additional site information: 2 acre site. 🐾 Cars can be parked by caravans and tents. Awnings permitted. No skates, scooters, bicycles etc. Car hire can be arranged.

Premier Park

Truro Caravan and Camping Park
▶▶▶▶▶ 85%

tel: 01872 560274 **TR4 8QN**
email: info@trurocaravanandcampingpark.co.uk
web: www.trurocaravanandcampingpark.co.uk
dir: *Exit A390 at Threemilestone roundabout onto unclassified road towards Chacewater. Site signed on right in 0.5 mile.*

An attractive south-facing and well-laid out park with spacious pitches, including good hardstandings, and quality modern toilets that are kept spotlessly clean. There are hardstanding pitches and most are fully serviced. It is situated on the edge of Truro yet close to many beaches, with St Agnes just 10 minutes away by car; it is equidistant from the rugged north coast and the calmer south coastal areas. There is a good bus service from the gate of the park to Truro.

Open: All year **Last arrival:** 18.00 **Last departure:** 10.30

Pitches: 🚐 🚐 ▲; 26 hardstanding pitches

Facilities: ☉ 🅟 ✳ 🔥 WiFi

Services: 🔌 🗑 🧺 ♨ 🔒 ⊘ ⊤

Within 3 miles: 🎣 🧲 ∪ ◎ 🎋 🏪

Additional site information: 8.5 acre site. 🐾 Cars can be parked by caravans and tents. Awnings permitted.

Summer Valley Touring Park
▶▶▶▶ 91%

tel: 07933 212643 **Shortlanesend TR4 9DW**
email: summervalleytruro@gmail.com web: www.summervalley.co.uk
dir: *From Truro take B3284 to Shortlanesend (approximately 3 miles). Through village, site on left.*

Summer Valley is situated in picturesque parkland that has far reaching views of farms and woodland yet is only two miles from Truro. Since taking over in 2017, the owners have focussed on providing high standards and very well maintained facilities to improve their guest's expectations; they like sharing their local knowledge so that everyone can get the best from their stay here. The park has seen significant investment with a new reception and a shop selling local produce. The refurbished amenity block is bright and modern, there's free WiFi across the park and a children's playground. Improved landscaping has been carried out to give more spacious pitch sizes, including grass super pitches (14 metres wide) and fully-serviced hardstanding pitches. There is also a new glamping pod with decking.

Open: 1 April to 30 September **Last arrival:** 20.00 **Last departure:** 10.30

Pitches: 🚐 from £18; 🚐 from £18; ▲ from £18 🏠; 5 hardstanding pitches; 6 seasonal pitches

Leisure: 🅐

Facilities: 🛁 ☉ 🅟 ✳ 🏪 🐾 WiFi

Services: 🔌 🗑 🧺 🔒 ⊘ ⊤

Within 3 miles: 🎣 🧲 ∪ ◎ 🛶 ☴

Additional site information: 3 acre site. 🐾 Cars can be parked by caravans and tents. Awnings permitted. No noise after 22.30. Campers' lounge, fresh provisions can be ordered daily.

Glamping available: Wooden pod. **Changeover days:** Any day

Additional glamping information: No smoking in pod. Cars can be parked by pod.

WADEBRIDGE
Map 2 SW97

Places to visit

Prideaux Place, PADSTOW, PL28 8RP, 01841 532411
prideauxplace.co.uk

Cornwall's Regimental Museum, BODMIN, PL31 1EG, 01208 72810
www.cornwalls-regimentalmuseum.org

Great for kids: Pencarrow, BODMIN, PL30 3AG, 01208 841369
www.pencarrow.co.uk

Crealy Theme Park & Resort, CLYST ST MARY, EX5 1DR, 01395 233200
www.crealy.co.uk

The Laurels Holiday Park
▶▶▶▶ 92%

tel: 01208 813341 & 07957 154578 **Padstow Road, Whitecross PL27 7JQ**
email: info@thelaurelsholidaypark.co.uk **web:** www.thelaurelsholidaypark.co.uk
dir: *A39 onto A389 signed Padstow, follow signs. Site entrance 1st right.*

A very smart and well-equipped park with individual pitches screened by hedges
and young shrubs. The enclosed dog walk is of great benefit to pet owners, and the
Camel (cycle) Trail and Padstow are not far away. An excellent base if visiting the
Royal Cornwall Showground. Four holiday cottages are also available.

Open: Easter or April to 31 October **Last arrival:** 20.00 (or by dark if earlier)
Last departure: 11.00

Pitches: 🚐 from £23; 🚍 from £23; ⛺ from £19; 15 hardstanding pitches;
10 seasonal pitches

Leisure: 🎢

Facilities: 🛁 ☉ ℘ ☼ 🎋 📶

Services: 🔌 🔾 🛒 🛢 🧼 🅣

Within 3 miles: 🎣 ℘ ∪ ⛷ 🚴 🎯 🏇 🛒

Additional site information: 2.2 acre site. 🐕 Cars can be parked by caravans and tents.
Awnings permitted. Family park, no group bookings, no commercial vehicles. Wet suit
dunking bath and drying area.

Lowarth Glamping

▶▶▶▶ 85% GLAMPING ONLY

tel: 01208 812011 & 07733 272148 **Chapel Farm, Edmonton PL27 7JA**
email: avrilrea@gmail.com **web:** www.lowarthglamping.co.uk
dir: *A39 from Wadebridge towards Truro. After roundabout take 1st right signed
Edmonton, pass Quarryman pub on right and cottages, 1st right, 300 yards, 1st right at
Lowarth sign.*

This site is in a secluded paddock in a peaceful location just outside Wadebridge
and enjoys stunning panoramic views across rolling countryside towards Bodmin
Moor. Avril Rea is the very proud owner and she does everything to ensure that a
stay here will be a glamping holiday with a difference; high levels of customer care
are assured. The six comfortable Lotus Belle tents, set in their own little garden
('lowarth' means garden in Cornish), are beautifully furnished in an understated,
contemporary style, with comfortable double beds with duvets, soft rugs, a wood-
burning stove plus a fully-equipped kitchen annexe. There is a separate wooden
cabin housing spotless unisex toilets and showers, a dish-washing room and
laundry, and a Shiatsu treatment cabin (with views across the Camel Estuary).
A fire pit with seating proves popular for evening get togethers.

Open: April to September **Last arrival:** 22.00 **Last departure:** 11.00

Leisure: 🏓

Facilities: 🛁 ☉ ℘ ☼ 🎋 📶

Within 3 miles: ℘ 🎯 🛒 🔾

Accommodation available: Lotus Belle tents from £45.

Changeover days: Mondays to Fridays, Saturdays and Sundays.

Additional site information: 0.5 acre site. 🚫 🐕 No pets. Social tent furnished with TV/
DVD. Cars can be parked by tents.

Little Bodieve Holiday Park
▶▶▶ 84%

tel: 01208 812323 **Bodieve Road PL27 6EG**
email: info@littlebodieve.co.uk **web:** www.littlebodieve.co.uk
dir: *From A39 roundabout on Wadebridge by-pass take B3314 signed Rock and Port
Isaac, site 0.25 mile on right.*

Rurally located with pitches in three large grassy paddocks, this family park is
close to the Camel Estuary. The licensed clubhouse provides bar meals, with an
entertainment programme in high season, and there is a swimming pool with sun
terrace plus a separate waterslide and splash pool. This makes a good base from
which to visit the Royal Cornwall Showground.

Open: mid March to October (restricted service: early and late season – shop, pool and
clubhouse closed) **Last arrival:** 21.00 **Last departure:** 11.00

Pitches: 🚐 🚍 ⛺ **Leisure:** 🏊 🎣 🎵

Facilities: ☉ ℘ ☼ ♿ 🚿 🎋 📶

Services: 🔌 🔾 🍴 🍽 🍺 🛒 🧼 🅣

Within 3 miles: 🎣 ℘ ∪ ◎ ⛷ 🎯

Additional site information: 22 acre site. 🐕 Cars can be parked by caravans and tents.
Awnings permitted. Families and couples only. Crazy golf.

WATERGATE BAY — Map 2 SW86

Places to visit

Carnewas at Bedruthan (NT), TRENANCE, PL27 7UW, 01637 860563
www.nationaltrust.org.uk/carnewas-at-bedruthan

Premier Park

Watergate Bay Touring Park
▶▶▶▶▶ 91% HOLIDAY CENTRE

tel: 01637 860387 **TR8 4AD**
email: email@watergatebaytouringpark.co.uk
web: www.watergatebaytouringpark.co.uk
dir: *From Bodmin on A30 follow Newquay airport signs. Continue past airport, left at T-junction, site 0.5 mile on right. (Note: for sat nav use TR8 4AE).*

A well-established park above Watergate Bay, where acres of golden sand, rock pools and surf are all contribute to making this a holidaymakers' paradise. The toilet facilities are appointed to a high standard and include top quality family/disabled rooms; there is a well-stocked shop and café, an inviting swimming pool, and a wide range of activities including tennis. There is regular entertainment in the clubhouse and outdoor facilities are tailored for all ages.

Open: March to November (restricted service: March to Spring Bank Holiday and September to October – restricted bar, café, shop and pool) **Last arrival:** 22.00
Last departure: noon

Pitches: 🚐 �"🚐 ⚊; 14 hardstanding pitches

Leisure: 🏊 🏊 ⚓ 🏐 🔍 ▢ 🎵 ⚽

Facilities: ☉ ☔ ❄ & ⑤ 🚿 WiFi

Services: 🔌 ⑤ 🍴 🍽 🚮 🛒 ⚌ 🔒 🪣 T

Within 3 miles: ⚓ ⚓ ◎ 🏊

Additional site information: 30 acre site. 🐕 Free mini bus to beach during main school holidays.

WHITE CROSS — Map 2 SW96

Places to visit

Trerice, TRERICE, TR8 4PG, 01637 875404
www.nationaltrust.org.uk/trerice

Great for kids: Dairy Land Farm World, NEWQUAY, TR8 5AA, 01872 510246
www.dairylandfarmworld.com

Platinum Park

Piran Meadows Resort and Spa
▶▶▶▶▶ HOLIDAY HOME PARK

tel: 01726 860415 **TR8 4LW**
email: enquiries@piranmeadows.co.uk web: www.piranmeadows.co.uk
dir: *From A30 take A392 toward Newquay. At crossroads in White Cross left, under rail bridge, site on right.*

A stunning development that provides excellent standards and facilities for couples and families. Generously spaced, superbly equipped lodges and static holiday homes are equipped with both practical and thoughtful extras and have unrivalled countryside views. The stylish main building, with a welcoming reception, is decorated and furnished with quality and comfort, and the many facilities include a modern swimming pool, special areas and attractions for children, and the excellent Serenity Spa offering a wide range of treatments. The 'Go Active' sports programme has its own instructors and the restaurant, with bar, has a spacious outdoor area for alfresco dining.

Open: All year

Holiday Homes: Sleep 8 Bedrooms 4 Bathrooms 3 Toilets 3 Two-ring burner Dishwasher Washing Machine Microwave Freezer TV Sky/Freeview DVD player WiFi Linen included Towels included Electricity included Gas included

Leisure: 🏊 ⚓ 🏐 🎵 ⚽

Facilities: & ⑤ WiFi

Within 3 miles: ⚓ U

Additional site information: 🐕

WIDEMOUTH BAY   Map 2 SS20

Places to visit

Penhallam Manor, WEEK ST MARY, EX22 6XW,
www.english-heritage.org.uk/visit/places/penhallam-manor

Cornish Coasts Caravan & Camping Park
►►► 88%

tel: 01288 361380 **Middle Penlean, Poundstock EX23 0EE**
email: admin@cornishcoasts.co.uk **web:** www.cornishcoasts.co.uk
dir: *From Bude take A39 towards Wadebridge. Approximately 5 miles to site on right (0.5 mile south of Rebel Cinema on left).*

Situated on the A39 midway between Padstow and the beautiful surfing beaches of Bude and Widemouth Bay, this is a quiet park with lovely terraced pitches that make the most of the stunning views over the countryside to the sea. The reception is in a 13th-century cottage, and the park is well equipped and tidy, with the well maintained and quirky toilet facilities (note the mosaic vanity units) housed in a freshly painted older-style building.

Open: April to October **Last arrival:** 22.00 **Last departure:** 10.30

Pitches: 🚐 🚍 ⛺; 8 hardstanding pitches

Facilities: ☺ 🗜 ☼ ♿ 🛍 🍴 ➤ WiFi

Services: 🔌 🖸 🔋 🔒 🔖 T

Within 3 miles: ⚓ 🎣 ∪ ◎ 🎿 🚿 🗓

Additional site information: 3.5 acre site. 🐕 Cars can be parked by caravans and tents. Awnings permitted. Quiet after 22.00. Post office.

Penhalt Farm Holiday Park
►►► 78%

tel: 01288 361210 & 07970 521549 **EX23 0DG**
email: info@penhaltfarm.co.uk **web:** www.penhaltfarm.co.uk
dir: *From Bude on A39 take 2nd right to Widemouth Bay road, left at end by Widemouth Manor signed Millook onto coastal road. Site 0.75 mile on left.*

Splendid views of the sea and coast can be enjoyed from all pitches on this sloping but partly level site, set in a lovely rural area on a working farm. About one mile away is one of Cornwall's finest beaches which proves popular with all the family as well as surfers.

Open: Easter to October **Last arrival:** 21.00 **Last departure:** 11.00

Pitches: * 🚐 from £15; 🚍 from £15; ⛺ from £12; 12 hardstanding pitches

Leisure: 🎣

Facilities: 🏠 ☺ 🗜 ☼ ♿ 🛍 🍴

Services: 🔌 🖸 🔋 🔒 🔖

Within 3 miles: ⚓ 🎣 ∪ 🎿 🚿 🗓

Additional site information: 8 acre site. 🐕 Cars can be parked by caravans and tents. Awnings permitted. No rollerblades, no noise after midnight. Pool table, netball, air hockey and table tennis.

Cumbria

Cumbria means the Lake District really – a rumpled, rugged landscape that is hard to beat for sheer natural beauty and grandeur. It is almost certainly England's best known and most scenic national park, famous for Lake Windermere, the country's largest lake, and Derwentwater, described as the 'Queen of the English Lakes.'

The Lake District is a region of Britain that leaves some visitors relaxed, others completely exhausted. The list of activities and places to visit is endless. The old adage 'always leave something to come back for' is certainly apt in this remote corner of the country.

This region has long been inextricably associated with poets, artists and writers. Not surprisingly, it was this beautiful countryside that inspired William Wordsworth, Samuel Taylor Coleridge, Arthur Ransome and Robert Southey. Born in the Cumbrian town of Cockermouth, Wordsworth and his sister Dorothy moved to Dove Cottage in Grasmere in 1799. Their annual rent was £5. The poet later moved to Rydal Mount in Ambleside, a family home with a 4-acre garden and a charming setting on the banks of Rydal Water. Today, both Dove Cottage and Rydal Mount are among the most visited of all the Lake District attractions. Another house with strong literary links is Hill Top, the 17th-century farmhouse home of Beatrix Potter who moved here in 1905. Located near Windermere, Hill Top and its surroundings sparked Potter's imagination and she painstakingly reproduced much of what she saw and cherished in her charming book illustrations. Tom Kitten, Samuel Whiskers and Jemima Puddleduck were all created here and the success of the 2006 film about Potter's life has introduced her extraordinary work to new audiences.

Walkers are spoilt for choice in Cumbria and the Lake District. The 70-mile Cumbria Way follows the valley floors rather than the mountain summits, while the 190-mile Coast to Coast has just about every kind of landscape and terrain imaginable. The route, pioneered by the well-known fell walker and writer Alfred Wainwright, cuts across the Lake District, the Yorkshire Dales and the North York Moors, spanning the width of England between St Bees on the Cumbrian west coast, and Robin Hood's Bay on the North Yorkshire and Cleveland Heritage Coast. The region is also popular with cyclists and there are a great many cycle hire outlets and plenty of routes available.

As with any popular scenic region of the country, the Lake District has an abundance of attractions but there are plenty of places within its boundaries and outside them where you can experience peace, tranquillity and a true sense of solitude. The southern half of Cumbria is often overlooked in favour of the more obvious attractions of the region. The Lune Valley, for example, remains as lovely as it was when Turner came here to paint. In the 19th century, writer John Ruskin described the view from 'The Brow', a walk running behind Kirkby Lonsdale's parish church, as 'one of the loveliest scenes in England.'

The Cumbrian coast is also one of the county's secret gems. Overlooking the Solway Firth and noted in the area for its wide cobbled streets and spacious green, the town of Silloth is one of the finest examples of a Victorian seaside resort in the north of England and yet outside Cumbria few people know its name. There are other historic towns along this coastline, including Whitehaven, Workington and Maryport. The Roman defences at Ravenglass are a reminder of the occupation, as is the Cumbrian section of Hadrian's Wall where it follows the county's northern coast. Well worth a visit is the ancient and historic city of Carlisle. Once a Roman camp – its wall still runs north of the city – it was captured during the Jacobean rising of 1745. The cathedral dates back to the early 12th century.

◁ Lake Windermere

CUMBRIA

AMBLESIDE
Map 18 NY30

Places to visit

The Armitt Museum & Library, AMBLESIDE, LA22 9BL, 015394 31212
www.armitt.com

Beatrix Potter Gallery, HAWKSHEAD, LA22 0NS, 015394 36355
www.nationaltrust.org.uk/beatrix-potter-gallery-and-hawkshead

Platinum Park

Skelwith Fold Caravan Park
▶ ▶ ▶ ▶ ▶

tel: 015394 32277 **LA22 0HX**
email: info@skelwith.com **web:** www.skelwith.com
dir: *From Ambleside on A593 towards Coniston, left at Clappersgate onto B5286
(Hawkshead road). Site 1 mile on right.*

In the grounds of a former mansion, this park is in a beautiful setting close to
Lake Windermere. Touring areas are dotted in paddocks around the extensively
wooded grounds, and the all-weather pitches are set close to the many facility
buildings; the premium pitches are quite superb. There is a five-acre family
recreation area, which has spectacular views of Loughrigg Fell. Two excellent
safari tents, suitable for a family of six, are for hire. An excellent children's play
area and astro-turfed five-a-side football pitch are great features. There is a
large well-stocked shop selling an extensive range of groceries.

Open: March to 15 November **Last arrival:** dusk **Last departure:** noon
Pitches: 🚐 🚃 🏠; 130 hardstanding pitches; 30 seasonal pitches
Leisure: 🎢 ♨ 🎱 ⚽ ⊕
Facilities: 🛁 ☺ ℱ ✳ ⅋ 🚿 🗐 🎋 🛒 ⷷ 🎪 WiFi
Services: 🔌 🗑 📶 ⅏ 🛒 ⊕ 📇 🚮 🝗 T
Within 3 miles: ⅃ ℘ ∪ ◎ ≋ ⅍ ⛳ 🎴

Additional site information: 130 acre site. 🐕 Cars can be parked by caravans.
Awnings permitted.

Glamping available: Safari tents

Hawkshead Hall Farm
▶ ▶ ▶   83%

tel: 015394 36221 **Hawkshead LA22 0NN**
email: enquiries@hawksheadhall-campsite.co.uk
web: www.hawksheadhall-campsite.co.uk
dir: *From Ambleside take A593 signed Coniston, then B5286 signed Hawkshead. Site
signed on left just before Hawkshead. Or from Coniston take B5285 to T-junction. Left,
then 1st right into site.*

A lovely site that is situated on a working Lakeland farm in a perfect location for
those looking for an active holiday in the heart of one of the most beautiful parts of
the Lake District National Park. The campsite lies just 10 minutes away, by foot,
from the small attractive village of Hawkshead; a path has been created to enable
guests to walk safely off-road into the village to shop or explore. There are pitches
for tourers and for tents, and this busy site has very good amenities, with spotlessly
clean, well-appointed toilets and a spacious, comfortable TV room, plus free WiFi.

Open: March to January **Last arrival:** 21.00 **Last departure:** noon

Pitches: 🚐 🚃 🛖
Leisure: ☐
Facilities: 🛁 ☺ ℱ ✳ WiFi
Services: 🔌 🗑
Within 3 miles: ℘ ∪ ≋ ⅍ 📇

Additional site information: 3 acre site. 🐕 Dogs must be kept on a lead at all times.
Cars can be parked by caravans and tents. Awnings permitted. No noise 23.00–07.00.

APPLEBY-IN-WESTMORLAND
Map 18 NY62

Places to visit

Acorn Bank Garden and Watermill, TEMPLE SOWERBY, CA10 1SP, 017683 61893
www.nationaltrust.org.uk/acorn-bank

Great for kids: Wetheriggs Animal Rescue, BARNARD CASTLE, DL12 9TY,
01833 627444, www.wetheriggsanimalrescue.co.uk

Premier Park

Wild Rose Park
▶ ▶ ▶ ▶ ▶   82%

tel: 017683 51077 **Ormside CA16 6EJ**
email: reception@wildrose.co.uk **web:** www.harrisonholidayhomes.co.uk
dir: *In Burrells on B6260 (between Appleby and Hoff) follow site signs. Left, site
signed.*

Situated in the Eden Valley, this large leisure group-run park has been carefully
landscaped and offers superb facilities maintained to an extremely high
standard, including four wooden wigwams for hire. There are several individual
pitches, and extensive views from most areas of the park. Traditional stone walls
and the planting of lots of indigenous trees help the site to blend into the
environment; wildlife is actively encouraged. There is a stylish reception with
adjacent internet café, the Pennine View bar with slate floor and pub games
(and where dogs are welcome) and a choice of adults-only and family
entertainment rooms are available. Please note, tents are not accepted.

Open: All year (restricted service: November to March – shop closed, restaurant
has reduced hours. Pool closed 6 September to 27 May) **Last arrival:** 22.00
Last departure: 11.00

Pitches: 🚐 🚃 🛖; 140 hardstanding pitches
Leisure: ⧖ ♨ ☐ ♫ ⊕
Facilities: 🛁 ☺ ℱ ✳ ⅋ 📇 WiFi
Services: 🔌 🗑 📶 🍴 ⅏ 🛒 ⊕ 📇 🚮 🝗 T
Within 3 miles: ⅃ ℘

Additional site information: 85 acre site. 🐕 No dangerous dogs. Cars can be parked
by caravans. Awnings permitted. No unaccompanied teenagers, no group bookings, no
noise after 22.30.

Glamping available: Wooden wigwams. **Changeover days:** Friday

LEISURE: 🏊 Indoor swimming pool 🏊 Outdoor swimming pool 🎢 Children's playground 🧒 Kids' club ♨ Tennis court 🎱 Games room ☐ Separate TV room
⅃ Golf course 🏌 Pitch n putt ⛵ Boats for hire 🚲 Bikes for hire 🎭 Entertainment ♫ Fishing ◎ Mini golf ⅍ Watersports 💪 Gym ⊕ Sports field ∪ Stables
FACILITIES: 🛁 Baths/Shower ☺ Electric shaver sockets ℱ Hairdryer ✳ Ice Pack Facility 👶 Baby facilities ⅋ Disabled facilities 📇 Shop on site or within 200yds
🎋 BBQ area 🎪 Picnic area WiFi WiFi

BARROW-IN-FURNESS
Map 18 SD26

Places to visit

The Dock Museum, BARROW-IN-FURNESS, LA14 2PW, 01229 876400
www.dockmuseum.org.uk

Furness Abbey, BARROW-IN-FURNESS, LA13 0PJ, 01229 823420
www.english-heritage.org.uk/visit/places/furness-abbey

Great for kids: South Lakes Safari Zoo, DALTON-IN-FURNESS, LA15 8JR
01229 466086, www.safarizoo.co.uk

South End Caravan Park
▶▶▶▶ 84%

tel: 01229 472823 **Walney Island LA14 3YQ**
email: enquiries@secp.co.uk web: www.walneyislandcaravanpark.co.uk
dir: *M6 junction 36, A590 to Barrow, follow signs for Walney Island. Cross bridge, turn left. Site 6 miles south.*

A friendly family-owned and run park next to the sea and close to a nature reserve, on the southern end of Walney Island. It offers an extensive range of quality amenities including an adult lounge, and high standards of cleanliness and maintenance.

Open: March to October (restricted service: March to Easter and October – pool closed)
Last arrival: 22.00 **Last departure:** noon
Pitches: 🚐 🚌; 15 hardstanding pitches; 34 seasonal pitches
Leisure: 🏊 ⛳ 🎣 ☐
Facilities: 🛁 ☺ ✳ ♿ **WiFi**

Services: 🔌 🗑 🍺 🏪 🔋 🔒 🌿 🚽
Within 3 miles: ⚓ 🎣 ⛳ 💲

Additional site information: 7 acre site. 🐕 Cars can be parked by caravans. Awnings permitted. Bowling green, snooker table.

BEWALDETH
Map 18 NY23

Places to visit

Mirehouse, KESWICK, CA12 4QE, 017687 72287
www.mirehouse.com

Wordsworth House and Garden, COCKERMOUTH, CA13 9RX, 01900 824805
www.nationaltrust.org.uk/wordsworthhouse

Great for kids: Lake District Wildlife Park, BASSENTHWAITE, CA12 4RD, 017687 76239, www.lakedistrictwildlifepark.com

Premier Park

Keswick Reach Lodge Retreat
▶▶▶▶▶ 93% HOLIDAY HOME PARK

tel: 01768 766510 **Bewaldeth CA13 9SY**
email: reception@keswickreach.co.uk web: www.keswickreach.co.uk
dir: *Signed from A591, south of Bothel.*

Opened following significant investment and renovation by Darwin Escapes several years ago, with creative architecture and landscaping, this former campsite has been transformed into an award-winning and must-visit destination for lovers of wildlife and outdoor activities. An ornamental lake and areas that attract wildlife was created, and the only distractions are running water and birdsong. The activities centre houses a smart reception, shop, a stylish bar and brasserie, and a well-equipped spa with treatments, sauna, gym and hot tub. The stylish one to four-bedroom lodges are very well spaced and angled to create optimum privacy as well as affording stunning views; some of the premier lodges feature private hot tub facilities. Keswick Reach is also very pet friendly offering pet packs on arrival and dog-washing facilities.

Open: All year **Last arrival:** 20.00 **Last departure:** 10:00

Holiday Homes: Sleep 8 Bedrooms 4 Bathrooms 2 Toilets 2 Two-ring burner Dishwasher Washing Machine Tumble dryer Microwave Freezer TV DVD player WiFi Linen included Towels included Electricity included Gas included Woodburner

Changeover days: 4 night breaks Monday – Thursday, 3 night breaks Friday – Sunday
Leisure: 🍴
Facilities: 🛁 ☺ 🎣 💲 **WiFi**
Additional site information: 🐕

BOWNESS-ON-WINDERMERE

See Windermere

CARLISLE
Map 18 NY35

Places to visit

Lanercost Priory, BRAMPTON, CA8 2HQ, 01697 73030
www.english-heritage.org.uk/visit/places/lanercost-priory

Tullie House Museum & Art Gallery Trust, CARLISLE, CA3 8TP, 01228 618718
www.tulliehouse.co.uk

Green Acres Caravan Park
▶▶▶▶▶ 92%

tel: 01228 675418 & 07720 343820 **High Knells, Houghton CA6 4JW**
email: info@caravanpark-cumbria.com **web:** www.caravanpark-cumbria.com
dir: *M6 junction 44, A689 east towards Brampton for 1 mile. Left at Scaleby sign. Site 1 mile on left.*

A small, adults-only touring park in rural surroundings close to the M6 with distant views of the fells. A convenient stopover, this pretty park is run by keen, friendly owners who maintain high standards throughout. The site has a caravan and motorhome pressure-washer area, a field and woodland dog walk and two superb unisex shower rooms which include a toilet and wash basin.

Open: April to October **Last arrival:** 20.00 **Last departure:** noon

Pitches: 🚐 🚙 ▲; 35 hardstanding pitches; 17 seasonal pitches

Leisure: ⚽

Facilities: 🛁 ☉ 🧴 ☀ 🚻 🛒 WiFi

Services: 🔌 🔲

Within 3 miles: ⚓ 🛒

Additional site information: 3 acre site. Adults only. 🐕 Cars can be parked by caravans and tents. Awnings permitted. No group bookings. Woodland walk (joins public footpath).

CARTMEL
Map 18 SD37

Places to visit

Holker Hall & Gardens, HOLKER, LA11 7PL, 015395 58328
www.holker.co.uk

Hill Top, NEAR SAWREY, LA22 0LF, 015394 36269
www.nationaltrust.org.uk/hilltop

Great for kids: Lakes Aquarium, LAKESIDE, LA12 8AS, 015395 30153
www.lakesaquarium.co.uk

Greaves Farm Caravan Park
▶▶▶ 83%

tel: 015395 36587 **Field Broughton LA11 6HR**
email: info@greavesfarmcaravanpark.co.uk **web:** www.greavesfarmcaravanpark.co.uk
dir: *M6 junction 36, A590 signed Barrow. Approximately 1 mile before Newby Bridge, turn left at end of dual carriageway signed Cartmel and Holker. Site 2 miles on left just before church.*

A small family-owned park close to a working farm in a peaceful rural area. Motorhomes are parked in a paddock which has spacious hardstandings, and there is a large field for tents and caravans. This basic park is carefully maintained, offers electric pitches (6amp), and there is always a sparkle to the toilet facilities. Static holiday caravans are available for hire. (Note: sat nav (including Garmin Camper) directions should not be used for accessing this site; follow directions given here).

Open: March to end October **Last arrival:** 21.00 **Last departure:** noon

Pitches: * 🚐 from £20; 🚙 from £20; ▲ from £18; 9 hardstanding pitches

Facilities: 🛁 ☉ 🧴 ☀

Services: 🔌 🔒

Within 3 miles: ⚓ 🎣 ⛳ 🏊 🎯 🛒

Additional site information: 3 acre site. 🐕 ☺ Cars can be parked by caravans and tents. Awnings permitted. Couples and families only. No open fires, no noise after 22.30. Separate chalet for dishwashing, small freezer and fridge available.

CROOKLANDS

Places to visit

Levens Hall, LEVENS, LA8 0PD, 015395 60321
www.levenshall.co.uk

RSPB Leighton Moss & Morecambe Bay Nature Reserve, SILVERDALE, LA5 0SW,
01524 701601, www.rspb.org.uk/leightonmoss

LEISURE: 🏊 Indoor swimming pool 🏊 Outdoor swimming pool 🎢 Children's playground 🧒 Kids' club 🎾 Tennis court 🎱 Games room 📺 Separate TV room ⛳ Golf course ⛳ Pitch n putt 🚣 Boats for hire 🚲 Bikes for hire 🎬 Cinema 🎵 Entertainment 🎣 Fishing 🏌 Mini golf 🏄 Watersports 🏋 Gym 🏟 Sports field ⛲ Stables
FACILITIES: 🛁 Baths/Shower ☉ Electric shaver sockets 🧴 Hairdryer ☀ Ice Pack Facility 🍼 Baby facilities ♿ Disabled facilities 🛒 Shop on site or within 200yds 🍖 BBQ area 🧺 Picnic area WiFi WiFi

CROOKLANDS
Map 18 SD58

Waters Edge Caravan Park
►►►► 84%

tel: 015395 67708 **LA7 7NN**
email: stay@watersedgecaravanpark.co.uk **web:** www.watersedgecaravanpark.co.uk
dir: M6 junction 36, A65 towards Kirkby Lonsdale, at 2nd roundabout follow signs for Crooklands and Endmoor. Site 1 mile on right at Crooklands garage, just after 40mph limit sign.

A truly lovely site bordered by streams and woodland. Despite being an oasis of calm, the site is just a short distance from the M6 and is ideal either as a stopover or for longer stays. There is a wonderful, reception that shares space with a small shop, behind which is a comfortable bar. The pitches are excellent and very well maintained, as are the spotlessly clean toilets.

Open: March to 14 November (restricted service: bar open daily 9–6 & evenings Friday to Sunday) **Last arrival:** 22.00 **Last departure:** noon
Pitches: * 🚐 from £19.96; 🚍 from £19.96; ▲ from £12; 26 hardstanding pitches; 10 seasonal pitches
Leisure: 🎣 ▢
Facilities: 🏠 ☺ ☞ ✳ ♿ 🔥 🚿 🚻 WiFi
Services: 🔌 🗑 🍴 🛢 ⌀ T
Within 3 miles: ⚲ ↻

Additional site information: 3 acre site. 🐕 Cars can be parked by caravans and tents. Awnings permitted. No noise after midnight.

CUMWHITTON
Map 18 NY55

Places to visit
Lanercost Priory, BRAMPTON, CA8 2HQ, 01697 73030
www.english-heritage.org.uk/visit/places/lanercost-priory

Cairndale Caravan Park
►►► 72%

tel: 01768 896280 **CA8 9BZ**
dir: Exit A69 at Warwick Bridge on unclassified road through Great Corby to Cumwhitton, left at village sign, site 1 mile.

Lovely grass site set in the tranquil Eden Valley with good views to distant hills. The all-weather touring pitches have electricity, and are located close to the immaculately maintained toilet facilities. Static holiday caravans for hire.

Open: March to October **Last arrival:** 22.00
Pitches: * 🚐 from £18; 🚍 from £18; 5 hardstanding pitches
Facilities: 🏠 ☺ ✳ **Services:** 🔌 🛢
Within 3 miles: ⚽ ⚲ ⛵ ✶

Additional site information: 2 acre site. 🐕 🚭 Cars can be parked by caravans. Awnings permitted.

FLOOKBURGH
Places to visit
Holker Hall & Gardens, HOLKER, LA11 7PL, 015395 58328
www.holker.co.uk

FLOOKBURGH
Map 18 SD37

Premier Park

Lakeland Leisure Park
►►►►► 88% HOLIDAY CENTRE

tel: 01539 558556 **Moor Lane LA11 7LT**
email: lakeland@haven.com **web:** www.haven.com/lakeland
dir: Off B5277 through Grange-over-Sands to Flookburgh. Left at village square, site in 1 mile.

A leisure park with full range of activities and entertainment, making this flat, grassy site ideal for families. The touring area, which includes 24 fully-serviced pitches, is quietly situated away from the main amenities, but the swimming pools and evening entertainment are just a short stroll away. In addition to a choice of takeaway food options, the stylish Lakeside Bay bar/bistro serves a wide range of hot and cold dishes and also features a section in memory of Arthur Wainwright. There is an adventure trail, aerial adventure activities and a lake offering non-motorised water sports.

Open: mid March to end October (restricted service: mid March to May and September to October – reduced activities, outdoor pool closed) **Last arrival:** anytime **Last departure:** 10.00
Pitches: 🚐 🚍 ▲; 24 hardstanding pitches
Leisure: 🏊 🏊 🎿 🐴 🎣 ⚲ 🎱 ⚽ 🎾
Facilities: 🏠 ☺ ☞ ✳ ♿ 🔥 🚿 🚻 🚲 WiFi
Services: 🔌 🗑 🍴 🍽 🔋 🛢 T
Within 3 miles: ⚲ ↻ ◎ ⛵

Additional site information: 105 acre site. 🐕 Maximum 2 dogs per booking, certain dog breeds banned. No commercial vehicles, no bookings by persons under 21 years unless a family booking.

HOLMROOK
Map 18 SD09

Places to visit
Great for kids: Ravenglass & Eskdale Railway, RAVENGLASS, CA18 1SW, 01229 717171, www.ravenglass-railway.co.uk

Seven Acres Caravan Park
►►► 79%

tel: 01946 822777 **CA19 1YD**
email: reception@seacote.com **web:** www.sevenacrespark.co.uk
dir: Site signed on A595 between Holmrook and Gosforth.

This sheltered park is close to quiet west Cumbrian coastal villages and beaches, and also handy for Eskdale and Wasdale. There is a good choice of pitches, some with hedged bays for privacy and some with coastal views. The park has a heated toilet block.

Open: All year **Last arrival:** 21.00 **Last departure:** 10.00
Pitches: 🚐 🚍 ▲; 20 hardstanding pitches
Facilities: 🏠 ☺ 🚻 **Services:** 🔌 🗑
Within 3 miles: ⚽ ⚲ ↻ ◎ 💲

Additional site information: 7 acre site. 🐕 Cars can be parked by caravans and tents. Awnings permitted.

PITCHES: 🚐 Caravans 🚍 Motorhomes ▲ Tents 🏠 Glamping accommodation **SERVICES:** 🔌 Electric hook-up 🗑 Launderette 🍴 Licensed bar 🛢 Calor Gas ⌀ Campingaz T Toilet fluid 🍽 Café/Restaurant 🔋 Fast Food/Takeaway 🔋 Battery charging ⚓ Motorhome service point * 2019 prices 🚫 No credit or debit cards 🐕 Dogs permitted ⊗ No dogs

KESWICK

Map 18 NY22

Places to visit

The Derwent Pencil Museum, KESWICK, CA12 5NG, 017687 73626
www.pencilmuseum.co.uk

Honister Slate Mine, BORROWDALE, CA12 5XN, 01768 777230
www.honister.com

Great for kids: Mirehouse, KESWICK, CA12 4QE, 017687 72287
www.mirehouse.com

Premier Park

Castlerigg Hall Caravan & Camping Park
▶▶▶▶▶ 92%

tel: 017687 74499 **Castlerigg Hall CA12 4TE**
email: info@castlerigg.co.uk **web:** www.castlerigg.co.uk
dir: *1.5 miles south-east of Keswick on A591, turn right at sign. Site 200 metres on right after Heights Hotel.*

Castlerigg Hall is situated in the heart of the Lake District with truly breathtaking views across Derwentwater to Catbells and other well-known

Lakeland fells, this really is a superb location for anyone interested in exploring the area on foot, bike or by vehicle. As well as superb toilet blocks and pitches there is a well-stocked shop and an excellent indoor campers' kitchen. In addition there are pods and caravans for hire. Castlerigg was a previous AA regional campsite winner for the outstanding quality across all aspects of the operation.

Castlerigg Hall Caravan & Camping Park

Open: mid March to 7 November **Last arrival:** 21.00 **Last departure:** 11.30

Pitches: 🚐 🚐 ▲ 🏠; 68 hardstanding pitches

Leisure: 🎣 🐾 **Facilities:** 🛁 ⊙ 🖙 ☀ 🖈 ⑤ WiFi

Services: 🔌 🖫 🛒 ⛽ 🖉 🖲 T **Within 3 miles:** ⅃ 🖉 U ◎ 🗙 🎣 ⊟

Additional site information: 8 acre site. 🐾 Cars can be parked by caravans and tents. Awnings permitted. Dogs must not be left unattended, no noise after 22.30. Campers' kitchen, sitting room, gallery. Car hire can be arranged.

Glamping available: Wooden pods.

Additional glamping information: Standard pods sleep 2 adults and 1 child; Family pods sleep 2 adults and 2 children; Castle pods sleep 2 adults and 2 children (no pets permitted). Maximum of 2 dogs permitted in standard and family pods. Cars can be parked by pods.

See advert below

LEISURE: 🏊 Indoor swimming pool 🏊 Outdoor swimming pool /🏔\ Children's playground 👧 Kids' club 🎾 Tennis court 🎱 Games room 📺 Separate TV room
⅃ Golf course 🚩 Pitch n putt ⛵ Boats for hire 🚲 Bikes for hire 🎬 Cinema 🎵 Entertainment 🎣 Fishing ◎ Mini golf 🏄 Watersports 🏋 Gym 🌐 Sports field U Stables
FACILITIES: 🛁 Baths/Shower ⊙ Electric shaver sockets 🖙 Hairdryer ☀ Ice Pack Facility 🍼 Baby facilities 🖈 Disabled facilities ⑤ Shop on site or within 200yds
🍖 BBQ area 🪑 Picnic area WiFi WiFi

Places to visit

Sizergh, SIZERGH, LA8 8DZ, 015395 60951
www.nationaltrust.org.uk/sizergh

Premier Park

Woodclose Caravan Park
►►►►► 89%

tel: 015242 71597 **High Casterton LA6 2SE**
email: info@woodclosepark.com **web:** www.woodclosepark.com
dir: On A65, 0.25 mile after Kirkby Lonsdale towards Skipton, park on left.

A peaceful, well-managed park set in idyllic countryside within the beautiful Lune Valley, and centrally located for exploring the Lakes and Dales. Ideal for that 'back to nature' experience, with riverside walks, on-site woodland walks for both families and dogs, and top notch amenity blocks with fully serviced cubicles – one is allocated for the Glamping Pod village and camping field. The generous pitches are surrounded by mature trees and seasonal planting. Parts of the site are havens for wildlife.

Open: March to early November **Last arrival:** 21.00 (no arrivals before 13.00) **Last departure:** noon

Pitches: ⊕ ⊕ ⋔; 20 hardstanding pitches; 22 seasonal pitches

Leisure: ⁄⁄\ ☺

Facilities: 🖾 ⊙ ℱ ✳ ☕ 🖭 🍴 🎋 🛒 WiFi

Services: 🔌 🖲 ⅄ 🔋 ⌀

Within 3 miles: ↧ ℘ ∪

Additional site information: 9 acre site. ⋔ Cars can be parked by caravans. Awnings permitted. Crock boxes for hire. Car hire can be arranged.

Glamping available: 10 wooden pods.

Additional glamping information: 2 night minimum stay. Variety of pods, some dog friendly, some fully en suite.

New House Caravan Park
►►►► 82%

tel: 015242 71590 **LA6 2HR**
email: colinpreece9@aol.com
dir: 1 mile south-east of Kirkby Lonsdale on A65, turn right into site entrance 300 yards after Whoop Hall Inn.

Colourful floral displays greet new arrivals, creating an excellent first impression at this former farm, which has been carefully changed to provide well-spaced pitches, with hardstandings sheltered by surrounding mature trees and shrubs. An ideal base for exploring the Yorkshire Dales and the Lake District.

Open: All year **Last arrival:** 21.00 **Last departure:** noon

Pitches: * ⊕ from £18.50; ⊕ from £18.50; 50 hardstanding pitches

Facilities: 🖾 ⊙ ℱ ✳ ☕ WiFi

Services: 🔌 🖲 ⅄ 🔋 ⌀ T

Within 3 miles: ↧ ℘ 🖗

Additional site information: 3 acre site. ⋔ ⊛ Cars can be parked by caravans. Awnings permitted. No cycling.

Places to visit

Jennings Brewery Tour and Shop, COCKERMOUTH, CA13 9NE, 01900 820362
www.jenningsbrewery.co.uk

Wordsworth House and Garden, COCKERMOUTH, CA13 9RX, 01900 824805
www.nationaltrust.org.uk/wordsworthhouse

Larches Caravan Park
►►►► 79%

tel: 016973 71379 **CA7 1LQ**
email: thelarches@hotmail.co.uk
dir: On A595 (Carlisle to Cockermouth road).

This over 18s-only park is set in wooded rural surroundings on the fringe of the Lake District National Park. Touring units are spread out over two sections. The friendly family-run park offers constantly improving facilities, including a well-stocked shop that also provides a very good range of camping and caravanning spares.

Open: March to October (restricted service: in early and late season) **Last arrival:** 21.30 **Last departure:** noon

Pitches: * ⊕ from £18.90; ⊕ from £18.90; ⋏ from £18.90; 30 hardstanding pitches

Facilities: 🖾 ⊙ ℱ ✳ ☕ 🖗

Services: 🔌 🖲 ⅄ 🔋 ⌀ T

Within 3 miles: ↧ ℘ ∪

Additional site information: 20 acre site. Adults only. ⋔ ⊛ Cars can be parked by caravans and tents. Awnings permitted.

PITCHES: ⊕ Caravans ⊕ Motorhomes ⋏ Tents ⋔ Glamping accommodation **SERVICES:** 🔌 Electric hook-up 🖲 Launderette 🍷 Licensed bar 🔋 Calor Gas ⌀ Campingaz T Toilet fluid 🍴 Café/Restaurant 🎋 Fast Food/Takeaway 🔋 Battery charging ⅄ Motorhome service point * 2019 prices ⊛ No credit or debit cards ⋔ Dogs permitted ⊗ No dogs

MILNTHORPE — Map 18 SD48

Places to visit

RSPB Leighton Moss & Morecambe Bay Nature Reserve, SILVERDALE, LA5 0SW, 01524 701601, www.rspb.org.uk/leightonmoss

Levens Hall, LEVENS, LA8 0PD, 015395 60321 www.levenshall.co.uk

Hall More Caravan Park

►►►► 81%

tel: 01524 781453 & 784221 **Hale LA7 7BP**
email: enquiries@pureleisure-holidays.co.uk **web:** www.pureleisure-holidays.co.uk
dir: M6 junction 35, A6 towards Milnthorpe for 4 miles. Left at Lakeland Wildlife Oasis, follow brown signs.

Major investment over the past few years has enhanced the facilities and improved standards on this long-established holiday destination, which is set on former meadowland and surrounded by mature trees. This rural park provides neat, well-spaced pitches with colourful hedged areas and pretty seasonal flowers, and clean, well-maintained toilet and shower facilities. The site is adjacent to a fishery where fly-fishing for trout is possible, and a farm with stables that offers pony trekking is nearby. There are seven wooden camping pods for hire.

Open: March to January **Last arrival:** 22.00 **Last departure:** 10.00
Pitches: ⌖ ⌖ ⌂; 7 hardstanding pitches
Leisure: ◣ ⛏
Facilities: ☺ ⌐ ☼
Services: ⊡ ⊡ ⊡ ⊻ ⌂ ⌀
Within 3 miles: ⌂ ⌂ ⌂ ⌂ ⌂

Additional site information: 4 acre site. Cars can be parked by caravans. Awnings permitted.

Glamping available: Wooden pods.

NETHER WASDALE — Map 18 NY10

Places to visit

Ravenglass & Eskdale Railway, RAVENGLASS, CA18 1SW, 01229 717171 www.ravenglass-railway.co.uk

Hardknott Roman Fort, BOOT, CA19 1TH, 0370 333 1181 www.english-heritage.org.uk/visit/places/hardknott-roman-fort

Church Stile Farm & Holiday Park

►►►► 84%

tel: 01946 726252 **Church Stile CA20 1ET**
email: info@churchstile.com **web:** www.churchstile.com
dir: M6 junction 36, (follow signs for Western Lakes) A590, A5092, A595 (towards Whitehaven). In Gosforth follow Nether Wasdale signs. Pass 2 pubs. Site immediately after church.

A superb, secluded park surrounded by mature trees, hedging and Lakeland-stone walls in a peaceful valley setting. The combination of indigenous trees and plants creates stunning displays to complement the beauty of the surrounding hills. A renowned farm shop with a wide range of local produce is situated within the stylish reception and café. The site offers two shepherd's huts and wooden pods for hire.

Open: March to 15 October **Last arrival:** 21.00 **Last departure:** 11.00
Pitches: ⌖ ⌂ ⌂; 16 hardstanding pitches
Leisure: ◬ ⌂
Facilities: ⌂ ☺ ⌐ ☼ ⌂ ⌂ ⌂ ⌂ ⌂ WiFi
Services: ⊡ ⊡ ⊡ ⌂ ⌀
Within 3 miles: ⌂ ⌂

Additional site information: 10 acre site. Cars can be parked by tents. Awnings permitted. No noise after 23.00. Picnic tables, table tennis, woodland walk.

Glamping available: Shepherd's hut, bell tent, pods. **Changeover days:** Friday, Saturday, Monday

Additional glamping information: Bell tent: minimum stay 2 nights (3 nights on bank holiday weekends). Pods: minimum stay 2 nights. Cars can be parked by units.

PATTERDALE — Map 18 NY31

Places to visit

Aira Force and Ullswater (NT), PENRITH, CA11 0JS, 017684 82067 www.nationaltrust.org.uk/aira-force-and-ullswater

Sykeside Camping & Caravan Park

►►► 81%

tel: 017684 82239 **Brotherswater CA11 0NZ**
email: info@sykeside.co.uk **web:** www.sykeside.co.uk
dir: Direct access from A592 (Windermere to Ullswater road) at foot of Kirkstone Pass.

A campers' delight, this family-run park is sited at the foot of Kirkstone Pass, under the 2,000ft Hartsop Dodd in a spectacular area with breathtaking views. The park has mainly grass pitches with a few hardstandings, and for those campers without a tent there is bunkhouse accommodation, yurts and tipis for hire. There's a small campers' kitchen and the bar serves breakfast and bar meals. There is abundant wildlife in the park.

Open: All year **Last arrival:** 22.30 **Last departure:** noon
Pitches: * ⌖ from £21; ⌖ from £21; ⌂ from £16.55 ⌂; 30 hardstanding pitches
Facilities: ⌂ ☺ ⌐ ☼ ⌂ ⌂ ⌂ WiFi
Services: ⊡ ⊡ ⊡ ⌂ ⌂ ⌂ ⌀ T
Within 3 miles: ⌂ ⌂ ⌂

Additional site information: 10 acre site. Cars can be parked by caravans and tents. Awnings permitted. No noise after 23.00. Laundry and drying room.

Glamping available: 2 yurts; tipis. **Changeover days:** Monday and Friday

Additional glamping information: Yurts: available from March to November, sleep 6, minimum stay 3 nights. Cars can be parked by units.

LEISURE: ⌂ Indoor swimming pool ⌂ Outdoor swimming pool ◬ Children's playground ⌂ Kids' club ⌂ Tennis court ◣ Games room ⌂ Separate TV room ⌂ Golf course ⌂ Pitch n putt ⌂ Boats for hire ⌂ Bikes for hire ⌂ Cinema ⌂ Entertainment ⌂ Fishing ◎ Mini golf ⌂ Watersports ⛏ Gym ⌂ Sports field ⌂ Stables
FACILITIES: ⌂ Baths/Shower ☺ Electric shaver sockets ⌐ Hairdryer ☼ Ice Pack Facility ⌂ Baby facilities ⌂ Disabled facilities ⌂ Shop on site or within 200yds ⌂ BBQ area ⌂ Picnic area WiFi WiFi

PENRITH
Map 18 NY53

Places to visit

Dalemain House & Gardens, DALEMAIN, CA11 0HB, 017684 86450
www.dalemain.com

Shap Abbey, SHAP, CA10 3NB, 0370 333 1181
www.english-heritage.org.uk/visit/places/shap-abbey

Great for kids: The Rheged Centre, PENRITH, CA11 0DQ, 01768 868000
www.rheged.com

Premier Park

Lowther Holiday Park
▶ ▶ ▶ ▶ ▶ 87%

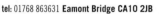

tel: 01768 863631 **Eamont Bridge CA10 2JB**
email: alan@lowther-holidaypark.co.uk **web:** www.lowther-holidaypark.co.uk
dir: 3 miles south of Penrith on A6.

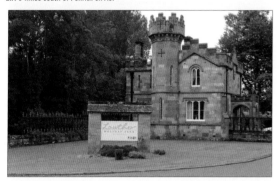

A secluded natural woodland site with lovely riverside walks and glorious countryside all around. The park is home to a rare colony of red squirrels, and trout fishing is available on the two-mile stretch of the River Lowther which runs through it. A birdwatch scheme, with a coloured brochure, invites guests to spot some of the 30 different species that can be seen on the park. Fully-serviced pitches are available.

Open: early March to mid November **Last arrival:** 22.00 **Last departure:** 22.00

Pitches: * 🚐 from £28; 🚐 from £28; ▲ from £28; 🏠 see price below;
50 hardstanding pitches; 80 seasonal pitches

Leisure: 🎱 🎣 ♪ ✎ ⚽

Facilities: 🏪 ☉ 🅿 ⚒ ⚐ ⑤ 🚻 🚮 WiFi

Services: 🔌 ⑤ 🍺 🍽 ⊞ 🔋 ↯ 🔋 🧴 🅣

Within 3 miles: ⚓ ∪ ◎ 🚣 🎿

Additional site information: 50 acre site. 🐕 Cars can be parked by caravans and tents. Awnings permitted. Families only. No commercial vehicles, rollerblades or skateboards, no cats.

Glamping available: Wooden pods from £38.

Additional glamping information: No pets. Cars can be parked by pods.

PENTON
Map 21 NY47

Places to visit

Lanercost Priory, BRAMPTON, CA8 2HQ, 01697 73030
www.english-heritage.org.uk/visit/places/lanercost-priory

Twin Willows
▶ ▶ ▶ 80%

tel: 01228 577313 & 07850 713958 **The Beeches CA6 5QD**
email: davidson_b@btconnect.com
dir: M6 junction 44, A7 signed Longtown, right into Netherby Street, 6 miles to Bridge Inn pub. Right then 1st left, site 300 yards on right.

Located close to Longtown, Twin Willows is a spacious park in a rural location on a ridge overlooking the Scottish border. All facilities, including all-weather pitches, are of a high quality. The park is suited to those who enjoy being away-from-it-all yet at the same time like to explore the area's rich history. A seasonal marquee is erected to hold regular barbecue and hog roast parties.

Open: All year **Last arrival:** 22.00 **Last departure:** 10.00

Pitches: 🚐 🚐 ▲ 🏠; 16 hardstanding pitches; 10 seasonal pitches

Leisure: 🎾 ⚽

Facilities: 🏪 ☉ 🅿 ⚒ ⚐ 🚮 🚻 WiFi

Services: 🔌 ⑤ 🍽 ↯ 🔋 🧴 🅣

Within 3 miles: ✎ ∪ ⑤

Additional site information: 3 acre site. 🐕 Cars can be parked by caravans and tents. Awnings permitted.

Glamping available: Wooden pods. **Changeover days:** Saturday

Additional glamping information: Cars can be parked by pods.

PITCHES: 🚐 Caravans 🚐 Motorhomes ▲ Tents 🏠 Glamping accommodation **SERVICES:** 🔌 Electric hook-up ⑤ Launderette 🍺 Licensed bar
🔋 Calor Gas ⚗ Campingaz 🅣 Toilet fluid 🍽 Café/Restaurant ⊞ Fast Food/Takeaway 🔋 Battery charging ↯ Motorhome service point
* 2019 prices ⊗ No credit or debit cards 🐕 Dogs permitted ⊗ No dogs

POOLEY BRIDGE

Map 18 NY42

Places to visit

Dalemain House & Gardens, DALEMAIN, CA11 0HB, 017684 86450
www.dalemain.com

Great for kids: The Rheged Centre, PENRITH, CA11 0DQ, 01768 868000
www.rheged.com

Premier Park

Park Foot Caravan & Camping Park

▶ ▶ ▶ ▶ ▶ 90% HOLIDAY CENTRE

tel: 017684 86309 **Howtown Road CA10 2NA**
email: holidays@parkfootullswater.co.uk **web:** www. parkfootullswater.co.uk
dir: *M6 junction 40, A66 towards Keswick, then A592 to Ullswater. Turn left for Pooley Bridge, right at church, right at crossroads signed Howtown. Alternatively from Penrith take A6 to Shap, then B5320 to Pooley Bridge, turn left towards Howton, site 1 mile on left.*

A gorgeous location right beside Ullswater and the wonderful fells, this site is perfect for those that wish to explore the many paths in the area; there is a lovely walk from the park's shorefront to picturesque Pooley Bridge from where the Ullswater steamer departs. There is a range of excellent touring pitches for caravans, motorhomes and tents, with high quality amenities in each of the touring areas. Pony-trekking is possible from the site and electric bicycles are available for those who think the hills are just a bit too steep. With a well-stocked shop, a very good restaurant and bar, as well as entertainment for all the family, this site certainly is a high quality, family-owned holiday centre.

Open: March to October (restricted service: March to April and mid September to October – clubhouse open weekends only) **Last arrival:** 22.00 **Last departure:** noon

Pitches: * 🚐 from £23; 🚃 from £23; ⛺ from £16; 50 hardstanding pitches

Leisure: ⋀ 🖐 ⧖ ♣ ▭ ⚓ ♫ ⌇ ⚽

Facilities: 🛁 ⊙ 𝒫 ✳ ⅋ ⑤ ⊟ 🚿 WiFi

Services: 🔌 🗑 🍴 ⑩ 🏭 🚮 ⟰ 🛢 ⌀ Ⓣ

Within 3 miles: ⋃ ⌇ ⌇

Additional site information: 40 acre site. 🐕 Families and couples only. Boat launch, pony-trekking, pool table, table tennis, kids' club in summer holidays, lakeside walk.

Waterfoot Caravan Park

▶ ▶ ▶ ▶ 86%

tel: 017684 86302 **CA11 0JF**
email: bookings@waterfootpark.co.uk **web:** www.waterfootpark.co.uk
dir: *M6 junction 40, A66 for 1 mile, A592 for 4 miles, site on right before lake. (Note: do not leave A592 until site entrance; sat nav is not compatible).*

A quality touring park with neat, hardstanding pitches (most are fully serviced) in a grassy glade within the wooded grounds of an elegant Georgian mansion. The toilet facilities are clean and well maintained, and the lounge bar, with a separate family room, enjoys lake views. An excellent new reception and shop, at the entrance, opened in 2019. A path leads to Ullswater, and Dalemain House and Gardens, Pooley Bridge and Aira Force waterfall are all close by. Wooden glamping pods and Hive Cabins (for two adults and two children) are available for hire. Please note that there is no access via Dacre.

Open: March to 14 November **Last arrival:** 21.30 **Last departure:** noon

Pitches: 🚐 🚃 🛖; 32 hardstanding pitches

Leisure: ⋀ ♣ ♫ ☺

Facilities: 🛁 ⊙ 𝒫 ✳ ⅋ ⑤ ⊟ 🚿 WiFi

Services: 🔌 🗑 🍴 🏭 🚮 ⟰ 🛢 ⌀ Ⓣ

Within 3 miles: ⌇ ⌇ ⋃ ☺ ☯ ⌇ ⌇ 🗓

Additional site information: 22 acre site. 🐕 Cars can be parked by caravans. Awnings permitted. No tents. Coffee lounge, fish and chips mobile unit (peak season only), table tennis, badminton nets, pool table. Car hire can be arranged.

Glamping available: Wooden wigwams **Changeover days:** Any day

Additional glamping information: Minimum stay 2 nights at weekends. Cars can be parked by wigwams.

SILLOTH
Map 18 NY15

Places to visit
RSPB Campfield Marsh, BOWNESS-ON-SOLWAY, CA7 5AG, 01697 351330
www.rspb.org.uk/reserves-and-events/reserves-a-z/campfield-marsh

Premier Park

Stanwix Park Holiday Centre
▶▶▶▶▶ 92% HOLIDAY CENTRE

tel: 016973 32666 **Greenrow CA7 4HH**
email: enquiries@stanwix.com **web:** www.stanwix.com
dir: 1 mile south-west on B5300. From A596 (Wigton bypass) follow signs to Silloth on B5302. In Silloth follow signs to site, approximately 1 mile on B5300.

A large well-run family park within easy reach of the Lake District. Attractively laid out, with lots of amenities to ensure a lively holiday, including a 4-lane automatic, 10-pin bowling alley, and a choice of indoor and outdoor swimming pools. There are excellent touring areas with hardstandings, one in a peaceful glade well away from the main leisure complex, a campers' kitchen and clean, well-maintained toilet facilities. Four camping pods are available to hire in Skiddaw touring field.

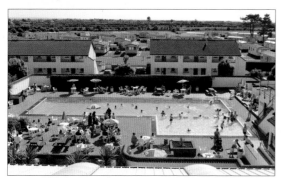

Open: All year (restricted service: closed 25-26 December for tourers; November to February (except New Year) – no entertainment, shop closed) **Last arrival:** 21.00 **Last departure:** 11.00

Pitches: * 🚐 from £22.50; 🚑 from £22.50; ▲ from £22.50; 🏠 see price below; 95 hardstanding pitches; 28 seasonal pitches

Leisure: 🏊 🏊 ⚙ 👋 🎱 ♦ ⛳ 🎯 🎵 🎯

Facilities: 🏠 ☉ ✳ 👤 🚻 🎮 ➜ WiFi
Services: 🔌 🧺 🍺 🍴 🛒 🔧 🔋 🚽
Within 3 miles: 🚶 ⛳ ◎

Additional site information: 26 acre site. 🐕 Families only. Amusement arcade, bowling alley, leisure centre.

Glamping available: Wooden pods from £30. **Changeover days:** Any day

Additional glamping information: Wooden pods sleep 4. Pet friendly pods available. No electric for pods. Own camping equipment required. Cars can be parked by pods.

See advert on page 118

Hylton Caravan Park
▶▶▶▶ 88%

tel: 016973 32666 **Eden Street CA7 4AY**
email: enquiries@stanwix.com **web:** www.stanwix.com
dir: On entering Silloth on B5302 follow signs for site, approximately 0.5 mile on left, at end of Eden Street.

A smart, modern touring park with excellent toilet facilities including several bathrooms. This high quality park is a sister site to Stanwix Park, which is just a mile away and offers all the amenities of a holiday centre, which are available to Hylton tourers.

Open: March to November **Last arrival:** 21.00 **Last departure:** 11.00

Pitches: * 🚐 from £19.40; 🚑 from £19.40; ▲ from £19.40; 23 hardstanding pitches; 20 seasonal pitches

Leisure: ⚙

Facilities: 🏠 ☉ 👤 WiFi
Services: 🔌 🧺 🚽
Within 3 miles: 🚶 ⛳ ◎ 🧺

Additional site information: 18 acre site. 🐕 Cars can be parked by caravans and tents. Awnings permitted. Families only. Use of facilities at Stanwix Park Holiday Centre.

SILLOTH *continued*

Solway Holiday Village
▶▶▶▶ 80% HOLIDAY CENTRE

tel: 01697 331236 **Skinburness Drive CA7 4QQ**
email: solway@hagansleisure.co.uk **web:** www.hagansleisure.co.uk
dir: *Phone for directions.*

A long established holiday destination set on a former wartime airfield with a wide range of indoor and outdoor activities. Both The Nags Head pub and Harley's entertainment bar serve bar food to supplement the stylish bistro. Children benefit from a wide range of activities including an indoor swimming pool, a soft ball room, great outdoor play equipment and the adjacent Silverstone animal farm. The touring and camping areas are located in a peaceful tree surrounded area with a dedicated warden to hand. Investment and improvements are planned by the owners, Hagans Leisure.

Open: March to 10 November **Last arrival:** 18.00 **Last departure:** 10.00

Pitches: ⊕ ⇔ ▲; 18 hardstanding pitches

Leisure: ☜ ⋀ ⬇ ◔ ⚽ ✪

Facilities: 🛁 ⊙ ⬤ ⑤ ⬇ WiFi

Services: ⊕ 🗑 ⊪ ⧫ 🍴 ⬛ ⬆ T

Additional site information: 130 acre site. 🐾 Dogs must be kept on leads at all times. Dog exercise area.

ULVERSTON

Places to visit

The Dock Museum, BARROW-IN-FURNESS, LA14 2PW, 01229 876400
www.dockmuseum.org.uk

Furness Abbey, BARROW-IN-FURNESS, LA13 0PJ, 01229 823420
www.english-heritage.org.uk/visit/places/furness-abbey

Great for kids: South Lakes Safari Zoo, DALTON-IN-FURNESS, LA12 0LU, 01229 466086, www.safarizoo.co.uk

---

Premier Park

Bardsea Leisure Park
▶▶▶▶▶ 89%

tel: 01229 584712 **Priory Road LA12 9QE**
email: reception@bardsealeisure.co.uk **web:** www.bardsealeisure.co.uk
dir: *M6 junction 36, A590 towards Barrow. At Ulverston take A5087, site 1 mile on right.*

This attractively landscaped former quarry creates a quiet and very sheltered site; set on the southern edge of the town, it is convenient for both the coast and the Lake District. Many of the generously-sized pitches offer all-weather, full facilities. The superb amenity blocks provide excellent privacy. The site has a well-stocked caravan accessories shop. Please note, this site does not accept tents.

Open: All year **Last arrival:** 22.00 **Last departure:** noon

Pitches: ⊕ ⇔; 83 hardstanding pitches; 50 seasonal pitches

Leisure: ✪

Facilities: 🛁 ⊙ 🖝 ✳ ⬤ ⑤ ⧓ WiFi

Services: ⊕ 🗑 ⬛ ⧫ ⬆ 🔒 ⊘ T

Within 3 miles: ⬇ 🎣 ∪ 🗏

Additional site information: 5 acre site. 🐾 Cars can be parked by caravans. Awnings permitted. No noise after 22.30.

LEISURE: ☜ Indoor swimming pool ☝ Outdoor swimming pool ⋀ Children's playground ⬇ Kids' club ◔ Tennis court ⬤ Games room ▭ Separate TV room ⬇ Golf course 🖝 Pitch n putt ⬳ Boats for hire 🚲 Bikes for hire ▤ Cinema ♫ Entertainment 🎣 Fishing ◎ Mini golf ⬳ Watersports ⚑ Gym ⚐ Sports field ∪ Stables
FACILITIES: 🛁 Baths/Shower ⊙ Electric shaver sockets 🖝 Hairdryer ✳ Ice Pack Facility ⬇ Baby facilities ⬤ Disabled facilities ⑤ Shop on site or within 200yds ⧓ BBQ area ⬚ Picnic area WiFi WiFi

WATERMILLOCK

Map 18 NY42

Places to visit

Aira Force and Ullswater (NT), PENRITH, CA11 0JS, 017684 82067
www.nationaltrust.org.uk/aira-force-and-ullswater

Dalemain House & Gardens, DALEMAIN, CA11 0HB, 017684 86450
www.dalemain.com

REGIONAL WINNER – NORTH WEST ENGLAND AA CAMPSITE OF THE YEAR 2020

Premier Park

The Quiet Site

 93%

tel: 07768 727016 **Ullswater CA11 OLS**
email: info@thequietsite.co.uk **web:** www.thequietsite.co.uk
dir: *M6 junction 40, A66 signed Workington. At next roundabout left onto A592 signed Ullswater. 5 miles (Ullswater on left), turn right at Brackenrigg Inn signed Bennethead. Approximately 1.5 miles to site on right.*

A lovely site with breathtaking views across Ullswater, and less than 20 minutes away by car there are access points to some of the best fell walking in the Lake District; maps of walks closer by are provided by the site including the 20-mile circular Ullswater Way that passes the impressive 20-metre high Aira Force. Caravans, motorhomes and tents enjoy very good level terraced pitches, and at the top of the site there are camping pods and comfortable Hobbit Holes for hire. This is a site justifiably proud of its green credentials; they have a biomass boiler that heats all the water for their well-appointed toilet block. Free WiFi is available across the whole site, and there is also a popular bar. A new shop and reception opened in 2019.

Open: All year (restricted service: low season – bar may close on weekdays)
Last arrival: 21.00 **Last departure:** noon (or 11.00 for pods)

Pitches: 🚐 🚌 ▲; 🏠; 60 hardstanding pitches; 15 seasonal pitches

Leisure: ♦ ☐ ⚽ ۞

Facilities: ☉ 🏴 ☀ ♿ ⑤ 🎋 📶

Services: 🔌 ⑤ 🍴 🛒 🔋 ⚡ 🔧 🔵 ⦿ Ⓣ

Within 3 miles: ✎ 🏊 🚴

Additional site information: 10 acre site. 🐕 Cars can be parked by caravans and tents. Awnings permitted. Quiet from 22.00. Pool table, soft play area for toddlers, caravan storage. Car hire can be arranged.

Glamping available: Bell tents, wooden pods, hobbit holes. **Changeover days:** Any day
Additional glamping information: Minimum stay – 2 nights at weekends. Cars can be parked by units.

Cove Caravan & Camping Park

▶▶▶▶ 89%

tel: 017684 86549 **Ullswater CA11 OLS**
email: info@cove-park.co.uk **web:** www.cove-park.co.uk
dir: *M6 junction 40, A66 signed Workington. At next roundabout left onto A592 signed Ullswater. 5 miles (Ullswater on left), turn right at Brackenrigg Inn signed Bennethead. Approximately 1.5 miles to site on left.*

A peaceful family site in an attractive and elevated position with extensive fell views and glimpses of Ullswater Lake. Extensive ground works have been carried out in order to provide spacious, mostly level pitches. Pretty, seasonal flowers are planted amid the wide variety of mature trees and shrubs.

Open: March to October **Last arrival:** 21.00 **Last departure:** noon

Pitches: 🚐 🚌 ▲; 27 hardstanding pitches; 10 seasonal pitches

Leisure: 🎋

Facilities: 🏴 ☉ 🏴 ☀ ♿ 🎋 🎋

Services: 🔌 ⑤ 🔵 ⦿

Within 3 miles: ✎ ∪ 🏊 🚴 ⑤

Additional site information: 3 acre site. 🐕 Cars can be parked by caravans and tents. Awnings permitted. No groups, no open fires, no noise after 22.30.

Ullswater Holiday Park

▶▶▶▶ 84%

tel: 017684 86666 **High Longthwaite CA11 OLR**
email: info@ullswaterholidaypark.co.uk **web:** www.ullswaterholidaypark.co.uk
dir: *M6 junction 40, A66 signed Workington. At next roundabout left onto A592 signed Ullswater. 5 miles. (Ullswater on left for 2 miles), turn right at phone box signed Longthwaite. Site 0.5 mile on right.*

A pleasant rural site with its own nearby boat launching and marine storage facility, making it ideal for sailors. The family-owned and run park enjoys fell and lake views, and there is a bar, a stylish café, a splendid undercover area for campers, and a shop on site. Many of the pitches are fully serviced and there are wooden cabins (some en suite) with barbecues. Please note that the Marine Park is one mile from the camping area.

Open: March to 14 November (restricted service: low season – bar open at weekends only)
Last arrival: 21.00 **Last departure:** noon

Pitches: * 🚐 from £17.50; 🚌 from £17.50; ▲ from £17.50; 🏠 see price below; 58 hardstanding pitches

Leisure: 🎋 ♦

Facilities: 🏴 ☉ 🏴 ☀ ♿ ⑤ 🎋 📶

Services: 🔌 ⑤ 🍴 🛒 🔋 🔵 ⦿ Ⓣ

Within 3 miles: ✎ ∪ 🏊 🚴

Additional site information: 12 acre site. 🐕 Cars can be parked by caravans and tents. Awnings permitted. No open fires, no noise after 23.30. Boat launching and moorings in 1 mile.

Glamping available: Cabins from £38. **Changeover days:** Any day
Additional glamping information: Some cabins are dog friendly. Cars can be parked by cabins.

WINDERMERE
Map 18 SD49

Places to visit

Holehird Gardens, WINDERMERE, LA23 1NP, 015394 46008
www.holehirdgardens.org.uk

Blackwell The Arts & Crafts House, BOWNESS-ON-WINDERMERE, LA23 3JT,
015394 46139, www.blackwell.org.uk

Great for kids: Brockhole on Windermere, WINDERMERE, LA23 1LJ,
015394 46601, www.brockhole.co.uk

Premier Park

Park Cliffe Camping & Caravan Estate
▶▶▶▶▶ 91%

tel: 015395 31344 **Birks Road, Tower Wood LA23 3PG**
email: info@parkcliffe.co.uk **web:** www.parkcliffe.co.uk
dir: M6 junction 36, A590. Right at Newby Bridge onto A592. 3.6 miles right into site.
(Note: due to difficult access from main road this is the only advised direction for
approaching the site).

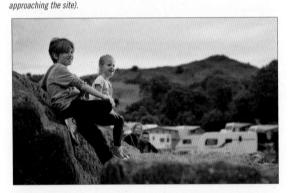

A lovely hillside park set in 25 secluded acres of fell land. The camping area is
sloping and uneven in places, but well drained and sheltered; some pitches
have spectacular views of Lake Windermere and the Langdales. The park offers
a high level of customer care and is very well equipped for families (including
family bathrooms), and there is an attractive bar and brasserie restaurant
serving quality food; 10 wooden pods, a shepherd's hut and three static holiday
caravans are for hire.

Open: March to mid November (weekends and school holidays – facilities fully open)
Last arrival: 22.00 **Last departure:** noon

Pitches: * ⊞ from £27; ⊞ from £27; ▲ from £22; ⋒ see prices below;
60 hardstanding pitches; 25 seasonal pitches

Leisure: ⋀ ✎ **Facilities:** ⬛ ☉ ⊞ ✳ ⅄ ⑤ ⋒ ⊒ ⛟ WiFi

Services: ⬛ ⑤ ⚐ ⦿ ⼢ ⬛ ⼢ ⼢ ⚐ ⊤

Within 3 miles: ⅃ ✎ ◎ ⼢ ⼢ ⊟

Additional site information: 25 acre site. ⼢ Cars can be parked by caravans and
tents. Awnings permitted. No noise 23.00–07.30. Off licence, bathrooms for hire.

Glamping available: Wooden pods from £44; 1 shepherd's hut from £72.
Changeover days: Varies depending on type of accommodation booked

Additional glamping information: Different size pods available – standard (no beds,
sleeps 2); standard dog friendly (no beds, sleeps 2 adults, 1 child and 1 dog); family
(no beds, sleeps 2 adults and 3 children); family plus (sleeps 2 adults and 2
children); premier (double bed, bunk beds, trundle bed, sleeps 2 adults and 3
children). Shepherd's hut (sleeps 2 adults). Cars can be parked by units.

Premier Park

Hill of Oaks & Blakeholme
▶▶▶▶▶ 86%

tel: 015395 31578 **LA12 8NR**
email: enquiries@hillofoaks.co.uk **web:** www.hillofoaks.co.uk
dir: M6 junction 36, A590 towards Barrow. At roundabout signed Bowness turn right
onto A592. Site approximately 3 miles on left.

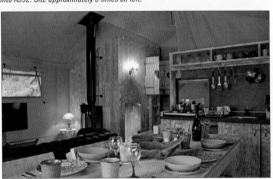

A secluded, heavily wooded park on the shores of Lake Windermere. Pretty
lakeside picnic areas, woodland walks and a play area make this a delightful
park that's perfect for families; there are excellent serviced pitches, a licensed
shop and a heated toilet block; both the ladies' and gents' amenities have
quality fittings and very good privacy options. There are very high spec pods
available for hire including two that are accessible. Three safari tents were
added for the 2019 season. WiFi is available throughout all areas of the park.
Watersport activities include sailing and canoeing, with private jetties for boat
launching. The private pier provides a regular ferry service to Bowness.

Open: March to 14 November (restricted service: Christmas and New Year self catering
only) **Last departure:** noon

Pitches: ⊞ ⊞ ⋒; 46 hardstanding pitches

Leisure: ⋀ ✎ ⚽

Facilities: ⬛ ☉ ⊞ ✳ ⅄ ⑤ ⋒ WiFi

Services: ⬛ ⑤ ⼢ ⬛ ⊤

Within 3 miles: ⅃ ∪ ◎ ⼢ ⼢ ⊟

Additional site information: 31 acre site. ⼢ Cars can be parked by caravans.
Awnings permitted. No tents (except trailer tents), no groups. Daily lake cruise in peak
season to Lakeside Pier connections to Ambleside, Bowness on Windermere. Car hire
can be arranged.

Glamping available: 5 lakeside glamping pods, safari tents.
Changeover days: Monday, Friday

Additional glamping information: Wooden pods sleep 4. Minimum stay 3 nights. Each
pod has underfloor heating, TV, shower, toilet, sofa bed, table, chairs, patio furniture
and a kitchen with two-ring cooker, microwave and fridge. Towels and linen are
included. Cars can be parked by pods.

LEISURE: 🏊 Indoor swimming pool 🏊 Outdoor swimming pool ⋀ Children's playground 🖐 Kids' club 🎾 Tennis court 🎱 Games room 📺 Separate TV room
⅃ Golf course ⛳ Pitch n putt ⛵ Boats for hire 🚲 Bikes for hire 🎬 Cinema 🎵 Entertainment 🎣 Fishing ◎ Mini golf 🏄 Watersports 💪 Gym ⚽ Sports field ∪ Stables
FACILITIES: 🛁 Baths/Shower ☉ Electric shaver sockets ⊞ Hairdryer ✳ Ice Pack Facility 🍼 Baby facilities ⅄ Disabled facilities ⑤ Shop on site or within 200yds
🍖 BBQ area 🧺 Picnic area WiFi WiFi

DERBYSHIRE

BAKEWELL
Map 16 SK26

Places to visit

Chatsworth, CHATSWORTH, DE45 1PP, 01246 565300
www.chatsworth.org

BUXTON
Map 16 SK07

Places to visit

Poole's Cavern (Buxton Country Park), BUXTON, SK17 9DH, 01298 26978
www.poolescavern.co.uk

Great for kids: Go Ape Buxton, BUXTON, SK17 9DH, 01603 895500
www.goape.co.uk/buxton

Greenhills Holiday Park
▶▶▶▶ 87%

tel: 01629 813052 & 813467 **Crowhill Lane DE45 1PX**
email: info@greenhillsholidaypark.co.uk **web:** www.greenhillsholidaypark.co.uk
dir: *1 mile north-west of Bakewell on A6. Signed before Ashford-in-the-Water, onto unclassified road on right.*

A well-established park set in lovely countryside within the Peak District National Park. Many pitches enjoy uninterrupted views, and there is easy access to all facilities, including the newly refurbished amenity block and games room not to mention the on-site pub and well-equipped children's play area and spacious football field. The park is very well situated for Bakewell, Chatsworth House and other local attractions.

Open: February to November (restricted service: February to April and October to November – bar and shop closed) **Last arrival:** 22.00 **Last departure:** noon

Pitches: * 🚐 from £25; 🚐 from £25; ▲ from £20; 85 hardstanding pitches; 50 seasonal pitches

Leisure: 🎱 ⚽

Facilities: 🏪 ☉ 🌳 ⚡ 🛁 💲 ☕ WiFi

Services: 🔌 🔄 🍴 🍲 🔋 ⚡ 🔋 ⊘ T

Within 3 miles: 🚶 🏇 ∪ ◎

Additional site information: 8 acre site. 🐕 Cars can be parked by caravans and tents. Awnings permitted.

AA MOST IMPROVED CAMPSITE OF THE YEAR 2020

Beech Croft Farm
▶▶▶▶ 94%

tel: 01298 85330 **Beech Croft, Blackwell in the Peak SK17 9TQ**
email: mail@beechcroftfarm.co.uk **web:** www.beechcroftfarm.co.uk
dir: *Exit A6 midway between Buxton and Bakewell. Site signed.*

A small, terraced farm site with lovely Peak District views. There's a fine stone-built toilet block with ultra-modern fittings, underfloor heating and additional unisex facilities. A new, dedicated reception and shop are now provided on site – the shop is fully stocked with camping essentials and an array of local produce plus a daily bakery delivery. Hardstanding caravan pitches, gravel roads, a campers' shelter, and a super tarmac pathway leading from the camping field to the toilet block are each maintained to a high standard. All the tent pitches have electrical hook-up via a pre-payment card system. There's a boot, dog and bike wash. This makes an ideal site for those touring or walking in the Peak District.

Open: All year (restricted service: November to February – tents not accepted)
Last arrival: 20.00 **Last departure:** noon

Pitches: * 🚐 from £23; 🚐 from £23; ▲ from £16; 30 hardstanding pitches

Leisure: 🎱 ⚽

Facilities: 🏪 ☉ ⚡ 🛁 💲 🚻 WiFi

Services: 🔌 🔄 ⚡ 🔋 ⊘ T

Additional site information: 3 acre site. 🐕 Cars can be parked by caravans and tents. Awnings permitted. No noise after 22.00.

BUXTON *continued*

Lime Tree Park

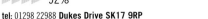

►►►► 92%

tel: 01298 22988 **Dukes Drive SK17 9RP**
email: info@limetreeparkbuxton.com **web:** www.limetreeparkbuxton.com
dir: *1 mile south of Buxton, between A515 and A6.*

A very attractive and well-designed site, set on the side of a narrow valley in an elevated location, with separate, neatly landscaped areas for statics, tents, touring caravans and motorhomes and four newly added glamping pods. There's good attention to detail throughout including the clean toilet and shower blocks. Its backdrop of a magnificent old railway viaduct and views over Buxton and the surrounding hills, make this a sought-after destination with easy access to the Peak Districts many attractions.

Open: March to October **Last arrival:** 18.00 **Last departure:** noon

Pitches: 🚐 🚌 ⛺; 22 hardstanding pitches

Leisure: ⅍ 🔍 ☐

Facilities: 🛁 ⊙ 🖍 ✳ ♿ ⑤ WiFi

Services: 🔌 🔄 🧺 🔒 🚿 Ⓣ

Within 3 miles: ↧ ∪ ◎ ⚓

Additional site information: 10.5 acre site. 🐾 Cars can be parked by caravans and tents. Awnings permitted. No noise after 22.00, no fires.

Glamping available: Glamping pods.

HOPE   Map 16 SK18

Places to visit

Peveril Castle, CASTLETON, S33 8WQ, 01433 620613
www.english-heritage.org.uk/visit/places/peveril-castle

Speedwell Cavern, CASTLETON, S33 8WA, 01433 623018
www.speedwellcavern.co.uk

Pindale Farm Outdoor Centre

►►► 80%

tel: 01433 620111 **Pindale Road S33 6RN**
email: info@pindalefarm.co.uk **web:** www.pindalefarm.co.uk
dir: *From A6187 in Hope follow Pindale sign between church and Woodroffe Arms. Site 1 mile on left.*

Set around a 13th-century farmhouse and a former lead mine pump house (now converted to a self-contained bunkhouse for up to 60 people), this simple, off-the-beaten-track site is an ideal base for walking, climbing, caving and various outdoor pursuits. Around the farm are several deeply wooded areas available for tents, and old stone buildings that have been converted to house modern toilet facilities.

Open: March to October

Pitches: * ⛺ from £8.50

Facilities: 🛁 ⊙ ✳ WiFi

Services: 🔌 🔄

Within 3 miles: ∪ ⑤

Additional site information: 4 acre site. 🐾 Cars can be parked by tents. Awnings permitted. No anti-social behaviour, noise must be kept to minimum after 21.00, no fires. Charge for WiFi.

MATLOCK   Map 16 SK35

Places to visit

Crich Tramway Village, CRICH, DE4 5DP, 01773 854321
www.tramway.co.uk

Haddon Hall, HADDON HALL, DE45 1LA, 01629 812855
www.haddonhall.co.uk

Great for kids: The Heights of Abraham, MATLOCK BATH, DE4 3NT, 01629 582365, www.heightsofabraham.com

Lickpenny Caravan Site

►►►► 92%

tel: 01629 583040 **Lickpenny Lane, Tansley DE4 5GF**
email: enquiries@lickpennycaravanpark.co.uk **web:** www.lickpennycaravanpark.co.uk
dir: *From Matlock take A615 towards Alfreton for 3 miles. Site signed to left, into Lickpenny Lane, right into site near end of road.*

A picturesque site in the grounds of an old plant nursery with areas broken up and screened by a variety of shrubs, and with spectacular views, which are best enjoyed from the upper terraced areas. The pitches, several fully serviced, are spacious, well screened and well marked, and facilities are kept to a very good standard. The bistro/coffee shop is popular with visitors.

Open: All year **Last arrival:** 20.00 **Last departure:** noon (later departures until 17.00 — charges apply)

Pitches: 🚐 from £22; 🚌 from £22; 80 hardstanding pitches; 20 seasonal pitches

Leisure: ⅍ ⚽

Facilities: 🛁 ⊙ 🖍 ♿ ⑤ 🪑 WiFi

Services: 🔌 🔄 🧺 ⚓ 🔒 Ⓣ

Within 3 miles: ↧ 🎣 ∪ ◎ ⚓

Additional site information: 16 acre site. 🐾 Cars can be parked by caravans. 1 car per pitch. Awnings permitted. No noise after 23.00. Child's bath available, woodland walk. Car hire can be arranged.

NEWHAVEN   Map 16 SK16

Places to visit

Haddon Hall, HADDON HALL, DE45 1LA, 01629 812855
www.haddonhall.co.uk

Newhaven Holiday Park
►►►► 85%

tel: 01298 84300 **SK17 ODT**
email: hello@newhavenholidaypark.co.uk **web:** www.newhavenholidaypark.co.uk
dir: *Between Ashbourne and Buxton at junction of A515 and A5012.*

Pleasantly situated within the Peak District National Park, this park has mature trees screening the three touring areas. Very good toilet facilities cater for touring vans and a large tent field, and there's a restaurant adjacent to the site. The static caravans on the site are privately owned.

Open: March to October **Last arrival:** Sunday to Thursday 19.30, Friday 20.00
Last departure: noon

Pitches: 🚐 🚐 ▲; 95 hardstanding pitches; 40 seasonal pitches

Leisure: ⚙ ✎

Facilities: 🏠 ☉ 🅿 ✳ 🅂 🍴 🎏

Services: 🔌 ⬛ 🔋 🪫 ⌀ 🚹

Within 3 miles: ✎ ∪ ⚓

Additional site information: 30 acre site. 🐕 Cars can be parked by caravans and tents. Awnings permitted. No noise after 23.00.

RIDDINGS   Map 16 SK45

Places to visit

Denby Pottery Village, DENBY, DE5 8NX, 01773 740799
www.denbypottery.com

Midland Railway Butterley, RIPLEY, DE5 3QZ, 01773 747674
www.midlandrailway-butterley.co.uk

Riddings Wood Caravan and Camping Park
►►►► 85%

tel: 01773 605160 **Bullock Lane DE55 4BP**
email: info@riddingswoodcaravanandcampingpark.co.uk
web: www.riddingswoodcaravanandcampingpark.co.uk
dir: *M1 junction 27, A608 signed Heanor. Right onto B600 signed Alfreton and Selston. Left onto B6016 signed Jacksdale. Through Jacksdale towards Ridding. Site on right.*

Located close to both Derby and Nottingham, this site's layout can be described as a sloping amphitheatre. It is surrounded by the mature trees of Riddings Wood on all sides and has a fabulous panoramic view looking down towards Jacksdale. Beyond the sweeping driveway and security barrier, you'll find a smart chalet-style reception, neat gravel hardstandings, manicured grass tent pitches, and a stylish amenity block with quality shower and toilet facilities. Picnic benches are scattered around the park for campers to use, and fully serviced pitches are available. Lodges, sleeping up to four people, are available for hire; exclusive use of a hot tub is included in the price. A local bus service runs every nine minutes from the site entrance to both Derby and Nottingham.

Open: March to December (for tourers) **Last arrival:** 22.00 **Last departure:** 11.30

Pitches: 🚐 🚐; ▲, 26 hardstanding pitches; 4 seasonal pitches

Leisure: ⚙ ✪

Facilities: 🏠 ☉ 🅿 ✳ 🅂 🍴 🎏 📶

Services: 🔌 ⬛ 🔋 🪫 🔒

Within 3 miles: ✦ ✎ ∪ 🅂

Additional site information: 11.5 acre site. 🐕 Dogs must be kept on leads at all times. Cars can be parked by caravans and tents. Awnings permitted. Children must be accompanied by an adult at all times. Rubbish must be placed in designated areas. No noise after 23.00.

RIPLEY   Map 16 SK35

Places to visit

Midland Railway Butterley, RIPLEY, DE5 3QZ, 01773 747674
www.midlandrailway-butterley.co.uk

Denby Pottery Village, DENBY, DE5 8NX, 01773 740799
www.denbypottery.com

Golden Valley Caravan & Camping Park
►►►► 87%

tel: 01773 513881 & 746786 **Coach Road DE55 4ES**
email: enquiries@goldenvalleycaravanpark.co.uk
web: www.goldenvalleycaravanpark.co.uk
dir: *M1 junction 26, A610 to Codnor. Right at lights. Right into Alfreton Road. In 1 mile left into Coach Road, park on left. (Note: it is advisable to ignore sat nav for last few miles and follow these directions).*

This superbly landscaped park is set within 30 acres of woodland in the Amber Valley. The fully serviced pitches are set out in informal groups in clearings amongst the trees. The park has a cosy bar and bistro with a new dining room and upstairs event space, and an outside patio, a fully-stocked fishing lake, an innovative and well-equipped play area, an on-site jacuzzi and fully-equipped fitness suite. There is also a wildlife pond and a nature trail; camping pods are available for hire.

Open: All year (restricted service: low season – bar and café open, children's activities at weekends only) **Last arrival:** 20.00 (call if any later) **Last departure:** noon

Pitches: 🚐 🚐 ▲ 🏠; 45 hardstanding pitches; 12 seasonal pitches

Leisure: ⚙ ✪ ▢ ✎ 🦅

Facilities: 🏠 ☉ 🅿 ✳ 🅂 🍴 🎏 📶

Services: 🔌 ⬛ 🔋 🍴 🪫 🔋 🪫 ⌀ 🚹

Within 3 miles: ✦ ∪ ◎ ⚓ 🎏

Additional site information: 30 acre site. 🐕 Cars can be parked by caravans and tents. Awnings permitted. No vehicles on grass, no open fires or disposable BBQs, no noise after 22.30. Zip slide, tractor train, log flume ride, bouncy castle, paddle boats, crazy golf, segways (high season only).

Glamping available: Wooden pod, wooden barrel pod.

Additional glamping information: Wooden pod sleeps 2, wooden barrel pod sleeps 4. No dogs, no smoking, no fires. Own sleeping equipment and camping accessories required.

ROSLISTON — Map 10 SK21

Places to visit

Ashby-de-la-Zouch Castle, ASHBY-DE-LA-ZOUCH, LE65 1BR, 01530 413343
www.english-heritage.org.uk/visit/places/ashby-de-la-zouch-castle

Great for kids: Conkers, MOIRA, DE12 6GA, 01283 216633
www.visitconkers.com

Beehive Woodland Lakes
►►►► 86%

tel: 01283 763981 **DE12 8HZ**
email: info@beehivefarm-woodlandlakes.co.uk
web: www.beehivefarm-woodlandlakes.co.uk
dir: From A444 in Castle Gresley into Mount Pleasant Road. Follow Rosliston signs for 3.5 miles through Linton. Left at T-junction signed Beehive Farms.

A small, informal and continually developing caravan area secluded from an extensive woodland park in the heart of the National Forest National Park. The toilet facilities include four family rooms. Young children will enjoy the playground, whilst anglers can pass many a happy hour fishing at the park's three lakes. There are also five camping pods available to hire.

Open: All year **Last arrival:** 19.00 (17.00 in low season) **Last departure:** noon

Pitches: from £21; from £21; from £21; see prices below; 46 hardstanding pitches; 18 seasonal pitches

Leisure:
Facilities:
Services:
Within 3 miles:

Additional site information: 2.5 acre site. Cars can be parked by caravans and tents. Awnings permitted. Gas BBQs only, no generators, no unaccompanied groups of young people. Takeaway food delivered to site.

Glamping available: Wooden pods from £40.

Additional glamping information: Wooden pods sleep 4 (suitable for families). No pets. Cars can be parked by pods.

SHARDLOW — Map 11 SK43

Places to visit

Melbourne Hall & Gardens, MELBOURNE, DE73 8EN, 01332 862502
www.melbournehall.com

Shardlow Marina Caravan Park
►►► 74%

tel: 01332 792832 **London Road DE72 2GL**
email: admin@shardlowmarina.co.uk
dir: M1 junction 24a, A50 signed Derby. Exit from A50 junction 1 at roundabout signed Shardlow. Site 1 mile on right.

A large marina site with restaurant facilities, situated on the Trent and Merseyside Canal. Pitches are on grass surrounded by mature trees, and for the keen angler, the site offers fishing within the marina. The attractive grass touring area overlooks the marina.

Open: March to January **Last arrival:** 17.00 **Last departure:** noon

Pitches: ; 26 hardstanding pitches; 10 seasonal pitches

Leisure:
Facilities:
Services:
Within 3 miles:

Additional site information: 25 acre site. Maximum of 2 dogs per unit, dogs must not be left unattended or tied up outside. Cars can be parked by caravans and tents. Awnings permitted. Office closed between 13.00–14.00.

PITCHES: 🚐 Caravans 🚐 Motorhomes ⛺ Tents ⛺ Glamping accommodation **SERVICES:** ⚡ Electric hook-up 🔲 Launderette 🍷 Licensed bar
🔋 Calor Gas ⊘ Campingaz T Toilet fluid 🍽 Café/Restaurant 🍟 Fast Food/Takeaway 🔋 Battery charging ⚡ Motorhome service point
* 2019 prices 🚫 No credit or debit cards 🐕 Dogs permitted 🚫 No dogs

Devon

With magnificent coastlines, two historic cities and the world-famous Dartmoor National Park, Devon sums up all that is best about the British landscape. For centuries it has been a fashionable and much loved holiday destination – especially south Devon's glorious English Riviera.

When the crime writer Agatha Christie was born in Torquay on Devon's glorious south coast, the town was a popular seaside resort. It was 1890, the start of Queen Victoria's last decade as monarch, and Torquay was a fashionable destination for all sorts of people; those looking for a permanent home by the sea as well as holidaymakers in search of long hours of sunshine and a mild climate. In many ways, Torquay remains much the same today and its impressive setting still evokes a sense of its Victorian heyday. A local steam train attraction adds to the atmosphere; you can travel from Paignton to Dartmouth, alighting on the way at the small station at Churston, just as Hercule Poirot does in Christie's 1930s detective novel *The ABC Murders*. The Queen of Crime herself used this station when she had a summer home nearby. The house, Greenway, overlooks a glorious sweep of the River Dart and is now managed as a popular visitor attraction by the National Trust.

Close to the English Riviera lies Dartmoor, one of the south-west's most spectacular landscapes. The contrast between the traditional attractions of the coast and this expanse of bleak, brooding moorland could not be greater. The National Park, which contains Dartmoor, covers 365 square miles and includes many fascinating geological features – isolated granite tors and two summits exceeding 2,000 feet among them. Dartmoor's waterfalls, including the tumbling Whitelady Waterfall at Lydford Gorge, can be seen in full spate even in the depths of winter. Everywhere you venture on Dartmoor, there are stone circles, burial chambers and mysterious clues to the distant past. The place oozes antiquity. Sir Arthur Conan Doyle set his classic Sherlock Holmes story *The Hound of the Baskervilles* on Dartmoor, and Agatha Christie stayed at a local hotel for two weeks at the height of the First World War in order to finish writing her first detective novel *The Mysterious Affair at Styles*, first published in 1920.

Not surprisingly, Dartmoor equates with walking and the opportunities are enormous. For something really adventurous, try the Two Moors Way. This long-distance route begins at Ivybridge and crosses the National Park to enter neighbouring Exmoor, which straddles the Devon/Somerset border. At Lynton and Lynmouth the trail connects with the South West Coast Path, which takes walkers on a breathtaking journey to explore north Devon's gloriously rugged coastline, renowned for its extraordinary collection of peaks and outcrops. Cycling in the two National Parks is also extremely popular and there is a good choice of off-road routes taking you to the heart of Dartmoor and Exmoor.

Devon's towns and cities offer a pleasing but stimulating alternative to the rigours of the countryside. There are scores of small market towns in the region – for example there is Tavistock with its popular farmers' market, one of many in the county. Plymouth lies in Devon's south-west corner and is a striking city and naval port. Much of its transformation over the years is a reminder of the devastation it suffered, together with Exeter, during the Second World War. The city places particular emphasis, of course, on the Spanish Armada and the voyage of the Pilgrim Fathers to America.

On the theme of sailing, Devon is synonymous with this most invigorating of boating activities. Salcombe, on the county's south coast, is a sailing playground. Situated on a tree-fringed estuary beneath lush rolling hills, the town thrives on boats – it hosts the week-long Salcombe Regatta in August. It's even suitable for swimming, with several sandy beaches and sheltered bays.

◁ Combe Martin Beach, Exmoor National Park

DEVON

ASHBURTON   Map 3 SX77

Places to visit

Compton Castle, COMPTON, TQ3 1TA, 01803 661906
www.nationaltrust.org.uk/comptoncastle

Great for kids: Buckfast Butterflies & Dartmoor Otter Sanctuary,
BUCKFASTLEIGH, TQ11 0DZ, 01364 642916
www.ottersandbutterflies.co.uk

Parkers Farm Holiday Park

►►►► 88%

tel: 01364 654869 **Higher Mead Farm TQ13 7LJ**
email: parkersfarm@btconnect.com web: www.parkersfarmholidays.co.uk
dir: *From Exeter on A38, 2nd left after Plymouth (29 miles) sign, signed Woodland and Denbury. From Plymouth on A38 take A383 Newton Abbot exit, turn right across bridge, rejoin A38, then as above.*

A well-developed site terraced into rising ground with stunning views across rolling countryside to the Dartmoor tors. Part of a working farm, this park offers excellent fully serviced hardstanding pitches, which make the most of the fine views; it is beautifully maintained and has good quality toilet facilities, a popular games room and a bar/restaurant that serves excellent meals. Large family rooms with two shower cubicles, a large sink and a toilet are especially appreciated by families with small children. There are regular farm walks when all the family can meet and feed the various animals.

Open: Easter to end October (restricted service: low season – bar and restaurant open at weekends only) **Last arrival:** 22.00 **Last departure:** 10.00
Pitches: * 🚐 from £15; 🚐 from £15; ▲ from £13; 20 hardstanding pitches
Leisure: 🅰 🏊 🎱 🔲 🎵 ⚽
Facilities: 🛁 ☺ 🎦 ✳ ♿ ⑤ 🍴 🎪 🐾 WiFi
Services: 🔌 🗑 🚐 🍴 ♨ 🛒 ⬇ 🔒 🌿 🆃
Within 3 miles: ✐

Additional site information: 25 acre site. 🐕 Cars can be parked by caravans and tents. Awnings permitted. Large field available for dog walking.

River Dart Country Park

►►►► 88%

tel: 01364 652511 **Holne Park TQ13 7NP**
email: info@riverdart.co.uk web: www.riverdart.co.uk
dir: *M5 junction 31, A38 towards Plymouth. In Ashburton at Peartree junction follow brown site signs. Site 1 mile on left. (Note: Peartree junction is 2nd exit at Ashburton; do not exit at Linhay junction as narrow roads are unsuitable for caravans).*

Set in 90 acres of magnificent parkland that was once part of a Victorian estate, with many specimen and exotic trees, this peaceful, hidden-away touring park occupies several camping areas, all served with good quality toilet facilities. In spring the park is a blaze of colour from the many azaleas and rhododendrons.

There are numerous outdoor activities for all ages including abseiling, caving and canoeing, plus high quality, well-maintained facilities. The open moorland of Dartmoor is only a few minutes away.

Open: April to September (restricted service: low and mid season – reduced opening hours at shop and café bar) **Last arrival:** 21.00 **Last departure:** 11.00
Pitches: * 🚐 from £17; 🚐 from £17; ▲ from £17; 34 hardstanding pitches
Leisure: 🅰 🏊 🎱 🎾 ✐
Facilities: 🛁 ☺ 🎦 ✳ ♿ ⑤ 🎪 WiFi
Services: 🔌 🗑 🚐 🍴 🛒 ⬇ 🔒 🌿 🆃
Within 3 miles: ⛳ 🐴

Additional site information: 90 acre site. 🐕 Dogs must be kept on leads at all times. Cars can be parked by caravans and tents. Awnings permitted. Adventure playground, dare devil activities, cycle track.

ASHILL   Map 3 ST01

Places to visit

Coldharbour Mill Working Wool Museum, UFFCULME, EX15 3EE, 01884 840960
www.coldharbourmill.org.uk

Leafy Fields Glamping

►►►► 80% GLAMPING ONLY

tel: 07842 320981 **Ingleton Farm, Ashill Moor EX15 3NP**
email: leafyfieldsglamping@yahoo.com web: www.leafyfieldsglamping.com
dir: *Phone for directions.*

Located in the small hamlet of Ashill deep on the Blackdown Hills, Leafy Fields is a very tranquil, well laid out and rural glamping site with a relaxing back-to-nature atmosphere and a good choice of accommodation. Two safari lodges, six bell tents and a shepherd's hut are neatly arranged in a pleasant meadow with toilet and shower facilities close at hand in a converted stable block. The bell tents are fully equipped and have a small kitchen unit outside, and there are six toilets/showers allocated to each bell tent. The larger safari lodges sleep six, have a kitchen area and are very well equipped, plus they have en suite toilets and showers and an alfresco decking area. The interiors are well presented and there is an electric radiator in all units. The site maintenance is excellent and there is a small children's play area and a family room with a sensory playroom. Fire pits and logs are also available.

Open: All year (restricted service: July to September) **Last arrival:** 18.00
Last departure: 11.00
Leisure: 🅰
Facilities: 🛁 ☺ ♿
Within 3 miles: ⑤

Accommodation available: 2 Safari lodges; a maximum of 6 Bell Tents; Shepherd's hut
Additional site information: ⊗ Sensory playroom, rainy day room. Cars can be parked by units.

LEISURE: 🏊 Indoor swimming pool 🏊 Outdoor swimming pool 🅰 Children's playground 🚣 Kids' club 🎾 Tennis court 🎱 Games room 🔲 Separate TV room
⛳ Golf course 🥅 Pitch n putt 🚣 Boats for hire 🚲 Bikes for hire 🎬 Cinema 🎵 Entertainment ✐ Fishing ⛳ Mini golf 🏄 Watersports 🏋 Gym 🏟 Sports field 🐴 Stables
FACILITIES: 🛁 Baths/Shower ☺ Electric shaver sockets 🎦 Hairdryer ✳ Ice Pack Facility 🍼 Baby facilities ♿ Disabled facilities ⑤ Shop on site or within 200yds
🎪 BBQ area 🎪 Picnic area WiFi WiFi

AXMINSTER
Map 4 SY29

Places to visit

Branscombe - The Old Bakery, Manor Mill and Forge, BRANSCOMBE, EX12 3DB, 01752 346585; www.nationaltrust.org.uk/branscombe

Allhallows Museum, HONITON, EX14 1PG, 01404 44966 www.honitonmuseum.co.uk

Platinum Park

Hawkchurch Resort & Spa
▶▶▶▶▶ HOLIDAY HOME PARK

tel: 01297 678402 **Hawkchurch EX13 5UL**
email: reception@hawkchurchresort.co.uk **web:** www.hawkchurchresort.co.uk
dir: *From A35 between Axminster and Charmouth take B3165 signed Crewkerne. Left signed Hawkchurch.*

This superb park is located in lovely countryside near Axminster and the Jurassic Coast and enjoys views over the Axe Valley. The luxury lodges are fully equipped and have en suite facilities. There are excellent leisure facilities – the Ezina Spa offering a wide range of luxury treatments, plus a spa pool and gym. In addition, there is a good restaurant, The Beeches, as well as an alfresco eating and drinking area.

Open: All year

Holiday Homes: Sleep 8 Two-ring burner Dishwasher Washing Machine Tumble dryer Microwave Freezer TV Sky/Freeview DVD player WiFi Linen included Towels included Electricity included Gas included

Leisure: ☜ ❣

Additional site information: ⌁

Andrewshayes Holiday Park
▶▶▶▶ 90%

tel: 01404 831225 **Dalwood EX13 7DY**
email: info@andrewshayes.co.uk **web:** www.andrewshayes.co.uk
dir: *3 miles from Axminster towards Honiton on A35, right at Taunton Cross signed Dalwood and Stockland. Site 150 metres on right.*

An attractive family park within easy reach of Lyme Regis, Seaton, Branscombe and Sidmouth in an ideal touring location. This popular park offers modern toilet facilities, a quiet, cosy bar and takeaway service, and an excellent play area for

children that's set beside the swimming pool, bar and restaurant area. There are three camping pods for hire.

Open: 24 March to 3 November (restricted service: off-peak season – shop and bar reduced hours and takeaway availability limited) **Last arrival:** 22.00 **Last departure:** 10.30

Pitches: ⌑ ⌑ ⌘ ⋔; 105 hardstanding pitches; 100 seasonal pitches

Leisure: ☜ ⋔ ☂ ✿

Facilities: ⌑ ⊙ ⌗ ✳ ⧼ ⑤ ⌻ ▥ WiFi

⌑⌑⌑⌑ ⌑ ⌂ ⌑ ⦿ ⌑ ⌑ ⌑ ⌑ ⌑

Within 3 miles: ⌑

Additional site information: 12 acre site. ⌁ Cars can be parked by caravans and tents. Awnings permitted. Children under 12 must be supervised by an adult in the pool. Table tennis, woodland walk.

Glamping available: Wooden pods.

Additional glamping information: Wooden pods: minimum stay 2 nights, offer lighting, heater, kettle, electric sockets, BBQ, picnic table and private decking area. No dogs allowed. Cars can be parked by pods.

BARNSTAPLE
Map 3 SS53

Places to visit

Exmoor Zoological Park, BLACKMOOR GATE, EX31 4SG, 01598 763352 www.exmoorzoo.co.uk

Arlington Court, ARLINGTON, EX31 4LP, 01271 850296 www.nationaltrust.org.uk/arlington-court

Hallsdown Farm Touring Site
▶▶▶▶ 82%

tel: 01271 850847 **Hallsdown Farm, Arlington EX31 4SW**
email: andrew.mather@yahoo.co.uk **web:** www.hallsdownfarm.co.uk
dir: *A361 signed South Molton-Barnstaple to A399 signed Blackmoorgate. Approximately 1 mile after junction with B3358 turn left signed Loxhore, campsite on right.*

Located on a working farm, this small and very peaceful, adults-only park is tucked away in a glorious part of north Devon, yet is close to Barnstaple, Exmoor and the dramatic coast. Some of the pitches are fully serviced hardstandings and there are four toilet and shower cubicles that are kept spotlessly clean. The site has a laundry room and dishwashing area, plus there is good access from the main road, neatly kept grass, shelter from the surrounding trees and CCTV security.

Open: 15 March to 31 October **Last arrival:** 22.00 **Last departure:** 11.30

Pitches: ⌑ ⌑; 11 hardstanding pitches; 5 seasonal pitches

Facilities: ⌑ ⌗ ⑤ WiFi

Services: ⌑ ⑤ ⌑ ⌑

Within 3 miles: ⌑ ↻

Additional site information: 2.5 acre site. Adults only. ⊗ Cars can be parked by caravans. Awnings permitted. No children under 18 years.

PITCHES: ⌑ Caravans ⌑ Motorhomes ⌘ Tents ⋔ Glamping accommodation **SERVICES:** ⌑ Electric hook-up ⑤ Launderette ⌻ Licensed bar
⌑ Calor Gas ⌀ Campingaz ⊤ Toilet fluid ⌑ Café/Restaurant ⌑ Fast Food/Takeaway ⌑ Battery charging ↯ Motorhome service point
* 2019 prices ⊛ No credit or debit cards ⌁ Dogs permitted ⊗ No dogs

BERRYNARBOR
Map 3 SS54

Places to visit

Great for kids: Watermouth Castle & Family Theme Park, ILFRACOMBE, EX34 9SL, 01271 867474, www.watermouthcastle.com

Combe Martin Wildlife Park & Dinosaur Park, COMBE MARTIN, EX34 0NG, 01271 882486, cmwdp.co.uk

Mill Park Touring Caravan & Camping Park

▶▶▶▶▶ 90%

tel: 01271 882647 **Mill Lane EX34 9SH**
email: enquiries@millpark.com **web:** www.millpark.com
dir: *M5 junction 27, A361 towards Barnstaple. Right onto A399 towards Combe Martin. At Sawmills Inn take turn opposite Berrynarbor sign.*

Under enthusiastic ownership, this well managed park is set in an attractive wooded valley with a stream that runs into a lake where coarse fishing is available. There is a quiet bar and restaurant with a family room, a very pleasant camping meadow, an excellent children's play area, and clean and tidy toilet facilities. The park has lakeside wooden pods (cocoons), wooden pods (glampods) and Lotus Belle tents for hire. The site is located two miles from Combe Martin and Ilfracombe and just a stroll across the road from the small harbour at Watermouth.

Open: March to October **Last arrival:** 21.00 **Last departure:** 10.00

Pitches: * 🚐 from £20; 🚎 from £20; ▲ from £20; 🏠 see prices below; 32 hardstanding pitches; 30 seasonal pitches

Leisure: 🛝 🎣 ✎
Facilities: 🛁 ⊙ 🌡 ✳ ⚬ 🛒 🚻 🐕 WiFi
Services: 🚮 🗑 🍴 🏪 🛗 🔒 🗑 T
Within 3 miles: 🎣 ∪ ◎ 🛶 🎯 🗓

Additional site information: 30 acre site. 🐕 Cars can be parked by caravans and tents. Awnings permitted. No open fires, no groundsheets/footprints under tents. Fresh coffee and croissants available everyday. Family bathroom, accessible wetroom.

Glamping available: Lotus Belle tents from £50; wooden cocoon from £40; wooden pods from £50.

Additional glamping information: Lotus Belle tents: no dogs allowed. Lotus Belle tents, wooden cocoons and wooden pods offer fridge, heater, kettle, light, electricity, BBQ and picnic table. Cars can be parked by units.

See advert opposite

BRAUNTON
Map 3 SS43

Places to visit

Marwood Hill Gardens, BARNSTAPLE, EX31 4EA, 01271 342528 www.marwoodhillgarden.co.uk

Great for kids: Combe Martin Wildlife Park & Dinosaur Park, COMBE MARTIN, EX34 0NG, 01271 882486, cmwdp.co.uk

Premier Park

Hidden Valley Park

▶▶▶▶▶▶ 94%

Best of British

tel: 01271 813837 **West Down EX34 8NU**
email: info@hiddenvalleypark.com **web:** www.hiddenvalleypark.com
dir: *Direct access from A361, 8 miles from Barnstaple and 2 miles from Mullacott Cross.*

A delightful, well-appointed family site set in a wooded valley, with superb toilet facilities and a café. The park is set in a very rural, natural location not far from the beautiful coast around Ilfracombe. The woodland is home to nesting buzzards and woodpeckers, and otters have taken up residence by the lake. WiFi is available. There are three fully equipped timber cabins for hire, and the Lakeside Restaurant and Bar serves good home-cooked meals.

Open: All year **Last arrival:** 21.00 **Last departure:** 10.30

Pitches: 🚐 🚎 ▲; 50 hardstanding pitches; 15 seasonal pitches

Leisure: 🛝
Facilities: 🛁 ⊙ 🌡 ✳ ⚬ 🛒 🚻 🐕 WiFi
Services: 🚮 🗑 🍴 🍽 🏪 🛗 🔒 🗑 T
Within 3 miles: 🎣 ✎ ∪ ◎ 🛶 🗓

Additional site information: 32 acre site. 🐕 Cars can be parked by caravans and tents. Awnings permitted.

Lobb Fields Caravan & Camping Park

►►► 85%

tel: 01271 812090 **Saunton Road EX33 1HG**
email: info@lobbfields.com **web:** www.lobbfields.com
dir: *At crossroads in Braunton take B3231 towards Croyde. Site signed on right.*

Located between Braunton and the miles of golden sands at Saunton, this bright, tree-lined park with gently-sloping grass pitches is a dog-friendly site and offers 180 pitches in two areas. There are seasonal pitches and caravan storage is available. Apart from relaxing and enjoying the views in this UNESCO World Biosphere area, there's plenty of surfing and cycling to be had with the 30-mile Tarka Trail cycle route nearby.

Open: March to October **Last arrival:** 22.00 **Last departure:** 10.30

Pitches: * from £16; from £16; from £11; 13 hardstanding pitches; 19 seasonal pitches

Leisure:

Facilities: WiFi

Services:

Within 3 miles:

Additional site information: 14 acre site. Cars can be parked by caravans and tents. Awnings permitted. No under 18s unless accompanied by an adult, no fires, no noise after 23.00. Surfing boards and wet suits for hire, wet suit washing areas.

Places to visit

Lydford Castle and Saxon Town, LYDFORD, EX20 4BH, 0370 333 1181
www.english-heritage.org.uk/visit/places/lydford-castle-and-saxon-town

Museum of Dartmoor Life, OKEHAMPTON, EX20 1HQ, 01837 52295
www.museumofdartmoorlife.org.uk

Bridestowe Caravan Park

►►► 77%

tel: 01837 861261 **EX20 4ER**
email: ali.young53@btinternet.com **web:** www.glebe-park.co.uk
dir: *Exit A30 at A386 and Sourton Cross junction, follow B3278 signed Bridestowe, left in 3 miles. In village centre, left onto unclassified road for 0.5 mile.*

A small, well-established park in a rural setting close to Dartmoor National Park. This mainly static park has a small, peaceful touring space, and there are many activities to enjoy in the area including fishing and riding. Part of the National Cycle Route 27 (the Devon Coast to Coast) passes close to this park.

Open: March to December **Last arrival:** 22.30 **Last departure:** noon

Pitches: ; 3 hardstanding pitches

Leisure: **Facilities:**

Services:

Additional site information: 1 acre site. Cars can be parked by caravans and tents. Awnings permitted.

BROADWOODWIDGER · Map 3 SX48

Roadford Lake
▶▶▶ 81%

tel: 01409 211507 **Lower Goodacre PL16 OJL**
email: info@swlakestrust.org.uk web: www.southwestlakes.co.uk
dir: *Exit A30 between Okehampton and Launceston at Roadford Lake signs, cross dam wall, site 0.25 mile on right.*

Located right at the edge of Devon's largest inland water, this popular rural park is well screened by mature trees and shrubs. There is an excellent watersports school for sailing, windsurfing, rowing and kayaking, with hire and day launch facilities. This is an ideal location for brown trout fly fishing.

Open: March to October **Last arrival:** late arrivals by prior arrangement **Last departure:** 11.00

Pitches: * 🚐 from £15; 🚍 from £15; ▲ from £15; 13 hardstanding pitches

Leisure: 🎣

Facilities: 🛁 ⊙ 🧴 🚿 🚿 🛗 BBQ WiFi

Services: 🛒 📵 🍴

Within 3 miles: 🚴 🎿 🛒

Additional site information: 3 acre site. 🐕 Cars can be parked by caravans and tents. Awnings permitted. Off-ground BBQs only, no open fires. Climbing wall, archery, high ropes, watersports.

BUCKFASTLEIGH · Map 3 SX76

Places to visit
Buckfast Abbey, BUCKFASTLEIGH, TQ11 0EE, 01364 645500
www.buckfast.org.uk

Great for kids: Buckfast Butterflies & Dartmoor Otter Sanctuary, BUCKFASTLEIGH, TQ11 0DZ, 01364 642916
www.ottersandbutterflies.co.uk

Churchill Farm Campsite
▶▶ 90%

tel: 01364 642844 & 07977 113175 **TQ11 0EZ**
email: apedrick@btinternet.com web: www.churchillfarmcampsite.com
dir: *From A38 follow Buckfast Abbey signs. Pass Abbey entrance on right, at top of hill left into no-through road. Pass Abbey entrance, up hill, left at crossroads to site entrance opposite Holy Trinity Church.*

A working family farm in a relaxed and peaceful setting, with keen, friendly owners. Set on the hills above Buckfast Abbey, this attractive park is maintained to a good standard. The spacious pitches in the neatly trimmed paddock enjoy extensive country views towards Dartmoor, and the clean, simple toilet facilities include smart showers and a family room. This is a hidden gem for those who love traditional camping. Close to a local bus service and within walking distance of Buckfastleigh, the Abbey and the South Devon Steam Railway. This site is within a Site of Special Scientific Interest (SSSI).

Open: Easter to September **Last arrival:** 20.00 **Last departure:** noon

Pitches: 🚐 from £15; 🚍 from £15; ▲ from £15

Facilities: 🛁 ⊙ 🚿 🚿 **Services:** 🛒 🛗

Within 3 miles: 🛒 **Additional site information:** 3 acre site. 🐕 🚗 Cars can be parked by caravans and tents. Awnings permitted. No ball games. BACS transfers possible.

Beara Farm Caravan & Camping Site
▶ 85%

tel: 01364 642234 **Colston Road TQ11 0LW**
dir: *From Exeter take Buckfastleigh exit at Dart Bridge, follow South Devon Steam Railway and Butterfly Farm signs. 200 metres after South Devon Steam Railway entrance take 1st left into Old Totnes Road, 0.5 mile, right at red brick cottages signed Beara Farm. Approximately 1 mile to site.*

A very good farm park, with clean unisex facilities, run by very keen and friendly owners. A well-trimmed camping field offers peace and quiet. Close to the River Dart and the Dart Valley Steam Railway line, within easy reach of the sea and moors. Please note that the approach to the site is narrow, with passing places, and care needs to be taken.

Open: All year **Last arrival:** 21.00 **Last departure:** anytime

Pitches: * 🚐 from £12; 🚍 from £12; ▲ from £12; 1 hardstanding pitch

Facilities: 🛁 ⊙ 🚿 🛗 🛗

Services: 🛗

Within 3 miles: 🎣 🛒

Additional site information: 3.63 acre site. 🐕 🚗 Cars can be parked by caravans and tents. Awnings permitted. No noise after 22.30. Access to River Dart.

CLAYHIDON · Map 4 ST11

Places to visit
Coldharbour Mill Working Wool Museum, UFFCULME, EX15 3EE, 01884 840960
www.coldharbourmill.org.uk

Kingsmead Centre Camping
▶▶▶▶ 77%

tel: 01823 421630 **EX15 3TR**
email: contact@kingsmeadcentre.com web: www.kingsmeadcentre.com
dir: *M5 junction 26 onto A38 signed Wellington, continue southbound. Turn left signed Ford Street, continue until crossroads at top of hill and turn left. Follow signs for Kingsmead Centre. From A303 at Eagle Cross junction follow signs for Wellington. Continue to T-junction, turn right (pass The Holman Clavel pub on left). After 3 miles, turn left signed Kingsmead Centre.*

Located in the middle of a forest, this well-maintained site offers two good, clean toilet blocks and caters for everyone, with a good mix of pitches for tents, caravans and motorhomes, plus the added attraction of a yurt, a Lotus Belle tent and a bell tent for hire. There are two fishing lakes on the site.

Open: All year (restricted service: end August to Easter – hardstandings and statics only) **Last arrival:** 21.00 **Last departure:** 11.00

Pitches: * 🚐 from £20; 🚍 from £20; ▲ from £20; 🏠; 7 hardstanding pitches

Leisure: 🎣 **Facilities:** 🛁 ⊙ 🚿 🚿 🛒 🛗 WiFi

Services: 🛒 📵 🛗 🔒 🅣

Within 3 miles: 🛒 🅄

Additional site information: 7 acre site. 🐕 Cars can be parked by caravans and tents. Awnings permitted. No amplified music; no noise after 21.00 (Monday to Friday) or after 22.00 (Saturday to Sunday). Firepits available for hire.

Glamping available: 1 Lotus Belle tent; 1 Bell tent; 1 yurt. **Changeover days:** Any day

Additional glamping information: 2 night minimum stay. Available between Easter and September. Cars can be parked by units

CLYST ST MARY
Map 3 SX99

Places to visit

Exeter Cathedral, EXETER, EX1 1HS, 01392 285983
www.exeter-cathedral.org.uk

Exeter's Underground Passages, EXETER, EX1 1GA, 01392 665887
www.exeter.gov.uk/passages

Great for kids: The World of Country Life, EXMOUTH, EX8 5BY, 01395 274533
www.worldofcountrylife.co.uk

Premier Park

Crealy Theme Park & Resort
90%

tel: 01395 234888 **Sidmouth Road EX5 1DR**
email: fun@crealy.co.uk **web:** www.crealy.co.uk
dir: *M5 junction 30, A3052 signed Exmouth. At roundabout take A3052 signed Seaton. Follow brown Crealy Theme & Resort signs. Turn right.*

A quality park with excellent toilet facilities, spacious, fully serviced pitches and good security, situated adjacent to the popular Crealy Theme Park; free or discounted entry is available for all campers. Pre-erected luxury safari cabins are for hire, and also in the Camelot Village there are medieval-style pavillion tents for a real glamping holiday. In addition there are 17 spacious lodges with hot tubs for all the family to enjoy. For children, there is a unique 'own pony' and 'character breakfast' experience, plus there's a multi-use games area and adventure golf. There is a clubhouse with bar and restaurant, located next to reception. Free WiFi is available and free kennel accommodation is offered on request. The park is within a short drive of Exeter and the seaside attractions at Sidmouth.

Open: All year **Last arrival:** 20.00 **Last departure:** 10.00
Pitches: from £19; from £19; ▲ from £19 ; 29 hardstanding pitches
Leisure:
Facilities:
Services:
Within 3 miles:

Additional site information: 14.65 acre site. Cars can be parked by caravans and tents. Awnings permitted. Underfloor heating in bathrooms. Crealy Theme Park within walking distance.
Glamping available: Safari cabins, medieval pavillions.
Changeover days: Monday and Friday
Additional glamping information: Maximum occupancy 8 persons. Cars can be parked by units.

COMBE MARTIN
Map 3 SS54

Places to visit

Arlington Court, ARLINGTON, EX31 4LP, 01271 850296
www.nationaltrust.org.uk/arlington-court

Great for kids: Combe Martin Wildlife Park & Dinosaur Park, COMBE MARTIN, EX34 0NG, 01271 882486, cmwdp.co.uk

Premier Park

Stowford Farm Meadows
93%

Best of British

tel: 01271 882476 **Berry Down EX34 0PW**
email: enquiries@stowford.co.uk **web:** www.stowford.co.uk
dir: *M5 junction 27, A361 to Barnstaple. Take A39 from town centre towards Lynton, in 1 mile left onto B3230. Right at garage at Lynton Cross onto A3123, site 1.5 miles on right.*

A very gently sloping, grassy, sheltered and south-facing site approached down a wide, well-kept driveway. This family-friendly site is set in 500 acres of rolling countryside and offers many quality amenities including a large swimming pool and horse riding. A woodland walk is an added attraction, as is the Petorama, an undercover mini zoo, with its variety of friendly animals. There's also a "new and used" caravan sales centre, a comprehensive caravan accessory shop, and VW campervan conversion centre.

Open: All year (restricted service: in winter at certain times – bars closed and catering not available) **Last arrival:** 20.00 **Last departure:** 11.00
Pitches: * from £34; from £36; ▲ from £34; 130 hardstanding pitches; 330 seasonal pitches
Leisure:
Facilities:
Services:
Within 3 miles:

Additional site information: 100 acre site. Maximum of 3 dogs permitted. Cars can be parked by caravans and tents. Awnings permitted. No noise after 23.00, 10mph speed limit on site. Caravan accessory shop, storage, workshop and sales.

COMBE MARTIN *continued*

Premier Park

Newberry Valley Park

►►►►► 89%

tel: 01271 882334 **Woodlands EX34 0AT**
email: relax@newberryvalleypark.co.uk **web:** www.newberryvalleypark.co.uk
dir: *M5 junction 27, A361 towards Barnstaple. Right at North Aller roundabout onto A399, through Combe Martin to sea. Left into site.*

A family owned and run touring park on the edge of Combe Martin, with all its amenities just a five-minute walk away. The park is set in a wooded valley with its own coarse fishing lake and has a stunning toilet block with underfloor heating and excellent unisex privacy cubicles. There is a wooden pod, named Lily, and a shepherd's hut, named Rose, located in a quite spot and available to hire. The safe beaches of Newberry and Combe Martin are reached by a short footpath opposite the park entrance, where the South West Coast Path passes.

Open: 15 March to October (restricted service: low season – office hours limited)
Last arrival: variable (last arrival time is dusk in winter) **Last departure:** 11.00

Pitches: * 🚐 from £20; 🚐 from £20; ▲ from £18; 🏠 see prices below; 40 hardstanding pitches; 18 seasonal pitches

Leisure: 🅰 ✐

Facilities: 🛁 ☉ 🐾 ✳ ⅁ ⑤ 🛒 🎋 **WiFi**

Services: 🔌 ⑤ 🛒 ⅃ Ⓣ

Within 3 miles: ↧ ∪ ⋚ ✈

Additional site information: 20 acre site. 🐾 Cars can be parked by caravans and tents. Awnings permitted. No camp fires. Kitchen preparation area, fridge and microwave available; fresh bread and butchery delivery. Car hire can be arranged.

Glamping available: Wooden hut from £34; shepherd's hut from £44.
Changeover days: Any day

Additional glamping information: Cars can be parked by units.

Places to visit

Marwood Hill Gardens, BARNSTAPLE, EX31 4EA, 01271 342528
www.marwoodhillgarden.co.uk

Great for kids: Watermouth Castle & Family Theme Park, ILFRACOMBE, EX34 9SL, 01271 867474
www.watermouthcastle.com

Bay View Farm Caravan & Camping Park

►►►► 87%

tel: 01271 890501 **EX33 1PN**
email: info@bayviewfarm.co.uk **web:** www.bayviewfarm.co.uk
dir: *M5 junction 27, A361, through Barnstaple to Braunton, left onto B3231. Site at entrance to Croyde.*

A very busy and popular park close to surfing beaches and rock pools, with a public footpath leading directly to the sea. Set in a stunning location with views out over the Atlantic to Lundy Island, it is just a short stroll from Croyde. The facilities are clean and well maintained; a family bathroom is available. There is a fish and chip shop on site. Please note that dogs are not permitted.

Open: March to October **Last arrival:** 21.30 **Last departure:** 11.00

Pitches: * 🚐 from £26; 🚐 from £26; ▲ from £26 🏠; 40 hardstanding pitches; 15 seasonal pitches

Leisure: 🅰

Facilities: 🛁 ☉ 🐾 ✳ ⅁ ⑤ **WiFi**

Services: 🔌 ⑤ 🛒 🛢 ⌀ Ⓣ

Within 3 miles: ↧ ∪ ◎ ⋚

Additional site information: 10 acre site. ⊗ Cars can be parked by caravans and tents. Awnings permitted. No noise after midnight. Fresh produce available in high season.

Glamping available: Wooden pods.

Additional glamping information: Cars can be parked by pods.

See Kentisbeare

Places to visit

Dartmouth Castle, DARTMOUTH, TQ6 0JN, 01803 834445
www.english-heritage.org.uk/visit/places/dartmouth-castle

LEISURE: 🏊 Indoor swimming pool 🏊 Outdoor swimming pool 🅰 Children's playground 👶 Kids' club ♨ Tennis court 🎱 Games room 📺 Separate TV room
↧ Golf course ⛳ Pitch n putt 🚣 Boats for hire 🚲 Bikes for hire 🎬 Cinema 🎵 Entertainment 🎣 Fishing ◎ Mini golf ⛴ Watersports 🏋 Gym 🏟 Sports field ∪ Stables
FACILITIES: 🛁 Baths/Shower ☉ Electric shaver sockets 🐾 Hairdryer ✳ Ice Pack Facility 🍼 Baby facilities ⅁ Disabled facilities ⑤ Shop on site or within 200yds
🎋 BBQ area 🎋 Picnic area **WiFi** WiFi

DARTMOUTH
Map 3 SX85

Premier Park

Woodlands Grove Caravan & Camping Park
Best of British
▶▶ ▶▶ ▶▶ 92%

tel: 01803 712598 **Blackawton TQ9 7DQ**
email: holiday@woodlandsgrove.com **web:** www.woodlandsgrove.co.uk
dir: *From Dartmouth take A3122, 4 miles. Or from A38 take A3808 to Totnes. Then A381 towards Salcombe, after Halwell take A3122 towards Dartmouth, site signed (brown tourist signs).*

A quality caravan and tent park with smart toilet facilities (including excellent family rooms), spacious pitches, including decent hardstandings and good attention to detail throughout, all set in an extensive woodland environment with a terraced grass camping area. Free entry to the adjoining Woodlands Theme Park makes an excellent package holiday for families, but also good for adults travelling without children who are perhaps seeking a low season break. Please check with the site with reference to their minimum stay policy. There is a bus stop at the entrance.

Open: 27 March to 1 November **Last arrival:** 21.30 **Last departure:** 11.00
Pitches: * 🚐 from £18; 🚐 from £18; ▲ from £18; 129 hardstanding pitches
Leisure: 🅰 🎣 ▢ 🎵 **Facilities:** 🚿 ☉ 🌡 ⚒ ♿ 🏧 🎂 📶
Services: 🔌 🔲 🍴 🍺 🚰 ⚓ ♻ Ⓣ **Within 3 miles:** 🚲 ◎

Additional site information: 16 acre site. 🐕 Cars can be parked by caravans and tents. Awnings permitted. No open fires, fire pits or chimeneas, quiet 22.30–08.00. Falconry centre, woodland walk, mini-golf, zoo-farm, dog kennels, free entry into Woodlands Family Theme Park.

DAWLISH
Map 3 SX97

Places to visit
Powderham Castle, POWDERHAM, EX6 8JQ, 01626 890243
www.powderham.co.uk

Premier Park

Cofton Holidays
▶▶ ▶▶ ▶▶ 92%

tel: 01626 890111 **Starcross EX6 8RP**
email: info@coftonholidays.co.uk **web:** www.coftonholidays.co.uk
dir: *On A379 (Exeter to Dawlish road), 3 miles from Dawlish.*

This park is set in a rural location surrounded by spacious open grassland, with plenty of well-kept flowerbeds throughout. Most pitches overlook either the swimming pool complex or the coarse fishing lakes and woodlands. Both new (in 2019) and refurbished purpose-built toilet blocks offer smart modern facilities and the on-site pub serves drinks, meals and snacks for all the family, and a mini-market caters for most shopping needs.

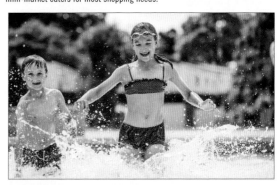

Open: All year **Last arrival:** 20.00 **Last departure:** 10.00
Pitches: * 🚐 from £18; 🚐 from £18; ▲ from £18; 60 hardstanding pitches; 110 seasonal pitches
Leisure: 🏊 🏊 🅰 🎣 🎵 🎾 ⛳ ⊕
Facilities: 🚿 ☉ 🌡 ⚒ ♿ 🏧 🎂 🐕 📶
Services: 🔌 🔲 🍺 🍴 🚰 ⚓ ⚓ ♻ Ⓣ **Within 3 miles:** 🚲 ◎ ⚓ ⚓ 🎣

Additional site information: 45 acre site. 🐕 Cars can be parked by caravans and tents. Awnings permitted. Soft play area, sauna and steam room, bowlingo.

PITCHES: 🚐 Caravans 🚐 Motorhomes ▲ Tents 🏠 Glamping accommodation **SERVICES:** 🔌 Electric hook-up 🔲 Launderette 🍺 Licensed bar
🔋 Calor Gas ⊘ Campingaz Ⓣ Toilet fluid 🍴 Café/Restaurant 🎂 Fast Food/Takeaway ⚓ Battery charging ⚓ Motorhome service point
* 2019 prices ⊘ No credit or debit cards 🐕 Dogs permitted ⊗ No dogs

DAWLISH *continued*

Premier Park

Lady's Mile Holiday Park
►►►►► 88%

tel: 01626 863411 **EX7 0LX**
email: info@ladysmile.co.uk **web:** www.ladysmile.co.uk
dir: *1 mile north of Dawlish on A379.*

A family owned and run touring park with a wide variety of pitches, including some that are fully serviced. There are plenty of activities for everyone, including two swimming pools with waterslides, a children's splash pool, a well-equipped gym, a sauna in the main season, a large adventure playground, extensive restaurant facilities, and a bar with entertainment in high season. Facilities are kept very clean, and the surrounding beaches are easily accessed. Holiday homes and high quality safari tents are also available.

Open: All year (restricted service: November to 22 March – facilities reduced)
Last arrival: 20.00 **Last departure:** 11.00

Pitches: * ⊞ from £14; ⊞ from £14; ▲ from £14 ⋒; 100 hardstanding pitches; 200 seasonal pitches

Leisure: 🏊 🏊 ⚏ ✋ 🔍 ♪ 🎯 ⚽

Facilities: 🛁 ☉ ⏛ ♿ ⑤ 🔥 ☕ WiFi

Services: 🔌 🗑 🐕 🍽 ⛽ ☕ ⛔ 🅃

Within 3 miles: ⚘ 🎣 ∪ ◉ ≋ ⚑

Additional site information: 60 acre site. 🐕 Cars can be parked by caravans and tents. Awnings permitted. No noise after 23.00. Bowling alley.

Glamping available: Safari tents. **Changeover days:** Friday, Saturday, Monday

Additional glamping information: Safari tents have a king-size four-poster bed and hot tub. Cars can be parked by safari tents

---

Leadstone Camping
►►►► 85%

tel: 01626 864411 **Warren Road EX7 0NG**
email: leadstonecampng@gmail.com **web:** www.leadstonecamping.co.uk
dir: *M5 junction 30, A379 to Dawlish. Before village turn left on brow of hill, signed Dawlish Warren. Site 0.5 mile on right.*

A traditional, mainly level, grassy camping park approximately a half-mile walk from the sands and dunes at Dawlish Warren – a nature reserve and Blue Flag

beach. This mainly tented park has been run by the same friendly family for many years, and is an ideal base for touring south Devon. A regular bus service from outside the gate takes in a wide area. The smart, well-equipped timber cabin toilet facility includes some privacy cubicles. There is a pub a short walk away.

Open: 22 May to 7 September **Last arrival:** 22.00 **Last departure:** noon

Pitches: ⊞ from £30; ⊞ from £25; ▲ from £20; 14 seasonal pitches

Leisure: ⚏

Facilities: 🛁 ☉ ⏛ ✳ ♿ WiFi

Services: 🔌 🗑 🐕 ⛽ ⛔ ☕ 🅃

Within 3 miles: ⚘ 🎣 ◉ ⑤

Additional site information: 8 acre site. 🐕 Cars can be parked by caravans and tents. Awnings permitted. No noise after 23.00. Only portable and disposable BBQs permitted.

DREWSTEIGNTON   Map 3 SX79

Places to visit

Castle Drogo, DREWSTEIGNTON, EX6 6PB, 01647 433306
www.nationaltrust.org.uk/castle-drogo

Finch Foundry, STICKLEPATH, EX20 2NW, 01837 840046
www.nationaltrust.org.uk/finch-foundry

Premier Park

Woodland Springs Adult Touring Park
▷▷▷▷ 92%

tel: 01647 231695 **Venton EX6 6PG**
email: enquiries@woodlandsprings.co.uk **web:** woodlandsprings.co.uk
dir: *Exit A30 at Whiddon Down junction onto A382 towards Moretonhampstead. Site 1.5 miles on left.*

An attractive and very well managed park in a rural area within Dartmoor National Park. This site is surrounded by woodland and farmland, and is very peaceful. The toilet block offers superb facilities, including four fully serviced cubicles, some suitable for disabled visitors. Guests can expect high levels of customer care. There are two glamping pods for hire. Please note, children are not accepted.

Open: All year **Last arrival:** 20.00 **Last departure:** 11.00

Pitches: * ⊞ from £21; ⊞ from £24; ▲ from £17.50; ⋒ see prices below; 50 hardstanding pitches; 20 seasonal pitches

Facilities: 🛁 ☉ ⏛ ✳ ♿ ⑤ WiFi

Services: 🔌 🗑 🐕 ⛽ ⛔ ☕ 🅃

Within 3 miles: 🎣

Additional site information: 6 acre site. Adults only. 🐕 Cars can be parked by caravans and tents. Awnings permitted. No fires, no noise 23.00–08.00. Day kennels, freezer, coffee vending machine.

Glamping available: Wooden pods from £40.

Additional glamping information: Maximum 2 adults. No cooking inside pod. Cars can be parked by pods.

LEISURE: 🏊 Indoor swimming pool   🏊 Outdoor swimming pool   ⚏ Children's playground   ✋ Kids' club   🎾 Tennis court   🎱 Games room   📺 Separate TV room   ⚘ Golf course   🏌 Pitch n putt   🚣 Boats for hire   🚲 Bikes for hire   🎬 Cinema   ♪ Entertainment   🎣 Fishing   ◉ Mini golf   🏄 Watersports   🏋 Gym   ⚽ Sports field   ∪ Stables
FACILITIES: 🛁 Baths/Shower   ☉ Electric shaver sockets   ⏛ Hairdryer   ✳ Ice Pack Facility   🐾 Baby facilities   ♿ Disabled facilities   ⑤ Shop on site or within 200yds   🔥 BBQ area   🧺 Picnic area   WiFi WiFi

EAST ALLINGTON
Map 3 SX74

Mounts Farm Touring Park
▶▶▶ 80%

tel: 01548 521591 **The Mounts TQ9 7QJ**
email: mounts.farm@lineone.net web: www.mountsfarm.co.uk
dir: *A381 from Totnes towards Kingsbridge (Note: ignore signs for East Allington). At 'Mounts' site 0.5 mile on left.*

A neat, grassy park divided into four paddocks by mature natural hedges. Three of the paddocks are for the tourers and campers, and the fourth is a children's play area. The laundry, toilets and well-stocked little shop are in converted farm buildings. There's an on-site snack bar and Calor Gas retailer.

Open: mid March to end October **Last arrival:** 22.00 **Last departure:** 16.00

Pitches: ⊞ ⊞ ▲; 10 seasonal pitches

Leisure: ⊙

Facilities: ⊙ ℘ ✵ ⑤

Services: ⊕ ⑤ ⊞ ⊞ ⊘ ⊺

Within 3 miles: ℘ ∪ ⊱ ⊹ ⊟

Additional site information: 7 acre site. ⚐ Cars can be parked by caravans and tents. Awnings permitted. Camping accessories shop on site.

EAST WORLINGTON
Map 3 SS71

Places to visit
Knightshayes, KNIGHTSHAYES, EX16 7RG, 01884 254665
www.nationaltrust.org.uk/knightshayes

Yeatheridge Farm Caravan Park

▶▶▶▶ 87%

tel: 01884 860330 **EX17 4TN**
email: info@yeatheridge.co.uk web: www.yeatheridge.co.uk
dir: *M5 junction 27, A361, at 1st roundabout at Tiverton take B3137 for 9 miles towards Witheridge. Fork left 1 mile after Nomansland onto B3042. Site on left in 3.5 miles. (Note: do not enter East Worlington).*

A well-kept park in a remote woodland setting on the edge of the Tamar Valley. It is peacefully located at the end of a private, half-mile, tree-lined drive; it offers superb on-site facilities, including an excellent restaurant and bar area with outside seating, a large children's play area, and high levels of customer care from the hands-on owners. The toilets are immaculate and well maintained, plus there is an indoor swimming pool, sauna and a good information and games room – all have a friendly atmosphere. Two fishing lakes are also available.

Open: 15 March to 1st weekend in October **Last arrival:** 22.00 **Last departure:** 10.00

Pitches: ⊞ from £14; ⊞ from £14; ▲ from £14; 11 hardstanding pitches

Leisure: ⊛ ⋀ ⬧ ℘ ⊙

Facilities: ⊞ ⊙ ℘ ✵ ⅋ ⑤ ⊞ ⊕ WiFi

Services: ⊕ ⑤ ⊞ ⊺⊙⊺ ⊞ ⊞ ⊍ ⊞ ⊘ ⊺

Within 3 miles: ∪

Additional site information: 12 acre site. ⚐ Cars can be parked by caravans and tents. Awnings permitted. Quiet after 22.30.

EXETER

See Kennford

HOLSWORTHY
Map 3 SS30

Places to visit
Dartington Crystal, GREAT TORRINGTON, EX38 7AN, 01805 626242
visitdartington.co.uk

RHS Garden Rosemoor, GREAT TORRINGTON, EX38 8PH, 01805 624067
www.rhs.org.uk/rosemoor

Great for kids: The Milky Way Adventure Park, CLOVELLY, EX39 5RY, 01237 431255, www.themilkyway.co.uk

Headon Farm Caravan Site
▶▶▶ 88%

tel: 01409 254477 **Headon Farm, Hollacombe EX22 6NN**
email: reader@headonfarm.co.uk web: www.headonfarm.co.uk
dir: *From Holsworthy A388 signed Launceston. 0.5 mile, at hill brow left into Staddon Road. 1 mile (follow site signs) turn right signed Ashwater. 0.5 mile, left at hill brow. Site in 25 yards.*

Set on a working farm in a quiet rural location. All pitches have extensive views of the Devon countryside, yet the park is only two and a half miles from the market town of Holsworthy, and within easy reach of roads to the coast and beaches of north Cornwall. New toilets and showers were added for the 2019 season.

Open: All year **Last arrival:** 19.00 **Last departure:** noon

Pitches: * ⊞ from £19; ⊞ from £19; ▲ from £19; 11 hardstanding pitches

Leisure: ⊙

Facilities: ⊞ ⊙ ✵ ⊞ ⊼ WiFi

Services: ⊕ ⊞

Within 3 miles: ↓ ℘ ∪ ⊱ ⑤ ⑤

Additional site information: 2 acre site. ⚐ Cars can be parked by caravans and tents. Awnings permitted. Breathable groundsheets only. Caravan and motorhome storage (outside or undercover). Car hire can be arranged.

Noteworthy Farm Caravan and Campsite

▶▶ 80%

tel: 01409 253731 & 07811 000071 **Noteworthy, Bude Road EX22 7JB**
email: enquiries@noteworthy-devon.co.uk web: www.noteworthy-devon.co.uk
dir: *On A3072 between Holsworthy and Bude. 3 miles from Holsworthy on right.*

This campsite is owned by a friendly young couple with their own children. There are good views from the quiet rural location, and simple toilet facilities. The local bus stops outside the gate on request.

Open: All year **Last departure:** 11.00

Pitches: ⊞ ⊞ ▲; 3 hardstanding pitches

Leisure: ℘ **Facilities:** ⊞ ⊙ ✵

Services: ⊕ ⑤

Within 3 miles: ↓ ∪ ⊱ ⑤

Additional site information: 5 acre site. ⚐ ⊛ Cars can be parked by caravans and tents. Awnings permitted. No open fires, no noise after 22.30. Dog grooming available.

PITCHES: ⊞ Caravans ⊞ Motorhomes ▲ Tents ⋒ Glamping accommodation SERVICES: ⊕ Electric hook-up ⑤ Launderette ⊞ Licensed bar
⊞ Calor Gas ⊘ Campingaz ⊺ Toilet fluid ⊺⊙⊺ Café/Restaurant ⊞ Fast Food/Takeaway ⊞ Battery charging ⊍ Motorhome service point
* 2019 prices ⊛ No credit or debit cards ⚐ Dogs permitted ⊗ No dogs

ILFRACOMBE
Map 3 SS54

Places to visit

Arlington Court, ARLINGTON, EX31 4LP, 01271 850296
www.nationaltrust.org.uk/arlington-court

Exmoor Zoological Park, BLACKMOOR GATE, EX31 4SG, 01598 763352
www.exmoorzoo.co.uk

Great for kids: Watermouth Castle & Family Theme Park, ILFRACOMBE,
EX34 9SL, 01271 867474
www.watermouthcastle.com

Premier Park

Hele Valley Holiday Park
▶▶▶▶▶ 87%

tel: 01271 862460 **Hele Bay EX34 9RD**
email: holidays@helevalley.co.uk **web:** www.helevalley.co.uk
dir: *M5 junction 27, A361, through Barnstaple and Braunton to Ilfracombe. Take A399 towards Combe Martin. Follow brown Hele Valley signs. In 400 metres sharp right to T-junction. Park on left.*

A deceptively spacious park set in a picturesque valley with glorious tree-lined hilly views from most pitches. High quality toilet facilities are provided, and the park is within walking distance of a lovely beach and on a regular bus route. Camping pods are available to hire. The harbour and other attractions of Ilfracombe are just a mile away.

Open: Easter to end October **Last arrival:** 18.00 **Last departure:** 11.00

Pitches: * 🚐 from £29; 🚐 from £24; ▲ from £24; 🛖 see price below; 20 hardstanding pitches

Leisure: ⚠ **Facilities:** 🛁 ⊙ 🕝 ☀ ♿ 🍽 🎪 WiFi

Services: 🔌 🗑 🚰 🛗 🚽 🖉

Within 3 miles: ♨ 🎣 ∪ ◎ 🚤 🎯 🗓 🛒

Additional site information: 17 acre site. 🐕 Cars can be parked by caravans and tents. Awnings permitted. Groups, motorhomes and tourers by arrangement only. Nature trail, postal collection and newspapers. Car hire can be arranged.

Glamping available: Wooden pods from £34. **Changeover days:** Any day

Additional glamping information: Wooden pods are double glazed, heated (electricity included in price) and have a small decking area with table, chairs and brazier. Cars can be parked by pods.

Sunnymead Farm Camping & Touring Site
▶▶▶▶ 80%

tel: 01271 879845 & 07826 184874 **Morthoe Road EX34 8NZ**
email: info@sunnymead-farm.co.uk **web:** www.sunnymead-farm.co.uk
dir: *From A361 between Ilfracombe and Braunton, at Mullacott Cross roundabout, take B3343 signed Woolacombe. Site approximately 1 mile on right, just after Veterinary Hospital; opposite Highways Guest House.*

Peace and tranquillity abound at this small farm site that's set in the beautiful north Devon countryside with easy reach to Ilfracombe and Woolacombe. 30 grass pitches are set around a well mown and tended paddock, most have electric hook-up and some enjoy superb sea views. Expect spotlessly clean toilet facilities and a traditional camping atmosphere.

Open: Easter to October (restricted service: low season – reduced hours at reception/shop) **Last arrival:** 19.00 (arrival up to 21.00 by prior arrangement only) **Last departure:** 10.30

Pitches: * 🚐 from £15; 🚐 from £15; ▲ from £15; 14 hardstanding pitches; 12 seasonal pitches

Leisure: ⚠ **Facilities:** 🛁 ⊙ ☀ ♿ 🛒 WiFi

Services: 🔌 🚰 **Within 3 miles:** ♨ 🎣 ∪ ◎ 🚤 🎯 🗓 🛒

Additional site information: 3 acre site. 🐕 Cars can be parked by caravans and tents. Awnings permitted. Booking advisable during school holidays. Storage facilities, 2 static caravans.

KENNFORD
Map 3 SX98

Places to visit

Canonteign Falls, CHUDLEIGH, EX6 7RH, 01647 252434
www.canonteignfalls.co.uk

Custom House Visitor Centre, EXETER, EX2 4AN, 01392 271611
www.exeter.gov.uk/customhouse

Great for kids: Crealy Theme Park & Resort, CLYST ST MARY, EX5 1DR,
01395 233200, www.crealy.co.uk

Premier Park

Kennford International Holiday Park
▶▶▶▶▶ 84%

tel: 01392 833046 **EX6 7YN**
email: ian@kennfordinternational.com **web:** www.kennfordinternational.co.uk
dir: *At end of M5 take A38, site signed at Kennford slip road.*

Screened from the A38 by trees and shrubs, this park offers pitches divided by hedging for privacy. A high quality toilet block complements the park's facilities. A good, centrally-located base for exploring the coast and touring the countryside of Devon, and Exeter is easily accessible via buses that stop nearby.

Open: All year **Last arrival:** 21.00 (winter – check with site for arrival times) **Last departure:** 11.00

Pitches: 🚐 🚐 ▲; 9 hardstanding pitches **Leisure:** ⚠

Facilities: 🛁 ⊙ ♿ WiFi **Services:** 🔌 🗑 🚰 🛗 🚽 T

Within 3 miles: ♨ 🎣 ∪ 🎯 🗓 🛒

Additional site information: 15 acre site. 🐕 Cars can be parked by caravans and tents. Awnings permitted.

LEISURE: 🏊 Indoor swimming pool 🏊 Outdoor swimming pool ⚠ Children's playground 🖐 Kids' club 🎾 Tennis court 🎱 Games room 📺 Separate TV room
♨ Golf course 🏌 Pitch n putt 🚤 Boats for hire 🚲 Bikes for hire 🎬 Cinema 🎵 Entertainment 🎣 Fishing ◎ Mini golf 🏄 Watersports 🏋 Gym 🏟 Sports field ∪ Stables
FACILITIES: 🛁 Baths/Shower ⊙ Electric shaver sockets 🕝 Hairdryer ☀ Ice Pack Facility 🍼 Baby facilities ♿ Disabled facilities 🛒 Shop on site or within 200yds
🍽 BBQ area 🏕 Picnic area WiFi WiFi

KENTISBEARE
Map 3 ST00

Places to visit

Killerton House & Garden, KILLERTON, EX5 3LE, 01392 881345
www.nationaltrust.org.uk/killerton

Custom House Visitor Centre, EXETER, EX2 4AN, 01392 271611
www.exeter.gov.uk/customhouse

Great for kids: Diggerland, COLLOMPTON, EX15 2PE, 0871 227 7007 (calls cost 10p per minute plus your phone company's access charge)
www.diggerland.com/days-out-in-devon

Forest Glade Holiday Park

►►►► 85%

tel: 01404 841381 **EX15 2DT**
email: enquiries@forest-glade.co.uk web: www.forest-glade.co.uk
dir: Tent traffic: from A373 turn left past Keepers Cottage Inn (2.5 miles east of M5 junction 28). (Note: due to narrow roads, touring caravans and larger motorhomes must approach from Honiton direction. Phone site for access details).

A quiet, attractive park in a forest clearing with well-kept gardens and beech hedge screening. One of the main attractions is the site's immediate proximity to the forest which offers magnificent hillside walks with surprising views over the valleys. There's an undercover heated swimming pool, a good children's play area and large games room; camping pods are available for hire. Please note, that because the roads are narrow around the site, it is best to phone the site for suitable route details.

Open: mid March to end October (restricted service: low season – limited shop hours)
Last arrival: 21.00 **Last departure:** noon

Pitches: ♥ ♥ Å ♠; 40 hardstanding pitches; 28 seasonal pitches

Leisure: ☜ 瓜 ♨ ♠ ⚽

Facilities: ♠ ⊙ ♂ ☀ ﴾ ⑤ 戸 ♥ WiFi

Services: ♥ ⑥ 世 ﯼ ⋃ ● ⌀ Ⓣ

Within 3 miles: ✐ ∪

Additional site information: 26 acre site. ✕ Cars can be parked by caravans and tents. Awnings permitted. Families and couples only. Adventure and soft play areas, wildlife information room, paddling pool.

Glamping available: Wooden pods. **Changeover days:** Any day

Additional glamping information: Wooden pods: no dogs permitted. Cars can be parked by pods.

KINGSBRIDGE

Places to visit

Kingsbridge Cookworthy Museum, KINGSBRIDGE, TQ7 1AW, 01548 853235
www.kingsbridgemuseum.org.uk

Overbeck's, SALCOMBE, TQ8 8LW, 01548 842893
www.nationaltrust.org.uk/overbecks

KINGSBRIDGE
Map 3 SX74

Premier Park

Parkland Caravan and Camping Site

►►►►► 86%

tel: 01548 852723 & 07968 222008 **Sorley Green Cross TQ7 4AF**
email: enquiries@parklandsite.co.uk web: www.parklandsite.co.uk
dir: A384 to Totnes, A381 towards Kingsbridge, 12 miles, at Stumpy Post Cross roundabout turn right, 1 mile. Site 200 yards on left after Sorley Green Cross.

Expect a high level of customer care at this family-run park set in the glorious South Hams countryside; it has panoramic views over Salcombe and the rolling countryside towards Dartmoor. The immaculately maintained grounds offer generous grass pitches, hardstandings and super pitches (RVs can be accommodated), and a dedicated touring field has 10 fully-serviced pitches. The on-site shop sells seasonal produce, everyday provisions, pre-ordered hampers and camping supplies. There is an excellent café; the toilet facilities feature quality cubicles, family washrooms, a bathroom and a fully-fitted disabled suite. Babysitting is available by arrangement. A bus stops close to the site entrance, which is handy for exploring the local towns and villages.

Open: All year **Last arrival:** 20.00 **Last departure:** 11.30

Pitches: ♥ from £27; ♥ from £27; Å from £27; ♠ see prices below; 30 hardstanding pitches; 25 seasonal pitches

Leisure: 瓜 ▭

Facilities: ♠ ⊙ ♂ ☀ ﴾ ⑤ 買 戸 ♥ WiFi

Services: ♥ ⑥ 世 ⋃ ● ⌀ Ⓣ

Within 3 miles: ⅃ ✐ ∪ ◎ ⚐ ⚑ 日

Additional site information: 3 acre site. ✕ Cars can be parked by caravans and tents. Awnings permitted. No camp fires, no noise after 22.30, site gates closed 23.00–07.00. Use of fridge freezers, campers' kitchen, freshly baked croissants, short term caravan storage facility, electric car-charging point. Car hire can be arranged.

Glamping available: Shepherd's hut from £45 (sleeps 2); small cabin from £45 (sleeps 2). **Changeover days:** Any day

Additional glamping information: Adults only, all linen provided, TV, microwave, kettle, toaster, utensils/crockery, en suite shower room, patio. Minimum 2 night stay. Cars can be parked by units.

KINGSBRIDGE *continued*

Premier Park

Island Lodge Caravan & Camping Site

►►►►► 83%

tel: 01548 852956 & 07968 222007 **Stumpy Post Cross TQ7 4BL**
email: islandlodgesite@gmail.com **web:** www.islandlodgesite.co.uk
dir: *Take A381 from Totnes towards Kingsbridge. In 12 miles, at roundabout (Stumpy Post Cross) right, 300 metres left into lane, site signed. 200 metres on left.*

A small, peaceful and well-established park, with extensive views over the South Hams, which has been run by the same family for many years. The site has a security barrier, low-level lighting around the park, good hardstanding pitches, and a motorhome service point. The immaculate toilet facilities are of good quality. A scenic 35-minute walk will take you to Kingsbridge, or the Kingsbridge bus stops close to the site. There are several dog-friendly beaches nearby.

Open: All year (restricted service: November to March – shop has basic supplies only) **Last arrival:** 19.00 **Last departure:** 11.30

Pitches: 🚐 from £25; 🚚 from £25; ▲ from £25; 4 hardstanding pitches; 24 seasonal pitches

Leisure: ⚠

Facilities: 🛁 ☉ 🖍 ❄ ఉ 🖆 🎄 📶

Services: 🖭 🔄 🛒 🛗 🛢 🖊 🖩

Within 3 miles: ⛵ 🖍 ♻ ◎ 🚤 🛶 🖩

Additional site information: 2 acre site. 🐾 Restrictions on certain dog breeds. 🐕 Cars can be parked by caravans and tents. Awnings permitted. No generators. Play area open 09.00–21.00. Electronic security barrier closed overnight. 24-hour CCTV, secure caravan storage yard, boat park, local brewery with off license 200 yards from site. Car hire can be arranged.

LYNTON

Places to visit

Arlington Court, ARLINGTON, EX31 4LP, 01271 850296
www.nationaltrust.org.uk/arlington-court

Great for kids: Exmoor Zoological Park, BLACKMOOR GATE, EX31 4SG, 01598 763352, www.exmoorzoo.co.uk

---

LYNTON   Map 3 SS74

Channel View Caravan and Camping Park

►►►► 72%

tel: 01598 753349 **Manor Farm EX35 6LD**
email: relax@channel-view.co.uk **web:** www.channel-view.co.uk
dir: *On A39 from Barbrook towards Hillsford Bridge. Approximately 0.5 mile to site on left.*

On the top of the cliffs overlooking the Bristol Channel, this is a well-maintained park on the edge of Exmoor, and close to both Lynton and Lynmouth. Pitches can be selected from either those in a hidden hedged area or those with panoramic views over the coast.

Open: 15 March to 15 November **Last arrival:** 22.00 **Last departure:** noon

Pitches: * 🚐 from £23; 🚚 from £23; ▲ from £17; 15 hardstanding pitches

Facilities: 🛁 ☉ 🖍 ❄ ఉ 🖆 📶

Services: 🖭 🔄 🛒 🖊 🛢 🖩 🖩

Within 3 miles: 🖍 ♻ ◎ 🚤 🖩

Additional site information: 6 acre site. 🐾 Cars can be parked by caravans and tents. Awnings permitted. Groups by prior arrangement only. Parent and baby room.

MODBURY   Map 3 SX65

Places to visit

Kingsbridge Cookworthy Museum, KINGSBRIDGE, TQ7 1AW, 01548 853235
www.kingsbridgemuseum.org.uk

Overbeck's, SALCOMBE, TQ8 8LW, 01548 842893
www.nationaltrust.org.uk/overbecks

Pennymoor Camping & Caravan Park

►►► 88%

tel: 01548 830542 **PL21 0SB**
email: enquiries@pennymoor-camping.co.uk **web:** www.pennymoor-camping.co.uk
dir: *Exit A38 at Wrangaton Cross. Left, then right at crossroads. After by-passing Ermington, turn left onto A379 Hollowcombe Cross, through Modbury, left at Harraton Cross. Site on left.*

Owned and run by the same family since 1935, this well-established, rural and lovingly tended park is tucked away in South Hams; it is close to glorious beaches and has good views over rolling countryside to Dartmoor in the distance. On part level, part gently sloping grass, Pennymoor is an ideal base for exploring south Devon and offers everything for a relaxing and peaceful family stay, with spotless, well-maintained toilets, a fully-equipped children's play area, a well-stocked shop, site-wide WiFi and a relaxing atmosphere.

Open: 15 March to 15 November (restricted service: 15 March to mid May – only one toilet and shower block open) **Last arrival:** 20.00 (later arrival times by prior arrangement) **Last departure:** 11.00

Pitches: * 🚐 from £14; 🚚 from £14; ▲ from £14; 3 hardstanding pitches; 14 seasonal pitches

Leisure: ⚠   **Facilities:** 🛁 ☉ 🖍 ❄ ఉ 🖆 📶

Services: 🖭 🔄 🍴 🖕 🛒 🖊 🖩 🖩

Within 3 miles: ⛵

Additional site information: 12.5 acre site. 🐾 Cars can be parked by caravans and tents. Awnings permitted. No skateboards or scooters, no noise after 22.00. Emergency phone, table tennis. Flogas. Caravans for hire and sale.

LEISURE: 🏊 Indoor swimming pool 🏊 Outdoor swimming pool ⚠ Children's playground 🖐 Kids' club 🎾 Tennis court 🎱 Games room 🖵 Separate TV room
⛳ Golf course 🏌 Pitch n putt 🚣 Boats for hire 🚲 Bikes for hire 🎬 Cinema 🎵 Entertainment 🎣 Fishing ◎ Mini golf 🏄 Watersports 🏋 Gym ⚽ Sports field ♻ Stables
FACILITIES: 🛁 Baths/Shower ☉ Electric shaver sockets 🖍 Hairdryer ❄ Ice Pack Facility 🍼 Baby facilities ఉ Disabled facilities 🖆 Shop on site or within 200yds
🍖 BBQ area 🎄 Picnic area 📶 WiFi

MORTEHOE
Map 3 SS44

See also Woolacombe

Places to visit

Marwood Hill Gardens, BARNSTAPLE, EX31 4EA, 01271 342528
www.marwoodhillgarden.co.uk

Great for kids Watermouth Castle & Family Theme Park, ILFRACOMBE,
EX34 9SL, 01271 867474
www.watermouthcastle.com

North Morte Farm Caravan & Camping Park
▶ ▶ ▶ ▶ 90%

tel: 01271 870381 **North Morte Road EX34 7EG**
email: info@northmortefarm.co.uk web: www.northmortefarm.co.uk
dir: *From B3343 into Mortehoe, right at post office. Site 500 yards on left.*

Set in spectacular coastal countryside close to National Trust land and 500 yards
from Rockham Beach. This attractive park is very well run and maintained by
friendly family owners, and the quaint village of Mortehoe with its cafés, shops and
pubs, is just a five-minute walk away.

Open: April to October **Last arrival:** 21.00 **Last departure:** noon

Pitches: ⬜ ⬜ ▲; 25 hardstanding pitches; 13 seasonal pitches

Leisure: �▲

Facilities: 🏠 ☺ ℱ ☀ ♿ ⑤ 🛒 WiFi

Services: 🔌 ⑤ 🎲 ☴ ⚒ 🔋 🧴 Ⓣ

Within 3 miles: 🎣 ✎ ∪ ◎ 🚌

Additional site information: 22 acre site. 🐕 Cars can be parked by caravans and tents.
Awnings permitted. No large groups.

NEWTON ABBOT

Places to visit

Bradley Manor, NEWTON ABBOT, TQ12 1LX, 01803 661907
www.nationaltrust.org.uk/bradley

Shaldon Wildlife Trust, SHALDON, TQ14 0HP, 01626 872234
www.shaldonwildlifetrust.org.uk

NEWTON ABBOT
Map 3 SX87

Platinum Park

Dornafield
▶ ▶ ▶ ▶ ▶

tel: 01803 812732 **Dornafield Farm, Two Mile Oak TQ12 6DD**
email: enquiries@dornafield.com web: www.dornafield.com
dir: *From Newton Abbot take A381 signed Totnes for 2 miles. At Two Mile Oak Inn right,
left at crossroads in 0.5 mile. Site on right.*

An immaculately kept park in a tranquil wooded valley between Dartmoor and
Torbay, divided into three areas. At the heart of the 30-acre site is Dornafield, a
14th-century farmhouse, adapted for campers' to use but still retaining much
charm. The friendly family owners are always available for help or to give advice.
The site has superb facilities in two ultra-modern toilet blocks. On site there is
the Quarry Café which provides takeaway food two nights a week. This is a quiet
and peaceful location convenient for Torbay, Dartmoor and the charming coastal
villages of the South Hams. A bus service to Totnes or Newton Abbot runs nearby.

Open: 14 March to 8 November **Last arrival:** 22.00 **Last departure:** 11.00

Pitches: * ⬜ from £13; ⬜ from £13; ▲ from £13; 119 hardstanding pitches;
26 seasonal pitches

Leisure: ⌏ ♨ 🔍 **Facilities:** 🏠 ☺ ℱ ☀ ♿ ⑤ 🛒 WiFi

Services: 🔌 ⑤ 🎲 ☴ ⚒ 🔋 🧴 Ⓣ **Within 3 miles:** 🎣 ✎ 🚌

Additional site information: 30 acre site. 🐕 Cars can be parked by caravans and
tents. Awnings permitted. No commercial vehicles; no sign-written vehicles. Table
tennis, secure caravan storage (all year), freshly baked bread.

PITCHES: ⬜ Caravans ⬜ Motorhomes ▲ Tents 🏠 Glamping accommodation **SERVICES:** 🔌 Electric hook-up ⑤ Launderette 🍺 Licensed bar
🔥 Calor Gas ⊘ Campingaz Ⓣ Toilet fluid 🍴 Café/Restaurant 🍔 Fast Food/Takeaway 🔋 Battery charging ⚒ Motorhome service point
* 2019 prices ⊘ No credit or debit cards 🐕 Dogs permitted 🚫 No dogs

NEWTON ABBOT *continued*

Platinum Park

Ross Park
▶▶▶▶▶

Best of British

tel: 01803 812983 **Park Hill Farm, Ipplepen TQ12 5TT**
email: enquiries@rossparkcaravanpark.co.uk **web:** www.rossparkcaravanpark.co.uk
dir: *North of Ipplepen on A381 follow brown site signs and sign for Woodland opposite Essar garage.*

A top-class park in every way, with large secluded pitches, high quality toilet facilities (which include excellent family rooms) and colourful flower displays throughout – note the wonderful floral walk to the toilets. The beautiful tropical conservatory also offers a breathtaking show of colour. There's a conservation walk through glorious wild flower meadows, replete with nature trail, a dog shower/grooming area, and six fully serviced pitches. This very rural park enjoys superb views of Dartmoor, and good quality meals to suit all tastes and pockets are served in the restaurant. Expect high levels of customer care – this park gets better each year. Home-grown produce and honey are sold in the shop. A bus, which stops close to the entrance, runs to Totnes and Newton Abbot.

Open: March to 2 January (restricted service: 1st 3 weeks in March, November and December (except Christmas and New Year) – restaurant and bar closed)
Last arrival: 21.00 **Last departure:** 11.00

Pitches: * ⚏ from £19.75; ⚏ from £19.75; ▲ from £19.75; 110 hardstanding pitches

Leisure: ⚏ ⚏ ⚏ ⚏

Facilities: ⚏ ⚏ ⚏ ⚏ ⚏ ⚏ ⚏ ⚏ WiFi

Services: ⚏ ⚏ ⚏ ⚏ ⚏ ⚏ ⚏ ⚏ ⚏ ⚏ T

Within 3 miles: ⚏ ⚏ ∪ ⚏

Additional site information: 32 acre site. ⚏ Cars can be parked by caravans and tents. Awnings permitted. Bikes, skateboards and scooters only permitted on leisure field. Snooker, table tennis, badminton.

Twelve Oaks Farm Caravan Park
▶▶▶▶ 84%

tel: 01626 335015 & 07976 440456 **Teigngrace TQ12 6QT**
email: info@twelveoaksfarm.co.uk **web:** www.twelveoaksfarm.co.uk
dir: *A38 from Exeter left signed Teigngrace (only), 0.25 mile before Drumbridges roundabout. 1.5 miles, through village, site on left. Or from Plymouth pass Drumbridges roundabout, take slip road for Chudleigh Knighton. Right over bridge, rejoin A38 towards Plymouth. Left for Teigngrace (only), then as above.*

An attractive small park on a working farm close to Dartmoor National Park, and bordered by the River Teign. The tidy pitches are located amongst trees and shrubs, and the modern facilities are very well maintained. A new motorhome service point was installed for 2019. There are two well-stocked fishing lakes and children will enjoy visiting all the farm animals. Close by is Stover Country Park and also the popular Templar Way walking route.

Open: All year **Last arrival:** 21.00 **Last departure:** 10.30

Pitches: ⚏ from £18; ⚏ from £18; ▲ from £18; 25 hardstanding pitches

Leisure: ⚏ ⚏ ⚏

Facilities: ⚏ ⚏ ⚏ ⚏ ⚏ ⚏ ⚏ ⚏ WiFi

Services: ⚏ ⚏ ⚏ ⚏ ⚏ T

Within 3 miles: ⚏ ∪ ⚏ ⚏ ⚏

Additional site information: 2 acre site. ⚏ Dogs must be kept on leads at all times and picked up after. Cars can be parked by caravans and tents. Awnings permitted. No noise after 23.00, no fire pits.

Map 3 SX86

PAIGNTON

Places to visit

Dartmouth Steam Railway & River Boat Company, PAIGNTON, TQ4 6AF, 01803 555872, www.dartmouthrailriver.co.uk

Kents Cavern, TORQUAY, TQ1 2JF, 01803 215136 www.kents-cavern.co.uk

Great for kids: Paignton Zoo Environmental Park, PAIGNTON, TQ4 7EU, 01803 697500, www.paigntonzoo.org.uk

Premier Park

Beverley Park Caravan & Camping Park
►►►►► 88%

Best of British

tel: 01803 843887 **Goodrington Road TQ4 7JE**
email: info@beverley-holidays.co.uk **web:** www.beverley-holidays.co.uk
dir: On A380, A3022, 2 miles south of Paignton left into Goodrington Road. Beverley Park on right.

A high quality family-run park with extensive views of the bay and plenty of on-site amenities. The park boasts indoor and outdoor heated swimming pools, plus good bars and restaurants. The toilet facilities are modern and very clean and include excellent fully serviced family rooms. The park complex is attractively laid out with the touring areas divided into nicely screened sections.

Open: All year **Last arrival:** 21.00 **Last departure:** 10.00

Pitches: 🚐 🚐 ⛺; 49 hardstanding pitches

Leisure: 🏊 🏊 ⛰ 🎣 🎱 ⬜ 🎵 🎯 ⚽

Facilities: 🏪 ☺ 🍳 ☀ ♿ 🅂 🚻 📶 WiFi

Services: 🔌 🅛 🍴 🍽️ 🍔 🔋 🏧 ⛽ 💈 ⊤

Within 3 miles: ⚓ 🎣 🗘 ◎ 🚣 🎿 🚲 🎯

Additional site information: 12 acre site. 🐕 Cars can be parked by caravans and tents. Awnings permitted. Hot tub, sauna, steam room, gym, play area, soft play, crazy golf.

Whitehill Country Park
►►►► 88%

tel: 01803 782338 **Stoke Road TQ4 7PF**
email: info@whitehill-park.co.uk **web:** www.whitehill-park.co.uk
dir: A385 through Totnes towards Paignton. Turn right by Parkers Arms into Stoke Road towards Stoke Gabriel. Site on left in approximately 1.5 miles.

A family-owned and run park set in rolling countryside, with many scenic beaches just a short drive away. This extensive country park covers 40 acres with woodland walks and nature trails, an excellent outdoor swimming pool with splash pad and poolside spa, a café, a bar and restaurant plus summer entertainment. A new addition for 2019 – a fully equipped gym with an impressive array of equipment. The park offers ideal facilities, including luxury caravans, lodges and camping pods (dog-friendly accommodation is available) for an excellent holiday.

Open: Easter to October **Last arrival:** 21.00 **Last departure:** 10.00

Pitches: 🚐 🚐 ⛺ 🏠; 30 hardstanding pitches; 40 seasonal pitches

Leisure: 🏊 ⛰ 🎣 ⬜ 🎵

Facilities: 🏪 🍳 ☀ ♿ 🅂 🚻 🚲 WiFi

Services: 🔌 🅛 🍴 🍽️ 🍔 🏧 ⛽ 💈 ⊤

Within 3 miles: ⚓ 🎣 🗘 ◎ 🚣 🎿 🚲 🎯

Additional site information: 40 acre site. 🐕 Cars can be parked by caravans and tents. Awnings permitted. Letter box trail, craft room, table tennis, soft play area, woodland walking trails, poolside spa and splash pad. Picnic area. Freshly baked bread available.

Glamping available: 6 wooden pods. **Changeover days:** Any day

Additional glamping information: Wooden pods offer fold-out beds, heating, lighting, plug socket and outdoor furniture.

PLYMOUTH | Map 3 SX45

Places to visit

Saltram, PLYMPTON, PL7 1UH, 01752 333500
www.nationaltrust.org.uk/saltram

Riverside Caravan Park
►►►► 85%

tel: 01752 344122 **Leigham Manor Drive PL6 8LL**
email: office@riversidecaravanpark.com **web:** www.riversidecaravanpark.com
dir: From A38 at Marsh Mills roundabout, follow signs for Plympton (B3416) and brown 'Riverside' signs. At lights left into Riverside Road signed 'Riverside'. 400 metres, right into Leighham Manor Drive (River Plym on right) to site on right.

A well-groomed site on the outskirts of Plymouth on the banks of the River Plym, in a surprisingly peaceful location surrounded by woodland. The toilet facilities are appointed to a very good standard, and include private cubicles, plus there's a good games room and bar/restaurant serving food. This park is an ideal stopover for the ferries to France and Spain, and makes an excellent base for touring Dartmoor and the coast. The local bus stop is just a 10-minute walk from the site.

Open: All year (restricted service: October to Easter – bar, restaurant, takeaway and pool closed) **Last arrival:** 22.00 **Last departure:** 11.00

Pitches: 🚐 🚗 Å; 63 hardstanding pitches

Leisure: ⊛ ◕ ▭

Facilities: ⊙ ℱ ✳ ♿ ⑤ WiFi

Services: ♨ 🔟 🍽 🍲 ⊞ 🛒 ♨ 🔒 ⊘ Ⓣ

Within 3 miles: 🎣 ℘ ∪ ◎ ⚓ 🚴 🎯

Additional site information: 11 acre site. 🐾 Cars can be parked by caravans and tents. Awnings permitted.

PRINCETOWN | Map 3 SX57

Places to visit

The Garden House, YELVERTON, PL20 7LQ, 01822 854769
www.thegardenhouse.org.uk

Merrivale Prehistoric Settlement, MERRIVALE, PL20 6ST, 0370 333 1181
www.english-heritage.org.uk/visit/places/merrivale-prehistoric-settlement

The Plume of Feathers Inn
►► 77%

tel: 01822 890240 **Plymouth Hill PL20 6QQ**
email: contact@theplumeoffeathersdartmoor.co.uk
web: www.theplumeoffeathersdartmoor.co.uk
dir: Site accessed from B3212 roundabout (by Plume of Feathers Inn) in centre of Princetown.

Set amidst the rugged beauty of Dartmoor, and behind the village pub, this campsite boasts good toilet facilities and all the amenities of the inn. The Plume of Feathers is Princetown's oldest building, and serves all day food in an atmospheric setting – try the 'camp and breakfast' deal that's on offer. This campsite is mainly for tents.

Open: All year **Last arrival:** 23.00 **Last departure:** noon

Pitches: 🚗 Å **Services:** 🍽 🍲

Additional site information: 5 acre site. 🐾

SALCOMBE | Map 3 SX73

Places to visit

Overbeck's, SALCOMBE, TQ8 8LW, 01548 842893
www.nationaltrust.org.uk/overbecks

Kingsbridge Cookworthy Museum, KINGSBRIDGE, TQ7 1AW, 01548 853235
www.kingsbridgemuseum.org.uk

Karrageen Caravan & Camping Park
►►►► 84%

tel: 01548 561230 **Bolberry, Malborough TQ7 3EN**
email: phil@karrageen.co.uk **web:** www.karrageen.co.uk
dir: At Malborough on A381, sharp right through village, in 0.6 mile right again, 0.9 mile, site on right.

A small friendly, family-run park with secluded hidden dells for tents and terraced grass pitches giving extensive sea and country views. There is a well-stocked shop and an excellent toilet block that has two cubicled units – one suitable for families and for less able visitors. This park is just one mile from the beach and pretty hamlet of Hope Cove and is a really peaceful park from which to explore the South Hams coast.

Open: Easter to September **Last arrival:** 21.00 **Last departure:** 11.30

Pitches: 🚐 🚗 Å

Facilities: 🛁 ⊙ ℱ ✳ ♿ ⑤ 🍴 WiFi

Services: ♨ 🔟 🛒 🔒 ⊘ Ⓣ

Within 3 miles: 🎣 ℘ 🚴 🎯

Additional site information: 7.5 acre site. 🐾 ☻ Cars can be parked by caravans and tents. Awnings permitted. Noise to be kept to a minimum after 22.00. Freshly baked bread and croissants available. BACS payments accepted.

Bolberry House Farm Caravan & Camping Park
►►► 83%

tel: 01548 561251 **Bolberry TQ7 3DY**
email: enquiries@bolberryparks.co.uk **web:** www.bolberryparks.co.uk
dir: At Malborough on A381 turn right signed Hope Cove and Bolberry. Take left fork after village signed Soar and Bolberry. Right in 0.6 mile. Site signed in 0.5 mile.

A very popular park in a peaceful setting on a coastal farm with sea views, fine cliff walks and nearby beaches. Customers are assured of a warm welcome and the nicely tucked-away portaloo facilities are smart and beautifully maintained. Hardstandings are available. A mobile fish and chip van calls weekly in high season. There's a super dog-walking area.

Open: Easter to October **Last arrival:** 20.00 **Last departure:** 11.30

Pitches: 🚐 🚗 Å; 7 hardstanding pitches

Facilities: ⊙ ℱ ✳ ⑤ WiFi

Services: ♨ 🔟 🛒

Within 3 miles: 🎣 ℘ ◎ 🚴 🎯

Additional site information: 6 acre site. 🐾 Dogs must not be left unattended. ☻ Cars can be parked by caravans and tents. Awnings permitted. Minimum noise 22.00–08.30. Shop on site (high season only).

Higher Rew Caravan & Camping Park

▶▶▶ 83%

tel: 01548 842681 **Higher Rew, Malborough TQ7 3BW**
email: enquiries@higherrew.co.uk **web:** www.higherrew.co.uk
dir: *A381 to Malborough. Right at Townsend Cross, follow signs to Soar. 1 mile, left at Rew Cross, 0.5 mile, site on right.*

A long-established park in a remote location within sight of the sea. The spacious, open touring field has some tiered pitches in the sloping grass, and there are lovely countryside or sea views from every pitch. The friendly family owners are continually improving the facilities.

Open: Easter to October **Last arrival:** 22.00 **Last departure:** noon

Pitches: ⚏ ⛌ 𝗔

Leisure: ⚲ ⚞ 🔍

Facilities: ☺ ⌒ ⚹ ⑤ WiFi

Services: ⚡ ⑤ ⛟ ⛽ 🔋 ⌀ T

Within 3 miles: ⚲ ⚞ ⚞

Additional site information: 5 acre site. ↰ ⊕ Cars can be parked by caravans and tents. Awnings permitted. Minimum noise after 23.00. Play barn with table tennis. Freshly baked bread and croissants available in high season.

SAMPFORD PEVERELL

Places to visit

Tiverton Castle, TIVERTON, EX16 6RP, 01884 253200
www.tivertoncastle.com

Tiverton Museum of Mid Devon Life, TIVERTON, EX16 6PJ, 01884 256295
www.tivertonmuseum.org.uk

SAMPFORD PEVERELL — Map 3 ST01

Premier Park

Minnows Touring Park

▷ ▷ ▷ ▷ ▷ 90%

tel: 01884 821770 **Holbrook Lane EX16 7EN**
email: admin@minnowstouringpark.co.uk **web:** www.minnowstouringpark.co.uk
dir: *M5 junction 27, A361 signed Tiverton and Barnstaple. In 600 yards take 1st slip road, right over bridge, site ahead.*

A small, well-sheltered park, peacefully located amidst fields and mature trees. The refurbished toilet facilities are of a high quality in keeping with the rest of the park, and there is a good laundry. The park has direct gated access to the canal towpath; a brisk 20-minute walk leads to a choice of pubs and a farm shop, and the bus stop is 15 minutes away. All pitches are hardstanding with some large enough for American RVs; fully serviced pitches are also available. The park has WiFi.

Open: 6 March to 6 November **Last arrival:** 20.00 (earliest arrival 13.00)
Last departure: noon

Pitches: ⚏ from £18.50; ⛌ from £18.50; 𝗔 from £8.50; 59 hardstanding pitches

Facilities: ⛺ ☺ ⌒ ⚹ ⚿ ⑤ ⧫ WiFi

Services: ⚡ ⑤ ⛟ ⚲ 🔋 T

Within 3 miles: ⚞ ⚲ ⚞

Additional site information: 5.5 acre site. ↰ Cars can be parked by caravans and tents. Awnings permitted. No cycling, no groundsheets on grass. Children aged 14 years and over accepted. Caravan storage, fishing and boating permits available. Car hire can be arranged.

SHALDON — Map 3 SX97

Places to visit

'Bygones', TORQUAY, TQ1 4PR, 01803 326108
www.bygones.co.uk

Babbacombe Model Village, TORQUAY, TQ1 3LA, 01803 315315
www.model-village.co.uk

Coast View Holiday Park
▶▶▶▶ 82% HOLIDAY HOME PARK

tel: 01626 818350 **Torquay Road TQ14 0BG**
email: holidays@coastview.co.uk **web:** www.southwestholidayparks.co.uk
dir: M5 junction 31, A38 then A380 towards Torquay. A381 towards Teignmouth. Right in 4 miles at lights, over Shaldon Bridge. In 0.75 mile, up hill, site on right.

Set high on the cliffs above Shaldon and with spectacular views across Teignmouth Bay and the Jurassic Coast, this popular holiday home park makes the most of the stunning location, with quality park homes spaciously laid out on neat terraces, each with a glass sheltered decked area from which to soak up the glorious sea views. Serious investment across the park has seen significant improvements in recent years including fully equipped statics and luxury lodges and the opening of an impressive and very smart complex featuring a restaurant and bar and indoor swimming pool.

Open: March to November **Last arrival:** 20.00 **Last departure:** 10.00

Holiday Homes: Sleep 4 Bedrooms 2 Bathrooms 2 Microwave TV WiFi Linen included Towels included Electricity included Gas included

Changeover days: Friday, Saturday, Monday

Leisure: 🏊

Facilities: WiFi

Within 3 miles: ↡ 🏌 🛒 🔲

Additional site information: 33 acre site. 🐕

SIDMOUTH

Places to visit

Branscombe - The Old Bakery, Manor Mill and Forge, BRANSCOMBE, EX12 3DB, 01752 346585
www.nationaltrust.org.uk/branscombe

Otterton Mill, OTTERTON, EX9 7HG, 01395 568521
www.ottertonmill.com

Great for kids: Pecorama Pleasure Gardens, BEER, EX12 3NA, 01297 21542
www.pecorama.co.uk

SIDMOUTH — Map 3 SY18

Platinum Park

Oakdown Country Holiday Park
▶▶▶▶▶

tel: 01297 680387 **Gatedown Lane, Weston EX10 0PT**
email: enquiries@oakdown.co.uk **web:** www.oakdown.co.uk
dir: Exit A3052, 2.5 miles east of junction with A375.

A quality, friendly, well-maintained park with good landscaping and plenty of maturing trees that make it well screened from the A3052. Pitches are grouped in groves surrounded by shrubs, with a 50-pitch development replete with an upmarket toilet block. The park has excellent facilities including a spacious reception building, a 9-hole par 3 golf course, a new dog wash facility, and a good shop and café. There are four-berth wooden pods and a toilet cabin for the pods, and two shepherd's huts for hire. The park's conservation areas, with their natural flora and fauna, offer attractive walks, and there is a hide by the Victorian reed bed for both casual and dedicated birdwatchers.

Open: March to November **Last arrival:** 22.00 **Last departure:** 10.30

Pitches: * 🚐 from £14.25; 🚗 from £14.25; ⛺ from £14.25; 🏠 see prices below; 90 hardstanding pitches; 35 seasonal pitches

Leisure: 🎠 🎣 🔲 ↡

Facilities: 🛁 ☉ 🖙 ✳ ♿ 🛒 🐕 WiFi

Services: 🔌 🔋 🍽 🏧 🎒 ⚓ 🛢 🧺 Ⓣ

Within 3 miles: 🏌 🎯 ◎ ⛷ ♨ 日

LEISURE: 🏊 Indoor swimming pool 🏊 Outdoor swimming pool 🎢 Children's playground ✋ Kids' club 🎾 Tennis court 🎱 Games room 🔲 Separate TV room
↡ Golf course 🏌 Pitch n putt ⛵ Boats for hire 🚲 Bikes for hire 🎬 Cinema 🎵 Entertainment 🎣 Fishing ◎ Mini golf 🏊 Watersports 🏋 Gym ⚽ Sports field U Stables
FACILITIES: 🛁 Baths/Shower ☉ Electric shaver sockets 🖙 Hairdryer ✳ Ice Pack Facility 👶 Baby facilities ♿ Disabled facilities 🛒 Shop on site or within 200yds
🍖 BBQ area 🏕 Picnic area WiFi WiFi

Additional site information: 16 acre site. 🐕 Cars can be parked by caravans and tents. Awnings permitted. No bikes, skateboards, drones or kite flying. Microwave available, field trail to donkey sanctuary.

Glamping available: Wooden pods from £40; shepherd's huts from £90.
Changeover days: Any day

Additional glamping information: Shepherd's huts: Linen supplied, TV and microwave. Patio area with table and chairs. Cars can be parked by units.

Premier Park

Salcombe Regis Caravan & Camping Park
▶ ▶ ▶ ▶ 90%

tel: 01395 514303 **Salcombe Regis EX10 0JH**
email: contact@salcombe-regis.co.uk **web:** www.salcombe-regis.co.uk
dir: *A375 to Sidford onto A3052 towards Lyme Regis, 1 mile, turn right at brown Salcombe Regis/campsite sign. From Lyme Regis towards Sidford on A3052 turn left after Donkey Sanctuary (Note: it is advisable to follow brown tourist signs not sat nav).*

Set in quiet countryside with glorious views, this spacious park has well-maintained facilities, including an impressive new, spacious and modern reception building, where guests will also find a good shop and excellent new toilet facilities. The park offers good mix of grass and hardstanding pitches and a footpath runs from the park to the coastal path and the beach. There is a self-catering holiday cottage and static caravans for hire. This is a perfect location for visiting Sidmouth, Lyme Regis and the coastal area of south-east Devon.

Open: Easter to end October **Last arrival:** 20.15 **Last departure:** noon
Pitches: 🚐 🚌 🛆; 40 hardstanding pitches; 30 seasonal pitches
Leisure: 🅿
Facilities: 🏠 ☺ ℗ ✳ ♿ ⑤ 🍴 🚻 WiFi
Services: 🔌 ⑥ 🔋 ⚒ 🔥 ⌀ T
Within 3 miles: 🔓 🐾 ∪ ◎ ⛷ ⛷ 🗓

Additional site information: 16 acre site. 🐕 Cars can be parked by caravans and tents. Awnings permitted. Quiet at 22.00, no noise from 23.00. No open fires, no drones or remote controlled planes or helicopters. Putting green, table tennis, goal posts, badminton. Croissants baked to order. Car hire can be arranged.

SOURTON CROSS
Map 3 SX59

Places to visit
Lydford Gorge, LYDFORD, EX20 4BH, 01822 820320
www.nationaltrust.org.uk/lydford-gorge

Okehampton Castle, OKEHAMPTON, EX20 1JA, 01837 52844
www.english-heritage.org.uk/visit/places/okehampton-castle

Bundu Camping & Caravan Park
▶ ▶ ▶ 84%

tel: 01837 861747 **EX20 4HT**
email: bundu@btconnect.com **web:** www.bundu.co.uk
dir: *From A30, west of Okehampton towards Launceston, left onto A386 signed Tavistock. 1st left and left again.*

The welcoming, friendly owners set the tone for this well-maintained site, ideally positioned on the border of the Dartmoor National Park. Along with fine views, well-maintained toilet facilities, level grassy pitches and two bell tents for hire, the Granite Way cycle track (from Lydford to Okehampton) that runs along the old railway line passes the edge of the park. There is a bus stop and cycle hire a few minutes' walk away. Dogs are accepted.

Open: All year **Last arrival:** 21.00 **Last departure:** noon
Pitches: * 🚐 from £18.50; 🚌 from £18.50; 🛆 from £10; 🏠 see prices below; 16 hardstanding pitches
Facilities: 🏠 ☺ ℗ ✳ ♿ 🍴 🚻 WiFi
Services: 🔌 ⑥ 🔋 🔥 ⌀ T
Within 3 miles: 🔓 🐾 ⑤

Additional site information: 4.5 acre site. 🐕 Cars can be parked by caravans and tents. Awnings permitted.

Glamping available: Bell tents from £40. **Changeover days:** Any day

Additional glamping information: No dogs in bell tents. Cars can be parked by bell tents.

SOUTH MOLTON

Map 3 SS72

Places to visit

Quince Honey Farm, SOUTH MOLTON, EX36 3RD, 01769 572401
www.quincehoneyfarm.co.uk

Cobbaton Combat Collection, CHITTLEHAMPTON, EX37 9RZ, 01769 540740
www.cobbatoncombat.co.uk

Great for kids: Exmoor Zoological Park, BLACKMOOR GATE, EX31 4SG,
01598 763352, www.exmoorzoo.co.uk

Premier Park

Riverside Caravan & Camping Park
▶▶▶▶▶ 92%

tel: 01769 579269 **Marsh Lane, North Molton Road EX36 3HQ**
email: relax@exmoorriverside.co.uk **web:** www.exmoorriverside.co.uk
dir: M5 junction 27, A361 towards Barnstaple. Site signed 1 mile before South Molton
on right.

A family-run park set alongside the River Mole and in 70 acres of landscaped
parkland with 10 acres of woodland trails. This is an ideal base for exploring

Exmoor, as well as north Devon's golden beaches. It offers 58 premium, fully-
serviced pitches for RVs, motorhomes, caravans and campervans, 40 jumbo grass
pitches with electricity for tents, a large camping field and rally field, an award-
winning shower block, the Country Club restaurant and bar, family entertainment,
caravan storage and a collection service. There is a public footpath linking the
park to South Molton and the local bus stops at park entrance.

Riverside Caravan & Camping Park

Open: All year **Last arrival:** 22.00 **Last departure:** 11.00
Pitches: 🚐 from £18; 🚍 from £18; ⛺ from £10; 54 hardstanding pitches
Leisure: 🎵 🎶 ⚽
Facilities: 🛁 ☉ 🗗 ✳ 🚿 🛒 🚾
Services: 🚰 🗑 🚽 🍽 🛒 🧺 🛢 🌿 🎫
Within 3 miles: 🎣 ∪ 🚣 🎋

Additional site information: 70 acre site. 🚗 Cars can be parked by caravans and
tents. Awnings permitted. Quiet after 23.00. Woodland and valley walks.

See advert below

LEISURE: 🏊 Indoor swimming pool 🏊 Outdoor swimming pool 🛝 Children's playground 🧒 Kids' club 🎾 Tennis court 🎱 Games room 📺 Separate TV room
🏌 Golf course ⛳ Pitch n putt 🚣 Boats for hire 🚲 Bikes for hire 🎬 Cinema 🎶 Entertainment 🎣 Fishing ◎ Mini golf 🏄 Watersports 💪 Gym 🏟 Sports field ∪ Stables
FACILITIES: 🛁 Baths/Shower ☉ Electric shaver sockets 🗗 Hairdryer ✳ Ice Pack Facility 🍼 Baby facilities 🚿 Disabled facilities 🛒 Shop on site or within 200yds
🍖 BBQ area 🪑 Picnic area 🚾 WiFi

STARCROSS

See Dawlish

STOKE GABRIEL — Map 3 SX85

Places to visit

Berry Pomeroy Castle, TOTNES, TQ9 6LJ, 01803 866618
www.english-heritage.org.uk/visit/places/berry pomeroy castle

Totnes Elizabethan House Museum, TOTNES, TQ9 5RU, 01803 863821
www.totnesmuseum.org

Great for kids: Paignton Zoo Environmental Park, PAIGNTON, TQ4 7EU, 01803 697500, www.paigntonzoo.org.uk

Higher Well Farm Holiday Park
▶▶▶ 86%

tel: 01803 782289 **Waddeton Road TQ9 6RN**
email: higherwell@talk21.com **web:** www.higherwellfarmholidaypark.co.uk
dir: From Exeter A380 to Paignton, turn right onto A385 for Totnes, in 0.5 mile left for Stoke Gabriel, follow signs.

Set on a quiet farm yet only four miles from Paignton, this rural holiday park is on the outskirts of the picturesque village of Stoke Gabriel. A toilet block, with some en suite facilities, is an excellent amenity, and tourers are sited in an open field with very good views.

Open: 4 April to 1 November **Last arrival:** 22.00 **Last departure:** 10.00

Pitches: 🚐 from £15; 🚍 from £15; ▲ from £15; 3 hardstanding pitches

Facilities: 🏪 ⊙ 🅿 ✳ ♿ ⓢ

Services: 🔌 🖭 🖚 ↴ 🗑 🅰 🚽 Ⓣ

Within 3 miles: 👶 🏌

Additional site information: 10 acre site. 🐕 Cars can be parked by caravans and tents. Awnings permitted. No commercial vehicles. Pets must not be left unattended in caravans, motorhomes or tents.

Broadleigh Farm Park
▶▶▶ 84%

tel: 01803 782110 **Coombe House Lane, Aish TQ9 6PU**
email: enquiries@broadleighfarm.co.uk **web:** www.broadleighfarm.co.uk
dir: From Exeter on A38 then A380 towards Torbay. Right onto A385 for Totnes. In 0.5 mile right at Whitehill Country Park. Site approximately 0.75 mile on left.

Set in a very rural location on a working farm bordering Paignton and Stoke Gabriel. The large sloping field with a timber-clad toilet block in the centre is sheltered and peaceful, surrounded by rolling countryside but handy for the beaches. There is also an excellent rally field with good toilets and showers.

Open: March to October **Last arrival:** 21.00 **Last departure:** 11.00

Pitches: 🚐 🚍 ▲

Facilities: 🏪 ⊙ 🅿 ✳ ♿ ⓢ 🖥 🎪 WiFi

Services: 🔌 🖭 🖚

Within 3 miles: 👶 🏌 ⊚ ⛵ 🎣 🎯

Additional site information: 7 acre site. 🐕 Cars can be parked by caravans and tents. Awnings permitted. Fish and chip van Saturdays in high season, basic essentials shop.

TAVISTOCK — Map 3 SX47

Places to visit

Morwellham Quay, MORWELLHAM, PL19 8JL, 01822 832766
www.morwellham-quay.co.uk

Premier Park

Woodovis Park
▶▶▶▶ 92%

tel: 01822 832968 **Gulworthy PL19 8NY**
email: info@woodovis.com **web:** www.woodovis.com
dir: A390 from Tavistock signed Callington and Gunnislake. At hill top right at roundabout signed Lamerton and Chipshop. Site 1 mile on left.

A well-kept park in a remote woodland setting on the edge of the Tamar Valley. Peacefully located at the end of a private, half-mile, tree-lined drive, it offers superb on-site facilities and high levels of customer care from the owners. The toilets are immaculate and well maintained, plus there is an indoor swimming pool, sauna and a good information and games room, all creating a friendly atmosphere. Facilities include electric bike hire and a charging point for electric cars. 2-berth and 4-berth wooden pods are available for hire.

Open: 13 March to 31 October **Last arrival:** 20.00 **Last departure:** 11.00

Pitches: * 🚐 from £21; 🚍 from £21; ▲ from £21; 🏠 see price below; 28 hardstanding pitches; 8 seasonal pitches

Leisure: 🏊 🎱 🎣 🏓 ⚽

Facilities: 🏪 ⊙ 🅿 ✳ ♿ ⓢ 🖥 🎪 WiFi

Services: 🔌 🖭 🖚 ↴ 🚽 🅰 🚽 Ⓣ

Within 3 miles: 👶 🏌 ⊚ ⛵ 🎯

Additional site information: 14.5 acre site. 🐕 Cars can be parked by caravans and tents. Awnings permitted. No open fires. Pétanque court, outdoor table tennis, archery, water-walking, infrared therapy cabin, hot tub, circus skills workshops and story telling (in school holidays).

Glamping available: Wooden pods from £54. **Changeover days:** Any day

Additional glamping information: Wooden pods: 1 night stay not possible for Fridays or Saturdays. Cars can be parked by pods.

TAVISTOCK *continued*

Harford Bridge Holiday Park
►►►►► 86%

tel: 01822 810349 **Peter Tavy PL19 9LS**
email: stay@harfordbridge.co.uk **web:** www.harfordbridge.co.uk
dir: *A386 from Tavistock towards Okehampton, 2 miles, right signed Peter Tavy, site 200 yards on right.*

This beautiful spacious park is set beside the River Tavy in the Dartmoor National Park. Pitches are located beside the river and around the copses, and the park is very well equipped for holidaymakers. An adventure playground and games room keep children entertained, and there is fly-fishing and a free tennis court. Studio lodges (S-pods) and a lovely, authentic shepherd's hut complete with fridge and woodburner are available to let.

Open: All year (restricted service: 14 November to 15 March — no camping or touring pitches available (holiday caravans, lodges and studio lodges only))
Last arrival: 18.00 **Last departure:** noon

Pitches: 🚐 🚏 ▲ 🏠; 20 hardstanding pitches; 10 seasonal pitches

Leisure: 🎠 ⛱ 🔍 ▢ ⚽

Facilities: 🛁 ⊙ 🧴 ❄ ⑤ 📦 🚰 🛒 WiFi

Services: 🔌 ◻ 🏭 🛒 ⚖ 🔒 🕰 🔟

Within 3 miles: ⛳ ∪ 🚵 🎣

Additional site information: 16 acre site. 🐕 Cars can be parked by caravans and tents. Awnings permitted. Baguettes, croissants, snacks, sweets, cold drinks, ices and grocery basics available. Expedition groups and rallies welcome by prior arrangement.

Glamping available: Shepherd's hut; studio lodges (S-pods) – sleeps 2 and 4.
Changeover days: Saturday

Additional glamping information: No smoking or vaping in holiday accommodation. Shepherd's hut and 2 person studio lodges are adult only. Cars can be parked by units.

Langstone Manor Camping & Caravan Park
►►►►► 83%

tel: 01822 613371 **Moortown PL19 9JZ**
email: jane@langstonemanor.co.uk **web:** www.langstonemanor.co.uk
dir: *Take B3357 from Tavistock to Princetown. Approximately 1.5 miles turn right at crossroads, follow signs. Over bridge, cattle grid, up hill, left at sign, left again to park (Note: do not follow sat nav).*

A secluded and very peaceful site set in the well-maintained grounds of a manor house in Dartmoor National Park. Many attractive mature trees provide screening within the park, yet the west-facing terraced pitches on the main park enjoy the superb summer sunsets. There are excellent toilet facilities plus a popular lounge bar offering a very good menu of reasonably priced evening meals. Plenty of activities and places of interest can be found within the surrounding moorland. Dogs are accepted. Twelve wooden pods in a woodland setting are available for hire; three mega-pods have en suite facilities.

Open: 21 March to 30 October (restricted service: Bar and restaurant seasonal opening times) **Last arrival:** 21.00 **Last departure:** 11.00

Pitches: 🚐 from £19; 🚏 from £19; ▲ from £19; 🏠 see prices below; 18 hardstanding pitches

Leisure: 🎠 🔍 ⚽ **Facilities:** 🛁 ⊙ 🧴 ❄ ♿ 🚰 🛒 🛍 WiFi

Services: 🔌 ◻ 🧺 🍽 🏭 🛒 ⚖ 🕰 🔟

Within 3 miles: ⛳ 🎣 ∪ ◎ 🚵 🎣 ⑤

Additional site information: 6.5 acre site. 🐕 Cars can be parked by caravans and tents. Awnings permitted. Cycle shed. Baguettes, croissants etc available. Car hire can be arranged.

Glamping available: Wooden pods from £45; mega pods from £90.
Changeover days: Any day

Additional glamping information: Cars can be parked by units

TIVERTON

See East Worlington

TORQUAY
Map 3 SX96

See also Newton Abbot

Places to visit

Torre Abbey Historic House & Gallery, TORQUAY, TQ2 5JE, 01803 293593
www.torre-abbey.org.uk

'Bygones', TORQUAY, TQ1 4PR, 01803 326108
www.bygones.co.uk

Widdicombe Farm Touring Park
►►►► 90%

tel: 01803 558325 **Marldon TQ3 1ST**
email: info@widdicombefarm.co.uk **web:** www.widdicombefarm.co.uk
dir: On A380, midway between Torquay and Paignton.

A friendly family-run park on a working farm with good quality facilities, extensive views and easy access as there are no narrow roads. The level pitches are terraced to take advantage of the views towards the coast and Dartmoor. This is the only adult touring park within Torquay, and is also handy for Paignton and Brixham. There's a bus service from the park to the local shopping centre and Torquay's harbour. It has a small shop, a restaurant and a bar with entertainment from Easter to the end of September. Club WiFi is available throughout the park and The Nippy Chippy van calls regularly.

Open: mid March to end October **Last arrival:** 20.00 **Last departure:** 11.00

Pitches: 🚐 �læ 𝐀; 180 hardstanding pitches; 20 seasonal pitches

Leisure: 🎵 **Facilities:** ☺ ℙ ✳ ☝ ⑤ 🛒 WiFi

Services: 🔌 ⑤ 🍺 🍽 🎂 🔋 🛠 🔋 🧪 🅣

Within 3 miles: ↓ ⌕ ◎ 🚣 ⚓ 🗓

Additional site information: 8 acre site. Adults only. 🐕 Most dog breeds accepted (contact site for details). Cars can be parked by caravans and tents. Awnings permitted. No groups.

WHIDDON DOWN
Map 3 SX69

Places to visit

Castle Drogo, DREWSTEIGNTON, EX6 6PB, 01647 433306
www.nationaltrust.org.uk/castle-drogo

Finch Foundry, STICKLEPATH, EX20 2NW, 01837 840046
www.nationaltrust.org.uk/finch-foundry

Dartmoor View Holiday Park
►►► 84%

tel: 01647 588026 **EX20 2QL**
email: dartmoorviewtouring@haulfryn.co.uk **web:** www.dartmoorviewtouring.co.uk
dir: From M5 junction 31, take A30 to Okehampton. At Whiddon Down take left junction through village. Turn right at small roundabout. Park is 400 metres on right.

Located just off the A30 near Okehampton, on the northern edge of Dartmoor, this immaculate 20-acre park certainly lives up to its name, and more. Although predominantly a static park, the 26 designated pitches (hardstandings with electric, and some with water and waste drainage) for touring caravans and motorhomes are secluded in a separate, well-landscaped field, replete with a spotlessly clean and well-equipped amenity block. Dogs and children are very welcome and there's a children's play area and a heated outdoor swimming pool, which has a sun-deck area. Dartmoor View is the ideal base for those keen to explore Dartmoor on foot or by bike.

Open: March to October **Last arrival:** 18.00 **Last departure:** 11.00

Pitches: 🚐 �æ; 26 hardstanding pitches; 26 seasonal pitches

Leisure: 🏊 ⚺ 🎣 ▱ ⌕ ⚽ **Facilities:** 🏪 ℙ ☝ 🌂 WiFi

Services: 🔌 ⑤ **Within 3 miles:** ⑤

Additional site information: 20 acre site. 🐕 Cars can be parked by caravans. Awnings permitted. 10mph speed limit.

PITCHES: 🚐 Caravans �æ Motorhomes 𝐀 Tents 🏕 Glamping accommodation **SERVICES:** 🔌 Electric hook-up ⑤ Launderette 🍺 Licensed bar 🔋 Calor Gas 🧪 Campingaz 🅣 Toilet fluid 🍽 Café/Restaurant 🎂 Fast Food/Takeaway 🔋 Battery charging 🛠 Motorhome service point
* 2019 prices 🚫 No credit or debit cards 🐕 Dogs permitted ⊗ No dogs

WOOLACOMBE

See also Mortehoe

Places to visit

Great for kids: Combe Martin Wildlife Park & Dinosaur Park, COMBE MARTIN, EX34 0NG, 01271 882486, cmwdp.co.uk

WOOLACOMBE	Map 3 SS44

Premier Park

Warcombe Farm Caravan & Camping Park

▶ ▶ ▶ ▶   92%

tel: 01271 870690 **Station Road, Mortehoe EX34 7EJ**
email: info@warcombefarm.co.uk **web:** www.warcombefarm.co.uk
dir: *On B3343 towards Woolacombe turn right towards Mortehoe. Site less than 1 mile on right.*

Extensive views over the Bristol Channel can be enjoyed from the open areas of this attractive park, while other pitches are sheltered in paddocks with maturing trees. The site has 14 excellent super pitches with hardstandings. The superb sandy, Blue Flag beach at Woolacombe Bay is only a mile and a half away, and there is a fishing lake with direct access from some pitches. The local bus stops outside the park entrance.

Open: 15 March to October **Last arrival:** 21.00 **Last departure:** 11.00

Pitches: * 🚐 from £22; 🚃 from £22; ▲ from £22; 82 hardstanding pitches; 12 seasonal pitches

Leisure: 🏕 ⚽ 🎿 **Facilities:** 🛁 ☉ 🏳 ✳ ♿ 🏪 🎪 WiFi

Services: 🔌 🔲 🏢 🧺 ♨ 🔒 🧼 T

Within 3 miles: 🎣 ∪ ◎ ⛵ ⛳ 🎡

Additional site information: 35 acre site. 🐾 Cars can be parked by caravans and tents. Awnings permitted. No noise after 22.30. Woodland walk. Fresh bread, pastries available. Car hire can be arranged.

Escape to North Devon

Explore three miles of golden sands and rolling waves in Woolacombe

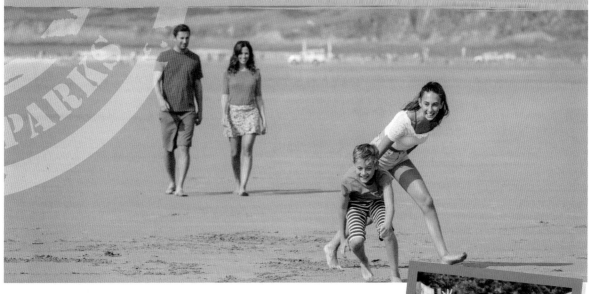

What we've got to offer...

- Sea view touring & super pitches
- Level pitches with easy access
- 400 all weather pitches
- 16 amp electric hookups
- Modern amenity blocks
- Over 40 activities included

 Stay at one Park and you get to use the facilities on all four of our award winning Holiday Parks...

Golden Coast | Woolacombe Bay | Twitchen House | Easewell Farm

Indoor & outdoor pool fun

Call **01271 872 302**
or visit **woolacombe.com**

We're here

WOOLAC◯MBE BAY
HOLIDAY PARKS

For more information please see our four Park listings.

PITCHES: 🚐 Caravans 🚍 Motorhomes ⛺ Tents 🏠 Glamping accommodation **SERVICES:** ⚡ Electric hook-up 🧺 Launderette 🍷 Licensed bar 🔋 Calor Gas ⛽ Campingaz 🅃 Toilet fluid 🍽 Café/Restaurant 🧺 Fast Food/Takeaway 🔌 Battery charging ⚙ Motorhome service point
* 2019 prices 🚫 No credit or debit cards 🐕 Dogs permitted 🚫 No dogs

WOOLACOMBE *continued*

Twitchen House Holiday Village
▶▶▶▶▶ 90% HOLIDAY CENTRE

tel: 01271 872302 **Mortehoe Station Road, Mortehoe EX34 7ES**
email: goodtimes@woolacombe.com **web:** www.woolacombe.com
dir: *M5 junction 27, A361 to Ilfracombe. From Mullacott Cross roundabout take B3343 (Woolacombe road) to Turnpike Cross junction. Take right fork, site 1.5 miles on left.*

Hidden in the trees with an historic Edwardian manor house. A woodland footpath leads to the sea, connecting to the South West Coastal Path. Those looking for a leisurely experience and quality family time will love Twitchen House. All-weather camping and touring pitches with exceptional woodland and coastal views, immaculate on-site facilities. Many fully serviced pitches; 80 that are available for tents. Super pitches have water, drainage, electricity, TV aerial and night light. Shower rooms are heated under-foot with individual cubicles. Saunas, steam room, launderette, washing up area and chemical disposal are also onsite.

Open: mid March to October (restricted service: mid March to mid May and September to October – outdoor pool closed) **Last arrival:** midnight **Last departure:** 10.00

Pitches: 🚐 from £10; 🚛 from £10; ▲ from £10; 110 hardstanding pitches. Seasonal pitches and storage available.

Leisure: 🏊 ⛵ 🅰 🖐 🎾 🔍 ▢ 🎵 ✏ ⛳ 🏋 🏁

Facilities: 🛁 ☉ 🗲 ✳ ♿ ⑤ 🏺 🛒 WiFi

Services: 🔌 🔋 🍴 🍽 🛢 🚮 🛁 🌿 🔲

Within 3 miles: ⚓ ∪ ◎ ⛷ ⛵ 🏁

Additional site information: 45-acre site. 🐾 Pets allowed. Play area, indoor and outdoor pools, two indoor waterslides. Cafe, bar with terrace and woodland walk on site. Adventure golf, amusement arcade, entertainment, climbing wall and many more included activities. Blockbuster cinema showing latest releases. The beach bus takes guests to the beach or to sister parks.

Woolacombe Bay Holiday Village & Spa
▶▶▶▶▶ 88% HOLIDAY HOME PARK

tel: 01271 872302 **Sandy Lane EX34 7AH**
email: goodtimes@woolacombe.com **web:** www.woolacombe.com
dir: *M5 junction 27, A361 to Ilfracombe. At Mullacott roundabout take 1st exit to Woolacombe. Follow Mortehoe signs.*

This is a premium seaside holiday home Park with the beach on its doorstep and spectacular sea views, boasting a lively atmosphere with a superb selection of activities and entertainment for all ages. There's a great selection of onsite accommodation including caravan Holiday Homes, apartments, Surf Lodges with private hot tubs and a unique Surf Pod. The Park has breathtaking coastal views overlooking one of Britain's best beaches. There's an excellent choice of sports facilities, exciting entertainment day and night plus lots of fun all-weather activities included, for all ages. There's also an indoor heated pool and toddler fun pool with an interactive indoor water play area, bright pirate-themed and coloured sculptures, fountains, slides and water jets. An outside heated pool with a toddler pool, flume and sun terrace feature.

Open: mid March to October (restricted service: mid March to mid May and September to October – outdoor pool closed) **Last arrival:** midnight **Last departure:** 10.00

Accommodation available: Caravans, apartments and surf lodges.

Leisure: 🏊 ⛵ 🅰 🖐 👶 🔍 ⚓ 🎵 ⛳ 🏋 ⊕ 🏁 ⛷ Spa

Facilities: 🛁 ☉ 🗲 ✳ ♿ ⑤ 🏺 🛒 WiFi

Services: 🔋 🍴 🍽 ⏛

Within 3 miles: ✏ ∪ ◎ ⛷ ⛵ 🏁

Additional site information: 8.5-acre site. 🐾 Pets friendly accommodation available. Site not ideal for guests with mobility issues, steep hills and steps. Segways, zorbing, Romano spa, gym, terrace, bars & restaurants and over 40 included activities. Blockbuster cinema showing latest releases. The beach bus takes guests to the beach or to sister parks.

Glamping: Surf pod located in Surf Village, sleeps 4.

Golden Coast Holiday Village
► ► ► ► ► 87% HOLIDAY CENTRE

tel: 01271 872302 **Station Road EX34 7HW**
email: goodtimes@woolacombe.com **web:** www.woolacombe.com
dir: *M5 junction 27, A361 to Ilfracombe. At Mullacott roundabout 1st exit to Woolacombe*

A seaside holiday park set beside a three-mile sandy beach. Home to an exhilarating surfing simulator and an all-weather sports complex, including high wires and climbing walls. It's perfect for families, especially those with teenagers. You'll love the warm and friendly atmosphere, fantastic entertainment day and night, excellent facilities and all-weather activities (many of them free) for all ages. A neat touring area includes a unisex toilet block with individual cubicles and underfloor heating, all maintained to a high standard. Super pitches have water, drainage, electricity, TV aerial and night light.

Open: February to November (restricted service: February to May and mid September to November – outdoor pool closed) **Last arrival:** midnight **Last departure:** 10.00

Pitches: 🚐 from £14; 🚍 from £14; ▲ from £14; 89 hardstanding pitches

Leisure: 🎣 🚣 ⚑ 🎳 🏊 ♨ 🎱 🎵 ✎ ⛳ 🏹 ☺

Facilities: 🛍 ☺ 🌳 ❄ ♿ 🛁 🚿 🚻 🚮 WiFi

Services: 🔌 🔘 🍴 🍽 🍟 🔋 ♨ ⌀ T

Within 3 miles: 🛒 ∪ ◎ ⛳ ⚓ 🎣 🎯

Additional site information: 10-acre site. 🐕 No pets allowed on caravan, motorhome or tent pitches. Dogs only allowed in pet friendly accommodation. Four heated pools, slides, entertainment, pub and restaurant, adventure play area. Three kid's clubs, high ropes course and surfing simulator. Adventure golf, amusement arcade and climbing wall. A bus provides handy access to the beach and other sister parks' facilities.

Easewell Farm Holiday Village
► ► ► 85%

tel: 01271 872302 **Mortehoe Station Road, Mortehoe EX34 7EH**
email: goodtimes@woolacombe.com **web:** www.woolacombe.com
dir: *M5 junction 27, A361 to Ilfracombe. At Mullacott roundabout 1st exit to Woolacombe. Follow Mortehoe signs.*

A peaceful cliff-top park in a coastal, rural setting, with superb views and full facility pitches for tents, caravans and motorhomes. Super pitches available, with water, drainage, electricity, TV aerial and night light. Shower rooms have individual cubicles, with washing up area, launderette and chemical disposal facilities. The Park offers a traditional countryside campsite experience which is very close to the beach. The South West Coast Path runs through the site and gives you access to miles of coastal trails and many hidden coves. The Park offers low-key entertainment during the school and bank holidays. For more excitement, pop over to Twitchen House (just across the road). There is also a professional sea view 9-hole (18 tee) par 33 golf course onsite.

Open: mid March to end October (restricted service: at Easter) **Last arrival:** 22.00 **Last departure:** 10.00

Pitches: 🚐 from £6; 🚍 from £6; ▲ from £6; 186 hardstanding pitches. Seasonal pitches and storage available.

Leisure: 🎣 ⚑ 🏊 ♨ 🎵

Facilities: 🛍 ☺ 🌳 ❄ ♿ 🛁 🚿 🚻 🚮 WiFi

Services: 🔌 🔘 🍴 🍽 🍟 🔋 ⌀ T

Within 3 miles: ✎ ∪ ◎ ⛳ ⚓ 🎯

Additional site information: 17-acre site. 🐕 Awnings permitted. Pool, arcade, pool table, bar & restaurant. Professional golf course, indoor bowls, darts and outdoor adventure play area. The beach bus takes guests to the beach or to sister parks.

Dorset

Dorset means rugged varied coastlines and high chalk downlands with more than a hint of Thomas Hardy, its most famous son. Squeezed in among the cliffs and set amid some of Britain's most beautiful scenery is a chain of picturesque villages and seaside towns.

Along the coast you'll find the Lulworth Ranges, which run from Kimmeridge Bay in the east to Lulworth Cove in the west. Walking is the most obvious and rewarding recreational activity here, but the British Army firing ranges mean that access to this glorious landscape is restricted. This is Britain's Jurassic Coast, a UNESCO World Heritage Site and Area of Outstanding Natural Beauty, noted for its layers of shale and numerous fossils embedded in the rock. Among the best-known natural landmarks on this stretch of the Dorset coast is Durdle Door, a rocky arch that has been shaped and sculpted to perfection by the elements. The whole area has the unmistakable stamp of prehistory. The landscape and coastal views may be spectacular but the up-and-down nature of the walking here is often physically demanding.

This designated coastline stretches from Swanage and the Isle of Purbeck to east Devon, offering miles of breathtaking scenery. Beyond the seaside town of Weymouth is Chesil Beach, a long shingle reef running for 10 miles between Portland and Abbotsbury. The beach is covered by a vast wall of shingle left by centuries of dramatic weather-induced activity along the Devon and Dorset coast. Beyond Bridport and West Bay, where the hugely successful TV series *Broadchurch* is filmed, lies quaint Lyme Regis, with its sturdy breakwater, known as The Cobb. It's the sort of place where Georgian houses and pretty cottages jostle with historic pubs and independently run shops. With its blend of architectural styles and old world charm, Lyme Regis looks very much like a film set. Perhaps that is why film producers chose this setting as a location for the making of *The French Lieutenant's Woman* in 1981. Jeremy Irons and Meryl Streep starred in the film, based on the novel by John Fowles.

Away from Dorset's magical coastline lies a landscape with a very different character and atmosphere, but one that is no less appealing. Here, winding, hedge-lined country lanes lead beneath lush, green hilltops to snug, sleepy villages hidden from view and the wider world. The main roads lead to the country towns of Sherborne, Blandford Forum, Wareham and Shaftesbury and in September these routes fill with even more traffic as the county prepares to host the annual Dorset Steam Fair. This famous event draws many visitors who come to admire the various vintage and classic vehicles on display. The same month is also set aside for the two-day County Show, an eagerly anticipated annual fixture.

Inland there are further links with literature. Dorset is justifiably proud of the achievements of Thomas Hardy, and much of the county is immortalised in his writing. He was born at Higher Bockhampton, near Dorchester, and this quaint old cob-and-thatch cottage was where the writer lived until he was 34. As a child, Hardy spent much of his time here reading and writing poems about the countryside. The cottage contains the desk where he wrote *Far from the Madding Crowd*. In later years Hardy lived at Max Gate on the edge of Dorchester and here he was visited by many distinguished writers of the day, including Rudyard Kipling and Virginia Woolf. Even the Prince of Wales called on him one day in 1923. Both homes are now in the care of the National Trust.

One of Thomas Hardy's great friends was T. E. (Thomas Edward) Lawrence, better known as Lawrence of Arabia, who lived nearby in a modest cottage known as Clouds Hill. The cottage, also managed by the National Trust, was Lawrence's secluded retreat from the world, where he could read and play music.

◁ Lyme Regis

DORSET

BERE REGIS   Map 4 SY89

Places to visit

Kingston Lacy, WIMBORNE, BH21 4EA, 01202 883402
www.nationaltrust.org.uk/kingston-lacy

Priest's House Museum and Garden, WIMBORNE, BH21 1HR, 01202 882533
www.priest-house.co.uk

Great for kids: Monkey World-Ape Rescue Centre, WOOL, BH20 6HH,
01929 462537, www.monkeyworld.org

Rowlands Wait Touring Park
►►► 88%

tel: 01929 472727 **Rye Hill BH20 7LP**
email: enquiries@rowlandswait.co.uk **web:** www.rowlandswait.co.uk
dir: *From A35 or A31 to Bere Regis, follow Bovington Tank Museum signs. 0.75 mile, at top of Rye Hill turn right. 200 yards to site.*

This park lies in a really attractive setting overlooking Bere Regis and the Dorset countryside, and is set amongst undulating areas of trees and shrubs. It is located within a few miles of The Tank Museum (Bovingdon Camp) with its mock battles, and is also very convenient for visiting the Dorchester, Poole and Swanage areas. The toilet facilities include two family rooms. The park has fully-equipped tents (a pop-up Glampotel as they call them) each with a shower, toilet and wash basin, as well as a wood-burning stove.

Open: mid March to October (winter by prior arrangement) (restricted service: November to February – own facilities required) **Last arrival:** 21.00 **Last departure:** noon

Pitches: 🚐 🚎 Å; 3 hardstanding pitches; 23 seasonal pitches

Leisure: 🅰 🔍

Facilities: 🛁 ⊙ 🇫 ✳ ♿ $ WiFi

Services: 🔌 ⑤ 🛒 ⚐ 🛢 🕭 T

Within 3 miles: 🔥

Additional site information: 8 acre site. 🐾 Cars can be parked by caravans and tents. Awnings permitted. No open fires. Pool table, table tennis, hot drinks, fresh bread to order, woodland walks, cycling trails from site.

Glamping available: 4 bell tents, 2 safari tents.

Additional glamping information: Bell tents and safari tents are en suite, fully equipped and have log-burners. Cars can be parked by units.

BLANDFORD FORUM   Map 4 ST80

Places to visit

Kingston Lacy, WIMBORNE, BH21 4EA, 01202 883402
www.nationaltrust.org.uk/kingston-lacy

Old Wardour Castle, TISBURY, SP3 6RR, 01747 870487
www.english-heritage.org.uk/visit/places/old-wardour-castle

Great for kids: Monkey World-Ape Rescue Centre, WOOL, BH20 6HH,
01929 462537, www.monkeyworld.org

The Inside Park
►►►► 86%

tel: 01258 453719 **Down House Estate DT11 9AD**
email: mail@theinsidepark.co.uk **web:** www.theinsidepark.co.uk
dir: *From Blandford Forum follow Winterborne Stickland signs. Site in 1.5 miles.*

An attractive, well-sheltered and quiet park, half a mile along a country lane in a wooded valley, yet close to Blandford Forum. The spacious pitches are divided by mature trees and shrubs, and the amenities are housed in an 18th-century coach house and stables. There are some lovely woodland walks within the park, an excellent fenced play area for children and a dog-free area; four dog kennels are available for daily hire. This site makes the perfect base for anyone visiting the Blandford Steam Fair in August, and there are over six miles of private waymarked farm walks for guests to enjoy.

Open: Easter to October **Last arrival:** 22.00 **Last departure:** noon

Pitches: 🚐 from £21; 🚎 from £21; Å from £21

Leisure: 🅰 🔍

Facilities: 🛁 ⊙ 🇫 ✳ ♿ $ WiFi

Services: 🔌 ⑤ 🛒 ⚐ 🛢 🕭 T

Within 3 miles: 🔥 🚲 ∪

Additional site information: 12 acre site. 🐾 Kennels (charges apply). Cars can be parked by caravans and tents. Awnings permitted.

FreshwaterBeach HOLIDAY PARK

Great family holidays
on Dorset's World Heritage Coast

AS SEEN ON TV
An ITV
BROADCHURCH
filming
location

FEATURING
JURASSIC FUN CENTRE

CAMPING · TOURING · HOLIDAY HOME HIRE

Previous Holiday Centre of the Year AA

Call **01308 897317**
www.freshwaterbeach.co.uk

WiFi

BRIDPORT   Map 4 SY49

Places to visit

Dinosaurland Fossil Museum, LYME REGIS, DT7 3PY, 01297 443541
www.dinosaurland.co.uk

Abbotsbury Subtropical Gardens, ABBOTSBURY, DT3 4LA, 01305 871387
abbotsbury-tourism.co.uk/gardens/

Great for kids: Abbotsbury Swannery, ABBOTSBURY, DT3 4JG, 01305 871858
www.abbotsbury-tourism.co.uk/swannery

Platinum Park

Highlands End Holiday Park

▶▶▶▶▶

tel: 01308 422139 & 426947 **Eype DT6 6AR**
email: holidays@wdlh.co.uk **web:** www.wdlh.co.uk
dir: *1 mile west of Bridport on A35, follow signs for Eype. Site signed.*

A well-screened site with magnificent cliff-top views over the Channel and the
Dorset coast, adjacent to National Trust land and overlooking Lyme Bay. The
pitches are mostly sheltered by hedging and are well spaced on hardstandings.
The excellent facilities include a stylish bar and restaurant, indoor pool, leisure
centre and The Cowshed Café, a very good coffee shop, and a soft-play area for
children. There is a mixture of statics and tourers, but the tourers enjoy the best
cliff-top positions, including gravel hardstanding pitches overlooking Lyme Bay.
Ten luxury lodges and wooden pods, that sleep four, are available for hire.

Open: March to November **Last arrival:** 22.00 **Last departure:** 11.00

Pitches: 🚐 🚌 ⛺ 🏠; 45 hardstanding pitches

Leisure: 🏊 ⛰ 🛝 🔍 🎣 🎵 🏌 🎾 ⚽

Facilities: 🚿 ☉ ⚡ ✳ 🛁 🚻 🅢 🍴 **WiFi**

Services: 🔌 🗑 🍴 🍽 🍺 🧺 🧷 🛒 🛢 🌿 🚕

Within 3 miles: 🚶 🏌 ⛳ 🎣

Additional site information: 9 acre site. 🐕 Cars can be parked by caravans and
tents. Awnings permitted. Steam room, sauna, pitch and putt.

Glamping available: Wooden pods. **Changeover days:** Monday, Friday, Saturday
(Saturday only in peak season)

Additional glamping information: Cars can be parked by units

Premier Park

Freshwater Beach Holiday Park

▶▶▶▶▶   92% HOLIDAY CENTRE

tel: 01308 897317 **Burton Bradstock DT6 4PT**
email: office@freshwaterbeach.co.uk **web:** www.freshwaterbeach.co.uk
dir: *Take B3157 from Bridport towards Burton Bradstock. Site 1.5 miles from Crown
roundabout on right.*

A family holiday centre sheltered by a sand bank and enjoying its own private
beach. The park offers a wide variety of leisure and entertainment programmes
for all the family, plus the Jurassic Fun Centre with indoor pool, gym, 6-lane
bowling alley, restaurant and bar is excellent. There is an adults-only Sunset
Lounge Bar and Cellar function room. The park is well placed at one end of the
Weymouth to Bridport coastal area with spectacular views of Chesil Beach.
There are three immaculate toilet blocks with excellent private rooms.

Open: mid March to mid November **Last arrival:** 22.00 **Last departure:** 10.00

Pitches: * 🚐 from £23; 🚌 from £23; ⛺ from £23; 25 hardstanding pitches

Leisure: 🏊 ⛱ ⛰ 🛝 🔍 🎵 🎣 🎾 ⚽

Facilities: 🚿 ☉ ⚡ ✳ 🛁 🅢 🛒 **WiFi**

Services: 🔌 🗑 🍴 🍽 🍺 🧺 🧷 🛒 🛢 🌿 🚕

Within 3 miles: 🚶 ⛳ 🎣

Additional site information: 40 acre site. 🐕 Families and couples only. Large TV,
kids' club in high season and bank holidays, ten-pin bowling alley.

See advert on page 159

LEISURE: 🏊 Indoor swimming pool 🏊 Outdoor swimming pool ⛰ Children's playground 🛝 Kids' club 🎾 Tennis court 🔍 Games room 🖵 Separate TV room
🏌 Golf course ⛳ Pitch n putt 🚣 Boats for hire 🚲 Bikes for hire 🎬 Cinema 🎵 Entertainment 🎣 Fishing ◎ Mini golf 🏄 Watersports 🏋 Gym 🏑 Sports field ⛎ Stables
FACILITIES: 🚿 Baths/Shower ☉ Electric shaver sockets ⚡ Hairdryer ✳ Ice Pack Facility 🍼 Baby facilities 🛁 Disabled facilities 🅢 Shop on site or within 200yds
🍴 BBQ area 🪑 Picnic area **WiFi** WiFi

Graston Copse Holiday Park

▶▶▶ 91%

tel: 01308 426912 & 422139 **Annings Lane, Burton Bradstock DT6 4QP**
email: holidays@wdlh.co.uk **web:** www.wdlh.co.uk
dir: *From Dorchester take A35 to Bridport. In Bridport follow 'Westbound through traffic' sign at mini-roundabout. At next roundabout left onto B3157 to Burton Bradstock. In village, left at Anchor Inn, 2nd right into Annings Lane. 1 mile to site.*

This small, peaceful site offering good facilities for families, is located near the village of Burton Bradstock making it a perfect base for visiting the stunning cliffs and beaches along the Jurassic coastline. The facilities are modern and spotlessly clean. Wooden pods that sleep four are available to hire. Please note, extra care is needed if driving through Burton Bradstock to the site.

Open: 28 April to 5 September **Last arrival:** 22.00 **Last departure:** 11.00

Pitches: 🚐 🚙 ▲ ⌂

Facilities: 🏠 ☺ 🏳 ✳ 🎄 WiFi

Services: 🔌 🔄 **Within 3 miles:** ↓ 🦮 ∪ ⊚ ≟ ⚓ 🗓 💲

Additional site information: 9 acre site. 🐾 Cars can be parked by caravans and tents. Awnings permitted.

Glamping available: Wooden pods. **Changeover days:** Monday, Friday, Saturday (Saturday only in peak season)

Additional glamping information: No dogs permitted in pods. Cars can be parked by pods.

CERNE ABBAS Map 4 ST60

Lyons Gate Caravan and Camping Park
▶▶▶▶ 81%

tel: 01300 345260 **DT2 7AZ**
email: info@lyons-gate.co.uk **web:** www.lyons-gate.co.uk
dir: *Direct access from A352, 3 miles north of Cerne Abbas, site signed.*

A peaceful park with pitches set out around the four attractive coarse fishing lakes. It is surrounded by mature woodland, with many footpaths and bridleways. A smart café and shop are proving a very popular additional facility. Other easily accessible attractions include the Cerne Giant carved into the hills, the old market town of Dorchester and the superb sandy beach at Weymouth.

Open: All year **Last arrival:** 20.00 **Last departure:** 11.30

Pitches: 🚐 from £17; 🚙 from £17; ▲ from £17; 24 hardstanding pitches

Leisure: 🎱 🎣

Facilities: 🏠 ☺ 🏳 ✳ ♿ 🚿 🚻 🎄 WiFi

Services: 🔌 🔄 🍴 🔋 T **Within 3 miles:** ↓ ∪

Additional site information: 10 acre site. 🐾 Cars can be parked by caravans and tents. Awnings permitted.

Giants Head Caravan & Camping Park
▶▶▶ 80%

tel: 01300 341242 & 07970 277730 **Giants Head Farm, Old Sherborne Road DT2 7TR**
email: holidays@giantshead.co.uk **web:** www.giantshead.co.uk
dir: *From Dorchester to Cerne Abbas avoiding bypass, at Top O'Town roundabout take A352 (Sherborne road), in 500 yards right fork at BP (Loder's) garage and Lidl store.*

A pleasant, though rather basic, park set in Dorset downlands near the Cerne Giant (the famous landmark figure cut into the chalk) and with stunning views. There are smart toilet and shower blocks which are kept very clean. This is a good stopover site especially for tenters and backpackers on The Ridgeway National Trail. The site also offers 'Treasure Trail' routes for Dorset. Holiday chalets are available to let.

Open: Easter to October **Last arrival:** 21.00 unless by prior arrangement **Last departure:** noon

Pitches: 🚐 from £14; 🚙 from £14; ▲ from £14

Facilities: 🏠 ☺ 🏳 ✳ 🎄

Services: 🔌 🔄 🔋 🛢 🚿

Within 3 miles: 🦮 💲

Additional site information: 4 acre site. 🐾 Dogs must be on leads at all times. Owners must clean up after their pets – bin provided. Cars can be parked by caravans and tents. Awnings permitted. Ice cream and catering vans on site at busy times.

CHARMOUTH
Map 4 SY39

Places to visit

Forde Abbey, THORNCOMBE, TA20 4LU, 01460 220231
www.fordeabbey.co.uk

Great for kids: Abbotsbury Swannery, ABBOTSBURY, DT3 4JG, 01305 871858
www.abbotsbury-tourism.co.uk/swannery

Premier Park

Wood Farm Caravan & Camping Park
▶▶▶▶▶ 94%

Best of British

tel: 01297 560697 **Axminster Road DT6 6BT**
email: reception@woodfarm.co.uk **web:** www.woodfarm.co.uk
dir: *Accessed directly from A35 roundabout, on Axminster side of Charmouth.*

This top quality park, the perfect place to relax, is set amongst mature native trees with the various levels of the ground falling away into a beautiful valley below. The park offers excellent facilities including family rooms and fully serviced pitches. Everything throughout the park is spotless. At the bottom end of the park there is an indoor swimming pool and leisure complex, plus the licensed, conservatory-style Offshore Café. There's a very good children's play room and excellent play area, in addition to tennis courts and a well-stocked, coarse-fishing lake. The park is well positioned on the Heritage Coast near Lyme Regis. Static holiday homes are also available for hire.

Open: Easter to October **Last arrival:** 19.00 **Last departure:** noon
Pitches: ⊞ from £21.50; ⊞ from £21.50; ▲ from £18.50;
175 hardstanding pitches; 20 seasonal pitches

Leisure: ⊜ ⋔ ⊛ ⚲ ⊡ ℘
Facilities: 🛁 ⊙ ℱ ✳ ⚹ ⑤ WiFi
Services: ⚡ ⊡ ⁞〇 ⊞ ⬆ 🔒 ⊘ Ⓣ
Within 3 miles: ⌇ ∪ ◎ ⚲ ⚲ ⚲ 🗓

Additional site information: 13 acre site. 🐾 Dog bowls provided at café terrace, dog shower, dog walks with waste bags provided. Cars can be parked by caravans and tents. Awnings permitted. No bikes, skateboards, scooters, roller skates, kites or drones.

See advert on page 165

Premier Park

Newlands Holidays
▶▶▶▶▶ 86%

tel: 01297 560259 **DT6 6RB**
email: enq@newlandsholidays.co.uk **web:** www.newlandsholidays.co.uk
dir: *6.4 miles west of Bridport on A35.*

A very smart site with excellent touring facilities, set on gently sloping ground in hilly countryside near the sea. Level and very spacious pitches are available. During the high season, the park offers a full entertainment programme, and boasts a clubhouse, an indoor swimming pool and an outdoor pool with water slide. Lodges, apartments and motel rooms are available, plus there are four camping pods for hire.

Open: mid March to October **Last arrival:** 21.00 **Last departure:** 10.00
Pitches: ⊞ ⊞ ▲; 🛖 see price below; 72 hardstanding pitches; 40 seasonal pitches
Leisure: ⊜ ⊛ ⋔ ⬇ ⚲ ⊡ ♫ ⊛
Facilities: 🛁 ⊙ ℱ ✳ ⚹ ⑤ ⊓ ⇶ WiFi
Services: ⚡ ⊡ ⁞〇 ⊞ 🛒 🔒 ⊘ Ⓣ
Within 3 miles: ⌇ ℘ ∪ ◎ ⚲ ⚲ ⚲ 🗓

Additional site information: 23 acre site. 🐾 Cars can be parked by caravans and tents. Awnings permitted. Kids' club during school holidays, freshly baked bread available. On-site nature trail. Car hire can be arranged.

Glamping available: Wooden pods from £56. **Changeover days:** Any day
Additional glamping information: Cars can be parked by pods.

Manor Farm Holiday Centre
▶▶▶▶ 85%

tel: 01297 560226 **DT6 6QL**
email: enquiries@manorfarmholidaycentre.co.uk
web: www.manorfarmholidaycentre.co.uk
dir: *From east: A35 into Charmouth, site 0.75 mile on right.*

Set just a short walk from the safe sand and shingle beach at Charmouth, this popular family park offers a good range of facilities. There is an indoor-outdoor swimming pool plus café, a fully-equipped gym and sauna. Children certainly enjoy the activity area and the park also offers a lively programme in the extensive bar and entertainment complex. In addition there are 16 luxury cottages available for hire and smart lodges for sale.

Open: All year (restricted service: mid March to end October – statics only)
Last arrival: 20.00 **Last departure:** 10.00
Pitches: * ⊞ from £17; ⊞ from £17; ▲ from £17; 80 hardstanding pitches;
100 seasonal pitches

Leisure: 🌊 🏊 🎱 🎣 🎵 🏇

Facilities: 🛁 ⊙ 🍴 ☼ ♿ 🚿 WiFi

Services: 🔌 🗑 🍴 🍽 🛒 🔧 🔋 🧺 T

Within 3 miles: 🎣 🚴 ∪ ◎ 🛶 🎣 ⛳ 🎯 $

Additional site information: 30 acre site. 🐕 Cars can be parked by caravans and tents. Awnings permitted. No skateboards.

CHIDEOCK
Map 4 SY49

Places to visit
Mapperton, BEAMINSTER, DT8 3NR, 01308 862645
www.mapperton.com

Premier Park

Golden Cap Holiday Park
▶▶▶▶▶ 86%

tel: 01308 422139 & 426947 **Seatown DT6 6JX**
email: holidays@wdlh.co.uk **web:** www.wdlh.co.uk
dir: On A35, in Chideock follow Seatown signs, site signed.

A grassy site, overlooking the sea and beach and surrounded by National Trust parkland. This uniquely placed park slopes down to the sea, although pitches are generally level. A slight dip hides the view of the beach from the back of the park, but this area benefits from having trees, scrub and meadows, unlike the barer areas closer to the sea which do have a spectacular outlook. There is a smart toilet and shower block, plus there's a shop and café and takeaway. Three luxury lodges, with outstanding views, and different types of glamping accommodation are available, including two impressive Premier Pods. This makes an ideal base for touring Dorset and Devon. Lake fishing is possible (a licence can be obtained locally).

Open: March to November **Last arrival:** 22.00 **Last departure:** 11.00

Pitches: 🚐 �
A 🏠; 24 hardstanding pitches

Leisure: 🎱

Facilities: 🛁 ⊙ 🍴 ☼ ♿ $ 🚿 WiFi

Services: 🔌 🗑 🛒 🔋 🧺 T

Within 3 miles: 🎣

Additional site information: 11 acre site. 🐕 Cars can be parked by caravans and tents. Awnings permitted.

Glamping available: Wooden pods; safari tents; Lotus Belle tents.
Changeover days: Monday, Friday, Saturday (Saturday only in peak)

Additional glamping information: Cars can be parked by units.

CHRISTCHURCH
Map 5 SZ19

Places to visit
Red House Museum & Gardens, CHRISTCHURCH, BH23 1BU, 01202 482860
www.hampshireculture.org.uk/red-house-museum-and-gardens

Great for kids: Oceanarium, BOURNEMOUTH, BH2 5AA, 01202 311993
www.oceanarium.co.uk

Premier Park

Meadowbank Holidays
▶▶▶▶▶ 88%

tel: 01202 483597 **Stour Way BH23 2PQ**
email: enquiries@meadowbankholidays.co.uk **web:** www.meadowbank-holidays.co.uk
dir: A31 onto A338 towards Bournemouth. 5 miles, left towards Christchurch on B3073. Right at 1st roundabout into St Catherine's Way, becomes River Way. 3rd right into Stour Way to site.

A very smart park on the banks of the River Stour, with a colourful display of hanging baskets and flower-filled tubs placed around the superb reception area. The toilet block is excellent, with modern, stylish facilities. There's a choice of pitch sizes including luxury, fully serviced ones. There is also an excellent play area, a cycle storage facility, a good shop on site and coarse fishing. Statics are available for hire. The park is well located in a peaceful area and very convenient for visiting nearby Christchurch, the south coast and the New Forest.

Open: March to October **Last arrival:** 21.00 **Last departure:** noon

Pitches: 🚐 �; 22 hardstanding pitches

Leisure: 🎱 🎣

Facilities: 🛁 ⊙ 🍴 ♿ $ 🚿 🔧 WiFi

Services: 🔌 🗑 🛒 🔋 🧺 T

Within 3 miles: 🎣 ∪ ◎ 🛶 🎣 ⛳ 🎯

Additional site information: 2 acre site. Cars can be parked by caravans. Awnings permitted. No pets. Table tennis, riverside walk. Car hire can be arranged.

CORFE CASTLE   Map 4 SY98

Places to visit

Brownsea Island, BROWNSEA ISLAND, BH13 7EE, 01202 707744
www.nationaltrust.org.uk/brownsea-island

Corfe Castle, CORFE CASTLE, BH20 5EZ, 01929 481294
www.nationaltrust.org.uk/corfecastle

Great for kids: Swanage Railway, SWANAGE, BH19 1HB, 01929 425800
www.swanagerailway.co.uk

Corfe Castle Camping & Caravanning Club Site
▶▶▶▶   94%

tel: 01929 480280 & 024 7647 5426 **Bucknowle BH20 5PQ**
email: corfecastle.site@campingandcaravanningclub.co.uk
web: www.campingandcaravanningclub.co.uk/corfecastle
dir: *A351 from Wareham towards Swanage for 4 miles. Right at foot of Corfe Castle signed Church Knowle. 0.75 mile, right at Corfe Castle C&CC Site sign.*

This lovely campsite, where non-members are also very welcome, is set in woodland near the famous Corfe Castle at the foot of the Purbeck Hills. It has a stone reception building, which has a really comfortable information lounge, on-site shop and modern toilet and shower facilities, which are spotless. Although the site is sloping, pitches are level and include spacious hardstandings. The site is perfect for anyone visiting the many attractions of the Purbeck area, including the award-winning beaches at Studland and Swanage, and the seaside towns of Poole, Bournemouth and Weymouth. There is also a station at Corfe for the Swanage Steam Railway. The site is pet friendly.

Open: March to October **Last arrival:** 20.00 (later arrivals by prior arrangement only) **Last departure:** noon

Pitches: * 🚐 from £19.25; 🚍; ▲; 43 hardstanding pitches

Leisure: ⚠

Facilities: 🛁 ☺ 🪒 ❄ 🦽 ⓢ

Services: 🔌 🔲 🚮 🛗 🔒 🗑 🅣

Within 3 miles: 🎣 ↻ ◎ ⛳ 🎯 🎪

Additional site information: 6 acre site. 🐾 Cars can be parked by caravans and tents. Awnings permitted. Site gates closed 23.00–07.00. Bread and newspapers can be ordered. Local sausages, bacon, ice cream and free-range eggs available.

Woodyhyde Camp Site

▶▶▶   81%

tel: 01929 480274 **Valley Road BH20 5HT**
email: camp@woodyhyde.co.uk **web:** www.woodyhyde.co.uk
dir: *From Corfe Castle towards Swanage on A351, site approximately 1 mile on right.*

A large grassy campsite in a sheltered location for tents and motorhomes only, divided into three paddocks – one is dog free. This site offers traditional camping in a great location between Corfe Castle and Swanage, and the Swanage steam railway that runs past the site adds interest for campers. There is a well-stocked shop on site, a modern toilet and shower block, and there's a regular bus service that stops near the site entrance. Electric hook-ups and some hardstandings are available and glamping accommodation is offered, consisting of yurts and a shepherd's hut.

Open: March to October **Last departure:** noon

Pitches: 🚍 ▲ 🏠; 25 hardstanding pitches

Facilities: 🛁 ☺ 🪒 ❄ 🦽 ⓢ 📶

Services: 🔌 🛒 🚮 🛗 🔒 🗑 🅣

Within 3 miles: 🎣 🏌 ↻ ◎ ⛳ 🎯 🎪 🎮

Additional site information: 13 acre site. 🐾 Cars can be parked by tents. Awnings permitted. No noise after 23.00, no open fires.

Glamping available: 1 shepherd's hut; 5 yurts.

See advert on page 167

DORCHESTER

See Cerne Abbas

DRIMPTON   Map 4 ST40

Places to visit

Forde Abbey, THORNCOMBE, TA20 4LU, 01460 220231
www.fordeabbey.co.uk

Mapperton, BEAMINSTER, DT8 3NR, 01308 862645
www.mapperton.com

Oathill Farm Touring and Camping Site
▶▶▶▶ 84%

tel: 01460 30234 & 07403 415986 **Oathill TA18 8PZ**
email: oathillfarm@btconnect.com **web:** www.oathillfarmleisure.co.uk
dir: *From Crewkerne take B3165. Site on left just after Clapton.*

This small peaceful park borders Somerset and Devon, with the Jurassic Coast at Lyme Regis, Charmouth and Bridport only a short drive away. The modern facilities are spotless and there are hardstandings and fully serviced pitches available. There is also a very pleasant camping area which has two additional hardstandings. Lucy's Tea Room serves breakfast and meals. The well-stocked, landscaped fishing ponds prove a hit with anglers. Three luxury lodges are available.

Open: All year (restricted service: winter – shop not fully stocked) **Last arrival:** 20.00
Last departure: noon

Pitches: 🚐 🚍 ▲; 18 hardstanding pitches; 8 seasonal pitches

Leisure: ⚽ ☺

Facilities: 🏠 ☺ 🍴 ☀ ⑤ ⊟ 🎍 WiFi

Services: 🔌 ⑥ 🍴 🎂 🛒 ⚓ 🛢 🧴 ⊤

Within 3 miles: ⚓ ∪

Additional site information: 10 acre site. 🐕 Cars can be parked by caravans and tents. Awnings permitted. No washing lines, no quad bikes, no noise after 23.00. Separate recreational areas, dog walking area.

PITCHES: 🚐 Caravans 🚍 Motorhomes ▲ Tents 🏠 Glamping accommodation **SERVICES:** 🔌 Electric hook-up ⑥ Launderette 🍷 Licensed bar 🛢 Calor Gas 🔥 Campingaz ⊤ Toilet fluid 🍴 Café/Restaurant 🎂 Fast Food/Takeaway ⚓ Battery charging ⚓ Motorhome service point * 2019 prices ⊘ No credit or debit cards 🐕 Dogs permitted ⊗ No dogs

FERNDOWN
Map 5 SU00

Places to visit

Kingston Lacy, WIMBORNE, BH21 4EA, 01202 883402
www.nationaltrust.org.uk/kingston-lacy

Great for kids: Oceanarium, BOURNEMOUTH, BH2 5AA, 01202 311993
www.oceanarium.co.uk

St Leonards Farm Caravan & Camping Park

►►►► 84%

tel: 01202 872637 **Ringwood Road, West Moors BH22 0AQ**
email: enquiries_stleonards@yahoo.co.uk **web:** www.stleonardsfarmpark.com
dir: From Ringwood on A31 (dual carriageway) towards Ferndown, exit left into slip road at site sign. From Wimborne Minster on A31 at roundabout (junction of A31 & A347) follow signs for Ringwood (A31) (pass Texaco garage on left) to next roundabout. 3rd exit (ie double back towards Ferndown) exit at slip road for site.

A private road accessed from the A31 leads to this well-screened park divided into paddocks that have spacious pitches. The site has an excellent, secure children's soft-play area and an indoor play barn. There is a toilet and shower block with excellent family/disabled rooms, and a late arrival point with electricity and water. A shepherd's hut, complete with a fully-equipped utility cabin, is available for hire. The park is also well located for visiting nearby Bournemouth and the New Forest National Park.

Open: 7 February to 6 January (restricted service: 31 October to 6 January, 7 February to 31 March – site open only from Friday to Sunday) **Last arrival:** late arrivals by prior arrangement **Last departure:** noon

---

Pitches: 🚐 🚎 🛄 🏠; 15 hardstanding pitches; 30 seasonal pitches
Leisure: 🅰 ⚽
Facilities: 🛁 ☉ 🖗 ✳ ♿ 🎇
Services: 🔌 🗓 🛒 🔒 🖉
Within 3 miles: ⅃ 🖉 ∪ 🖺

Additional site information: 12 acre site. 🐾 No dogs in July and August. Cars can be parked by caravans and tents. Awnings permitted. No large groups, no noise after 23.00, no disposable BBQs, no gazebos.

Glamping available: Shepherd's hut. **Changeover days:** Monday

Additional glamping information: Cars can be parked by shepherd's hut.

HOLDITCH
Map 4 ST30

Places to visit

Forde Abbey, THORNCOMBE, TA20 4LU, 01460 220231
www.fordeabbey.co.uk

Premier Park

Crafty Camping

►►►►► 85% GLAMPING ONLY

tel: 01460 477771 **Woodland Workshop, Yonder Hill TA20 4NL**
email: enquiries@mallinson.co.uk **web:** www.mallinson.co.uk
dir: From A358 between Axminster and Chard, in Tytherleigh into Broom Lane signed Holditch (becomes Holditch Lane). Through Holditch, after Manor Farm, after sharp left bend, car park on left in 200 yards. (Note: it is advisable not to use sat nav).

Crafty Camping offers a unique holiday adventure in peaceful and beautiful surroundings. If you have a desire to experience a different type of holiday, then this adults-only site could fit the bill. Choose from fully-equipped yurts, each with their own toilet and shower facilities, or bell tents and a tipi, which share excellent communal facilities, or book 'the jewel in the crown', a spectacular tree house. Here there's a double bed, toilet and shower facilities, including a copper bath, a wood-burning stove, and a decked area with table and chairs, hammock, pizza oven and even an open-air shower. There is a spiral staircase to an upper level, which has a sauna and a hot tub – you can even get to the forest floor via a slide! There is also a communal kitchen and eating area, and woodland craft courses are also available. Although hidden away in the hamlet of Holditch, it is close to Axminster, Lyme Regis and the Jurassic Coast. The Woodman's Treehouse was filmed for George Clarke's 'Amazing Spaces' programme for Channel 4 and has been shortlisted for various design awards.

Open: All year **Last arrival:** After 15.00 **Last departure:** 11.00

Leisure: 🎣 🖉
Facilities: 🛁 ✳ 🎇 🎇
Within 3 miles: ⅃ 🖺 🗓

Accommodation available: Bell tents from £97; tipi from £139; yurts from £139; treehouse from £495.

Changeover days: Monday, Wednesday, Friday

Additional site information: 14 acre site. Adults only. No pets, no children, no noise. Wood-fired pizza oven, sauna yurt.

LYME REGIS
Map 4 SY39

See also Charmouth

Places to visit

Shute Barton (NT), SHUTE, EX13 7PT, 01752 346585
www.nationaltrust.org.uk/shute-barton

Great for kids: Pecorama Pleasure Gardens, BEER, EX12 3NA, 01297 21542
www.pecorama.co.uk

Shrubbery Touring Park

▶▶▶▶ 91%

tel: 01297 442227 **Rousdon DT7 3XW**
email: info4shrubberypark@yahoo.co.uk **web:** www.shrubberypark.co.uk
dir: *3 miles west of Lyme Regis on A3052 (coast road).*

Mature trees enclose this peaceful park, which has distant views of the lovely countryside. The modern facilities are well kept and include well designed family rooms, the hardstanding pitches are spacious, and there is plenty of space for children to play in the grounds. There is a small area set aside for adults only and there are two camping pods for hire. Well located for visiting Lyme Regis, Sidmouth and Seaton, the park is right on the Jurassic Coast bus route, which is popular with visitors to this area.

Open: April to October **Last arrival:** 21.00 **Last departure:** 11.00

Pitches: 🚐 🚍 Å; 40 hardstanding pitches; 12 seasonal pitches

Leisure: 🎠

Facilities: 🛁 ⊙ 🎣 ☀ ♿ ⑤ 📶

Services: ⚡ 🔵 ⬆ 🔋 ⊘ Ⓣ

Within 3 miles: 🚶 ⚴ ∪ ◎ ⌇ ⚑

Additional site information: 10 acre site. 🐕 Cars can be parked by caravans and tents. Awnings permitted. No groups (except rallies), no motor scooters, roller skates or skateboards. Crazy golf.

Glamping available: 2 wooden pods.

Additional glamping information: Wooden pods – one with double bed and two singles. Both offer electric sockets, heating, lighting and picnic bench. No pets permitted. Cars can be parked by pods.

PITCHES: 🚐 Caravans 🚍 Motorhomes Å Tents 🏠 Glamping accommodation **SERVICES:** ⚡ Electric hook-up 🔵 Launderette 🍺 Licensed bar 🔋 Calor Gas ⊘ Campingaz Ⓣ Toilet fluid 🍽 Café/Restaurant 🍔 Fast Food/Takeaway 🔌 Battery charging ⬆ Motorhome service point * 2019 prices ⊗ No credit or debit cards 🐕 Dogs permitted ⊗ No dogs

LYME REGIS *continued*

Hook Farm Caravan & Camping Park

▶▶▶ 87%

tel: 01297 442801 **Gore Lane, Uplyme DT7 3UU**
email: info@hookfarmcamping.com **web:** www.hookfarmcamping.com
dir: *A35 onto B3165 towards Lyme Regis and Uplyme at Hunters Lodge pub. In 2 miles right into Gore Lane, site 400 yards on right.*

Set in a peaceful and very rural location, this popular farm site enjoys lovely views of Lym Valley and is just a mile from the seaside at Lyme Regis. There are modern toilet facilities at the top and bottom of the site, and good on-site amenities. Most pitches are level due to excellent terracing — it is a great site for tents but also suited to motorhomes and caravans. A shepherd's hut is now available for hire. Please note, it is advised that if arriving in a motorhome or if towing a caravan that sat nav is not used; there are many narrow roads that only have a few passing places.

Open: March to October **Last arrival:** 20.00 **Last departure:** 10.30
Pitches: ⊞ ⇌ ▲ ⋒; 4 hardstanding pitches
Leisure: ⚠
Facilities: 🛁 ☉ 🖃 ☀ ♿ ⑤ WiFi
Services: ⊕ 🔄 ♨ 🔒 ⌀ T
Within 3 miles: ⚓ ⚘ ∪ 🎣 ⛴ ♨ 🏕 ⊟
Additional site information: 5.5 acre site. 🐕 No dangerous dog breeds. Cars can be parked by caravans and tents. Awnings permitted. No groups of 4 adults or more. Freshly baked bread and pastries available, visiting takeaway food in peak season. River walk into Lyme Regis. Car hire can be arranged.

LYTCHETT MATRAVERS   Map 4 SY99

Places to visit
Brownsea Island, BROWNSEA ISLAND, BH13 7EE, 01202 707744
www.nationaltrust.org.uk/brownsea-island

Poole Museum, POOLE, BH15 1BW, 01202 262600
poolemuseum.org.uk/

Great for kids: Swanage Railway, SWANAGE, BH19 1HB, 01929 425800
www.swanagerailway.co.uk

Huntick Farm Caravan Park
▶▶▶▶ 82%

tel: 01202 622222 **Huntick Road BH16 6BB**
email: huntickcaravans@btconnect.com **web:** www.huntick.co.uk
dir: *Between Lytchett Minster & Lytchett Matravers. From A31 take A350 towards Poole. Follow Lytchett Minster signs, then Lytchett Matravers signs. Into Huntick Road by Rose & Crown pub.*

A really attractive, small park surrounded by woodland and located a mile from the village of Lytchett Matravers. There are excellent toilet and shower facilities as well as a warm welcome from the friendly staff in the reception building. The park's delightful rural location makes it a peaceful base for touring in this lovely county.

Open: April to October **Last arrival:** 21.00 **Last departure:** noon
Pitches: ⊞ ⇌ ▲; 13 seasonal pitches
Leisure: ⚽
Facilities: 🛁 ☉ ☀ WiFi

Services: ⊕ 🔒
Within 3 miles: ⚓ ∪ ⑤ ⊙
Additional site information: 4 acre site. 🐕 Cars can be parked by caravans and tents. Awnings permitted. No gazebos. Ball games permitted only on games field, no noise 22.00–08.00.

OWERMOIGNE   Map 4 SY78

Places to visit
RSPB Nature Reserve Radipole Lake and Wild Weymouth Discovery Centre, WEYMOUTH, DT4 7TZ, 01305 778313
www.rspb.org.uk/reserves-and-events/reserves-a-z/radipole-lake/

Clouds Hill, BOVINGTON CAMP, BH20 7NQ, 01929 405616
www.nationaltrust.org.uk/clouds-hill

Great for kids: Weymouth Sea Life Adventure Park & Marine Sanctuary, WEYMOUTH, DT4 7SX, www2.visitsealife.com/weymouth

---

Sandyholme Holiday Park
▶▶▶ 87%

tel: 01308 422139 & 426947 **Moreton Road DT2 8HZ**
email: holidays@wdlh.co.uk **web:** www.wdlh.co.uk
dir: *From A352 (Wareham to Dorchester road) turn towards Owermoigne. Site on left in 1 mile.*

A pleasant quiet site surrounded by trees and within easy reach of the coast at Lulworth Cove, and handy for several seaside resorts, including Weymouth, Portland, Purbeck and Swanage. The facilities are good, including a children's play area, small football pitch, shop and tourist information. Glamping accommodation features a well-appointed safari lodge and a Lotus Belle tent.

Open: 18 March to 6 November (restricted service: at Easter) **Last arrival:** 22.00 **Last departure:** 11.00
Pitches: ⊞ ⇌ ▲ ⋒; 20 seasonal pitches
Leisure: 🎱 ⚽
Facilities: 🛁 ☉ 🖃 ☀ ♿ ⑤ ⊟ WiFi
Services: ⊕ 🔄 ♨ ♨ 🔒 ⌀ T
Within 3 miles: 🖃
Additional site information: 6 acre site. 🐕 Cars can be parked by caravans and tents. Awnings permitted. Table tennis, wildlife lake, football pitch.
Glamping available: Safari tent; Lotus Belle tent.

POOLE

See also Wimborne Minster

Places to visit
Brownsea Island, BROWNSEA ISLAND, BH13 7EE, 01202 707744
www.nationaltrust.org.uk/brownsea-island

Poole Museum, POOLE, BH15 1BW, 01202 262600
poolemuseum.org.uk/

Great for kids: Oceanarium, BOURNEMOUTH, BH2 5AA, 01202 311993
www.oceanarium.co.uk

LEISURE: 🏊 Indoor swimming pool 🏊 Outdoor swimming pool ⚠ Children's playground 👦 Kids' club 🎾 Tennis court ♣ Games room ⊟ Separate TV room ⛳ Golf course 🏌 Pitch n putt ⛵ Boats for hire 🚲 Bikes for hire 🎬 Cinema 🎵 Entertainment 🎣 Fishing ◎ Mini golf ⛵ Watersports 🏋 Gym ⚽ Sports field ∪ Stables
FACILITIES: 🛁 Baths/Shower ☉ Electric shaver sockets 🖃 Hairdryer ☀ Ice Pack Facility ♨ Baby facilities ♿ Disabled facilities ⑤ Shop on site or within 200yds 🍖 BBQ area 🧺 Picnic area WiFi WiFi

POOLE

Map 4 SZ09

Platinum Park

South Lytchett Manor Caravan & Camping Park

▶▶▶▶▶

tel: 01202 622577 Dorchester Road, Lytchett Minster BH16 6JB
email: info@southlytchettmanor.co.uk web: www.southlytchettmanor.co.uk
dir: Exit A35 onto B3067, 1 mile east of Lytchett Minster, 600 yards on right after village.

Year-on-year improvements are made here in order to exceed guest expectations, including upgrading of the amenity blocks with air conditioning and the addition of a stylish, mobile coffee pod, which also offers fresh croissants and pastries from the on-site bakery. Situated in the grounds of a historic manor house, the site has modern facilities that are spotless and well maintained. There's a TV hook-up on every pitch and free WiFi across the park. A warm and friendly welcome awaits at this lovely site which is well located for visiting Poole and Bournemouth; the Jurassic X53 bus route (Exeter to Poole) has a stop just outside the park. Four stylishly furnished and well-equipped Romany caravans, replete with double bed and two singles plus kitchen and fridge, are available for hire.

Open: March to 2 January Last arrival: 21.00 Last departure: 11.00
Pitches: 🚐 🚍 ▲; 🏠 see price below; 90 hardstanding pitches; 4 seasonal pitches
Leisure: ⚄ 🎣 ▢ ⚽ ⚙
Facilities: 🖥 ☺ ⚐ ✳ ♿ 🖻 🚻 📡 WiFi

Services: 🔌 🖥 🍽 🏪 🔋 ⚒ 🔒 🍃 Ⓣ
Within 3 miles: ⚓ ⚲ ∪ ⚄ 🎌

Additional site information: 22 acre site. ⋈ Cars can be parked by caravans and tents. Awnings permitted. No camp fires or Chinese lanterns, no noise after 22.30. Table tennis, football nets. Bread and croissants available, café and takeaway food in high season. Car hire can be arranged.

Glamping available: Romany caravans from £60.

Additional glamping information: 2 units dog friendly. Please advise site in advance of any allergies. Cars can be parked by units.

See advert on page 170

Premier Park

Rockley Park

▶ ▶ ▶ ▶ ▶ 94% HOLIDAY HOME PARK

tel: 0800 197 2075 & 01202 679393 Hamworthy BH15 4LZ
email: rockleypark@haven.com web: www.haven.com/rockleypark
dir: M27 junction 1, A31 to Poole centre, then follow signs to site.

A complete holiday experience, including a wide range of day and night entertainment, and plenty of sports and leisure activities, notably watersports. There is also mooring and launching from the park. A great base for all the family, set in a good location for exploring Poole and Bournemouth, offering something for all ages, and there are a wide choice of quality eating outlets.

Open: March to 2 January Last arrival: 24 hours Last departure: 10.00

Holiday Homes: Sleep 8 Bedrooms 3 Bathrooms 2 Toilets 2 Two-ring burner Dishwasher Microwave Freezer TV Sky/Freeview DVD player WiFi Towels included Electricity included Gas included

Prices: Low season from £121 High season from £499

Changeover days: Fridays, Saturdays, Mondays

Leisure: ⚄ 🏊 ⚄ 👆 ⚄ 🎵
Facilities: 🖥 🚻 🚮 WiFi
Within 3 miles: ⚲ ◎ ⚄ 🎌

Additional site information: ⋈ Most dog breeds accepted (please check when booking). Dogs must be kept on leads at all times. The facilities provided in the holiday homes may differ depending on the grade.

PORTESHAM
Map 4 SY68

Places to visit

Tutankhamun Exhibition, DORCHESTER, DT1 1UW, 01305 269571
www.tutankhamun-exhibition.co.uk

Maiden Castle, DORCHESTER, DT2 9EY, 0370 333 1181
www.english-heritage.org.uk/visit/places/maiden-castle

Great for kids: Teddy Bear Museum, DORCHESTER, DT1 1JU, 01305 266040
www.teddybearmuseum.co.uk

Portesham Dairy Farm Campsite
▶▶▶▶ 83%

tel: 01305 871297 **DT3 4HG**
email: info@porteshamdairyfarm.co.uk **web:** www.porteshamdairyfarm.co.uk
dir: *From Dorchester take A35 towards Bridport. In 5 miles left at Winterbourne Abbas, follow Portesham signs. Through village, left at Kings Arms pub, site 350 yards on right.*

Located at the edge of the picturesque village of Portesham close to the Dorset coast, this family-run, level park is part of a small working farm in a quiet rural location. Fully serviced and seasonal pitches are available. There is an excellent pub and a country store just a short walk from the site, and a bus stop outside of the park. This quiet site is close to Abbotsbury Swannery and well situated for visiting many areas of the west Dorset coast.

Open: All year **Last arrival:** 21.00 **Last departure:** 11.00

Pitches: * 🚐 from £15; 🚎 from £15; ▲ from £15; 70 hardstanding pitches; 60 seasonal pitches

Leisure: 🛝

Facilities: 🛁 ☺ 🚿 ✳ 💲 **WiFi**

Services: 🚐 🗑 🔒

Within 3 miles: 🖋

Additional site information: 8 acre site. 🐾 Cars can be parked by caravans and tents. Awnings permitted. No commercial vehicles, groups accepted by prior arrangement only, no camp fires, minimum noise after 22.00. Caravan storage.

PUNCKNOWLE

Places to visit

Hardy's Cottage, DORCHESTER, DT2 8QJ, 01305 262366
www.nationaltrust.org.uk/hardys-cottage

Abbotsbury Swannery, ABBOTSBURY, DT3 4JG, 01305 871858
www.abbotsbury-tourism.co.uk/swannery

Great for kids: Dinosaur Museum, DORCHESTER, DT1 1EW, 01305 269880
www.thedinosaurmuseum.com

LEISURE: 🏊 Indoor swimming pool 🏊 Outdoor swimming pool 🛝 Children's playground 🙌 Kids' club 🎾 Tennis court 🎱 Games room 📺 Separate TV room
⛳ Golf course 🚩 Pitch n putt ⛵ Boats for hire 🚲 Bikes for hire 🎦 Cinema 🎵 Entertainment 🎣 Fishing ⛳ Mini golf 🏄 Watersports 🏋 Gym 🏐 Sports field ♻ Stables
FACILITIES: 🛁 Baths/Shower ☺ Electric shaver sockets 🚿 Hairdryer ✳ Ice Pack Facility 🚼 Baby facilities ♿ Disabled facilities 💲 Shop on site or within 200yds
🍖 BBQ area 🛆 Picnic area **WiFi** WiFi

PUNCKNOWLE
Map 4 SY58

Home Farm Caravan and Campsite
▶▶▶ 81%

tel: 01308 897258 **Home Farm, Rectory Lane DT2 9BW**
web: www.caravanandcampingwestdorset.co.uk
dir: *From Dorchester towards Bridport on A35, left at start of dual carriageway, at hill bottom right to Litton Cheney. Through village, 2nd left to Puncknowle (Hazel Lane). Left at T-junction, left at phone box. Site 150 metres on right. Caravan route: approach via A35 Bridport, then Swyre on B3157, continue to Swyre Lane and Rectory Lane.*

This quiet site, hidden away on the edge of a little hamlet, has good facilities and is an excellent place to camp; hardstanding pitches are available. It offers sweeping views of the Dorset countryside from most pitches, and is just five miles from Abbotsbury, and one and a half miles from the South West Coast Path. This is a really good base from which to tour this attractive area. There is an excellent pub in the village, just a short walk from the campsite.

Open: April to 6 October **Last arrival:** 20.00 (arrivals until 21.00 by prior arrangement only) **Last departure:** noon

Pitches: * 🚐 from £17; 🚐 from £17; ▲ from £14; 2 hardstanding pitches; 14 seasonal pitches

Facilities: 🚿 ☉ 🎤 ⚒ 🎪 **Services:** 🔌 🔒 🗑 **Within 3 miles:** 🎣 🏪

Additional site information: 6.5 acre site. 🐕 Dogs must be kept on leads at all times. 🚗 Cars can be parked by caravans and tents. Awnings permitted. No cats, no wood-burning fires, skateboards, rollerblades, motorised toys, drones or loud music. Calor Gas exchange.

ST LEONARDS
Map 5 SU10

Premier Park

Shamba Holidays
▶▶▶▶▶ 88%

tel: 01202 873302 **230 Ringwood Road BH24 2SB**
email: enquiries@shambaholidays.co.uk **web:** www.shambaholidays.co.uk
dir: *From Poole on A31, pass Woodman Pub on left, straight on at roundabout (keep in left lane), immediately left into East Moors Lane. Site 1 mile on right.*

This top quality park is situated in a popular location near the south coast and is handy for visiting Bournemouth, Poole or Christchurch, as well as the New Forest. The toilet and shower block is excellent and offers some of the best facilities you will find in the country. There is a lovely indoor-outdoor swimming pool as well as a very tasteful clubhouse which serves food, and has entertainment in the main season. You can always be assured of a warm welcome.

Open: All year (restricted service: low and mid season – some facilities only open at weekends) **Last arrival:** 20.00 (later arrivals by prior arrangement only) **Last departure:** 11.00

Pitches: 🚐 🚐 ▲; 10 hardstanding pitches; 40 seasonal pitches

Leisure: 🏊 🏊 🎡 🎣 🎵 ⚽ **Facilities:** 🚿 ☉ 🎤 ⚒ & ⓢ 🛒 **WiFi**

Services: 🔌 🗑 🍴 🍽️ 🛒 🔋 🔒 🗑 🅣

Within 3 miles: 🏇 🎣 🎯

Additional site information: 7 acre site. 🐕 Cars can be parked by caravans and tents. Awnings permitted. No large groups or commercial vehicles, no noise after 23.00. Fresh bread delivered daily. Entertainment 4 nights in low season, 5 nights in high season.

Back of Beyond Touring Park
▶▶▶▶ 94%

tel: 01202 876968 **234 Ringwood Rd BH24 2SB**
email: info@backofbeyondtouringpark.co.uk **web:** www.backofbeyondtouringpark.co.uk
dir: *From north and east: M3 junction 13 follow signs onto M27 westbound, onto A31 (signed Ringwood) to St Leonards, pass St Leonard's Hotel, at next roundabout U-turn into lane immediately left. Site at end of lane. From west: on A31 pass Texaco garage and Woodman Inn, immediately left to site.*

This lovely adults-only park, a member of the Tranquil Parks group, is set in 30 acres of woodland and offers plenty of pleasant walks. Visitors are sure to receive a warm welcome from the owners and their team. In addition to good caravan and motorhome pitches, there are some excellent areas for tents. The site has a fishing lake and a picnic area, and the whole area is a haven for wildlife. The facilities are well appointed and very clean. There are fish and chip and pizza nights as well as BBQ evenings, and guests will find an excellent shop stocked with local produce. A secluded and separate glamping area offers camping pods, a yurt, bell tents, two new shepherd's huts, and cabins for hire – all have their own spacious decking areas.

Open: March to October **Last arrival:** 19.00 **Last departure:** 11.00

Pitches: * 🚐 from £20; 🚐 from £20; ▲ from £15; 🏠 see prices below; 34 seasonal pitches

Leisure: 🎣 🎯 🎣

Facilities: 🚿 ☉ 🎤 ⚒ & ⓢ 🎪 **WiFi**

Services: 🔌 🗑 🛒 🔋 🔒 🗑 🅣

Within 3 miles: 🏇 ◎ 🎣 🎯

Additional site information: 30 acre site. Adults only. 🐕 Cars can be parked by caravans and tents. Awnings permitted. No commercial vehicles, no groups, no noise after 22.30. Visiting food vans, coffee and tea available, morning bakery. Licensed to sell alcohol. Car hire can be arranged.

Glamping available: Pods (furnished) from £45; yurt (furnished) from £45; lodges (furnished) from 45; shepherd's hut (furnished) from £45. **Changeover days:** Any day

Additional glamping information: Dogs allowed in lodges and shepherd's hut. Wood burner in yurt and shepherd's hut. Cars can be parked by units.

SHAFTESBURY
Map 4 ST82

Places to visit

Shaftesbury Abbey Museum & Garden, SHAFTESBURY, SP7 8JR, 01747 852910
www.shaftesburyabbey.org.uk

Premier Park

Dorset Country Holidays
►►►►► 88% GLAMPING ONLY

tel: 01747 851523 & 01225 290924 **Sherborne Causeway SP7 9PX**
email: info@dche.co.uk **web:** www.blackmorevalecaravanandcampingpark.co.uk
dir: *From Shaftesbury's Ivy Cross roundabout take A30 signed Sherborne. Site 2 miles on right.*

Dorset Country Holidays is next to Blackmore Vale Caravan & Camping Park site (see next entry). The glamping area is screened from the main park and is run by its own 24/7, dedicated team. The accommodation varies, two luxury yurts, of British design and manufacture offer excellent insulation, heating and lighting; they have double beds, two single futons, some have fridges and TV and rugs. Set on wooden decking, each comes with picnic benches and a BBQ and guests receive a welcome breakfast pack and towelling gowns. In addition, there are bell tents, a geo dome plus a 'country kabin' – all are fully equipped to a high standard. There's a modern and well-appointed toilet and shower room block. Customer service here is excellent and guests are welcomed with refreshments and can be collected from the local railway station. Deluxe glamping packages and massage breaks are now also available.

Open: All year **Last arrival:** 21.00 **Last departure:** noon

Accommodation available: Bell tents, yurts, cabin, geo dome.

Additional site information: 1 acre site. 🐾

Blackmore Vale Caravan & Camping Park
►►►► 86%

tel: 01747 851523 & 01225 290924 **Sherborne Causeway SP7 9PX**
email: info@dche.co.uk **web:** www.blackmorevalecaravanpark.co.uk
dir: *From Shaftesbury's Ivy Cross roundabout take A30 signed Sherborne. Site 2 miles on right.*

This small park set in open countryside just outside Shaftesbury (famous for the steep, cobbled street known as Gold Hill) offers a wide range of camping opportunities, including touring pitches (some with large hardstandings). The facilities are modern and very clean, and a fully-equipped gym is available to all customers. There is a separate glamping area with a dedicated team to look after guests (see entry above).

Open: All year **Last arrival:** 21.00

Pitches: 🚐 🚃 ▲; 7 hardstanding pitches

Leisure: 🎣 🎯

Facilities: 🛁 ⊙ 🗲 ✳ ♿ ⑤ 🍴 ㅠ

Services: 🔌 🗑 🛒 🛢 🧴 🅣

Additional site information: 3 acre site. 🐾 Cars can be parked by caravans and tents. Awnings permitted. No noise after 23.00. Caravan sales and accessories.

Lower Liston Farm Touring Park
►►► 80%

tel: 01747 851865 & 07725 500963 **Lower Liston Farm, Semley Hollow SP7 9AG**
email: lowerlistoncamping@outlook.com **web:** www.lowerlistonfarm.co.uk
dir: *From Shaftesbury towards Warminster on A350, 2 miles from Shaftesbury. Gate on left after rail bridge.*

A small, well managed, family run, adults-only site located on a working sheep farm and equestrian centre. Accessed via a private drive visible from the A350, it passes through the farm and opens into a secluded campsite with large individual pitches with electric points and water. All pitches have been arranged to make the most of the views. The site has immaculately clean toilet and shower facilities and provides a peaceful rural base for exploring the north Dorset and Wiltshire countryside. Natural, organic meadows with an abundance of wildlife surround this farm site and a network of footpaths radiate from the farm. Dogs are very welcome.

Open: February to 1 December **Last arrival:** 19.00 (later arrival by prior arrangement) **Last departure:** noon

Pitches: * 🚐 from £20; 🚃 from £20; 10 hardstanding pitches

Facilities: 🛁 ⊙ 🍴 ㅠ 🆆ℹ🅵ℹ

Services: 🔌 🗑 🛒 🛢 🅣

Within 3 miles: 🎣 ♿ 🍴 ⑤

Additional site information: 2 acre site. Adults only. 🐾 Cars can be parked by caravans. Awnings permitted. No commercial vehicles. Woodland walks. Free range eggs available.

SIXPENNY HANDLEY

Places to visit

Larmer Tree Gardens, TOLLARD ROYAL, SP5 5PT, 01725 516971
www.larmertree.co.uk

Shaftesbury Abbey Museum & Garden, SHAFTESBURY, SP7 8JR, 01747 852910
www.shaftesburyabbey.org.uk

Great for kids: Moors Valley Country Park and Forest, RINGWOOD, BH24 2ET, 01425 470721, www.moors-valley.co.uk

LEISURE: 🏊 Indoor swimming pool 🏊 Outdoor swimming pool /Λ\ Children's playground 👶 Kids' club 🎾 Tennis court 🎱 Games room 📺 Separate TV room
🏌 Golf course ⛳ Pitch n putt ⛵ Boats for hire 🚲 Bikes for hire 🎬 Cinema 🎵 Entertainment 🎣 Fishing ◎ Mini golf 🏄 Watersports 💪 Gym 🏈 Sports field ♨ Stables
FACILITIES: 🛁 Baths/Shower ⊙ Electric shaver sockets 🗲 Hairdryer ✳ Ice Pack Facility 👶 Baby facilities ♿ Disabled facilities ⑤ Shop on site or within 200yds
🍴 BBQ area ㅠ Picnic area 🆆ℹ🅵ℹ WiFi

SIXPENNY HANDLEY   Map 4 ST91

Church Farm Caravan & Camping Park
▶▶▶▶ 80%

tel: 01725 552563 & 07766 677525 **The Bungalow, Church Farm SP5 5ND**
email: churchfarmcandcpark@hotmail.co.uk web: www.churchfarmcandcpark.co.uk
dir: *1 mile south of Handley Hill roundabout. Exit for Sixpenny Handley, right by school, site 300 yards by church.*

A spacious park located within the Cranborne Chase Area of Outstanding Natural Beauty; the site is split into several camping areas including one for adults only. There is a first-class facility block with good private facilities, an excellent café and restaurant, and a function room, Hanlega's. The pretty village of Sixpenny Handley, with all its amenities, is just 200 yards away, and the site is well positioned for visiting the Great Dorset Steam Fair, the New Forest National Park, Bournemouth, Poole and Stonehenge.

Open: All year (restricted service: November to March – 10 vans maximum)
Last arrival: 21.00 **Last departure:** 11.00
Pitches: 🚐 🚚 🏕; 4 hardstanding pitches; 5 seasonal pitches
Facilities: 🚿 ☺ ✳ ⚲ 🎋 WiFi
Services: 🔌 🌀 🍺 🍴 🛍 🔋 🛠 🛢 🖋 T
Within 3 miles: ⚡ 🏧

Additional site information: 10 acre site. Cars can be parked by caravans and tents. Awnings permitted. Quiet after 23.00. Use of fridge freezer and microwave.

SWANAGE

Places to visit

Corfe Castle, CORFE CASTLE, BH20 5EZ, 01929 481294
www.nationaltrust.org.uk/corfecastle

Brownsea Island, BROWNSEA ISLAND, BH13 7EE, 01202 707744
www.nationaltrust.org.uk/brownsea-island

Great for kids: Swanage Railway, SWANAGE, BH19 1HB, 01929 425800
www.swanagerailway.co.uk

SWANAGE   Map 5 SZ07

Premier Park

Ulwell Cottage Caravan Park
▶▶▶▶▶ 89%

tel: 01929 422823 **Ulwell Cottage, Ulwell BH19 3DG**
email: enq@ulwellcottagepark.co.uk web: www.ulwellcottagepark.co.uk
dir: *From Bournemouth via Sandbanks chain ferry onto B3351 towards Swanage. Through Studland, fork left follow Swanage sign. Site on right. Or from Wareham on A351 to Swanage, left on seafront towards Studland (Shore Road becomes Ulwell Road). Approximately 2 miles, left at campsite sign.*

Sitting under the Purbeck Hills and surrounded by scenic walks, this park is only two miles from the beach. It is a family-run and caters well for families and couples, and offers a toilet and shower block complete with good family rooms (heated in winter), all appointed to a high standard. There are fully serviced pitches and a good indoor swimming pool; the village inn offers a good range of meals. There is a camping pod for hire and, suitable for a couple, a stylish self-contained S-pod with a decking area.

Open: March to 7 January (restricted service: Easter to 31 October – shop has variable opening times) **Last arrival:** 22.00 **Last departure:** 11.00
Pitches: 🚐 🚚 🏕; 23 hardstanding pitches
Leisure: 🏊 🎱 ⚽ **Facilities:** 🚿 ☺ 🅿 ✳ ⚲ 🛁 🎋 🛒 WiFi
Services: 🔌 🌀 🍺 🍴 🔋 🛢 🖋
Within 3 miles: ⚡ 🎣 ∪ ◎ ⛷ ✈ 🎯

Additional site information: 13 acre site. Cars can be parked by caravans and tents. Awnings permitted. No bonfires or fireworks.

Glamping available: Wooden pods, cabin (S-pod). **Changeover days:** Variable
Additional glamping information: Linen only supplied if requested. Cars can be parked by pods.

Herston Caravan & Camping Park
▶▶▶ 85%

tel: 01929 422932 **Washpond Lane BH19 3DJ**
email: office@herstonleisure.co.uk web: www.herstonleisure.co.uk
dir: *From Wareham on A351 towards Swanage. Washpond Lane on left just after 'Welcome to Swanage' sign.*

Set in a rural area, with extensive views of the Purbecks, this tree-lined park has fully serviced pitches plus large camping areas. There is a toilet and shower block with excellent family rooms, a bar and restaurant, takeaway and barbecue food, and entertainment in the high season. Herston Halt, a stop for the famous Swanage Steam Railway between the town centre and Corfe Castle, is within walking distance. Lodges and 20 glamping bell tents area are now available for hire.

Open: All year **Pitches:** * 🚐 from £20; 🚚 from £20; 🏕 from £10; 🏠;
17 hardstanding pitches
Facilities: 🚿 ☺ 🅿 ✳ ⚲ 🛁 🎋 🛒 WiFi
Services: 🔌 🌀 🍺 🍴 🔋 🛠 T
Within 3 miles: ⚡ 🎣 ∪ ◎ ⛷ ✈ 🎯

Additional site information: 10 acre site. Cars can be parked by caravans and tents. Awnings permitted. No noise after 23.00.

Glamping available: Bell tents. **Changeover days:** Any day
Additional site information: Cars can be parked by units.

SWANAGE *continued*

Acton Field Camping Site
▶▶ 80%

tel: 01929 424184 **Acton Field, Langton Matravers BH19 3HS**
email: enquiries@actonfieldcampsite.co.uk **web:** www.actonfieldcampsite.co.uk
dir: *From A351 right after Corfe Castle onto B3069 to Langton Matravers, 2nd right after village (bridleway sign).*

This informal campsite, bordered by farmland on the outskirts of Langton Matravers, offers good toilet facilities. There are superb views of the Purbeck Hills and towards the Isle of Wight, and a footpath leads to the coastal path. The site occupies what was once a stone quarry so rock pegs may be required. Its location and views make it a wonderful place to camp.

Open: Early May Bank Holiday weekend, Spring Bank Holiday weekend, early July to end August (organised groups from Easter to end October) **Last arrival:** 22.00 **Last departure:** noon

Pitches: ⊞ ⊞ Å

Facilities: ⊙ ✳

Services: 🔌 ≟

Within 3 miles: ♪ ✐ ∪ ◎ ≋ ⚓ 目 ⑤ ⌕

Additional site information: 7 acre site. ⌁ 🐾 Cars can be parked by caravans and tents. Awnings permitted. No open or wood fires, no noise after 23.00. Mobile grocer calls during school summer holidays, phone charger on site.

THREE LEGGED CROSS   Map 5 SU00

Places to visit

Moors Valley Country Park and Forest, RINGWOOD, BH24 2ET, 01425 470721
www.moors-valley.co.uk

Woolsbridge Manor Farm Caravan Park
▶▶▶▶ 85%

tel: 01202 826369 **BH21 6RA**
email: woolsbridge@btconnect.com **web:** www.woolsbridgemanorcaravanpark.co.uk
dir: *From Ringwood take A31 towards Ferndown. Approximately 1 mile, follow signs for Three Legged Cross and Horton. Site 2 miles on right.*

A small farm site with spacious pitches on a level field. This quiet site is an excellent central base for touring the New Forest National Park, Salisbury and the south coast, and is close to Moors Valley Country Park for outdoor family activities. The facilities are good and very clean and there are excellent family rooms available.

Open: March to October **Last arrival:** 20.00 **Last departure:** 10.30

Pitches: ⊞ ⊞ Å

Leisure: ⚠ ✐

Facilities: 🛁 ⊙ ℱ ✳ ⚕ ⑤ ⌕ WiFi

Services: 🔌 ⑤ ≟ 🛢 ⌀ Ⓣ

Within 3 miles: ♪ ∪

Additional site information: 6.75 acre site. ⌁ Cars can be parked by caravans and tents. Awnings permitted. Car hire can be arranged.

WAREHAM

Places to visit

Brownsea Island, BROWNSEA ISLAND, BH13 7EE, 01202 707744
www.nationaltrust.org.uk/brownsea-island

LEISURE: 🏊 Indoor swimming pool 🏊 Outdoor swimming pool ⚠ Children's playground 👶 Kids' club ⑨ Tennis court 🎱 Games room ⬜ Separate TV room ♪ Golf course ⛳ Pitch n putt ⛵ Boats for hire 🚲 Bikes for hire 🎬 Cinema 🎵 Entertainment 🎣 Fishing ◎ Mini golf 🏄 Watersports 🏐 Sports field ∪ Stables
FACILITIES: 🛁 Baths/Shower ⊙ Electric shaver sockets ℱ Hairdryer ✳ Ice Pack Facility 👶 Baby facilities ⚕ Disabled facilities ⑤ Shop on site or within 200yds 🍖 BBQ area 🍽 Picnic area WiFi WiFi

WAREHAM

Map 4 SY98

Platinum Park

Wareham Forest Tourist Park
▶▶▶▶▶

tel: 01929 551393 **North Trigon BH20 7NZ**
email: holiday@warehamforest.co.uk **web:** www.warehamforest.co.uk
dir: *From A35 between Bere Regis and Lytchett Minster follow Wareham sign into Sugar Hill. Site on left.*

A woodland park within the tranquil Wareham Forest, with its many walks and proximity to Poole, Dorchester and the Purbeck coast. Two luxury blocks, with combined washbasin and toilets for total privacy, are maintained to a high standard of cleanliness. A heated outdoor swimming pool, off licence, shop and games room add to the enjoyment of a stay on this top quality park. There is a bike wash and a separate dog wash with hot water. Year-on-year investment ensures optimum privacy within touring areas coupled with excellent security, which includes barriers and CCTV. Its location and high standards make this one of the leading parks in the country.

Open: All year (restricted service: limited services available in off-peak season)
Last arrival: 21.00 **Last departure:** 11.00

Pitches: 🚐 🚍 ⛺; 70 hardstanding pitches; 70 seasonal pitches

Leisure: 🏊 ⏛ 🎱 **Facilities:** 🏪 ⊙ 🍴 ✳ ♿ 🔥 🚿 WiFi

Services: 🔌 🔴 🔋 ⚲ 🛢 ⊘ T **Within 3 miles:** 🎣 🚴 ∪ 🛶 🚶

Additional site information: 55 acre site. 🐕 Cars can be parked by caravans and tents. Awnings permitted. Families and couples only, no group bookings. Table tennis. Fresh bread and croissants available in high season.

Birchwood Tourist Park
▶▶▶▶ 86%

tel: 01929 554763 **Bere Road, Coldharbour BH20 7PA**
email: birchwoodtouristpark@hotmail.com **web:** www.birchwoodtouristpark.co.uk
dir: *From Poole (A351) or Dorchester (A352) on north side of railway line at Wareham, follow Bere Regis signs. 2nd park after 2.25 miles.*

Set in 50 acres of parkland located within Wareham Forest, this site offers direct access to areas that are ideal for walking, mountain biking and horse and pony riding. This is a spacious open park, ideal for families, with plenty of room for young people to play games, including football, and there is a small pool for children and a games room. The modern facilities are in two central locations and are very clean. The site has a good security barrier system. The park is only a short drive from Bournemouth and Swanage.

Open: All year **Last arrival:** 21.00 **Last departure:** 11.00 (until 16.00 – fee applies)
Pitches: * 🚐 from £20; 🚍 from £20; ⛺ from £20; 25 hardstanding pitches; 50 seasonal pitches

Leisure: ⏛ 🎱 ⚽

Facilities: 🏪 ⊙ ✳ 🔥 WiFi

Services: 🔌 🔴 🍴 🍟 🔋 ⚲ 🛢 ⊘ T

Within 3 miles: 🎣 🚴 🛶 🚶

Additional site information: 25 acre site. 🐕 Dogs must be kept on leads. Cars can be parked by caravans and tents. Awnings permitted. No groups on bank holidays, no generators or camp fires. No noise after 22.00, barrier entry system. Paddling pool, table tennis. Shop/reception open for 2-3 hours daily.

See advert on page 176

PITCHES: 🚐 Caravans 🚍 Motorhomes ⛺ Tents 🏠 Glamping accommodation **SERVICES:** 🔌 Electric hook-up 🔴 Launderette 🍸 Licensed bar 🛢 Calor Gas ⊘ Campingaz T Toilet fluid 🍴 Café/Restaurant 🍟 Fast Food/Takeaway 🔋 Battery charging ⚲ Motorhome service point
* 2019 prices 🚫 No credit or debit cards 🐕 Dogs permitted 🚫 No dogs

WAREHAM *continued*

Norden Farm Touring Caravan and Camping Site
▶▶▶▶ 83%

tel: 01929 480098 **Norden Farm, Corfe Castle BH20 5DS**
email: campsite@nordenfarm.com **web:** www.nordenfarm.com
dir: *On A351 from Wareham towards Swanage, 3.5 miles to site on right.*

This delightful farm site offers traditional camping but with excellent toilet and shower facilities. It is a very dog-friendly site and is ideally suited for those who enjoy country pursuits. Its location is very close to Corfe Castle so it's very convenient for visiting the Isle of Purbeck and Swanage (the Swanage Railway now runs seasonal trains from Swanage through to Wareham). There is a holiday cottage and Norden House (exclusive use) for hire.

Open: March to October (weather depending) (restricted service: early March to late October – 1 shower block may be closed) **Last arrival:** 22.00 **Last departure:** 11.00 (flexible departure times available in low season)

Pitches: 🚐 from £11; 🚃 from £11; ▲ from £8

Leisure: 🏔 ✐ ☺ **Facilities:** 🏠 ☉ 🅿 ✳ ⚐ ⑤ 🚽 WiFi

Services: 🔌 ⑤ 🛒 ⤵ 🛢 ⌀ Ⓣ **Within 3 miles:** ⌁ ⚏ ⊟

Additional site information: 10 acre site. 🐾 Cars can be parked by caravans and tents. Awnings permitted. Strict 5mph speed limit on site, no noise after 23.00. Fresh bakery deliveries daily, hot shower washroom for dogs, footpaths to local attractions.

East Creech Farm Campsite
▶▶▶ 86%

tel: 01929 480519 **East Creech Farm, East Creech BH20 5AP**
email: farmhouse@eastcreechfarm.co.uk **web:** www.eastcreechfarm.co.uk
dir: *From Wareham on A351 south towards Swanage. On bypass at 3rd roundabout take Furzebrook/Blue Pool Road exit, site approximately 2 miles on right.*

This grassy park set in a peaceful location beneath the Purbeck Hills, with extensive views towards Poole and Brownsea Island. The park boasts bright, clean toilet facilities, a woodland play area, a farm shop selling milk, eggs and bread, and a children's play area. There are also four coarse fishing lakes teeming with fish. A

good tearoom, The Cake Room, adjacent to the site, is open in the main season. The park is close to Norden Station on the Swanage to Norden steam railway line, and is well located for visiting Corfe Castle, Swanage and the Purbeck coast.

Open: April to October **Last arrival:** 20.00 **Last departure:** noon

Pitches: * 🚐 from £16.50; 🚃 from £16.50; ▲ from £16.50 **Leisure:** 🏔 ✐
Facilities: 🏠 ☉ 🅿 ✳ **Services:** 🔌 ⑤ 🍴 **Within 3 miles:** ⌁ ⚏ ⚐ ⊟ ⑤

Additional site information: 4 acre site. 🐾 Cars can be parked by caravans and tents. Awnings permitted. No camp fires, no loud noise.

Glamping available: 2 wooden pods

Additional glamping information: Minimum 2 nights stay. No pets. No smoking. No stag/hen parties. Cars can be parked by units.

Ridge Farm Camping & Caravan Park
▶▶▶ 81%

tel: 01929 556444 **Barnhill Road, Ridge BH20 5BG**
email: enquiries@ridgefarm.co.uk **web:** www.ridgefarm.co.uk
dir: *From Wareham take B3075 towards Corfe Castle, cross river, into Stoborough, left to Ridge. Follow site signs for 1.5 miles.*

A quiet rural park, adjacent to a working farm and surrounded by trees and bushes. This away-from-it-all park is ideally located for touring this part of Dorset, and especially for birdwatchers, or those who enjoy walking and cycling. This site is perfect for visiting the Arne Nature Reserve, the Blue Pool and Corfe Castle. There are good supermarkets and shops in nearby Wareham.

Open: April to 29 September **Last arrival:** 21.00 **Last departure:** noon

Pitches: * 🚐 from £19; 🚃 from £19; ▲ from £15; 2 hardstanding pitches; 20 seasonal pitches

Facilities: 🏠 ☉ 🅿 ✳ ⑤ **Services:** 🔌 ⑤ 🛒 Ⓣ
Within 3 miles: ⌁ ✐ ⟲ ⚏ ⊟

Additional site information: 3.47 acre site. 🐾 Dogs by arrangement. 🚗 Cars can be parked by caravans and tents. Awnings permitted.

LEISURE: 🏊 Indoor swimming pool 🏊 Outdoor swimming pool 🏔 Children's playground 🪁 Kids' club 🎾 Tennis court 🎱 Games room 📺 Separate TV room ⌁ Golf course 🏌 Pitch n putt 🚣 Boats for hire 🚲 Bikes for hire 🎬 Cinema 🎭 Entertainment ✐ Fishing ◎ Mini golf 🏄 Watersports 🏋 Gym ⚽ Sports field ⟲ Stables **FACILITIES:** 🏠 Baths/Shower ☉ Electric shaver sockets 🅿 Hairdryer ✳ Ice Pack Facility 🍼 Baby facilities ♿ Disabled facilities ⑤ Shop on site or within 200yds 🍖 BBQ area 🪑 Picnic area WiFi WiFi

WEYMOUTH

Map 4 SY67

Places to visit

RSPB Nature Reserve Radipole Lake and Wild Weymouth Discovery Centre, WEYMOUTH, DT4 7TZ, 01305 778313
www.rspb.org.uk/reserves-and-events/reserves-a-z/radipole-lake/

Portland Castle, PORTLAND, DT5 1AZ, 01305 820539
www.english-heritage.org.uk/visit/places/portland-castle

Great for kids: Weymouth Sea Life Adventure Park & Marine Sanctuary, WEYMOUTH, DT4 7SX, www2.visitsealife.com/weymouth

REGIONAL WINNER – SOUTH WEST ENGLAND
AA CAMPSITE OF THE YEAR 2020

Platinum Park

East Fleet Farm Touring Park

▶▶▶▶▶

tel: 01305 785768 **Chickerell DT3 4DW**
email: enquiries@eastfleet.co.uk **web:** www.eastfleet.co.uk
dir: On B3157 (Weymouth to Bridport road), 3 miles from Weymouth.

Set on a working organic farm and in a unique location on the shores of the Fleet Lagoon, overlooking Chesil Beach and the sea, with direct access to the South West Coast Path. There is a wide variety of pitches, including hardstandings and fully serviced pitches, and the largest family tents can be accommodated. This park offers excellent new toilet and shower facilities with family rooms - added for 2019 season. There are good play facilities for children, including an excellent fenced play area for younger ones and a separate play barn with table tennis and other activities. The Old Barn has a tasteful bar and lovely patio area, where customers are welcome to take their own food, or order locally and have the food delivered to the bar. In addition, there is 'Festival Food', an area for pizzas and fish and chips, which is very popular with guests. The park is well positioned for visiting Weymouth and Portland, as well as other local attractions, such as the Abbotsbury Swannery and the Abbotsbury Subtropical Gardens. There is a fine drive along the coast road from East Fleet to Bridport with spectacular views of Chesil Beach.

Open: 16 March to end October **Last arrival:** 22.00 **Last departure:** 10.30

Pitches: * ⊞ from £21.36; ⊞ from £21.36; ▲ from £18.30; 90 hardstanding pitches; 5 seasonal pitches

Leisure: ⚲ ⚽ ☺

Facilities: 🛢 ☉ ℉ ❊ & 🛢 🚻 ⊓ WiFi

Services: 🔌 🗑 🍺 🛒 ⚡ ⛽ 🔋 🛢 🅟 T

Within 3 miles: ↧ ⚓ ∪ ◎ ≋ ⚓ 🍴

Additional site information: 21 acre site. 🐕 Cars can be parked by caravans and tents. Awnings permitted. Camping and caravan accessories shop. Car hire can be arranged.

Premier Park

Weymouth Bay Holiday Park

▶▶▶▶▶   93% HOLIDAY HOME PARK

tel: 01305 832271 **Preston DT3 6BQ**
email: weymouthbay@haven.com **web:** www.haven.com/weymouthbay
dir: From A35 towards Dorchester take A354 signed Weymouth. Follow Preston signs onto A353. At Chalbury roundabout 1st left into Preston Road. Park on right.

This well-located holiday park, just a short drive away from Weymouth beach, offers the complete holiday experience for the whole family. It has excellent indoor and outdoor pools complete with a Lazy River attraction. There is a good choice of eating outlets as well as a full entertainment programme, and an excellent range of sporting activities for all ages. Although a large holiday park, it is of exceptional quality and very well cared for, and guests can expect top customer service throughout their stay. The holiday homes are well appointed throughout. The park is conveniently placed for visiting Portland Bill, Lulworth Cove and Chesil Beach.

Open: mid March to October

Holiday Homes: Sleep 8 Bedrooms 2 Bathrooms 1 Toilet 1 Microwave Freezer TV Sky/Freeview DVD player WiFi Linen included Towels included Electricity included

Leisure: ⚲ ⚲ ⚲ 🖐   **Facilities:** ⊓ WiFi   **Within 3 miles:** 🅟 💲 ◎

Additional site information: 🐕 Most dog breeds accepted (please check when booking). Dogs must be kept on leads at all times. The facilities provided in the holiday homes may differ depending on the grade. Restaurant, Papa John's, high chairs for hire, entertainment and sports area.

Premier Park

Littlesea Holiday Park

▶▶▶▶▶   88% HOLIDAY CENTRE

tel: 01305 774414 **Lynch Lane DT4 9DT**
email: littlesea@haven.com **web:** www.haven.com/littlesea
dir: A35 onto A354 signed Weymouth. Right at 1st roundabout, 3rd exit at 2nd roundabout towards Chickerell. Left into Lynch Lane after lights. Site at far end of road.

Just three miles from Weymouth with its lovely beaches and many attractions, Littlesea has a cheerful family atmosphere and fantastic facilities. Indoor and outdoor entertainment and activities are on offer for all the family, and the toilet facilities on the touring park are modern and spotlessly clean as well as being nice and warm. The touring section of this holiday complex is at the far end of the site adjacent to the South West Coast Path in a perfect location. An excellent base for visiting the many attractions close to Weymouth and Portland.

Open: end March to end October (restricted service: end March to May and September to end October – facilities may be reduced) **Last arrival:** 20.30 **Last departure:** 10.00

Pitches: ⊞ ⊞ ▲; 17 hardstanding pitches

Leisure: ⚲ ⚲ ⚲ 🖐 ☺ ⚓ ♫ ⚽ ☺

Facilities: 🛢 ☉ ℉ ❊ & 🛢 🚻 ⊓ ♿ WiFi

Services: 🔌 🗑 🍺 🍽 🛒 🛢 🅟 T

Within 3 miles: ↧ ⚓ ∪ ◎ ≋ ⚓ 🍴

Additional site information: 100 acre site. 🐕 Maximum 2 dogs per booking, certain dog breeds banned. No commercial vehicles, no bookings by persons under 21 years unless a family booking, no boats. Bakery, Starbucks, Papa John's, Fish and chips, adventure golf. Touring hardstandings – pea gravel topped.

PITCHES: ⊞ Caravans ⊞ Motorhomes ▲ Tents 🏕 Glamping accommodation **SERVICES:** 🔌 Electric hook-up 🗑 Launderette 🍺 Licensed bar 🛢 Calor Gas ⚡ Campingaz T Toilet fluid 🍽 Café/Restaurant 🛒 Fast Food/Takeaway 🔋 Battery charging ⚡ Motorhome service point * 2019 prices ⊘ No credit or debit cards 🐕 Dogs permitted 🚫 No dogs

WEYMOUTH *continued*

Premier Park

Seaview Holiday Park
▶▶▶▶▶ 87% HOLIDAY CENTRE

tel: 01305 832271 **Preston DT3 6DZ**
email: seaview@haven.com **web:** www.haven.com/parks/dorset/seaview/
dir: *A354 to Weymouth, follow signs for Preston and Wareham onto A353. Site 3 miles on right just after Weymouth Bay Holiday Park.*

A fun-packed holiday centre especially suited to families and for all ages, with plenty of activities and entertainment during the day or evening. Guests can use the facilities offered at the sister park, Weymouth Bay Holiday Park, which can be reached via a walkway from Seaview Holiday Park. There is a touring section for caravans, motorhomes and tents, the upper area having all fully serviced pitches, whilst the lower section is mainly for tents. There are also six fully-equipped safari tents in this area for anyone wishing to try a glamping experience.

Open: mid March to end October (restricted service: mid March to May and September to end October – some facilities may be reduced) **Last arrival:** midnight **Last departure:** 10.00

Pitches: 🚐 🚌 ▲; 🏠 see price below; 35 hardstanding pitches

Leisure: 🏊 🏊 🅿 🖐 🎵 ⚽

Facilities: 🛁 ☉ 🗲 ☀ ⚒ 🛒 🍴 🛗 🌐

Services: 🔌 🗑 🍽 🍴 🛒 🔒

Within 3 miles: ⛳ 🎣 ∪ 🚣 🚴 🗓

Additional site information: 20 acre site. 🐕 Maximum 2 dogs per booking, certain dog breeds banned. No commercial vehicles, no bookings by persons under 21 years unless a family booking.

Glamping available: Safari tents from £125. **Changeover days:** Fridays and Mondays

Additional glamping information: Safari tents: minimum stay 3 nights (price for 3 nights). Kitchen equipment included.

Pebble Bank Caravan Park
▶▶▶▶ 90%

tel: 01305 774844 **Camp Road, Wyke Regis DT4 9HF**
email: info@pebblebank.co.uk **web:** www.pebblebank.co.uk
dir: *A354 to Weymouth, B3155 signed Portland. At lights into Wyke Road signed Wyke Regis. Straight on at roundabout, 1st left into Camp Road. Site on left. Or from Portesham take B3157 signed Weymouth. Right onto B3156 (Lanehouse Rocks Road). Right into Camp Road.*

This site, although only one and a half miles from Weymouth, is in a peaceful location overlooking Chesil Beach and The Fleet, and is an excellent place to stay. The refurbished bar and restaurant has an alfresco decking area and enjoys fabulous views. The toilet and shower block is very modern and spotlessly clean and there are now 12 hardstandings available. The park is adjacent to the South West Coast Path, making it a good base for walkers.

Open: Easter to mid October (restricted service: bar open in high season and at weekends only) **Last arrival:** 18.00 **Last departure:** 11.00

Pitches: * 🚐 from £21; 🚌 from £21; ▲ from £15

Leisure: 🅿

Facilities: 🛁 ☉ 🗲 ☀ ⚒ 🌐

Services: 🔌 🗑 🍽 🍴 🛒 🔒

Within 3 miles: ⛳ 🎣 ∪ ◎ 🚣 🚴 🗓 💲

Additional site information: 4 acre site. 🐕 Cars can be parked by caravans and tents. Awnings permitted.

Bagwell Farm Touring Park
▶▶▶▶ 89%

tel: 01305 782575 **Knights in the Bottom, Chickerell DT3 4EA**
email: aa@bagwellfarm.co.uk **web:** www.bagwellfarm.co.uk
dir: *From A354 follow signs for Weymouth town centre, then B3157 to Chickerell and Abbotsbury, 1 mile after Chickerell turn left into site 500 yards after Victoria Inn.*

This well located park is set in a small valley with access to the South West Coast Path and is very convenient for visiting Weymouth and Portland. It has excellent facilities including a good shop, pets' corner, children's play area plus the Red Barn bar and restaurant. A good range of hardstandings is available, including 25 super pitches, which are very spacious and can take the longest units. This is an excellent place to stay at any time of the year.

Open: All year (restricted service: winter – bar closed) **Last arrival:** 21.00 **Last departure:** 11.00

Pitches: * 🚐 from £17.50; 🚌 from £17.50; ▲ from £17.50; 40 hardstanding pitches; 70 seasonal pitches

Leisure: 🅿

Facilities: 🛁 ☉ 🗲 ☀ ⚒ 🛒 🍴 🌐

Services: 🔌 🗑 🍽 🍴 🛒 🛗 🔒 🐾 🅣

Additional site information: 14 acre site. 🐕 Cars can be parked by caravans and tents. Awnings permitted. Families and couples only, no noise after 23.00. Wet suit shower, campers' shelter, dog wash. Car hire can be arranged.

West Fleet Holiday Farm

▶ ▶ ▶ 92%

tel: 01305 782218 **Fleet DT3 4EF**
email: aa@westfleetholidays.co.uk **web:** www.westfleetholidays.co.uk
dir: *From Weymouth take B3157 towards Abbotsbury for 3 miles. Past Chickerell turn left at mini roundabout to Fleet, site 1 mile on right.*

A spacious farm site with both level and sloping pitches divided into paddocks and screened by hedges. This site has good views of the Dorset countryside, and is a relaxing place for a family holiday, particularly suited to tents, especially family-sized tents, and small motorhomes or campervans. The Barn Clubhouse has a bar, restaurant and entertainment area. There is an excellent and very popular outdoor swimming pool, which is great for families, and modern, toilet facilities. WiFi is also available.

Open: Easter to September (restricted service: mid and low season – clubhouse closed; low season – pool closed) **Last arrival:** 21.00 **Last departure:** 11.00 (late departures only out of high season)

Pitches: 🚐 🚐 �†

Leisure: ⚬ 🎢 🎵 ⚽

Facilities: 🛁 ☺ 🌁 ✲ ♿ ⑤ **WiFi**

Services: ⚡ ⑤ 🍺 🍽 🎯 ⚓ 🔋 🛢 ⚙ Ⓣ

Within 3 miles: ⚓

Additional site information: 12 acre site. 🐕 Dogs restricted to certain areas. Cars can be parked by caravans and tents. Awnings permitted. Non-family groups by arrangement only.

See advert below

Rosewall Camping

▶ ▶ ▶ 90%

tel: 01305 832248 **East Farm Dairy, Osmington Mills DT3 6HA**
email: holidays@weymouthcamping.com **web:** www.weymouthcamping.com
dir: *Take A353 towards Weymouth. At Osmington Mills sign (opposite garage) turn left, 0.25 mile, site on 1st right.*

This well-positioned sloping tent site, just a few miles to the east of Weymouth, is adjacent to the South West Coast Path and affords great sea views from virtually every pitch. There are excellent toilet and shower facilities including a block at the bottom of the campsite. There is a well-stocked shop and for those that like horse riding or are thinking of learning how to ride, there is Rosewall Equestrian near the site entrance. This is a great place to bring a tent and makes a good base for exploring this area.

Open: Easter to October (restricted service: April to May and September to October – shop opening times vary) **Last arrival:** 22.00 **Last departure:** 11.00

Pitches: 🚐 from £18; �† from £18

Leisure: 🎢 🎣

Facilities: 🛁 ☺ ✲ ♿ ⑤

Services: ⑤ 🔋 🛢 ⚙

Within 3 miles: ∪ 🎣 ⚓ 🎯

Additional site information: 13 acre site. 🐕 Cars can be parked by tents. Awnings permitted. Families and couples only, no noise after 23.00. Riding stables and coarse fishing.

PITCHES: 🚐 Caravans 🚐 Motorhomes �† Tents 🏠 Glamping accommodation **SERVICES:** ⚡ Electric hook-up ⑤ Launderette 🍺 Licensed bar 🛢 Calor Gas ⚙ Campingaz Ⓣ Toilet fluid 🍽 Café/Restaurant ⚓ Fast Food/Takeaway 🔋 Battery charging ⚓ Motorhome service point
* 2019 prices 🚫 No credit or debit cards 🐕 Dogs permitted ⊗ No dogs

WEYMOUTH *continued*

Sea Barn Farm
▶▶▶ 83%

tel: 01305 782218 **Fleet Road, Fleet DT3 4ED**
email: aa@seabarnfarm.co.uk **web:** www.seabarnfarm.co.uk
dir: *From Weymouth take B3157 towards Abbotsbury for 3 miles. Past Chickerell turn left at mini-roundabout into Fleet Road, site 1 mile on left.*

This site is set high on the Dorset coast and has spectacular views over Chesil Beach, The Fleet and Lyme Bay, and it is also on the South West Coast Path. Optional use of the clubhouse and swimming pool (in high seaon) at West Fleet Holiday Farm is available. The pitches are sheltered by hedging, and there is an excellent toilet facility block, and plenty of space for outdoor games. This site is suitable mainly for tents, especially large family tents, and small motorhomes or campervans.

Open: 15 March to October **Last arrival:** 21.00 **Last departure:** 11.00

Pitches: ⊡ ⊡ ▲

Facilities: ⊡ ☉ ⌁ ✳ ⅋ ⑤ ⊟ WiFi

Services: ⊡ ⑤ ⬛ ∅ ⊤

Within 3 miles: ⌁

Additional site information: 12 acre site. ⌁ Dogs must be kept on leads at all times. Cars can be parked by caravans and tents. Awnings permitted. Non-family groups by prior arrangement only. Use of West Fleet facilities including outdoor pool, motorhome service point, bar and restaurant (open in high season – dates on request).

See advert on page 179

See advert on page 179

WIMBORNE MINSTER

Places to visit

Kingston Lacy, WIMBORNE, BH21 4EA, 01202 883402
www.nationaltrust.org.uk/kingston-lacy

Priest's House Museum and Garden, WIMBORNE, BH21 1HR, 01202 882533
www.priest-house.co.uk

Charris Camping & Caravan Park
▶▶▶▶ 91%

tel: 01202 885970 **Candys Lane, Corfe Mullen BH21 3EF**
email: bookings@charris.co.uk **web:** www.charris.co.uk
dir: *From A31 (Wimborne bypass) at roundabout (junction with B3078, south of Wimborne Minster) into Wimborne Road signed Corfe Mullen. Right at crossroads into Candys Lane. Site on right.*

A sheltered park of grassland lined with trees on the edge of the Stour Valley, with Poole and the south coast resorts only a short drive away. Customers can be assured of a warm welcome at this well located park. The facilities are very clean, some hardstandings are available, and social get-togethers are held for customers including barbecues which prove very popular. In addition to the top quality toilet and shower block, the park has seen major improvements making it a top place to stay.

Open: All year **Last arrival:** 21.00 (earliest arrival 11.00) **Last departure:** 11.00

Pitches: ⊡ ⊡ ▲; 12 hardstanding pitches; 10 seasonal pitches

Facilities: ⊡ ☉ ⌁ ✳ ⅋ ⑤ ⊟ WiFi

Services: ⊡ ⑤ ⬛ ⬛ ∅ ⊤

Within 3 miles: ⌁ ⌁ ∪

Additional site information: 3.5 acre site. ⌁ Cars can be parked by caravans and tents. Awnings permitted. No noise after 23:00.

Glamping available: Shepherd's hut.

Additional glamping information: Cars can be parked by shepherd's hut.

Springfield Touring Park
▶▶▶ 86%

tel: 01202 881719 **Candys Lane, Corfe Mullen BH21 3EF**
email: john.clark18@btconnect.com **web:** www.springfieldtouringpark.co.uk
dir: *From Wimborne Minster towards Dorchester on A31 (Wimborne bypass) after Caravan Sales and Accessories shop, then garage, take 1st left in Candys Lane. Follow brown campsite signs.*

A small touring park with extensive views over the Stour Valley and a quiet and friendly atmosphere. It is well positioned for visiting Poole, Bournemouth or the really lovely town of Wimborne. The park is well maintained, has a well-stocked shop, and is a great place to stay.

Open: April to end October **Last arrival:** 21.00 **Last departure:** 11.00

Pitches: ⊡ from £22; ⊡ from £22; ▲ from £20; 38 hardstanding pitches

Leisure: ⋀

Facilities: ⊡ ☉ ⌁ ✳ ⅋ ⑤

Services: ⊡ ⑤ ⬛

Within 3 miles: ⌁ ⌁ ∪ ⅋ ⊟

Additional site information: 3.5 acre site. ⌁ ⊛ Cars can be parked by caravans and tents. Awnings permitted. No skateboards.

WOOL
Map 4 SY88

Places to visit
Lulworth Castle & Park , LULWORTH, BH20 5QS, 01929 400352
www.lulworth.com/visit/places-to-visit/castle-and-park

Great for kids: Monkey World-Ape Rescue Centre, WOOL, BH20 6HH,
01929 462537, www.monkeyworld.org

Whitemead Caravan Park
▶▶▶▶ 89%

tel: 01929 462241 **East Burton Road BH20 6HG**
email: book@whitemeadcaravanpark.co.uk
dir: *From A352 (opposite petrol station) in Wool into East Burton Road signed East Burton. Site on right.*

This quality park situated in the village of Wool is well placed for visiting the many attractions of the area and also has the advantage of a train station within walking distance – a great alternative to driving and easy for visiting Poole or Weymouth. The facilities are excellent and spotlessly clean. There is a good shop selling basic provisions, wine and camping accessories. The site is also close to Bovington Tank Museum.

Open: 14 March to 31 October **Last arrival:** 19.00 **Last departure:** 11.00
Pitches: * 🚐 from £21; 🚍 from £21; ⛺ from £16.50; 10 hardstanding pitches; 24 seasonal pitches
Leisure: ⚖ 🎣
Facilities: 🏪 ☺ ℙ ✳ ♿ ⓢ ☐ WiFi
Services: 🔌 🗃 ⚓ 🛢 ⊘ Ⓣ
Within 3 miles: ⚓ ↺

Additional site information: 🐕 Cars can be parked by caravans and tents. Awnings permitted. No pit fires, no ball games. River walks, bridle path.

COUNTY DURHAM

BARNARD CASTLE
Map 19 NZ01

Places to visit
Barnard Castle, BARNARD CASTLE, DL12 8PR, 01833 638212
www.english-heritage.org.uk/visit/places/barnard-castle

The Bowes Museum, BARNARD CASTLE, DL12 8NP, 01833 690606
www.thebowesmuseum.org.uk

Pecknell Farm Caravan Park
▶▶▶ 83%

tel: 01833 638357 **Lartington DL12 9DF**
dir: *1.5 miles from Barnard Castle. From A66 take B6277. Site on right 1.5 miles from junction with A67.*

A small well laid out site on a working farm in beautiful rural meadowland, with spacious marked pitches on level ground. There are many walking opportunities that start directly from this friendly site.

Open: April to October **Last arrival:** 20.00 **Last departure:** noon
Pitches: 🚐 from £16; 🚍 from £16; 5 hardstanding pitches
Facilities: 🏪 ☺ ℙ
Services: 🔌 ⚓
Within 3 miles: ⚓ ℙ ↺ ◎ 🅗 ⓢ 🗃

Additional site information: 1.5 acre site. 🐕 Maximum of 2 dogs. ⊘ Cars can be parked by caravans. Awnings permitted. No noise after 22.30.

ESSEX

BRADFIELD
Map 13 TM13

Places to visit
RSPB Stour Estuary, RAMSEY, CO12 5ND, 01206 391153
www.rspb.org.uk/reserves-and-events/reserves-a-z/stour-estuary

Strangers Home
▶▶▶ 82%

tel: 01255 870304 & 07762 956134 **The Street CO11 2US**
email: joannmeri@aol.com **web:** www.strangershome.co.uk
dir: *From Manningtree take B1352 towards Harwich. Strangers Home pub and campsite on right in village centre.*

A level, well maintained and improving, small campsite located behind the Strangers Home pub on the edge of pretty Bradfield, close to the Stour Estuary, Flatford Mill and historic Harwich. There are 10 spacious hardstandings, electricity to all pitches, modern toilets in rustic outbuildings, and summer bike storage is available. Children can use the excellent village play area, 100 yards along the road.

Open: March to 14 January **Last arrival:** flexible **Last departure:** flexible
Pitches: 🚐 🚍 ⛺; 22 seasonal pitches
Leisure: ⚖ 🎵 **Facilities:** 🏪 🍽 ☐
Services: 🔌 🗃 🍽 🍟 **Within 3 miles:** ℙ ↺ ⓢ

Additional site information: 4 acre site. 🐕 Cars can be parked by caravans and tents. Awnings permitted. No noise after 23.00. Seasonal live entertainment in pub.

MERSEA ISLAND
Map 7 TM01

Places to visit

Layer Marney Tower, LAYER MARNEY, CO5 9US, 01206 330784
www.layermarneytower.co.uk

Premier Park

Waldegraves Holiday Park
►►►►► 82% HOLIDAY CENTRE

tel: 01206 382898 & 381195 **CO5 8SE**
email: holidays@waldegraves.co.uk **web:** www.waldegraves.co.uk
dir: A12 junction 26, B1025 to Mersea Island across The Strood. Left to East Mersea, 2nd right, follow tourist signs to site.

A spacious and pleasant site located between farmland and its own private beach on the Blackwater Estuary. There are well-maintained standard grass pitches and a limited selection of hardstanding and serviced pitches – some have hedges to offer a greater level of privacy; the pitches are flat and spacious. There are excellent facilities including the restaurant, bar, shop, coarse fishing lakes, entertainment, a boat slipway, a heated outdoor swimming pool and fibre optic WiFi.

Open: March to November (touring); 15 February to 15 January (static) (restricted service: March to June and September to November (except bank holidays and school half terms) – pool, shop and clubhouse reduced opening hours; pool open May to September weather permitting) **Last arrival:** 22.00 **Last departure:** 13.00 (touring); 10.00 (static)

Pitches: 🚐 from £20; 🚌 from £20; ▲ from £20; 26 hardstanding pitches; 100 seasonal pitches

Leisure: 🏊 🅰 🤾 🔍 🎣 🎯 🎵 🎿 ⚽

Facilities: 🚿 ⊙ 🧴 ❄ ♿ 🛒 🍴 🏕 🚽 **WiFi**

Services: 🔌 🔵 🚰 🍴 ♨ 🛒 ⬆ 🛒 🛢 🗑 🗊

Within 3 miles: ⛵ ◎ 🎿 🏌

Additional site information: 25 acre site. 🐕 No groups of under 21s. Boating lake, slipway, driving range, crazy golf, foot golf, family games room, family entertainment. Car hire can be arranged.

Fen Farm Caravan Site
►►►► 86%

tel: 01206 383275 **Moore Lane, East Mersea CO5 8FE**
email: havefun@fenfarm.co.uk **web:** www.fenfarm.co.uk
dir: B1025 from Colchester to Mersea Island, left signed East Mersea. 1st right after Dog and Pheasant pub into Moore Lane. (Note: road is tidal, please check tide times).

The first tents were pitched at Fen Farm in 1923 and over the years the farm gave way entirely to becoming a caravan park. Enjoying an enviable location beside the Blackwater Estuary, it has unique atmosphere with a mixture of meadow, woodland and marine shore, and varied wildlife to match each environment. There are two excellent solar-heated toilet blocks, which include three family rooms and privacy cubicles, with the newest block constructed in the local style of black clapboard and a red tile roof. There is a woodland dog walk and two well-equipped play areas, while crabbing in the beach pools is also a popular pastime. The site also includes an electric car charger.

Open: Mid March to end October **Last arrival:** dusk

Pitches: * 🚐 from £19; 🚌 from £19; ▲ from £19; 3 hardstanding pitches; 65 seasonal pitches

Leisure: 🅰 ⚽

Facilities: 🚿 ⊙ 🧴 ❄ ♿ 🛒 **WiFi**

Services: 🔌 🔵 ⬆ 🛢 ♨ 🗊

Within 3 miles: 🎣 ◎

Additional site information: 25 acre site. 🐕 Cars can be parked by caravans and tents. Awnings permitted. No open fires, no noise after 23.00. Electric car charger.

LEISURE: 🏊 Indoor swimming pool 🏊 Outdoor swimming pool 🅰 Children's playground 👶 Kids' club 🎾 Tennis court 🎱 Games room ☐ Separate TV room 🏌 Golf course 🚩 Pitch n putt ⛵ Boats for hire 🚲 Bikes for hire 🎬 Cinema 🎵 Entertainment 🎣 Fishing ◎ Mini golf 🏄 Watersports 💪 Gym ⚽ Sports field ⛵ Stables
FACILITIES: 🚿 Baths/Shower ⊙ Electric shaver sockets 🧴 Hairdryer ❄ Ice Pack Facility 🚼 Baby facilities ♿ Disabled facilities 💲 Shop on site or within 200yds 🍴 BBQ area 🏕 Picnic area **WiFi** WiFi

Seaview Holiday Park

▶▶▶ 80%

tel: 01206 382534 & 07733 333940 **Seaview Avenue, West Mersea CO5 8DA**
web: www.seaviewholiday.co.uk
dir: *From A12 (Colchester) onto B1025 (Mersea Island), cross causeway, left towards East Mersea, 1st right, follow signs.*

With sweeping views across the Blackwater Estuary, this well-established park has its own private beach, complete with boat slipway and attractive beach cabins, a shop, café and a stylish clubhouse that offers evening meals and drinks in a quiet family atmosphere. The touring area is well maintained and has 40 fully serviced pitches.

Open: April to October **Last arrival:** 18.00 (phone site if late arrival expected)
Last departure: noon

Pitches: 🚐 🚎; 40 hardstanding pitches

Facilities: 🏪 ♿ 🖺 WiFi

Services: 🔌 🗑 🍽 🍴 🛒 🔧

Within 3 miles: ⚓ ✎ ∪ ⚓

Additional site information: 30 acre site. 🐾 Cars can be parked by caravans. Awnings permitted. No noise after midnight, no boats or jet skis. Private beach.

The Orchards Holiday Park

▶▶▶▶ 83% HOLIDAY CENTRE

tel: 01255 820651 **CO16 8LJ**
email: theorchards@haven.com **web:** www.haven.com/theorchards
dir: *From Clacton-on-Sea take B1027 towards Colchester. Left after petrol station, straight on at crossroads in St Osyth. Follow signs to Point Clear. Park in 3 miles.*

The Orchards offers good touring facilities with a centrally heated toilet block which includes a laundry, play area and two very spacious family rooms. The touring pitches are generously sized. There's also direct access to all the leisure, entertainment and dining outlets available on this large popular holiday park on the Essex coast.

Open: end March to end October (restricted service: end March to May and September to October – some facilities may be reduced) **Last arrival:** anytime **Last departure:** 10.00

Pitches: 🚐 🚎 ▲

Leisure: 🏊 🏖 ⚓ ♪ 🎵 ✎ ⚽

Facilities: 🏪 ☺ 🚿 ♿ 🖺 🧺 🍴 WiFi

Services: 🔌 🗑 🍽 🍴 🛒

Within 3 miles: ∪ ◎ ⚓

Additional site information: 140 acre site. 🐾 Maximum of 2 dogs per booking, certain dog breeds banned. No commercial vehicles, no bookings by persons under 21 years unless a family booking.

Hogsdown Farm Caravan & Camping Park

▶▶▶ 80%

tel: 01453 810224 **Hogsdown Farm, Lower Wick GL11 6DD**
web: www.hogsdownfarm.co.uk
dir: *M5 junction 14 (Falfield), A38 towards Gloucester. Through Stone and Woodford. After Newport turn right signed Lower Wick.*

A pleasant site with good toilet facilities, located between Bristol and Gloucester. It is well positioned for visiting Berkeley Castle and the Cotswolds, and makes an excellent overnight stop when travelling to or from the West Country.

Open: All year **Last arrival:** 21.00 **Last departure:** 16.00

Pitches: * 🚐 from £14; 🚎 from £14; ▲ from £11.50; 12 hardstanding pitches

Leisure: ⚞

Facilities: 🏪 ☺ ❄

Services: 🔌 🗑 🔋 🔒

Within 3 miles: ⚓ ✎ ∪ 🖺

Additional site information: 5 acre site. 🐾 Cars can be parked by caravans and tents. Awnings permitted. No skateboards or bikes.

CHELTENHAM	Map 10 SO92

Places to visit

Holst Birthplace Museum, CHELTENHAM, GL52 2AY, 01242 524846
www.holstmuseum.org.uk

Sudeley Castle & Gardens, WINCHCOMBE, GL54 5JD, 01242 604244
www.sudeleycastle.co.uk

Briarfields Motel & Touring Park
▶▶▶▶ 90%

tel: 01242 235324 **Gloucester Road GL51 0SX**
email: reception@briarfields.net **web:** www.briarfields.net
dir: *M5 junction 11, A40 towards Cheltenham. At roundabout left onto B4063, site 200 metres on left.*

This is a well-designed, level, adults-only park, with a motel, where the facilities are modern and very clean. It is well-positioned between Cheltenham and Gloucester, with easy access to the Cotswolds. And, being close to the M5, it makes a perfect overnight stopping point.

Open: All year **Last arrival:** 20.00 **Last departure:** 11.00

Pitches: * 🚐 from £19; 🚐 from £19; ▲ from £17; ⌂ see price below;
72 hardstanding pitches

Leisure:

Facilities: 🛁 ☉ ℙ ✳ ♿ ⑤ 🍴 WiFi

Services: 🔌 ⑤ ↯

Within 3 miles: ⌓ ✎ ↻ ≋ 🎱

Additional site information: 5 acre site. Adults only. 🐕 Cars can be parked by caravans and tents. Awnings permitted. No noise 22.00–08.00. Car hire can be arranged.

Glamping available: Pods from £50 per night.

Additional glamping information: Pods sleep two and include double or twin beds, electric sockets, USB sockets, fridge, microwave, kettle, table and chairs. Outdoor picnic area. Arrivals from 13.00, departures by 11.00. Cars can be parked by pods.

CIRENCESTER	Map 5 SP00

Places to visit

New Brewery Arts, CIRENCESTER, GL7 1JH, 01285 657181
www.newbreweryarts.org.uk

Corinium Museum, CIRENCESTER, GL7 2BX, 01285 655611
www.coriniummuseum.org

Mayfield Park
▶▶▶▶ 90%

tel: 01285 831301 & 07483 327535 **Cheltenham Road GL7 7BH**
email: enquiries@mayfieldpark.co.uk **web:** www.mayfieldpark.co.uk
dir: *In Cirencester at roundabout junction of A429 and A417, take A417 signed Cheltenham and A435. Right onto A435 signed Cheltenham, follow brown camping signs, pass golf course, site on left.*

A much improved and gently sloping park on the edge of the Cotswolds that offers level pitches and a warm welcome. Popular with couples and families, it has a reception area, a small shop selling essentials and offers well-appointed fully serviced hardstanding pitches and caravans for hire. A children's play area and dog exercising space were added for 2019. This lovely park makes an ideal base for exploring the Cotswolds and its many attractions, and for walking the nearby Monarch's Way and the Cotswold Way long-distance paths.

Open: All year

Pitches: 🚐 🚐 ▲; 22 hardstanding pitches; 21 seasonal pitches

Leisure: ⚞

Facilities: 🛁 ☉ ℙ ✳ ♿ ⑤ 🪑 WiFi

Services: 🔌 ⑤ ⛴ ↯ 🔒 🧺 Ⓣ

Within 3 miles: ⌓

Additional site information: 13 acre site. 🐕 Cars can be parked by caravans and tents. Awnings permitted. No bikes, scooters or skateboards, no noise after 23.00, minimum 3 nights stay for bank holidays.

NEWENT
Map 10 SO72

Places to visit

Odda's Chapel, DEERHURST, GL19 4BX, 0370 333 1181
www.english-heritage.org.uk/visit/places/oddas-chapel

Westbury Court Garden, WESTBURY-ON-SEVERN, GL14 1PD, 01452 760461
www.nationaltrust.org.uk/westbury-court-garden

Great for kids: International Centre for Birds of Prey, NEWENT, GL18 1JJ,
01531 820286, www.icbp.org

Pelerine Caravan and Camping
▶▶▶ 86%

tel: 01531 822761 & 07909 914262 **Ford House Road GL18 1LQ**
email: pelerine@hotmail.com **web:** www.newent.biz
dir: 1 mile from Newent.

A pleasant, French-themed site divided into separate areas (Rue de Pelerine and Avenue des Familles), plus one for adults only; there are some hardstandings and electric hook-ups in each area. Facilities are very good, especially for families. It is close to several vineyards, and well positioned in the north of the Forest of Dean with Tewkesbury, Cheltenham and Ross-on-Wye within easy reach.

Open: March to November **Last arrival:** 22.00 **Last departure:** 16.00

Pitches: 🚐 🚐 ▲; 2 hardstanding pitches; 20 seasonal pitches

Facilities: 🏠 ☉ 🏳 ☼ ♿ 🍴 WiFi

Services: 🔌 🗑 🎒

Within 3 miles: 🔦 🎣 ∪ 🏇 💲

Additional site information: 5 acre site. 🐕 Dogs must be kept on leads at all times. Cars can be parked by caravans and tents. Awnings permitted. Woodburners, chimneas, burning pits available.

SLIMBRIDGE
Map 4 SO70

Places to visit

WWT Slimbridge Wetland Centre, SLIMBRIDGE, GL2 7BT, 01453 891900
www.wwt.org.uk/slimbridge

Great for kids: Berkeley Castle & Butterfly House, BERKELEY, GL13 9BQ,
01453 810303, www.berkeley-castle.com

Tudor Caravan & Camping
▶▶▶▶ 88%

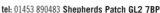

tel: 01453 890483 **Shepherds Patch GL2 7BP**
email: aa@tudorcaravanpark.co.uk **web:** www.tudorcaravanpark.com
dir: M5 junctions 13 and 14, follow WWT Slimbridge Wetland Centre signs. Site at rear of Tudor Arms pub.

This park benefits from one of the best locations in the county, situated right alongside the Sharpness to Gloucester canal and just a short walk from the famous Wildfowl & Wetlands Trust at Slimbridge. The site has two areas, one for adults only, and a more open area with a facility block. There are both grass and gravel pitches complete with electric hook-ups. Being beside the canal, there are excellent walks plus the National Cycle Network route 41 can be accessed from the site. There is a pub and restaurant adjacent to the site.

Open: All year **Last arrival:** 20.00 **Last departure:** 11.00

Pitches: 🚐 🚐 ▲; 48 hardstanding pitches; 4 seasonal pitches

Leisure: 🎣

Facilities: 🏠 ☉ 🏳 ☼ ♿ 💲 🍴 🛒 WiFi

Services: 🔌 🗑 🍺 🍴 🍔 🎒 ⚡ 🛢 ⊘ T

Within 3 miles: ∪ 🎿

Additional site information: 8 acre site. 🐕 Cars can be parked by caravans and tents. Awnings permitted. Debit cards accepted (no credit cards).

STONEHOUSE

Map 4 SO80

Places to visit

Painswick Rococo Garden, PAINSWICK, GL6 6TH, 01452 813204
www.rococogarden.org.uk

WWT Slimbridge Wetland Centre, SLIMBRIDGE, GL2 7BT, 01453 891900
www.wwt.org.uk/slimbridge

Apple Tree Park Caravan and Camping Site
►►►► 89%

tel: 01452 742362 & 07708 221457 **A38, Claypits GL10 3AL**
email: appletreepark@hotmail.co.uk **web:** www.appletreepark.co.uk
dir: *M5 junction 13, A38. Take 1st exit at roundabout. Site in 0.7 mile on left (400 metres beyond filling station).*

This is a family-owned park conveniently located on the A38, not far from the M5. A peaceful site with glorious views of the Cotswolds, it offers modern and spotlessly clean toilet facilities with underfloor heating. The park is well located for visiting Wildfowl & Wetlands Trust Slimbridge and makes an excellent stopover for M5 travellers. There is a bus stop directly outside the park which is handy for those with motorhomes who wish to visit nearby Gloucester and Cheltenham.

Open: All year **Last arrival:** 21.00 **Last departure:** noon

Pitches: 🚐 🚏 ▲; 14 hardstanding pitches; 10 seasonal pitches

Leisure: ⚙

Facilities: 🛁 ⊙ ℱ ✳ ⅃ ⑤ WiFi

Services: 🔌 ⅄ 🛢 ⌀ T

Within 3 miles: ✎ ⚲ ⚶

Additional site information: 6.5 acre site. ✈ Cars can be parked by caravans and tents. Awnings permitted. Minimum noise after 22.30.

GREATER MANCHESTER

LITTLEBOROUGH

Map 16 SD91

Places to visit

Standedge Tunnel and Visitor Centre, MARSDEN, HD7 6NQ, 01484 844298
canalrivertrust.org.uk/places-to-visit/standedge-tunnel-and-visitor-centre

Hollingworth Lake Caravan Park
►►► 74%

tel: 01706 378661 **Round House Farm, Rakewood Road OL15 0AT**
email: info@hollingworthlakecaravanpark.com
dir: *From Littleborough or Milnrow (M62 junction 21), follow Hollingworth Lake Country Park signs to Fishermans Inn and The Wine Press. Take 'No Through Road' to Rakewood, then 2nd right.*

A popular park adjacent to Hollingworth Lake, at the foot of the Pennines, within easy reach of many local attractions. Backpackers walking the Pennine Way are welcome at this family-run park, and there are also large rally fields.

Open: All year **Last arrival:** 20.00 **Last departure:** noon

Pitches: 🚐 🚏 ▲; 25 hardstanding pitches

Leisure: ⚙

Facilities: 🛁 ⊙ ✳ ⅃ ⑤ 🍖

Services: 🔌 ⑤ 🛒 ⅄ 🛢 ⌀ T

Within 3 miles: ⚓ ✎ ∪ ⚲ ⚶

Additional site information: 5 acre site. ✈ Maximum of 1 dog per pitch. ⊛ Cars can be parked by caravans and tents. Awnings permitted. Family groups only. Pony trekking.

LEISURE: 🏊 Indoor swimming pool 🏊 Outdoor swimming pool ⚠ Children's playground 🖐 Kids' club ⚲ Tennis court 🎱 Games room ⬛ Separate TV room ⚑ Golf course ⚐ Pitch n putt ⚓ Boats for hire 🚲 Bikes for hire 🎬 Cinema 🎵 Entertainment ✎ Fishing ◉ Mini golf 🏄 Watersports 🏋 Gym ⚙ Sports field ∪ Stables
FACILITIES: 🛁 Baths/Shower ⊙ Electric shaver sockets ℱ Hairdryer ✳ Ice Pack Facility 🍼 Baby facilities ⅃ Disabled facilities ⑤ Shop on site or within 200yds 🍖 BBQ area 🌲 Picnic area WiFi WiFi

HAMPSHIRE

BRANSGORE
Map 5 SZ19

Places to visit

Sammy Miller Museum, NEW MILTON, BH25 5SZ, 01425 620777
www.sammymiller.co.uk

Red House Museum & Gardens, CHRISTCHURCH, BH23 1BU, 01202 482860
www.hampshireculture.org.uk/red-house-museum-and-gardens

Great for kids: Moors Valley Country Park and Forest, RINGWOOD, BH24 2ET, 01425 470721, www.moors-valley.co.uk

Harrow Wood Farm Caravan Park
▶▶▶ 86%

tel: 01425 672487 **Harrow Wood Farm, Poplar Lane BH23 8JE**
email: harrowwood@caravan-sites.co.uk **web:** www.caravan-sites.co.uk
dir: *From Ringwood take B3347 towards Christchurch. At Sopley, left for Bransgore, to T-junction. Turn right. Straight on at crossroads. Left in 400 yards (just after garage) into Poplar Lane.*

A well laid-out, well-drained and spacious site in a pleasant rural position adjoining woodland and fields. Facilities are well appointed and very clean. Free on-site coarse fishing is available at this peaceful park. Well located for visiting Christchurch, the New Forest National Park and the south coast.

Open: March to 6 January **Last arrival:** 22.00 **Last departure:** noon
Pitches: 🚐 🚍 ⋀; 60 hardstanding pitches
Leisure: ⌁
Facilities: 🏠 ☉ 🅿 ✳ ⅙ WiFi
Services: 🔌 ◎ 🛒 ⅄ 🛢
Within 3 miles: ⑤

Additional site information: 6 acre site. ⊗ Cars can be parked by caravans and tents. Awnings permitted. No open fires.

HAMBLE-LE-RICE
Map 5 SU40

Riverside Holidays
▶▶▶▶ 85%

tel: 023 8045 3220 **Satchell Lane SO31 4HR**
email: enquiries@riversideholidays.co.uk **web:** www.riversideholidays.co.uk
dir: *M27 junction 8, follow signs to Hamble on B3397. Left into Satchell Lane, site in 1 mile.*

A small, peaceful park set alongside the River Hamble and next to a marina that offers a unique place to stay in this attractive area. There is a well-appointed central facility block with separate and spacious fully serviced rooms for ladies and gents. There is a convenient pub and restaurant right beside the site plus good river walks along the river. Bell tents will be available for hire from 2020.

Open: March to October **Last arrival:** 22.00 **Last departure:** 11.00
Pitches: 🚐 from £25; 🚍 from £25; ⋀ from £22
Facilities: 🏠 ☉ 🅿 ✳ ⅙ WiFi
Services: 🔌 ◎ 🛒 🛢 ⓣ
Within 3 miles: ⅃ 🅿 ∪ ≋ ✦ ⑤

Additional site information: 3 acre site. 🐾 Cars can be parked by caravans and tents. Awnings permitted. Quiet between 22.00–07.00. Chargeable WiFi.

PITCHES: 🚐 Caravans 🚍 Motorhomes ⋀ Tents 🏠 Glamping accommodation **SERVICES:** 🔌 Electric hook-up ◎ Launderette 🍺 Licensed bar 🛢 Calor Gas ⌀ Campingaz Ⓣ Toilet fluid 🍽 Café/Restaurant 🍔 Fast Food/Takeaway 🛒 Battery charging ⅄ Motorhome service point * 2019 prices ⊘ No credit or debit cards 🐾 Dogs permitted ⊗ No dogs

LINWOOD
Map 5 SU10

Places to visit

The New Forest Centre, LYNDHURST, SO43 7NY, 023 8028 3444
www.newforestcentre.org.uk

Furzey Gardens, MINSTEAD, SO43 7GL, 023 8081 2464
www.furzey-gardens.org

Great for kids: Paultons Park, OWER, SO51 6AL, 023 8081 4442
www.paultonspark.co.uk

Red Shoot Camping Park

▶▶▶ 90%

tel: 01425 473789 **BH24 3QT**
email: enquiries@redshoot-campingpark.com **web:** www.redshoot-campingpark.com
dir: A31 onto A338 towards Fordingbridge and Salisbury. Right at brown signs for caravan park towards Linwood on unclassified roads, site signed.

Located behind the Red Shoot Inn in one of the most attractive parts of the New Forest, this park is in an ideal spot for nature lovers and walkers. It is personally supervised by friendly owners, and offers many amenities including a children's play area. There are modern and spotless facilities plus a smart reception and shop selling fresh bread, croissants and local farm produce.

Open: March to October **Last arrival:** 19.00 **Last departure:** 13.00

Pitches: * 🚐 from £18; 🚐 from £18; ▲ from £18 🏠 see prices below

Leisure: ⋀

Facilities: 🛁 ☺ 🪒 ✳ ♿ ⑤

Services: 🔌 🗑 🛗 🍴 🎇 ⬆ 🛢 ⊘ Ⓣ

Within 3 miles: 🎣 ⛳ ⛵

Additional site information: 3.5 acre site. 🐾 Cars can be parked by caravans and tents. Awnings permitted. Quiet after 22.30. Dogs must be on leads at all times. No wood burning. Freshly baked bread and croissants available. Car hire can be arranged.

Glamping available: River keeper's hut from £40 per night. **Changeover days:** Any day
Additional glamping information: Sleeps 2 adults & 2 children under 10 years. No running water. Kettle, toaster, microwave and utensils provided. Cars can be parked by units.

RINGWOOD

See St Leonards (Dorset)

ROMSEY
Map 5 SU32

Places to visit

Sir Harold Hillier Gardens, AMPFIELD, SO51 0QA, 01794 369318
www.hilliergardens.org.uk

Mottisfont, MOTTISFONT, SO51 0LP, 01794 340757
www.nationaltrust.org.uk/mottisfont

Great for kids: Longdown Activity Farm, ASHURST, SO40 7EH, 023 8029 2837
www.longdownfarm.co.uk

Green Pastures Farm Camping & Touring Park

▶▶▶ 85%

tel: 023 8081 4444 **Ower SO51 6AJ**
email: enquiries@greenpasturesfarm.com **web:** www.greenpasturesfarm.com
dir: M27 junction 2. Follow Salisbury signs, 0.5 mile, follow brown tourist signs for Green Pastures. Also signed from A36 and A3090 at Ower.

This pleasant site offers a variety of easily accessed pitches, including those with electric hook-up. There is a code access security barrier to the site. Green Pastures is well located for visiting Paultons Park, Southampton and the New Forest National Park, and being close to the M27 it is convenient for overnight stops. There are kennels where dogs can be left while you visit the theme park or go shopping.

Open: 13 March to October **Last arrival:** 20.00 **Last departure:** 11.00

Pitches: 🚐 🚐 ▲; 6 hardstanding pitches

Facilities: 🛁 ✳ ♿ ⑤ 📶

Services: 🔌 🗑 🛗 ⬆ 🛢 ⊘ Ⓣ

Within 3 miles: 🎣 🎣

Additional site information: 6 acre site. 🐾 Cars can be parked by caravans and tents. Awnings permitted. No water games, no fire pits, only off-ground BBQs permitted. Coffee van on Saturday mornings.

WARSASH
Map 5 SU40

Places to visit
Explosion Museum of Naval Firepower, GOSPORT, PO12 4LE, 023 9283 9766 www.historicdockyard.co.uk/site-attractions/off-site-attractions/explosion-museum-of-naval-firepower

Portchester Castle, PORTCHESTER, PO16 9QW, 023 9237 8291 www.english-heritage.org.uk/visit/places/portchester-castle

Great for kids: Blue Reef Aquarium, PORTSMOUTH, PO5 3PB, 023 9287 5222 www.bluereefaquarium.co.uk/portsmouth

Dibles Park
▶▶▶▶ 88%

tel: 01489 575232 **Dibles Rd SO31 9SA**
email: dibles.park@btconnect.com **web:** www.diblespark.co.uk
dir: *M27 junction 9, at roundabout 5th exit (Parkgate A27), 3rd roundabout 1st exit, 4th roundabout 2nd exit. Site 500 yards on left. Or M27 junction 8, at roundabout 1st exit (Parkgate), next roundabout 3rd exit (Brook Lane), 4th roundabout 2nd exit. Site 500 yards on left.*

A small peaceful touring park adjacent to a private residential park. The facilities are excellent and spotlessly clean, and the spacious pitches are hardstanding with electric and can take the largest RVs. A warm welcome awaits visitors to this well-managed park, which is very convenient for the Hamble, the Solent and very well positioned for an overnight stay if heading for the cross-channel ferry port at Portsmouth, which is about 14 miles away. WiFi is available. The park also offers free leaflets of the many excellent walks around the area.

Open: All year **Last arrival:** Anytime **Last departure:** 11.00
Pitches: 🚐 🚎 🛆; 11 hardstanding pitches
Facilities: 🖥 ⊙ 🎏 ☼ 📶
Services: 🔌 🗑 ᗐ 🔋 🧴
Within 3 miles: 🧭 ∪ 🚵 🎣 🗓 ⑤

Additional site information: 0.75 acre site. 🐕 No dog walking on site. Cars can be parked by caravans and tents. Awnings permitted. No noise after 23.00, no children's ball games, no cycling, no scooters.

HERTFORDSHIRE

HODDESDON
Map 6 TL30

Places to visit
RSPB Rye Meads, STANSTEAD ABBOTTS, SG12 8JS, 01992 708383 www.rspb.org.uk/reserves-and-events/reserves-a-z/rye-meads

Lee Valley Caravan Park Dobbs Weir
▶▶▶▶ 83%

tel: 03000 030 619 **Charlton Meadows, Essex Road EN11 0AS**
email: dobbsweircampsite@vibrantpartnerships.co.uk
web: www.visitleevalley.org.uk/en/content/cms/where-to-stay-and-short-breaks
dir: *From A10 follow Hoddesdon signs, at 2nd roundabout left signed Dobbs Weir. At next roundabout take 3rd exit. 1 mile to site on right.*

This site provides much needed camping facilities close to London. Situated on level ground beside the River Lee, the park has a modernised toilet block with good facilities, a large timber chalet housing the reception and shop, an extremely innovative motorhome service point. 12 wooden wigwams, three family safari tents and two luxury lodges are available for hire. On-site fishing is available and there's free WiFi.

Open: March to January **Last arrival:** 20.00 **Last departure:** 11.00 (late departures by prior arrangement)

Pitches: 🚐 🚎 🛆; 🏠 see prices below; 21 hardstanding pitches
Leisure: ♨ 🎾 🎣
Facilities: 🖥 ⊙ ☼ ♿ ⑤ 🔋 🎏 📶
Services: 🔌 🗑 ᗐ 🔋 🧴 ⊤
Within 3 miles: 🚵 🎣

Additional site information: 11 acre site. 🐕 Cars can be parked by caravans and tents. Awnings permitted. No commercial vehicles. Under 18's must be accompanied by an adult. Fire pit hire. Fresh produce in shop.

Glamping available: Wooden wigwams from £75; safari tents from £105.

Additional glamping information: Safari tents have cooking galleys. Cars can be parked by units.

Isle of Wight

There is a timeless quality to the Isle of Wight. For many it embodies the spirit and atmosphere of English seaside holidays over the years, and being an island, it has a unique and highly distinctive identity. Small and intimate – it's just 23 miles by 13 miles – it's a great place to get away-from-it-all, and with its mild climate, long hours of sunshine and colourful architecture, it has something of a continental flavour.

The Isle of Wight is probably most famous for the world's premier sailing regatta. Cowes Week, which takes place at the height of summer, is a key annual fixture in the country's sporting calendar, with the regatta drawing more than 1,000 boats and around 100,000 spectators. It is a hugely colourful event attracting Olympic veterans, weekend sailors and top names from the worlds of sport and the media. Various spectator boats offer good views of the action, but for something less hectic and more sedate, take to the island's 65-mile Coast Path, which offers a continual, unfolding backdrop of magnificent coastal scenery and natural beauty. The sea is seen at numerous points along the route and during Cowes Week, you get constant views of the energetic sailing activity. The regatta is held in the first week of August.

The Isle of Wight Coast Path is a good way to explore the island's varied coastline at any time of the year. Even in the depths of winter, the weather conditions are often favourable for walking. Much of the trail in the southern half of the island represents a relatively undemanding walk over majestic chalk downs. Beyond Freshwater Bay the coast is largely uninhabited with a palpable air of isolation. It is on this stretch that walkers can appreciate how the elements have shaped and weathered the island over many centuries. Away from the coast an intricate network of paths offers the chance to discover a rich assortment of charming villages, hidden valleys and country houses. In all, the Isle of Wight has more than 500 miles of public rights of way and over half the island is acknowledged as an Area of Outstanding Natural Beauty. There is an annual walking festival in May and a weekend walking festival in October. Cycling is also extremely popular here, with the Round the Island Cycle Route attracting many enthusiasts. The route runs for 49 miles and there are starting points at Yarmouth, Cowes and Ryde.

Away from walking and cycling, the Isle of Wight offers numerous attractions and activities. You could plan a week's itinerary on the island and not set foot on the beach. The island's history is a fascinating and crucial aspect of its story. It was long considered as a convenient stepping stone for the French in their plan to invade the mainland, and various fortifications – including Fort Victoria and Yarmouth Castle – reflect its key strategic role in the defence of our coastline. Carisbrooke Castle at Newport – the island's capital – is where Charles I was held before his execution in 1649.

The Isle of Wight has been a fashionable destination for the rich and famous over the years, and members of royalty made their home here. Queen Victoria and Prince Albert boosted tourism hugely when they chose the island as the setting for their summer home, Osborne House, which is now open to the public. Elsewhere, there are echoes of the Isle of Wight's fascinating literary links. Charles Dickens is said to have written six chapters of *David Copperfield* in the village of Bonchurch, near Ventnor, and the Victorian Poet Laureate Alfred Lord Tennyson lived at Faringford House, near Freshwater Bay. He claimed that the air on the coast here was worth 'sixpence a pint.'

◁ Bembridge

ISLE OF WIGHT

BRIGHSTONE
Map 5 SZ48

Places to visit
Mottistone Gardens, MOTTISTONE, PO30 4ED, 01983 741302
www.nationaltrust.org.uk/mottistone-gardens-and-estate

Grange Farm

►►►► 75%

tel: 01983 740296 **Grange Chine PO30 4DA**
email: grangefarmholidays@gmail.com **web:** www.grangefarmholidays.com
dir: *From Freshwater Bay take A3055 towards Ventnor, 5 miles (pass Isle of Wight Pearl). Site in approximately 0.5 mile on right.*

This family-run site is set in a stunning location on the south-west coast of the island in Brighstone Bay. The range of facilities is very good. For children there is an imaginative play area and a wide range of animals to see including llamas, goats and a donkey. This site is right on the coastal path and ideally located for those who like walking and cycling. There are camping pods for hire plus static homes on a lower level by the beach.

Open: March to October **Last arrival:** noon **Last departure:** noon

Pitches: ⊕ ⊕ ⅄ ⋔; 8 hardstanding pitches

Facilities: ⊙ ℙ ✳ ⑤ ⌹ ⌷ WiFi

Services: ⊕ ⑤ ⇌ ⬇ ⬛ ⌀ Ⓣ

Within 3 miles: ✐ ⅀

Additional site information: 8 acre site. ⌁ Cars can be parked by caravans and tents. Awnings permitted. No fires. Bakery.

Glamping available: Wooden pods.

FRESHWATER
Map 5 SZ38

Places to visit
Yarmouth Castle, YARMOUTH, PO41 0PB, 01983 760678
www.english-heritage.org.uk/visit/places/yarmouth-castle

Dimbola Museum & Galleries, FRESHWATER, PO40 9QE, 01983 756814
www.dimbola.co.uk

Great for kids: The Needles Park, ALUM BAY, PO39 0JD, 01983 752401
www.theneedles.co.uk

Heathfield Farm Camping

►►►► 88%

tel: 01983 407822 **Heathfield Road PO40 9SH**
email: web@heathfieldcamping.co.uk **web:** www.heathfieldcamping.co.uk
dir: *2 miles west from Yarmouth ferry port on A3054, left to Heathfield Road, entrance 200 yards on right.*

A well located park in the far west of the island, perfect for visiting the Needles, Freshwater, Totland and Tennyson Down. There are large grass pitches (many over 200 square metres) giving plenty of space, and the facilities are modern, well appointed and very clean. There is also a good backpackers' area for camping with picnic tables, and a good children's play area. The local town of Freshwater has an excellent supermarket and good range of shops. The closest ferry point is at Yarmouth but the site is easily reached from all ferry ports.

Open: May to September **Last arrival:** 20.00 **Last departure:** 11.00

Pitches: ⊕ ⊕ ⅄

Leisure: ⚠ ⚽

Facilities: ⌂ ⊙ ℙ ✳ ⅋ ⌹ ⌷ WiFi

Services: ⊕ ⑤ ⬇ ⌀

Within 3 miles: ↓ ✐ ∪ ◎ ⅀ ≒ ⑤

Additional site information: 10 acre site. ⌁ Cars can be parked by caravans and tents. Awnings permitted. Car hire can be arranged.

LEISURE: 🏊 Indoor swimming pool 🏊 Outdoor swimming pool ⚠ Children's playground 🪁 Kids' club 🎾 Tennis court 🎱 Games room ▭ Separate TV room ↓ Golf course ⛳ Pitch n putt ⛵ Boats for hire 🚲 Bikes for hire 🎬 Cinema 🎵 Entertainment 🎣 Fishing ◎ Mini golf 🏄 Watersports 🏋 Gym 🏟 Sports field ∪ Stables
FACILITIES: 🛁 Baths/Shower ⊙ Electric shaver sockets ℙ Hairdryer ✳ Ice Pack Facility 🍼 Baby facilities 🦽 Disabled facilities ⑤ Shop on site or within 200yds 🍴 BBQ area ⌷ Picnic area WiFi WiFi

NEWBRIDGE
Map 5 SZ48

Places to visit
Newtown Old Town Hall, NEWTOWN, PO30 4PA, 01983 531785
www.nationaltrust.org.uk/newtown-national-nature-reserve-and-old-town-hall

Great for kids: Yarmouth Castle, YARMOUTH, PO41 0PB, 01983 760678
www.english-heritage.org.uk/visit/places/yarmouth-castle

Platinum Park

The Orchards Holiday Caravan Park
►►►►►

tel: 01983 531331 & 531350 **Main Road PO41 0TS**
email: info@orchards-holiday-park.co.uk **web:** www.orchards-holiday-park.co.uk
dir: *A3054 from Yarmouth, right in 3 miles at Horse & Groom Inn. Follow signs to Newbridge. Entrance opposite post office. Or from Newport, 6 miles, via B3401.*

A really excellent, well-managed park set in a peaceful village location amid downs and meadowland, with glorious downland views. The pitches are terraced and offer a good provision of hardstandings, including those that are water serviced. There is a high quality facility centre offering excellent, spacious showers and family rooms, plus there is access for less able visitors to all site facilities and disabled toilets. The park has indoor and outdoor swimming pools, a takeaway and licensed shop. Static homes are available for hire and 'ferry plus stay' packages are on offer. The site is just 10 minutes from the Wightlink ferry terminal in Yarmouth and there are buses that stop at the site entrance every hour.

Open: 31 March to 30 October (restricted service: March to late May and mid/late September to October – outdoor pool closed) **Last arrival:** 23.00 **Last departure:** 11.00

Pitches: * 🚐 from £19; 🚍 from £19; 🅰 from £19; 52 hardstanding pitches

Leisure: 🏊 ⛱ 🎱 🎯 ⚽

Facilities: 🛁 ⊙ 🎣 ✳ ♿ 🖐 🚾 🚮 WiFi

Services: 🔌 🛢 🍴 🎰 🛒 🚰 🔋 Ⓣ

Within 3 miles: ↧

Additional site information: 15 acre site. 🐕 Cars can be parked by caravans and tents. Awnings permitted. No cycling, no noise after midnight. Table tennis room, fin2fit mermaid experience, poolside coffee shop, pool room, arcade, play areas, football, live music on Tuesday evenings. Car hire can be arranged.

RYDE

Places to visit
Nunwell House & Gardens, BRADING, PO36 0JQ, 01983 407240
www.nunwellhouse.co.uk

Bembridge Windmill, BEMBRIDGE, PO35 5SQ, 01983 873945
www.nationaltrust.org.uk/bembridge-windmill

Great for kids: Robin Hill Country Park, ARRETON, PO30 2NU, 01983 527352
www.robin-hill.com

RYDE
Map 5 SZ59

Platinum Park

Whitefield Forest Touring Park
►►►►►

tel: 01983 617069 **Brading Road PO33 1QL**
email: pat&louise@whitefieldforest.co.uk **web:** www.whitefieldforest.co.uk
dir: *From Ryde follow A3055 towards Brading, after Tesco roundabout site in 0.5 mile on left.*

This park is beautifully laid out in the Whitefield Forest, and offers a wide variety of pitches, including 30 fully serviced pitches, as well as family rooms. The site is conveniently located on a bus route. It offers excellent modern facilities which are kept spotlessly clean. The park takes great care to retain the natural beauty of the forest, and is a haven for wildlife; red squirrels can be spotted throughout the park, including along the nature walk. Activities such as foraging, bushcraft and cycle rides for children and adults are available at certain times of the year.

Open: 3 April to 5 October **Last arrival:** 21.00 **Last departure:** 11.00

Pitches: * 🚐 from £19; 🚍 from £19; 🅰 from £19; 40 hardstanding pitches

Leisure: 🎱 **Facilities:** 🛁 ⊙ 🎣 ✳ ♿ 🖐 WiFi

Services: 🔌 🛢 🛒 🚰 🔋 🕭 Ⓣ

Within 3 miles: ↧ 🎣 ∪ ⛵ 🚴 🎯 🚌

Additional site information: 23 acre site. 🐕 Cars can be parked by caravans and tents. Awnings permitted.

SANDOWN
Map 5 SZ58

Places to visit
Nunwell House & Gardens, BRADING, PO36 0JQ, 01983 407240
www.nunwellhouse.co.uk

Bembridge Windmill, BEMBRIDGE, PO35 5SQ, 01983 873945
www.nationaltrust.org.uk/bembridge-windmill

Great for kids: Dinosaur Isle, SANDOWN, PO36 8QA, 01983 404344
www.dinosaurisle.com

Old Barn Touring Park
►►►► 79%

tel: 01983 866414 **Cheverton Farm, Newport Road PO36 9PJ**
email: mail@oldbarntouring.co.uk **web:** www.oldbarntouring.co.uk
dir: *On A3056 from Newport, site on left after Apse Heath roundabout.*

A terraced site with several secluded camping areas that are divided by hedges. This site is well positioned for visiting the eastern side of the island, and customers can be sure of a warm welcome from the friendly staff. Rallies are very welcome.

Open: Easter to September **Last arrival:** 21.00 **Last departure:** noon

Pitches: 🚐 🚍 🅰; 9 hardstanding pitches; 6 seasonal pitches

Leisure: 🎱 🏓 **Facilities:** 🛁 ⊙ 🎣 ✳ ♿ WiFi

Services: 🔌 🛢 🛒 🚰 🔋 🕭

Within 3 miles: ↧ 🎣 ∪ ◎ ⛵ 🚴 🎯 🕭

Additional site information: 5 acre site. 🐕 Cars can be parked by caravans and tents. Awnings permitted. Car hire can be arranged.

PITCHES: 🚐 Caravans 🚍 Motorhomes 🅰 Tents 🏕 Glamping accommodation **SERVICES:** 🔌 Electric hook-up 🛢 Launderette 🍴 Licensed bar 🔋 Calor Gas 🌀 Campingaz Ⓣ Toilet fluid 🍴 Café/Restaurant 🎰 Fast Food/Takeaway 🔋 Battery charging 🚰 Motorhome service point * 2019 prices 🚫 No credit or debit cards 🐕 Dogs permitted 🚫 No dogs

SHANKLIN
Map 5 SZ58

Places to visit

Shanklin Chine, SHANKLIN, PO37 6BW, 01983 866432
www.shanklinchine.co.uk

Ventnor Botanic Garden, VENTNOR, PO38 1UL, 01983 855397
www.botanic.co.uk

Great for kids: Dinosaur Isle, SANDOWN, PO36 8QA, 01983 404344
www.dinosaurisle.com

Ninham Country Holidays
▶▶▶▶ 90%

tel: 01983 864243 **Ninham PO37 7PL**
email: office@ninham-holidays.co.uk **web:** www.ninham-holidays.co.uk
dir: *Signed from A3056 (Newport to Sandown road). (Note: for sat nav use PO36 9PJ).*

Enjoying a lofty rural location with fine country views, this delightful, spacious park occupies two separate, well-maintained areas in a country park setting near the sea and beach. It has an excellent toilet and shower block in The Orchards that has a good layout of pitches; there is also a good outdoor pool, a games room and an excellent children's play area. Willow Brook is a separate camping area with a toilet and newly refurbished shower block. In between Willow Brook and The Orchards are two fishing lakes. This is a great place for families and close to Shanklin and Sandown.

Open: May to September **Last arrival:** 20.00 **Last departure:** 10.00

Pitches: * ⊞ from £19.50; ⊞ from £19.50; ▲ from £16.50

Leisure: ⊚ ⋀ ◕ ▭ ◉
Facilities: ▣ ⊙ ℱ ✳ ⅃ WIFI
Services: ▣ ▣ ▭ ⌄ ▐ ⌀
Within 3 miles: ⌁ ∪ ◎ ⌇ ⌇ ⅀

Additional site information: 12 acre site. ⌁ Cars can be parked by caravans and tents. Awnings permitted. Recycling obligatory.

See advert opposite

TOTLAND BAY
Map 5 SZ38

Places to visit

Dimbola Museum & Galleries, FRESHWATER, PO40 9QE, 01983 756814
www.dimbola.co.uk

Mottistone Gardens, MOTTISTONE, PO30 4ED, 01983 741302
www.nationaltrust.org.uk/mottistone-gardens-and-estate

Great for kids: Yarmouth Castle, YARMOUTH, PO41 0PB, 01983 760678
www.english-heritage.org.uk/visit/places/yarmouth-castle

Stoats Farm Camping
▶▶▶ 78%

tel: 01983 755258 **PO39 0HE**
email: hello@adventureactivitiesuk.com **web:** www.stoats-farm.co.uk
dir: *0.75 mile south of Totland. (Note: it is advisable for caravans and motorhomes to approach via Moons Hill; do not approach via Weston Lane which is narrow).*

Recently acquired by Adventure Activity Holidays, this long-established camping site, and now activity centre, is located in an attractive area near Freshwater. Alongside the camping facilities, including a refurbished office and toilet block (wooden clad to blend in with the surrounding environment), multiple activities based in the water, on the hills and in the woodland are offered. These include, to name but a few, kayak surfing sessions, archery in the woods, and jumping off cliffs and swimming through the caves whilst coasteering. Families and groups are welcomed here.

Open: April to October
Pitches: ⊞ ⊞ ▲
Facilities: ▣ ⊙ ℱ ✳ ⅃ ⑤ ♨
Services: ▣ ▣ ▭ ⌄ ⌀
Within 3 miles: ⌁ ℱ ∪ ◎ ⌇ ⅀

Additional site information: 10 acre site. ⌁ Cars can be parked by caravans and tents. Awnings permitted. No loud noise after 23.00. No camp fires unless appropriate equipment used (check with site manager). Campers' fridge available, service wash laundry.

WHITECLIFF BAY

Places to visit

Bembridge Windmill, BEMBRIDGE, PO35 5SQ, 01983 873945
www.nationaltrust.org.uk/bembridge-windmill

Great for kids: Dinosaur Isle, SANDOWN, PO36 8QA, 01983 404344
www.dinosaurisle.com

LEISURE: ⊛ Indoor swimming pool ⊛ Outdoor swimming pool ⋀ Children's playground ⅃ Kids' club ⌇ Tennis court ◕ Games room ▭ Separate TV room
⌁ Golf course ⊓ Pitch n putt ⌇ Boats for hire ⊗ Bikes for hire ▯ Cinema ♫ Entertainment ℱ Fishing ◎ Mini golf ⌇ Watersports ⅄ Gym ◉ Sports field ∪ Stables
FACILITIES: ▣ Baths/Shower ⊙ Electric shaver sockets ℱ Hairdryer ✳ Ice Pack Facility ⊌ Baby facilities ⅃ Disabled facilities ⑤ Shop on site or within 200yds
♨ BBQ area ☐ Picnic area WIFI WiFi

WHITECLIFF BAY
Map 5 SZ68

Premier Park

Whitecliff Bay Holiday Park
▶▶▶▶▶ 89% HOLIDAY CENTRE

tel: 01983 872671 **Hillway Road, Bembridge PO35 5PL**
email: holiday.sales@awayresorts.co.uk **web:** www.wight-holidays.com
dir: *1 mile south of Bembridge, signed from B3395 in village.*

This is a large seaside complex on two sites, with camping on one and self-catering chalets and luxury static holiday homes on the other. There is an indoor pool with flume and spa pool, and an outdoor pool with a kiddies' pool, a family entertainment club, and plenty of traditional on-site activities including crazy golf and table tennis, plus an indoor soft play area, a restaurant and a choice of bars. Activities include a programme for all the family in partnership with Fit4Life. There is access to a secluded beach from the park. The site also has a canvas village for a glamping holiday with safari lodges and bell tents to hire.

Open: All year (restricted service: off-peak season – facilities reduced)
Last arrival: flexible **Last departure:** 10.00

Pitches: 🚐 🚍 ▲; 50 hardstanding pitches; 400 seasonal pitches

Leisure: 🏊 🎣 🎮 🖐 🎯 ▭ 🎱 🎵 🎡

Facilities: 🛁 ☺ 🍳 ✳ 🚿 🛒 🚻 🪑 🛒 WiFi

Services: 🔌 🧺 🍺 🍴 🏧 ⛽ ⛽ 🔋 🛢 🚐 Ⓣ

Within 3 miles: ⚓ ⛵ ∪ 🎯 ⚾ 🎿

Additional site information: 49 acre site. 🐕 Adults and families only. Sports TV lounge, outdoor cinema.

Glamping available: Bell tents, safari tents.
Changeover days: Monday, Friday, Saturday

Additional glamping information: Bell tents and safari tents – minimum stay 3 nights. Cars can be parked by units.

WOOTTON BRIDGE
Map 5 SZ59

Places to visit
Osborne House, OSBORNE HOUSE, PO32 6JT, 01983 200022
www.english-heritage.org.uk/visit/places/osborne

Carisbrooke Castle, CARISBROOKE, PO30 1XY, 01983 522107
www.english-heritage.org.uk/visit/places/carisbrooke-castle

Great for kids: Robin Hill Country Park, ARRETON, PO30 2NU, 01983 527352
www.robin-hill.com

Platinum Park

Woodside Bay Lodge Retreat
▶▶▶▶▶ HOLIDAY HOME PARK

tel: 01983 885220 **Lower Woodside Road PO33 4JT**
email: reception@woodside-bay.co.uk **web:** www.woodside-bay.co.uk
dir: *From A3054 between Ryde and Newport, turn right into New Road, becomes Lower Woodside Road.*

This luxury park is located on the north-east shore of the Isle of Wight near Wootton Bridge – the setting is absolutely fabulous and the sloping terrain offers lovely views over the Solent. The restaurant and its position on the park is ideal and if the weather's good you can enjoy your meal or drinks on a covered veranda along with the views. There is a quality spa and gym plus an alfresco eating area, The Braai. Accommodation offered is a variety of luxury fully-equipped lodges sleeping 4, 6 or 8 plus and two spectacular tree houses that sleep two. Do not follow sat nav, follow brown signs or ring for directions.

Open: All year

Holiday Homes: Two-ring burner Dishwasher Washing Machine Tumble dryer Microwave Freezer TV Sky/Freeview DVD player WiFi Linen included Towels included Electricity included Gas included

Leisure: 🏋 **Facilities:** 🛒 WiFi

Within 3 miles: ∪ 🖇

Additional site information: 🐕

01983 864243

NINHAM COUNTRY HOLIDAYS

WOOTTON BRIDGE *continued*

Kite Hill Farm Caravan & Camping Park
►►► 88%

tel: 01983 883261 **Firestone Copse Road PO33 4LE**
email: welcome@kitehillfarm.co.uk **web:** www.kitehillfarm.co.uk
dir: *Signed from A3054 at Wootton Bridge, between Ryde and Newport.*

The park, on a gently sloping field, is tucked away behind the owners' farm, just a short walk from the village and attractive river estuary. The facilities are excellent and very clean. This park provides a pleasant relaxing atmosphere for a stay on the island and is well located for visiting Cowes and the many attractions on this part of the island. Rallies are welcome here.

Open: All year **Last arrival:** anytime **Last departure:** noon

Pitches: 🚐 from £18.50; 🚎 from £18.50; ▲ from £18.50

Leisure: 🄰

Facilities: 🛁 ☉ ✳ ♿

Services: 🐕 🔋 🍴 🛒 ⌀

Within 3 miles: 🎣 🏌 ∪ 🎱 🚴 ✈ 📅 🖧

Additional site information: 12.5 acre site. 🐾 Owners must clean up after their pets. Cars can be parked by caravans and tents. Awnings permitted.

YARMOUTH

See Newbridge

KENT

ASHFORD
Map 7 TR04

Places to visit

Kent & East Sussex Railway, TENTERDEN, TN30 6HE, 01580 765155
www.kesr.org.uk

Great for kids: Port Lympne Reserve, LYMPNE, CT21 4LR, 01303 264647
www.aspinallfoundation.org/portlympne

Premier Park

Broadhembury Caravan & Camping Park
►►►►► 90%

tel: 01233 620859 **Steeds Lane, Kingsnorth TN26 1NQ**
email: holidaypark@broadhembury.co.uk **web:** www.broadhembury.co.uk
dir: *M20 junction 10, A2070 towards Brenzett. Straight on at 1st roundabout. Left at 2nd roundabout (ignore fork left). Straight on at next roundabout. Left at 2nd crossroads in village.*

A well-run and well-maintained small family park surrounded by open pasture; it is neatly landscaped with pitches sheltered by mature hedges. There is a well-equipped campers' kitchen adjacent to the spotless toilet facilities, and children will love the play areas, games room and football pitch. The adults-only area, close to the excellent reception building, includes popular fully serviced hardstanding pitches; this area has its own first-class, solar heated toilet block.

Open: All year **Last arrival:** 21.00 (late arrivals to use designated area)
Last departure: noon

Pitches: 🚐 from £22; 🚐 from £22; ⛺ from £22; 🏠 see price below; 20 hardstanding pitches

Leisure: 🅰 🎣 ▭ ✪ **Facilities:** 🚻 ☉ ⌗ ✲ 🚿 ⚘ ⓢ WiFi

Services: 🔌 🗑 🍺 🔋 ⚘ 🔧 ⓣ

Within 3 miles: ⌘ ⚓ ∪ ◎ ≋ ⚲ 目

Additional site information: 10 acre site. 🐕 Cars can be parked by caravans and tents. Awnings permitted. No noise after 22.00. Bakery, table tennis, pool, skittle alley and air hockey. Car hire can be arranged.

Glamping available. Lotus Belle tents from £66. Changeover days: Sunday to Friday

Additional glamping information: Lotus Belle tents: minimum stay 2 nights. Double bed, 2 single beds or 1 double bed. Fully equipped. Bed linen can be hired. BBQ and picnic table. Cars can be parked by units.

AYLESFORD | Map 6 TQ75

Places to visit

Aylesford Priory, AYLESFORD, ME20 7BX, 01622 717272
www.thefriars.org.uk

Premier Park

Kits Coty Glamping 🏠

▶▶▶▶▶ 88% GLAMPING ONLY

tel: 01634 685862 **84 Collingwood Road, Kits Coty Estate ME20 7ER**
email: info@kitscotyglamping.co.uk **web:** www.kitscotyglamping.co.uk
dir: *M2 junction 3, A229 towards Maidstone, follow Eccles and Burham signs. Under motorway bridge, 1st right signed Kits Coty Estate. 1st left into Salisbury Road (before joining M2). 2nd left into Beresford Road. Right at T-junction to site at end.*

Established in a lush paddock opposite the owners' house, Kits Coty Glamping is located in glorious North Downs countryside between Maidstone and Chatham, with far-reaching views across the Medway Valley. The well landscaped paddock is home to a shepherd's hut (traditionally decorated and with a double bed and log-burning stove), three spacious bell tents and 'Gretel', a woodland-themed cabin. Careful thought has been given to the space between the units and the attention to detail is excellent, as is the customer care from hands-on owners Ami and Mark, who are passionate about their unique glamping patch. The bell tents have quality mattresses, chest of drawers, electric lighting and stove, Egyptian cotton sheets, cosy duvets, throws and blankets – these are very colourful in the spacious and fun Festival and Marrakesh tents; the Marmadou tent just sleeps two. Each unit has a decked area outside, with chairs, a picnic bench and rustic log seats around a brazier. The facility cabin houses a well-equipped washing-up area that also contains every conceivable cooking utensil plus a fridge and freezer, kettle, microwave and toaster. There are also two spacious fully serviced wet rooms and two extra toilet and washbasin cubicles. There's a great outdoor space for ball games in a separate paddock, which also contains the communal eating area, chill-out room and a large fire pit.

Open: May to October **Last arrival:** 22.00 **Last departure:** 10.30

Leisure: 🅰 ⚽ ✪ **Facilities:** 🚻 ☉ ⌗ ✲ 🚿 ⚘ ☕ 🍴 🚙 WiFi

Within 3 miles: ⌘ ∪ ≋ ⓢ

Accommodation available: Bell tents, shepherd's huts and camping cabin from £100.

Additional site information: 1 acre site. ⊗ Guests must abide by site's code of conduct (available on website).

DETLING | Map 7 TQ75

Places to visit

Leeds Castle, MAIDSTONE, ME17 1PL, 01622 765400
www.leeds-castle.com

Maidstone Museum, MAIDSTONE, ME14 1LH, 01622 602838
www.museum.maidstone.gov.uk

Great for kids: Kent Life, MAIDSTONE, ME14 3AU, 01622 763936
www.kentlife.org.uk

Oak View Caravan Park

▶▶▶ 87%

tel: 01622 631298 **Scragged Oak Road ME14 3HB**
email: bookings@scraggedoak.co.uk
dir: *From M20 junction 7, A429 towards Ramsgate. After Detling left signed Bredhurst into Scragged Oak Road.*

Situated on top of the North Downs, adjacent to the Kent Showground, this peaceful park has a smart toilet block and provides a handy overnight stop for the ferries and Channel Tunnel. The experienced and enthusiastic wardens are gradually improving the park, adding hardstanding pitches and refurbishing the water/waste stations.

Open: March to October **Last arrival:** 22.00 **Last departure:** noon

Pitches: 🚐 🚐 ⛺; 22 hardstanding pitches

Facilities: 🚻 ☉ ⌗ ✲ 🚿 ⚘ ⓢ 🍺 WiFi

Services: 🔌 🗑 🔋 🔧 ⚘ 🔧 ⓣ **Within 3 miles:** ⌘

Additional site information: 6 acre site. 🐕 Cars can be parked by caravans and tents. Awnings permitted. No unaccompanied children in toilet block, no noise after 22.30, no gazebos, no wood burning. Freshly baked bread, croissants and sausage rolls available; dog shower.

LEYSDOWN-ON-SEA | Map 7 TR07

Priory Hill

▶▶▶ 75%

tel: 01795 510267 **Wing Road ME12 4QT**
email: touringpark@prioryhill.co.uk **web:** www.prioryhill.co.uk
dir: *M2 junction 5, A249 signed Sheerness, then A2500 to Eastchurch, then B2231 to Leysdown, follow brown tourist signs.*

A small well-maintained touring area on an established family-run holiday park close to the sea, with views of the north Kent coast. Amenities include a clubhouse and a swimming pool. The pitch price includes membership of the clubhouse with live entertainment, and use of the indoor swimming pool.

Open: March to October **Last arrival:** 18.00 **Last departure:** noon

Pitches: * 🚐 from £20; 🚐 from £20; ⛺ from £20

Leisure: 🏊 🎣 ▭ 🎵 ✪

Facilities: 🚻 ☉ ⚘ ⓢ 🚙 WiFi

Services: 🔌 🗑 🍴 🍽 🍺 ⚘ 🔧

Within 3 miles: ⌘ ◎

Additional site information: 1.5 acre site. 🐕 Cars can be parked by caravans and tents. Awnings permitted. Cakes and fresh coffee available. Fresh bread and pastries baked daily.

PITCHES: 🚐 Caravans 🚐 Motorhomes ⛺ Tents 🏠 Glamping accommodation **SERVICES:** 🔌 Electric hook-up 🗑 Launderette 🍺 Licensed bar
🔋 Calor Gas ⚘ Campingaz ⓣ Toilet fluid 🍽 Café/Restaurant 🍴 Fast Food/Takeaway 🔋 Battery charging 🔧 Motorhome service point
* 2019 prices ⊘ No credit or debit cards 🐕 Dogs permitted ⊗ No dogs

MARDEN
Map 6 TQ74

Places to visit

Scotney Castle, LAMBERHURST, TN3 8JN, 01892 893820
www.nationaltrust.org.uk/scotneycastle

Premier Park

Tanner Farm Touring Caravan & Camping Park

▶▶▶▶▶ 90%

tel: 01622 832399 **Tanner Farm, Goudhurst Road TN12 9ND**
email: enquiries@tannerfarmpark.co.uk **web:** www.tannerfarmpark.co.uk
dir: *From A21 or A229 onto B2079. Midway between Marden and Goudhurst.*

At the heart of a 150-acre Wealden farm, this extensive, long-established touring park is peacefully tucked away down a quiet farm drive deep in unspoilt Kent countryside, yet close to Sissinghurst Castle and within easy reach of London (Marden station is three miles away). Perfect for families, as it has farm animals, two excellent play areas and a recreation/wet weather room (with TV); it offers quality toilet blocks with privacy cubicles, a good shop, spacious hardstandings (12 fully serviced), and high levels of security and customer care. Two camping pods are available.

Open: All year (restricted service: winter months – no tents accepted)
Last arrival: 20.00 **Last departure:** noon

Pitches: ♥ ⚏ ▲ 🏠; 34 hardstanding pitches; 13 seasonal pitches
Leisure: ⚏ ● ▢ ⚽
Facilities: 🛁 ☉ 🗲 ✳ ♿ 🖫 WiFi
Services: ♥ 🗓 ↴ 🦮 🗑 🍴 Ⓣ
Within 3 miles: 🎣

Additional site information: 15 acre site. ⬤ Cars can be parked by caravans and tents. Awnings permitted. No groups, 1 car per pitch, no commercial vehicles. Recreation room with table football and TV. Woodland walks.

Glamping available: Wooden pods.

Additional glamping information: Wooden pods sleep 2. Minimum stay 2 nights Friday to Sunday. Cars can be parked by pods.

MINSTER ON SEA
Map 7 TQ97

Plough Leisure Caravan Park
▶▶▶ 75%

tel: 01795 872895 & 07788 986547 **Plough Road ME12 4JF**
email: andyjames@live.co.uk **web:** www.ploughleisurecaravanpark.com
dir: *M2 junction 5, A429 signed Sheerness. Right at roundabout signed Leysdown onto A2500. Left signed Minster onto B2008. At roundabout take 1st exit. Right at phone box and brown camping sign into Plough Road. Site on left.*

Tucked away on the edge of Minster-on-Sea and well placed to visit the island's marshes and coastline, this small touring site is part of a neatly maintained static

park and offers well-spaced pitches, a good play area and a games field for children, and much improved toilet, shower and dishwashing facilities were added for the 2019 season.

Open: March to 1 October **Last arrival:** anytime **Last departure:** anytime
Pitches: ♥ ⚏ ▲
Leisure: ⚏ ⚽
Facilities: 🛁 ☉ ✳ ♿ 🖫 🏕
Services: ♥ 🗓 ↴ 🦮 🗑 ⚏
Within 3 miles: 🚴 🎣 Ⓢ

Additional site information: 4 acre site. ⬤ Dogs must be kept on leads at all times. No dangerous dogs permitted. Cars can be parked by caravans and tents. Awnings permitted. Noise to a minimum after 22.00. No fires on grass.

ROCHESTER
Map 6 TQ76

Places to visit

Guildhall Museum, ROCHESTER, ME1 1PY, 01634 332900
www.visitmedway.org/attractions/rochester-guildhall-museum-2132/

Upnor Castle, UPNOR, ME2 4XG, 01634 718742
www.english-heritage.org.uk/visit/places/upnor-castle

Great for kids: Diggerland, STROOD, ME2 2NU, 0871 227 7007 *(calls cost 10p per minute plus your phone company's access charge)*
www.diggerland.com/days-out-in-kent/

Allhallows Leisure Park

▶▶▶▶ 82% HOLIDAY HOME PARK

tel: 01634 270385 **Allhallows-on-Sea ME3 9QD**
email: allhallows@haven.com **web:** www.haven.com/allhallows
dir: *M25 junction 2, A2 signed Rochester, A289 signed Gillingham. A228 signed Grain. Follow site signs.*

Located in a peaceful country park setting close to Rochester, Allhallows is a static-only holiday park offering a wide range of sporting and leisure activities for all the family, including swimming pools, tennis courts, a 9-hole golf course and fencing. Children will love the kids' club and play area, while there is a restaurant and bar with evening entertainment for adults.

Open: March to October **Last arrival:** 24-hour check in **Last departure:** 10.00

Holiday Homes: Sleep 8 Bedrooms 2 Bathrooms 1 Toilet 1 Two-ring burner Dishwasher Microwave Freezer TV Sky/Freeview DVD player WiFi Linen included Electricity included Gas included

Leisure: ⚏ ⚏ ⚏ 🎣 ⚏ ♣ 🎵 ⚽
Facilities: ♿ Ⓢ 🏕 WiFi
Within 3 miles: ◎ ⚏

Additional site information: 188 acre site. ⬤ Most dog breeds accepted (please check when booking). Dogs must be kept on leads at all times. The facilities provided in the holiday homes may differ depending on the grade. Towels and garden furniture available for hire.

LEISURE: 🏊 Indoor swimming pool 🏊 Outdoor swimming pool ⚏ Children's playground 🏊 Kids' club 🎾 Tennis court ● Games room ▢ Separate TV room 🏌 Golf course ⛳ Pitch n putt 🚣 Boats for hire 🚲 Bikes for hire 🎬 Cinema 🎵 Entertainment 🎣 Fishing ◎ Mini golf 🏄 Watersports 💪 Gym ⚽ Sports field ♨ Stables
FACILITIES: 🛁 Baths/Shower ☉ Electric shaver sockets 🗲 Hairdryer ✳ Ice Pack Facility 🏕 Baby facilities ♿ Disabled facilities Ⓢ Shop on site or within 200yds 🍴 BBQ area 🏕 Picnic area WiFi WiFi

WHITSTABLE
Map 7 TR16

Places to visit

One Pound Lane, CANTERBURY, CT1 2BZ, 01227 458629
www.onepoundlane.co.uk

The Canterbury Tales, CANTERBURY, CT1 2TG, 01227 696002
www.canterburytales.org.uk

Great for kids: Druidstone Park, CANTERBURY, CT2 9JR, 01227 765168
www.druidstone.net

Homing Park

►►►► 85%

tel: 01227 771777 **Church Lane, Seasalter CT5 4BU**
email: info@homingpark.co.uk **web:** www.homingpark.co.uk
dir: *Exit A299 for Whitstable and Canterbury, left at brown camping-caravan sign into Church Lane. Site entrance has 2 large flag poles.*

A small touring park close to Seasalter Beach and Whitstable, which is famous for its oysters. All pitches are generously sized and fully serviced, and most are separated by hedging and shrubs. A clubhouse and swimming pool are available on site with a small cost for the use of the swimming pool. Wooden camping pods, for four or six people, are available for hire; their outwardly sloping walls adds to the internal space.

Open: Easter to October **Last arrival:** 20.00 **Last departure:** 11.00

Pitches: * ➡ from £23; ➡ from £23; ▲ from £23; ⋒ see price below

Leisure: ⬳ ⌂ ⬳

Facilities: 🏚 ⊙ ⌱ ⁕ & 📶

Services: 🔌 ▣ ⍩ 🍽 🔋

Within 3 miles: ↧ ⌿ ⬳ 💲

Additional site information: 12.6 acre site. 🐾 Cars can be parked by caravans and tents. Awnings permitted. No commercial vehicles, no tents larger than 8 berths or 5 metres wide, no unaccompanied minors, no cycles or scooters.

Glamping available: Wooden pods from £35. **Changeover days:** Any day

Additional glamping information: Minimum stay 2 nights (3 nights at bank holiday weekends). Cars can be parked by units

WROTHAM HEATH
Map 6 TQ65

Places to visit

Ightham Mote, IGHTHAM, TN15 0NT, 01732 810378
www.nationaltrust.org.uk/ightham-mote

St Leonard's Tower, WEST MALLING, ME19 6PD, 0370 333 1181
www.english-heritage.org.uk/visit/places/st-leonards-tower

Great for kids: Kent Life, MAIDSTONE, ME14 3AU, 01622 763936
www.kentlife.org.uk

Gate House Wood Touring Park
►►► 82%

tel: 01732 843062 **Ford Lane TN15 7SD**
email: contact@gatehousewoodtouringpark.com
web: www.gatehousewoodtouringpark.com
dir: *M26 junction 2a, A20 south towards Maidstone, through lights at Wrotham Heath. 1st left signed Trottiscliffe, left at next junction into Ford Lane. Site 100 yards on left.*

A well-sheltered and mature site in a former quarry surrounded by tall deciduous trees and gorse banks. The well-designed facilities include a reception, shop and smart toilets, 11 hardstandings, and there is good entrance security and high levels of customer care. The colourful flower beds and hanging baskets are impressive and give a positive first impression. Conveniently placed for the M20 and M25 and a fast rail link to central London.

Open: March to October **Last arrival:** 21.00 **Last departure:** noon

Pitches: * ➡ from £16.50; ➡ from £16.50; ▲ from £16.50

Leisure: ⌂

Facilities: 🏚 ⊙ ⌱ ⁕ & 💲 🛋

Services: 🔌 ▣ ⬆ 🔋 ⬳ T

Within 3 miles: ↧ ⌿ ∪ ⬳ ⊹

Additional site information: 3.5 acre site. 🐾 Cars can be parked by caravans and tents. Awnings permitted. No commercial vehicles, no noise after 23.00, no camp fires, soft balls only. Car hire can be arranged.

LANCASHIRE

See also sites under Greater Manchester and Merseyside

BLACKPOOL

Map 18 SD33

See also Lytham St Annes and Thornton

Places to visit

Madame Tussauds Blackpool, BLACKPOOL, FY1 5AA,
www.madametussauds.com/Blackpool

Great for kids: Blackpool Zoo, BLACKPOOL, FY3 8PP, 01253 830830
www.blackpoolzoo.org.uk

Premier Park

Marton Mere Holiday Village
▶▶▶▶▶ 88% HOLIDAY CENTRE

tel: 01253 767544 **Mythop Road FY4 4XN**
email: martonmere@haven.com **web:** www.haven.com/martonmere
dir: *M55 junction 4, A583 towards Blackpool. Right at Clifton Arms lights into Mythop Road. Site 150 yards on left.*

A very attractive holiday centre in an unusual setting on the edge of the mere, with plenty of birdlife to be spotted. The site has a stylish Mediterranean seaside-themed Boathouse Restaurant and the on-site entertainment is tailored for all ages, and includes a superb show bar. There's a regular bus service into Blackpool for those who want to explore further afield. The separate touring area is well equipped with hardstandings and electric pitches, and there are good quality facilities, including a superb amenity block.

Open: mid March to end October (restricted service: March to end May and September to October – reduced facilities, splash zone closed) **Last arrival:** 22.00 **Last departure:** 10.00

Pitches: 🚐 🚙; 82 hardstanding pitches

Leisure: 🏊 🎢 🚣 🎵

Facilities: 🛁 ☉ 🪒 ✳ ♿ 🔒 🛒 WiFi

Services: 🔌 🗑 🛒 🍴 🎱 💰 🅿

Within 3 miles: 🎣 ⛳ U ◎ 🎿 🐴 🗓

Additional site information: 30 acre site. 🐕 Maximum of 2 dogs per booking, certain dog breeds banned. No commercial vehicles, no bookings by persons under 21 years unless a family booking. 24-hour on-site team.

Manor House Caravan Park
▶▶▶▶ 83%

tel: 01253 764723 **Kitty Lane, Marton Moss FY4 5EG**
email: manorhousecaravanpark@outlook.com **web:** www.manorhousecaravanpark.co.uk
dir: *At roundabout at end of M55 junction 4, take A5230 signed Squires Gate. At next roundabout take 3rd exit (Blackpool/Squires Gate/A5230). In 0.5 mile left at lights into Midgeland Road. 500 yards, straight on at crossroads. 250 yards, right into Kitty Lane. In 250 yards, site on right. (Note: it is advisable not to follow sat nav).*

A sympathetically converted former small holding close to both Lytham St Annes and Blackpool, this peacefully located adults-only park is surrounded by high neat hedges and generous sized hardstanding pitches ensure optimum privacy. A warm welcome is assured by the resident owners and although there is no shop or launderette, both services are within a 10-minute drive. There are caravan pitches and motorhome pitches. Please note that tents are not accepted.

Open: February to November **Last arrival:** 20.00 **Last departure:** 11.30

Pitches: 🚐 from £23; 🚙 from £23; 10 hardstanding pitches

Facilities: 🛁 🌲

Services: 🔌 🅿

Within 3 miles: 🎣 ⛳ U ◎ 🎿 🗓 🛒 🗺

Additional site information: 1 acre site. Adults only. 🐕 Pets accepted by prior arrangement only. Cars can be parked by caravans. Awnings permitted. No ball games or loud music.

BOLTON LE SANDS

Places to visit

Lancaster Maritime Museum, LANCASTER, LA1 1RB, 01524 382264
www.lancaster.gov.uk/sport-and-leisure/museums/maritime-museum

Lancaster City Museum, LANCASTER, LA1 1HT, 01524 64637
www.lancaster.gov.uk/sport-and-leisure/museums/city-museum

Great for kids: Lancaster Castle, LANCASTER, LA1 1YJ, 01524 64998
www.lancastercastle.com

BOLTON LE SANDS   Map 18 SD46

Premier Park

Bay View Holiday Park
►►►►► 85%

tel: 01524 732854 & 701508 **LA5 9TN**
email: info@holgates.co.uk **web:** www.holgates.co.uk
dir: *M6 junction 25, A6 through Carnforth to Bolton-le-Sands. Site on right.*

A high quality, family-oriented seaside destination with fully serviced
all-weather pitches, many of which have views of Morecambe Bay and the
Cumbrian hills. A stylish bar/restaurant, featuring local produce and providing a
dog-friendly area, is just one of the park's amenities, and there is a wide range
of activities and attractions on offer within a few miles. This makes a good
choice for a family holiday by the sea; two family pods are available to hire.

Open: All year (restricted service: at quieter times – restaurant and bar reduced
hours) **Last arrival:** 20.00 **Last departure:** noon
Pitches: 🚐 🚍 ⛺; 50 hardstanding pitches; 127 seasonal pitches

Leisure: ⚠ 🎣 ▭ ⚽
Facilities: 🛁 ⊙ ✳ ♿ 🄂 ⋔ 🚮 WiFi
Services: 🔌 🗇 🍺 🍽 🍔 🔋 ⚓ 🛢 🧼 🗂
Within 3 miles: ↓ 🎣 ↻ ≥ ⟟ ⥫

Additional site information: 40 acre site. 🐕 No dogs in pods. Cars can be parked by
caravans and tents. Awnings permitted. No noise after 23.00. Car hire can be
arranged.

Glamping available: 2 wooden pods. **Changeover days:** Saturday

Additional glamping information: Wooden pods (sleep 2 adults and 3 children) offer
light, heater, electrical sockets and pull-out bed/sofa.

See advert on page 205

Red Bank Farm
►►► 81%

tel: 01524 823196 **LA5 8JR**
email: mark.archer@hotmail.co.uk **web:** www.redbankfarm.co.uk
dir: *From Morecambe take A5015 towards Carnforth. After Hest Bank left into Pastures
Lane (follow brown site sign). Over rail bridge, right (follow site sign). At T-junction left
into The Shore to site at end.*

A gently sloping grassy field with mature hedges, close to the sea shore and a RSPB
reserve. This farm site has smart toilet facilities, a superb view across Morecambe
Bay to the distant Lake District hills, and is popular with tenters. Archers Café
serves a good range of cooked food, including home-reared marsh lamb dishes.

Open: March to October **Last arrival:** 22.00

Pitches: * 🚍 from £14; ⛺ from £14

Facilities: 🛁 ⊙ 🅿 ✳ WiFi

Services: 🔌 🗇 🍽 🍔

Within 3 miles: ↓ 🎣 ≥ ⟟ ⥫ 🄂

Additional site information: 3 acre site. 🐕 Cars can be parked by tents. Awnings
permitted. No noise after 22.30. Pets' corner.

PITCHES: 🚐 Caravans 🚍 Motorhomes ⛺ Tents 🏕 Glamping accommodation **SERVICES:** 🔌 Electric hook-up 🗇 Launderette 🍺 Licensed bar
🛢 Calor Gas ⊘ Campingaz 🗂 Toilet fluid 🍽 Café/Restaurant 🍔 Fast Food/Takeaway 🔋 Battery charging ⚓ Motorhome service point
* 2019 prices ⊘ No credit or debit cards 🐕 Dogs permitted ⊗ No dogs

CAPERNWRAY   Map 18 SD57

Places to visit

Leighton Hall, CARNFORTH, LA5 9ST, 01524 734474
www.leightonhall.co.uk

RSPB Leighton Moss & Morecambe Bay Nature Reserve, SILVERDALE, LA5 0SW,
01524 701601, www.rspb.org.uk/leightonmoss

Premier Park

Old Hall Caravan Park

▶▶▶▶▶ 92%

tel: 01524 733276 **LA6 1AD**
email: hello@oldhallcaravanpark.co.uk **web:** www.oldhallcaravanpark.co.uk
dir: *M6 junction 35, A601(M) follow signs for Over Kellet, at T-junction left onto B6254. In Over Kellet left at village green signed Capernwray. Site 1.5 miles on right.*

A lovely secluded park set in a clearing amongst trees at the end of a half-mile long drive. This peaceful park is home to a wide variety of wildlife, and there are marked walks in the woods. A pathway over a meandering brook through woodland separates the reception from the touring area. All pitches are fully serviced and the stylish amenity block contains superb combined shower, toilet and washbasin rooms with excellent fixtures and fittings. The facilities are well maintained by the friendly owners, and booking is advisable. Please note, on bank holidays a minimum stay of three nights is required.

Open: March to January (restricted service: November to January – seasonal tourers can stay longer by prior arrangement) **Last arrival:** 9.30 **Last departure:** noon

Pitches: * 🚐 from £25; 🚊 from £25; 38 hardstanding pitches; 30 seasonal pitches

Leisure: ⚠

Facilities: 🛁 ☉ 🇫 🕭 WiFi

Services: 🔌 🔄 🚽 🔯 🛢

Within 3 miles: 🚣 U 🛶 🎣 🕟

Additional site information: 3 acre site. ✇ Cars can be parked by caravans. Awnings permitted. No skateboards, scooters, rollerblades or roller boots. Woodland walk, information room.

COCKERHAM   Map 18 SD45

Places to visit

Lancaster Cathedral, LANCASTER, LA1 3BT, 01524 384820
www.lancastercathedral.org.uk

Moss Wood Caravan Park

▶▶▶▶ 88%

tel: 01524 791041 **Crimbles Lane LA2 0ES**
email: info@mosswood.co.uk **web:** www.mosswood.co.uk
dir: *M6 junction 33, A6, approximately 4 miles to site. From Cockerham take west A588. Left into Crimbles Lane to site.*

A tree-lined grassy park with sheltered, level pitches, located on peaceful Cockerham Moss. A spacious air-conditioned licensed shop at the entrance stocks a variety of local produce including cheeses, smoked bacon and ales. The modern toilet block is attractively clad in stained wood, and the facilities include cubicle washing units and a launderette. A private lake is also available for coarse fishing enthusiasts.

Open: March to October **Last arrival:** 20.00 **Last departure:** 16.00

Pitches: * 🚐 from £24; 🚊 from £24; 31 hardstanding pitches; 12 seasonal pitches

Leisure: 🖋 ⚽

Facilities: 🛁 ☉ 🇫 🕭 ⑤ WiFi

Services: 🔌 🔄 🛢 🔯 🕕

Within 3 miles: 🚣 U

Additional site information: 25 acre site. ✇ Cars can be parked by caravans. Awnings permitted. Woodland walks, fishing lake, nature trail.

CROSTON   Map 15 SD41

Places to visit

Harris Museum & Art Gallery, PRESTON, PR1 2PP, 01772 258248
www.harrismuseum.org.uk

Rufford Old Hall, RUFFORD, L40 1SG, 01704 821254
www.nationaltrust.org.uk/ruffordoldhall

Royal Umpire Caravan Park

▶▶▶▶ 82%

tel: 01772 600257 **Southport Road PR26 9JB**
email: info@royalumpire.co.uk **web:** www.harrisonholidays.com
dir: *From north: M6 junction 28 (from south: M6 junction 27), onto B5209, right onto B5250.*

A large park with tree- or hedge-lined bays for touring caravans and motorhomes, plus a large camping field in open countryside. There are many areas for children's activities and several pubs and restaurants within walking distance. Four camping pods are available for hire, including a Gemini Pod which can accommodate large family groups.

Open: All year **Last arrival:** 20.00 **Last departure:** 16.00

Pitches: * 🚐 from £10; 🚊 from £10; ▲ from £8.50; 180 hardstanding pitches; 100 seasonal pitches

Leisure: ⚂ ⚽

Facilities: 🏪 ☺ 🏳 ✳ 👶 ♨

Services: 🔌 🛢 🔼 🔋 🗑

Within 3 miles: 🏇 🎣 ♻ 🏌 ⛸ 🎿 💲

Additional site information: 60 acre site. 🐾 Cars can be parked by caravans and tents. Awnings permitted. No campfires, vans or commercial vehicles.

Glamping available: Wooden pods. **Changeover days:** Any day

Additional glamping information: Wooden pods offer fridge, microwave, toaster, kettle, crockery, electric heater, TV. Own bedding and towels required. Pets accepted in 2 pods only. BBQs must be raised off ground away from decking. Cars can be parked by pods.

ESPRICK | Map 18 SD43

Places to visit
Blackpool Zoo, BLACKPOOL, FY3 8PP, 01253 830830
www.blackpoolzoo.org.uk

AA SMALL CAMPSITE OF THE YEAR 2020

Charoland Farm
►►►► 81%

tel: 07876 196434 & 01253 836595 **Greenhalgh Lane, Greenhalgh PR4 3HL**
email: enquiries@charolandfarm.co.uk **web:** www.charolandfarm.co.uk
dir: Exit M55 junction 3 onto A585 signed Fleetwood. Left into Greenhalgh Lane.

A hedge-screened, adults-only touring park based on an award-winning beef cattle and sheep farm, ideally located for touring the many Fylde Coast attractions. All pitches are firm and surrounded by attractive seasonal shrubs and flowers, and level approaches to facilities benefit less mobile visitors. Please note that there is no laundry facility at this park.

Open: March to October **Last arrival:** 20.00 **Last departure:** 17.00

Pitches: 🚐 🚍 🛆; 10 hardstanding pitches

Facilities: 🏪 ☺ ✳ 👶 ♨ 🍴 ♨

Services: 🔌

Within 3 miles: ♻ 💲

Additional site information: 0.5 acre site. Adults only. 🐾 Pets by prior arrangement. ⊘ Cars can be parked by caravans and tents. Awnings permitted. No commercial vehicles. No ball games.

FAR ARNSIDE

Places to visit
Rufford Old Hall, RUFFORD, L40 1SG, 01704 821254
www.nationaltrust.org.uk/ruffordoldhall

RSPB Leighton Moss & Morecambe Bay Nature Reserve, SILVERDALE, LA5 0SW, 01524 701601, www.rspb.org.uk/leightonmoss

---

FAR ARNSIDE | Map 18 SD47

Premier Park

Hollins Farm Camping & Caravanning
►►►►► 88%

tel: 01524 701767 & 701508 **LA5 0SL**
email: reception@holgates.co.uk **web:** www.holgates.co.uk
dir: M6 junction 35, A601 (Carnforth). Left in 1 mile at roundabout to Carnforth. Right in 1 mile at lights signed Silverdale. Left in 1 mile into Sands Lane, signed Silverdale. 2.4 miles over auto-crossing, 0.3 mile to T-junction. Right, follow signs to site, in approximately 3 miles take 2nd left after passing Holgates.

Hollins Farm is a long established park that continues to be upgraded by the owners. There are fully serviced hardstanding pitches for tourers and fully serviced tent pitches; the excellent amenity block provides very good facilities and privacy options. It has a traditional family camping feel and offers high standard facilities; most pitches have views towards Morecambe Bay, and WiFi is available throughout the park. Two family pods (Daisy and Buttercup) are available for hire. The leisure and recreation facilities of the nearby, much larger, sister park (Silverdale Caravan Park at Silverdale) can be accessed by guests here.

Open: 14 March to 7 November **Last arrival:** 20.00 **Last departure:** noon
Pitches: 🚐 🚍 🛆 🏠; 5 hardstanding pitches; 38 seasonal pitches
Leisure: ⚂ 🎱 🏓 **Facilities:** 🏪 ☺ ✳ 👶 ♨ WiFi
Services: 🔌 🛢 🔼 🔋 🗑 🛠 Ⓣ **Within 3 miles:** 🏇 ♻ 🏌 ◎ ⛸ 💲
Additional site information: 30 acre site. 🐾 Cars can be parked by caravans and tents. Awnings permitted. No unaccompanied children, no fire pits or chimeneas, no gazebos, no commercial vehicles at reception after unloading, no noise after 22.30.
Glamping available: Wooden pods.
Additional glamping information: Wooden pods offer sofa bed and heater.

FLEETWOOD
Map 18 SD34

Places to visit
Blackpool Zoo, BLACKPOOL, FY3 8PP, 01253 830830
www.blackpoolzoo.org.uk

Premier Park

Cala Gran Holiday Park
►►►►► 86% HOLIDAY HOME PARK

tel: 01253 872555 **Fleetwood Road FY7 8JY**
email: calagran@haven.com **web:** www.haven.com/calagran
dir: M55 junction 3, A585 signed Fleetwood. At 4th roundabout (Nautical College on left) take 3rd exit. Park 250 yards on left.

Cala Gran is a lively holiday park close to Blackpool with a range of quality holiday caravans and apartments. The park is all about fun, and the entertainment includes live music, comedy shows and resident DJs, while for children there are swimming pools and a SplashZone, a pick and paint room, climbing wall, and also a sports range for supervised archery and fencing.

Open: mid March to 30 October

Holiday Homes: Sleep 8 Bedrooms 2 Bathrooms 1 Toilet 1 Microwave Freezer TV Sky/Freeview

Leisure: ☜ ⚠ ✋ 🎾 ♫

Facilities: ⑤ ☎ WiFi

Within 3 miles: ⚷ ◎ 日

Additional site information: 🐕 Most dog breeds accepted (please check when booking). Dogs must be kept on leads at all times. The facilities provided in the holiday homes may differ depending on the grade. All-weather sports court.

GARSTANG

Places to visit
Lancaster Maritime Museum, LANCASTER, LA1 1RB, 01524 382264
www.lancaster.gov.uk/sport-and-leisure/museums/maritime-museum

Lancaster City Museum, LANCASTER, LA1 1HT, 01524 64637
www.lancaster.gov.uk/sport-and-leisure/museums/city-museum

Great for kids: Lancaster Castle, LANCASTER, LA1 1YJ, 01524 64998
www.lancastercastle.com

GARSTANG
Map 18 SD44

Bridge House Marina & Caravan Park
►►►► 83%

tel: 01995 603207 **Nateby Crossing Lane, Nateby PR3 0JJ**
email: info@bridgehousemarina.co.uk **web:** www.bridgehousemarina.co.uk
dir: Exit A6 at pub and Knott End sign, immediately right into Nateby Crossing Lane, over canal bridge to site on left.

Set in attractive countryside by the Lancaster Canal, you drive through an extensive boatyard with lots of historical interest, to arrive at this carefully landscaped park. It has excellent pitches, including some that are fully serviced, and an excellent motorhome service point. The stylish Bridge 64 Cafe Bar is open during the day and evenings at weekends.

Open: March to 4 January **Last arrival:** 22.00 **Last departure:** 13.00

Pitches: 🚐 🚗; 42 hardstanding pitches; 20 seasonal pitches

Leisure: ⚠ ⚽ **Facilities:** ☎ ☺ ℱ ✳ ⚷ ⑤ WiFi

Services: ⚡ ⑤ ▮┤ ⏽ 📶 ⚓ ∅ ⊤ **Within 3 miles:** ⚷ ℱ ≽

Additional site information: 4 acre site. 🐕 Cars can be parked by caravans. Awnings permitted.

LANCASTER
Map 18 SD46

Places to visit
Lancaster Maritime Museum, LANCASTER, LA1 1RB, 01524 382264
www.lancaster.gov.uk/sport-and-leisure/museums/maritime-museum

Lancaster City Museum, LANCASTER, LA1 1HT, 01524 64637
www.lancaster.gov.uk/sport-and-leisure/museums/city-museum

Great for kids: Lancaster Castle, LANCASTER, LA1 1YJ, 01524 64998
www.lancastercastle.com

New Parkside Farm Caravan Park
►►► 83%

tel: 015247 70723 **Denny Beck, Caton Road LA2 9HH**
email: enquiries@newparksidefarm.co.uk **web:** www.newparksidefarm.co.uk
dir: M6 junction 34, A683 towards Caton and Kirkby Lonsdale. Site 1 mile on right.

A few minutes from M6 and an ideal stopover en route to or from Scotland, this rural and peaceful park is set in the Lune Valley and is near the historic city of

Lancaster and the Forest of Bowland. This is friendly, family-run park is part of a working farm and has generously sized pitches (both grass and hardstanding) and a smart amenity block. Please note there is no laundry at this site.

Open: March to October **Last arrival:** 20.00 **Last departure:** 16.00

Pitches: * 🚐 from £17; 🚌 from £17; ▲ from £8; 40 hardstanding pitches

Facilities: 🏪 ☉ ⚐

Services: 🔌 🔒

Within 3 miles: 🚴 ✎ 🎯 🎪 🛒 🔄

Additional site information: 4 acre site. 🐕 🐾 Cars can be parked by caravans and tents. Awnings permitted. No football.

LONGRIDGE

Places to visit

Brockholes Nature Reserve, SAMLESBURY, PR5 0AG, 01772 872000
www.brockholes.org

LONGRIDGE Map 18 SD63

Beacon Fell View Holiday Park
▶▶▶▶ 81% HOLIDAY CENTRE

tel: 01772 783233 **110 Higher Road PR3 2TF**
email: beacon@hagansleisure.co.uk **web:** www.hagansleisure.co.uk
dir: *At junction of Dilworth Road (B6243) and King Street in Longridge into Higher Road. Site on right.*

Located on the outskirts of Longridge with fine views of the surrounding fells, this long-established family holiday destination has a good range of all-weather attractions for both adults and children. In addition to holiday homes, the touring areas have good hardstanding pitches for caravans or motorhomes with electric hook-ups to all.

Open: March to 11 November **Last arrival:** 22.00 **Last departure:** 11.00

Pitches: 🚐 🚌 ▲; 56 hardstanding pitches; 12 seasonal pitches

Leisure: 🏊 🎡 🏌 🎣 🎵 ⛳

Facilities: 🏪 ☉ ♿ 🔄 🚿 🚻 📶 WiFi

Services: 🔌 🔄 🍴 🍟 🔋 🔒

Within 3 miles: 🚴 ◎ 🎯

Additional site information: 32 acre site. 🐕 Dogs must be kept on leads at all times. Quiet between 22.00–07.00.

PITCHES: 🚐 Caravans 🚌 Motorhomes ▲ Tents 🏕 Glamping accommodation **SERVICES:** 🔌 Electric hook-up 🔄 Launderette 🍴 Licensed bar 🔋 Calor Gas 🔥 Campingaz T Toilet fluid 🍴 Café/Restaurant 🍟 Fast Food/Takeaway 🔋 Battery charging 🔧 Motorhome service point * 2019 prices 🚫 No credit or debit cards 🐕 Dogs permitted 🚫 No dogs

Places to visit

Blackpool Zoo, BLACKPOOL, FY3 8PP, 01253 830830
www.blackpoolzoo.org.uk

Eastham Hall Holiday Park
►►►► 86%

tel: 01253 737907 **Saltcotes Road FY8 4LS**
email: info@easthamhall.co.uk **web:** www.easthamhall.co.uk
dir: *M55 junction 3. Straight over 3 roundabouts onto B5259. Through Wrea Green and Moss Side, site 1 mile after level crossing.*

A large family-run park in a tranquil rural setting, surrounded by trees and mature shrubs. A major replanting programme including bee-attracting buddleia has been undertaken in recent years and the increase in wildlife is encouraging. The pitch density is very good and most are fully serviced, plus the amenity blocks have been appointed to a high standard. Please note, this site does not accept tents.

Open: March to 1 December (restricted service: 20 February to 1 March and 2 December to 3 January holiday homes only) **Last arrival:** 20.00 **Last departure:** noon

Pitches: 🚐 from £19; 🚚 from £19; 103 hardstanding pitches; 76 seasonal pitches

Leisure: 🛝 ⚽

Facilities: 🛁 ☉ 𝓕 ✳ ⅙ 🛒 WiFi
Services: 🔌 🗑 ↯ 🛢 🧹 🆃
Within 3 miles: ↓ 🏌 ∪ ◎ 🚣 ⚓

Additional site information: 30 acre site. 🐕 Dogs must be kept on leads at all times, dog exercise area. Cars can be parked by caravans. Awnings permitted. No tents, no noise after 23.00, 10mph speed limit. Football field, wildlife walk. Local produce, newspapers available. 27 night touring pitches.

Places to visit

Leighton Hall, CARNFORTH, LA5 9ST, 01524 734474
www.leightonhall.co.uk

Lancaster City Museum, LANCASTER, LA1 1HT, 01524 64637
www.lancaster.gov.uk/sport-and-leisure/museums/city-museum

Venture Caravan Park
►►►► 80%

tel: 01524 412986 **Langridge Way, Westgate LA4 4TQ**
email: mark@venturecaravanpark.co.uk **web:** www.venturecaravanpark.co.uk
dir: *M6 junction 34, A683, follow Morecambe signs. At 1st roundabout 1st exit, at 2nd roundabout 1st exit. At major crossroads (at lights) turn right into Morecambe Road. At next roundabout 1st left into Westgate. After fire station (on right) turn right into Langridge Way.*

A large family park close to the town centre, with good modern facilities, including a small indoor heated pool, a licensed clubhouse and a family room with children's entertainment. The site has many statics, some of which are for holiday hire. Please note, tents are not accepted.

Open: All year (restricted service: in winter – only one toilet block open)
Last arrival: 22.00 **Last departure:** noon

Pitches: * 🚐 from £25; 🚚 from £25; 40 hardstanding pitches; 25 seasonal pitches

Leisure: 🏊 🛝 🔍 ⚽
Facilities: 🛁 ☉ 𝓕 ✳ ⅙ 🛒 WiFi
Services: 🔌 🗑 🍽 🧺 🛒 ↯ 🛢 🆃
Within 3 miles: ↓ 🏌 🎱

Additional site information: 17.5 acre site. 🐕 Cars can be parked by caravans. Awnings permitted. Amusement arcade, off licence, seasonal entertainment.

Places to visit

Leighton Hall, CARNFORTH, LA5 9ST, 01524 734474
www.leightonhall.co.uk

Great for kids: RSPB Leighton Moss & Morecambe Bay Nature Reserve, SILVERDALE, LA5 0SW, 01524 701601
www.rspb.org.uk/leightonmoss

LEISURE: 🏊 Indoor swimming pool 🏊 Outdoor swimming pool 🛝 Children's playground 🎣 Kids' club 🎾 Tennis court 🔍 Games room 📺 Separate TV room
↓ Golf course 🏌 Pitch n putt 🚣 Boats for hire 🚲 Bikes for hire 🎬 Cinema 🎵 Entertainment 🎣 Fishing ◎ Mini golf 🚣 Watersports 🏋 Gym ⊕ Sports field ∪ Stables
FACILITIES: 🛁 Baths/Shower ☉ Electric shaver sockets 𝓕 Hairdryer ✳ Ice Pack Facility 👶 Baby facilities ⅙ Disabled facilities 🛒 Shop on site or within 200yds
🍴 BBQ area 🎍 Picnic area WiFi WiFi

SILVERDALE
Map 18 SD47

Platinum Park

Silverdale Caravan Park

► ► ► ► ►

tel: 01524 701508 **Middlebarrow Plain, Cove Road LA5 0SH**
email: reception@holgates.co.uk **web:** www.holgates.co.uk
dir: M6 junction 35, A601(M) follow Kirkby Lonsdale (B6254) signs. At T-junction right to Carnforth. In Carnforth centre at crossroads, straight on (Silverdale). 1 mile, left into Sands Lane (Silverdale). 2.4 miles, over automatic level crossing. Right at T-junction, follow Holgates sign. 1 mile left, 0.5 mile right into Cove Road, 0.7 mile to site.

A superb family holiday destination, enveloped in the wooded countryside and overlooking Morecambe Bay. All areas of the park are maintained in excellent condition with mature trees, shrubs and seasonal flowers; creating a peaceful and relaxing atmosphere. The pitch density is generous and the spotlessly clean amenity blocks are conveniently located. There's a 17-metre indoor heated swimming pool, a well-stocked licensed shop, fully stocked bar and restaurant, bowling alley with amusements and a toddlers' soft play area. Free Wi-Fi is also available within the main leisure complex.

Open: All year **Last arrival:** 20.00 **Last departure:** noon
Pitches: 🚐 🚍 ⅄ ⋒; 80 hardstanding pitches; 2 seasonal pitches
Leisure: 🏊 ⅍ 🔍 🎵 ⚾ ⚽ ☉

Facilities: 🖥 ⊙ 𝒫 ☼ ♿ ⑤ 🚿 🛒 WiFi
Services: 🔌 ⑤ 🍴 🍽 🍴 🚰 ↯ 🔋 ⌀ T
Within 3 miles: ⅃ ⌒ U ◎ ⌇

Additional site information: 100 acre site. 🐕 Cars can be parked by caravans and tents. Awnings permitted. No unaccompanied children, no gazebos, no fire pits or chimeneas, no noise after 22.30. Sauna, spa pool, steam room, bowling alley, ice cream parlour, indoor play area. Freshly baked bread.

Glamping available: Wooden pods.

Additional glamping information: Wooden pods offer a sofa bed, heater and lighting.

See advert on page 205

THORNTON
Map 18 SD34

Places to visit
Blackpool Zoo, BLACKPOOL, FY3 8PP, 01253 830830
www.blackpoolzoo.org.uk

Premier Park

Kneps Farm Holiday Caravan Park

► ► ► ► ► 84%

tel: 01253 823632 **River Road, Stanah FY5 5LR**
email: enquiries@knepsfarm.co.uk **web:** www.knepsfarm.co.uk
dir: Exit A585 at roundabout onto B5412 to Little Thornton. Right at mini-roundabout after school into Stanah Road, over 2nd mini-roundabout, leading to River Road.

This is a long established holiday destination which has been in the same family ownership for over 50 years. It is a quality park quietly located adjacent to the River Wyre and the Wyre Estuary Country Park, and handily placed for the attractions of Blackpool and the Fylde coast. It offers a well-stocked shop, an excellent toilet block with immaculate facilities, and a mixture of hard and grass pitches (no tents are accepted), plus there are 4-berth and 6-berth wooden pods for hire.

Open: March to mid November (restricted service: March and early November – shop closed) **Last arrival:** 20.00 **Last departure:** noon

Pitches: * 🚐 from £22; 🚍 from £22; ⋒ see price below; 40 hardstanding pitches; 12 seasonal pitches

Leisure: ⅍

Facilities: 🖥 ⊙ 𝒫 ☼ ♿ ⑤ 🚿 WiFi
Services: 🔌 ⑤ 🔋 ↯ 🔋 ⌀ T
Within 3 miles: ⅃ ⌒ ⌇ 目

Additional site information: 10 acre site. 🐕 Maximum of 3 dogs (chargeable) per unit. Cars can be parked by caravans. Awnings permitted. No commercial vehicles. No gazebos or shade sails, complete quiet after midnight.

Glamping available: Wooden pods from £35. **Changeover days:** Any day

Additional glamping information: Wooden pods: minimum advanced booking 2 nights (3 for bank holidays). Arrival 15:00, depart noon. Standard pods sleep 3; family pods sleep 4. Own bedding and other equipment required. No smoking/vaping, no pets, no unaccompanied teenagers. Cars can be parked by pods.

LEICESTERSHIRE

See also Wolvey (Warwickshire)

CASTLE DONINGTON   Map 11 SK42

Places to visit

Calke Abbey, CALKE, DE73 7JF, 01332 863822
www.nationaltrust.org.uk/calke-abbey

Ashby-de-la-Zouch Castle, ASHBY-DE-LA-ZOUCH, LE65 1BR, 01530 413343
www.english-heritage.org.uk/visit/places/ashby-de-la-zouch-castle

Donington Park Farmhouse
▶▶▶ 76%

tel: 01332 862409 **Melbourne Road, Isley Walton DE74 2RN**
email: info@parkfarmhouse.co.uk **web:** www.parkfarmhouse.co.uk
dir: *M1 junction 24, pass airport to Isley Walton, right towards Melbourne. Site 0.5 mile on right.*

A secluded touring site, at the rear of a hotel beside Donington Park Racing Circuit, which is very popular on race days so booking is essential. Reception for the campsite is at the hotel. Please note that there are no laundry facilities and both day and night flights from nearby East Midlands Airport may cause disturbance.

Open: 23–27 December (restricted service: closed for 7 days in early June; winter – hardstanding only) **Last arrival:** 21.00 **Last departure:** noon

Pitches: 🚐 🚎 ▲; 50 hardstanding pitches

Facilities: 🛁 ⊙ ☼ ⚙

Services: 🔌 🗑 🍴 ⬇ 🔒 ⊤

Within 3 miles: ⚓ ◢ 🛒

Additional site information: 10 acre site. 🐕 Dogs on lead at all times. Cars can be parked by caravans and tents. Awnings permitted. No noise between 23.00–08.00. Family camping. Bread and milk available, on-site hotel with bar and WiFi.

MELTON MOWBRAY   Map 11 SK71

AA CAMPSITE OF THE YEAR FOR ENGLAND 2020

Platinum Park

Eye Kettleby Lakes
▶▶▶▶▶

tel: 01664 565900 **Eye Kettleby LE14 2TN**
email: info@eyekettlebylakes.com **web:** www.eyekettlebylakes.com
dir: *A607 from Melton Mowbray towards Leicester for approximately 2 miles. Left signed Great Dalby and Eye Kettleby Lakes. Site 1 mile on left.*

A haven for lovers of coarse fishing and walking, this long-established leisure destination, located in the hamlet of Eye Kettleby, provides very high standards. There are eight fishing lakes as well as designated walking areas and accommodation located in lodges, a glamping forest and touring fields. Touring pitches are fully serviced and divided by mature hedges to provide optimum privacy. The top-notch amenity blocks provide excellent standards in respect of fittings and privacy. A large Scandinavian log building houses a reception, shop, café and clubhouse where regular entertainment is provided.

Open: All year **Last arrival:** 22.00 **Last departure:** noon

Pitches: * 🚐 from £25.50; 🚎 from £25.50; ▲ from £25.50; 🏠 see price below; 130 hardstanding pitches

Leisure: ◣ ▢ 🎾 🎵 ◢

Facilities: 🛁 ⊙ 🗲 ☼ ⚙ ⑤ 🎪 📶

Services: 🔌 🗑 🗑 🍴 🔒 ⊤

Within 3 miles: ⚓ ♻ 🏛

Additional site information: 150 acre site. Adults only. 🐕 Cars can be parked by caravans and tents. Awnings permitted. Cycle routes, coarse/specimen fishing.

Glamping available: Wooden pods from £62.50. **Changeover days:** Any day (July to August – arrive Monday to Thursday; 3-day mini breaks Friday to Sunday).

Additional glamping information: Wooden pods have en suite bathroom.

LINCOLNSHIRE

ANCASTER
Map 11 SK94

Places to visit
Belton House Park & Gardens, BELTON, NG32 2LS, 01476 566116
www.nationaltrust.org.uk/belton-house

Woodland Waters
►►►► 84%

tel: 01400 230888 **Willoughby Road NG32 3RT**
email: info@woodlandwaters.co.uk web: www.woodlandwaters.co.uk
dir: *On A153 west of junction with B6403.*

On an impressive estate, with a wide variety of mature trees and five beautifully landscaped fishing lakes, this popular holiday destination provides lodges including Wood View lodges, lodge rooms and level touring areas with smart modern amenity blocks. A pub and clubhouse, with restaurant, are additional benefits.

Open: All year **Last arrival:** 20.00 **Last departure:** noon
Pitches: * 🚐 from £19.50; 🚐 from £19.50; 20 hardstanding pitches
Leisure: 🎣 🔍 ⌇
Facilities: ☉ ℗ ⅙ ⑤ 🚿 🗻 WiFi
Services: 🔌 ⑤ 🍺 🍽 ♨ 🔋 ⚡ 🔋 ⌀
Within 3 miles: ⌁ ∪

Additional site information: 72 acre site. 🐕 Cars can be parked by caravans and tents. Awnings permitted. No noise after 23.00.

BOSTON
Map 12 TF34

Places to visit
Battle of Britain Memorial Flight Visitor Centre, CONINGSBY, LN4 4SY, 01522 782040, www.lincolnshire.gov.uk/bbmf

Tattershall Castle, TATTERSHALL, LN4 4LR, 01526 342543
www.nationaltrust.org.uk/tattershall-castle

Long Acres Touring Park
►►►► 92%

Best of British

tel: 01205 871555 **Station Road, Old Leake PE22 9RF**
email: info@long-acres.co.uk web: www.long-acres.co.uk
dir: *From A16 take B1184 at Sibsey (by church); approximately 1 mile at T-junction turn left. 1.5 miles, after level crossing take next right into Station Road. Park entrance approximately 0.5 mile on left.*

A small, rural, adults-only park in an attractive setting within easy reach of Boston, Spalding and Skegness. Excellent shelter is provided by the high, mature boundary hedging. The park has a smart toilet block which is very clean and has an appealing interior with modern, upmarket fittings and a laundry room. A holiday cottage is available to let. Long Acres is a member of the Tranquil Parks group.

Open: March to 8 January **Last arrival:** 20.00 **Last departure:** 11.00
Pitches: 🚐 🚐 ⅄; 40 hardstanding pitches
Facilities: ⛟ ☉ ℗ ⅙ ⅙ WiFi

Services: 🔌 ⑤ ⚡ 🔒
Within 3 miles: ⌇ ⑤

Additional site information: 3 acre site. Adults only. 🐕 Cars can be parked by caravans and tents. Awnings permitted.

Orchard Park
►►►► 86%

tel: 01205 290328 **Frampton Lane, Hubbert's Bridge PE20 3QU**
email: info@orchardpark.co.uk web: www.orchardpark.co.uk
dir: *On B1192 between A52 (Boston to Grantham road) and A1121 (Boston to Sleaford road).*

Ideally located for exploring the unique Fenlands, this continually improving park has two lakes – one for fishing and the other set aside for conservation. The attractive restaurant and bar are popular with visitors and Jan's Café is open for snacks during the day.

Open: All year (restricted service: December to February – bar closed) **Last arrival:** 20.00 **Last departure:** 16.00
Pitches: * 🚐 from £20; 🚐 from £20; ⅄ from £10; 15 hardstanding pitches
Leisure: 🎣 🎵 ⌇ ⚽
Facilities: ⛟ ☉ ℗ ⅙ ⅙ ⑤ 🚿 🗻 WiFi
Services: 🔌 ⑤ 🍺 🍽 ♨ 🔋 ⚡ 🔒 ⌀ Ⓣ
Within 3 miles: ⌁ ∪ ◎

Additional site information: 51 acre site. Adults only. 🐕 Dogs must be kept on leads at all times. Cars can be parked by caravans and tents. Awnings permitted. No washing lines.

CAISTOR
Map 17 TA10

Platinum Park

Caistor Lakes Leisure Park
►►►►►

tel: 01472 859626 **99a Brigg Road LN7 6RX**
email: info@caistorlakes.co.uk web: www.caistorlakes.co.uk
dir: *From Caistor bypass follow Immingham and Humber Bridge signs onto A1173. 1st left signed Brigg (A1084) into Grimsby Road (becomes High Street, then Brigg Road). Site on left.*

This is a stunning seven-acre park that was developed beside established fishing lakes. The passionate owners have created a very impressive park – there's excellent landscaping and first-class facilities that include 29 smart hardstanding pitches and modern, low-level buildings housing the professionally-run reception, the top-notch toilets and showers, a shop selling fishing supplies, and a smart 100-seat restaurant with views across the lakes and Lincolnshire Wolds. There are five luxury lodges with hot tubs available for hire.

Open: All year **Last arrival:** 17.00 **Last departure:** 15.00
Pitches: 🚐 🚐; 28 hardstanding pitches
Leisure: ⌇
Facilities: ⛟ ℗ ⅙ WiFi
Services: 🔌 🍺 🍽 ♨
Within 3 miles: ∪ ⑤

Additional site information: 7 acre site. Adults only. 🐕 Cars can be parked by caravans. Awnings permitted. No swimming in lakes, no bikes.

CAISTOR *continued*

Wolds View Touring Park
▶▶▶▶ 88%

tel: 01472 851099 **115 Brigg Road LN7 6RX**
email: woldsviewcaistor@gmail.com web: www.woldsviewtouringpark.co.uk
dir: *From A46, at Caistor, follow Brigg and A1084 signs. 1st left signed Brigg and Caistor. Through Caistor, continue on A1084. Approximately 1 mile, site on left.*

Set in the Lincolnshire Wolds with spectacular views, Wolds View is extremely welcoming, really modern and tidy, with good wide access, stoned roads, and good shrubbery and hedging throughout. The facilities block is a beautiful, purpose-designed wooden building, painted cornflower blue – at one end is a fabulous café and coffee shop serving a variety of drinks, breakfasts and home-made cakes, and at the other end are light, modern and spotless toilet and shower facilities, and a professionally managed reception.

Open: All year **Last arrival:** 20.00 (18.00 weekdays) **Last departure:** 13.00

Pitches: ⊕ ⊕ Å ⋒; 20 hardstanding pitches

Facilities: 🛁 ⊙ ℱ ✳ ⚓ ⑤ 🛏 ⋔ WiFi

Services: ⚡ 🔋 🍴 ⊞ ⚒ 🔒 🔲

Within 3 miles: ℘ ∪

Additional site information: 4.5 acre site. Adults only. 🐾 Cars can be parked by caravans and tents. Awnings permitted. No groups. No noise after 23.00.

Glamping available: 1 wooden pod. **Changeover days:** Any day

Additional glamping information: Wooden pod: minimum stay 2 nights. King-size bed, TV, toaster, microwave, tea and coffee making facilities, oil radiator, 2 chairs, outdoor patio set. Own bedding required. Cars can be parked by pod.

CLEETHORPES

Places to visit

Grimsby Fishing Heritage Centre, GRIMSBY, DN31 1UZ, 01472 323345
www.thefishingheritagecentre.com

CLEETHORPES   Map 17 TA30

Premier Park

Thorpe Park Holiday Centre
▶▶▶▶▶ 85% HOLIDAY CENTRE

tel: 01472 813395 **DN35 0PW**
email: thorpepark@haven.com web: www.haven.com/thorpepark
dir: *From A180 at Cleethorpes take unclassified road signed 'Humberstone and Holiday Park'.*

A large static site, adjacent to the beach, with touring facilities, including fully serviced pitches and pitches with hardstandings. This holiday centre offers excellent recreational and leisure activities including an indoor pool, archery range, climbing wall, lake coarse fishing and a 9-hole golf course. The Carousel bar and restaurant with its unique fairground theme is popular, along with several very good takeaway food options.

Open: mid March to end October (restricted service: mid March to May and September to end October – some facilities may be reduced) **Last arrival:** anytime **Last departure:** 10.00

Pitches: ⊕ ⊕ Å; 81 hardstanding pitches

Leisure: 🏊 🏊 ⋒ ♨ ⚲ ♪ ℘

Facilities: 🛁 ⊙ ℱ ⚓ ⑤ 🛏

Services: ⚡ 🔋 🍴 🍴 ⊞ 🔒 🔘

Within 3 miles: ∪ ◎ ⛵ 🏐

Additional site information: 300 acre site. 🐾 Maximum 2 dogs per booking, certain dog breeds banned. No commercial vehicles, no bookings by persons under 21 years unless a family booking.

GREAT CARLTON   Map 17 TF48

Places to visit

Cadwell Park Circuit, LOUTH, LN11 9SE, 01507 343248
www.cadwellpark.co.uk

West End Farm
▶▶▶ 87%

tel: 01507 450949 **Salters Way LN11 8BF**
email: info@westendfarm.co.uk web: www.skegnessmablethorpecaravancamping.com
dir: *From Gayton Top on A157 follow Great Carlton signs. Follow brown sign for West End Farm. Site on right in 0.5 mile.*

A neat and well-maintained four-acre touring park situated on the edge of the Lincolnshire Wolds. Surrounded by mature trees and bushes and well away from the busy main roads, yet connected by walking and cycling paths, it offers enjoyable peace and quiet close to the popular holiday resort of Mablethorpe. The site has good, clean facilities throughout and there's a passionate approach to everything 'green', with a reed bed sewage system, wild areas, bird and bat boxes and wildlife identification charts.

Open: 28 March to 2 October **Last arrival:** 20.30 **Last departure:** 14.00

Pitches: ⊕ ⊕ Å; 4 seasonal pitches

LEISURE: 🏊 Indoor swimming pool 🏊 Outdoor swimming pool ⋔ Children's playground 🧒 Kids' club ⚲ Tennis court 🎱 Games room ▭ Separate TV room ⛳ Golf course ⛳ Pitch n putt ⛵ Boats for hire 🚲 Bikes for hire 🎬 Cinema ♪ Entertainment ℘ Fishing ◎ Mini golf ⛵ Watersports 🏋 Gym 🏐 Sports field ∪ Stables **FACILITIES:** 🛁 Baths/Shower ⊙ Electric shaver sockets ℱ Hairdryer ✳ Ice Pack Facility 🍼 Baby facilities ⚓ Disabled facilities ⑤ Shop on site or within 200yds 🛏 BBQ area 🛏 Picnic area WiFi WiFi

Facilities: ⌂ ⌐ ⁕ ☷ ⊓

Services: ⊕ ◙ ☰ ⊍ T

Within 3 miles: ⅃ ✐ ∪ ◎ ⑤

Additional site information: 4 acre site. ⊁ Cars can be parked by caravans and tents. Awnings permitted. No fires, quiet after 22.30. Fridge available.

LANGWORTH   Map 17 TF07

Places to visit

The Collection: Art & Archaeology in Lincolnshire, LINCOLN, LN2 1LP, 01522 782040, www.thecollectionmuseum.com

Lincoln Cathedral, LINCOLN, LN2 1PL, 01522 561600 lincolncathedral.com

Barlings Country Holiday Park
► ► ► ► 85%

tel: 01522 753200 & 07931 227673 **Barlings Lane LN3 5DF**
email: info@barlingscountrypark.co.uk **web:** www.barlingscountrypark.co.uk
dir: *From Lincoln take A158 towards Horncastle. In Langworth right into Barlings Lane signed Barlings and Reepham.*

Set in rural Lincolnshire and only a short car journey from Lincoln, this idyllic 26-acre site offers both seasonal and touring pitches positioned around four lakes. With wildlife in abundance, the park is well landscaped, with beautifully mown grass and trimmed shrubs, a wooden reception chalet, spotlessly clean, older-style toilet facilities, including family rooms, and fishing from purpose-built jetties on two of the lakes. Lodges, static caravans and glamping cabins, with hot tubs, are available to hire.

Open: All year **Last arrival:** 18.00 (late arrivals can be arranged) **Last departure:** noon

Pitches: ⊞ ⊟ ⋀ ⋔; 43 hardstanding pitches; 40 seasonal pitches

Leisure: ✐ ✪

Facilities: ⌂ ⊙ ⅃ ⊓ WiFi

Services: ⊕ ◙ ☰ ⊍ ⌂ ⊘ T

Within 3 miles: ⑤

Additional site information: 26 acre site. ⊁ Cars can be parked by caravans and tents. Awnings permitted. No music after 22.00, quiet 23.00–08.00. Mobile shop Friday 11–11.30 only, ice cream van (summer).

Glamping available: 2 small cabins. **Changeover days:** Any day

Additional glamping information: Small cabins offer hot tubs. Cars can be parked by cabins.

MABLETHORPE   Map 17 TF58

Places to visit

Great for kids: Skegness Natureland Seal Sanctuary, SKEGNESS, PE25 1DB, 01754 764345, www.skegnessnatureland.co.uk

Premier Park

Golden Sands Holiday Park
► ► ► ► ► 85% HOLIDAY CENTRE

tel: 01507 477871 **Quebec Road LN12 1QJ**
email: goldensands@haven.com **web:** www.haven.com/goldensands
dir: *From centre of Mablethorpe left into Quebec Road (seafront road). Site on left.*

A large, well-equipped seaside holiday park with many all-weather attractions and a good choice of entertainment and eating options, including the stylish Quayside Bar and Restaurant. The large touring area is serviced by two amenity blocks and is close to the mini market and laundry. Just across the road is The Marblethorpe Seal Sanctuary and Wildlife Centre.

Open: mid March to end October **Last arrival:** anytime **Last departure:** 10.00

Pitches: ⊞ ⊟ ⋀; 20 hardstanding pitches

Leisure: ⧀ ⌇ ⋔ ⅃ ◕ ⅃ ✐

Facilities: ⌂ ⊙ ⅃ ⁕ ⅃ WiFi

Services: ⊕ ◙ ☰ ⌁ ⊞ ☰ ⊍ T

Within 3 miles: ⅃ ◎ ⌂ ⑤

Additional site information: 23 acre site. ⊁ Maximum 2 dogs per booking, certain dog breeds banned. No commercial vehicles, no bookings by persons under 21 years unless a family booking. Mini bowling alley, snooker and pool, amusement arcade.

Kirkstead Holiday Park
► ► ► 85%

tel: 01507 441483 **North Road, Trusthorpe LN12 2QD**
email: kirksteadholidaypark@outlook.com **web:** www.kirkstead.co.uk
dir: *From Mablethorpe town centre take A52 south towards Sutton-on-Sea. 1 mile, sharp right by phone box into North Road. Site signed in 300 yards.*

A well-established family-run park catering for all age groups, just a few minutes' walk from Trusthorpe and the sandy beaches of Mablethorpe. The main touring area, which is serviced by good quality toilet facilities, has 37 fully serviced pitches on what was once the football pitch. A small café and shop for essentials are also provided.

Open: March to November **Last arrival:** 21.00 **Last departure:** 11.00

Pitches: ⊞ ⊟ ⋀; 3 hardstanding pitches; 30 seasonal pitches

Leisure: ⋔ ◕ ⅃ ✪

Facilities: ⌂ ⊙ ⅃ ⁕ ⅃ ⑤ ⊓ WiFi

Services: ⊕ ◙ ☰ ⌁ ⊞ ☰ ⊍

Within 3 miles: ⅃ ✐ ∪ ◎ ⌂ ⊟

Additional site information: 12 acre site. ⊁ No dogs in tents. Cars can be parked by caravans and tents. Awnings permitted.

SKEGNESS   Map 17 TF56

Places to visit

Skegness Natureland Seal Sanctuary, SKEGNESS, PE25 1DB, 01754 764345
www.skegnessnatureland.co.uk

The Village-Church Farm Museum, SKEGNESS, PE25 2HF, 01754 766658
www.churchfarmvillage.org.uk

Eastview Caravan Park
►►►► 81%

tel: 01754 875324 **Trunch Lane, Chapel St Leonards PE24 5UA**
email: enquiries@eastviewcaravans.co.uk **web:** www.eastviewcaravans.co.uk
dir: *A52 from Skegness to Chapel St Leonards. Turn left into Trunch Lane. 2nd caravan park on left.*

Set in 15 acres and only a short walk from one of Lincolnshire's finest beaches, Eastview Caravan Park is neat and tidy and a good all-round campsite. It has beautifully mown grass, well-trimmed shrubbery and spotlessly clean and practical toilet facilities. There is a children's playground and a shop. It is well placed for exploring both the coast and the countryside, especially the beautiful Lincolnshire Wolds.

Open: March to October **Last arrival:** 17.00 (Friday 20.00) **Last departure:** 10.30 (later departures until 17.00 – fee applies).

Pitches: * ⊞ from £20.50; ⊞ from £20.50; ▲ from £19; 56 hardstanding pitches; 116 seasonal pitches

Facilities: ⊙ ✳ ⅊ ♿ ⊟ WiFi

Services: ⊕ ⊡ ⬆ 🔒 Ⓣ

Within 3 miles: ⌿ ⁄ ♻ ◎ ⬆ 目 Ⓢ

Additional site information: 15 acre site. 🐾 Maximum 2 dogs per pitch. Cars can be parked by caravans and tents. Awnings permitted. No motorised scooters, BB guns or kites. BBQs to be at least 1 foot off ground, quiet after 22.30. Dog wash.

TATTERSHALL   Map 17 TF25

Places to visit

Tattershall Castle, TATTERSHALL, LN4 4LR, 01526 342543
www.nationaltrust.org.uk/tattershall-castle

Tattershall Lakes Country Park
►►►► 90%

tel: 01526 348800 **Sleaford Road LN4 4LR**
email: tattershall.holidays@awayresorts.co.uk **web:** www.tattershall-lakes.com
dir: *Access from A153 in Tattershall.*

Set amongst woodlands, lakes and parkland on the edge of Tattershall in the heart of the Lincolnshire Fens, this mature country park has been created from old gravel pits and the flat, well-drained and maintained touring area offers plenty of space for campers. There's a lot to entertain the youngsters as well as the grown-ups, with good fishing on excellent lakes, a 9-hole golf course, water-skiing and jet-skiing lakes and an indoor heated pool with spa facilities. A newly created beach is an added attraction as is the indoor and outdoor splash zone.

Open: end March to end October (restricted service: off-peak season – reduced services) **Last arrival:** 19.00 **Last departure:** 10.00

Pitches: ⊞ ⊞ ▲ ⋒; 2 hardstanding pitches

Leisure: 🏊 ⛵ ♦ ⊡ ♪ ⚽ ⚽

Facilities: ⊙ ⅊ ♿ Ⓢ 🍴 ⊟ 🚼 WiFi

Services: ⊕ ⊡ 🍴 🍴 ⬆ 🔒

Within 3 miles: ⌿ ⁄ ⬆ ⬆ 目

Additional site information: 365 acre site. 🐾 Cars can be parked by caravans and tents. Awnings permitted. No excessive noise after midnight.

Glamping available: Bell tents; safari tents (canvas cottage).

Additional glamping information: Safari tents: includes hot tub.

WADDINGHAM

Places to visit

Gainsborough Old Hall, GAINSBOROUGH, DN21 2NB, 01522 782040
www.english-heritage.org.uk/visit/places/gainsborough-old-hall

LEISURE: 🏊 Indoor swimming pool 🏊 Outdoor swimming pool ⋀ Children's playground 👶 Kids' club 🎾 Tennis court 🎱 Games room ⬜ Separate TV room ⛳ Golf course ⛳ Pitch n putt ⛵ Boats for hire 🚲 Bikes for hire 🎬 Cinema ♪ Entertainment 🎣 Fishing ◎ Mini golf 🏄 Watersports 💪 Gym ⚽ Sports field 🐴 Stables
FACILITIES: 🛁 Baths/Shower ⊙ Electric shaver sockets 💇 Hairdryer ✳ Ice Pack Facility 🚼 Baby facilities ♿ Disabled facilities Ⓢ Shop on site or within 200yds 🍴 BBQ area 🪑 Picnic area WiFi WiFi

WADDINGHAM
Map 17 SK99

Brandy Wharf Leisure Park
►►► 72%

tel: 01673 818010 **Brandy Wharf DN21 4RT**
email: brandywharflp@freenetname.co.uk **web:** www.brandywharfleisurepark.co.uk
dir: *From A15 onto B1205 through Waddingham. Site in 3 miles.*

A small site in a very rural area on the banks of the River Ancholme, where fishing is available. The toilet block has unisex rooms with combined facilities as well as a more conventional ladies and gents with washbasins and toilets. All the grassy pitches have electricity, and there's a play and picnic area. This site will appeal to bikers, groups, music lovers, and families – children's natural play is encouraged. Advance booking is necessary for weekend pitches.

Open: All year (restricted service: November to Easter – no tents) **Last arrival:** dusk
Last departure: 17.00

Pitches: 🚐 🚍 ▲

Leisure: ⚐ 🎾 🎣

Facilities: 🛁 ☉ ✳ ♿ 🏠 🛋 WiFi

Services: 🔌 🗑 🛒 🔋 🛶

Within 3 miles: 🎣 ♒ 🛒 📮

Additional site information: 5 acre site. 🐕 Cars can be parked by caravans and tents. Awnings permitted. No disposable BBQs on grass, no music after 23.00. Boat mooring and slipway, canoe hire, pedalos, pets' corner. Camping – children under 10 are free of charge.

PITCHES: 🚐 Caravans 🚍 Motorhomes ▲ Tents ⛺ Glamping accommodation **SERVICES:** 🔌 Electric hook-up 🗑 Launderette 🍺 Licensed bar 🔥 Calor Gas 🔥 Campingaz T Toilet fluid 🍴 Café/Restaurant 🍔 Fast Food/Takeaway 🔋 Battery charging ⚡ Motorhome service point * 2019 prices 🚫 No credit or debit cards 🐕 Dogs permitted 🚫 No dogs

WOODHALL SPA

Map 17 TF16

Places to visit

Tattershall Castle, TATTERSHALL, LN4 4LR, 01526 342543
www.nationaltrust.org.uk/tattershall-castle

Battle of Britain Memorial Flight Visitor Centre, CONINGSBY, LN4 4SY,
01522 782040
www.lincolnshire.gov.uk/bbmf

Premier Park

Woodhall Country Park

▶ ▶ ▶ ▶ 93%

tel: 01526 353710 **Stixwould Road LN10 6UJ**
email: info@woodhallcountrypark.co.uk web: www.woodhallcountrypark.co.uk
dir: *In Woodhall Spa at roundabout in High Street take Stixwould Road. 1 mile, site on right, just before Village Limits pub.*

A peaceful and attractive touring park situated just a short walk from Woodhall Spa. The owners transformed part of the woodland area into a countryside retreat for campers who wish to get away from a hectic lifestyle. Well organised and well laid out, the park offers fishing lakes, three superb log cabin amenity blocks, fully serviced pitches and high levels of customer care. There's a strong ethos towards sustainability and a bio-mass boiler provides all the heating and hot water to the amenity blocks, plus there are several walks and trails on site. Two and four-berth camping pods and four luxury lodges are available for hire. A mobile van, offering wood-fired pizzas, is a feature on Friday nights.

Open: March to November **Last arrival:** 20.00 **Last departure:** noon

Pitches: * 🚐 from £23; 🚙 from £23; ⛺ from £19; 🏠 see prices below; 88 hardstanding pitches

Leisure: ⚞ 🎾 ⚽ ⚘

Facilities: 🛁 ☺ 🚿 ❄ 🚻 🅂 🍴 🐕 WiFi

Services: 🔌 🔘 🔒 🚮 Ⓣ

Within 3 miles: ⚓ ∪ ◎ 🎯

Additional site information: 80 acre site. 🚗 Cars can be parked by caravans and tents. Awnings permitted. No fires, Chinese lanterns or fireworks, no noise between 23.00–07.00. BBQs must be off ground. Walking and cycling trail, food preparation room including worktops, fridge/freezer, kettle, sinks and microwave available. Herb garden.

Glamping available: Wooden pods from £30; cabins from £40.
Changeover days: Any day

Additional glamping information: Minimum stay 2 nights; check-in from 15.00, check out by 11.00. Cabins have their own kitchenette and shower/toilet. Cabins allow dogs. No dogs in wooden pods. Bedding and towel packs available for hire. Cars can be parked by units.

See advert on page 213

Petwood Caravan Park

▶ ▶ ▶ ▶ 90%

tel: 01526 354799 **Off Stixwould Road LN10 6QH**
email: info@petwoodcaravanpark.co.uk web: www.petwoodcaravanpark.com
dir: *From Lincoln take A15 towards Sleaford. Left onto B1188 signed Woodhall Spa. In approximately 7.5 miles at Metheringham left onto B1189 (signed Billinghay). 3.7 miles, left onto B1191 (Woodhall Spa). In approximately 6 miles at roundabout in Woodhall Spa, 1st exit into Stixwould Road. In 0.3 mile left into Jubilee Park, follow site signs.*

Covering seven immaculate acres of beautifully manicured grounds, Petwood Caravan Park is a hidden gem located behind a much larger touring park in the heart of Woodhall Spa. There are 98 pitches, each with electric hook-ups and fresh water taps; 16 have spacious hardstandings suitable for caravans and motorhomes. There is a modern reception and shop, and two excellent heated toilet blocks, each containing a spotlessly maintained disabled/family room. Dogs are welcome at no extra charge.

Open: 5 April to 20 October **Last arrival:** 20.00 **Last departure:** noon

Pitches: 🚐 from £20; 🚙 from £20; ⛺ from £20; 16 hardstanding pitches; 20 seasonal pitches

Facilities: 🛁 ☺ 🚿 ❄ 🚻 🅂 WiFi

Services: 🔌 🔘 🔛

Within 3 miles: ⚓ 🎣 ◎ 🎯

Additional site information: 7 acre site. 🚗 Cars can be parked by caravans and tents. Awnings permitted. No rollerblades, skateboards, hoverboards or segways. No noise after 22.00.

LEISURE: 🏊 Indoor swimming pool 🏊 Outdoor swimming pool ⚞ Children's playground 🙌 Kids' club 🎾 Tennis court 🎱 Games room 📺 Separate TV room ⚓ Golf course 🏌 Pitch n putt ⛵ Boats for hire 🚲 Bikes for hire 🎬 Cinema 🎵 Entertainment 🎣 Fishing ◎ Mini golf 🏄 Watersports 💪 Gym ⚘ Sports field ∪ Stables
FACILITIES: 🛁 Baths/Shower ☺ Electric shaver sockets 🚿 Hairdryer ❄ Ice Pack Facility 🐣 Baby facilities 🚻 Disabled facilities 🅂 Shop on site or within 200yds 🍴 BBQ area 🧺 Picnic area WiFi WiFi

LONDON

E4 CHINGFORD
Map 6 TQ39

Places to visit

Waltham Abbey Gatehouse, Bridge & Entrance to Cloisters, WALTHAM ABBEY, EN9 1XQ, 08456 770 600
www.english-heritage.org.uk/visit/places/waltham-abbey-gatehouse-and-bridge

Lee Valley Campsite
▶▶▶▶ 81%

tel: 020 8529 5689 **Sewardstone Road, Chingford E4 7RA**
email: sewardstonecampsite@vibrantpartnerships.co.uk
web: www.visitleevalley.org.uk/wheretostay
dir: *M25 junction 26, A112. Site signed.*

Overlooking King George's Reservoir and close to Epping Forest, this popular and very peaceful park features very good modern facilities and excellent hardstanding pitches including nine that are able to accommodate larger motorhomes. This impressive park is maintained to a high standard and there is glamping accommodation (2-berth cocoons and 4-berth small cabins) in a separate shady glade. A bus calls at the site hourly to take passengers to the nearest tube station, and Enfield is easily accessible.

Open: March to January **Last arrival:** 20.00 **Last departure:** 11.00 (late departures by prior arrangement)
Pitches: 🚐 🚍 ⛺ 🏠; 65 hardstanding pitches
Leisure: 🎱 ⛲ **Facilities:** 🍴 ☉ ☂ ❄ ♿ ⑤ 📶
Services: 🔌 🗑 🔋 ⚡ 🛢 🗑 Ⓣ
Within 3 miles: 🚣 🎣 ↻ 🛶 🎠

Additional site information: 12 acre site. 🐕 Cars can be parked by caravans and tents. Awnings permitted. Under 18s must be accompanied by an adult, no commercial vehicles. Fresh produce, bike hire, fire pit.

Glamping available: Wooden pods.

Additional glamping information: 2 and 4 berth wooden pods. Cars can be parked by pods.

N9 EDMONTON
Map 6 TQ39

Places to visit

Queen Elizabeth's Hunting Lodge, LONDON, E4 7QH, 020 7332 1911
www.cityoflondon.gov.uk/things-to-do/green-spaces/epping-forest/visitor-information/Pages/queen-elizabeths-hunting-lodge.aspx

Lee Valley Camping & Caravan Park
▶▶▶▶ 81%

tel: 020 8803 6900 **Meridian Way N9 0AR**
email: edmontoncampsite@vibrantpartnerships.co.uk
web: www.visitleevalley.org.uk/wheretostay
dir: *M25 junction 25, A10 south, 1st left onto A1055, approximately 5 miles to Leisure Complex. From A406 (North Circular), north on A1010, left after 0.25 mile, right into Pickets Lock Lane.*

A pleasant, open site within easy reach of London yet peacefully located close to two large reservoirs. There are excellent gravel access roads to the camping field,

good signage and lighting and smart toilets. The site has the advantage of being next to an 18-hole golf course and a multi-screen cinema. There are also camping pods (cocoons), ready-erected tents and small timber cabins for hire. A convenient bus stop provides a direct service to central London.

Open: All year **Last arrival:** 20.00 **Last departure:** 11.00 (late departure by prior arrangement)
Pitches: 🚐 🚍 ⛺ 🏠; 54 hardstanding pitches
Leisure: 🎱 ⚽ **Facilities:** 🍴 ☉ ☂ ❄ ♿ ⑤ 📶
Services: 🔌 🗑 🍴 🔋 ⚡ 🛢 Ⓣ **Within 3 miles:** 🛶

Additional site information: 7 acre site. 🐕 Cars can be parked by caravans and tents. Awnings permitted. Under 18s must be accompanied by an adult. Foot golf. Fresh produce available.

Glamping available: Wooden pods (cocoons and cabins).

Additional glamping information: Cars can be parked by pods and cabins.

MERSEYSIDE

SOUTHPORT
Map 15 SD31

Places to visit

RSPB Marshside, SOUTHPORT, PR9 9PJ, 01704 211690
www.rspb.org.uk/reserves-and-events/reserves-a-z/marshside

British Lawnmower Museum, SOUTHPORT, PR8 5AJ, 01704 501336
www.lawnmowerworld.com

Great for kids: Dunes Splash World, SOUTHPORT, PR8 1RX, 01704 537160
www.splashworldsouthport.com

Premier Park

Riverside Holiday Park
▶▶▶▶▶ 86% HOLIDAY CENTRE

tel: 01704 228886 **Southport New Road PR9 8DF**
email: reception@harrisonleisureuk.com web: www.riversideleisurecentre.co.uk
dir: *M6 junction 27, A5209 towards Parbold and Burscough, right onto A59. Left onto A565 at lights in Tarleton. Continue to dual carriageway. At roundabout straight across, site 1 mile on left.*

A family-friendly park north of Southport, with many indoor attractions, including a swimming pool, sauna, steam room and jacuzzi, plus a clubhouse. The generously sized pitches are located on neat landscaped grounds and served by a conveniently located modern amenity block. Free WiFi is provided in an attractive café.

Open: 14 February to January **Last arrival:** 17.00 **Last departure:** 11.00
Pitches: 🚐 🚍 🏠; 130 hardstanding pitches
Leisure: 🏊 🎱 🎣
Facilities: 🍴 ☂ ♿ ⑤ 🍴 📶
Services: 🔌 🗑 🍴 🍴 🍟
Within 3 miles: 🚣 ↻ 🎠

Additional site information: 80 acre site. 🐕 One car per pitch. Cash payments not accepted.

Glamping available: Glamping hives **Changeover days:** Any day

Additional glamping information: Cars can be parked by units.

SOUTHPORT *continued*

Willowbank Holiday Home & Touring Park
▶▶▶▶ 88%

tel: 01704 571566 **Coastal Road, Ainsdale PR8 3ST**
email: info@willowbankcp.co.uk **web:** www.willowbankcp.co.uk
dir: *From A565 between Formby and Ainsdale exit at Woodvale lights onto coast road, site 150 metres on left. From north: M6 junction 31, A59 towards Preston, A565, through Southport and Ainsdale, right at Woodvale lights.*

Set in woodland on a nature reserve next to sand dunes, this constantly improving park is a peaceful and relaxing holiday destination with mature trees, shrubs and colourful seasonal flowers surrounding neat pitches and modern amenity blocks.

Open: 14 February to 31 January **Last arrival:** 20.30 **Last departure:** noon

Pitches: * 🚐 from £18.15; 🚐 from £18.15; 61 hardstanding pitches

Leisure: 🎢 ⚽

Facilities: 🛁 ☉ 🗲 ✳ ⚑ 🎪 **WiFi**

Services: 🚰 🗄 ⚒ 🔒 🧴

Within 3 miles: 🎣 🏌 ∪ ◎ 🎿 🎯 🎪 ⑤

Additional site information: 8 acre site. 🐕 No dangerous dog breeds, maximum of 2 dogs, no cats. Cars can be parked by caravans. Awnings permitted. Cannot accommodate continental door entry units, no commercial vehicles, only one car parked by caravan. Cycling trail.

Hurlston Hall Country Caravan Park
▶▶▶▶ 80%

tel: 01704 840400 & 842829 **Southport Road L40 8HB**
email: info@hurlstonhall.co.uk **web:** www.hurlstonhallcaravanpark.co.uk
dir: On A570, 3 miles from Ormskirk towards Southport.

A peaceful tree-lined touring park next to a static site in attractive countryside about 10 minutes' drive from Southport. The park is maturing well, with fairly large trees and a coarse fishing lake, and the excellent on-site facilities include golf, a bistro, a well-equipped health centre, a bowling green and model boat lake. Please note, neither tents nor dogs are accepted at this site.

Open: 1 March to 31 October **Last arrival:** 20.30 (last arrival 18.30 at weekends and bank holidays) **Last departure:** 17.00

Pitches: * 🚐 from £30; 🚐 from £30

Leisure: 🎣 ⚲ ✐ ✦

Facilities: 🛁 ☉ ⚹

Services: 🔌 🔲 🔌 🍽 🔒

Within 3 miles: 🏪

Additional site information: 5 acre site. ⊗ Cars can be parked by caravans. Awnings permitted.

Norfolk

Think of Norfolk, and the theme of water – in particular the Norfolk Broads, a complex network of mostly navigable rivers and man-made waterways – usually springs to mind. This delightfully unspoiled region attracts thousands of visitors every year, as does the North Norfolk Coast, designated an Area of Outstanding Natural Beauty and probably the finest of its kind in Europe.

'A long way from anywhere' and 'a remote corner of England that has been able to hold on to its traditions and ancient secrets,' are two of the apt descriptions that apply to this spacious corner of the country that still seems a separate entity, as if it is strangely detached from the rest of the country.

The coastline here represents a world of lonely beaches, vast salt marshes and extensive sand dunes stretching to the far horizon. It remains essentially unchanged, a stark reminder of how this area has long been vulnerable to attack and enemy invasion.

The highly successful thriller writer Jack Higgins chose this theme as the subject of his hugely popular adventure yarn *The Eagle has Landed*, published in 1975. The book, about a wartime Nazi plot to kidnap and assassinate Winston Churchill while he is spending the weekend at a country house near the sea in this part of East Anglia, vividly conveys the strange, unsettling atmosphere of the North Norfolk Coast.

Walking is the best way to gain a flavour of that atmosphere and visit the story's memorable setting. The 93-mile Peddars Way and North Norfolk Coast Path is one of Britain's most popular national trails. Made up of two paths strung together to form one continuous route, the trail begins near Thetford on the Suffolk/Norfolk border and follows ancient tracks and sections of Roman road before reaching the coast near Hunstanton. Cycling is another popular pastime in this region and in places you can combine it with a local train ride. One option, for example, is to cycle beside the Bure Valley Railway on a 9-mile trail running from Aylsham to Wroxham, returning to the start by train. There is also the North Norfolk Coast Cycleway between King's Lynn and Cromer, among other routes.

Norfolk prides itself on its wealth of historic houses, the most famous being Sandringham, where Her Majesty the Queen and her family spend Christmas. The Grade II-listed house, which is surrounded by 20,000 acres, has been the private home of four generations of monarchs since 1862. 'Dear old Sandringham, the place I love better than anywhere in the world,' wrote King George V. The house and gardens are open to visitors. Among the other great houses in the region are Holkham Hall – the magnificent Palladian home of the Earls of Leicester – and the National Trust properties of Blickling Hall and Felbrigg Hall.

Many of Norfolk's towns have a particular charm and a strong sense of community. The quiet market towns of Fakenham and Swaffham are prime examples, and there is also Thetford, with its popular museum focusing on the iconic TV comedy series *Dad's Army*. Much of the filming for this cherished BBC production took place in the town and in nearby Thetford Forest. On the coast, you'll find a string of quaint villages and small towns. Wells-next-the-Sea is a popular destination for many visitors to Norfolk, as is Blakeney, renowned for its mudflats and medieval parish church, dedicated to the patron saint of seafarers, standing guard over the village and the estuary of the River Glaven. With its iconic pier, a key feature of coastal towns, Cromer is a classic example of a good old fashioned seaside resort where rather grand Victorian hotels look out to sea. Together with Sheringham, Cromer hosts a Crab and Lobster Festival in May.

◁ Thetford Forest

NORFOLK

BARNEY
Map 13 TF93

Places to visit

Baconsthorpe Castle, BACONSTHORPE, NR25 9LN, 0370 333 1181
www.english-heritage.org.uk/visit/places/baconsthorpe-castle

Holkham Hall, HOLKHAM, NR23 1AB, 01328 710227
www.holkham.co.uk

Great for kids: Roarr! Dinosaur Adventure, LENWADE, NR9 5JW, 01603 876310
www.roarrdinosauradventure.co.uk

Platinum Park

The Old Brick Kilns
▶▶▶▶▶

tel: 01328 878305 **Little Barney Lane NR21 0NL**
email: enquiries@old-brick-kilns.co.uk **web:** www.old-brick-kilns.co.uk
dir: *From A148 (Fakenham to Cromer road) follow brown tourist signs to Barney, left into Little Barney Lane. Site at end of lane.*

This award-winning, secluded and peaceful park is approached via a quiet, leafy country lane. The park is on two levels with its own boating and fishing pool and many mature trees. Excellent, well-planned and beautifully appointed toilet facilities include a smart new washroom block for 2019, and there is a short dog walk around the site. In Barney's Restaurant & Bar, food and drink (including takeaways) are available on selected nights of the week (ask on check-in). The shop sells basic essentials including freshly baked bread and newspapers. Please note, due to a narrow access road, no arrivals are accepted until after 1.30pm. There are also four self-catering holiday cottages and B&B available.

Open: 15 March to 2 January (restricted service: Easter to September – bar food and takeaway available on selected nights only) **Last arrival:** 21.00 **Last departure:** 11.00
Pitches: ⊞ ⊟ ▲; 65 hardstanding pitches; 7 seasonal pitches
Leisure: ⚠ ⚓ ⬚ ✐
Facilities: ⌂ ⊙ ℱ ✳ ⚐ ⑤ ⍍ ⍟ ⤆ WiFi
Services: ⚡ ⑤ ⍭ ⍢ ⛟ ⚏ ⚐ ⚏ ⌂ ∅ Ⓣ
Additional site information: 12.73 acre site. ➤ Cars can be parked by caravans and tents. Awnings permitted. No gazebos. Outdoor draughts, chess and family games. Freshly baked bread available.

BELTON
Map 13 TG40

Places to visit

Burgh Castle, BURGH CASTLE, NR31 9QB, 0370 333 1181
www.english-heritage.org.uk/visit/places/burgh-castle

Premier Park

Rose Farm Touring & Camping Park
▶▶▶▶▶ 86%

tel: 01493 738292 **Stepshort NR31 9JS**
email: office@rosefarmtouringpark.com **web:** www.rosefarmtouringpark.com
dir: *From A143 follow signs to Belton. In Belton, from mini-roundabout on New Road into Stepshort, site on right.*

A former railway line is the setting for this very peaceful, beautifully presented site which enjoys rural views. It is brightened with many flower and herb beds. The toilet facilities are smart, spotlessly clean, inviting to use and include family rooms. The customer care here is exceptional and there is a wooden cabin (The Summer House) available for hire.

Open: All year **Last arrival:** 21.00 **Last departure:** 14.00
Pitches: ⊞ ⊟ ▲ ⋔; 26 hardstanding pitches; 60 seasonal pitches
Leisure: ⚓ ⬚
Facilities: ⌂ ⊙ ℱ ✳ ⚐ WiFi
Services: ⚡ ⑤ ⌂ ∅
Within 3 miles: ⚲ ✐ ∪ ⊚ ⚐ ⑤
Additional site information: 10 acre site. ➤ Cars can be parked by caravans and tents. Awnings permitted. No dog fouling, dogs on leads.

Glamping available: Cabins (summerhouses).

Additional glamping information: Summerhouses: cabin for daily, weekly, or seasonal hire (includes fridge, TV, microwave, wardrobe, bunk beds, sofa bed, toaster, kettle). Cars can be parked by units

Wild Duck Holiday Park
▶▶▶▶ 81% HOLIDAY CENTRE

tel: 01493 780268 **Howards Common NR31 9NE**
email: wildduck@haven.com **web:** www.haven.com/wildduck
dir: *A47 to Great Yarmouth, 3rd exit at Asda roundabout, straight on at next 2 roundabouts. Left onto A143 signed Beccles. Right at lights, 2 miles to dual carriageway, right at roundabout signed Belton. Straight on at mini-roundabout. Right at T-junction, left at next T-junction. Park 200 yards on right.*

This a large holiday complex with plenty to do for all ages both indoors and out. It's a level grassy site with well laid-out facilities and set in a forest with small, cleared areas for tourers. Clubs for children and teenagers, sporting activities and evening shows all add to the fun of a stay here. There are 10 fully-equipped safari tents for hire, each with its own stone-built barbecue and facility block.

Open: 16 March to 5 November (restricted service: mid March to May and September to early November – some facilities may be reduced) **Last arrival:** 21.00 **Last departure:** 10.00
Pitches: ⊞ ⊟ ▲; ⋔ see prices below
Leisure: ⚝ ⚝ ⚠ ⚐ ⚓ ♫
Facilities: ⌂ ⊙ ℱ ✳ ⚐ ⑤ ⍍ WiFi

Services: 🔌 🔲 🍺 🍴 🍔 🔒

Within 3 miles: 🎣 🚴 ⛳ ◎ ≈

Additional site information: 97 acre site. 🐕 Maximum 2 dogs per booking, certain dog breeds banned. No commercial vehicles, no bookings by persons under 21 years unless a family booking.

Glamping available: Safari tents from £119. **Changeover days:** Mondays, Fridays

Additional glamping information: Safari tents: minimum stay 3 nights.

DURHAM DEEPDALE   Map 13 TF84

Places to visit

Brancaster Estate (NT), BRANCASTER STAITHE, PE31 8BW, 01263 740241
www.nationaltrust.org.uk/brancaster-estate

RSPB Nature Reserve Titchwell Marsh, TITCHWELL, PE31 8BB, 01485 210779
www.rspb.org.uk/reserves-and-events/reserves-a-z/titchwell-marsh

Great for kids: Wells & Walsingham Light Railway, WELLS-NEXT-THE-SEA, NR23 1QB, 01328 711630, www.wwlr.co.uk

Deepdale Backpackers & Camping
►►►► 88%

tel: 01485 210256 **Deepdale Farm PE31 8DD**
email: stay@deepdalebackpackers.co.uk **web:** www.deepdalebackpackers.co.uk
dir: *On south side of A149 (coast road), opposite church, between Hunstanton and Wells-next-the-Sea.*

Within the heart of this notable tourist destination, near craft and food shops, a petrol station and visitor centre, which are all part of the Deepdale Estate, this park is a must for lovers of peace and tranquillity. The touring areas, spread over four distinctive fields, all offering generous pitch sizes, and most are equipped with electric hook-ups. There are also five fully serviced pitches capable of accommodating RVs. Three separate amenity blocks provide superb decor, fixtures and fittings and have excellent privacy options. The site is located a short stroll from the coastal path.

Deepdale Backpackers & Camping

Open: All year **Last arrival:** 21.00 **Last departure:** 11.00

Pitches: 🚐 ⛺; 7 hardstanding pitches

Leisure: 🎯 🎵   **Facilities:** 🚿 ☉ 🅟 ❄ ♿ 🅢 WiFi

Services: 🔌 🔲 🍴 🍔 🔋 ⛽ 🔒 🚰 T   Within 3 miles: 🎣 🚴 ≈ ◎

Additional site information: 8 acre site. 🐕 Cars can be parked by tents. Awnings permitted. Quiet policy after 22.00. See website for terms and conditions. Visitor information centre.

CAISTER-ON-SEA   Map 13 TG51

Places to visit

Caister Roman Fort, CAISTER-ON-SEA, NR30 5RN, 0370 333 1181
www.english-heritage.org.uk/visit/places/caister-roman-fort

Thrigby Hall Wildlife Gardens, FILBY, NR29 3DR, 01493 369477
www.thrigbyhall.co.uk

Premier Park

Caister-on-Sea Holiday Park
►►►►► 88% HOLIDAY CENTRE

tel: 01493 728931 **Ormesby Road NR30 5NH**
email: caister@haven.com **web:** www.haven.com/caister
dir: *A1064 signed Caister-on-Sea. At roundabout 2nd exit onto A149, at next roundabout 1st exit onto Caister bypass, at 3rd roundabout 3rd exit to Caister-on-Sea. Park on left.*

An all-action holiday park located beside the beach north of the resort of Great Yarmouth, yet close to the attractions of the Norfolk Broads. The touring area offers 46 fully serviced pitches and a modern, well-appointed, purpose-built toilet block. Customer care is of an extremely high standard with a full time, experienced and caring warden. Please note, this park does not accept tents.

Open: mid March to end October **Last arrival:** anytime **Last departure:** 10.00

Pitches: 🚐 🚐; 49 seasonal pitches

Leisure: 🏊 🎣 🏊 🎯 🎵

Facilities: 🚿 ☉ 🅟 ♿ 🅢 🎪 🛒 WiFi

Services: 🔌 🔲 🍺 🍴 🍔 🔒   Within 3 miles: 🎣 🚴 ⛳ ◎

Additional site information: 138 acre site. 🐕 Maximum 2 dogs per booking, certain dog breeds not accepted. No tents, no commercial vehicles, no bookings by persons under 21 years unless a family booking.

PITCHES: 🚐 Caravans 🚐 Motorhomes ⛺ Tents 🏠 Glamping accommodation **SERVICES:** 🔌 Electric hook-up 🔲 Launderette 🍺 Licensed bar 🔒 Calor Gas ⌀ Campingaz T Toilet fluid 🍴 Café/Restaurant 🍔 Fast Food/Takeaway 🔋 Battery charging ⚡ Motorhome service point
* 2019 prices ⊘ No credit or debit cards 🐕 Dogs permitted ⊗ No dogs

CLIPPESBY — Map 13 TG41

Places to visit

Fairhaven Woodland & Water Garden, SOUTH WALSHAM, NR13 6DZ, 01603 270449, www.fairhavengarden.co.uk

Caister Roman Fort, CAISTER-ON-SEA, NR30 5RN, 0370 333 1181
www.english-heritage.org.uk/visit/places/caister-roman-fort

REGIONAL WINNER – HEART OF ENGLAND
AA CAMPSITE OF THE YEAR 2020

Platinum Park

Clippesby Hall
►►►►►

tel: 01493 367800 **Hall Lane NR29 3BL**
email: holidays@clippesby.com **web:** www.clippesbyhall.com
dir: From A47 follow tourist signs for The Broads. At Acle roundabout take A1064, in 2 miles left onto B1152, 0.5 mile left opposite village sign, site 400 yards on right.

A lovely country house estate with secluded pitches hidden among the trees or in sheltered sunny glades – guests can expect spacious pitches and good privacy. The toilet facilities, appointed to a very good standard, provide a wide choice of cubicles. New for 2019 is the fabulous 'Basecamp' amenity area, replete with new-look reception, a stylish bar and café area, and a well-stocked mini-market. Excellent hardstanding pitches are available as the park is open all year. There are pine lodges, cottages and four new shepherd's huts for holiday lets.

Open: All year (restricted service: November to March – coffee shop, bar and restaurant closed) **Last arrival:** 17.30 **Last departure:** 11.00
Pitches: 🚐 �30 ⚠; 41 hardstanding pitches
Leisure: 🏊 ⚠ ⚽ ⚓ 🏌 🎵 ⚽
Facilities: 🛁 ⊙ ℱ ✳ ♿ ⑤ ⊞ 🚿 📶
Services: 🔌 🔋 🔲 🍴 ⬛ 🛒 🛗 🔒 🐕 Ⓣ
Within 3 miles: ⚲ ⛳ ∪ ◎ ⛸ ⚓

Additional site information: 30 acre site. 🐕 Cars can be parked by caravans and tents. Awnings permitted. No groups, no noise after 23.00, no camp fires. Table tennis, cycle trail.

CROMER — Map 13 TG24

Places to visit

RNLI Henry Blogg Museum, CROMER, NR27 9ET, 01263 511294
www.rnli.org/henryblogg

Felbrigg Hall, FELBRIGG, NR11 8PR, 01263 837444
www.nationaltrust.org.uk/felbrigg-hall

Forest Park
►►►► 84%

tel: 01263 513290 **Northrepps Road NR27 0JR**
email: info@forest-park.co.uk **web:** www.forest-park.co.uk
dir: A140 from Norwich, left at T-junction signed Cromer, right signed Northrepps, right then immediately left, left at T-junction, site on right.

Surrounded by forest, this gently sloping park offers a wide choice of pitches. Visitors have the use of a heated indoor swimming pool, a stylish café and a large clubhouse which provides entertainment. Glamping options include wooden wigwams, some with en suite facilities, and a shepherd's hut in its own enclosed area.

Open: 15 March to 15 January **Last arrival:** 21.00 **Last departure:** 11.00
Pitches: 🚐 �30 ⚠ 🏠; 5 hardstanding pitches
Leisure: 🏊 ⚠ 🎵
Facilities: 🛁 ⊙ ℱ ✳ ♿ ⑤ 🚿 📶
Services: 🔌 🔋 🔲 🍴 ⬛ 🛒 🛗 🔒 🐕 Ⓣ
Within 3 miles: ⚲ ⛳ ◎ ⛸ ⚓ 🎾

Additional site information: 100 acre site. 🐕 Cars can be parked by caravans and tents. Awnings permitted. Freshly baked bread and croissants available. Woodland walk.

Glamping available: Wooden wigwams. **Changeover days:** Any day

Additional glamping information: Wooden wigwams: very short walk to dedicated car park.

Manor Farm Caravan & Camping Site
►►►► 83%

tel: 01263 512858 **East Runton NR27 9PR**
email: stay@manorfarmcampsite.co.uk **web:** www.manorfarmcaravansite.co.uk
dir: 1 mile west of Cromer, exit A148 or A149 (recommended towing route) at Manor Farm sign.

A well-established family-run site on a working farm enjoying panoramic sea views. There are good modern facilities across the site, including three smart toilet blocks that include two quality family rooms and privacy cubicles, two good play areas and a large expanse of grass for games – the park is very popular with families. Care must be taken on approaching the site, which is along a 0.5 mile long farm track; if required, please ask for directions from reception.

Open: Easter to September **Last arrival:** 20.30 **Last departure:** noon
Pitches: * 🚐 from £15.50; �30 from £15.50; ⚠ from £15.50 **Leisure:** ⚠ 🎾 ⚽
Facilities: 🛁 ⊙ ✳ ♿
Services: 🔌 🔋 🛗 🔒 🐕
Within 3 miles: ⚲ ⛳ ◎ ⛸ 🎾 ⑤

Additional site information: 17 acre site. 🐕 Cars can be parked by caravans and tents. Awnings permitted. No groups, no noise after 23.00. 1 dog-free field available.

LEISURE: 🏊 Indoor swimming pool 🏊 Outdoor swimming pool ⚠ Children's playground 🧒 Kids' club 🎾 Tennis court ⚲ Games room ⬜ Separate TV room ⚲ Golf course ⛳ Pitch n putt ⚓ Boats for hire 🚲 Bikes for hire 🎬 Cinema 🎵 Entertainment 🎣 Fishing ◎ Mini golf 🤿 Watersports 💪 Gym ⚽ Sports field ∪ Stables
FACILITIES: 🛁 Baths/Shower ⊙ Electric shaver sockets ℱ Hairdryer ✳ Ice Pack Facility 🚿 Baby facilities ♿ Disabled facilities ⑤ Shop on site or within 200yds 🍴 BBQ area 🔲 Picnic area 📶 WiFi

DOWNHAM MARKET
Map 12 TF60

Places to visit

WWT Welney Wetland Centre, WELNEY, PE14 9TN, 01353 860711
www.wwt.org.uk/welney

Oxburgh Hall, OXBOROUGH, PE33 9PS, 01366 328258
www.nationaltrust.org.uk/oxburgh-hall

Lakeside Caravan Park & Fisheries
►►►► 83%

tel: 01366 383491 & 387074 **Sluice Rd, Denver PE38 0DZ**
email: bookings@westhallfarmholidays.co.uk **web:** www.westhallfarmholidays.co.uk
dir: *Exit A10 towards Denver, follow signs to Denver Windmill, site on right.*

A peaceful park set around five pretty fishing lakes. There are several grassy touring areas which are sheltered by mature hedging and trees, a function room for social get-togethers, a shop, laundry and children's play area. Electric hook-up pitches are available and rallies are welcome.

Open: All year (restricted service: October to March) **Last arrival:** 21.00
Last departure: 10.30

Pitches: 🚐 🚍 ⚊

Leisure: ⚐ ✎
Facilities: 🖼 ☉ ⌒ ☼ ♿ ⑤ 🎌 **WiFi**
Services: 🔌 ⑤ 🛒 🛢 ⌀ T
Within 3 miles: ⚓ ≋ ⚘

Additional site information: 30 acre site. 🐕 Cars can be parked by caravans and tents. Awnings permitted. No noise after 23.00. Fishing tackle and bait, caravan accessories, caravan storage. Newspapers, bread and milk available.

FAKENHAM
Map 13 TF92

Places to visit

Houghton Hall & Gardens, HOUGHTON, PE31 6UE, 01485 528569
www.houghtonhall.com

Great for kids: Pensthorpe Natural Park, FAKENHAM, NR21 0LN, 01328 851465
www.pensthorpe.co.uk

Caravan Club M.V.C. Site
►►► 84%

tel: 01328 862388 **Fakenham Racecourse NR21 7NY**
email: caravan@fakenhamracecourse.co.uk **web:** www.fakenhamracecourse.co.uk
dir: *From B1146, south of Fakenham follow brown Racecourse signs (with tent and caravan symbols) leads to site entrance.*

A very well laid-out site set around the racecourse, with a grandstand offering smart, modern toilet facilities. Tourers move to the centre of the course on race days, and enjoy free racing, and there's a wide range of sporting activities in the club house.

Open: All year **Last arrival:** 21.00 **Last departure:** noon

Pitches: * 🚐 from £19.50; 🚍 from £19.50; ⚊ from £9; 25 hardstanding pitches; 22 seasonal pitches

Leisure: ⚑ ⚓
Facilities: 🖼 ☉ ⌒ ☼ ♿ ⑤ 🎌 **WiFi**
Services: 🔌 ⑤ 🛒 🍴 ⚒ 🛢 ⌀ T
Within 3 miles: ✎ ⊟

Additional site information: 11.4 acre site. 🐕 Maximum 2 dogs per pitch. Cars can be parked by caravans and tents. Awnings permitted. TV aerial hook-ups.

GREAT YARMOUTH — Map 13 TG50

Places to visit

Time and Tide Museum of Great Yarmouth Life, GREAT YARMOUTH, NR30 3BX, 01493 743930
www.museums.norfolk.gov.uk/time-tide

Great for kids: Sea Life Great Yarmouth, GREAT YARMOUTH, NR30 3AH, 01493 330631
www.visitsealife.com/great-yarmouth

Premier Park

Seashore Holiday Park
▶▶▶▶▶ 88% HOLIDAY HOME PARK

tel: 01493 851131 **North Denes NR30 4HG**
email: seashore@haven.com **web:** www.haven.com/seashore
dir: *A149 from Great Yarmouth to Caister. Right at 2nd lights signed seafront and racecourse. Continue to sea, turn left. Park on left.*

Bordered by sand dunes and with direct access to a sandy beach, Seashore Holiday Park is located in Great Yarmouth with easy access to the peaceful Norfolk Broads. Facilities include excellent water activities, with the swimming pool upgraded for 2019, bike hire for children and lively evening entertainment for adults. There is a good range of holiday homes for hire to suit both couples and families. New facilities, the Coast House Bar and Grill and the adjoining Cakery, were opened in 2019.

Open: mid March to end October

Holiday Homes: Sleep 8 Bedrooms 3 Bathrooms 1 Toilet 1 Two-ring burner Microwave Freezer TV Sky/Freeview WiFi

Changeover days: Friday, Monday

Leisure: 🏊 🎠 🧑‍🤝‍🧑 🎾 🎵 ⚽

Facilities: 🚿 💲 WiFi

Within 3 miles: 🎣 ⛳ ◎ 🎡

Additional site information: The facilities provided in the holiday homes may differ depending on the grade. 🐕 Most dog breeds accepted (please check when booking). Dogs must be kept on leads at all times.

The Grange Touring Park
▶▶▶▶ 81%

tel: 01493 730306 & 730023 **Yarmouth Road, Ormesby St Margaret NR29 3QG**
email: info@grangetouring.co.uk **web:** www.grangetouring.co.uk
dir: *From A149, 3 miles north of Great Yarmouth. Site at junction of A149 and B1159, signed.*

A mature park with a stunning display of shrubs and trees, located just one mile from the sea and within easy reach of both coastal attractions and the Norfolk Broads. The level pitches have WiFi and electric hook-ups and include hardstanding pitches. There are clean toilets including three spacious family rooms, and an electric car charging point.

Open: Easter to October **Last arrival:** 21.00 **Last departure:** 14.00

Pitches: 🚐 �caravan 🏕; 7 hardstanding pitches; 2 seasonal pitches

Leisure: 🎠

Facilities: 🚿 ☉ 🗞 ❄ 🚿 WiFi

Services: 🔌 🗄 🍽 🚿 🪣 🛒 🌿

Within 3 miles: 🎣 ⛳ ⛲ ◎ 💲

Additional site information: 3.5 acre site. 🐕 Cars can be parked by caravans and tents. Awnings permitted. No football, no open fires. Table tennis, bar/restaurant adjoining.

HOPTON ON SEA — Map 13 TM59

Places to visit

St Olave's Priory, ST OLAVES, NR31 9HE, 0370 333 1181
www.english-heritage.org.uk/visit/places/st-olaves-priory

Premier Park

Hopton Holiday Village
▶▶▶▶▶ 94% HOLIDAY HOME PARK

tel: 01502 730214 **NR31 9BW**
email: hopton@haven.com **web:** www.haven.com/hopton
dir: *Site signed from A47 between Great Yarmouth and Lowestoft.*

Located between Lowestoft and Great Yarmouth, close to beaches and the town attractions, this lively holiday park offers excellent sport activities, including a 9-hole golf course and tennis coaching, plus popular evening entertainment in the form of shows, music and dancing. A wide range of quality holiday homes is available for letting.

Open: mid March to 30 October

Holiday Homes: Sleep 8 Bedrooms 2 Bathrooms 1 Toilet 1 Microwave Freezer TV Sky/Freeview

Prices: Low season from £79

Changeover days: Monday, Friday, Saturday

Leisure: 🏊 🏊 🎠 🧑‍🤝‍🧑 🎾 🎣 🎵

Facilities: 🚿 💲 🛍 🚐 WiFi

Within 3 miles: ◎ 🎡

Additional site information: The facilities provided in the holiday homes may differ depending on the grade. 🐕 Most dog breeds accepted (please check when booking). Dogs must be kept on leads at all times.

LEISURE: 🏊 Indoor swimming pool 🏊 Outdoor swimming pool 🎠 Children's playground 🧑‍🤝‍🧑 Kids' club 🎾 Tennis court 🎱 Games room 📺 Separate TV room 🎣 Golf course 🏌 Pitch n putt ⛵ Boats for hire 🚲 Bikes for hire 🎬 Cinema 🎵 Entertainment 🎣 Fishing ◎ Mini golf 🌊 Watersports 💪 Gym ⚽ Sports field ⛲ Stables
FACILITIES: 🚿 Baths/Shower ☉ Electric shaver sockets 💈 Hairdryer ❄ Ice Pack Facility 🚼 Baby facilities ♿ Disabled facilities 💲 Shop on site or within 200yds 🍖 BBQ area 🪑 Picnic area WiFi WiFi

HUNSTANTON   Map 12 TF64

Places to visit

Lynn Museum, KING'S LYNN, PE30 1NL, 01553 775001
www.museums.norfolk.gov.uk/lynn-museum

Norfolk Lavender, HEACHAM, PE31 7JE, 01485 570384
www.norfolk-lavender.co.uk

Great for kids: Hunstanton Sea Life Sanctuary, HUNSTANTON, PE36 5BH,
01485 533576
www.visitsealife.com/hunstanton

Premier Park

Searles Leisure Resort

▶▶▶▶▶ **93%** HOLIDAY CENTRE

tel: 01485 534211 **South Beach Road PE36 5BB**
email: bookings@searles.co.uk **web:** www.searles.co.uk
dir: *A149 from King's Lynn to Hunstanton. At roundabout follow signs for South Beach. Straight on at 2nd roundabout. Site on left.*

A large seaside holiday complex with well managed facilities, adjacent to sea and beach. The tourers have their own areas, including two excellent toilet blocks, and pitches are individually marked by small maturing shrubs for privacy. A wide range of food options is available from takeaway choices to more formal dining and wide ranging indoor and outdoor activities include a full entertainment programme for all ages.

Open: All year (restricted service: December to March (except February half term) – limited facilities. Outdoor pool open May to September only)

Pitches: * 🚐 from £15; 🚍 from £15; ▲ from £15; 🏠 see prices below; 91 hardstanding pitches

Leisure: 🏊 🏊 🎱 🛶 🎣 🔍 ⛳ 🎶 🎿 🎯 ⚽

Facilities: 🚿 ❄ ⚷ 🏧 🍴 🚻 WiFi

Services: 🔌 🔋 🍺 🍴 🛒 ⚓ 🔌 🛢 ⊘ T

Within 3 miles: ∪ ◎ 🛶

Additional site information: 50 acre site. 🐕 Restrictions on certain dog breeds (contact site for details).

Glamping available: Wooden pods from £24.

Additional glamping information: Cars can be parked by units

KING'S LYNN   Map 12 TF62

See also Stanhoe

Places to visit

Bircham Windmill, GREAT BIRCHAM, PE31 6SJ, 01485 578393
www.birchamwindmill.co.uk

Castle Rising Castle, CASTLE RISING, PE31 6AH, 01553 631330
www.english-heritage.org.uk/visit/places/castle-rising-castle

Premier Park

King's Lynn Caravan and Camping Park

▶▶▶▶▶ 86%

tel: 01553 840004 **New Road, North Runcton PE33 0RA**
email: klcc@btconnect.com **web:** www.kl-cc.co.uk
dir: *From King's Lynn take A47 signed Swaffham and Norwich, in 1.5 miles turn right signed North Runcton. Site 100 yards on left.*

Set in approximately 10 acres of parkland, this developing camping park is situated on the edge of North Runcton, just a few miles south of the historic town of King's Lynn. The three very extensive touring fields are equipped with 150 electric hook-ups and one field is reserved for rallies. There is an eco-friendly toilet block which is powered by solar panels and an air-sourced heat pump which also recycles rainwater – this in itself proves a source of great interest to visitors. There are eight high quality camping pods and 14 superb pine lodges for hire.

Open: All year **Last arrival:** flexible **Last departure:** flexible

Pitches: 🚐 from £15; 🚍 from £15; ▲ from £12 🏠; 12 hardstanding pitches; 54 seasonal pitches

Leisure: 🎿 ⧠

Facilities: 🚿 ☺ ⚷ ❄ ⚷ � WiFi

Services: 🔌 🔋 🍴 🛒 ⚓ 🛢 ⊘ T

Within 3 miles: 🎣 ⛳ ∪ 🛶

Additional site information: 9 acre site. 🐕 Cars can be parked by caravans and tents. Awnings permitted. No skateboards or fires.

Glamping available: Wooden pods.

Additional glamping information: No smoking in wooden pods; no dogs in wooden pods.

PITCHES: 🚐 Caravans 🚍 Motorhomes ▲ Tents 🏠 Glamping accommodation **SERVICES:** 🔌 Electric hook-up 🔋 Launderette 🍺 Licensed bar 🛢 Calor Gas ⊘ Campingaz T Toilet fluid 🍴 Café/Restaurant 🚚 Fast Food/Takeaway ⚓ Battery charging ⚡ Motorhome service point * 2019 prices 🚫 No credit or debit cards 🐕 Dogs permitted 🚫 No dogs

NORTH WALSHAM   Map 13 TG23

Places to visit

Blickling Estate, BLICKLING, NR11 6NF, 01263 738030
www.nationaltrust.org.uk/blickling

Mannington Gardens, SAXTHORPE, NR11 7BB, 01263 584175
www.manningtongardens.co.uk

Premier Park

Two Mills Touring Park
▶▶▶▶▶ 88%

tel: 01692 405829 **Yarmouth Road NR28 9NA**
email: enquiries@twomills.co.uk **web:** www.twomills.co.uk
dir: *In North Walsham at lights on A149 follow Norwich sign into Norwich Road. At mini-roundabout, right into Grammar School Road. At mini-roundabout (Lidl supermarket opposite) right into Yarmouth Road. Site on left in approximately 1 mile (after police station and hospital).*

An intimate, beautifully presented park set in superb countryside in a peaceful, rural spot, which is also convenient for touring. The 'Top Acre' section is maturing and features fully serviced pitches with panoramic views over the site, an immaculate toilet block and good planting, plus the layout of pitches and facilities is excellent. A cabin-style building houses a fully-equipped disabled room. The very friendly owners keep the park in immaculate condition. Please note, this park is for adults only.

Open: March to 3 January **Last arrival:** 18.00 **Last departure:** noon

Pitches: * 🚐 from £21.95; 🚐 from £21.95; ▲ from £21.95;
81 hardstanding pitches; 30 seasonal pitches

Facilities: 🛁 ⊙ 🌀 ✳ ⅙ ⑤ 🎋 WiFi

Services: ⊕ 🔄 🛒 ⅏ 🔒 🥗 T

Within 3 miles: ✐

Additional site information: 7 acre site. Adults only. 🐾 Cars can be parked by caravans and tents. Awnings permitted. Maximum 2 dogs per pitch. Library, DVDs, tea and coffee facilities.

SCRATBY

Places to visit

Time and Tide Museum of Great Yarmouth Life, GREAT YARMOUTH, NR30 3BX, 01493 743930
www.museums.norfolk.gov.uk/time-tide

Great for kids: Caister Roman Fort, CAISTER-ON-SEA, NR30 5RN, 0370 333 1181
www.english-heritage.org.uk/visit/places/caister-roman-fort

SCRATBY   Map 13 TG51

Scratby Hall Caravan Park
▶▶▶▶ 86%

tel: 01493 730283 **NR29 3SR**
email: scratbyhall@aol.com **web:** www.scratbyhall.co.uk
dir: *5 miles north of Great Yarmouth. Exit A149 onto B1159, site signed.*

A beautifully maintained park situated on former gardens and farmland with high wall or hedge surroundings to improve privacy and wind resistance. The well-spaced lush grass pitches include many with full services, and the amenity block includes unisex shower toilet and washbasin rooms. The park also benefits from a well-stocked shop, popular children's play area and outdoor swimming pool.

Open: Easter to end September (restricted service: Easter to 3rd week July and September — pool closed; shop hours reduced outside peak season) **Last arrival:** 21.00 **Last departure:** noon

Pitches: * 🚐 from £11; 🚐 from £11; ▲ from £11

Leisure: ⩊ ⅏

Facilities: 🛁 ⊙ 🌀 ✳ ⅙ ⑤ WiFi

Services: ⊕ 🔄 🛒 🔒 🥗 T

Within 3 miles: ⅃ ✐ ⅂ ⅎ

Additional site information: 5 acre site. 🐾 Cars can be parked by caravans and tents. Awnings permitted. No commercial vehicles, no noise after 23.00. Food preparation room, family/privacy bathroom.

STANHOE — Map 13 TF83

Places to visit

Norfolk Lavender, HEACHAM, PE31 7JE, 01485 570384
www.norfolk-lavender.co.uk

Walsingham Abbey Grounds & Shirehall Museum, LITTLE WALSINGHAM,
NR22 6BP, 01328 820510
www.walsinghamabbey.com

The Rickels Caravan & Camping Park
►►► 85%

tel: 01485 518671 **Bircham Road PE31 8PU**
email: therickelscaravanandcampingpark@hotmail.co.uk
dir: Take A149 (south of King's Lynn) signed Cromer (and A148). Right at roundabout onto A148 signed Fakenham and Cromer. Left on B1153 signed Flitcham and Great Bircham. In Great Bircham right onto B115 signed Stanhoe. At crossroads (junction with B1454) straight across (Stanhoe). Site on left.

Set in three acres of grassland, with sweeping country views this adults-only park has a pleasant, relaxing atmosphere. The meticulously maintained grounds and facilities are part of the attraction, and the slightly sloping land has some level areas and sheltering for tents. A field is available to hire for rallies.

Open: All year **Last arrival:** 21.00 **Last departure:** 11.00
Pitches: * ♠ from £16; ♠ from £16; ▲ from £12
Leisure: ▭
Facilities: ▭ ☉ ☼ WiFi
Services: ♠ ▢ ▰ ▪ ∅
Within 3 miles: ⌔ ⑤
Additional site information: 3 acre site. Adults only. ✚ ⊛ Cars can be parked by caravans and tents. Awnings permitted. No groundsheets.

SWAFFHAM

Places to visit

Gressenhall Farm and Workhouse, GRESSENHALL, NR20 4DR, 01362 869263
www.museums.norfolk.gov.uk/Gressenhall

Castle Acre Priory, CASTLE ACRE, PE32 2XD, 01760 755394
www.english-heritage.org.uk/visit/places/castle-acre-castle-acre-priory

SWAFFHAM — Map 13 TF80

Breckland Meadows Touring Park
►►►► 83%

tel: 01760 721246 **Lynn Road PE37 7PT**
email: info@brecklandmeadows.co.uk **web:** www.brecklandmeadows.co.uk
dir: In Swaffham from A1065 northbound at lights turn into Lynn Street (pass Asda on left, petrol station on right). Site on right in approximately 1 mile. Or from A47 eastbound: follow Swaffham sign. Site on left in 0.75 mile after Swaffham village sign. Or from A47 westbound, at roundabout (east of Swaffham) left signed Norwich Road. Straight on at lights in Swaffham centre into Lynn Street (pass Asda on left, petrol station on right). Site on right in approximately 1 mile.

An immaculate, well-landscaped little park on the edge of Swaffham. The toilet block is a very impressive facility, replete with quality fixtures and fittings, spacious cubicles, including a family and disabled room, a large, well-equipped laundry, and a high tech, and very efficient, hot water system. Planned planting creates optimum privacy and the hardstandings are particularly spacious. Leading directly from the site is Swaefas Way, a pleasant walk with, or without, a dog.

Open: All year **Last arrival:** 19.00 **Last departure:** noon
Pitches: ♠ ♠ ▲; 35 hardstanding pitches; 5 seasonal pitches
Facilities: ▭ ☉ ☼ ⑤ ▪ ⌗ WiFi
Services: ♠ ▢ ▰ ▪ ∅ ⓣ
Within 3 miles: ⌔ ⌔
Additional site information: 3 acre site. Adults only. ✚ Dogs must be on leads at all times and exercised off site. Newspaper deliveries. Cars can be parked by caravans and tents. Awnings permitted.

SYDERSTONE — Map 13 TF83

Places to visit

Creake Abbey, NORTH CREAKE, NR21 9LF, 0370 333 1181
www.english-heritage.org.uk/visit/places/creake-abbey

The Garden Caravan Site
►►► 80%

tel: 07788 438968 **Barmer Hall Farm PE31 8SR**
email: nlmason@tiscali.co.uk **web:** www.gardencaravansite.co.uk
dir: Signed from B1454 at Barmer between A148 and Docking, 1 mile north of Syderstone.

In the tranquil setting of a former walled garden beside a large farmhouse, with mature trees and shrubs, this is a secluded site surrounded by woodland. The site is run mainly on trust, with a daily notice indicating which pitches are available, and an honesty box for basic foods. An ideal site for the discerning camper, and well placed for touring north Norfolk.

Open: March to November **Last arrival:** 21.00 **Last departure:** noon
Pitches: ♠ ♠ ▲
Facilities: ▭ ☉ ⌗ ☼ ⌗
Services: ♠ ▰ ⌔ ▪
Within 3 miles: ⌔ ◎ ⊟ ⑤
Additional site information: 3.5 acre site. ✚ Maximum 2 dogs per pitch. ⊛ Cars can be parked by caravans and tents. Awnings permitted. Maximum tent width 5 metres. Cold drinks, ice creams and eggs available.

NORTHAMPTONSHIRE

BULWICK
Map 11 SP99

Places to visit

Kirby Hall, DEENE, NN17 3EN, 01536 203230
www.english-heritage.org.uk/visit/places/kirby-hall

Deene Park, DEENE, NN17 3EW, 01780 450 278
www.deenepark.com

Great for kids: Nene Valley Railway, WANSFORD, PE8 6LR, 01780 784444
www.nvr.org.uk

Premier Park

New Lodge Farm Caravan & Camping Site
▶▶▶▶▶ 86%

tel: 01780 450493 **New Lodge Farm NN17 3DU**
email: shop@newlodgefarm.com **web:** www.newlodgefarm.com
dir: *On A43 between Corby (5 miles) and Stamford (8 miles) turn right at Laxton and Harringworth junction. Site signed.*

Simon and Sarah Singlehurst have worked hard to create this beautiful adults-only site on their working farm in rural Northamptonshire. The result is impressive – large, fully serviced and level pitches (26 with hardstandings), all with views over the farm and rolling countryside. The heated toilet and amenity block is located in a beautifully restored stone barn, as is the site reception. There's an award-winning farm shop that sells home-reared meats, bread, cakes and locally grown fruit and vegetables. Attached to the shop is a cosy licensed café with a patio area overlooking the site – here breakfasts, lunches and afternoon teas are served. Nobbies Nook is a landscaped riverside chill-out area. The site is situated in the heart of Rockingham Forest, making this a good base for visiting Stamford, Oundle and Uppingham.

Open: 13 March to 31 October **Last arrival:** 20.00 **Last departure:** noon

Pitches: 🚐 🚏 ▲ 🏠; 26 hardstanding pitches; 10 seasonal pitches

Facilities: 🛁 ⊙ 🗭 ✳ 🔥 ⓢ 🍴 🛋 WiFi

Services: 🔌 🗑 🛒 🍴 🏧 🛒 ⬆ 🛢 🧽 🆃

Within 3 miles: ⚘ 🎣 ∪

Additional site information: 4 acre site. Adults only. 🐾 Cars can be parked by caravans and tents. Awnings permitted. No noise after 23.00. Farm shop and butchery. Car hire can be arranged.

Glamping available: 2 wooden pods.

Additional glamping information: Sleep 2. No dogs permitted. Wet room includes toilet, shower and basin. Guests to supply own towels and bedding.

NORTHUMBERLAND

BAMBURGH
Map 21 NU13

Places to visit

Chillingham Wild Cattle Park, CHILLINGHAM, NE66 5NP, 01668 215250
www.chillinghamwildcattle.com

Bamburgh Castle, BAMBURGH, NE69 7DF, 01668 214208
www.bamburghcastle.com

Great for kids: Alnwick Castle, ALNWICK, NE66 1NG, 01665 511100
www.alnwickcastle.com

Waren Caravan & Camping Park
▶▶▶▶ 91%

tel: 01668 214366 & 214224 **Waren Mill NE70 7EE**
email: waren@meadowhead.co.uk **web:** www.meadowhead.co.uk
dir: *2 miles east of town. From A1 onto B1342 signed Bamburgh. Take unclassified road past Waren Mill, signed Budle.*

An especially attractive, family- and dog-friendly park sheltered within the grassy embankments of a former quarry and with truly stunning sea views over the beautiful Burdle Bay. As well as a footpath leading to the sandy beach there are excellent walking and cycling opportunities in the surrounding area. The park offers excellent facilities – fully serviced pitches, an on-site restaurant serving a good breakfast and smartened up toilet and shower blocks, which include several family bathrooms. There are also wooden wigwams for hire.

Open: March to October (restricted service: March to Spring Bank Holiday and October – splash pool closed) **Last arrival:** 20.00 **Last departure:** noon

Pitches: 🚐 from £15.30; 🚏 from £15.30; ▲ from £10.94; 🏠 see prices below; 41 hardstanding pitches

Leisure: 🏊 🎠 🎣 🎵 ☼

Facilities: 🛁 ⊙ 🗭 ✳ 🔥 ⓢ 🍴 🛋 🐾 WiFi

Services: 🔌 🗑 🛒 🍴 🏧 🛒 ⬆ 🛢 🧽 🆃

Within 3 miles: ⚘ 🎣 ∪ ◎ 🏊

Additional site information: 4 acre site. 🐾 Cars can be parked by caravans and tents. Awnings permitted. No noise after 23.00. 100 acres of private heathland. Fire pits for hire, BBQ hut for hire, freshly baked bread available. Car hire can be arranged.

Glamping available: Wooden wigwams from £15.50. **Changeover days:** Any day

Additional glamping information: Wooden wigwams sleep 5. Cars can be parked by units

Glororum Caravan Park

▶▶▶▶ 90%

tel: 01670 860256 **Glororum Farm NE69 7AW**
email: enquiries@northumbrianleisure.co.uk **web:** www.northumbrianleisure.co.uk
dir: *Exit A1 at junction with B1341 (Purdy's Lodge). In 3.5 miles left onto unclassified road. Site 300 yards on left.*

Glororum Caravan Park continues to go from strength to strength following serious recent investment in the amenities and the infrastructure across the park. Pleasantly situated in open countryside the park offers good views of Bamburgh Castle. A popular holiday destination where tourers have their own separate area — 43 excellent, well-spaced, fully serviced pitches have a lush grass area in addition to the hardstanding. This field also has an excellent purpose-built amenity block with a smartly clad interior and modern, efficient fittings. Children will love the new modern play area.

Open: March to end November **Last arrival:** 18.00 **Last departure:** noon

Pitches: ⊕ ⇔; 43 hardstanding pitches; 30 seasonal pitches

Leisure: ⊕ ⋀

Facilities: ⊙ ℱ ⋇ ⅙ ⑤ ⊓

Services: ⊕ ⑤ ⊘ ⊤

Within 3 miles: ↓ ⌇ ∪ ⇞ ⋇

Additional site information: 6 acre site. ➤ Cars can be parked by caravans. Awnings permitted. No commercial vehicles, no noise after 23.00.

BELFORD

Places to visit

Bamburgh Castle, BAMBURGH, NE69 7DF, 01668 214208
www.bamburghcastle.com

Lindisfarne Castle, HOLY ISLAND [LINDISFARNE], TD15 2SH, 01289 389244
www.nationaltrust.org.uk/lindisfarne-castle

Great for kids: Alnwick Castle, ALNWICK, NE66 1NG, 01665 511100
www.alnwickcastle.com

BELFORD
Map 21 NU13

Platinum Park

South Meadows Caravan Park

▶▶▶▶▶

tel: 01668 213326 **South Road NE70 7DP**
email: info@southmeadows.co.uk **web:** www.southmeadows.co.uk
dir: *From A1 between Alnwick and Berwick-upon-Tweed take B6349 towards Belford, at right bend site signed, turn left, site on right.*

An excellent, justifiably very popular site that is ideally situated to exploit the many beauties and attractions of the nearby Northumbrian coast. It is set in open countryside with generous, very well laid out pitches set amongst attractive newly-planted beech hedging. There is a great adventure playground for children of all ages and even two very good dog walks on site, one through bluebell woodland. A first class toilet block was added in 2018, beside increased numbers of touring pitches, and investment in the park continues to impress.

Open: All year **Last departure:** 16.00

Pitches: * ⊕ from £19.75; ⇔ from £19.75; ⋏ from £19.75; ⋒ see prices below; 57 hardstanding pitches; 65 seasonal pitches

Leisure: ⋀ ⊕

Facilities: ⊡ ⊙ ℱ ⋇ ⅙ ⑤ ⊟ ⊓ WiFi

Services: ⊕ ⑤ ⊑ ⊻ ⬛ ⊘ ⊤

Within 3 miles: ↓ ∪

Additional site information: 50 acre site. ➤ Cars can be parked by caravans and tents. Awnings permitted. Minimum noise after 23.00, under 12s must be supervised in toilet blocks. Woodland walk, football and recreation field.

Glamping available: 5 wooden pods from £65 per night.

Additional glamping information: Pods sleep up to 4 adults or 2/3 adults + 2/3 children. 5 people maximum per pod. Fully equipped including BBQ. Must bring own bedding. 1 dog allowed per pod. Cars can be parked by units

---

BELLINGHAM · Map 21 NY88

Places to visit

Wallington, CAMBO, NE61 4AR, 01670 773600
www.nationaltrust.org.uk/wallington

Premier Park

Bellingham Camping & Caravanning Club Site
▶▶▶▶▶ 90%

tel: 01434 220175 & 024 7647 5426 **Brown Rigg NE48 2JY**
email: bellingham.site@campingandcaravanningclub.co.uk
web: www.campingandcaravanningclub.co.uk/bellingham
dir: From A69 take A6079 north to Chollerford and B6320 to Bellingham. Pass Forestry Commission land, site 0.5 mile south of Bellingham.

A beautiful and peaceful campsite set in the glorious Northumberland National Park. It is exceptionally well managed by the enthusiastic owners who offer high levels of customer care, maintenance and cleanliness. The excellent toilet facilities are spotlessly clean, and there are family washrooms, a recreation room, a campers' kitchen, a drying room, and star-gazing equipment for customers to use. There are four camping pods for hire. This is a perfect base for exploring an undiscovered part of England, and it is handily placed for visiting the beautiful Northumberland coast.

Open: March to 4 January **Last arrival:** 20.00 **Last departure:** noon

Pitches: 🚐 � 🅰; 🏠 see prices below; 42 hardstanding pitches

Leisure: 🎡 🎣 🖵

Facilities: 🚿 ⊙ 🝙 ✳ ⅙ ⑤ 🎍 📶

Services: 🔌 ⑤ 🚽 ⇞ 🛢 🥗 🗊

Within 3 miles: 🏌 🖋

Additional site information: 5 acre site. 🐾 Cars can be parked by caravans and tents. Awnings permitted. Site gates closed and quiet time from 23.00–07.00. BBQ's allowed, no open fires. Only accept septic tank soft (green) toilet fluids. Communal modern fitted kitchen, central heated indoor social space, drying room.

Glamping available: Wooden pods from £45.

Additional glamping information: Wooden pods: minimum stay 2 nights, sleeps either 3 adults or 2 adults and 2 children. Pods are well insulated and carpeted with electric heating and lighting. They have no fixed beds. Pods have no electric sockets but there are plenty in the indoor social space and kitchen. Deals available for selected stays.

BERWICK-UPON-TWEED

Places to visit

Berwick-upon-Tweed Barracks, BERWICK-UPON-TWEED, TD15 1DF, 01289 304493
www.english-heritage.org.uk/visit/places/berwick-upon-tweed-barracks-and-main-guard

BERWICK-UPON-TWEED · Map 21 NT95

Premier Park

Ord House Country Park
▶▶▶▶▶ 92%

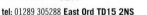

tel: 01289 305288 **East Ord TD15 2NS**
email: enquiries@ordhouse.co.uk **web:** www.maguirescountryparks.co.uk
dir: From A1 (Berwick bypass), or from A698, at roundabout (south of River Tweed) follow East Ord sign, then brown site signs.

Set within the grounds of 18th-century Ord House, this very well-run park takes great pride in the quality of its landscaping and in the siting and spacing of touring pitches, some of which are fully serviced. The newly refurbished toilet blocks are truly superb. Youngsters are well catered for with a fantastic adventure playground, mini golf and a football field. A broad range of meals is available in Maguires Bar & Grill where there is also a soft toy play area for children. Wooden wishbone lodges, each sleeping four, are available for hire.

Open: All year **Last arrival:** 23.00 **Last departure:** noon

Pitches: * 🚐 from £23; � from £23; 🅰 from £15; 🏠 see price below; 46 hardstanding pitches; 30 seasonal pitches

Leisure: 🎣 🎡 **Facilities:** 🚿 ⊙ 🝙 ✳ ⅙ ⑤ 🎍 📶

Services: 🔌 ⑤ 🚽 🍴 🍺 ⇞ 🛢 🥗 **Within 3 miles:** 🏌 🖋 ◎ ⚲ 📅

Additional site information: 42 acre site. 🐾 Cars can be parked by caravans and tents. Awnings permitted. No noise after 22.30. Crazy golf, table tennis, football field, soft play area, woodland walk.

Glamping available: Wooden wishbone lodges from £48.

Additional glamping information: Wishbone lodges include bunk beds, camp beds, electricity and heating. No group bookings. Cars can be parked by units.

Premier Park

Berwick Holiday Park
▶▶▶▶▶ 89% HOLIDAY HOME PARK

tel: 01289 307113 **Magdalene Fields TD15 1NE**
email: berwick@haven.com **web:** www.haven.com/berwick
dir: From A1 follow Berwick-upon-Tweed signs. At Morrisons/McDonalds roundabout take 2nd exit. At mini-roundabout straight on, into North Road (pass Shell garage on left). At next mini-roundabout 1st exit into Northumberland Avenue. Park at end.

A very friendly, welcoming static-only holiday park with excellent entertainment and leisure facilities for all ages, and with direct access to the beach on the edge of Berwick. Exciting family activities and entertainment include the FunWorks Amusement Centre, Nature Rockz and a multisports court. Everything here is of a high standard – the holiday homes, the landscaping and the facilities – customer feedback on their holiday experience is very positive.

Open: mid March to 30 October

Holiday Homes: Sleep 8 Bedrooms 2 Bathrooms 1 Toilet 1 Microwave Freezer TV Sky/Freeview DVD player Linen included Electricity included Gas included

Changeover days: Monday, Friday, Saturday

Leisure: 🏊 🏊 🎣 🎡 🏌 ⚽

Facilities: ⑤ 📶 **Within 3 miles:** ⑤

Additional site information: 🐾 The facilities provided in the holiday homes may differ depending on the grade. Most dog breeds accepted (please check when booking). Dogs must be kept on leads at all times.

Premier Park

Haggerston Castle Holiday Park

▶▶▶▶▶ 84% HOLIDAY CENTRE

tel: 01289 381333 **Beal TD15 2PA**
email: haggerstoncastle@haven.com **web:** www.haven.com/haggerstoncastle
dir: *On A1, 7 miles south of Berwick-upon-Tweed, site signed.*

A large holiday centre along with a touring park, offering comprehensive holiday activities. The entertainment complex contains amusements for the whole family, and there are several bars, an adventure playground, boating on the lake, a children's club, a 9-hole golf course, tennis courts, and various eating outlets. Please note that this site does not accept tents.

Open: mid March to end October (restricted service: mid March to May and September to October – some facilities may be reduced) **Last arrival:** anytime **Last departure:** 10.00

Pitches: 🚐 🚙; 140 hardstanding pitches

Leisure: 🏊 ⚲ ✋ 🎣 🏓 🎵 ✏ 🎯

Facilities: 🏪 ⊙ 🅿 ✳ 🖙 🖆 🍴 🚻 WiFi

Services: 🔌 🔘 🍺 🍽 🚮 🔧 🔒 🚾

Within 3 miles: ∪ ◎ 🎣

Additional site information: 100 acre site. 🐕 Maximum 2 dogs per booking, certain dog breeds banned. No commercial vehicles, no bookings by persons under 21 years unless a family booking.

Old Mill Caravan Site

▶▶ 80%

tel: 01289 381295 & 07791 976535 **West Kyloe Farm, Fenwick TD15 2PF**
email: info@westkyloe.co.uk **web:** www.westkyloe.co.uk
dir: *A1 onto B6353 (9 miles south of Berwick-upon-Tweed) signed Lowick and Fenwick. Site 1.5 miles signed on left.*

Small, secluded site accessed through a farm complex, and overlooking a mill pond complete with resident ducks. Some pitches are in a walled garden, and the amenity block is basic but well kept. Delightful walks can be enjoyed on the 600-acre farm. A holiday cottage is also available.

Open: April to October **Last arrival:** 19.00 **Last departure:** 11.00

Pitches: 🚐 from £20; 🚙 from £20; 🏕 from £15

Facilities: 🏪 ⊙ 🖙

Services: 🔌

Within 3 miles: ⓢ

Additional site information: 2.5 acre site. 🐕 🚫 Cars can be parked by caravans and tents. Awnings permitted. No gazebos or open fires. Wet room, farm walks (600 acres).

HALTWHISTLE Map 21 NY76

Places to visit

Corbridge Roman Town – Hadrian's Wall, CORBRIDGE, NE45 5NT, 01434 632349
www.english-heritage.org.uk/visit/places/corbridge-roman-town-hadrians-wall

Chesters Roman Fort, WALWICK, NE46 4EU, 01434 681379
www.english-heritage.org.uk/visit/places/chesters-roman-fort-and-museum-hadrians-wall

Premier Park

Herding Hill Farm Touring & Camping Site

▶▶▶▶▶ 90%

tel: 01434 320175 **Shield Hill NE49 9NW**
email: bookings@herdinghillfarm.co.uk **web:** www.herdinghillfarm.co.uk
dir: *A69 to Haltwhistle. Follow the brown campsite signs. If towing a caravan – from west: exit A69 at Greenhead onto B6318. Follow brown campsite signs, right at Milecastle Inn; from east: exit A69 at Corbridge onto A68 north, left onto B6318 towards Chollerford. Follow brown campsite signs, left at Milecastle Inn.*

In an idyllic moorland location above Haltwhistle, close to Hadrian's Wall, this beautifully developed working farm site is geared to families and offers a mix of accommodation – excellent tent pitches, quality hardstandings, a 6-berth lodge, and a glamping area. The upmarket amenity block is really ultra-modern – the internal red and grey partitioning really sets off the very high standard of fixtures and fittings, and the underfloor heating is very welcoming. A drying room, barbecues and fire baskets, a playground and petting farm, an excellent shop, and activities such as star-gazing, geocaching, and walking along Hadrian's Wall complete the package. This is a top-class site.

Open: All year. **Last arrival:** 20.00 (late arrival with prior arrangement) **Last departure:** noon

Pitches: 🚐 from £20; 🚙 from £20; 🏕 from £20; 13 hardstanding pitches

Leisure: ⚲

Facilities: 🏪 ⊙ 🅿 ✳ 🖙 🚿 🚻 WiFi

Services: 🔌 🔘 🚮 🔋 🔧 🔒 ⌀ 🚾

Within 3 miles: ⚲ ✏ ∪ ⓢ

Additional site information: 4.86 acre site. 🐕 Cars can be parked by caravans and tents. Awnings permitted. No noise after 22.30. Unisex sauna. Takeaway pizza Friday and Saturday in season. BBQ meat packs available. Dog walk.

PITCHES: 🚐 Caravans 🚙 Motorhomes 🏕 Tents 🏕 Glamping accommodation **SERVICES:** 🔌 Electric hook-up 🔘 Launderette 🍺 Licensed bar 🔋 Calor Gas ⌀ Campingaz 🚾 Toilet fluid 🍽 Café/Restaurant 🚮 Fast Food/Takeaway 🔋 Battery charging 🔧 Motorhome service point * 2019 prices 🚫 No credit or debit cards 🐕 Dogs permitted 🚫 No dogs

HALTWHISTLE *continued*

Premier Park

Herding Hill Farm, Glamping site
►►►►► 88% GLAMPING ONLY

tel: 01434 320175 **Shield Hill NE49 9NW**
email: bookings@herdinghillfarm.co.uk web: www.herdinghillfarm.co.uk
dir: *A69 to Haltwhistle. Follow the brown campsite signs. If towing a caravan – from west: exit A69 at Greenhead onto B6318. Follow brown campsite signs, right at Milecastle Inn; from east: exit A69 at Corbridge onto A68 north, left onto B6318 towards Chollerford. Follow brown campsite signs, left at Milecastle Inn.*

Located above the town of Haltwhistle and very close to Hadrian's Wall, this developing glamping site is ideally suited for walkers, ramblers and historians alike. Separate from the touring area at the bottom of the site on a rolling hillside, the wooden wigwams, tipis and Lotus Belle tents enjoy panoramic views. Each unit has electric heating and seven of the wigwams have their own toilet and washbasin; all units have full use of the modern amenity block located between the glamping and touring areas. Bedding is provided in the Lotus Belle tents only. BBQs and fire pits can be hired, and there is a sauna too.

Open: All year. **Last arrival:** 20.00 **Last departure:** 10.00

Leisure: /A\

Facilities: 🛁 ☉ ℰ ✳ ♿ 🪑 ⟑ WiFi

Services: ⊡ 🎯

Within 3 miles: ⑤

Accommodation available: 17 wooden wigwams from £50; 4 Lotus Belle tents from £45; 3 'Tentipi' tents from £35.

Changeover days: Any day

Additional site information: 4 acre site. 🐾 Minimum stay 2 nights. (1 night possible if pre-arranged). Wooden wigwams offer electricity, full size fridge, microwave, kettle and heater; some wigwams have hot tubs; some have en suite facilities; BBQs and fire pits for hire. Cars cannot be parked by Lotus Belle tents or tipis. No pets in Lotus Belle tents. Home-made pizza nights (in season), BBQ meat packs. Dog walk. Unisex sauna.

HEXHAM

Places to visit

Vindolanda (Chesterholm), BARDON MILL, NE47 7JN, 01434 344277
www.vindolanda.com

Temple of Mithras (Hadrian's Wall), CARRAWBROUGH, NE46 4DB, 0370 333 1181
www.english-heritage.org.uk/visit/places/temple-of-mithras-carrawburgh-hadrians-wall

Great for kids: Housesteads Roman Fort, HOUSESTEADS, NE47 6NN,
01434 344363
www.english-heritage.org.uk/visit/places/housesteads-roman-fort-hadrians-wall

HEXHAM   Map 21 NY96

Hexham Racecourse Caravan Site
►►► 79%

tel: 01434 606847 & 606881 **Hexham Racecourse NE46 2JP**
email: hexrace.caravan@btconnect.com
dir: *From Hexham take B6305 signed Allendale and Alston. Left in 3 miles signed to racecourse. Site 1.5 miles on right.*

A part-level and part-sloping grassy site, Hexham Racecourse Caravan Site offers commanding views from its elevated position, overlooking the Northumberland and Hexham Moors. Good, new amenities had opened for our early inspection visit but further work and development of the site was still to be carried out and due for completion in 2019. The site is still very much a work in process but great improvements have been made to date.

Open: May to September **Last arrival:** 20.00 **Last departure:** noon

Pitches: 🚐 �", 🛖 ⚠; 20 seasonal pitches

Leisure: /A\ ♖

Facilities: 🛁 ☉ ℰ ✳ ⟑ WiFi

Services: ⊕ ⊡ 🎯 🛒 🖴 ⊘

Within 3 miles: ⚐ ℰ ◎ ⚷ 日 ⑤

Additional site information: 4 acre site. 🐾 Cars can be parked by caravans and tents. Awnings permitted. No noise after 23.00.

NOTTINGHAMSHIRE

CHURCH LANEHAM   Map 17 SK87

Places to visit

Newark Air Museum, NEWARK-ON-TRENT, NG24 2NY, 01636 707170
www.newarkairmuseum.org

Doddington Hall, LINCOLN, LN6 4RU, 01522 694308
www.doddingtonhall.com

Trentfield Farm
►►► 85%

tel: 01777 228651 **DN22 ONJ**
email: post@trentfield.co.uk web: www.trentfield.co.uk
dir: *A1 onto A57 towards Lincoln for 6 miles. Left signed Laneham, 1.5 miles, through Laneham and Church Laneham (pass Ferryboat pub on left). Site 300 yards on right.*

A delightfully rural and level grass park tucked away on the banks of the River Trent. The park has its own river frontage with free coarse fishing available to park residents. The cosy local pub, which serves food, is under the same ownership.

Open: Easter to November **Last arrival:** 20.00 **Last departure:** noon

Pitches: 🚐 �", 🛖 ⚠; 20 seasonal pitches

Facilities: 🛁 ☉ ℰ ✳ ♿ ⑤ ⟑ WiFi

Services: ⊕ ⊡ 🎯 🛒 🖴

Within 3 miles: ⚐ ℰ ∪

Additional site information: 34 acre site. 🐾 Cars can be parked by caravans and tents. Awnings permitted. No open fires or fire pits. 24-hour mini shop.

LEISURE: 🏊 Indoor swimming pool 🏊 Outdoor swimming pool /A\ Children's playground 👶 Kids' club 🎾 Tennis court ♖ Games room ⬜ Separate TV room ⚐ Golf course ⛳ Pitch n putt 🚣 Boats for hire 🚲 Bikes for hire 🎬 Cinema 🎵 Entertainment ℰ Fishing ◎ Mini golf 🏄 Watersports 💪 Gym ⚽ Sports field ∪ Stables
FACILITIES: 🛁 Baths/Shower ☉ Electric shaver sockets ℰ Hairdryer ✳ Ice Pack Facility 🚼 Baby facilities ♿ Disabled facilities ⑤ Shop on site or within 200yds ⟑ BBQ area ⟑ Picnic area WiFi WiFi

MANSFIELD   Map 16 SK56

Places to visit

Sherwood Forest National Nature Reserve, EDWINSTOWE, NG21 9RN,
01623 677321, www.visitsherwood.co.uk

Tall Trees Touring Park
►►► 77%

tel: 01623 620203 **Old Mill Lane, Forest Town NG19 0JP**
email: info@talltreestouringpark.co.uk **web:** www.talltreestouringpark.co.uk
dir: A60 from Mansfield towards Worksop. In 1 mile turn right at lights into Old Mill Lane.
Site in approximately 0.5 mile on left.

A pleasant park situated just on the outskirts of Mansfield and within easy walking
distance of shops and restaurants. It is surrounded on three sides by trees and
shrubs, and securely set at the back of the residential park. This site has a modern
amenity block, a fishing lake to the rear of the site and an extra grassed area to
give more space for caravans and tents.

Open: All year **Last arrival:** anytime **Last departure:** 11.00

Pitches: 🚐 from £15; 🚍 from £15; ⛺ from £15; 12 hardstanding pitches;
15 seasonal pitches

Leisure: ⚓ 🎣 ⚽

Facilities: 🏪 ☺ 🅿 ※ ♿ 🍴 WiFi

Services: 🔌 🔘

Within 3 miles: ↕ ∪ ⚡ 🎯 🅿

Additional site information: 10 acre site. 🐕 Cars can be parked by caravans and tents.
Awnings permitted. No noise after 22.00.

NEWARK

See Southwell

RADCLIFFE ON TRENT

Places to visit

Wollaton Hall, Gardens & Deer Park, NOTTINGHAM, NG8 2AE, 0115 876 3100
www.wollatonhall.org.uk

Great for kids: Green's Windmill, NOTTINGHAM, NG2 4QB, 0115 915 6878
www.nottinghamcity.org.uk/greenswindmill

RADCLIFFE ON TRENT   Map 11 SK63

Thornton's Holt Camping Park
►►►► 85%

tel: 0115 933 2125 & 933 4204 **Stragglethorpe Road, Stragglethorpe NG12 2JZ**
email: camping@thorntons-holt.co.uk **web:** www.thorntons-holt.co.uk
dir: At lights on A52 (3 miles east of Nottingham) follow Cropwell Bishop signs. Site
0.5 mile on left. Or from A46 (southeast of Nottingham) at Stragglethorpe junction
follow Cropwell Bishop signs. Site 2.5 miles on right.

A well-run family site in former meadowland, with pitches (hardstanding and also
grass from April to October) located amid maturing trees and bushes that create a
rural and peaceful setting. There is a children's play area, a laundry and a new
café, shop and reception building opened in 2019. The newly completed toilet
block is spacious and has plenty of hot water. The indoor swimming pool is a
popular attraction.

Open: All year (restricted service: November to March – swimming pool and shop closed)
Last arrival: 20.00 **Last departure:** noon

Pitches: * 🚐 from £21.75; 🚍 from £21.75; ⛺ from £18; 35 hardstanding pitches;
20 seasonal pitches

Leisure: 🏊 ⚓

Facilities: 🏪 ☺ 🅿 ※ ♿ 🅂 WiFi

Services: 🔌 🔘 ⛽ ⚑ 🔋 ⚗ 🅃

Within 3 miles: ↕ 🅿 ∪ ◎ ⚡ 🎯 🅿

Additional site information: 14 acre site. 🐕 Cars can be parked by caravans and tents.
Awnings permitted. No noise after 22.00.

SOUTHWELL   Map 17 SK65

Places to visit

The Workhouse, SOUTHWELL, NG25 0PT, 01636 817260
www.nationaltrust.org.uk/theworkhouse

New Hall Farm Touring Park
►►► 84%

tel: 01623 883041 **New Hall Farm, New Hall Lane NG22 8BS**
email: enquiries@newhallfarm.co.uk **web:** www.newhallfarm.co.uk
dir: From A614 at White Post Modern Farm Centre follow Southwell signs. Immediately
after Edingley into New Hall Lane to site.

A park on a working stock farm with the elevated pitching area enjoying
outstanding panoramic views. It is within a short drive of medieval Newark and
Sherwood Forest. A log cabin viewing gantry offers a place to relax and take in the
spectacular scenery.

Open: March to October **Last arrival:** 21.00 **Last departure:** noon

Pitches: * 🚐 from £16; 🚍 from £16; ⛺ from £15; 10 hardstanding pitches;
7 seasonal pitches

Facilities: 🏪 ☺ ※ 🔋 🅿

Services: 🔌 🔘 🔋

Within 3 miles: ↕ 🅿 ∪ 🅿

Additional site information: 2.5 acre site. Adults only. 🐕 🚭 Cars can be parked by
caravans and tents. Awnings permitted. Quiet after 22.00. Walking trail, cycling trail,
viewing gantry, ice cream for sale on site.

TEVERSAL — Map 16 SK46

Places to visit

Hardwick Hall, HARDWICK HALL, S44 5QJ, 01246 850430
www.nationaltrust.org.uk/hardwick

Premier Park

Teversal Camping & Caravanning Club Site

▶▶▶▶▶ 93%

tel: 01623 551838 & 024 7647 5426 **Silverhill Lane NG17 3JJ**
email: teversal.site@campingandcaravanningclub.co.uk
web: www.campingandcaravanningclub.co.uk/teversal
dir: *M1 junction 28, A38 towards Mansfield. Left at lights onto B6027. At top of hill straight over at lights, left at Tesco Express. Right onto B6014, left at Carnarvon Arms, site on left.*

A top notch park with excellent purpose-built facilities and innovative, hands-on owners. Each pitch is spacious, the excellent toilet facilities are state-of-the-art, and there are views of, and access to, the countryside and nearby Silverhill Community Woods. Both the attention to detail and the all-round quality are truly exceptional – there is a special area for washing dogs and bikes. The site has a shop, and buses for Sutton-in-Ashfield and Chesterfield stop just a five-minute walk from the site. A six-berth holiday caravan, luxury ready-erected safari tents and a log cabin are available for hire. Good pub food can be found only a few minutes' walk from the site.

Open: All year **Last arrival:** 20.00 **Last departure:** noon

Pitches: 🚐 🚃 ▲; 🏠 see prices below; 92 hardstanding pitches

Leisure: ⚠ ⚽ ☸

Facilities: 🛁 ☉ ☞ ☀ ᕽ 🖥 WiFi

Services: 🔌 🗑 ⛏ 🛢 🐾 🅣

Within 3 miles: ♨ ⚲ ∪

Additional site information: 6 acre site. 🐕 Cars can be parked by caravans and tents. Awnings permitted. Site gates close from 23.00–07.00. Cycle trails nearby. Car hire can be arranged.

Glamping available: Safari tents from £44; Log cabin from £200 (for 3 nights).
Changeover days: Any day for safari tents; Monday and Friday for log cabin.

Additional glamping information: Safari tents: minimum stay 3 nights. Log cabin: minimum stay 3 nights (Friday to Monday), 4 nights (Monday to Friday). Cars can be parked by units.

OXFORDSHIRE

BANBURY — Map 11 SP44

Places to visit

Banbury Museum, BANBURY, OX16 2PQ, 01295 236165
www.banburymuseum.org

Broughton Castle, BROUGHTON, OX15 5EB, 01295 276070
www.broughtoncastle.com

Great for kids: Deddington Castle, DEDDINGTON, 0370 333 1181
www.english-heritage.org.uk/visit/places/deddington-castle

Barnstones Caravan & Camping Site

▶▶▶▶ 84%

tel: 01295 750289 **Great Bourton OX17 1QU**
dir: *Take A423 from Banbury signed Southam. In 3 miles turn right signed Great Bourton and Cropredy, site 100 yards on right.*

A popular, neatly laid-out site with plenty of hardstandings, some fully serviced pitches, a smart up-to-date toilet block, and excellent rally facilities. Well run by a very personable owner, this is an excellent value park. The site is well positioned for stopovers or for visiting nearby Banbury.

Open: All year **Last arrival:** by arrangement **Last departure:** by arrangement

Pitches: * 🚐 from £14; 🚃 from £14; ▲ from £12; 44 hardstanding pitches

Leisure: ⚠ ☸

Facilities: 🛁 ☉ ☀ ᕽ 🖥 🎋 WiFi

Services: 🔌 🗑 ⛏ 🛢 ⛟ 🐾

Within 3 miles: ♨ ⚲ ∪ ◎ 🏌 ᙏ 🕳 🛒

Additional site information: 3 acre site. 🐕 ☸ Cars can be parked by caravans and tents. Awnings permitted. No rollerblades. No noise after midnight.

BLETCHINGDON

Places to visit

Rousham House, ROUSHAM, OX25 4QX, 01869 347110
www.rousham.org

History of Science Museum, OXFORD, OX1 3AZ, 01865 277293
hsm.ox.ac.uk

Great for kids: Oxford University Museum of Natural History, OXFORD, OX1 3PW, 01865 272950, www.oum.ox.ac.uk

LEISURE: 🏊 Indoor swimming pool 🏊 Outdoor swimming pool ⚠ Children's playground 🧒 Kids' club ⚲ Tennis court 🎱 Games room ▭ Separate TV room
⛳ Golf course 🏌 Pitch n putt 🚣 Boats for hire 🚲 Bikes for hire ▤ Cinema ♫ Entertainment 🎣 Fishing ◎ Mini golf 🏄 Watersports 🏋 Gym ☸ Sports field ∪ Stables
FACILITIES: 🛁 Baths/Shower ☉ Electric shaver sockets ☞ Hairdryer ☀ Ice Pack Facility ᕽ Baby facilities ♿ Disabled facilities 🛒 Shop on site or within 200yds
🔥 BBQ area ᙏ Picnic area WiFi WiFi

BLETCHINGDON   Map 11 SP51

Greenhill Leisure Park
▶▶▶▶ 91%

tel: 01869 351600 **Greenhill Farm, Station Road OX5 3BQ**
email: info@greenhill-leisure-park.co.uk **web:** www.greenhill-leisure-park.co.uk
dir: *M40 junction 9, A34 south for 3 miles. Take B4027 to Bletchingdon. Site 0.5 mile after village on left.*

An all-year round park with spacious pitches, set in open countryside near the village of Bletchingdon and well placed for visiting Oxford and the Cotswolds. Fishing is available at the park's two well-stocked lakes and nearby river. This is a family-friendly park and certainly maintains the owner's 'where fun meets the countryside' philosophy. The facilities are very good and include an excellent reception, shop, candle and home fragrance shop and a café-bar, a beauty salon and photographic studio, and 12 fully serviced pitches.

Open: All year (restricted service: October to March – no dogs permitted, games room closed) **Last arrival:** 21.00 (20.00 in winter) **Last departure:** noon

Pitches: * 🚐 from £17; 🚍 from £17; ▲ from £17; 44 hardstanding pitches; 20 seasonal pitches

Leisure: ⚄ 🔍 ✐

Facilities: 🏠 ☺ 🎣 ☼ 🔥 🕭 🖰 WiFi

Services: 🔌 🗑 🍴 ⦿ 🚼 🛒 ⚲ 🔋 ⊘ T

Within 3 miles: ⌴

Additional site information: 7 acre site. 🐕 Cars can be parked by caravans and tents. Awnings permitted. No campfires or fire pits.

Diamond Caravan & Camping Park
▶▶▶▶ 86%

tel: 01869 350909 **Islip Road OX5 3DR**
email: warden@diamondpark.co.uk **web:** www.diamondpark.co.uk
dir: *M40 junction 9, A34 signed Oxford and Newbury. In 3 miles take B4027 to Bletchingdon. Site 1 mile on left.*

A well-run, quiet rural site in good level surroundings, and ideal for touring the Cotswolds, situated seven miles north of Oxford in the heart of the Thames Valley. This popular park is open all year, has excellent facilities, and offers a heated outdoor swimming pool, a games room for children and a small bar.

Open: All year (restricted service: September to May – bar and swimming pool closed) **Last arrival:** dusk **Last departure:** 11.00

Pitches: 🚐 🚍 ▲; 20 hardstanding pitches

Leisure: ⚄ ⚄ 🔍

Facilities: 🏠 ☺ 🎣 ☼ 🕭 🖰 WiFi

Services: 🔌 🗑 🍴 ⦿ 🛒 ⚲ 🔋 ⊘ T

Within 3 miles: ⌴ ✐

Additional site information: 3 acre site. 🐕 ⊗ Cars can be parked by caravans and tents. Awnings permitted. No campfires, no groups occupying more than 3 pitches, no noise after 22.30.

PITCHES: 🚐 Caravans 🚍 Motorhomes ▲ Tents ⚄ Glamping accommodation **SERVICES:** 🔌 Electric hook-up 🗑 Launderette 🍴 Licensed bar 🔋 Calor Gas ⊘ Campingaz T Toilet fluid ⦿ Café/Restaurant 🛒 Fast Food/Takeaway 🚼 Battery charging ⚲ Motorhome service point
* 2019 prices ⊘ No credit or debit cards 🐕 Dogs permitted ⊗ No dogs

BURFORD
Map 5 SP21

Places to visit

Minster Lovell Heritage Centre, MINSTER LOVELL, OX29 0RB, 01993 775262 minsterlovell.com

Cotswold Woollen Weavers, FILKINS, GL7 3JJ, 01367 860660 www.cotswoldwoollenweavers.co.uk

Wysdom Touring Park
▶▶ 86%

tel: 01993 823207 **Cheltenham Road OX18 4JG**
web: www.wysdomtouringpark.co.uk
dir: *From roundabout on A40 in Burford take A361 towards Lechdale-on-Thames. Turn right signed Burford School. 100 yards to site.*

Owned by Burford School, this small adults-only park is very much a hidden gem being just a five-minute walk from Burford, one of prettiest towns in the Cotswolds. The pitches have good privacy; all have electricity and there are many hardstandings for caravans and motorhomes. The unisex toilet facilities are very clean. This makes a good base from which to explore the Cotswolds.

Open: All year **Last arrival:** 21.00 **Last departure:** noon

Pitches: * 🚐 from £18; 🚐 from £18; 25 hardstanding pitches

Facilities: 🛁 ⊙ WIFI

Services: 🔌

Within 3 miles: ⅃ ⑤ 🎕

Additional site information: 2.5 acre site. Adults only. 🐕 Cars can be parked by caravans. Awnings permitted. Free book swap.

FRINGFORD

Places to visit

Rousham House, ROUSHAM, OX25 4QX, 01869 347110 www.rousham.org

Stowe House, STOWE, MK18 5EH, 01280 818002 www.stowehouse.org

Great for kids: Buckinghamshire Railway Centre, QUAINTON, HP22 4BY, 01296 655720, www.bucksrailcentre.org

FRINGFORD
Map 11 SP62

Glebe Leisure
▶▶▶ 80%

tel: 01869 277800 **Stratton Lane OX27 8RJ**
email: ann.herring@btinternet.com **web:** www.glebeleisure.co.uk
dir: *M40 junction 10, A43 (signed Northampton). At next roundabout take B4100 signed Bicester. 2nd right onto unclassified road signed Hethe and Stoke Lyne. Follow brown site signs.*

Glebe Leisure is a small, peaceful park in a good countryside location just a few miles from Bicester and the M40, making it an ideal overnight stopover site. It is also very popular with fishing enthusiasts due to the well-stocked lake, and with keen shoppers wishing to spend time at the Bicester Village shopping outlet, three miles away. The park comprises two well-tended fields – one with hardstandings and four camping pods, the other with neat, grassy pitches. The main toilet block offers clean, well-maintained facilities and there's a good motorhome service point.

Open: All year (restricted service: Site closes at 19.00) **Last arrival:** March to September 19.00; October to February 18.00 **Last departure:** anytime (subject to request)

Pitches: * 🚐 from £24; 🚐 from £24; ⛺ from £10; 🏠 see prices below; 15 hardstanding pitches

Leisure: ✎

Facilities: 🛁 ⁂ ⅃ 🗲 WIFI

Services: 🔌 ⑤ 🛒 ⅄

Within 3 miles: ⅃ ∪ 🎕 ⑤

Additional site information: 5 acre site. 🐕 Cars can be parked by caravans and tents. Awnings permitted. No noise or taxis after 23.00, no unaccompanied children in toilet block or around lakes. Dog walks.

Glamping available: Wooden pods from £35 and £45 per night.
Changeover days: Any day

Additional glamping information: Cars can be parked by units.

HENLEY-ON-THAMES

Places to visit

Greys Court, HENLEY-ON-THAMES, RG9 4PG, 01491 628529 www.nationaltrust.org.uk/greys-court

Great for kids: River & Rowing Museum, HENLEY-ON-THAMES, RG9 1BF, 01491 415600, www.rrm.co.uk

HENLEY-ON-THAMES	Map 5 SU78

Platinum Park

Swiss Farm Touring & Camping
▶▶▶▶▶

tel: 01491 573419 **Marlow Road RG9 2HY**
email: info@swissfarmhenley.co.uk web: www.swissfarmhenley.co.uk
dir: *From Henley on Thames take A4155 towards Marlow. 1st left after rugby club*

This park enjoys an excellent location within easy walking distance of the town and is perfect for those visiting the Henley Regatta (but booking is essential at that time). Pitches are spacious and well appointed, and include some that are fully serviced. There is a tasteful coffee shop and bar plus a nice outdoor swimming pool. There are wooden pods and a luxury lodge for hire.

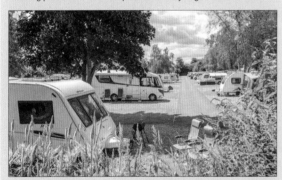

Open: March to November (restricted service: March to May and October to November – pool closed) **Last arrival:** 21.00 **Last departure:** noon
Pitches: ⛺ 🚐 ⛺ 🏠 see price below; 100 hardstanding pitches
Leisure: 🏊 Ⓜ ⚲ **Facilities:** 🚿 ☺ 🅿 ✳ ♿ Ⓢ 🚻 WiFi
Services: 🔌 🔄 🍴 🍺 🔋 ♨ 🔧 📍 Ⓣ
Within 3 miles: ⬇ ⬇ ⬇

Additional site information: 6 acre site. ⌁ Cars can be parked by caravans and tents. Awnings permitted. No groups. No dogs during spring half term and summer holidays.

Glamping available: Wooden pods from £85. **Changeover days:** Friday and Monday

See advert on page 235

STANDLAKE	Map 5 SP30

Places to visit
Buscot Park, BUSCOT, SN7 8BU, 01367 240786
www.buscotpark.com

Harcourt Arboretum, OXFORD, OX44 9PX, 01865 610305
www.harcourt-arboretum.ox.ac.uk

Great for kids: Cotswold Wildlife Park and Gardens, BURFORD, OX18 4JP, 01993 823006, www.cotswoldwildlifepark.co.uk

REGIONAL WINNER – SOUTH EAST ENGLAND AA CAMPSITE OF THE YEAR 2020

Platinum Park

Lincoln Farm Park Oxfordshire
▶▶▶▶▶

tel: 01865 300239 **High Street OX29 7RH**
email: info@lincolnfarmpark.co.uk web: www.lincolnfarmpark.co.uk
dir: *Exit A415 between Abingdon and Witney (5 miles southeast of Witney). Follow brown campsite sign in Standlake.*

This attractively landscaped family-run park, located in a quiet village near the River Thames, offers a truly excellent camping or caravanning experience. There are top class facilities throughout the park and through the combination of sound investment by the owner, passionate and caring new managers, the park has seen significant improvements over the past year. It has excellent leisure facilities in the Standlake Leisure Centre complete with two pools plus a gym and sauna, and there's a spa/massage facility. This is the perfect base for visiting the many attractions in Oxfordshire and the Cotswolds. A warm welcome is assured from the friendly staff.

Open: February to November **Last arrival:** 20.00 **Last departure:** noon
Pitches: ⛺ 🚐 ⛺ 🏠; 75 hardstanding pitches
Leisure: 🏊 Ⓜ ⚲ 🎾
Facilities: 🚿 ☺ 🅿 ✳ ♿ Ⓢ 🚻 WiFi
Services: 🔌 🔄 🍺 🔋 ♨ 🔧 Ⓣ
Within 3 miles: ⬇ ⬇ U ⬇ ⬇

Additional site information: 9 acre site. ⌁ Cars can be parked by caravans and tents. Awnings permitted. No noise after 22.00. Information/reading room, games.

RUTLAND

GREETHAM   Map 11 SK91

Places to visit

Rutland County Museum & Visitor Centre, OAKHAM, LE15 6HW, 01572 758440
rutlandcountymuseum.org.uk

Oakham Castle, OAKHAM, LE15 6DR, 01572 757578
www.oakhamcastle.org

Premier Park

Rutland Caravan & Camping
►►►►► 88%

tel: 01572 813520 **Park Lane LE15 7FN**
email: info@rutlandcaravanandcamping.co.uk
web: www.rutlandcaravanandcamping.co.uk
dir: *From A1 onto B668 towards Greetham. Before Greetham turn right at crossroads, left to site.*

This pretty caravan park, built to a high specification and surrounded by well-planted banks, continues to improve year after year due to the enthusiasm and vision of its owner. The site has a swimming pool, 40 fully serviced pitches and luxury lodges. From the spacious reception, café and the innovative play area to the high-spec toilet block, everything is of a very high standard. This spacious, grassy site is close to the Viking Way and other footpath networks, and is well situated for visiting Rutland Water and the many picturesque villages in the area.

Open: All year **Last arrival:** 20.00
Pitches: 🚐 �caravan 🛖; 65 hardstanding pitches; 20 seasonal pitches
Leisure: 🏊 ⚏ 🎱
Facilities: 🛁 ☉ 🚿 ✳ ♿ 🛍 🍴 WiFi
Services: 🔌 🗑 🍴 🛒 ⚒ 🛢 ⚗ T
Within 3 miles: 🏌 🎣 ⛳ ◎ ≋ 🚴

Additional site information: 5 acre site. 🐕 Cars can be parked by caravans and tents. Awnings permitted. No noise after 23.00. Dog shower. Car hire can be arranged.

WING   Map 11 SK80

Places to visit

Lyddington Bede House, LYDDINGTON, LE15 9LZ, 01572 822438
www.english-heritage.org.uk/visit/places/lyddington-bede-house

Great for kids: Oakham Castle, OAKHAM, LE15 6DR, 01572 757578
www.oakhamcastle.org

Wing Hall Caravan & Camping
►►► 74%

tel: 01572 737283 & 737090 **Wing Hall LE15 8RQ**
email: winghall1891@aol.com web: www.winghall.co.uk
dir: *From A1 take A47 towards Leicester, 14 miles, follow Morcott signs. In Morcott follow Wing signs. 2.5 miles, follow site signs.*

A deeply tranquil and rural park set in the grounds of an old manor house. The four grassy fields with attractive borders of mixed, mature deciduous trees have

exceptional views across the Rutland countryside and are just a mile from Rutland Water. There's a good farm shop which specialises in locally sourced produce, a licensed café, and there are high quality showers and a fully-equipped laundry. Shepherd's huts are now available too. Children and tents are very welcome – it's a safe environment where there is space to roam.

Open: All year (restricted service: November to March – large motorhomes advised not to arrive if weather is very wet) **Last arrival:** 21.00 **Last departure:** noon
Pitches: 🚐 � 🛖; 4 hardstanding pitches
Facilities: 🚿 ✳ 🛍 WiFi
Services: 🔌 🗑 🍴 🛢 ⚗
Within 3 miles: 🏌 🎣 ⛳ ≋ 🚴

Additional site information: 11 acre site. 🐕 Cars can be parked by caravans and tents. Awnings permitted. Coarse fishing.

SHROPSHIRE

BRIDGNORTH   Map 10 SO79

Places to visit

Benthall Hall, BENTHALL, TF12 5RX, 01952 882159
www.nationaltrust.org.uk/benthall-hall

Great for kids: Dudmaston Estate, QUATT, WV15 6QN, 01746 780866
www.nationaltrust.org.uk/dudmaston-estate

Premier Park

Stanmore Hall Touring Park
►►►►► 88%

tel: 01746 761761 **Stourbridge Road WV15 6DT**
email: stanmore@morris-leisure.co.uk web: www.morris-leisure.co.uk
dir: *2 miles east of Bridgnorth on A458.*

An excellent park in peaceful surroundings offering outstanding facilities. The pitches, many fully serviced (with Freeview TV), are arranged around the lake close to Stanmore Hall. Arboretum standard trees include some magnificent Californian Redwoods and an oak that is nearly 700 years old. The site is handy for visiting Ironbridge, the Severn Valley Railway and the attractive market town of Bridgnorth.

Open: All year **Last arrival:** 20.00 (late arrival pitches available) **Last departure:** noon
Pitches: * 🚐 from £27.10; � from £27.10; 🛖 from £27.10; 68 hardstanding pitches; 12 seasonal pitches
Leisure: ⚏ ☸
Facilities: 🛁 ☉ 🚿 ✳ ♿ 🛍 🍴 🖟 WiFi
Services: 🔌 🗑 🛒 🛢 ⚗ T
Within 3 miles: 🏌 🎣 ⛳ 🚴 🖟

Additional site information: 12.5 acre site. 🐕 Cars can be parked by caravans and tents. Awnings permitted. Maximum of 2 dogs per pitch. Adult only section. Dog walk.

Places to visit

Old Oswestry Hill Fort, OSWESTRY, SY11 1HT, 0370 333 1181
www.english-heritage.org.uk/visit/places/old-oswestry-hillfort

Great for kids: Hawkstone Historic Park & Follies, WESTON-UNDER-REDCASTLE,
SY4 5JY, 01948 841777, www.hawkstoneparkfollies.co.uk

Fernwood Caravan Park

▶▶▶▶ 87%

tel: 01948 710221 **SY12 0QF**

email: enquiries@fernwoodpark.co.uk **web:** www.fernwoodpark.co.uk
dir: *From A495 in Welshampton take B5063, over canal bridge, turn right, follow signs.*

A peaceful park set in wooded countryside, with a screened, tree-lined touring area
and coarse fishing lake. The approach to the park passes colourful shrubs and
flower beds, and part of the static area is tastefully arranged around a children's
play area. There is a small child-free touring area for those wanting complete
relaxation, and the park has 40 acres of woodland where there are many walks
to enjoy.

Open: March to November (restricted service: March and November – shop closed)
Last arrival: 21.00 **Last departure:** 17.00

Pitches: 🚐 🚌; 8 hardstanding pitches; 30 seasonal pitches

Leisure: 🛝 ✐

Facilities: 🏠 ☉ ℘ ☼ ⛐ ⑤

Services: 🔌 ⑤ ⛟ 🔋 🄣

Within 3 miles: ⚓

Additional site information: 26 acre site. ✳ Cars can be parked by caravans. Awnings
permitted. No noise after 23.00. Guest WiFi available by site office.

Places to visit

Powis Castle & Garden, WELSHPOOL, SY21 8RF, 01938 551944
www.nationaltrust.org.uk/powis-castle-and-garden

Great for kids: Stiperstones National Nature Reserve, SHREWSBURY,
01743 792294
www.gov.uk/government/publications/shropshires-national-nature-reserves/
shropshires-national-nature-reserves

Old School Campsite
▶▶▶ 87%

tel: 01588 650351 **Shelve SY5 0JQ**

email: bookings@theoldschoolcampsite.com **web:** www.theoldschoolcampsite.com
dir: *6.5 miles south-west of Minsterley on A488. Site on left, 2 miles after village sign
for Hope.*

Situated in the Shropshire Hills, an Area of Outstanding Natural Beauty, with many
excellent walks starting directly from the site, Old School Campsite is ideally
located for exploring both mid-Wales and historic Shrewsbury. Although a small site
of just 1.5 acres, it is well equipped. It is a really beautiful park, often described as

'a gem', with excellent facilities and offering all the requirements for a relaxing
countryside holiday. In addition to well maintained pitches, three bell tents are
located in an enclosed high-hedged area with fire pit, cooking equipment and
utensils supplied. The friendly owners also run active and creative classes for
individuals or groups of all ages, with children especially welcomed. A shop
features local produce and the superb high hedges surrounding the touring and
camping areas, assist in creating very good privacy.

Open: March to January **Last arrival:** 21.00 **Last departure:** 11.00

Pitches: 🚐 🚌 🅰 🛖; 10 hardstanding pitches; 6 seasonal pitches

Facilities: 🏠 ⚊ ☼ ⛐

Services: 🔌

Within 3 miles: ℘ ∪ ⑤

Additional site information: 1.5 acre site. ✳ 🚫 Cars can be parked by caravans and
tents. Awnings permitted. No ball games or cycle riding. Archery, climbing, canoeing,
jewellery making, crocheting, printing

Glamping available: Bell tents

Places to visit

Attingham Park Estate Town Walls (NT), SHREWSBURY, SY1 1TN, 01743 708162
www.nationaltrust.org.uk/attingham-park-estate-town-walls-tower

Great for kids: Wroxeter Roman City, WROXETER, SY5 6PH, 01743 761330
www.english-heritage.org.uk/visit/places/wroxeter-roman-city

Beaconsfield Farm Caravan Park
▶▶▶▶▶ 91%

tel: 01939 210370 & 210399 **Battlefield SY4 4AA**

email: mail@beaconsfieldholidaypark.co.uk **web:** www.beaconsfieldholidaypark.co.uk
dir: *At Hadnall, 1.5 miles northeast of Shrewsbury. Follow sign for Astley from A49.*

A purpose-built, adults-only (21 years and over) family-run park on farmland in
open countryside. This pleasant park offers quality in every area, including
superior toilets, heated indoor swimming pool, luxury lodges for hire and
attractive landscaping. Fly and coarse fishing are available from the park's own
lake. A large new restaurant with separate bar, replacing the popular Bothy
Bistro, will open in December 2019. Car hire is available directly from the site,
and there's a steam room, plus free WiFi. 12 luxury lodges are available for hire
or sale.

Open: All year **Last arrival:** 19.00 **Last departure:** 11.00

Pitches: * 🚐 from £27; 🚌 from £27; 50 hardstanding pitches; 10 seasonal pitches

Leisure: 🏊 🎯 ℘

Facilities: 🏠 ℘ ☼ ⛐ 🚻 WiFi

Services: 🔌 ⑤ 🍴 ⛟ 🔋

Within 3 miles: ⚘ 🎱 ⑤

Additional site information: 16 acre site. Adults only. ✳ Cars can be parked by
caravans. Awnings permitted.

PITCHES: 🚐 Caravans 🚌 Motorhomes 🅰 Tents 🛖 Glamping accommodation **SERVICES:** 🔌 Electric hook-up ⑤ Launderette 🍺 Licensed bar
🔋 Calor Gas ✐ Campingaz 🄣 Toilet fluid 🍴 Café/Restaurant 🍟 Fast Food/Takeaway 🔋 Battery charging ⛟ Motorhome service point
* 2019 prices 🚫 No credit or debit cards ✳ Dogs permitted 🚫 No dogs

SHREWSBURY *continued*

Oxon Hall Touring Park
▶▶▶▶▶ 91%

Best of British

tel: 01743 340868 **Welshpool Road SY3 5FB**
email: oxon@morris-leisure.co.uk **web:** www.morris-leisure.co.uk
dir: *Exit A5 (ring road) at junction with A458. Site shares entrance with Oxon Park and Ride.*

A delightful park with quality facilities, including a top-notch toilet block and a choice of grass and fully serviced pitches. The adults-only section proves very popular, and there is an inviting patio area next to reception and the shop, overlooking a small lake. This site is ideally located for a visit to Shrewsbury and the surrounding countryside, and the site also benefits from the Oxon Park and Ride being just a short walk away.

Open: All year **Last arrival:** 20.00 **Last departure:** noon

Pitches: * 🚐 from £27.10; 🚚 from £27.10; ▲ from £27.10;
72 hardstanding pitches; 12 seasonal pitches

Leisure: ⚠

Facilities: 🛁 ⊙ 𝓅 ♿ ⑤ 🎪 📶

Services: 🔌 ⑥ ⚡ ⛽ 🔒 ⌀ Ⓣ

Within 3 miles: ♪ ✎ ♺ ♬

Additional site information: 15 acre site. 🚗 Cars can be parked by caravans and tents. Awnings permitted. Maximum of 2 dogs per pitch. No children in adults only area.

Cartref Caravan & Camping
▶▶▶▶ 92%

tel: 01743 821688 & 07803 907061 **Cartref, Ford Heath SY5 9GD**
email: info@cartrefcaravansite.co.uk **web:** www.cartrefcaravansite.co.uk
dir: *From north: A5 from Oswestry. Exit off A5 onto A458 to Welshpool, in village of Ford turn left after petrol station (brown sign). 2nd right, campsite on left. From south: exit A5 onto B4386, approximately 2 miles turn right (brown sign), take 2nd left.*

Located in the peaceful hamlet of Ford Heath, less than five miles from Shrewsbury, this carefully designed, relaxing holiday destination provides separate adults-only and family areas suitable for caravans, motorhomes and tents. Pitches, most fully serviced, are enclosed by mature hedges and colourful shrubs to create optimum privacy. A vintage caravan with a converted horsebox housing the en suite facilities creates that unique Glamping experience. In addition to a well-equipped amenity block, a rustic-themed bar provides a wide range of wines, spirits and local ales, and the well-stocked shop offers the best local produce. Additional features include a safe meadow area for dog walking and a wildlife pond carefully planted to attract a variety of birds and animals including great crested newts.

Open: 6 March to 1 November **Last arrival:** 21.00 **Last departure:** 11.00 (later by prior arrangement)

Pitches: 🚐 from £30; 🚚 from £30; ▲ from £30; 🏠 see prices below;
31 hardstanding pitches; 13 seasonal pitches

Leisure: ⚠

Facilities: 🛁 ⊙ 𝓅 ✳ ♿ ⑤ 🎪 🛒 📶

Services: 🔌 ⑥ 🍴 🍽 ♨ 🛒 ⚡ 🔒 Ⓣ

Within 3 miles: ✎

Additional site information: 7.7 acre site. 🚗 Cars can be parked by caravans and tents. Awnings permitted. No ball games or cycling. Strict no noise policy between 23.00–8.00. Fresh baked bread to order, breakfast baps and fresh baked pizza on Friday and Saturday evenings. Local information available. Local walk details available. Car hire can be arranged.

Glamping available: Vintage caravan from £100 per night (includes continental breakfast). **Changeover days:** Any day

Additional glamping information: Sleeps 2. Includes coffee machine, combination microwave and fridge. Wet room in converted horse box. No dogs or BBQs. Cars can be parked by units

Places to visit

Lilleshall Abbey, LILLESHALL, TF10 9HW, 0370 333 1181
www.english-heritage.org.uk/visit/places/lilleshall-abbey

Ironbridge Gorge Museums, IRONBRIDGE, TF8 7DQ, 01952 433424
www.ironbridge.org.uk

Severn Gorge Park
▶▶▶▶▶ 81%

tel: 01952 684789 **Bridgnorth Road, Tweedale TF7 4JB**
email: info@severngorgepark.co.uk **web:** www.severngorgepark.co.uk
dir: *South of Telford take A442 towards Bridgnorth. Onto A4169 signed Telford Town Centre. Right at Cuckoo Oak roundabout into Bridgnorth Road (follow site signs). Site on right.*

A very pleasant wooded site in the heart of Telford, well screened and well maintained. The sanitary facilities are fresh and immaculate, and landscaping of the grounds is carefully managed. Although the touring section is small, this is a really delightful park to stay at, and it is also well positioned for visiting nearby Ironbridge and its museums. The Telford bus stops at the end of the drive.

Open: All year **Last arrival:** 20.00 by prior arrangement **Last departure:** noon

Pitches: 🚐 🚚; 12 hardstanding pitches

Facilities: 🛁 ⊙ 𝓅 ✳ ♿

Services: 🔌 ⑥ 🛒 ⚡ 🔒 ⌀

Within 3 miles: ♪ ✎ ♺ ◎ 🏊 ♬ ⑤

Additional site information: 6 acre site. Adults only. 🚗 Cars can be parked by caravans. Awnings permitted. Well behaved dogs only.

WEM — Map 15 SJ52

Places to visit

Hawkstone Historic Park & Follies, WESTON-UNDER-REDCASTLE, SY4 5JY, 01948 841777
www.hawkstoneparkfollies.co.uk

Attingham Park Estate Town Walls (NT), SHREWSBURY, SY1 1TN, 01743 708162
www.nationaltrust.org.uk/attingham-park-estate-town-walls-tower

Great for kids: Stiperstones National Nature Reserve, SHREWSBURY, 01743 702204
www.gov.uk/government/publications/shropshires-national-nature-reserves/shropshires-national-nature-reserves

Lower Lacon Caravan Park
▶▶▶ 81%

tel: 01939 232376 **SY4 5RP**
email: info@llcp.co.uk **web:** www.llcp.co.uk
dir: A49 onto B5065. Site 3 miles on right.

A large, spacious park with lively club facilities and an entertainment barn, set safely away from the main road. The park is particularly suited to families, with an outdoor swimming pool and many farm animals including alpacas and kune kune pigs. Family-size wooden pods are available for hire, and spacious fully serviced hardstanding pitches are suitable for larger units.

Open: All year (restricted service: in winter – entertainment barn and café closed)
Last arrival: anytime **Last departure:** 17.00

Pitches: 🚐 🚃 🛆 🏠; 30 hardstanding pitches; 100 seasonal pitches
Leisure: 🏊 🎱 ♨ 🔍 ▢
Facilities: 🏪 ⊙ 🅿 ✳ ⟁ ⑤ WiFi
Services: 🔌 🗑 🚆 🍴 ⚙ 🔋 🛢 🚿 Ⓣ
Within 3 miles: 🚶 🚲 ◎

Additional site information: 57 acre site. 🐕 Cars can be parked by caravans and tents. Awnings permitted. No skateboards, no commercial vehicles, no sign-written vehicles. Crazy golf.
Glamping available: Wooden pods.
Additional glamping information: Cars can be parked by units

WENTNOR

Places to visit

Montgomery Castle, MONTGOMERY, 03000 256000
cadw.gov.wales/visit/places-to-visit/montgomery-castle

Great for kids: Shropshire Hills Discovery Centre, CRAVEN ARMS, SY7 9RS, 01588 676060, www.shropshirehillsdiscoverycentre.co.uk

WENTNOR — Map 15 SO39

The Green Caravan Park
▶▶▶ 81%

tel: 01588 650605 **SY9 5EF**
email: lin@greencaravanpark.co.uk **web:** www.greencaravanpark.co.uk
dir: 1 mile north-east of Bishop's Castle on A489. Right at brown tourist sign.

A pleasant family-run site adjacent to a village pub, in a peaceful setting that's convenient for visiting Ludlow or Shrewsbury. The site is very family orientated, and has good facilities. The grassy pitches are mainly level – some hardstandings are available.

Open: Easter to October **Last arrival:** 21.00 **Last departure:** noon (fee charged for late departures)

Pitches: * 🚐 from £18; 🚃 from £18; 🛆 from £18; 6 hardstanding pitches; 42 seasonal pitches
Leisure: 🎱 📶
Facilities: 🏪 ⊙ 🅿 ✳ ⑤
Services: 🔌 🗑 🚆 🍴 ⚙ 🔋 🛢 🚿 Ⓣ

Additional site information: 15 acre site. 🐕 Cars can be parked by caravans and tents. Awnings permitted. No open fires, quiet from 23.00–08.00, dogs must be kept on leads at all times except in exercise area. Car hire can be arranged.

WHEATHILL — Map 10 SO68

Places to visit

Ludlow Castle, LUDLOW, SY8 1AY, 01584 873355
www.ludlowcastle.com

Premier Park

Wheathill Touring Park
▶▶▶▶ 91%

tel: 01584 823456 **WV16 6QT**
email: info@wheathillpark.co.uk **web:** www.wheathillpark.co.uk
dir: On B4364 between Ludlow and Bridgnorth. (NB Sat Nav may give directions to exit B4364, this should be ignored). Site entrance well signed from B4364. Site entrance adjacent to Three Horseshoes Pub.

Ideally located in open countryside between the historic towns of Bridgnorth and Ludlow, this development provides spacious, fully serviced pitches, most with stunning views. There is a top-notch amenity block in each field with quality fittings and good privacy options. The park is situated adjacent to a pub serving a good range of ales and food. Please note, the on-site shop only sells caravan and camping spares, but there's a licensed village shop within a 10-minute drive. The park also provides excellent and secure caravan and motorhome storage facilities.

Open: 15 March to 15 December **Last arrival:** 19.00 **Last departure:** noon

Pitches: 🚐 🚃; 50 hardstanding pitches; 5 seasonal pitches
Facilities: 🏪 ⊙ 🅿 ⟁ 🚿 🚻 WiFi
Services: 🔌 🗑 🔋 🛠 🛢 🚿 Ⓣ
Within 3 miles: 📶 ⛳ ⑤

Additional site information: 4 acre site. Adults only. 🐕 Cars can be parked by caravans. Awnings permitted.

Somerset

Somerset means 'summer pastures' – appropriate given that so much of this county remains rural and unspoiled. Ever popular areas to visit are the limestone and red sandstone Mendips Hills rising to over 1,000 feet, and by complete contrast, to the south and southwest, the flat landscape of the Somerset Levels.

At the heart of Somerset lies the city of Wells, one of the smallest in the country and surely one of the finest. The jewel in the city's crown is its splendid cathedral, with a magnificent Gothic interior; adorned with sculptures, the West Front is a masterpiece of medieval craftsmanship. Nearby are Vicar's Close, a delightful street of 14th-century houses, and the Bishop's Palace, which is 13th century and moated.

Radiating from Wells are numerous paths and tracks, offering walkers the chance to escape the noise and bustle of the city and discover Somerset's rural delights. Deep within the county are the Mendip Hills, 25 miles long by 5 miles wide, that have a distinctive character and identity.

One of Somerset's more adventurous routes, and a long-term favourite with walkers, is the West Mendip Way, running for 50 miles between the coast and the town of Frome. The starting point at Uphill is spectacular – a ruined hilltop church overlooking the coast near the classic seaside resort of Weston-Super-Mare. The town's famous pier replaces a previous structure destroyed by fire in 2008. Weston and Minehead, which lie on the edge of Exmoor National Park, are two traditional, much-loved holiday destinations on this stretch of coastline.

From Uphill, the West Mendip Way makes for Cheddar Caves and Gorge where stunning geological formations attract countless visitors who are left with a lasting impression of unique natural beauty. For almost a mile the gorge's limestone cliffs rise vertically above the road, in places giving Cheddar a somewhat sinister and oppressive air. Beyond Cheddar the trail heads for Wells. The choice of walks in Somerset is impressive, as is the range of cycle routes.

Descend to the Somerset Levels, an evocative lowland landscape that was the setting for the Battle of Sedgemoor in 1685. In the depths of winter this is a desolate place and famously prone to extensive flooding. There is also a palpable sense of the distant past among these fields and scattered communities. It is claimed that Alfred the Great retreated here after his defeat by the Danes.

One of Somerset's most famous features is the ancient, enigmatic Glastonbury Tor. Steeped in early Christian and Arthurian legend, the Isle of Avalon is one of a number of 'islands' rising above the Somerset Levels. This was once the site of the largest and richest monastery in medieval England and it is claimed that in this setting, Joseph of Arimathea founded the first Christian church in the country. Today, near this spot, modern-day pilgrims come for worship of a very different kind – every summer Glastonbury's legendary festival attracts big names from the world of music and large crowds who brave the elements to support them.

Away from the flat country are the Quantocks, once the haunt of poets. Samuel Taylor Coleridge wrote *The Ancient Mariner* while living in the area and William Wordsworth and his sister Dorothy visited on occasion and often accompanied their friend Coleridge on his country rambles among these hills. The Quantocks are noted for their gentle slopes, heather-covered moorland expanses and red deer. From the summit, the Bristol Channel is visible where it meets the Severn Estuary. So much of this hilly landscape has a timeless quality about it and large areas have hardly changed since Coleridge and William and Dorothy Wordsworth explored it on foot around the end of the 18th century.

◁ Selworthy Beacon, Exmoor National Park

SOMERSET

BATH
Map 4 ST76

See also Bishop Sutton

Places to visit

The Herschel Museum of Astronomy, BATH, BA1 2BL, 01225 446865
www.herschelmuseum.org.uk

Sally Lunn's Historic Eating House & Museum, BATH, BA1 1NX, 01225 461634
www.sallylunns.co.uk

Great for kids: Roman Baths & Pump Room, BATH, BA1 1LZ, 01225 477785
www.romanbaths.co.uk

Premier Park

Bath Mill Lodge Retreat
▶▶▶▶▶ 94% HOLIDAY HOME PARK

tel: 01225 333909 **Newton Road BA2 9JF**
email: reception@bathmill.co.uk **web:** www.bathmill.co.uk
dir: *From A36 from Bath towards Bristol at roundabout into Pennyquick Road signed Newton St Loe (Globe Inn on right). In 1 mile left into Newton Road. 1st left to park.*

Bath Mill offers very high quality lodge accommodation in a beautifully landscaped park close to Bath. The lodges are fully equipped to a very high standard and are available with two, three or four bedrooms, plus there are 'Studio Lodges', suitable for a couple, with king-size bed, sofa, a well-appointed excellent bathroom and kitchen. There is an excellent bar and bistro and a well-equipped gym. It's a peaceful location that makes a perfect base for visiting Bath, Bristol and the Mendip Hills.

Open: All year

Holiday Homes: Sleep 8 Bedrooms 4 Two-ring burner Dishwasher Washing Machine Microwave Freezer TV Sky/Freeview WiFi Linen included Towels included Electricity included Gas included

Leisure: /A ✲
Facilities: WiFi
Services: ⛲ ⛳
Within 3 miles: Ⓢ
Changeover days: Monday, Friday, Saturday
Additional site information: ⇥

BISHOP SUTTON
Map 4 ST55

Places to visit

Wookey Hole, WOOKEY HOLE, BA5 1BB, 01749 672243
www.wookey.co.uk

Platinum Park

Bath Chew Valley Caravan Park
▶▶▶▶▶

tel: 01275 332127 **Ham Lane BS39 5TZ**
email: enquiries@bathchewvalley.co.uk **web:** www.bathchewvalley.co.uk
dir: *From A4 towards Bath take A39 towards Weston-super-Mare. Right onto A368. 6 miles, right opposite The Red Lion into Ham Lane, site 250 metres on left.*

This peaceful adults-only park can be described as 'a park in a garden', with caravan pitches set amidst lawns, shrubs and trees. There are excellent private facilities – rooms with showers, wash basins and toilets – all are spotlessly clean and well maintained. There is a good woodland walk on the park, and a stylish fully-equipped lodge is available for hire. WiFi is available throughout the site and there is a free internet workstation. This site is well situated for visiting Bath, Bristol, Wells, Cheddar and Wookey Hole, and for walking in the Mendip Hills. Chew Valley Lake, noted for its top quality fishing, is close by.

Open: All year **Last arrival:** 19.00 **Last departure:** 11.00

Pitches: * ⛺ from £22; ⛺ from £22; ▲ from £22 ⌂; 4 seasonal pitches
Facilities: 🚿 ⊙ 🖤 ✲ 🚻 Ⓢ 🛒 🏕 WiFi
Services: 🔌 🗄 🛒 ⚡ 🚿 🚽 T
Within 3 miles: ◢ ⛳

Additional site information: 4.5 acre site. Adults only. ⇥ Awnings permitted. Lending library. Shop, pub/restaurant 200 metres from site. Car hire can be arranged.

Glamping available: 1 luxury contemporary lodge and 1 luxury cedar lodge.
Changeover days: Any day
Additional glamping information: Both lodges fully equipped. No dogs.

BREAN

Places to visit

King John's Hunting Lodge, AXBRIDGE, BS26 2AP, 01934 732012
www.kingjohnshuntinglodge.co.uk

Weston Museum, WESTON-SUPER-MARE, BS23 1PR, 01934 621028
www.westonmuseum.org

Great for kids: The Helicopter Museum, WESTON-SUPER-MARE, BS24 8PP, 01934 635227, www.helicoptermuseum.co.uk

BREAN   Map 4 ST25

Platinum Park

Warren Farm Holiday Centre
▶▶▶▶▶ HOLIDAY CENTRE

tel: 01278 751227 **Brean Sands TA8 2RP**
email: info@warrenfarm.co.uk **web:** www.warrenfarm.co.uk
dir: *M5 junction 22 , B3140 through Burnham-on-Sea to Berrow and Brean. Site 1.5 miles past Brean Leisure Park.*

A large family-run holiday park just a short walk from the beach and divided up into several fields (pet-friendly and pet-free), each with its own designated facilities. The pitches are spacious and level and both grass pitches and hardstandings are available; there are good panoramic views of the Mendip Hills and Brean Down. The park has its own Beachcomber Inn with bar, restaurant and entertainment area. The site is perfect for families and has an indoor play barn. Lake fishing is available on site and there is also a fishing tackle and bait shop. Luxury 'En suite Super Pitches' are also now available.

Open: April to October **Last arrival:** 20.00 **Last departure:** 11.00

Pitches: * ⊞ from £12; ⊞ from £12; ⛺ from £12; 136 hardstanding pitches; 400 seasonal pitches

Leisure: ⛰ 🎣 🎵 🎮 ⚽   **Facilities:** 🏪 ☉ 🅿 ✳ ♿ ⑤ 🚿 🚻 ⛽ 📶

Services: 🔌 ⑤ 🍺 🍽 🍟 🛒 ⬆ 🔋 🐕 ⊤   **Within 3 miles:** ♨ ◎

Additional site information: 100 acre site. 🐕 No commercial vehicles. Arcade, farm walk, clubhouse, entertainment. Luxury 'En suite Super Pitches' available.

See advert on page 246

Premier Park

Holiday Resort Unity
▶▶▶▶ 93% HOLIDAY CENTRE

tel: 01278 751235 **Coast Road, Brean Sands TA8 2RB**
email: admin@hru.co.uk **web:** www.hru.co.uk
dir: *M5 junction 22, B3140 through Burnham-on-Sea, through Berrow to Brean. Site on left just before Brean Leisure Park.*

This is an excellent, family-run holiday park offering very good touring facilities plus a wide range of family-oriented activities including bowling, RJ's entertainment club and the new Brean Country Club, which opened in 2019. There's plenty of eating outlets – The Tavern, RJ's, an American-themed diner, the beach-themed Bucket & Spade (especially suitable for smaller children), cafés and takeaway options. Brean Splash Waterpark is situated directly opposite this touring park – a discounted entry price is available. Wooden camping pods, yurts, two ready-erected, fully-equipped safari tents, and six Euro tents are also available for hire. The park also holds 'themed' weekends and rallies are also welcome.

Open: February to November (restricted service: New Year) **Last arrival:** 21.00 **Last departure:** 10.00

Pitches: * ⊞ from £14; ⊞ from £14; ⛺ from £14; ⛺ see prices below; 158 hardstanding pitches; 168 seasonal pitches

Leisure: 🏊 🎣 ⛰ 🎮 🎣 🎱 🎵 📚 🎯 ⚽

Facilities: 🏪 ☉ 🅿 ♿ ⑤ 🚿 📶

Services: 🔌 ⑤ 🍺 🍽 🍟 ⬆ 🔋 🐕 ⊤

Within 3 miles: ♨ ◎ 🏇

Additional site information: 200 acre site. 🐕 Family parties of 3 or more must be over 21 years (young persons' policy applies), late departures available (charge applies). Arcade, soft play, dog walk.

Glamping available: Safari tents from £48; wooden pods from £35.
Changeover days: contact site for details

Additional glamping information: Safari tents: sleep 4. Wooden pods: sleep 2 adults and 2 children. Only some units have own kitchen. Cars can be parked by units

---

LEISURE: Indoor swimming pool Outdoor swimming pool Children's playground Kids' club Tennis court Games room Separate TV room Golf course Pitch n putt Boats for hire Bikes for hire Cinema Entertainment Fishing Mini golf Watersports Gym Sports field Stables

FACILITIES: Baths/Shower Electric shaver sockets Hairdryer Ice Pack Facility Baby facilities Disabled facilities Shop on site or within 200yds BBQ area Picnic area WiFi

BREAN *continued*

Northam Farm Caravan & Touring Park

▷▷▷▷ 95%

tel: 01278 751244 **TA8 2SE**
email: stay@northamfarm.co.uk **web:** www.northamfarm.co.uk
dir: *M5 junction 22, B3140 to Burnham-on-Sea and Brean. Park on right 0.5 mile after Brean Leisure Park.*

An attractive site that's just a short walk from the sea and a long sandy beach. This quality park has lots of children's play areas, and also owns the Seagull Inn about 600 yards away, which includes a restaurant and entertainment. There is a top quality fishing lake on site, which is very popular and has been featured on TV. The facilities on this park are excellent. A DVD of the site is available on request, free of charge. The park has a main caravan dealership plus full workshop and repair facility.

Open: March to October (restricted service: March and October – reduced hours for shop, café and takeaway) **Last arrival:** 20.00 **Last departure:** 10.30

Pitches: * ⊞ from £13; ⊞ from £13; ⊼ from £14.50; 300 hardstanding pitches; 300 seasonal pitches

Leisure: ⚐ ▱ ☺

Facilities: 🛆 ☉ ⌁ ⚹ ⚹ & ⑤ 🗂 WiFi

Services: ⚡ ⑤ 🗑 ⑩ 🍺 🔋 ⚡ 🛆 ⊘ Ⓣ

Within 3 miles: ⌂ ◎ 🗓

Additional site information: 30 acre site. 🐕 Cars can be parked by caravans and tents. Awnings permitted. Families and couples only, no commercial vehicles. Car hire can be arranged.

See advert opposite

BRIDGETOWN Map 3 SS93

Places to visit

Dunster Castle, DUNSTER, TA24 6SL, 01643 821314
www.nationaltrust.org.uk/dunstercastle

Cleeve Abbey, WASHFORD, TA23 0PS, 01984 640377
www.english-heritage.org.uk/visit/places/cleeve-abbey

Premier Park

Exe Valley Caravan Site

▷▷▷▷ 90%

tel: 01643 851432 **Mill House TA22 9JR**
email: paulbridgetown@gmail.com **web:** www.exevalleycamping.co.uk
dir: *From south: M5 junction 27, A361 signed Tiverton. 7 miles, right at roundabout signed Bampton. Left at Exeter Inn roundabout, 2 miles, take A396. Through Exebridge to Bridgetown, left after Badgers Holt Inn, site on right. (NB for Sat Nav use TA22 9JN).*

Set in the Exmoor National Park, this adults-only park occupies an enchanting, peaceful spot in a wooded valley alongside the River Exe. There is free fly-fishing, an abundance of wildlife and excellent walks leading directly from the park. The site has good, spotlessly clean facilities. The inn opposite serves meals at lunchtime and in the evening.

Open: 13 March to 19 October **Last arrival:** 22.00 **Last departure:** 11.00

Pitches: * ⊞ from £15; ⊞ from £15; ⊼ from £15; 13 hardstanding pitches; 1 seasonal pitch

Leisure: ▱

Facilities: 🛆 ☉ ⌁ ⚹ & ⑤ 🗂 WiFi

Services: ⚡ ⑤ 🔋 ⚡ 🛆 ⊘ Ⓣ

Within 3 miles: ⌂ 🗓 🗓

Additional site information: 4 acre site. Adults only. 🐕 ⊗ Cars can be parked by caravans and tents. Awnings permitted. 17th-century mill, TV sockets and cables, dog wash.

PITCHES: ⊞ Caravans ⊞ Motorhomes ⊼ Tents ⛺ Glamping accommodation SERVICES: ⚡ Electric hook-up ⑤ Launderette 🍺 Licensed bar 🛆 Calor Gas ⊘ Campingaz Ⓣ Toilet fluid ⑩ Café/Restaurant 🍔 Fast Food/Takeaway 🔋 Battery charging ⚡ Motorhome service point
* 2019 prices ⊗ No credit or debit cards 🐕 Dogs permitted ⊗ No dogs

BRIDGWATER
Map 4 ST23

Places to visit

Hestercombe Gardens, TAUNTON, TA2 8LG, 01823 413923
www.hestercombe.com

Coleridge Cottage, NETHER STOWEY, TA5 1NQ, 01278 732662
www.nationaltrust.org.uk/coleridgecottage

Great for kids: Tropiquaria Zoo, WASHFORD, TA23 0QB, 01984 640688
www.tropiquaria.co.uk

Mill Farm Caravan & Camping Park
►►►► 86%

tel: 01278 732286 **Fiddington TA5 1JQ**
web: www.millfarm.biz
dir: *From Bridgwater take A39 west, left at Cannington roundabout, 2 miles, right just beyond Apple Tree Inn towards Fiddington. Follow camping signs.*

A large holiday park with plenty to interest all the family, including indoor and outdoor pools, a boating lake, a gym, horse riding and a BMX track. There is also a newly refurbished clubhouse with bar, and a full entertainment programme in the main season. Although lively and busy in the main season, the park also offers a much quieter environment at other times; out of season, some activities and entertainment may not be available.

Open: mid March to mid November (restricted service: shop and takeaway closed in low season) **Last arrival:** 23.00 **Last departure:** 10.00

Pitches: * 🚐 from £14.50; 🚏 from £14.50; ▲ from £14.50; 75 seasonal pitches

Leisure: 🏊 🏖 ⛰ 🎱 ❑ ♫ ⚽

Facilities: 🛁 ☉ ⌕ ✳ ⟐ 🛍 🅰 WiFi

Services: 🔌 🔵 🚽 🍴 ♨ ⛽ 🧺 ⊺

Within 3 miles: 🎣 ⚑ ∪

Additional site information: 6 acre site. 🐾 Cars can be parked by caravans and tents. Awnings permitted. No noise after 23.00. Canoeing, pool table, trampolines, fitness classes, saunas.

See advert on page 251

BURNHAM-ON-SEA
Map 4 ST34

Places to visit

The Helicopter Museum, WESTON-SUPER-MARE, BS24 8PP, 01934 635227
www.helicoptermuseum.co.uk

King John's Hunting Lodge, AXBRIDGE, BS26 2AP, 01934 732012
www.kingjohnshuntinglodge.co.uk

Premier Park

Burnham-on-Sea Holiday Village
►►►►► 91% HOLIDAY CENTRE

tel: 01278 783391 **Marine Drive TA8 1LA**
email: burnhamonsea@haven.com **web:** www.haven.com/burnhamonsea
dir: *M5 junction 22, A38 towards Highbridge. Over mini-roundabout, right onto B3139 to Burnham. After petrol station, left into Marine Drive. Park 400 yards on left.*

A large, family-orientated holiday village complex with a separate touring park containing 43 super pitches. There is a wide range of activities, including excellent indoor and outdoor pools, plus bars, restaurants and entertainment for all the family – there is plenty to do for all ages without even leaving the park. The coarse fishing lake is very popular, and the seafront at Burnham is only half a mile away. A wide range of well laid out holiday homes is available for hire; including Safari Village with fully-equipped safari tents.

Open: mid March to end October (restricted service: mid March to May and September to end October – some facilities may be reduced) **Last arrival:** anytime **Last departure:** 10.00

Pitches: 🚐 🚏 ▲; 🏠 see prices below; 46 hardstanding pitches

Leisure: 🏊 🏖 ⛰ 🤸 🏒 ♫ ⚑ ⚽

Facilities: 🛁 ⌕ ✳ ⟐ 🛍 🅰 WiFi

Services: 🔌 🔵 🚽 🍴 ♨ ⊟

Within 3 miles: 🎣 ∪ ◉ ⊞

Additional site information: 94 acre site. 🚫 No pets, no commercial vehicles, no bookings by persons under 21 years unless a family booking.

Glamping available: Safari tents from £125. **Changeover days:** Fridays and Mondays

Additional glamping information: Safari tents: minimum stay 3 nights. Price is for 3 nights. Includes 2 ring cooker, kettle, toaster, microwave and fridge.

CHEDDAR
Map 4 ST45

Places to visit

Cheddar Gorge (NT), CHEDDAR, BS27 3QE, 01934 744689
www.nationaltrust.org.uk/cheddar-gorge

Glastonbury Abbey, GLASTONBURY, BA6 9EL, 01458 832267
www.glastonburyabbey.com

Great for kids: Wookey Hole, WOOKEY HOLE, BA5 1BB, 01749 672243
www.wookey.co.uk

Platinum Park

Cheddar Woods Resort & Spa
▶▶▶▶▶ HOLIDAY HOME PARK

tel: 01934 742610 **Axbridge Road BS27 3DB**
email: enquiries@cheddarwoods.co.uk
web: www.darwinescapes.co.uk/parks/cheddar-woods-resort-spa
dir: From M5 junction 22 follow signs for 'Cheddar Gorge & Caves' (8 miles). Site midway between Cheddar and Axbridge on A371.

Situated in the beautiful Mendip Hills, Cheddar Woods is the perfect place to relax and unwind, and this state-of-the-art park is an ideal location for family holidays. Both large and smaller lodges are available for hire, all offering top quality accommodation. There are excellent leisure facilities including a gym, spa and swimming pool plus a 'Go Active' programme, and a pizza bar. In addition, there is a very tasteful bar and good restaurant. The park is just outside the village of Cheddar with its famous caves and is well positioned for visiting Wells, Weston-super-Mare and many other attractions of the area. It should be noted this is a lodge-only park.

Open: All year **Last arrival:** midnight **Last departure:** 10.00

Holiday Homes: Sleep 8 Bedrooms 4 Bathrooms 2 Toilets 2 Two-ring burner Dishwasher Washing Machine Tumble dryer Microwave Freezer TV Sky/Freeview DVD player WiFi Linen included Towels included Electricity included Gas included Woodburner

Prices: Low season from £130 High season from £2500 Weekly from £600

Leisure: 🏊 ⛰ 👣 ⌕ 🎣 🏹 ⚽

Facilities: ♿ 🚿 WiFi

Services: 🍽 🍺

Within 3 miles: 🎣 ⛳ 🎿 ↻

Additional site information: 🐕

COWSLIP GREEN
Map 4 ST46

Places to visit

Clevedon Court, CLEVEDON, BS21 6QU, 01275 872257
www.nationaltrust.org.uk/clevedon-court

Bristol Museum & Art Gallery, BRISTOL, BS8 1RL, 0117 922 3571
www.bristolmuseums.org.uk/bristol-museum-and-art-gallery

Brook Lodge Farm Camping & Caravan Park
▶▶▶ 92%

tel: 01934 862311 & 07538 055859 **Cowslip Green, Redhill BS40 5RB**
email: info@brooklodgefarm.com **web:** www.brooklodgefarm.com
dir: M5 junction 22, A38 to Churchill. Site 4 miles on right opposite Holiday Inn. Or M5 junction 18, follow Bristol Airport signs. From A38 towards Bridgwater (airport on right). Site 3 miles on left at bottom of hill.

A naturally sheltered country touring park sitting in a valley of the Mendip Hills, surrounded by trees and a historic walled garden. A friendly welcome is always assured by the family owners who are particularly keen on preserving the site's environment and have won a green tourism award. This park is particularly well placed for visiting the Bristol Balloon Festival, held in August, plus the many country walks in the area. There is also a separate glamping area, with bell tents, which has become very popular.

Open: March to October **Last arrival:** 20.00 **Last departure:** 11.30

Pitches: * 🚐 from £21; 🚍 from £20; 🏕 from £19; 🏠 see prices below; 5 hardstanding pitches

Leisure: 🎱

Facilities: 🛁 ☺ ⚑ ❄ ♿ 🚿 🚽 ⍰ WiFi

Services: 🔌 🗑 🔋 🚽

Within 3 miles: 🎣 ⛳

Additional site information: 5 acre site. 🐕 Cars can be parked by caravans and tents. Awnings permitted. Dogs by prior arrangement only. Car hire can be arranged.

Glamping available: Bell tents from £150 (minimum 2 night stay); Shepherd's hut from £100 per night

Additional glamping information: No pets, no stag parties. Cars can be parked by units.

CREWKERNE

See Drimpton (Dorset)

CROWCOMBE
Map 3 ST13

Places to visit

Cleeve Abbey, WASHFORD, TA23 0PS, 01984 640377
www.english-heritage.org.uk/visit/places/cleeve-abbey

Great for kids: Dunster Castle, DUNSTER, TA24 6SL, 01643 821314
www.nationaltrust.org.uk/dunstercastle

Premier Park

Quantock Orchard Caravan Park
►►►►► 79%

tel: 01984 618618 **Flaxpool TA4 4AW**

email: info@quantockorchard.co.uk **web:** www.quantock-orchard.co.uk
dir: Take A358 from Taunton, follow Minehead and Williton signs. In 8 miles left just
past Flaxpool Garage. Site immediately on left.

This small family-run park is set at the foot of the beautiful Quantock Hills and
makes an ideal base for touring Somerset, Exmoor and north Devon. It is also
close to the West Somerset Railway. There is a lovely heated outdoor swimming
pool, plus gym and fitness centre; bike hire is also available. There are static
homes for hire.

Open: All year (restricted service: 10 September to 20 May – swimming pool closed)
Last arrival: 22.00 **Last departure:** noon

Pitches: 🚐 � 🛆; 30 hardstanding pitches

Leisure: 🏊 🎢 🎯 🖵 🎱 🎾

Facilities: 🛁 ⊙ 🖤 ❄ 🕭 🛍 🍴 🏕 WiFi

Services: 🔌 🗑 🛒 ♨ 🛢 ⊘ 🚽

Within 3 miles: 🎯 🎣 ♻

Additional site information: 3.5 acre site. 🐾 Cars can be parked by caravans and
tents. Awnings permitted. Off licence.

DULVERTON
Map 3 SS92

Places to visit

Knightshayes, KNIGHTSHAYES, EX16 7RG, 01884 254665
www.nationaltrust.org.uk/knightshayes

Great for kids: Tiverton Castle, TIVERTON, EX16 6RP, 01884 253200
www.tivertoncastle.com

Wimbleball Lake
►►► 85%

tel: 01398 371460 & 371116 **Brompton Regis TA22 9NU**
email: wimbleball@swlakestrust.org.uk **web:** www.swlakestrust.org.uk
dir: From A396 (Tiverton to Minehead road) take B3222 signed Dulverton Services, follow
signs to Wimbleball Lake. Ignore 1st entry (fishing), take 2nd entry signed tea room and
camping. (Note care needed due to narrow roads).

A grassy site overlooking Wimbleball Lake, set high up on Exmoor National Park. The
camping area is adjacent to the visitor centre and café, which also includes the
camping toilets and showers. A new toilet block opened for the 2019 season. The
camping field, with 14 electric hook-ups and two hardstandings, is in a quiet and
peaceful setting with good views of the lake, which is nationally renowned for its
trout fishing; boats can be hired with advance notice. There are two camping pods
and three Lotus Belle tents for hire.

Open: March to October **Last arrival:** 22.00 **Last departure:** 11.00

Pitches: * 🚐 from £18; 🚐 from £18; 🛆 from £18 🏕; 2 hardstanding pitches

Leisure: ⚽

Facilities: 🛁 ⊙ 🖤 🕭 🛍 🍴 🏕

Services: 🔌 🗑 🍴 🚽

Within 3 miles: 🎣 ♻ ≋ ⚓

Additional site information: 1.25 acre site. 🐾 Cars can be parked by caravans and
tents. Awnings permitted. No open fires, off-ground BBQs only, no swimming in lake. Dogs
must be kept on leads at all times and are not permitted in lake. Watersports and activity
centre, birdwatching, cycling, lakeside walks and bushcraft.

Glamping available: 2 wooden pods; 3 Lotus Belle tents.

Additional glamping information: Cars can be parked by units.

EXFORD

Places to visit

Dunster Castle, DUNSTER, TA24 6SL, 01643 821314
www.nationaltrust.org.uk/dunstercastle

West Somerset Railway, MINEHEAD, TA24 5BG, 01643 704996
www.west-somerset-railway.co.uk

Great for kids: Exmoor Zoological Park, BLACKMOOR GATE, EX31 4SG,
01598 763352, www.exmoorzoo.co.uk

LEISURE: 🏊 Indoor swimming pool 🏊 Outdoor swimming pool 🎢 Children's playground 🧒 Kids' club 🎾 Tennis court 🎱 Games room 🖵 Separate TV room
🏌 Golf course 🎯 Pitch n putt 🚣 Boats for hire 🚲 Bikes for hire 🎬 Cinema 🎵 Entertainment 🎣 Fishing 🏌 Mini golf 🏄 Watersports 💪 Gym 🏉 Sports field ♻ Stables
FACILITIES: 🛁 Baths/Shower ⊙ Electric shaver sockets 🖤 Hairdryer ❄ Ice Pack Facility 🍼 Baby facilities 🕭 Disabled facilities 🛍 Shop on site or within 200yds
🍴 BBQ area 🏕 Picnic area WiFi WiFi

EXFORD
Map 3 SS83

Westermill Farm
▶▶▶ 87%

tel: 01643 831238 & 07970 594808 **TA24 7NJ**
email: info@westermill.com **web:** www.westermill.com
dir: *In Exford follow Porlock sign. Left in 0.25 mile, left to Westermill, sign on tree. Fork left. (NB this is the only recommended route).*

This is an idyllic site for those seeking peace and quiet — it is in a sheltered valley in the heart of Exmoor and has won many awards for conservation. Highly recommended for traditional camping, although a few hardstandings and electric hook ups are available. There are four waymarked walks over the 500-acre working farm and two miles of shallow water of the River Exe to bathe or fish in (not coarse fishing). Self-catering accommodation is also available. Please note, this site should only be approached from Exford (other approaches are difficult).

Open: March to October (restricted service: November to May — smaller toilet block and shop closed)

Pitches: 🚐 🚐 🛖

Leisure: 🎣

Facilities: 🏠 ⊙ 🍴 ☼ 🔥 🛒 🚿 WiFi

Services: 🔄 🔋 🛢 🌀

Additional site information: 12 acre site. ⛔ Cars can be parked by caravans and tents. Awnings permitted. No noise after 23.00. Well behaved dogs accepted. 4 waymarked walks, 500 acre farm.

FROME
Map 4 ST74

Places to visit
Stourhead, STOURHEAD, BA12 6QD, 01747 841152
www.nationaltrust.org.uk/stourhead

Nunney Castle, NUNNEY, BA11 4LW, 0370 333 1181
www.english-heritage.org.uk/visit/places/nunney-castle

Great for kids: Longleat, LONGLEAT, BA12 7NW, 01985 844400
www.longleat.co.uk

Seven Acres Caravan & Camping Site
▶▶▶ 85%

tel: 01373 464222 **Seven Acres, West Woodlands BA11 5EQ**
dir: *From roundabout on A361 (Frome bypass) onto B3092 towards Maiden Bradley, 0.75 mile to site.*

A level meadowland site beside the shallow River Frome, with a bridge across to an adjacent field, and plenty of scope for families. The facilities are spotless. Set on the edge of the Longleat Estate with its stately home, wildlife safari park and many other attractions.

Open: March to October

Pitches: * 🚐 from £18; 🚐 from £18; 🛖 from £13; 16 hardstanding pitches

Facilities: 🏠 ⊙ 🍴 ☼ 🍽 **Services:** 🔄 **Within 3 miles:** 🎣 🐎 ⛳ 🎯 🛒 🔄

Additional site information: 3 acre site. ⛔ 🐾 Cars can be parked by caravans and tents. Awnings permitted.

PITCHES: 🚐 Caravans 🚐 Motorhomes 🛖 Tents 🏠 Glamping accommodation **SERVICES:** 🔌 Electric hook-up 🔄 Launderette 🍺 Licensed bar 🛢 Calor Gas 🔵 Campingaz 🚽 Toilet fluid 🍴 Café/Restaurant 🍟 Fast Food/Takeaway 🔋 Battery charging 🚐 Motorhome service point
* 2019 prices 🚫 No credit or debit cards ⛔ Dogs permitted 🚫 No dogs

GLASTONBURY
Map 4 ST53

Places to visit

Lytes Cary Manor, KINGSDON, TA11 7HU, 01458 224471
www.nationaltrust.org.uk/lytes-cary-manor

Fleet Air Arm Museum, YEOVILTON, BA22 8HT, 01935 840565
www.fleetairarm.com

Great for kids: Haynes International Motor Museum, SPARKFORD, BA22 7LH,
01963 440804, www.himm.co.uk

Platinum Park

Old Oaks Touring & Glamping

►►►►►

tel: 01458 831437 **Wick Farm, Wick BA6 8JS**
email: info@theoldoaks.co.uk **web:** www.theoldoaks.co.uk
dir: M5 junction 23, A39 to Glastonbury. After Street take A39 towards Wells. At 3rd
roundabout follow Wick and Brindham signs. Site 1.5 miles on right. (NB it is
advisable not to use Sat Nav for last part of journey).

An exceptional adults-only park offering larger than average landscaped pitches
(premier pitches have satellite HD TV), impeccably maintained grounds and
wonderful views. The perfect 'get away from it all' spot where you can enjoy
walking, cycling, fishing and touring or simply relaxing amid the abundant
wildlife. The top class facilities include a well-stocked shop selling locally-
sourced produce and home-baked cakes, a smart shower block with excellent
wet rooms, WiFi, free walking and cycling maps, a half-acre fishing lake, a daily
mini bus service to nearby towns and even a hot doggy shower! Glamping now
comprises six 2-person, heated wooden 'camping cabins', two shepherd's huts
and four new mini lodges, all beautifully equipped to a high standard.

Open: March to mid November (restricted service: March and October to
November – reduced opening hours at shop and reception) **Last arrival:** 20.00
Last departure: noon

Pitches: ⊖ from £23.50; ⇌ from £23.50; ▲ from £23.50; ⋒ see prices below;
88 hardstanding pitches

Leisure: ⊡ ✐

Facilities: ⌂ ⊙ ⌁ ✳ ⚿ ⑤ WiFi

Services: ⊕ ⊚ ⊞ ≛ ↯ ⌷ ∅ ⓣ

Additional site information: 15 acre site. Adults only. ⌲ Cars can be parked by
caravans and tents. Awnings permitted. No groups, no noise after 22.30. Off licence,
local produce boxes, caravan cleaning, dog owners' information pack, fish and chip
nights, minibus. Car hire can be arranged.

Glamping available: Wooden pods from £65; shepherd's hut from £95; shepherd's hut
with hot tub from £105; mini cedar lodges from £99; mini cedar lodges with hot tub
from £125. **Changeover days:** any day

Additional glamping information: Each glamping unit has a fire pit and picnic bench
and are dog friendly. Cars can be parked by units.

Isle of Avalon Touring Caravan Park
►►►► 87%

tel: 01458 833618 **Godney Road BA6 9AF**
email: candicehatwell@hotmail.co.uk **web:** www.avaloncaravanpark.co.uk
dir: M5 junction 23, A39 to outskirts of Glastonbury, 2nd exit signed Wells at B&Q
roundabout, straight on at next roundabout, 1st exit at next roundabout (B3151), site
200 yards on right.

A popular site, on the south side of this historic town, and within easy walking
distance of the centre. It is a level park, with a separate tent field, that offers a
quiet environment. It makes an ideal spot from which to explore the many local
attractions that include Glastonbury Tor, Wells, Wookey Hole and Clarks Village.
Approved caravan storage is available.

Open: All year **Last arrival:** 21.00 **Last departure:** 11.00

Pitches: ⊖ ⇌ ▲; 70 hardstanding pitches

Facilities: ⊙ ⌁ ✳ ⚿ ⑤ ⌂ ⊟ WiFi

Services: ⊕ ⊚ ⊞ ≛ ↯ ⌷ ∅ ⓣ

Within 3 miles: ✐ ∪ ⊟

Additional site information: 8 acre site. ⌲ Cars can be parked by caravans and tents.
Awnings permitted. No ball games.

HIGHBRIDGE
Map 4 ST34

Places to visit

Huntspill River National Nature Reserve, WEST HUNTSPILL, 08708 506 506
www.gov.uk/government/publications/somersets-national-nature-reserves/
somersets-national-nature-reserves#huntspill-river

Greenacre Place Touring Caravan Park
►►► 86%

tel: 01278 785227 & 07717 822852 **Bristol Road, Edithmead TA9 4HA**
email: info@greenacreplace.com **web:** www.greenacreplace.com
dir: M5 junction 22, A38 signed Weston-Super-Mare and Burnham-on-Sea. At roundabout
take A38 signed Highbridge and Bridgwater. Site on right.

An excellent small adults-only park, very well located near to the M5 junction 22,
making it great for visiting the Somerset Levels, Burnham-on-Sea, Brean, Cheddar
or Clarks Village. It also makes an excellent stopover when travelling to and from
the West Country. All 10 pitches have electric hook-ups and the small facility block
is very well appointed and clean. There is free WiFi and also a two-bedroom cottage
available for hire where children are accepted. The park is also well placed for
anyone visiting the Somerset Carnivals held in November. Dogs are welcome.

Open: March to November **Last arrival:** 22.00 **Last departure:** 11.00

Pitches: ⊖ ⇌

Facilities: ⌂ ⊙ ⚿ WiFi

Services: ⊕

Within 3 miles: ⌁ ✐ ∪ ◎ ≛ ⅄ ⊟ ⑤ ⊚

Additional site information: 0.5 acre site. Adults only. ⌲ Cars can be parked by
caravans. Awnings permitted. Breathable groundsheets only, no ball games.

MARTOCK
Map 4 ST41

Places to visit

Montacute House, MONTACUTE, TA15 6XP, 01935 823289
www.nationaltrust.org.uk/montacute-house

Great for kids: Fleet Air Arm Museum, YEOVILTON, BA22 8HT, 01935 840565
www.fleetairarm.com

Southfork Caravan Park

▶▶▶▶ 86%

tel: 01935 825661 **Parrett Works TA12 6AE**
email: info@southforkcaravans.co.uk **web:** www.southforkcaravans.co.uk
dir: From A303: approximately 2 miles after Cargate roundabout exit left A303, over fly-over, signed A356 Martock. At junction left, then after sharp bend, next right. Site approximately 1 mile on right. M25 junction 25: follow A358 signed Yeovil. At roundabout junction of A303/A358, 1st exit signed Andover/London. Follow A303, to junction then left to Martock.

A neat, level mainly grass park in a quiet rural area, just outside the pretty village of Martock. Some excellent spacious hardstandings are available. The facilities are always spotless and the whole site is well cared for by the friendly owners, who will ensure your stay is a happy one, a fact borne out by the many repeat customers. The park is unique in that it also has a fully-approved caravan repair and servicing centre with accessory shop. There are also static caravans, a camping pod and a new lodge available for hire. Caravan storage is also available.

Open: All year **Last arrival:** 22.30 **Last departure:** noon

Pitches: 🚐 from £16; 🚙 from £16; ▲ from £16; 🏠 see prices below;
5 hardstanding pitches

Facilities: 🏠 ☺ 🅿 ✳ ⑤ **WiFi**

Services: 🔌 🗑 🔋 ⌀ Ⓣ

Within 3 miles: ⅃ 🖋

Additional site information: 2 acre site. 🐕 Cars can be parked by caravans and tents. Awnings permitted. No loud noise after 22.30, dogs must be kept on short leads at all times.

Glamping available: Wooden pod from £35. **Changeover days:** Any day

Additional glamping information: 12 volt supply only, double beds, picnic table outside. Cars can be parked by units.

MINEHEAD
Map 3 SS94

Places to visit

West Somerset Railway, MINEHEAD, TA24 5BG, 01643 704996
www.west-somerset-railway.co.uk

Dunster Castle, DUNSTER, TA24 6SL, 01643 821314
www.nationaltrust.org.uk/dunstercastle

Great for kids: Tropiquaria Zoo, WASHFORD, TA23 0QB, 01984 640688
www.tropiquaria.co.uk

Minehead & Exmoor Caravan & Camping Park
▶▶▶ 78%

tel: 01643 703074 **Porlock Road TA24 8SW**
email: enquiries@mineheadandexmoorcamping.co.uk
web: www.mineheadandexmoorcamping.co.uk
dir: 1 mile west of Minehead town centre take A39 towards Porlock. Site on right.

A small family-run terraced park, on the edge of Exmoor, spread over five small paddocks and screened by the mature trees that surround it. The level pitches provide a comfortable space for each unit. The site is very conveniently placed for visiting Minehead and the Exmoor National Park.

Open: March to October (restricted service: November to February – open certain weeks only (contact site for details)) **Last arrival:** 21.00 **Last departure:** 11.00

Pitches: 🚐 🚙 ▲; 9 hardstanding pitches; 10 seasonal pitches

Leisure: ⚠

Facilities: 🏠 ☺ 🅿 ✳ ♿

Services: 🔌 🔋 🔋 ⌀

Within 3 miles: ⅃ 🖋 ◎ ⚓ 🍴 ⑤ 🗑

Additional site information: 3 acre site. 🐕 🐕 Cars can be parked by caravans and tents. Awnings permitted. No open fires or loud music. Tumble dryer available.

PORLOCK   Map 3 SS84

Places to visit

West Somerset Railway, MINEHEAD, TA24 5BG, 01643 704996
www.west-somerset-railway.co.uk

Dunster Castle, DUNSTER, TA24 6SL, 01643 821314
www.nationaltrust.org.uk/dunstercastle

Great for kids: Tropiquaria Zoo, WASHFORD, TA23 0QB, 01984 640688
www.tropiquaria.co.uk

Burrowhayes Farm Caravan & Camping Site & Riding Stables

▶▶▶▶ 94%

tel: 01643 862463 **West Luccombe TA24 8HT**
email: info@burrowhayes.co.uk **web:** www.burrowhayes.co.uk
dir: *A39 from Minehead towards Porlock for 5 miles. Left at Red Post to Horner and West Luccombe, site 0.25 mile on right, immediately before humpback bridge.*

A delightful site on the edge of Exmoor that slopes gently down to Horner Water. The farm buildings have been converted into riding stables from where escorted rides onto the moors can be taken; the excellent toilet facilities are housed in timber-clad buildings. Hardstandings are available – some are fully serviced and many of the hook-ups have TV points. There is a popular, well-stocked shop and many countryside walks can be accessed directly from the site.

Open: 15 March to 31 October (restricted service: before Easter – caravan hire and riding not available) **Last arrival:** 22.00 **Last departure:** 11.00
Pitches: * ⊞ from £20; ⊟ from £20; ▲ from £16; 16 hardstanding pitches
Facilities: 🛁 ⊙ 🗜 ✳ ₺ ⑤ 🍴 WiFi
Services: 🔌 🗑 🚰 ⚒ 🔒 ⊘ Ⓣ
Within 3 miles: ⚓ ✐ ⋃ ◎

Additional site information: 8 acre site. 🐾 Cars can be parked by caravans and tents. Awnings permitted. Croissants and baguettes can be ordered.

PRIDDY   Map 4 ST55

Places to visit

Glastonbury Abbey, GLASTONBURY, BA6 9EL, 01458 832267
www.glastonburyabbey.com

The Helicopter Museum, WESTON-SUPER-MARE, BS24 8PP, 01934 635227
www.helicoptermuseum.co.uk

Great for kids: Wookey Hole, WOOKEY HOLE, BA5 1BB, 01749 672243
www.wookey.co.uk

Cheddar Mendip Heights Camping & Caravanning Club Site

▶▶▶▶ 89%

tel: 01749 870241 & 024 7647 5426 **Townsend BA5 3BP**
email: cheddar.site@campingandcaravanningclub.co.uk
web: www.campingandcaravanningclub.co.uk/cheddar
dir: *From A39 take B3135 to Cheddar. Left in 4.5 miles. Site 200 yards on right, signed.*

A gently sloping site set high on the Mendip Hills and surrounded by trees. This excellent campsite offers really good facilities, including top notch family rooms and private cubicles which are spotlessly maintained. Fresh bread is baked daily and, along with pastries, can be ordered each morning from the well-stocked shop. The site is well positioned for visiting local attractions such as Cheddar, Wookey Hole, Wells and Glastonbury, and is popular with walkers. Self-catering caravans are available for hire.

Open: March to January **Last arrival:** 20.00 **Last departure:** noon
Pitches: ⊞ ⊟ ▲; 38 hardstanding pitches
Leisure: ⚏
Facilities: 🛁 ⊙ 🗜 ✳ ₺ ⑤ WiFi
Services: 🔌 🗑 🚰 🔒 ⊘ Ⓣ
Within 3 miles: ⚓ ⋃

Additional site information: 4.5 acre site. 🐾 Cars can be parked by caravans and tents. Awnings permitted. Site gates closed 23.00–07.00. No fires, BBQs must be raised off the ground. Dogs must be on leads at all times. Quiet after 23.00. Freshly baked bread and pastries, local preserves, bacon, sausages, lamb, beef, beer, cider and cheese available at site shop. Car hire can be arranged.

SHEPTON MALLET

Map 4 ST64

Places to visit

East Somerset Railway, CRANMORE, BA4 4QP, 01749 880417
www.eastsomersetrailway.com

The Bishop's Palace, WELLS, BA5 2PD, 01749 988111
www.bishopspalace.org.uk

Great for kids: Wookey Hole, WOOKEY HOLE, BA5 1BB, 01749 672243
www.wookey.co.uk

Greenacres Camping

▶ ▶ 96%

tel: 01749 890497 **Barrow Lane, North Wootton BA4 4HL**
email: stay@greenacres-camping.co.uk **web:** www.greenacres-camping.co.uk
dir: *Approximately halfway between Glastonbury and Shepton Mallet on A361 turn at Steanbow Farm signed North Wootton. Or from A39 between Upper Coxley and Wells (at Brownes Garden Centre) into Woodford Lane. Follow North Wootton and site signs.*

An immaculately maintained site peacefully set within sight of Glastonbury Tor. It is mainly family orientated and there is plenty of space for children to play games in a very safe environment; many thoughtful extra facilities are provided such as play houses and a children's entertainment team in the high season. There is even a 'glow worm safari' at certain times of the year. Facilities are exceptionally clean and cycle hire is available. Please note, caravans and large motorhomes are not accepted.

Open: May to September **Last arrival:** 21.00 **Last departure:** 11.00

Pitches: * 🚐 from £20; ▲ from £20

Leisure: 🅰 ⚽ ⚙

Facilities: 🏠 ☉ ☂ ☀ 🛁 🛏 WiFi

Services: 🔌 🛒 🔋 🥫

Within 3 miles: ⚓ 🏌 ⟳ 🅗 🏪 🌀

Additional site information: 4.5 acre site. 🚫 Cars can be parked by tents. Awnings permitted. No noise between 23.00–07.00. Fire pits, campfires, free use of fridges and freezers, book library. Car hire can be arranged.

SPARKFORD

Map 4 ST62

Places to visit

Lytes Cary Manor, KINGSDON, TA11 7HU, 01458 224471
www.nationaltrust.org.uk/lytes-cary-manor

Haynes International Motor Museum, SPARKFORD, BA22 7LH, 01963 440804
www.himm.co.uk

Long Hazel Park

▶ ▶ ▶ ▶ 88%

tel: 01963 440002 **High Street BA22 7JH**
email: longhazelpark@hotmail.com **web:** www.longhazelpark.co.uk
dir: *Exit A303 at Hazlegrove roundabout, follow signs for Sparkford. Site 400 yards on left.*

A very neat, adults-only park next to the village inn in the high street. This attractive park is run by friendly owners to a very good standard. Many of the spacious pitches have hardstandings. There are also luxury lodges on site for hire or purchase. The site is close to the Haynes International Motor Museum and the Fleet Air Arm Museum.

Open: All year **Last arrival:** 21.00 **Last departure:** 11.00

Pitches: * 🚐 from £26; 🚍 from £26; ▲ from £25; 30 hardstanding pitches

Facilities: 🏠 ☉ ☂ ☀ 🛁 🛏 WiFi

Services: 🔌 🛒 🔋 🔋 🥫 🔧

Within 3 miles: ⚓ 🏌 🏪

Additional site information: 3.5 acre site. Adults only. 🐕 Dogs must be kept on leads at all times and exercised outside the park. 🚗 Cars can be parked by caravans and tents. Awnings permitted. No open fires or fire pits, no noise after 22.00. Picnic tables available, camping spares.

TAUNTON
Map 4 ST22

Places to visit

Hestercombe Gardens, TAUNTON, TA2 8LG, 01823 413923
www.hestercombe.com

Barrington Court, BARRINGTON, TA19 0NQ, 01460 241938
www.nationaltrust.org.uk/barrington-court

Cornish Farm Touring Park
▶▶▶▶ 90%

tel: 01823 327746 **Shoreditch TA3 7BS**
email: info@cornishfarm.com **web:** www.cornishfarm.com
dir: *M5 junction 25, A358 towards Taunton. Left at lights. 3rd left into Ilminster Road (follow Corfe signs). Right at roundabout, left at next roundabout. Right at T-junction, left into Killams Drive, 2nd left into Killams Avenue. Over motorway bridge. Site on left, access via 2nd entrance.*

This smart park provides really top quality facilities throughout. Only two miles from Taunton, it is set in open countryside and is a very convenient base for visiting the many attractions of the area such as Clarks Village, Glastonbury and Cheddar Gorge. Also makes an excellent base for watching county cricket at the nearby Somerset County Ground.

Open: All year **Last arrival:** anytime **Last departure:** 11.30
Pitches: 🚐 from £19; 🚏 from £19; ▲ from £10; 25 hardstanding pitches
Facilities: 🛁 ☉ ℘ ♿ 🍴 WiFi
Services: 🔌 🔋 🛁 🔒 T
Within 3 miles: ⌕ ℘ ∪ ◎ 目 ⑤

Additional site information: 3.5 acre site. 🐾 Cars can be parked by caravans and tents. Awnings permitted.

Ashe Farm Camping & Caravan Site
▶▶▶▶ 82%

tel: 01823 443764 & 07891 989482 **Thornfalcon TA3 5NW**
email: info@ashefarm.co.uk **web:** www.ashefarm.co.uk
dir: *M5 junction 25, A358, east for 2.5 miles. Right at Nags Head pub. Site 0.25 mile on right.*

A well-screened site surrounded by mature trees and shrubs, with two large touring fields. The modern, upgraded facilities block includes toilets and showers plus a separate laundry room. This site is not far from the bustling market town of Taunton, and handy for both south and north coasts. Also makes a good stopover for people travelling on the nearby M5.

Open: April to October **Last arrival:** 22.00 **Last departure:** noon
Pitches: 🚐 🚏 ▲; 11 hardstanding pitches
Leisure: ⋀ ⌕
Facilities: 🛁 ☉ ℘ ☀ ♿
Services: 🔌 🔋
Within 3 miles: ⌕ ℘ ∪ ◎ 目 ⑤

Additional site information: 7 acre site. 🐾 ⊛ Cars can be parked by caravans and tents. Awnings permitted. No camp fires, no noise after 22.00.

LEISURE: 🏊 Indoor swimming pool 🏊 Outdoor swimming pool ⋀ Children's playground 👶 Kids' club ⌕ Tennis court 🎱 Games room ▭ Separate TV room ⌕ Golf course ⚐ Pitch n putt ⛵ Boats for hire 🚲 Bikes for hire 目 Cinema ♫ Entertainment ℘ Fishing ◎ Mini golf 🏄 Watersports 🏋 Gym 🌐 Sports field ∪ Stables **FACILITIES:** 🛁 Baths/Shower ☉ Electric shaver sockets ℘ Hairdryer ☀ Ice Pack Facility 🍼 Baby facilities ♿ Disabled facilities ⑤ Shop on site or within 200yds 🍴 BBQ area 🪑 Picnic area WiFi WiFi

WATCHET   Map 3 ST04

Places to visit

West Somerset Railway, MINEHEAD, TA24 5BG, 01643 704996
www.west-somerset-railway.co.uk

Dunster Castle, DUNSTER, TA24 6SL, 01643 821314
www.nationaltrust.org.uk/dunstercastle

Great for kids: Tropiquaria Zoo, WASHFORD, TA23 0QB, 01984 640688
www.tropiquaria.co.uk

Premier Park

Doniford Bay Holiday Park
▶ ▶ ▶ ▶ ▶   92% HOLIDAY HOME PARK

tel: 01984 632423 **TA23 0TJ**
email: donifordbay@haven.com **web:** www.haven.com/donifordbay
dir: M5 junction 23, A38 towards Bridgwater, A39 towards Minehead. 15 miles, at
West Quantoxhead, right after St Audries garage. Park 1 mile on right.

This well-appointed holiday park, situated adjacent to a shingle and sand
beach, offers a wide range of activities for the whole family. The holiday homes
are spacious and well-appointed and there is plenty to keep children (of all
ages) interested, including great indoor and outdoor pools, a multi-sports
centre, slides and archery. The park has good eating outlets including a nice
café/restaurant. Being close to the Exmoor National Park, it offers visitors the
chance to seek out some of the best scenery in the county.

Open: mid March to end October **Last departure:** 10.00

Holiday Homes: Sleep 8 Bedrooms 2 Bathrooms 1 Toilet 1 Microwave Freezer TV Sky/
Freeview

Leisure: 🏊 🏊 🎮 ✋ 👤 🚴
Facilities: WiFi   **Services:** 🔌

Additional site information: 🐕 Most dog breeds accepted (please check when
booking). Dogs must be kept on leads at all times.

Home Farm Holiday Centre
▶ ▶ ▶ ▶   83%

tel: 01984 632487 **St Audries Bay TA4 4DP**
email: dib@homefarmholidaycentre.co.uk **web:** www.homefarmholidaycentre.co.uk
dir: From Bridgwater take A39 to West Quantoxhead (approximately 15 miles), after
garage, right onto B3191 signed Doniford, 0.25 mile, 1st right.

In a hidden valley beneath the Quantock Hills, this park overlooks its own private
beach. The atmosphere is friendly and quiet, and there are lovely sea views from
the level pitches. Flowerbeds, woodland walks and the Koi carp pond all enhance
this very attractive site, along with a lovely indoor swimming pool, an excellent
children's play area, and a beer garden.

Open: All year (restricted service: November to 1 March — no tents accepted; shop and bar
closed. Takeaway available in main season.) **Last arrival:** dusk **Last departure:** noon

Pitches: 🚐 from £12; 🚍 from £12; ⛺ from £12; 35 hardstanding pitches
Leisure: 🏊 🎮 🏌   **Facilities:** 🏪 ☺ 🌡 ✳ ♿ 🅂 WiFi
Services: 🔌 🔘 🍴 🚮 🔋 🔒 🗑 🔲

Additional site information: 45 acre site. 🐕 Cards can be parked by tents. Awnings
permitted. No noise after 23.00. Table tennis, sea fishing, woodland walk, coastal path;
baguettes, croissants and pain au chocolat available.

WELLS   Map 4 ST54

Places to visit

Glastonbury Abbey, GLASTONBURY, BA6 9EL, 01458 832267
www.glastonburyabbey.com

The Bishop's Palace, WELLS, BA5 2PD, 01749 988111
www.bishopspalace.org.uk

Premier Park

Wells Touring Park
▶ ▶ ▶ ▶ ▶   94%

tel: 01749 676869 **Haybridge BA5 1AJ**
email: info@wellstouringpark.co.uk **web:** www.wellstouringpark.co.uk
dir: On A371 between Wells and Westbury-sub-Mendip.

This well established, adults-only holiday park has first-class toilet facilities
and many hardstandings, some of which are fully serviced. It is a restful park
set in countryside on the outskirts of Wells, and is within easy walking distance
of the city centre, with its spectacular cathedral and Bishop's Palace. Cheddar
Gorge, Bath, Bristol, Weston-Super-Mare, Wookey Hole and Glastonbury are all
within easy driving distance. The site has a function room, The Lounge, which
has free WiFi and an excellent coffee shop, plus a hire car and an excellent
doggy shower. Holiday cottages are available for hire and luxury lodges for sale.

Open: All year **Last arrival:** 20.00 **Last departure:** noon

Pitches: 🚐 🚍; 54 hardstanding pitches; 10 seasonal pitches
Leisure: 🎣 ▭
Facilities: 🏪 ☺ 🌡 ✳ ♿ 🅂 🚿 ⛱ WiFi
Services: 🔌 🔘 🍴 🍽 🚮 🔋 🔒 🗑 🔲
Within 3 miles: 🚴 🏌 ⛳ ◉ 🎯

Additional site information: 7.5 acre site. Adults only. 🐕 Cars can be parked by
caravans. Awnings permitted. No tents. Pétanque. Car hire can be arranged.

WESTON-SUPER-MARE
Map 4 ST36

Places to visit

Weston Museum, WESTON-SUPER-MARE, BS23 1PR, 01934 621028
www.westonmuseum.org

Great for kids: The Helicopter Museum, WESTON-SUPER-MARE, BS24 8PP,
01934 635227, www.helicoptermuseum.co.uk

Country View Holiday Park
▶▶▶▶ 88%

tel: 01934 627595 **Sand Road, Sand Bay BS22 9UJ**
email: info@cvhp.co.uk **web:** www.cvhp.co.uk
dir: *M5 junction 21, A370 towards Weston-Super-Mare. Immediately into left lane, follow Kewstoke and Sand Bay signs. Straight over 3 roundabouts onto Lower Norton Lane. At Sand Bay right into Sand Road, site on right.*

A pleasant open site in a rural area a few hundred yards from Sandy Bay and the beach. The park is also well placed for energetic walks along the coast at either end of the beach and is only a short drive away from Weston-Super-Mare. There is a touring section for tents, caravans and motorhomes with a toilet and shower block. There are hardstanding pitches plus grass pitches all with electricity. The facilities are excellent and well maintained, including a nice outdoor swimming pool and small tasteful bar. There is also a separate seasonal touring section with its own facility block.

Open: March to January **Last arrival:** 20.00 **Last departure:** noon

Pitches: * 🚐 from £20; 🚍 from £20; ▲ from £20; 150 hardstanding pitches; 90 seasonal pitches

Leisure: 🏊 🎱 🎵 ⚽ 🎯

Facilities: 🛁 ⊙ 🌡 ✳ ⚐ 🛒 🥤 WiFi

Services: 🔌 🔟 🍽 ⊺ T

Within 3 miles: ↓ 🏌 ∪ ◎ 🚤 ⛸ ⛷ 🗓 ⑤

Additional site information: 20 acre site. 🐾 Cars can be parked by caravans and tents. Awnings permitted.

WINSFORD
Map 3 SS93

Places to visit

Dunster Castle, DUNSTER, TA24 6SL, 01643 821314
www.nationaltrust.org.uk/dunstercastle

Cleeve Abbey, WASHFORD, TA23 0PS, 01984 640377
www.english-heritage.org.uk/visit/places/cleeve-abbey

Great for kids: Tropiquaria Zoo, WASHFORD, TA23 0QB, 01984 640688
www.tropiquaria.co.uk

Halse Farm Caravan & Camping Park
▶▶▶▶ 82%

tel: 01643 851259 **TA24 7JL**
email: info@halsefarm.co.uk **web:** www.halsefarm.co.uk
dir: *Signed from A396 at Bridgetown. In Winsford turn left, bear left past pub. 1 mile up hill, entrance on left immediately after cattle grid.*

A peaceful little site on Exmoor overlooking a wooded valley with glorious views. This moorland site is quite remote, but it provides good modern toilet facilities which are kept immaculately clean. This is a good base for exploring the Exmoor National Park, and Minehead, Porlock and Lynton are only a short drive away.

Open: 23 March to 31 October **Last arrival:** 22.00 **Last departure:** noon

Pitches: * 🚐 from £14.50; 🚍 from £14.50; ▲

Leisure: 🛝

Facilities: 🛁 ⊙ 🌡 ✳ ⚐ WiFi

Services: 🔌 🔟 🛒 ⚕

Within 3 miles: 🏌 ∪ ⑤

Additional site information: 3 acre site. 🐾 Cars can be parked by caravans and tents. Awnings permitted.

WIVELISCOMBE
Map 3 ST02

Places to visit

Cleeve Abbey, WASHFORD, TA23 0PS, 01984 640377
www.english-heritage.org.uk/visit/places/cleeve-abbey

Hestercombe Gardens, TAUNTON, TA2 8LG, 01823 413923
www.hestercombe.com

Premier Park

Waterrow Touring Park
▷▷ ▷▷ ▷▷ ▷▷ ▷▷ 94%

tel: 01984 623464 **TA4 2AZ**
email: info@waterrowpark.co.uk **web:** www.waterrowpark.co.uk
dir: *M5 junction 25, A358 signed Minehead (bypassing Taunton), B3227 through Wiveliscombe. Site in 3 miles at Waterrow, 0.25 mile past Rock Inn.*

Under pro-active ownership, this really delightful park for adults has spotless facilities, plenty of spacious hardstandings, including fully serviced pitches and a motorhome service point. The River Tone runs along a valley beneath the park, accessed by steps to a nature area created by the owners, where fly-fishing is permitted. Watercolour painting workshops and other activities are available, and the local pub is a short walk away. There is also a bus stop just outside the site.

Open: All year **Last arrival:** 19.00 **Last departure:** 11.30

Pitches: ⊞ ⊞ ▲; 40 hardstanding pitches

Facilities: ☉ ☞ ✳ ⅋ ♨ ☶ WiFi

Services: ☯ ⊡ ≛ ⅄ 🔒 🅣

Within 3 miles: ⌁ ⑤

Additional site information: 8 acre site. Adults only. ⛵ Maximum 3 dogs per unit. Cars can be parked by caravans and tents. Awnings permitted. No gazebos. Caravan storage.

STAFFORDSHIRE

LONGNOR
Map 16 SK06

Places to visit

Poole's Cavern (Buxton Country Park), BUXTON, SK17 9DH, 01298 26978
www.poolescavern.co.uk

Haddon Hall, BAKEWELL, DE45 1LA, 01629 812855
www.haddonhall.co.uk

Premier Park

Longnor Wood Holiday Park
▷▷ ▷▷ ▷▷ ▷▷ ▷▷ 92%

tel: 01298 83648 **Newtown SK17 0NG**
email: info@longnorwood.co.uk **web:** www.longnorwood.co.uk
dir: *From A53 follow Longnor sign. Site signed from village, 1.25 miles.*

Enjoying a secluded and very peaceful setting in the heart of the Peak District National Park, this spacious adults-only park is a hidden gem. It is surrounded by beautiful rolling countryside and sheltered by woodland where there is a variety of wildlife to observe. Expect a warm welcome from the O'Neill family and excellent, well-maintained facilities, including spotlessly clean modern toilets, good hardstanding pitches, high levels of security, a putting green, badminton courts, a 4-acre dog walk (a dog wash is available too) and super walks from the park gate. The reception building includes a small shop. There are two fully-equipped log pods and six statics for hire.

Open: March to 10 January **Last arrival:** 19.00 **Last departure:** noon

Pitches: * ⊞ from £26.50; ⊞ from £26.50; ▲ from £24; ⋒ see prices below; 47 hardstanding pitches; 13 seasonal pitches

Facilities: 🛒 ☉ ☞ ✳ ⑤ ☶ WiFi

Services: ☯ ⊡ ≛ ⅄ 🔒 ⌀ 🅣

Within 3 miles: ⅃ ⌁ ∪ ⌇ ✦

Additional site information: 10.5 acre site. Adults only. ⛵ Cars can be parked by caravans and tents. Awnings permitted. No fires, no noise after 23.00. Car hire can be arranged.

Glamping available: 2 pods from £60. **Changeover days:** Any time

Additional glamping information: Pods: en suite bathroom, under floor heating, double bed and linen, fully equipped kitchen unit, TV/DVD, large external deck, outside furniture. Cars can be parked by units

Suffolk

Suffolk is Constable country, where the county's crumbling, time-ravaged coastline spreads itself under wide skies to convey a wonderful sense of remoteness and solitude. Highly evocative and atmospheric, this is where rivers wind lazily to the sea and notorious 18th-century smugglers hid from the excise men.

It was the artist John Constable who was responsible for raising the region's profile in the 18th century. Constable immortalised these expansive flatlands in his paintings and today the marketing brochures and websites usually refer to the area as Constable Country. Situated on the River Stour at Flatford, Constable's mill is now a major tourist attraction in the area but a close look at the surroundings confirms rural Suffolk is little changed since the family lived here. Constable himself maintained that the Suffolk countryside 'made me a painter and I am grateful.'

Facing the European mainland and with easy access by the various rivers, the county's open, often bleak, landscape made Suffolk vulnerable in early times to attack from waves of invaders. In the Middle Ages, however, it prospered under the wool merchants: it was their wealth that built the great churches which dominate the countryside.

Walking is one of Suffolk's most popular recreational activities. It may be flat but the county has much to discover on foot – not least the isolated Heritage Coast, which can be accessed via the Suffolk Coast Path. Running along the edge of the shore, between Felixstowe and Lowestoft, the trail is a fascinating blend of ecology and military history. Near its southerly start, the path passes close to one of the National Trust's most unusual acquisitions – Orford Ness. Acquired by the Trust in 1993, and officially opened in 1995, this spectacular stretch of coastline had previously been closed to the public since 1915 when the Royal Flying Corps chose Orford Ness as the setting for military research. These days, it is a Site of Special Scientific Interest, recognised in particular for its rare shingle habitats. Visitors to Orford Ness cross the River Ore by National Trust ferry from Orford Quay.

Beyond Orford, the Suffolk Coast Path parts company with the North Sea, albeit briefly, to visit Aldeburgh. Nearby are Snape Maltings, renowned internationally as the home of the Aldeburgh Festival that takes place in June. Benjamin Britten lived at Snape and wrote *Peter Grimes* here. The Suffolk coast is where both the sea and the natural landscape have influenced generations of writers, artists and musicians. An annual literary festival is staged at Aldeburgh on the first weekend in March.

Back on the Suffolk coast, the trail makes for Southwold, with its distinctive, white-walled lighthouse standing sentinel above the town and its colourful beach huts and attractive pier that feature on many a promotional brochure. The final section of the walk is one of the most spectacular, with low, sandy cliffs, several shallow Suffolk broads and the occasional church tower peeping through the trees. Much of Suffolk's coastal heathland is protected as a designated Area of Outstanding Natural Beauty and shelters several rare creatures including the adder, the heath butterfly and the nightjar.

In addition to walking, there is a good choice of cycling routes. There is the Heart of Suffolk Cycle Route, which extends for 78 miles, while the National Byway, a 4,000-mile cycle route around Britain takes in part of Suffolk and is a very enjoyable way to explore the county.

For something less demanding, visit some of Suffolk's best-known towns. Bury St Edmunds, Sudbury and Ipswich feature prominently on the tourist trail, while Lavenham, Kersey and Debenham are a reminder of the county's important role in the wool industry and the vast wealth it yielded the wool merchants. In these charming old towns look out for streets of handsome, period buildings and picturesque, timber-framed houses.

◁ Dunwich coast

SUFFOLK

BUNGAY

Map 13 TM38

Places to visit

Norfolk & Suffolk Aviation Museum, FLIXTON, NR35 1NZ, 01986 896644
www.aviationmuseum.net

Outney Meadow Caravan Park

►►► 79%

tel: 01986 892338 **Outney Meadow NR35 1HG**
email: c.r.hancy@ukgateway.net **web:** www.outneymeadow.co.uk
dir: In Bungay, site signed from roundabout junction of A143 and A144.

Three pleasant grassy areas beside the River Waveney, with screened pitches. The central toilet block offers good modern facilities, especially in the ladies' section, and is open at all times. The views from the site across the wide flood plain could be straight out of a Constable painting. Canoeing and boating, coarse fishing and cycling are all available here.

Open: March to October **Last arrival:** 21.00 **Last departure:** 16.00

Pitches: 🚐 🚃 ▲; 7 hardstanding pitches; 15 seasonal pitches

Facilities: 🛁 ⊙ 🇵 ✳ ♿ ⑤

Services: 🕳 ⑤ 🛒 🔒 🕳 ⊤

Within 3 miles: ↓ 🎣 ≋ ≋

Additional site information: 6 acre site. 🐾 Cars can be parked by caravans and tents. Awnings permitted. Boat and canoe.

DUNWICH

Places to visit

RSPB Minsmere, WESTLETON, IP17 3BY, 01728 648281
www.rspb.org.uk/minsmere

DUNWICH

Map 13 TM47

Premier Park

Haw Wood Farm Caravan Park

►►►►► 92%

tel: 01502 359550 **Hinton IP17 3QT**
email: info@hawwoodfarm.co.uk **web:** www.hawwoodfarm.co.uk
dir: Exit A12, 1.5 miles north of Darsham level crossing at Darsham shop and café. Site 0.5 mile on right.

An unpretentious family-orientated park set in two large fields surrounded by low hedges. The amenity block is appointed to a very high standard – it includes an excellent reception with café, a good play area and excellent toilet and shower facilities. With year-on-year investment and high levels of customer care assured, the visitor's experience is constantly improving.

Open: March to 14 January **Last arrival:** 21.00 **Last departure:** 11.00

Pitches: 🚐 🚃 ▲; 14 hardstanding pitches; 30 seasonal pitches

Leisure: 🅰 🚲

Facilities: 🛁 ⊙ 🇵 ✳ ♿ ⑤ 🍽 🍴 🐾 WiFi

Services: 🕳 ⑤ 🛒 🍴 🛒 🛒 🔒 🕳 ⊤

Within 3 miles: ↓ 🎣 ∪

Additional site information: 15 acre site. 🐾 Cars can be parked by caravans and tents. Awnings permitted. No noise after 22.00. Fresh bread and pastries available. Rainy day craft tent, nature trail, books and board games, table tennis.

LEISURE: 🏊 Indoor swimming pool 🏊 Outdoor swimming pool 🅰 Children's playground 👧 Kids' club 🎾 Tennis court 🎱 Games room 📺 Separate TV room ↓ Golf course ⛳ Pitch n putt 🚣 Boats for hire 🚲 Bikes for hire 🎬 Cinema 🎵 Entertainment 🎣 Fishing ◉ Mini golf 🏄 Watersports 🏋 Gym ⚽ Sports field ∪ Stables
FACILITIES: 🛁 Baths/Shower ⊙ Electric shaver sockets 🇵 Hairdryer ✳ Ice Pack Facility 🐾 Baby facilities ♿ Disabled facilities ⑤ Shop on site or within 200yds 🍖 BBQ area 🍴 Picnic area WiFi WiFi

FELIXSTOWE   Map 13 TM33

Places to visit

Ipswich Museum, IPSWICH, IP1 3QH, 01473 433551
www.cimuseums.org.uk/Ipswich-Museum

Christchurch Mansion, IPSWICH, IP4 2BE, 01473 433554
www.cimuseums.org.uk/Christchurch-Mansion

Peewit Caravan Park

►►► 86%

tel: 01394 284511 **Walton Avenue IP11 2HB**
email: enquiries@peewitcaravanpark.co.uk web: www.peewitcaravanpark.co.uk
dir: *A14 junction 62, follow sign for town centre. Site 100 metres on left.*

A grass touring area fringed by trees, with well-maintained grounds and a colourful floral display. This handy urban site is not overlooked by houses, and the toilet and shower facilities are clean and tidy. A function room contains a TV and library. The beach is a few minutes away by car.

Open: April (or Easter if earlier) to October **Last arrival:** 21.00 **Last departure:** 11.00 (later departures possible)

Pitches: 🚐 from £17; 🚙 from £17; 🛆 from £16; 4 hardstanding pitches

Leisure: ⚑

Facilities: 🏠 ☉ ℗ ✳ ♿ WiFi

Services: 🔌 🗑 🔒

Within 3 miles: 🛁 🎣 ◎ ≋ ≈ 🎌 🛒

Additional site information: 13 acre site. ⌀ Dogs must be kept on a lead. Cars can be parked by caravans and tents. Awnings permitted. 5mph speed restriction on site, only foam footballs permitted. Boules area, bowling green, small play area. Car hire can be arranged.

HOLLESLEY

Places to visit

The Tide Mill Living Museum, WOODBRIDGE, IP12 1BY, 01394 388202
www.woodbridgetidemill.org.uk

Sutton Hoo, WOODBRIDGE, IP12 3DJ, 01394 389700
www.nationaltrust.org.uk/suttonhoo

HOLLESLEY   Map 13 TM34

Run Cottage Touring Park

►►►► 88%

tel: 01394 411309 **Alderton Road IP12 3RQ**
email: info@runcottage.co.uk web: www.runcottage.co.uk
dir: *From A12 (Ipswich to Saxmundham road) onto A1152 at Melton. 1.5 miles, right at roundabout onto B1083. 0.75 mile, left to Hollesley. In Hollesley right into The Street, through village, down hill, over bridge, site 100 yards on left.*

Located in the peaceful village of Hollesley on the Suffolk coast, this landscaped adults-only park is set behind the owners' house. The generously-sized pitches, which include six new super pitches, are serviced by a well-appointed and immaculately maintained toilet block which includes two fully serviced cubicles. Another landscaped field offers 22 extra pitches, each with an electric hook-up and TV point, and seven hardstanding pitches. Two camping pods are available for hire. This site is handy for the National Trust's Sutton Hoo, and also by travelling a little further north, the coastal centre and beach at Dunwich Heath, and the RSPB bird reserve at Minsmere.

Open: All year **Last arrival:** 20.00 **Last departure:** 11.00

Pitches: 🚐 from £24; 🚙 from £24; 🛆 from £24; 🏠 see prices below; 20 hardstanding pitches

Facilities: 🏠 ☉ ℗ ✳ ♿ WiFi

Services: 🔌 🗑 🔋 T

Within 3 miles: 🛁 🎣 ∪ ≋ 🛒

Additional site information: 4.25 acre site. Adults only. ⌀ Cars can be parked by caravans and tents. Awnings permitted. No groundsheets. Satellite TV point on some pitches, 6 touring hardstandings serviced from £27 per night.

Glamping available: Wooden pods from £50.

Additional glamping information: Wooden pods: minimum stay 2 nights in summer. Microwave, toaster, tea and coffee, BBQ stand, bedding included. Cars can be parked by units.

KESSINGLAND
Map 13 TM58

Places to visit

East Anglia Transport Museum, LOWESTOFT, NR33 8BL, 01502 518459
www.eatransportmuseum.co.uk

Lowestoft Maritime Museum, LOWESTOFT, NR32 1XG, 01502 561963
www.lowestoftmaritimemuseum.co.uk

Great for kids: Africa Alive!, KESSINGLAND, NR33 7TF, 01502 740291
www.africa-alive.co.uk

Heathland Beach Holiday Park
▶▶▶▶ 91%

tel: 01502 740337 **London Road NR33 7PJ**
email: reception@heathlandbeach.co.uk **web:** www.heathlandbeach.co.uk
dir: *From roundabout on A12 (1 mile north of Kessingland) take B1437 signed Kessingland (and brown camping signs). Site 1st left.*

A well-run and maintained park offering superb toilet facilities. The park is set in meadowland, with level grass pitches, and mature trees and bushes. There is direct access to the sea and beach, and good provisions for families on site with a heated swimming pool and three play areas. New for 2019 – the Fitness Gym Trail; a cluster of outdoor exercise stations, for guests to use whilst taking in the fresh air. There is a well-stocked fishing lake, and sea fishing is also possible.

Open: April to October **Last arrival:** 21.00 **Last departure:** 11.00

Pitches: 🚐 🚙 ▲; 7 hardstanding pitches

Leisure: 🏊 🛝 ⚅ 🎾 📹 ⚽

Facilities: 🛁 ⊙ 🅿 ✳ ⚒ 🛉 🍴 🎍 WiFi

Services: 🔌 🗑 🍴 🍽 ⚏ ⚓ 🔒 🧴 T

Within 3 miles: ⚓ U ⊚ 🚲 ⛸ 🎍

Additional site information: 5 acre site. 🐕 Only 1 dog per unit during peak times. Cars can be parked by caravans and tents. Awnings permitted. Table tennis. Fresh bread available.

LEISTON

Places to visit

The Long Shop Museum, LEISTON, IP16 4ES, 01728 832189
www.longshopmuseum.co.uk

Leiston Abbey, LEISTON, IP16 4TD
www.english-heritage.org.uk/visit/places/leiston-abbey

Great for kids: Easton Farm Park, EASTON, IP13 0EQ, 01728 746475
www.eastonfarmpark.co.uk

LEISTON
Map 13 TM46

Premier Park

Cakes & Ale
▶▶▶▶▶ 90%

tel: 01728 831655 **Abbey Lane, Theberton IP16 4TE**
email: reception@cakesandale.co.uk **web:** www.cakesandale.co.uk
dir: *From Saxmundham east on B1119. 3 miles, follow minor road over level crossing, turn right, in 0.5 mile straight on at crossroads, entrance 0.5 mile on left.*

A large, well spread out and beautifully maintained site on a former World War II airfield that has many trees and bushes. The spacious touring area includes plenty of hardstandings and 55 super pitches, and there is a good bar. There is a high-quality, solar-powered toilet block containing four fully serviced family rooms, seven cubicled toilet and washbasin rooms, dishwashing facilities, laundry and underfloor heating.

Open: April to end October (restricted service: low season – club, shop and reception reduced opening hours) **Last arrival:** 19.00 **Last departure:** 13.00

Pitches: 🚐 from £32; 🚙 from £32; ▲ from £32; 55 hardstanding pitches

Leisure: 🛝 ⚅ ⚽ **Facilities:** 🛁 ⊙ 🅿 ✳ ⚒ 🛉 WiFi

Services: 🔌 🗑 🍴 ⚓ 🔒 🧴 T

Within 3 miles: ⚓ 📹 U 🚲 🎍

Additional site information: 45 acre site. 🐕 Cars can be parked by caravans and tents. Awnings permitted. No group bookings, no noise between 21.00–08.00. Golf practice range, football pitch, boules, table tennis.

See advert opposite

PITCHES: Caravans Motorhomes Tents Glamping accommodation **SERVICES:** Electric hook-up Launderette Licensed bar
Calor Gas Campingaz Toilet fluid Café/Restaurant Fast Food/Takeaway Battery charging Motorhome service point
* 2019 prices No credit or debit cards Dogs permitted No dogs

LOWESTOFT

See Kessingland

SAXMUNDHAM

Map 13 TM36

Places to visit

The Long Shop Museum, LEISTON, IP16 4ES, 01728 832189
www.longshopmuseum.co.uk

Leiston Abbey, LEISTON, IP16 4TD
www.english-heritage.org.uk/visit/places/leiston-abbey

Great for kids: RSPB Minsmere, WESTLETON, IP17 3BY, 01728 648281
www.rspb.org.uk/minsmere

Marsh Farm Caravan Site

▶▶ 91%

tel: 01728 602168 **Sternfield IP17 1HW**
web: www.marshfarm-caravansite.co.uk
dir: *A12 onto A1094 (Aldeburgh road), at Snape crossroads left signed Sternfield, follow signs to site.*

A very pretty site overlooking reed-fringed lakes which offer excellent coarse fishing. The facilities are very well maintained and includes a basic but fully-equipped facility block; five new toilets were added in 2018. The park truly is a peaceful haven but no tents are allowed.

Open: February to November (weather dependant) **Last arrival:** 21.00 **Last departure:** 14.00

Pitches: 🚐 🚍

Leisure: 🎣

Facilities: 🛁 ❄ 🖥 🍴 🎪

Services: 🔌 ⚡

Within 3 miles: ⚓ ♻ 🎯

Additional site information: 30 acre site. 🐕 🚭 Cars can be parked by caravans. Awnings permitted. Campers must report to reception on arrival. Site closed when freezing temperatures are forecast. Only 1 car per caravan on site. No tents accepted.

THEBERTON

Map 13 TM46

Places to visit

Leiston Abbey, LEISTON, IP16 4TD,
www.english-heritage.org.uk/visit/places/leiston-abbey

RSPB Minsmere, WESTLETON, IP17 3BY, 01728 648281
www.rspb.org.uk/minsmere

Sycamore Park

▶▶▶ 80%

tel: 01728 635830 & 01502 380129 **Rearoff Pump Cottages, Main Road IP16 4RA**
email: enquiries@sycamorepark.co.uk **web:** www.sycamorepark.co.uk
dir: *From A12 at Yoxford take B1122 towards Theberton.*

Sycamore Park is a very peaceful site in the village of Theberton, within easy reach of Southwold and Aldeburgh, and only three miles from RSPB Minsmere. There are 20 electric hook-ups on grass pitches set out in a compact field surrounded by mature trees. The small, but high quality and very stylish, toilet block contains combined cubicled facilities and has underfloor heating.

Open: 3 March to 28 January **Last departure:** noon

Pitches: 🚐 🚍 ⛺; 5 hardstanding pitches

Facilities: 🛁 🎪 WiFi

Services: 🔌

Within 3 miles: ⚓ ♻ 🎯 🍴 🖥 🗑

Additional site information: 2 acre site. Adults only. 🐕 🚭 Cars can be parked by caravans and tents. Awnings permitted.

WOODBRIDGE

Places to visit

Sutton Hoo, WOODBRIDGE, IP12 3DJ, 01394 389700
www.nationaltrust.org.uk/suttonhoo

Orford Castle, ORFORD, IP12 2ND, 01394 450472
www.english-heritage.org.uk/visit/places/orford-castle

Great for kids: Easton Farm Park, EASTON, IP13 0EQ, 01728 746475
www.eastonfarmpark.co.uk

WOODBRIDGE

Map 13 TM24

Premier Park

Moon & Sixpence

▶▶▶▶▶ 92%

tel: 01473 736650 **Newbourn Road, Waldringfield IP12 4PP**
email: info@moonandsixpence.co.uk web: www.moonandsixpence.co.uk
dir: From roundabout on A12 (east of Ipswich) follow brown Moon & Sixpence signs (Waldringfield). In 1.5 miles left at crossroads, follow signs.

A well-planned site, with tourers occupying a sheltered valley position around an attractive boating lake with a sandy beach. Toilet facilities are housed in a smart Norwegian-style cabin, and there is a laundry and dishwashing area. Leisure facilities include tennis courts, a bowling green, fishing, boating and a games room; there's also a lake, woodland trails, a cycle trail and 9-hole golf. The park has an adult-only area, and a strict 'no groups and no noise after 9pm' policy. Please note, tents are not accepted.

Open: April to October (restricted service: low season – reduced opening hours at club, shop and reception) **Last arrival:** 20.00 **Last departure:** noon

Pitches: * 🚐 from £26; 🚍 from £26; 6 hardstanding pitches

Leisure: 🎱 🏊 🎣 ⚽ **Facilities:** 🏠 ☉ ☂ ❄ 🅂 ♨ WiFi

Services: ⚡ 🗑 ⌾ 🍴 🏪 🛒 ⛽ 🐕 🚿 **Within 3 miles:** ☂ 🚴 🚶

Additional site information: 5 acre site. 🐕 Cars can be parked by caravans. Awnings permitted. No tents. No group bookings or commercial vehicles, quiet from 21.00–08.00. 10-acre sports area, 110-acre woods, lake and sandy beaches.

See advert on page 265

Moat Barn Touring Caravan Park

▶▶▶ 85%

tel: 01473 737520 **Dallinghoo Road, Bredfield IP13 6BD**
web: www.moatbarn.co.uk
dir: *Exit A12 at Bredfield, 1st right at village pump. Through village, 1 mile site on left.*

An attractive small park for adults only, set in idyllic Suffolk countryside, perfectly located for touring the heritage coastline and for visiting the National Trust's Sutton Hoo. The modern toilet block is well equipped and maintained. There are 10 tent pitches and the park is located on the popular Hull to Harwich cycle route; cycle hire is available.

Open: March to 15 January **Last arrival:** 22.00 **Last departure:** noon

Pitches: 🚐 from £20; 🚍 from £20; 🛖 from £20; 10 seasonal pitches

Leisure: 🚴

Facilities: 🏠 ☉ ☂ ❄ WiFi

Services: ⚡ 🛒

Within 3 miles: ↡ ☂ ⛳ ◎ 🚴 🚶 🏇 💷 ⛳

Additional site information: 2 acre site. Adults only. 🐕 🚫 Cars can be parked by caravans and tents. Awnings permitted. No ball games, only breathable groundsheets permitted.

Sussex

East and West Sussex are adjoining counties packed with interest. This is a land of stately homes and castles, miles of breezy chalk cliffs overlooking the English Channel, pretty rivers, picturesque villages and links to our glorious past. Since 2011 it has been the home of Britain's newest national park – the South Downs

Mention Sussex to many people and images of the South Downs immediately spring to mind – 'vast, smooth, shaven, serene,' as the writer Virginia Woolf described them. She and her husband lived at Monk's House in the village of Rodmell, near Lewes, and today, her modest home is managed by the National Trust and open to the public.

Close by, on the downs, is Charleston Farmhouse where Woolf's sister, the artist Vanessa Bell, lived a bohemian life as part of the renowned Bloomsbury group, whose members were mainly notable writers, artists and thinkers. Rudyard Kipling resided at Bateman's, near Burwash, and described the house as 'a good and peaceable place,' after moving there in 1902. 'We have loved it ever since our first sight of it,' he wrote later. Bateman's is also in the care of the National Trust, as is Uppark House at South Harting, near Petersfield. The writer H. G. Wells stayed at Uppark as a boy while his mother was employed there as housekeeper. Away to the east, inland from Hastings, lies Great Dixter, an ancient house in a magical garden. This was the home of the pioneering gardening writer Christopher Lloyd and today both Great Dixter and its garden are open to visitors.

There are a great many historic landmarks within Sussex, but probably the most famous is the battlefield where William, Duke of Normandy defeated Harold and his Saxon army to become William the Conqueror of England. By visiting Battle, near Hastings, you can, with a little imagination, picture the bloody events that led to his defeat. Before the Battle of Hastings, William vowed that if God gave him victory that day, he would build an abbey on the site of the battle at Senlac Field. This he did, with the high altar set up on the spot where Harold died. The abbey was enlarged and improved over the years and today is maintained by English Heritage.

In terms of walking in Sussex, this county is spoilt for choice. Studying the map reveals a multitude of routes – many of them to be found within the boundaries of the South Downs National Park – and an assortment of scenic long-distance trails leading towards distant horizons; all of them offer a perfect way to get to the heart of 'Sussex by the sea,' as it has long been known. The Monarch's Way, one of the region's most popular trails, broadly follows Charles II's escape route in 1651, while the most famous of them, the South Downs Way, follows hill paths and cliff-top tracks all the way from Winchester to Eastbourne. As well as a good range of walks, Sussex offers exhilarating cycle rides through the High Weald, along the South Downs Way and via coastal routes between Worthing and Rye. There is also the Forest Way through East Grinstead to Groombridge. If you enjoy cycling with the salty tang of the sea for company, try the ride between Chichester and West Wittering. You can vary the return journey by taking the Itchenor ferry to Bosham.

Sussex is renowned for its many pretty towns, of course. There is Arundel, littered with period buildings and dominated by the castle, the family home of the Duke of Norfolk, that dates back nearly 1,000 years. Midhurst, Lewes, Rye and Uckfield also have their charms, while the cities of Chichester and Brighton offer countless museums and fascinating landmarks. Brighton's best-known and grandest feature is surely the Royal Pavilion, created as the seaside palace of the Prince Regent (later George IV). The town's genteel Regency terraces and graceful crescents reflect his influence on Brighton. Often referred to as 'London by the sea,' the city has long enjoyed a colourful reputation and has been used as a location in many high profile and highly successful films, including *Brighton Rock* and *Quadrophenia*.

EAST SUSSEX

BATTLE   Map 7 TQ71

Places to visit

1066 Battle of Hastings Abbey & Battlefield, BATTLE, TN33 0AE, 01424 775705
www.english-heritage.org.uk/visit/places/1066-battle-of-hastings-abbey-and-battlefield

Great for kids: The Observatory Science Centre, HERSTMONCEUX, BN27 1RN,
01323 832731, www.the-observatory.org

Senlac Wood
►►► 84%

tel: 01424 773969 **Catsfield Road, Catsfield TN33 9LN**
email: enquiries@senlacwood.co.uk **web:** www.senlacwood.co.uk
dir: A271 from Battle onto B2204 signed Bexhill. Site on left.

A woodland site with many secluded hardstanding bays and two peaceful grassy glades for tents. The toilet facilities have been upgraded and are clean and tidy and there's a super little tea room on site. The site is ideal for anyone looking for seclusion and shade and it is well placed for visiting nearby Battle and the south coast beaches.

Open: March to October **Last arrival:** 22.00 **Last departure:** noon

Pitches: 🚐 🚍 ▲; 16 hardstanding pitches

Leisure: 🔍

Facilities: 🛁 ⊙ ☞ ⚙ 🍴 WiFi

Services: 🔌 🍴 ⭐ 🛒 🧺

Within 3 miles: ↕ ◢ ∪ ⑤

Additional site information: 20 acre site. 🐕 Cars can be parked by caravans and tents. Awnings permitted. No camp fires, no noise after 23.00. Caravan storage.

BEXHILL   Map 6 TQ70

Places to visit

RSPB Fore Wood, CROWHURST, TN33 9AG, 01892 752430
www.rspb.org.uk/reserves-and-events/reserves-a-z/fore-wood

Great for kids: The Observatory Science Centre, HERSTMONCEUX, BN27 1RN,
01323 832731, www.the-observatory.org

Premier Park

Kloofs Caravan Park
►►►►► 85%

tel: 01424 842839 **Sandhurst Lane TN39 4RG**
email: camping@kloofs.com **web:** www.kloofs.com

Hidden away down a quiet lane, just inland from Bexhill and the coast, Kloofs is a friendly, family-run park surrounded by farmland and oak woodlands, with views extending to the South Downs from hilltop pitches. Developed by the Griggs family over the past 20 years, the site is well landscaped and thoughtfully laid out, with excellent hardstandings (some large enough for RVs and fully serviced) and spacious pitches, each with mini patio, bench and brick barbecue. Toilet facilities include a family shower room and a unisex block with privacy cubicles, a dog shower and drying room.

Open: All year

Leisure: ⚘

Facilities: 🛁 ⑤

Additional site information: Quiet between 22.00–7.00

HASTINGS & ST LEONARDS

Places to visit

Shipwreck Museum, HASTINGS & ST LEONARDS, TN34 3DW, 01424 437452
www.shipwreckmuseum.co.uk

Great for kids: Blue Reef Aquarium, HASTINGS, TN34 3DW, 01424 718776
www.bluereefaquarium.co.uk/hastings
www.discoverhastings.co.uk

HASTINGS & ST LEONARDS

Map 7 TQ80

Premier Park

Combe Haven Holiday Park
▶▶▶▶▶ 87% HOLIDAY HOME PARK

tel: 01424 427891 **Harley Shute Road, St Leonards-on-Sea TN38 8BZ**
email: combehaven@haven.com web: www.haven.com/combehaven
dir: *A21 towards Hastings. In Hastings take A259 towards Bexhill. Park signed on right.*

Close to a beach and the resort attractions of Hastings, this holiday park has been designed with families in mind. Activities include a pirates' adventure playground, heated swimming pools and a wealth of sports and outdoor activities.

Open: mid March to October

Holiday Homes: Sleep 8 Bedrooms 3 Bathrooms 1 Toilet 1 Microwave Freezer TV Sky/Freeview

Leisure: 🏊 🏊 🎱 👋 🎯

Additional site information: The facilities provided in the holiday homes may differ depending on the grade. 🐕 Most dog breeds accepted (please check when booking). Dogs must be kept on leads at all times.

WEST SUSSEX

ARUNDEL

Map 6 TQ00

Places to visit

Arundel Castle, ARUNDEL, BN18 9AB, 01903 882173
www.arundelcastle.org

Harbour Park, LITTLEHAMPTON, BN17 5LH, 01903 721200
www.harbourpark.com

Great for kids: WWT Arundel Wetland Centre, ARUNDEL, BN18 9PB, 01903 883355
www.wwt.org.uk/wetland-centres/arundel

Ship & Anchor Marina
▶▶ 79%

tel: 01243 551262 **Station Road, Ford BN18 0BJ**
email: enquiries@shipandanchormarina.co.uk
dir: *From A27 at Arundel take road south signed Ford. Site 2 miles on left after level crossing.*

Neatly maintained by the enthusiastic, hard working owner, this small, well located site has dated but spotlessly clean toilet facilities, a secluded tent area, and enjoys a pleasant position beside the Ship & Anchor pub and the tidal River Arun. There are good walks from the site to Arundel and the coast. River fishing is possible.

Open: March to October **Last arrival:** 21.00 **Last departure:** noon

Pitches: 🚐 from £23; 🚌 from £23; ▲ from £20; 11 hardstanding pitches; 40 seasonal pitches

Leisure: 🎱

Facilities: 📷 ⊙ 🍴 ✳ ♿ 🛒

Services: 🔌 🎱 🍴 🛒 🔋 🔒 🗑 T

Within 3 miles: 🎣 ▱ ∪ ◎ ◉ ⚷ 🍴 🛶

Additional site information: 12 acre site. 🐕 Cars can be parked by caravans and tents. Awnings permitted. No music audible to others, no visitors, no ball games. Pub on site, river walk.

BARNS GREEN

Map 6 TQ12

Places to visit

Parham House & Gardens, PULBOROUGH, RH20 4HS, 01903 742021
www.parhaminsussex.co.uk

Great for kids: Bignor Roman Villa, BIGNOR, RH20 1PH, 01798 869259
www.bignorromanvilla.co.uk

Sumners Ponds Fishery & Campsite
▶▶▶▶ 90%

tel: 01403 732539 **Chapel Road RH13 0PR**
email: bookings@sumnersponds.co.uk web: www.sumnersponds.co.uk
dir: *From A272 at Coolham crossroads, north towards Barns Green. In 1.5 miles take 1st left at small crossroads. 1 mile, over level crossing. Site on left just after right bend.*

Dedication to provide high quality camping continues at this working farm set in attractive surroundings on the edge of the quiet village of Barns Green. There are three touring areas; one continues to develop and includes camping pods and extra hardstandings, and another, which has a stunning modern toilet block, has excellent pitches on the banks of one of the well-stocked fishing lakes. For a glamping holiday there are wooden pods, an impressive fully-equipped safari tent, lodges and shepherd's huts. There are many cycle paths on site and a woodland walk has direct access to miles of footpaths. The Café by the Lake serves meals from breakfast onwards. Horsham and Brighton are within easy reach.

Open: All year **Last arrival:** 20.00 **Last departure:** noon

Pitches: * 🚐 from £21; 🚌 from £21; ▲ from £21; 🏠 see prices below; 45 hardstanding pitches

Leisure: 🎱 ▱

Facilities: 📷 ⊙ 🍴 ✳ ♿ 🛒 🍴 WiFi

Services: 🔌 🗑 🍴 🛒 🔋 🔒 🗑 T

Within 3 miles: 🎣 ∪ 🛶

Additional site information: 100 acre site. 🐕 Well behaved dogs. Cars can be parked by caravans and tents. Awnings permitted. 1 car per pitch. No noise after 22.30. Fishing lakes, footpaths.

Glamping available: 6 sleeping pods from £36; 4 shepherd's huts from £100; 1 safari tent from £255.

Additional glamping information: Sleeping pods: minimum stay 1 night (2 nights at weekends, school holidays), 3 nights at bank holiday weekends; Shepherd's huts: minimum stay 2 nights (3 at weekends; 4 nights at Easter weekend); Safari tent minimum stay 3 nights Friday to Monday (4 nights Monday to Friday; 7 nights Friday to Friday or Monday to Monday) All units – electricity; no smoking. Shepherd's huts and safari tent – log burners; no dogs. Sleeping pods – electric heater. Cars can be parked by units.

PITCHES: 🚐 Caravans 🚌 Motorhomes ▲ Tents 🏠 Glamping accommodation **SERVICES:** 🔌 Electric hook-up 🗑 Launderette 🍴 Licensed bar 🔒 Calor Gas ⚬ Campingaz T Toilet fluid 🍴 Café/Restaurant 🛒 Fast Food/Takeaway 🔋 Battery charging 🛶 Motorhome service point * 2019 prices ⊗ No credit or debit cards 🐕 Dogs permitted ⊗ No dogs

CHICHESTER
Map 5 SU80

Places to visit
Pallant House Gallery, CHICHESTER, PO19 1TJ, 01243 774557
www.pallant.org.uk

Chichester Cathedral, CHICHESTER, PO19 1PX, 01243 782595
www.chichestercathedral.org.uk

Platinum Park

Concierge Camping

▶ ▶ ▶ ▶ ▶

The Best of British

tel: 01243 573118 **Ratham Estate, Ratham Lane PO18 8DL**
email: service@conciergecamping.co.uk **web:** www.conciergecamping.co.uk
dir: *From A27 onto A259 to Bosham. In Bosham at roundabout into Station Road. Over railway line, over A27. At T-junction left onto B2146 signed West Ashling. 1st left into Ratham Lane.*

Developing this stunning park in a field adjoining their home has been a labour of love for owners, Tracey and Guy. It is a first-class, small park for 27 units offering large fully serviced pitches with some suitable for American RVs, and the attention to detail throughout is very impressive. Everything is high spec, from very spacious pitches and the reception, complete with a shop that sells daily-delivered local produce, coffee, drinks, late-arrival and breakfast hampers, and smart alfresco tables and chairs for all to use, to the state-of-the-art amenity block. Here you'll find full-length mirrors, ultra-efficient rain showers, an air-blade hand drier, stylish washbasins and showers with temperature controls, piped radio and Ratham Estate toiletries plus an excellent room for families or disabled guests.

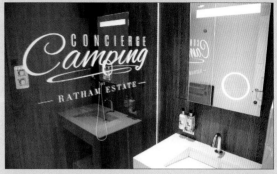

Concierge Camping

Open: All year **Last arrival:** 18.00 (later arrival times by prior arrangement)
Last departure: noon

Pitches: 🚐 🚍; 27 hardstanding pitches

Facilities: 🚿 ☉ 🏳 ♿ 🗑 🧺 🛋 WiFi

Services: 🔌 🔋 🚽 🍴 ♻ T

Within 3 miles: 🎣 🚴 ∪ 🏌 ⛳ 日

Additional site information: 4 acre site. 🐕 Cars can be parked by caravans. Awnings permitted. No bookings accepted by under 18 years. No noise after 23.00. Earliest arrival 13.00. No awnings on the grass. Fresh pastries available each morning.

See advert opposite

Premier Park

Concierge Glamping

▶ ▶ ▶ ▶   93% GLAMPING ONLY

tel: 01243 573118 **Ratham Estate, Ratham Lane PO18 8DL**
email: service@conciergecamping.co.uk **web:** www.conciergecamping.co.uk
dir: *From A27 onto A259 to Bosham. In Bosham at roundabout into Station Road. Over railway line, over A27. At T-junction left onto B2146 signed West Ashling. 1st left into Ratham Lane.*

Quality and attention to detail are very evident at Guy and Tracey Hodgkin's park near Chichester. They offer four stunning safari tents, idyllically situated in an adjoining meadow to the main site, beside a babbling chalk stream. These impressive 'lodges' are made from wood and top-quality canvas — they ooze style and comfort, with a range cooker, dishwasher, fridge-freezer, TV, underfloor

---

heating and a Nespresso machine in the fully-fitted kitchen, a smart en suite shower room (with piped radio), and two good-size bedrooms; the twin-bedded room is situated at the top of a wooden staircase. Each tent has a large veranda, replete with stylish seating, picnic bench and barbecue, and overlooks a stream.

Open: All year **Last arrival:** 18.00 **Last departure:** 10.00

Facilities: 🏠 ⊙ 🅿 ✳ ♨ 🗲 WiFi

Within 3 miles: ⑤

Accommodation available: Safari Lodge from £633

Changeover days: Monday and Friday

Additional site information: 4 acre site. 🐕 Booking advisable. Minimum stay 3 nights.

Ellscott Park
▶▶▶ 84%

tel: 01243 512003 **Sidlesham Lane, Birdham PO20 7QL**
email: camping@ellscottpark.co.uk **web:** www.ellscottpark.co.uk
dir: *From Chichester take A286 towards West Wittering. In approximately 4 miles left at Butterfly Farm sign, site 500 yards right.*

A well-kept park set in sheltered meadowland behind the owners' nursery and van storage area. The park attracts a peace-loving clientele, has spotless, well-maintained toilet facilities, and is handy for the beach, Chichester, Goodwood House, the racing at Goodwood and walking on the South Downs.

Open: April to 2nd week October **Last arrival:** in daylight **Last departure:** variable
Pitches: ⌕ from £17; ⌕ from £17; ▲ from £14; 26 seasonal pitches
Leisure: ♨ ⚽
Facilities: 🏠 ⊙ ✳ ♿ ♨ 🗲 WiFi
Services: 🔌 🔋 🛒 ⌀
Within 3 miles: ⌕ ⚲ ∪ ◎ ⚑ ⚑ ⑤

Additional site information: 6 acre site. 🐕 🐾 Cars can be parked by caravans and tents. Awnings permitted. No commercial vehicles, site closed between 22.30–07.00. Car hire can be arranged.

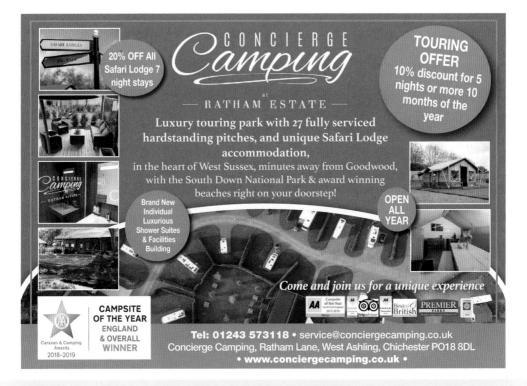

HENFIELD   Map 6 TQ21

Places to visit

Bolney Wine Estate, BOLNEY, RH17 5NB, 01444 881575
www.bolneywineestate.com

Blacklands Farm Caravan & Camping
►►► 74%

tel: 01273 493528 **Wheatsheaf Road BN5 9AT**
email: info@blacklandsfarm.co.uk **web:** www.blacklandsfarm.co.uk
dir: *A23, B2118, B2116 towards Henfield. Site approximately 4 miles on right.*

Tucked away, just off the B2116 east of Henfield, and well placed for visiting
Brighton and exploring the South Downs National Park, this simple, grassy site has
great potential and is gradually developing. There are spacious pitches down by
fishing lakes and the basic portaloos, smartly clad in wood, are clean and tidy – the
owners still have plans for a new toilet block.

Open: March to January **Last arrival:** 20.00 **Last departure:** anytime

Pitches: 🚐 🚙 ▲; 10 hardstanding pitches

Leisure: ⚠ ⌒ ⚽

Facilities: 🛁 ☔ ✳ 㕭 ⑤ 🚿 ᴒ WiFi

Services: 🔌 🔘 🚽 T

Within 3 miles: ⚓ ∪

Additional site information: 5 acre site. 🐕 Cars can be parked by caravans and tents.
Awnings permitted. No commercial vehicles, no noise after 23.00. Coffee machine.

HORSHAM

See Barns Green

PAGHAM   Map 6 SZ89

Places to visit

RSPB Pagham Harbour LNR, SIDLESHAM, PO20 7NE, 01243 641508
www.rspb.org.uk/reserves-and-events/reserves-a-z/pagham-harbour-local-
nature-reserve

Premier Park

Church Farm Holiday Park
►►►►► 92% HOLIDAY HOME PARK

tel: 01243 262635 **Church Lane PO21 4NR**
email: churchfarm@haven.com **web:** www.haven.com/churchfarm
dir: *At roundabout on A27 (south of Chichester) take B2145 signed Hunston and
Selsey. At mini-roundabout take 1st left signed North Mundham, Pagham and Bognor
Regis. Site in approximately 3 miles.*

Close to Portsmouth, Chichester and south coast beaches, this relaxing and
fun-packed holiday park is located on the edge of Pagham Harbour Nature
Reserve. On-site activities include golf on the 9-hole course, tennis coaching,
shopping, kids' play areas, excellent indoor and outdoor swimming pools, a new
pool-side bar and pizzeria, and evening entertainment. There are a range of
holiday caravans and apartments.

Open: 15 March to 31 October

Holiday Homes: Sleep 8 Bedrooms 2 Bathrooms 1 Toilet 1 Microwave Freezer TV
Sky/Freeview

Leisure: 🏊 🏊 ⚠ 👶 🐎

Additional site information: 🐕

SELSEY
Map 6 SZ89

Places to visit

RSPB Pagham Harbour LNR, SIDLESHAM, PO20 7NE, 01243 641508
www.rspb.org.uk/reserves-and-events/reserves-a-z/pagham-harbour-local-nature-reserve

Fishbourne Roman Palace, FISHBOURNE, PO19 3QR, 01243 785859
sussexpast.co.uk/properties-to-discover/fishbourne-roman-palace

---

Warner Farm
▶▶▶▶ 85% HOLIDAY CENTRE

tel: 01243 604499 **Warner Lane, Selsey PO20 9EL**
email: touring@bunnleisure.co.uk **web:** www.warnerfarm.co.uk
dir: *From B2145 in Selsey turn right into School Lane, follow signs.*

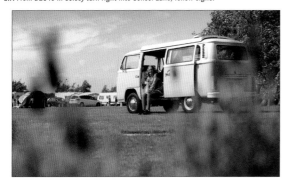

A well-screened touring site that adjoins the three static parks under the same ownership. A courtesy bus runs around the complex to entertainment areas and supermarkets. The park backs onto open grassland and offers modern toilet facilities and an excellent children's play area, and the leisure facilities with bar, amusements and bowling alley, and swimming pool/sauna complex are also accessible to tourers. A new top quality leisure complex with swimming pool and restaurants was opened on neighbouring White Horse Park in April 2019.

Open: March to January **Last arrival:** 17.30 **Last departure:** 10.00
Pitches: 🚐 🚍 ⚊ ; 60 hardstanding pitches; 25 seasonal pitches

---

Leisure: 🏊 🏊 🎱 🎣 ⚲ 🎯 🎵 🏇 ⚽ ☉
Facilities: 🚪 ☉ 🚿 ❄ ⚹ 🖫 🍴 🛒 WiFi
Services: 🔌 🛢 🍴 🍽 🍺 ⛽ 🔋 ⚙ T
Within 3 miles: 🚴 ⚲ ∪ ◎ 🚵 🎣
Additional site information: 10 acre site. 🐕

See advert opposite

TYNE & WEAR

SOUTH SHIELDS
Map 21 NZ36

Places to visit

Arbeia Roman Fort & Museum, SOUTH SHIELDS, NE33 2BB, 0191 277 1410
arbeiaromanfort.org.uk

Souter Lighthouse & The Leas, WHITBURN, SR6 7NH, 0191 529 3161
www.nationaltrust.org.uk/souter-lighthouse-and-the-leas

Great for kids: Blue Reef Aquarium, TYNEMOUTH, NE30 4JF, 0191 258 1031
www.bluereefaquarium.co.uk/tynemouth

Lizard Lane Caravan & Camping Site
▶▶▶ 87%

tel: 0191 455 4455 & 455 1732 **Lizard Lane NE34 7AB**
email: lizardlanecaravanpark@gmail.com **web:** www.meridianparks.co.uk
dir: *2 miles south of town centre on A183 (Sunderland road).*

Lizard Lane Caravan and Camping Site was in the midst of a full investment programme across the whole site with fantastic results seen at the time of our inspection visit. This work was close to being finished for the start of the 2019 season. This ever improving site is located in an elevated position with good sea views. All touring pitches are fully serviced and the modern smart amenity block is equipped with superb fixtures and fittings. A shop is also provided.

Open: February to 28 January **Last arrival:** 18.00 **Last departure:** 11.00
Pitches: 🚐 🚍 ⚊ ; 16 hardstanding pitches
Facilities: 🚿 ❄ ⚹ 🖫 🍴 WiFi
Services: 🔌 🛢 🔋 🔋 ⚙
Within 3 miles: 🚴 ⚲ ∪ ◎ 🚵 🎣 🎯
Additional site information: 2 acre site. 🐕 Cars can be parked by caravans and tents.

WARWICKSHIRE

HARBURY
Map 11 SP35

Places to visit

Warwick Castle, WARWICK, CV34 4QU, 01926 495421
www.warwick-castle.com

Farnborough Hall, FARNBOROUGH, OX17 1DU, 01295 670266
www.nationaltrust.org.uk/farnborough-hall

Great for kids: British Motor Museum, GAYDON, CV35 0BJ, 01926 641188
www.britishmotormuseum.co.uk

Premier Park

Harbury Fields
►►►►► 85%

tel: 01926 612457 **Harbury Fields Farm CV33 9JN**
email: rdavis@harburyfields.co.uk **web:** www.harburyfields.co.uk
dir: M40 junction 12, B4451 (signed Kineton and Gaydon). 0.75 mile, right signed Lightborne. 4 miles, right at roundabout onto B4455 (signed Harbury). 3rd right by petrol station, site in 700 yards by two cottages.

This peaceful park is in a peaceful farm setting with lovely countryside views. All pitches are hardstanding and fully serviced, the reception is housed in an attractive wooden chalet, and the facility block has fully serviced cubicles. The park is well positioned for visiting Warwick and Royal Leamington Spa as well as NEC Birmingham and Stoneleigh Park. Stratford is just 10 miles away, and Upton House (NT) and Compton Valley Art Gallery are nearby.

Open: February to 1 December **Last arrival:** 20.00 **Last departure:** noon
Pitches: * ⊞ from £19.50; ⊞ from £19.50; 59 hardstanding pitches
Facilities: 🛁 ♿ 📶
Services: 🔌 🔲 ⬇
Within 3 miles: ⅃ ↗ 🛒

Additional site information: 6 acre site. 🐕 Cars can be parked by caravans. Awnings permitted. No traffic noise midnight to 07.30.

KINGSBURY

Places to visit

Drayton Manor Theme Park, TAMWORTH, B78 3TW
www.draytonmanor.co.uk

Tamworth Castle, TAMWORTH, B79 7NA, 01827 709626
www.tamworthcastle.co.uk

Great for kids: Ash End House Children's Farm, MIDDLETON, B78 2BL,
0121 329 3240, www.childrensfarm.co.uk

KINGSBURY
Map 10 SP29

Tame View Caravan Site
► 69%

tel: 01827 873853 **Cliff Hall Lane B78 2DR**
dir: From A51 (Tamworth to Kingsbury road). Approximately 1 mile north of Kingsbury into Cliff Hall Lane (opposite pub), 400 yards to site.

A secluded spot overlooking the Tame Valley and river, sheltered by high hedges. Sanitary facilities are minimal but clean on this small park. The site is popular with many returning visitors who like a peaceful, basic site.

Open: All year **Last arrival:** 23.00 **Last departure:** 23.00
Pitches: ⊞ ⊞ ▲
Leisure: ✎
Facilities: 🛁 ✳ 🍳 🛋
Services: 🔌 🚽
Within 3 miles: ⅃ ↻ ◎ 🚣 ✈ 🗓 🛒 🎣

Additional site information: 3 acre site. 🐕 ⊛ Cars can be parked by caravans and tents. Awnings permitted. No noise after midnight. Fishing, takeaway food can be ordered for delivery.

WOLVEY
Map 11 SP48

Places to visit

Arbury Hall, NUNEATON, CV10 7PZ, 01676 540529
www.arburyestate.co.uk

Lunt Roman Fort, COVENTRY, CV8 3AJ, 024 7623 7575
www.luntromanfort.org

Great for kids: Coventry Transport Museum, COVENTRY, CV1 1JD, 024 7623 4270
www.transport-museum.com

Wolvey Villa Farm Caravan & Camping Park
►►► 80%

tel: 01455 220493 **LE10 3HF**
web: www.wolveycaravanpark.itgo.com
dir: M6 junction 2, B4065 follow Wolvey signs. Or M69 junction 1 and follow Wolvey signs.

A level grass site, surrounded by trees and shrubs, on the border of Warwickshire and Leicestershire. This quiet country site has its own popular fishing lake, and is convenient for visiting Coventry and Leicester. There are limited pitches available between October and March and park closes from November to February.

Open: 1 March to 31 October **Last arrival:** 22.00 **Last departure:** noon
Pitches: ⊞ ⊞ ▲; 24 hardstanding pitches
Leisure: 🎱 ✎ ⚽
Facilities: 🛁 ⊙ 🍳 ✳ ♿ 🛒 🛋
Services: 🔌 🔲 🛒 🧺 ⓣ
Within 3 miles: ⅃ ↻ ◎ 🗓

Additional site information: 7 acre site. 🐕 ⊛ Cars can be parked by caravans and tents. Awnings permitted. No noise after 23.00. No fire pits, no twin axle vehicles. Putting green, off licence.

WEST MIDLANDS

Places to visit

Blakesley Hall, BIRMINGHAM, B25 8RN, 0121 348 8120
www.birminghammuseums.org.uk/blakesley

Packwood House, LAPWORTH, B94 6AT, 01564 782024
www.nationaltrust.org.uk/packwood-house

MERIDEN   Map 10 SP28

Somers Wood Caravan Park

▶▶▶▶ 92%

tel: 01676 522978 **Somers Road CV7 7PL**
email: enquiries@somerswood.co.uk **web:** www.somerswood.co.uk
dir: *M42 junction 6, A45 signed Coventry. Keep left, do not take flyover. Right onto A452 signed Meriden and Leamington. At next roundabout left onto B4102 (Hampton Lane). Site in 0.5 mile on left.*

A peaceful adults-only park set in the heart of England with spotless facilities. The park is well positioned for visiting the National Exhibition Centre (NEC), the NEC Arena and National Indoor Arena (NIA), and Birmingham is only 12 miles away. The park also makes an ideal touring base for Stratford-upon-Avon, Warwick and Coventry. Please note, tents are not accepted.

Open: All year **Last arrival:** variable **Last departure:** variable

Pitches: 🚐 from £24; 🚍 from £24; 48 hardstanding pitches

Facilities: 🛁 ⊙ ℙ ♿ 📶

Services: 🔌 🗄 🛒 ⚡ Ⓣ

Within 3 miles: 🎣 ✎ ∪ 🎡 🏪

Additional site information: 4 acre site. Adults only. 🐕 Cars can be parked by caravans. Awnings permitted. No noise 22.30–08.00.

WILTSHIRE

AMESBURY

Places to visit

Stonehenge, STONEHENGE, SP4 7DE, 0370 333 1181
www.english-heritage.org.uk/visit/places/stonehenge

Heale Garden, MIDDLE WOODFORD, SP4 6NT, 01722 782504
www.healegarden.co.uk

Great for kids: Wilton House, WILTON [NEAR SALISBURY], SP2 0BJ, 01722 746728, www.wiltonhouse.com

AMESBURY   Map 5 SU14

Stonehenge Touring Park

▶▶▶ 91%

tel: 01980 620304 **Orcheston SP3 4SH**
email: stay@stonehengetouringpark.com **web:** www.stonehengetouringpark.com
dir: *From A360 towards Devizes turn right, follow lane, site at bottom of village on right.*

A quiet site adjacent to the small village of Orcheston near the centre of Salisbury Plain. There are modern and very clean facilities and an excellent on-site shop; some hardstandings are available and new cabins were added for 2019. This is a well located site for visiting Stonehenge and nearby Salisbury plus it's less that an hour's drive from the heart of the New Forest National Park.

Open: All year **Last arrival:** 19.00 **Last departure:** 11.00

Pitches: 🚐 🚍 ⚡; 13 hardstanding pitches

Leisure: ⚹

Facilities: 🛁 ⊙ ℙ ✳ ♿ 🖥 🛒 📶

Services: 🔌 🗄 🛒 ⚡ 🅰 ⊘ Ⓣ

Within 3 miles: ∪

Additional site information: 2 acre site. 🐕 Cars can be parked by caravans and tents. Awnings permitted. No noise after 23.00.

BERWICK ST JAMES   Map 5 SU03

Places to visit

Stonehenge, STONEHENGE, SP4 7DE, 0370 333 1181
www.english-heritage.org.uk/visit/places/stonehenge

Stonehenge Campsite & Glamping Pods

▶▶▶▶ 82%

tel: 07786 734732 **SP3 4TQ**
email: stay@stonehengecampsite.co.uk **web:** www.stonehengecampsite.co.uk
dir: *From Stonehenge Visitor Centre take A303 west, 2 miles. Through Winterbourne Stoke. Left onto B3083 towards Berwick St James. Site on left in 0.5 mile.*

This small campsite is split into three areas and has good modern toilets and showers including a laundry facility. The lower end of the site has hardstandings for caravans and motorhomes plus six glamping pods, including the novel Festival Pod. The middle field is for tents, both for families and individuals, whilst the top area is for larger groups who can enjoy some of their holiday time sitting around open fires or fire pits. The site is close to Stonehenge and Longleat; there are plenty of excellent walks from the campsite and two good pubs nearby.

Open: All year **Last arrival:** 20.00 **Last departure:** 10.45

Pitches: 🚐 🚍 ⚡ 🏕; see prices below; 12 hardstanding pitches

Facilities: 🛁 ⊙ ℙ ✳ 🖥 🪑 📶

Services: 🔌 🗄 🍺

Within 3 miles: ✎ ∪ 🏪

Additional site information: 4 acre site. 🐕 Cars can be parked by caravans and tents. Awnings permitted. No noise 22.00–08.00, no music at any time. Camp fire and mobile fire pits.

Glamping available: Luxury wooden pods from £45, basic festival and hobbit pods from £25.

Additional glamping information: Continental breakfast.

Blackland Lakes Holiday & Leisure Centre
▶▶▶ 83%

tel: 01249 810943 **Stockley Lane SN11 0NQ**
email: enquiries@blacklandlakes.co.uk **web:** www.blacklandlakes.co.uk
dir: *From Calne take A4 towards Beckhampton and Avebury for 1.5 miles. In Quemerford right at brown camp sign and Stockley/Headington sign into Stockley Lane. Site 1 mile on left.*

A rural site surrounded by the North and West Downs. The park offers 15 fully serviced pitches and is divided into several paddocks separated by hedges, trees and fences, and there are two well-stocked carp fisheries for the angling enthusiast. There are some excellent walks close by, and the interesting market town of Devizes is just a few miles away.

Open: All year (restricted service: 30 October to 1 March – pre-paid bookings only)
Last arrival: 22.00 **Last departure:** noon

Pitches: * 🚐 from £18.50; 🚌 from £18.50; ▲ from £18.50; 16 hardstanding pitches; 25 seasonal pitches

Leisure: 🎱 ✎

Facilities: 🚿 ☉ 🥾 ✳ ♿ ⑤ 🍴 🪑

Services: 🔌 🔋 🍽 🚮 ⬆ 🛢 ⊘ ⊤

Within 3 miles: 🎣 ↻

Additional site information: 15 acre site. 🐕 Cars can be parked by caravans and tents. Awnings permitted. No groups of under 25s. No noise after 22.30, no loud music. Wildfowl sanctuary, cycle trail, nature trail, pygmy goats. Licensed bar on bank holidays, Friday and Saturday in peak season.

Summerlands Caravan Park
▶▶▶ 80%

tel: 01722 718259 & 07718 014343 **College Farm, Rockbourne Road SP5 4LP**
email: enquiries@summerlandscaravanpark.co.uk
web: www.summerlandscaravanpark.co.uk
dir: *Signed from junction of A354 and Rockbourne Road. Approximately 6 miles south of Salisbury.*

Approached via a long private drive and situated well off the beaten track within Cranborne Chase, yet close to Salisbury, this small, family-run park offers peace and quiet and superb views across rolling countryside. 26 level grass pitches are located in a neat meadow and the well-maintained toilet and shower facilities are

kept spotlessly clean. There is also a well-equipped bell tent for hire. Dogs are welcome and there's plenty of space for children to play.

Open: April to October **Last arrival:** 21.00 **Last departure:** noon

Pitches: * 🚐 from £17; 🚌 from £17; ▲ from £17

Facilities: 🚿 ☉ 🥾 ✳ ♿

Services: 🔌 🚮 ⬆

Within 3 miles: ⑤

Additional site information: 3.3 acre site. 🐕 Cars can be parked by caravans and tents. Awnings permitted. No noise after 23.00. Vehicle access restrictions 23.00–07.00.

Piccadilly Caravan Park
▶▶▶▶ 85%

tel: 01249 730260 **Folly Lane West SN15 2LP**
email: info@piccadillylacock.co.uk **web:** www.piccadillylacock.co.uk
dir: *4 miles south of Chippenham just past Lacock. Exit A350 signed Gastard. Site 300 yards on left.*

A peaceful, pleasant site, well established and beautifully laid-out, close to the village of Lacock and Lacock Abbey. Both the facilities and the grounds are immaculately maintained; there is very good screening. A section of the park has been developed to provide spacious pitches especially for tents, complete with its own toilet and shower block.

Open: Easter and April to October **Last arrival:** 20.00 **Last departure:** noon

Pitches: 🚐 from £20; 🚌 from £20; ▲ from £20; 12 hardstanding pitches

Leisure: 🎱 ⊛

Facilities: 🚿 ☉ 🥾 ✳ 📶

Services: 🔌 🔋 🚮 🛢 ⊘

Within 3 miles: 🎣 ✎ ↻ 🍴 ⑤

Additional site information: 2.5 acre site. 🐕 ⊛ Cars can be parked by caravans and tents. Awnings permitted. No excessive noise.

LANDFORD
Map 5 SU21

Places to visit

Furzey Gardens, MINSTEAD, SO43 7GL, 023 8081 2464
www.furzey-gardens.org

Mottisfont, MOTTISFONT, SO51 0LP, 01794 340757
www.nationaltrust.org.uk/mottisfont

Great for kids: Paultons Park, OWER, SO51 6AL, 023 8081 4442
www.paultonspark.co.uk

Premier Park

Greenhill Farm Caravan & Camping Park
▶▶▶▶▶ 87%

tel: 01794 324117 **Greenhill Farm, New Road SP5 2AZ**
email: info@greenhillfarm.co.uk **web:** www.greenhillfarm.co.uk
dir: M27 junction 2, A36 towards Salisbury. Approximately 3 miles after Hampshire-Wiltshire border, pass Shoe Inn pub on right, BP garage on left, left into New Road, signed Nomansland, 0.75 mile on left.

A tranquil, well-landscaped park hidden away in unspoilt countryside on the edge of the New Forest National Park. Pitches overlooking the fishing lake include hardstandings and are for adults only. The other section of the park is for families and includes a play area and games room. The site provides excellent toilet and shower blocks in both the family area and adults-only area. This site is also well placed for visiting Paultons Park at Ower.

Open: All year **Last arrival:** 21.30 **Last departure:** 11.00

Pitches: 🚐 🚙 ▲ 🏠; 50 hardstanding pitches

Leisure: 🄰 🎣 🎱 ⚽ 🎯

Facilities: 🏚 ☺ 🌡 ⚒ & $

Services: 🔌 🔄 🍽 ⚙ 🚰 🔋 🛢 🚿 T

Within 3 miles: ⚓ ◎

Additional site information: 13 acre site. 🐕 Cars can be parked by caravans and tents. Awnings permitted. No noise after 23.00. Disposable BBQs, freshly baked bread available.

Glamping available: Log pods.

Additional glamping information: Log pods accomodate up to 4 people, no dogs. Cars can be parked by units.

SALISBURY

See also Amesbury

Places to visit

The Salisbury Museum, SALISBURY, SP1 2EN, 01722 332151
www.salisburymuseum.org.uk

Salisbury Cathedral, SALISBURY, SP1 2EJ, 01722 555120
www.salisburycathedral.org.uk

SALISBURY
Map 5 SU12

Coombe Touring Park
▶▶▶▶ 92%

tel: 01722 328451 **Race Plain, Netherhampton SP2 8PN**
email: enquiries@coombecaravanpark.co.uk **web:** www.coombecaravanpark.co.uk
dir: From Salisbury take A345 towards Blandford. Onto A3094 then follow Stratford Tony and site signs. After racecourse turn left. 700 yards to site on right. Or from A36 (west of Salisbury) onto A3094 (signed Bournemouth), at Netherhampton Corner follow Stratford Tony and racecourse signs. After racecourse turn left, 700 yards to site on right.

A very neat and attractive site adjacent to the racecourse with views over the downs. The park is well landscaped with shrubs and maturing trees, and the very colourful beds are stocked from the owner's own greenhouse. This is a lovely quiet and peaceful park to stay on with an excellent toilet and shower block, plus a fully-equipped function room with a kitchen that makes for a welcome campers' retreat. There are four static homes available for hire.

Open: All year (restricted service: October to April – shop closed) **Last arrival:** 21.00 **Last departure:** noon

Pitches: * 🚐 from £20; 🚙 from £20; ▲ from £20; 6 hardstanding pitches

Leisure: 🄰

Facilities: 🏚 ☺ 🌡 ⚒ & $ 🚻 🎪

Services: 🔌 🔄 🔋 🚿

Within 3 miles: ⚓ ↺

Additional site information: 8 acre site. 🐕 ◎ Cars can be parked by caravans and tents. Awnings permitted. No open fires, no mini motorbikes, no drones, no noise between 23.00–07.00. Table tennis, campers' kitchen, children's bathroom.

PITCHES: 🚐 Caravans 🚙 Motorhomes ▲ Tents 🏠 Glamping accommodation **SERVICES:** 🔌 Electric hook-up 🔄 Launderette 🍽 Licensed bar 🛢 Calor Gas 🚿 Campingaz T Toilet fluid 🍽 Café/Restaurant ⚙ Fast Food/Takeaway 🔋 Battery charging 🚰 Motorhome service point * 2019 prices ◎ No credit or debit cards 🐕 Dogs permitted 🚫 No dogs

TROWBRIDGE   Map 4 ST85

Places to visit

Great Chalfield Manor and Garden, BRADFORD-ON-AVON, SN12 8NH,
01225 782239
www.nationaltrust.org.uk/great-chalfield-manor-and-garden

The Courts Garden, HOLT, BA14 6RR, 01225 782875
www.nationaltrust.org.uk/the-courts-garden

Great for kids: Longleat, LONGLEAT, BA12 7NW, 01985 844400
www.longleat.co.uk

Stowford Manor Farm
► ► 76%

tel: 01225 752253 **Stowford, Wingfield BA14 9LH**
email: camping@stowfordmanorfarm.co.uk **web:** www.stowfordmanorfarm.co.uk
dir: *From Trowbridge take A366 west towards Radstock. Site on left in 3 miles.*

A very simple farm site set on the banks of the River Frome behind the farm
courtyard. The owners are friendly and relaxed and the park enjoys a similarly
comfortable ambience. Cream teas are available at the farmhouse. The unisex
facilities are kept clean and tidy. Farleigh & District Swimming Club, one of the few
remaining river swimming clubs, is just half a mile from the site.

Open: Easter to October **Last departure:** noon

Pitches: 🚐 from £24; 🚍 from £24; ▲ from £24

Leisure: 🖊

Facilities: 🛁 ⊙ ✳ WiFi

Services: 🔌 🍴 🛒

Within 3 miles: ⛳ ∪ 🚣 🎣 🎬 ⑤ 🗒

Additional site information: 1.5 acre site. 🅿 Cars can be parked by caravans and tents.
Awnings permitted. No open fires. Fishing, boating, river swimming. Fire bowl hire.

WESTBURY   Map 4 ST85

Places to visit

Great Chalfield Manor and Garden, BRADFORD-ON-AVON, SN12 8NH,
01225 782239
www.nationaltrust.org.uk/great-chalfield-manor-and-garden

The Courts Garden, HOLT, BA14 6RR, 01225 782875
www.nationaltrust.org.uk/the-courts-garden

Brokerswood Country Park
► ► ► ► 85% HOLIDAY HOME PARK

tel: 01373 822238 **Brokerswood BA13 4EH**
email: brokerswood.info@haulfryn.co.uk **web:** www.brokerswoodcountrypark.co.uk
dir: *M4 junction 17, south on A350. Right at Yarnbrook to Rising Sun pub at North
Bradley, left at roundabout. Left on bend approaching Southwick, 2.5 miles, site on right.*

A popular site on the edge of an 80-acre woodland park with nature trails, fishing
lakes and a good range of activities including archery, tree-top high rope course
and kayaking. The adventure playground offers plenty of fun for all ages, and there
is a miniature railway, an undercover play area and a breakfast bar. The park no
longer offers touring facilities; there are now 41 lodges and 10 glamping pods, plus
high quality toilet facilities.

Open: 7 April to 31 October **Last arrival:** 17.30 (later arrivals by prior arrangement only)
Last departure: 11.00

Leisure: 🎪 🖊

Facilities: 🛁 🖊 ✳ ♿ ⑤ 🚿 🪑 🛒 WiFi

Additional site information: 80 acre site. 🅿 Maximum of 3 pitches per booking.
Seasonal café/restaurant and takeaway food. Car hire can be arranged.

LEISURE: 🏊 Indoor swimming pool 🏊 Outdoor swimming pool 🛝 Children's playground Kids' club Tennis court 🎱 Games room 📺 Separate TV room
⛳ Golf course ⛳ Pitch n putt 🚣 Boats for hire 🚲 Bikes for hire 🎬 Cinema 🎵 Entertainment 🎣 Fishing ⊙ Mini golf 🏄 Watersports Gym ⚽ Sports field ∪ Stables
FACILITIES: 🛁 Baths/Shower ⊙ Electric shaver sockets 🖊 Hairdryer ✳ Ice Pack Facility 🍼 Baby facilities ♿ Disabled facilities ⑤ Shop on site or within 200yds
🚿 BBQ area 🪑 Picnic area WiFi WiFi

WORCESTERSHIRE

HONEYBOURNE
Map 10 SP14

Places to visit
Kiftsgate Court Garden, MICKLETON, GL55 6LN, 01386 438777
www.kiftsgate.co.uk

Hidcote Manor Garden, MICKLETON, GL55 6LR, 01386 438333
www.nationaltrust.org.uk/hidcote

Great for kids: Anne Hathaway's Cottage, SHOTTERY, CV37 9HH, 01789 338532
www.shakespeare.org.uk/visit/anne-hathaways-cottage

Premier Park

Ranch Caravan Park
▶▶▶▶▶ 91%

tel: 01386 830744 **Station Road WR11 7PR**
email: enquiries@ranch.co.uk **web:** www.ranch.co.uk
dir: From village crossroads towards Bidford, site 400 metres on left.

An attractive, well-run and improving park set amidst farmland in the Vale of Evesham and landscaped with trees and bushes. Tourers have their own excellent facilities in two locations, and the use of an outdoor heated swimming pool in peak season. The extended and refurbished facilities block really does have the wow factor, with underfloor heating to the laundry, wash up area and the showers and toilets, which includes family/accessible fully serviced cubicles. There is also a licensed club serving meals. Please note that this site does not accept tents.

Open: March to November (restricted service: March to May and September to November – swimming pool closed, shorter club hours) **Last arrival:** 20.00 **Last departure:** noon
Pitches: * 🚐 from £27; 🚍 from £27; 23 seasonal pitches
Leisure: 🏊 �️ 🎣 🗗 🎵 ⚽ ⚽
Facilities: 🚿 ⊙ 🌊 ✳ ♿ 💲
Services: 🔌 🗑 🍺 🍽 🎱 🔋 ♨ 🔋 ⚿ T
Within 3 miles: ↧ 🎣 ∪

Additional site information: 12 acre site. 🐕 Cars can be parked by caravans. Awnings permitted. No unaccompanied minors. 46 touring pitches. Car hire can be arranged.

WORCESTER
Map 10 SO85

Places to visit
Worcester Art Gallery & Museum, WORCESTER, WR1 1DT, 01905 25371
www.museumsworcestershire.org.uk/museums/worcester-city-art-gallery-museum

Greyfriars' House and Garden, WORCESTER, WR1 2LZ, 01905 23571
www.nationaltrust.org.uk/greyfriars

Great for kids: West Midland Safari & Leisure Park, BEWDLEY, DY12 1LF, 01299 402114, www.wmsp.co.uk

Peachley Leisure Touring Park
▶▶▶ 87%

tel: 01905 641309 & 07764 540803 **Peachley Lane, Lower Broadheath WR2 6QX**
email: peachleyleisure@live.co.uk **web:** www.peachleyleisure.com
dir: M5 junction 7, A44 (Worcester ring road) towards Leominster. Exit at sign for Elgar's Birthplace Museum. Pass museum, at crossroads turn right. In 0.75 mile at T-junction turn left. Park signed on right.

The park is set in its own area in the grounds of Peachley Farm and has all hardstanding and fully serviced pitches. The 25 super pitches have 16 amp electricity, mains water and sewer. There are two fishing lakes, a really excellent quad bike course and outdoor giant draughts, chess and jenga. The park is a peaceful haven, and an excellent base from which to explore the area, which includes The Elgar Birthplace Museum, Worcester Racecourse and the Worcester Victorian Christmas Fayre (in late November); it is also convenient for Malvern's Three Counties Showground.

Open: All year **Last arrival:** 21.30 **Last departure:** 15.00
Pitches: * 🚐 from £20; 🚍 from £20; ⚑ from £14; 82 hardstanding pitches; 50 seasonal pitches
Leisure: 🎣 ⚽
Facilities: 🚿 ⊙ 🌊 ♿ 🚿 🗂 WiFi
Services: 🔌 🗑 🍽 🔋
Within 3 miles: ↧ ∪ ◎ 🚴 ⚽ 🗓 💲

Additional site information: 8 acre site. 🐕 Cars can be parked by caravans and tents. Awnings permitted. No skateboards, no riding on motorbikes or scooters. Table tennis. Woodland walk.

Yorkshire

There is nowhere in the British Isles quite like Yorkshire. With such scenic and cultural diversity, it is almost a country within a country. For sheer scale, size and grandeur, there is nowhere to beat it. Much of it in the spectacular Pennines, Yorkshire is a land of glorious moors, gentle dales, ruined abbeys and picturesque market towns.

'My Yorkshire, a land of pure air, rocky streams and hidden waterfalls,' was how the celebrated vet Alf Wight described his adopted home. Wight was born in Sunderland but moved to the North Yorkshire market town of Thirsk soon after the outbreak of the Second World War. He fell in love with the place and in later years his affection for the beauty, spirit and character of this great county translated to the printed page when Wight, writing under the name of James Herriot, wrote eight best-selling volumes of memoirs about the life of a Yorkshire vet, which spawned two films and a long-running TV series. Today, thousands of visitors from near and far travel to the landscape he loved so dearly to see it all for themselves. His veterinary practice, and original home, in Thirsk is open to the public.

Not surprisingly, walking features prominently on the list of things to do in Yorkshire. There are countless footpaths and bridleways to explore and miles of long-distance trails across vast open moorland and through tranquil meandering valleys. The 81-mile Dales Way is a perfect way to discover the magnificent scenery of Wharfedale, Ribblesdale and Dentdale, while the Calderdale Way offers a fascinating insight into the Pennine heartland of industrial West Yorkshire. Most famous of all the region's longer routes is surely the Pennine Way, which opened 50 years ago in April 1965. Its inception was the most important achievement in the history of the Ramblers' Association, marking Britain's first national long-distance footpath.

The Pennine Way was the brainchild of Tom Stephenson, one-time secretary of the Association but his vision for a trail for everyone was a long time in the planning. Landowners regularly thwarted his attempts to make the landscape accessible to walkers and there were countless prosecutions for trespassing 'I could never understand how anyone could own a mountain,' Stephenson wrote. 'Surely it was there for everybody.'

One of the more surprising features to be found on the route of the Pennine Way is the ruined house known as Top Withins. This is thought to be the inspiration for *Wuthering Heights*, the Earnshaw home in Emily Brontë's stirring novel of the same name. The Brontë sisters knew the area well, and their home, now the Brontë Parsonage Museum, lies just a few miles from the ruins in the village of Haworth. The parsonage draws thousands of visitors every year; its atmospheric setting amid bleak moorland and gritstone houses vividly captures the spirit of this uniquely talented trio of writers.

An easier, more comfortable way of exploring much of Yorkshire's scenic landscape is by train. A ride on the famous Settle to Carlisle railway represents one of the region's most memorable train journeys. For a while during the late 1980s the future of this line was in serious doubt, when it seemed British Rail might close it because of soaring maintenance costs. Thanks to Michael Portillo, a noted railway enthusiast who was Secretary of State for Transport at the time, the line was saved. Essentially, the Settle to Carlisle railway is a lifeline for commuters and the people of the more remote communities of the western Dales, but it is also an extremely popular tourist attraction. Carriages are regularly filled with summer visitors in search of stunning scenery and they are not disappointed. Elsewhere in Yorkshire, a very different train recalls a very different age. In the National Railway Museum at York you'll find countless locomotives, including a replica of Stephenson's Rocket and the much-loved *Flying Scotsman*.

◁ Lower Wharfedale

EAST RIDING OF YORKSHIRE

BRANDESBURTON
Map 17 TA14

Places to visit

Beverley Guildhall, BEVERLEY, HU17 9XX, 01482 392783
www.eastriding.gov.uk/museums

Burton Constable Hall, SPROATLEY, HU11 4LN, 01964 562400
www.burtonconstable.com

Blue Rose Caravan Country Park
▶▶▶▶ 91%

tel: 01964 543366 & 07504 026899 **Star Carr Lane YO25 8RU**
email: info@bluerosepark.com **web:** www.bluerosepark.com
dir: *From A165 at roundabout into New Road, signed Brandesburton, which becomes Star Carr Lane. In approximately 1 mile, site on left.*

High standards of customer care are assured at this neat and well-maintained adults-only site that is well placed for visiting Hornsea and the Yorkshire coastline. The park is within walking distance of Brandesburton and offers an idyllic stopover for caravanners wanting a peaceful break in the countryside.

Open: All year **Last arrival:** 20.00 **Last departure:** noon

Pitches: * 🚐 from £23; 🚐 from £23; 59 hardstanding pitches; 35 seasonal pitches

Facilities: 🛁 ☉ 🖤 ⅋ 🛗 🚽 🍴 WiFi

Services: 🔌 🗑 🚰 🔒 🔗 Ⓣ

Within 3 miles: ⅃ 🎣 ∪ ◎ 🏊 ⛷ 🖫

Additional site information: 113 acre site. Adults only. 🐕 Cars can be parked by caravans. Awnings permitted.

Dacre Lakeside Park
▶▶▶ 88%

tel: 0800 180 4556 & 01964 543704 **YO25 8RT**
email: dacrepark@btconnect.com **web:** www.dacrepark.co.uk
dir: *From A165 (bypass) midway between Beverley and Hornsea, follow Brandesburton and brown site sign.*

A large lake popular with watersports enthusiasts is the focal point of this grassy site, which offers predominantly seasonal pitches – there are just three tent pitches and five caravan/motorhome pitches available. The stylish Bert's Pizzeria & Café, overlooking the lake, serves a wide range of food and beverages and the clubhouse provides indoor activities. The six-acre lake is used for windsurfing, sailing, kayaking, canoeing and fishing. Camping pods are available for hire.

Open: March to October **Last arrival:** 21.00 **Last departure:** noon

Pitches: 🚐 🚐 🛖 🏠; 2 hardstanding pitches; 107 seasonal pitches

Leisure: 🎢 🏊 🎣 🖵 🏓 🎵 🎣 ⚽ ✪

Facilities: 🛁 ☉ ⅋ ❄ 🛗 WiFi

Services: 🔌 🗑 🚰 🍴 🔒

Within 3 miles: ⅃ ∪ 🏊 ⛷ 🖫

Additional site information: 8 acre site. 🐕 Cars can be parked by caravans and tents. Awnings permitted. No noise 23.00–08.00, no craft with engines permitted on lake.

Glamping available: Wooden pods.

BRIDLINGTON
Map 17 TA16

See also Rudston

Places to visit

Sewerby Hall & Gardens, BRIDLINGTON, YO15 1EA, 01262 673769
www.sewerbyhall.co.uk

RSPB Bempton Cliffs, BEMPTON, YO15 1JF, 01262 422212
www.rspb.org.uk/bemptoncliffs

Great for kids: Burton Agnes Hall, BURTON AGNES, YO25 4NE, 01262 490324
www.burtonagnes.com

Fir Tree Caravan Park
▶▶▶▶ 81%

tel: 01262 676442 **Jewison Lane, Sewerby YO16 6YG**
email: info@flowerofmay.com **web:** www.flowerofmay.com
dir: *1.5 miles from centre of Bridlington. Left onto B1255 at Marton Corner. Site 600 yards on left.*

Fir Tree Caravan Park is a large, mainly static park that has a well laid out touring area with its own facilities. It has an excellent swimming pool complex and the adjacent bar-cum-conservatory serves meals. There is also a family bar, games room and outdoor children's play area. Please note, this park only offers seasonal touring pitches.

Open: March to October (restricted service: early and late season – bar and entertainment restrictions)

Pitches: 🚐; 45 hardstanding pitches; 45 seasonal pitches

Leisure: 🏊 🎢 🎣 🖵 🎵 ✪

Facilities: 🛁 ☉ ❄ 🛗 🖫 🚽 🍼 WiFi

Services: 🔌 🗑 🚰 🍴 🍺 🔒 🔗 Ⓣ

Within 3 miles: ⅃ 🎣 ∪ ◎ 🏊 ⛷ 🖫

Additional site information: 22 acre site. 🐕 Cars can be parked by caravans. Awnings permitted. No noise after midnight. Dogs accepted by prior arrangement only. Football area and dog walking area.

FLAMBOROUGH
Map 17 TA27

Places to visit
RSPB Bempton Cliffs, BEMPTON, YO15 1JF, 01262 422212
www.rspb.org.uk/bemptoncliffs

Premier Park

Thornwick Bay Holiday Village
►►►►► 88% HOLIDAY CENTRE

tel: 01262 850569 **North Marine Road YO15 1AU**
email: thornwickbay@haven.com **web:** www.haven.com/parks/yorkshire/thornwick-bay
dir: *From Flamborough take B1255 (Tower Street) signed North landing. Site entrance on left in approximately 1 mile.*

A large holiday village close to the beach, with a superb range of attractions including indoor swimming pools, lake fishing and a sports zone. Eating options include the stylish Lighthouse Bar & Grill and The Yorkshire Café that serves espressos, lattes and muffins. The large cliff-top touring and camping areas are mainly level and grassed; there are a few hardstandings and fully serviced pitches plus two smart amenity blocks with family rooms.

Open: mid March to end October **Last arrival:** 22.00 **Last departure:** 10.00
Pitches: ♥ ♥ ▲; 57 hardstanding pitches
Leisure: ♨ ♨ ⚐ ♞ ♟ ♪ ♪ ⚽
Facilities: ♨ ☺ ⚐ ⚙ ⚒ ⑤ ♨ ♨ WiFi
Services: ♥ ⑤ ♨ ♨ ♨ ♨ ♨ ♨
Within 3 miles: ♨ ◎ ♨

Additional site information: 4 acre site. ♥ 2 dogs per booking, certain dog breeds banned. No commercial vehicles, no bookings by person under 21 years unless a family booking. Bakery, fishing lake, sports and nature activities, nature trails. Car hire can be arranged.

KINGSTON UPON HULL

See Sproatley

RUDSTON
Map 17 TA06

Places to visit
Sewerby Hall & Gardens, BRIDLINGTON, YO15 1EA, 01262 673769
www.sewerbyhall.co.uk

Thorpe Hall Caravan & Camping Site
►►►► 84%

tel: 01262 420393 & 420574 **Thorpe Hall YO25 4JE**
email: info@thorpehall.co.uk **web:** www.thorpehall.co.uk
dir: *From Bridlington take B1253 west for 5 miles.*

A delightful, peaceful small park within the walled gardens of Thorpe Hall yet within a few miles of the bustling seaside resort of Bridlington. The site offers a games field, its own coarse fishery, and a games and TV lounge. There are numerous walks locally.

Open: March to October **Last arrival:** 22.00 **Last departure:** noon
Pitches: ♥ ♥ ▲
Leisure: ♨ ♞ ⚐ ⚽ ⚙
Facilities: ♨ ☺ ⚐ ⚒ ⚙ ⑤ ♨ WiFi
Services: ♥ ⑤ ♨ ♨ ♨ ⚙ T
Within 3 miles: ♨

Additional site information: 4.5 acre site. ♥ well behaved dogs only. Cars can be parked by caravans and tents. Awnings permitted. No ball games except on designated field, no noise 23.00–08.00, shop/reception open 09.00–11.30 and 16.30–8.30 (longer hours when busy). 4.5-acre golf practice area/games field. Car hire can be arranged.

SKIPSEA
Map 17 TA15

Places to visit
Hornsea Museum, HORNSEA, HU18 1AB, 01964 533443
www.hornseamuseum.com

Sewerby Hall & Gardens, BRIDLINGTON, YO15 1EA, 01262 673769
www.sewerbyhall.co.uk

Premier Park

Skirlington Leisure Park
►►►►► 89% HOLIDAY CENTRE

tel: 01262 468213 & 468466 **YO25 8SY**
email: info@skirlington.com **web:** www.skirlington.com
dir: *From M62 towards Beverley then Hornsea. Between Skipsea and Hornsea on B1242.*

A large, well-run seaside park set close to the beach in partly-sloping meadowland with young trees and shrubs. The site has five toilet blocks, a supermarket and an amusement arcade, plus occasional entertainment in the clubhouse. The wide range of family amenities includes an indoor heated swimming pool complex with sauna, steam room and gym. A 10-pin bowling alley and indoor soft play area for children are added attractions.

Open: March to October (restricted service: diner and some facilities open from Friday to Sunday only (except school holidays and bank holidays)) **Last arrival:** 20.00 **Last departure:** 11.00
Pitches: ♥ ♥; 15 hardstanding pitches; 180 seasonal pitches
Leisure: ♨ ♪ ⚐ ⚽
Facilities: ☺ ⚐ ⚙ ⑤ ♨ WiFi
Services: ♥ ⑤ ♨ ♨ ♨ ♨ ♨ ⚙
Within 3 miles: ♨ ⚐ ♨ ◎ ♨ ♨

Additional site information: 140 acre site. ♥ No noise after 22.00. Putting green, fishing lake, arcade, mini bowling alley, Sunday market.

SPROATLEY   Map 17 TA13

Places to visit

Burton Constable Hall, SPROATLEY, HU11 4LN, 01964 562400
www.burtonconstable.com

Streetlife Museum Hull, KINGSTON UPON HULL, HU1 1PS, 01482 300300
www.hcandl.co.uk/museums-and-galleries/streetlife-museum

Great for kids: The Deep, KINGSTON UPON HULL, HU1 4DP, 01482 381000
www.thedeep.co.uk

Premier Park

Burton Constable Holiday Park & Arboretum
► ► ► ► ► 87%

tel: 01964 562508 **Old Lodges HU11 4LJ**
email: info@burtonconstable.co.uk **web:** www.burtonconstableholidaypark.co.uk
dir: *A165 onto B1238 to Sproatley. Use Sat Nav HU11 4PG, follow Park Road alongside the Constable Arms for approximately 500 yards, follow signs to holiday park ahead.*

Within the extensive estate of Burton Constable Hall, this large and secluded holiday destination provides a wide range of attractions including fishing and boating on the two 10-acre lakes, a snooker room, Mr Constable's Country Kitchen, and a licensed bar with a designated family room. The grounds are immaculately maintained and generous pitch density offers good privacy. Two luxury lodges and nine pods (two with en suite facilities) are available for hire.

Open: March to beginning of November (restricted service: November to mid February)
Last arrival: 18.00 (later by prior arrangement) **Last departure:** 11.00

Pitches: * 🚐 from £26; � from £26; ▲ from £20; ⛺ see price below; 26 hardstanding pitches; 14 seasonal pitches

Leisure: 🎢 🎵 🎣 ⚽

Facilities: 🛁 ☺ 🪒 ♿ 🔋 🏞 WiFi

Services: 🔌 🔲 🚽 🍽 🛒 🚮 ♿ 🔒 ✂ T

Within 3 miles: 🚴 ⛳

Additional site information: 90 acre site. 🐾 Cars can be parked by caravans and tents. Awnings permitted. No fires, skateboards or rollerblades. Snooker, table tennis, woodland walks, cycling, toddlers' play area, night security warden. Beer garden and events at Lakeside bar.

Glamping available: Wooden pods from £40. **Changeover days:** Any day

Additional glamping information: Deluxe pods with shower, toilet, washbasin and kitchen are available, sleeps 5. Cars can be parked by units

TUNSTALL   Map 17 TA33

Places to visit

Burton Constable Hall, SPROATLEY, HU11 4LN, 01964 562400
www.burtonconstable.com

Premier Park

Sand le Mere Holiday Village
► ► ► ► ► 88% HOLIDAY CENTRE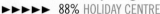

tel: 01964 670403 **Southfield Lane HU12 0JF**
email: info@sand-le-mere.co.uk **web:** www.sand-le-mere.co.uk
dir: *From Hull A1033 signed Withernsea, B1362 (Hull Road) signed Hedon. In Hedon continue on B3162 towards Withernsea. Turn left signed Roos. In Roos take B1242. Turn left at brown sign for site. In Tunstall right at T-junction, right into Seaside Lane to site.*

Ideally located between Withernsea and Bridlington, this impressive development provides first-class indoor leisure facilities with swimming pool, entertainment and a kiddies' soft ball area. Excellent level touring pitches, including six that have their own private en suite wet room pods, are surrounded by mature trees, and a lovely nature walk ensures that this rural destination can be fully appreciated. Please note, this site does not accept tents.

Open: March to November **Last arrival:** 23.00 **Last departure:** 11.00

Pitches: * 🚐 from £10; � from £10; 60 hardstanding pitches; 24 seasonal pitches

Leisure: 🏊 🎢 ⛹ 🎱 🔲 🎵 🎣 🎯 ⚽ 🏐

Facilities: 🛁 🪒 ☀ ♿ 🔋 🏞 🏞 🚮 WiFi

Services: 🔌 🔲 🚽 🍽 🛒 ♿ 🔒

Within 3 miles: 🚴 ◎

Additional site information: 135 acre site. 🐾 No noise after 23.00, speed limits around site to be observed, no camp fires. Nature trail and sensory room.

LEISURE: 🏊 Indoor swimming pool 🏊 Outdoor swimming pool 🎢 Children's playground ⛹ Kids' club 🎾 Tennis court 🎱 Games room 🔲 Separate TV room ⛳ Golf course ⛳ Pitch n putt ⛵ Boats for hire 🚲 Bikes for hire 🎬 Cinema 🎵 Entertainment 🎣 Fishing 🏌 Mini golf 🏄 Watersports 🏋 Gym ⚽ Sports field ♞ Stables
FACILITIES: 🛁 Baths/Shower ☺ Electric shaver sockets 🪒 Hairdryer ❄ Ice Pack Facility 🍼 Baby facilities ♿ Disabled facilities 🔋 Shop on site or within 200yds 🏞 BBQ area 🏞 Picnic area WiFi WiFi

NORTH YORKSHIRE

ACASTER MALBIS
Map 16 SE54

Places to visit

National Railway Museum, YORK, YO26 4XJ, 03330 161010
www.nrm.org.uk

York Minster, YORK, YO1 7HH, 01904 557200
www.yorkminster.org

Great for kids: Jorvik Viking Centre, YORK, YO1 9WT, 01904 615505
www.jorvik-viking-centre.com

Moor End Farm
 ►► 76%

tel: 01904 706727 & 07860 405872 **YO23 2UQ**
email: dawnhhall@hotmail.co.uk **web:** www.moor-end-farm.co.uk
dir: *At junction of A64 and A1237 at Copmanthorpe follow Acaster Malbis signs. In Copmanthorpe left into Station Road signed Acaster Malbis. In approximately 1.8 miles site on left.*

A very pleasant farm site with modernised facilities including a heated family/disabled shower room. A river boat pickup to York is 150 yards from the site entrance, and the village inn and restaurant are a short stroll away. A very convenient site for visiting York Racecourse.

Open: Easter or April to October **Last arrival:** 22.00 **Last departure:** noon
Pitches: * 🚐 from £22; 🚐 from £22; 🛖 from £22
Facilities: 🛁 ⊙ 🅿 ※ ♿ 🎋 WiFi
Services: 🔌 🗑 🔋
Within 3 miles: 🎣 📅 🏪

Additional site information: 1 acre site. 🐕 🚭 Cars can be parked by caravans and tents. Awnings permitted. Fridge, freezer and microwave available.

ALLERSTON
Map 19 SE88

Places to visit

Scarborough Castle, SCARBOROUGH, YO11 1HY, 01723 372451
www.english-heritage.org.uk/visit/places/scarborough-castle

Pickering Castle, PICKERING, YO18 7AX, 01751 474989
www.english-heritage.org.uk/visit/places/pickering-castle

Great for kids: Flamingo Land Resort, KIRBY MISPERTON, YO17 6UX,
0800 408 8840 www.flamingoland.co.uk

Vale of Pickering Caravan Park

►► ►► ►► 94%

tel: 01723 859280 **Carr House Farm YO18 7PQ**
email: info@valeofpickering.co.uk **web:** www.valeofpickering.co.uk
dir: *On B1415, 1.75 miles from A170 (Pickering to Scarborough road).*

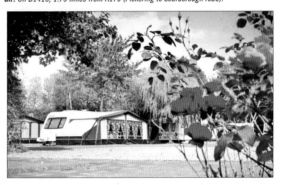

A well-maintained, spacious family park with excellent facilities including a well-stocked shop, immaculate toilet facilities, and an interesting woodland walk. A superb café is open during the day. A beautifully designed extension to the toilet block houses five family bathrooms and a wet room for less mobile visitors. Younger children will enjoy the attractive play area, while the large ball sports area will appeal to older ones. Three tastefully furnished and very well-equipped bell tents are also available for a glamping experience. The park is set in open countryside bounded by hedges, has manicured grassland and stunning seasonal floral displays, and is handy for the North Yorkshire Moors and the attractions of Scarborough.

Open: 6 March to 3 January **Last arrival:** 21.00 **Last departure:** 11.30
Pitches: 🚐 🚐 🛖 🏕; 100 hardstanding pitches; 70 seasonal pitches
Leisure: 🎱 ⚙ **Facilities:** 🛁 ⊙ 🅿 ※ ♿ 🗑 🎋 🎋 WiFi
Services: 🔌 🗑 🍽 🚰 ⚡ 🔋 🚿 T
Within 3 miles: 🎣 ⛳ ∪ ◎

Additional site information: 13 acre site. 🐕 Cars can be parked by caravans and tents. Awnings permitted. No open fires or Chinese lanterns, no noise after 23.00. Microwave available.

Glamping available: Bell tents.

Additional glamping information: No pets. Cars can be parked by units.

ALNE
Map 19 SE46

Places to visit

Beningbrough Hall, Gallery & Gardens, BENINGBROUGH, YO30 1DD, 01904 472027
www.nationaltrust.org.uk/beningbrough

Sutton Park, SUTTON-ON-THE-FOREST, YO61 1DP, 01347 810249
www.statelyhome.co.uk

Great for kids: National Railway Museum, YORK, YO26 4XJ, 03330 161010
www.nrm.org.uk

Premier Park

Alders Caravan Park
►►►►► 87%

tel: 01347 838722 **Home Farm YO61 1RY**
email: enquiries@homefarmalne.co.uk **web:** www.alderscaravanpark.co.uk
dir: From A19 exit at Alne sign, in 1.5 miles left at T-junction, 0.5 mile site on left in village centre.

A tastefully developed park on a working farm with screened pitches laid out in horseshoe-shaped areas. This well-designed park offers excellent toilet facilities including a bathroom and fully-serviced washing and toilet cubicles. A woodland area and a water meadow are pleasant places to walk. A summer house with comfortable seating is located at the edge of the village cricket grounds. Wooden pods are generously spaced in a separate enclosed area and a large, covered communal area for eating and relaxation is also provided.

Open: March to October **Last arrival:** 21.00 **Last departure:** 14.00
Pitches: * ⊞ from £22; ⊞ from £22; ▲ from £22; ⛺ see prices below; 6 hardstanding pitches; 71 seasonal pitches
Facilities: 🚿 ⊙ ℱ ✳ ♿ ☰ WiFi
Services: ⊞ 🗑 ☰ ⛟ ♠
Within 3 miles: ⌕ ℘ 🛒

Additional site information: 12 acre site. 🐕 Maximum 2 dogs per pitch. Cars can be parked by caravans and tents. Awnings permitted. Summer house. Farm produce for sale. Woodland walk, cricket club, Sustrans cycle track route 65. Car hire can be arranged.
Glamping available: Wooden pods from £40. **Changeover days:** Any day
Additional glamping information: No dogs in pods. Parking 20 metres from pods.

BISHOP MONKTON

Places to visit

Newby Hall & Gardens, RIPON, HG4 5AE, 01423 322583
www.newbyhall.com

Fountains Abbey & Studley Royal, RIPON, HG4 3DY, 01765 608888
www.nationaltrust.org.uk/fountains-abbey

Great for kids: Lightwater Valley Theme Park, NORTH STAINLEY, HG4 3HT, 01765 635321, www.lightwatervalley.co.uk

BISHOP MONKTON
Map 19 SE36

Church Farm Caravan Park
►►► 76%

tel: 01765 676578 & 07861 770164 **Knaresborough Road HG3 3QQ**
email: churchfarmcaravan@btinternet.com **web:** www.churchfarmcaravanpark.co.uk
dir: From A61 at crossroads follow Bishop Monkton signs. 1.25 miles to village. At crossroads right into Knaresborough Road, site approximately 500 metres on right.

A very pleasant rural site on a working farm, on the edge of the attractive village of Bishop Monkton with its well-stocked shop and pubs. Whilst very much a place to relax, there are many attractions close by, including Fountains Abbey, Newby Hall, Ripon and Harrogate.

Open: March to October **Last arrival:** 22.30 **Last departure:** noon
Pitches: ⊞ ⊞ ▲; 1 hardstanding pitches
Facilities: 🚿 ⊙ ✳ ♿
Services: ⊞ ☰ ⛟
Within 3 miles: ⌕ ℘ ∪ ◎ ⺼ 🛒 🍴

Additional site information: 4 acre site. 🐕 ⊛ Cars can be parked by caravans and tents. Awnings permitted. No ball games.

BOLTON ABBEY
Map 19 SE05

Places to visit

Bolton Abbey, SKIPTON, BD23 6EX, 01756 718000
www.boltonabbey.com

Embsay and Bolton Abbey Steam Railway, BOLTON ABBEY, BD23 6AF, 01756 710614
www.embsayboltonabbeyrailway.org.uk

Great for kids: Hesketh Farm Park, SKIPTON, BD23 6HA, 01756 710444
www.heskethfarmpark.co.uk

Howgill Lodge
►►►► 80%

tel: 01756 720655 **Barden BD23 6DJ**
email: info@howgill-lodge.co.uk **web:** www.howgill-lodge.co.uk
dir: From Bolton Abbey take B6160 signed Burnsall. In 3 miles at Barden Tower right signed Appletreewick. 1.5 miles, at phone box right into lane to site.

A beautifully-maintained and secluded site offering panoramic views of Wharfedale. The spacious hardstanding pitches are mainly terraced, and there is a separate tenting area with numerous picnic tables. There are three amenity blocks available with a larger well-equipped one at the top end and a simpler unit on the camping area to avoid travelling long distances to use the toilet facilities. There is also a well-stocked shop.

Open: mid March to October **Last arrival:** 20.00 **Last departure:** noon
Pitches: ⊞ ⊞ ▲; 20 hardstanding pitches
Leisure: ⊛ **Facilities:** ⊙ ℱ ✳ 🛒
Services: ⊞ 🗑 ☰ ♠ ⊘ T
Within 3 miles: ℘

Additional site information: 4 acre site. 🐕 Cars can be parked by caravans and tents. Awnings permitted.

LEISURE: 🏊 Indoor swimming pool 🏊 Outdoor swimming pool 🛝 Children's playground 🎣 Kids' club ⚾ Tennis court 🎱 Games room 📺 Separate TV room ⌕ Golf course ⛳ Pitch n putt 🚣 Boats for hire 🚲 Bikes for hire 🎬 Cinema 🎭 Entertainment 🎣 Fishing ◎ Mini golf 🏄 Watersports 💪 Gym 🏟 Sports field ∪ Stables
FACILITIES: 🚿 Baths/Shower ⊙ Electric shaver sockets ℱ Hairdryer ✳ Ice Pack Facility 🍼 Baby facilities ♿ Disabled facilities 🛒 Shop on site or within 200yds 🍴 BBQ area 🪑 Picnic area WiFi WiFi

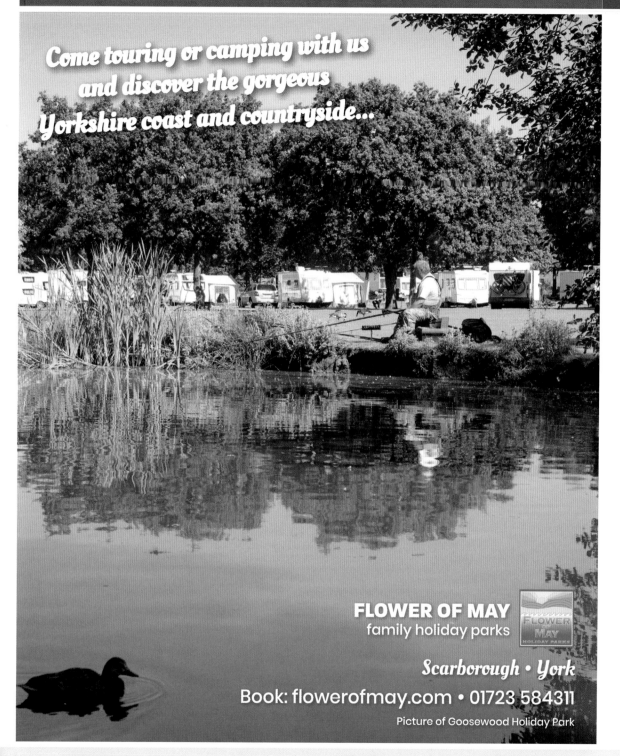

Come touring or camping with us and discover the gorgeous Yorkshire coast and countryside...

FLOWER OF MAY
family holiday parks

Scarborough • York

Book: flowerofmay.com • 01723 584311

Picture of Goosewood Holiday Park

CHOP GATE — Map 19 SE59

Places to visit

Mount Grace Priory, OSMOTHERLEY, DL6 3JG, 01609 883494
www.english-heritage.org.uk/visit/places/mount-grace-priory

Captain Cook Schoolroom Museum, GREAT AYTON, TS9 6NB
captaincookschoolroommuseum.co.uk

Lordstones Country Park
►►►► 86%

tel: 01642 778482 **Carlton Bank TS9 7JH**
email: info@lordstones.com **web:** www.lordstones.com
dir: *From A172 between Stokesley and Osmotherley follow signs to Carlton-in-Cleveland. Through Carlton-in-Cleveland to Lordstones entrance.*

Situated in the North York Moors National Park and commanding one of the highest spots in the county, Lordstones has glorious views that extend over 40 miles. It is a privately-owned country park that has been developed to become a distinctive visitor venue. There is a first-class restaurant (The Belted Bull), a quality farm shop selling estate produce and a small camping-cum-glamping park. There are 20 pitches, some with electricity, enclosed by woodland, and two fully-equipped bell tents, two bothy tents, yurts and five luxury wooden pods, each with a wood-burning stove, kitchenette, toilet and outside decking with barbecue and seating. There is a purpose-built amenity building housing showers and toilet facilities. The Cleveland Way national trail and the coast-to-coast walk both pass close to the site.

Open: All year **Last arrival:** 17.00 **Last departure:** 11.00
Pitches: Å 🏠
Facilities: ⊙ ♿ ⑤ 🚿 🎪 WiFi
Services: ♨ 🔌 🍽 ♨
Additional site information: 150 acre site. 🐾 Cars can be parked by tents. Awnings permitted.
Glamping available: Bell tents; wooden pods; yurts. **Changeover days:** Monday, Friday

CONSTABLE BURTON — Map 19 SE19

Places to visit

Middleham Castle, MIDDLEHAM, DL8 4QG, 01969 623899
www.english-heritage.org.uk/visit/places/middleham-castle

Great for kids: Bedale Museum, BEDALE, DL8 1AA, 01677 427516
www.bedalemuseum.org.uk

Constable Burton Hall Caravan Park
►►►► 83%

tel: 01677 450428 **DL8 5LJ**
email: caravanpark@constableburton.com **web:** www.cbcaravanpark.co.uk
dir: *From Leyburn on A684 towards Bedale, approximately 3 miles to site on left.*

A pretty site in the former deer park of the adjoining Constable Burton Hall, screened from the road by the park walls and surrounded by mature trees in a quiet rural location. The laundry is housed in a converted 18th-century deer barn and there is a pub and restaurant opposite; seasonal pitches are available. Please note that this site does not accept tents.

Open: April to October **Last arrival:** 20.00 **Last departure:** noon
Pitches: * 🚐 from £22; 🚗 from £22
Facilities: 🛁 ⊙ ℱ ✳ ♿ WiFi
Services: ♨ 🔌 🚚 ♨
Within 3 miles: ⚓ ⑤
Additional site information: 10 acre site. 🐾 Cars can be parked by caravans. Awnings permitted. No commercial vehicles, no games. Family shower room.

FILEY

Places to visit

Scarborough Castle, SCARBOROUGH, YO11 1HY, 01723 372451
www.english-heritage.org.uk/visit/places/scarborough-castle

Great for kids: Scarborough Sea Life Sanctuary, SCARBOROUGH, YO12 6RP, www.sealife.co.uk/scarborough

FILEY Map 17 TA18

Premier Park

Flower of May Holiday Park

▶ ▶ ▶ ▶ ▶ **92%** HOLIDAY CENTRE

tel: 01723 584311 **Lebberston Cliff YO11 3NU**
email: info@flowerofmay.com **web:** www.flowerofmay.com
dir: *Take A165 from Scarborough towards Filey. Site signed.*

A well-run, high quality family holiday park with top class facilities. This large landscaped park offers a full range of recreational activities, with plenty to occupy everyone. Grass and hard pitches are available – all are on level ground, and arranged in avenues screened by shrubs. Enjoy the 'Scarborough Fair' museum, with its collection of restored fairground attractions, including rides, organs and vintage cars. There are 4-berth and 5-berth wooden camping pods, each with a decking area. Please note that prices for caravans, motorhomes and tent pitches are for a maximum of 4 people and 1 car (electricity not included).

Open: Easter to October (restricted service: early and late season – restricted opening hours in café, shop and bars) **Last arrival:** dusk **Last departure:** noon

Pitches: * 🚐 from £26; 🚙 from £26; 🛆 from £26; 🏠 see prices below; 250 hardstanding pitches; 200 seasonal pitches

Leisure: 🏊 🎢 🎣 🎱 🎵 ⚽

Facilities: 🏪 ☺ 🅿 ❄ ♿ 🖐 🚿 🧺 🛒 [WiFi]

Services: 🔌 🗄 🍴 🍽 ⚙ 🔋 🦮 [T]

Within 3 miles: 🎣 💰 ↻ ◎ ⛵ ♨ 🎯 🎲

Additional site information: 13 acre site. 🐕 1 dog per pitch by prior arrangement only. No noise after midnight. Squash, basketball court, skate park, table tennis.

Glamping available: Wooden pods 4 berth from £45; 5 berth from £55.
Changeover days: Any day

Additional glamping information: Wooden pods: (sleep 4 or 5) minimum stay 2 nights (3 nights at bank holidays and in school holidays). Microwave, kettle, beds with mattresses, sockets, lighting and decking area included. Cars can be parked by units

See advert on page 289

Crows Nest Caravan Park

▶ ▶ ▶ ▶ **91%**

tel: 01723 582206 **Gristhorpe YO14 9PS**
email: enquiries@crowsnestcaravanpark.com **web:** www.crowsnestcaravanpark.com
dir: *5 miles south of Scarborough and 2 miles north of Filey. On seaward side of A165, signed from roundabout, near petrol station.*

A beautifully situated park on the coast between Scarborough and Filey, with excellent panoramic views. This large and mainly static park offers lively entertainment, and two bars. A small touring area is close to the attractions, and the main touring and camping section is at the top of the park overlooking the sea; this area is equipped with some excellent fully serviced pitches and a superb amenity block.

Open: March to October **Last departure:** noon

Pitches: 🚐 🚙 🛆; 50 hardstanding pitches

Leisure: 🏊 🎢 🎣 🎵 ⚽

Facilities: 🏪 ☺ 🅿 ❄ ♿ 🖐 🚿 🛒 [WiFi]

Services: 🔌 🗄 🍴 ⚙ ⚙ 🔋 🦮 [T]

Within 3 miles: 🎣 💰 ↻ ◎ ⛵

Additional site information: 20 acre site. 🐕 Dog park. Cars can be parked by caravans and tents. Awnings permitted. Prices based on 1 car and 4 adults.

FILEY *continued*

Primrose Valley Holiday Park
▶▶▶▶ 88% HOLIDAY CENTRE

tel: 01723 513771 **YO14 9RF**
email: primrosevalley@haven.com **web:** www.haven.com/primrosevalley
dir: *Signed from A165 (Scarborough to Bridlington road), 3 miles south of Filey.*

A large all-action holiday centre with a wide range of sports and leisure activities to suit everyone, from morning until late in the evening. The touring area is completely separate from the main park and has its own high quality amenity block. All touring pitches are fully serviced hardstandings with grassed awning strips. The lakeside development near the touring area provides a dine-in and takeaway bistro and watersport activities.

Open: mid March to end October **Last arrival:** anytime **Last departure:** 10.00

Pitches: 🚐 🚎; 34 hardstanding pitches

Leisure: 🏊 🏊 ✋ 🎾 🎱 🎵 🎣 ⚽ 🎠

Facilities: 🛁 ☂ ♿ 🏧 🛒 🍴 WiFi

Services: 🔌 🔲 🍴 🍽 🛒 🔒 🌿

Within 3 miles: ⛳ ◎ 🎿

Additional site information: 160 acre site. 🐕 Maximum 2 dogs per booking, certain dog breeds banned. No commercial vehicles, no bookings by persons under 21 years unless a family booking.

Orchard Farm Holiday Village
▶▶▶▶ 87%

tel: 01723 891582 **Stonegate, Hunmanby YO14 0PU**
email: info@orchardfarmholidayvillage.co.uk **web:** www.orchardfarmholidayvillage.co.uk
dir: *A165 from Scarborough towards Bridlington. Turn right signed Hunmanby, site on right just after rail bridge.*

Pitches are arranged around a large coarse fishing lake at this grassy park. The superb amenity block is equipped with quality fixtures and fittings and provides good privacy options. The enthusiastic owners are friendly, and offer a wide range of facilities including an indoor heated swimming pool and a licensed bar.

Open: March to October (restricted service: off-peak season – some facilities reduced) **Last arrival:** 23.00 **Last departure:** 11.00

Pitches: 🚐 🚎 ⛺; 48 hardstanding pitches

Leisure: 🏊 ⛹ 🎱 ◻ 🎵 🎣

Facilities: 🛁 ☉ ☂ ✳ ♿ 🛒 🍴 WiFi

Services: 🔌 🔲 🍴 🍽 🛒 ▨ 🔒 T

Within 3 miles: ⛳ ◎ 🎿

Additional site information: 14 acre site. 🐕 Cars can be parked by caravans and tents. Awnings permitted. No scooters, skateboards or similar.

Blue Dolphin Holiday Park
▶▶▶▶ 83% HOLIDAY CENTRE

tel: 01723 515155 **Gristhorpe Bay YO14 9PU**
email: bluedolphin@haven.com **web:** www.haven.com/bluedolphin
dir: *On A165, 2 miles north of Filey.*

There are great cliff-top views to be enjoyed from this fun-filled holiday centre with an extensive and separate touring area. The emphasis is on non-stop entertainment, with organised sports and clubs, all-weather leisure facilities, heated swimming pools (with multi-slide), and plenty of well-planned amusements. Pitches are mainly on level or gently-sloping grass plus there are some fully serviced hardstandings. The beach is just two miles away.

Open: mid March to end October (restricted service: mid March to May and September to end October – outdoor pool closed and some facilities may be reduced) **Last arrival:** midnight **Last departure:** 10.00

Pitches: 🚐 🚎 ⛺; 33 hardstanding pitches; 20 seasonal pitches

Leisure: 🏊 ⛹ 🎢 ✋ 🎵 🎣 ⚽

Facilities: 🛁 ☉ ✳ ♿ 🛒 🍴 🍼 WiFi

Services: 🔌 🔲 🍴 🍽 🛒 ▨ ⬆ 🔒 🌿 T

Within 3 miles: ⛳ ◎

Additional site information: 85 acre site. 🐕 Maximum 2 dogs per booking, certain dog breeds banned. No commercial vehicles, no bookings by persons under 21 years unless a family booking.

Reighton Sands Holiday Park
▶▶▶▶ 81% HOLIDAY CENTRE

tel: 01723 890476 **Reighton Gap YO14 9SH**
email: reightonsands@haven.com **web:** www.haven.com/reightonsands
dir: *On A165, 5 miles south of Filey at Reighton Gap, signed.*

A large, lively holiday centre with a wide range of entertainment and all-weather leisure facilities (including an indoor play area), located just a 10-minute walk from a long sandy beach. Although tents are not accepted, there are good all-weather pitches with panoramic sea views. The site is particularly geared towards families with young children.

Open: mid March to end October (restricted service: mid March to May and September to end October – some facilities may be reduced) **Last arrival:** 22.00 **Last departure:** 10.00

Pitches: 🚐 🚎; 47 hardstanding pitches

Leisure: 🏊 ⛹ 🎢 ✋ 🎱 ⛳ 🎵

Facilities: 🛁 ☉ ☂ ♿ 🛒 🍴 WiFi

Services: 🔌 🔲 🍴 🍽 🛒 ⬆

Within 3 miles: 🎣 U ◎ 🎯

Additional site information: 229 acre site. 🐕 Maximum 2 dogs per booking, certain dog breeds banned. No commercial vehicles, no bookings by persons under 21 years unless a family booking.

LEISURE: 🏊 Indoor swimming pool 🏊 Outdoor swimming pool 🎢 Children's playground 🧒 Kids' club 🎾 Tennis court 🎱 Games room ◻ Separate TV room ⛳ Golf course 🏌 Pitch n putt 🚣 Boats for hire 🚲 Bikes for hire 🎬 Cinema 🎵 Entertainment 🎣 Fishing ◎ Mini golf 🎿 Watersports 🏋 Gym 🏆 Sports field U Stables
FACILITIES: 🛁 Baths/Shower ☉ Electric shaver sockets ☂ Hairdryer ✳ Ice Pack Facility 🍼 Baby facilities ♿ Disabled facilities 🛒 Shop on site or within 200yds 🍴 BBQ area 🍽 Picnic area WiFi WiFi

Centenary Way Camping & Caravan Park
▶▶▶ 85%

tel: 01723 516415 **YO14 0HU**
dir: *From A165 onto A1039 signed Filey. 1st right to site.*

A friendly, owner-managed family park with a direct link to the beach and close to town centre. The pretty landscaped grounds ensure a peaceful and relaxing stay, and a fairy garden with pop-up café is open during school holidays and at other peak periods. It is advisable to use Sat Nav rather than Google Earth when locating this park.

Open: March to October **Last arrival:** 21.00 **Last departure:** noon

Pitches: 🚐 🚌 ⛺; 25 hardstanding pitches

Leisure: ⚞

Facilities: 🏠 ☺ ✳ ♿ ⑤

Services: 🔌 ⑤ 🍽 ⚡ ⚒

Within 3 miles: ⚓ 🏌 ◎ ✈

Additional site information: 3 acre site. 🐾 🚫 Cars can be parked by caravans and tents. Awnings permitted. No group bookings in peak period, no 9–12 berth tents, no gazebos, no noise after 23.00.

Filey Brigg Touring Caravan & Country Park
▶▶▶ 83%

tel: 01723 513852 & 512512 **North Cliff YO14 9ET**
email: fileybrigg@scarborough.gov.uk **web:** www.fileybriggcaravanpark.com
dir: *A165 from Scarborough to Filey. Left onto A1039, at roundabout into Church Cliff Drive, to site.*

A municipal park overlooking Filey Brigg with splendid views along the coast, and set in a country park. The beach is just a short walk away, as is the resort of Filey. There are two good amenity blocks and 50 all-weather pitches are available. A well-stocked shop, café and an excellent children's playground are adjacent to the touring areas.

Open: end February to 2 January **Last arrival:** 18.00 **Last departure:** noon

Pitches: 🚐 🚌 ⛺; 82 hardstanding pitches

Leisure: ⚞ ⚽ **Facilities:** 🏠 ☺ ✳ ♿ ⑤ ⚞

Services: 🔌 ⑤ 🍽 🍔 🔋 Ⓣ

Within 3 miles: ⚓ 🏌 ∪ ◎ ✈

Additional site information: 9 acre site. 🐾 Cars can be parked by caravans and tents. Awnings permitted. No ball games.

HARROGATE   Map 19 SE35

Places to visit

RHS Garden Harlow Carr, HARROGATE, HG3 1QB, 01423 565418
www.rhs.org.uk/harlowcarr

The Royal Pump Room Museum, HARROGATE, HG1 2RY, 01423 556188
www.harrogate.gov.uk/info/20151/royal_pump_room_museum

Great for kids: Brimham Rocks, BRIMHAM, HG3 4DW, 01423 780688
www.nationaltrust.org.uk/brimham-rocks

Premier Park

Ripley Caravan Park
▶▶▶▶▶ 87%

tel: 01423 770050 **Knaresborough Road, Ripley HG3 3AU**
email: info@ripleycaravanpark.com **web:** www.ripleycaravanpark.com
dir: *3 miles north of Harrogate on A61. Right at roundabout onto B6165 signed Knaresborough. Site 300 yards left.*

A well-run rural site in attractive meadowland which has been landscaped with mature tree plantings. The resident owners lovingly maintain the facilities, and there is a heated swimming pool and sauna, a games room, and a covered nursery playroom for small children. A bus calls every 15 minutes which gives easy access to Ripon and Leeds, and a cycleway/walkway leads from the site directly to Harrogate, a distance of approximately three miles. A former tractor shed has been tastefully converted in to a holiday home cottage, available for hire.

Open: 2nd week March to 31 October **Last arrival:** 21.00 **Last departure:** noon

Pitches: 🚐 🚌 ⛺; 60 hardstanding pitches; 75 seasonal pitches

Leisure: ⛱ ⚞ 🔍 ⚽

Facilities: 🏠 ☺ 📯 ✳ ♿ ⑤ WiFi

Services: 🔌 ⑤ 🔋 ⚒ 🛢 🚿 Ⓣ

Within 3 miles: ⚓ 🏌 ∪ ◎ ✈ 🎫

Additional site information: 24 acre site. 🐾 Cars can be parked by caravans and tents. Awnings permitted. Family camping only. No open fires, off-ground BBQs only, no skateboards or rollerblades. No motorised scooters. No noise after 22.00. Football, volleyball, table tennis, pool table.

HARROGATE *continued*

Premier Park

Rudding Holiday Park
▶▶▶▶▶ 86%

tel: 01423 870439 **Follifoot HG3 1JH**
email: holiday-park@ruddingpark.com **web:** www.ruddingholidaypark.co.uk
dir: *From A1 take A59 to A658 signed Bradford. 4.5 miles, right and follow signs.*

A spacious park set in and beautiful mature parkland of Rudding Park. The setting has been tastefully enhanced with terraced pitches and dry-stone walls. A separate area houses super pitches where all services are supplied, including picnic tables and two amenity blocks. An 18-hole golf course, 6-hole short course, driving range, golf academy, destination spa, heated outdoor swimming pool, the Deer House Family Pub and a children's play area complete the picture.

Open: March to January (restricted service: November to January — reduced opening hours at shop and Deer House Pub. Outdoor heated swimming pool — only open in summer) **Last arrival:** 22.00 **Last departure:** 11.00

Pitches: 🚐 from £20; 🚍 from £20; ▲ from £20; 20 hardstanding pitches; 50 seasonal pitches

Leisure: 🏊 🎢 🎱 ⚓ 🎵 ⚽

Facilities: 🛁 ☉ 🗲 ❄ ♿ 💲 🛒 🍽 🚼 📶

Services: 🔌 🗑 🚽 🍽 🏧 🎪 ⛺ 🔒 🧴 🆃

Within 3 miles: 🎣 ∪ ◉ ⛳ 🎌

Additional site information: 50 acre site. 🐕 Cars can be parked by caravans and tents. Awnings permitted. Under 18s must be accompanied by an adult. Car hire can be arranged.

High Moor Farm Park
▶▶▶▶ 86%

tel: 01423 563637 **Skipton Road HG3 2LT**
email: highmoorfarmpark@btconnect.com **web:** www.highmoorfarmpark.co.uk
dir: *4 miles west of Harrogate on A59 towards Skipton.*

A family site with very good facilities, set beside a small wood and surrounded by thorn hedges. The pitches are located in meadowland and fields and one area is fully serviced. A large heated indoor swimming pool, games room, 9-hole golf course, full-sized crown bowling green, and a bar serving meals and snacks are all popular. Please note that this park does not accept tents.

Open: Easter or April to October **Last arrival:** 21.00 **Last departure:** 15.00

Pitches: 🚐 🚍; 51 hardstanding pitches; 57 seasonal pitches

Leisure: 🏊 🎱 ⚽

Facilities: ☉ 🗲 ❄ ♿ 💲 🛒 📶

Services: 🔌 🗑 🚽 🍽 🎪 ⛺ 🔒 🧴 🆃

Within 3 miles: 🎣 🏌 ∪ 🎌

Additional site information: 15 acre site. 🐕 Cars can be parked by caravans. Awnings permitted. No noise after midnight, no electric scooters, hover or skate boards.

LEISURE: 🏊 Indoor swimming pool 🏊 Outdoor swimming pool 🎢 Children's playground 👦 Kids' club 🎾 Tennis court 🎱 Games room 📺 Separate TV room 🏌 Golf course 🏑 Pitch n putt 🚣 Boats for hire 🚲 Bikes for hire 🎬 Cinema 🎵 Entertainment 🎣 Fishing ◉ Mini golf 🏄 Watersports 🏋 Gym 🏟 Sports field ∪ Stables
FACILITIES: 🛁 Baths/Shower ☉ Electric shaver sockets 🗲 Hairdryer ❄ Ice Pack Facility 🚼 Baby facilities ♿ Disabled facilities 💲 Shop on site or within 200yds 🍖 BBQ area 🪑 Picnic area 📶 WiFi

Harrogate Caravan Park
▶▶▶▶ 83%

tel: 01423 546145 **Great Yorkshire Showground HG2 8NZ**
email: info@harrogatecaravanpark.co.uk **web:** www.harrogatecaravanpark.co.uk
dir: A1(M) junction 47, A59 to Harrogate. A658, then A661. At Sainsbury's lights turn left into Railway Road.

Located on the perimeter of the Yorkshire Showground and owned by the Yorkshire Agricultural Society, this very peaceful park offers easy main road access and is popular at weekends and during the days of the shows. The site has a high standard amenity block (including a dog wash), extensive tree planting and smart, gravelled hardstanding pitches. There is a direct walkway to adjacent Fodders farmer's market and café with shopping discounts for site users. This is a good base for visiting Harrogate and the Yorkshire Dales.

Open: early March to early November **Last arrival:** 20.00 **Last departure:** 11.00
Pitches: * 🚐 from £23; 🚐 from £23; ▲ from £23; 57 hardstanding pitches
Leisure: ⚙
Facilities: 🏠 ⊙ 🏳 ⅃ ⑤ 🛒 🎋 WiFi
Services: 🔌 ⑤ 🛒 🛠
Within 3 miles: ⅃ 🎣 ∪ ◎ 🍴 ⛅

Additional site information: 3.56 acre site. ⌀ Cars can be parked by caravans and tents. Awnings permitted. No fires or fire pits. Shop and café adjacent, supermarket at end of road.

Shaws Trailer Park
▶▶ 69%

tel: 07921 761066 **Knaresborough Road HG2 7NE**
dir: On A59, 1 mile from town centre. Site 0.5 mile southwest of Starbeck railway crossing.

A long-established site just a mile from the centre of Harrogate. The all-weather pitches are arranged around a carefully kept grass area, and the toilets are basic but functional and clean. The entrance is on the bus route to Harrogate.

Open: All year **Last arrival:** 20.00 **Last departure:** 14.00
Pitches: 🚐 🚐 ▲; 29 hardstanding pitches
Facilities: 🏠 ⊙ ⅃
Services: 🔌 ⑤ 🍴
Within 3 miles: ⅃ 🎣 ⛅ ⛅ ⑤

Additional site information: 11 acre site. Adults only. ⌀ ⊗ Cars can be parked by caravans and tents. Awnings permitted.

HELMSLEY

Places to visit

Duncombe Park, HELMSLEY, YO62 5EB, 01439 770213
www.duncombepark.com

Helmsley Castle, HELMSLEY, YO62 5AB, 01439 770442
www.english-heritage.org.uk/visit/places/helmsley-castle

Great for kids: Flamingo Land Resort, KIRBY MISPERTON, YO17 6UX, 0800 408 8840, www.flamingoland.co.uk

HELMSLEY
Map 19 SE68

Premier Park

Golden Square Caravan & Camping Park
▶▶▶▶▶ 88%

tel: 01439 788269 **Oswaldkirk YO62 5YQ**
email: reception@goldensquarecaravanpark.com
web: www.goldensquarecaravanpark.com
dir: From York take B1363 to Oswaldkirk. Left onto B1257, 2nd left onto unclassified road signed Ampleforth, site 0.5 mile on right. Or A19 from Thirsk towards York. Left, follow 'Caravan Route avoiding Sutton Bank' signs, through Ampleforth to site in 1 mile.

An excellent, popular and spacious site with very good facilities. This friendly, immaculately maintained park is set in a quiet rural situation with lovely views over the North York Moors. Terraced on three levels and surrounded by mature trees, it caters particularly for families, with excellent play areas and space for ball games. Country walks and mountain bike trails start here and an attractive holiday home area is also available. Please note that caravans are prohibited on the A170 at Sutton Bank between Thirsk and Helmsley.

Open: March to October (restricted service: November to 1 January statics only)
Last arrival: 21.00 **Last departure:** noon
Pitches: * 🚐 from £19; 🚐 from £19; ▲ from £19; 30 hardstanding pitches; 50 seasonal pitches
Leisure: 🎢 🎯 ⚙ **Facilities:** 🏠 ⊙ 🏳 ❄ ⅃ ⑤ 🎋 WiFi
Services: 🔌 ⑤ 🛒 🛠 🍴 ∅ Ⓣ **Within 3 miles:** ⅃ 🎣 ∪ ◎ ⛅

Additional site information: 12 acre site. ⌀ Cars can be parked by caravans and tents. Awnings permitted. No skateboards, fires, Chinese lanterns or hover boards. No noise after 23.00. Microwave available, storage compound, table tennis, pool table, woodland walks, cycle trails. Bread and cakes available.

HELMSLEY *continued*

Foxholme Caravan Park
▶▶▶ 81%

tel: 01439 772336 **Gale Lane, Nawton YO62 7SD**
email: stay@foxholmecaravanpark.co.uk web: www.foxholmecaravanpark.co.uk
dir: *From Helmsley, east on A170, signed Scarborough. Continue to Beadlam, in centre of village turn right into Gale Lane.*

A quiet adults-only park set in beautiful northern Ryedale countryside, with a pleasant open aspect to all pitches and views toward both the Yorkshire Wolds and the Howardian Hills area of outstanding natural beauty. The facilities are well maintained, and the site is ideal as a touring base or a place to relax. Please note that caravans are prohibited on the A170 at Sutton Bank between Thirsk and Helmsley.

Open: Easter to November **Last arrival:** 23.00 **Last departure:** noon

Pitches: 🚐 from £25; 🚚 from £25; ▲ from £25; 30 seasonal pitches

Facilities: 🛁 ☉ 🅿 ❄ ♿

Services: 🔌 🔲 🛒 ⚒ 🔒 🗑 🆃

Within 3 miles: ⅃ ♻ 🆂

Additional site information: 13 acre site. Adults only. 🐕 Cars can be parked by caravans and tents. Awnings permitted.

HIGH BENTHAM

Places to visit

Lancaster Maritime Museum, LANCASTER, LA1 1RB, 01524 382264
www.lancaster.gov.uk/sport-and-leisure/museums/maritime-museum

Lancaster City Museum, LANCASTER, LA1 1HT, 01524 64637
www.lancaster.gov.uk/sport-and-leisure/museums/city-museum

HIGH BENTHAM   Map 18 SD66

Riverside Caravan Park
▶▶▶▶▶ 91%

tel: 015242 61272 **LA2 7FJ**
email: info@riversidecaravanpark.co.uk web: www.riversidecaravanpark.co.uk
dir: *M6 junction 34, A683 towards Kirkby Lonsdale, right onto B6480 signed Bentham. Site signed from High Bentham town centre.*

A well-managed riverside park developed to a high standard, with level grass pitches set in avenues separated by trees, and there are excellent facilities for children, who are made to feel as important as the adults. It has an excellent, modern amenity block, including a family bathroom, and a well-stocked shop, laundry and information room. The superb games room and adventure playground are hugely popular, and the market town of High Bentham is close by. Please note that this site does not accept tents. Bentham Golf Club (within one mile) is also under same ownership with facilities available for Riverside customers.

Open: March to 2 January **Last arrival:** 20.00 **Last departure:** noon

Pitches: * 🚐 from £23; 🚚 from £23; 27 hardstanding pitches; 50 seasonal pitches

Leisure: 🅰 🔍 🖊

Facilities: 🛁 ☉ 🅿 ♿ 🆂 📶

Services: 🔌 🔲 ⚒ 🔒 🆃

Within 3 miles: ⅃ ♻

Additional site information: 12 acre site. 🐕 Cars can be parked by caravans. Awnings permitted. No hoverboards, segways or drones. Chargeable permits for private fishing, discounted green fees at Bentham Golf Club.

Lowther Hill Caravan Park
▶ 84%

tel: 015242 61657 **Clapham Road LA2 7FH**
web: www.caravancampingsites.co.uk/northyorkshire/lowtherhill/lowtherhill.html
dir: *A65 at Clapham onto B6480 signed Bentham. 3 miles to site on right. Or from M6 junction 34, A643 to Kirkby Lonsdale. In 6 miles turn right onto B6480 to Bentham. 9 miles, site on left between High Bentham and Clapham.*

A basic site with stunning panoramic views from every pitch. Peace reigns on this little park, though the tourist villages of Ingleton, Clapham and Settle are not far away. All pitches have electricity, and there is a heated toilet and washroom and dishwashing facilities.

Open: All year **Last arrival:** 21.00 **Last departure:** 14.00

Pitches: * 🚐 from £17.50; 🚚 from £17.50; ▲ from £6; 4 hardstanding pitches; 7 seasonal pitches

Facilities: 🛁 ♿

Services: 🔌

Within 3 miles: ⅃ 🖊 🆂 🔲

Additional site information: 1 acre site. 🐕 🦢 Cars can be parked by caravans and tents. Awnings permitted. Payment on arrival, no noise after midnight.

LEISURE: 🏊 Indoor swimming pool 🏊 Outdoor swimming pool 🅰 Children's playground 👶 Kids' club 🎾 Tennis court 🔍 Games room ☐ Separate TV room
⅃ Golf course 🏌 Pitch n putt 🚣 Boats for hire 🚲 Bikes for hire 🎬 Cinema 🎵 Entertainment 🎣 Fishing ⊚ Mini golf 🏄 Watersports 💪 Gym 🏟 Sports field ♻ Stables
FACILITIES: 🛁 Baths/Shower ☉ Electric shaver sockets 🅿 Hairdryer ❄ Ice Pack Facility ⚒ Baby facilities ♿ Disabled facilities 🆂 Shop on site or within 200yds
🍖 BBQ area 🏕 Picnic area 📶 WiFi

HUTTON-LE-HOLE — Map 19 SE79

Places to visit

Nunnington Hall, NUNNINGTON, YO62 5UY, 01439 748283
www.nationaltrust.org.uk/nunnington-hall

Rievaulx Abbey, RIEVAULX, YO62 5LB, 01439 798228
www.english-heritage.org.uk/visit/places/rievaulx-abbey

Great for kids: Pickering Castle, PICKERING, YO18 7AX, 01751 474989
www.english-heritage.org.uk/visit/places/pickering-castle

Hutton-le-Hole Caravan Park

▶▶▶▶ 86%

tel: 01751 417261 **Westfield Lodge YO62 6UG**
email: info@huttonleholecaravanpark.co.uk **web:** www.huttonleholecaravanpark.co.uk
dir: From A170 at Keldholme follow Hutton-le-Hole signs. Approximately 2 miles, over cattle grid, left in 500 yards into Park Drive, site signed.

A small, high quality park on a working farm in the North York Moors National Park. The purpose-built toilet block offers en suite family rooms, and there is a choice of hardstanding or grass pitches within a well-tended area surrounded by hedges and shrubs. The pretty village with its facilities is a 10-minute walk away and the park is centrally located for visiting York, The Dales and other notable areas of interest. Please note, caravans are prohibited on the A170 at Sutton Bank between Thirsk and Helmsley.

Open: Easter to October **Last arrival:** 21.00 **Last departure:** noon

Pitches: 🚐 🚐 🅰; 4 hardstanding pitches

Facilities: 🛁 ☺ 🅟 ☀ ♿ 🍴 WiFi

Services: 🔌 🔋 🅣

Within 3 miles: 🎣 ∪ ◎ ⑤

Additional site information: 5 acre site. 🐕 Cars can be parked by caravans and tents. Awnings permitted. Boot, bike and dog washing area, farm walks.

KETTLEWELL — Map 18 SD97

Places to visit

Grassington Folk Museum, GRASSINGTON, BD23 5AQ
grassingtonfolkmuseum.org.uk

Great for kids: Kilnsey Park Estate, KILNSEY, BD23 5PS, 01756 752150
www.kilnseypark.co.uk

Kettlewell Camping

▶▶▶▶ 80%

tel: 07930 379079 & 01756 761684 **Conistone Lane BD23 5RE**
email: info@kettlewellcamping.co.uk **web:** www.kettlewellcamping.co.uk
dir: From roundabout on A65 (north of Skipton) take B6265 signed Grassington. Through Threshfield (do not turn right for Grassington). Road becomes B6160. In Kettlewell, first signed Scargill. Follow brown tourist signs.

Created from former farm fields, this superb camping site has stunning countryside views and is enclosed by well-maintained stone walls. It has the benefit of being just a few minutes' walk from Kettlewell with its craft shops, pubs, tea rooms and a village shop. A top-notch amenity block, fed by a bio-mass boiler, has underfloor heating and modern quality fixtures and fittings, and includes a family room with shower, toilet and washbasin. Free WiFi is available and a separate field, suitable for large families or groups, is also available in a more isolated location; it is enclosed by dry stone walling, is adjacent to a trickling stream and has a heated toilet and shower block, electric hook-ups and a picnic area. Please note, there is no laundry at this site. Winner of the AA Small Campsite of the Year 2018-19.

Open: Easter to October half term (restricted service: only open from November to end March for special occasions) **Last arrival:** 20.30 **Last departure:** 11.00

Pitches: 🅰

Facilities: 🛁 ☺ 🅟 ☀ ♿ 🍴 WiFi

Services: 🔌 **Within 3 miles:** 🎣 ∪ ⑤

Additional site information: 0.6 acre site. 🐕 Dogs must be kept on leads at all times. Cars can be parked by tents. Awnings permitted. Quiet after 22.00. Fires permitted in raised fire pits only. Field available for exclusive hire with private facilities.

KIRKLINGTON — Map 16 SE38

Places to visit

Thirsk Birds of Prey Centre, THIRSK, YO7 4EU, 01845 587522
www.falconrycentre.co.uk

Great for kids: The Big Sheep and Little Cow Farm, BEDALE, DL8 1AW, 01677 422125, www.bigsheeplittlecow.co.uk

Camp Kátur

▶▶▶▶ 80% GLAMPING ONLY

tel: 01845 202100 **The Camphill Estate DL8 2LS**
email: info@campkatur.com **web:** www.campkatur.com
dir: A1(M) junction 50, A6055 towards Bedale. Left at 1st roundabout, 1st right to Kirklington. Through Kirklington, approximately 1.5 miles to site on left.

Located within The Camp Estate, a popular centre for equestrian pursuits, quad biking, orienteering and corporate team building, Camp Kátur is a unique glamping destination with a choice of glamping units set in meadowland or wooded areas that comprise a wide variety of indigenous and imported trees. All the units are spaced well apart ensuring optimum privacy, and all have the benefit of fire pits, barbecues and outside seating areas. The safari tents and geo domes have en suite facilities and other units are serviced by a communal shower, toilet and wash basin block. There is a great focus on upcycling materials here with fire pits created from washing machine drums and galvanised bucket wash basins to name just two ideas. There's a campers' kitchen, a barbecue pod seating 16 around a central cooking area, and a rustic outdoor area ideal for gatherings such as a wedding reception or an anniversary or birthday celebration. The eco spa has a sauna and hot tub fuelled by wood-burning stoves. A unique Yogo Geodome was introduced for 2019.

Open: April to October **Last arrival:** 22.00 **Last departure:** 11.00

Leisure: ⚑ 🎱 ⚽

Facilities: 🛁 ☀ ♿ 🍴 WiFi

Within 3 miles: 🎣 🅟 ∪ ◎ ⑤

Accommodation available: Bell tents; safari tents; tipis; cabins; geo domes; wooden unidomes; retro caravan; log cabin.

Changeover days: Monday, Wednesday, Friday, Sunday

Additional site information: 20 acre site. 🐕 Groups permitted only with management permission. No noise after 22.00.

KNARESBOROUGH
Map 19 SE35

Places to visit

RHS Garden Harlow Carr, HARROGATE, HG3 1QB, 01423 565418
www.rhs.org.uk/harlowcarr

Aldborough Roman Site, ALDBOROUGH, YO51 9ES, 01423 322768
www.english-heritage.org.uk/visit/places/aldborough-roman-site

Kingfisher Caravan Park
►►►► 81%

tel: 01423 869411 **Low Moor Lane, Farnham HG5 9JB**
email: enquiries@kingfisher-caravanpark.co.uk **web:** www.kingfisher-caravanpark.co.uk
dir: *From Knaresborough take A6055. Left in 1 mile towards Farnham, follow signs for Kingfisher. Park entrance on left.*

A large grassy site with open spaces set in a wooded area in rural countryside. Whilst Harrogate, Fountains Abbey and York are within easy reach, visitors can if they wish just relax and enjoy the grounds and lake, which are a magnet for an increasing variety of wildlife. The park has a separate, flat tenting field with electric hook-ups available.

Open: March to October **Last arrival:** 20.00 **Last departure:** 14.00

Pitches: ⌂ ⌂ ▲; 30 seasonal pitches

Leisure: ⌂

Facilities: ⌂ ⊙ ⌂ ❄ ⌂ ⌂ ⌂ ⌂

Services: ⌂ ⌂ ⌂ ⌂

Within 3 miles: ⌂ ⌂ ⌂ ⌂

Additional site information: 14 acre site. ⌂ ⌂ Cars can be parked by caravans and tents. Awnings permitted. No football.

MASHAM

Places to visit

Theakston Brewery & Visitor Centre, MASHAM, HG4 4YD, 01765 680000
www.theakstons.co.uk

Norton Conyers, RIPON, HG4 5EQ, 01765 640333
www.nortonconyers.org.uk

Great for kids: Lightwater Valley Theme Park, NORTH STAINLEY, HG4 3HT, 01765 635321, www.lightwatervalley.co.uk

MASHAM
Map 19 SE28

Old Station Holiday Park
►►►► 81%

tel: 01765 689569 **Old Station Yard, Low Burton HG4 4DF**
email: info@oldstation-masham.co.uk **web:** www.oldstation-masham.co.uk
dir: *From south: A1(M) junction 50, B6267, left in 8 miles. From north: A1(M) junction 51, A684 to Bedale, then B6268, 4 miles to site.*

An interesting site at a former station that still retains a railway theme. The enthusiastic and caring family owners have created a park with high quality facilities. The reception and café are situated in a carefully restored wagon shed and here a range of meals, using local produce, is offered. The small town of Masham, with its Theakston and Black Sheep Breweries, is within easy walking distance of the park. Holiday cottages and log cabins are also available for hire.

Open: March to November **Last arrival:** 20.00 **Last departure:** 11.00

Pitches: ⌂ ⌂ ▲ ⌂; 12 hardstanding pitches; 16 seasonal pitches

Facilities: ⌂ ⊙ ⌂ ❄ ⌂ ⌂ ⌂ ⌂ **WiFi**

Services: ⌂ ⌂ ⌂ ⌂ ⌂ ⌂ ⌂ ⌂ ⌂ ⌂

Within 3 miles: ⌂ ⌂ ⌂

Additional site information: 3.75 acre site. ⌂ Cars can be parked by caravans. Awnings permitted. No cycling around site, no campfires. No ball games near caravans, motorhomes or tents.

Glamping available: BBQ cabins.

Additional glamping information: BBQ cabins (sleep either 4 or 6) offer electricity, kettle and heater. Own bedding, crockery and cutlery required. Cars can be parked by units

NORTHALLERTON
Map 19 SE39

Places to visit

Thirsk Museum, THIRSK, YO7 1PQ, 01845 527707
www.thirskmuseum.org

Thirsk Birds of Prey Centre, THIRSK, YO7 4EU, 01845 587522
www.falconrycentre.co.uk

Otterington Park
►►►► 87%

tel: 01609 780656 **Station Farm, South Otterington DL7 9JB**
email: info@otteringtonpark.com **web:** www.otteringtonpark.com
dir: *From A168 midway between Northallerton and Thirsk onto unclassified road signed South Otterington. Site on right just before South Otterington.*

A high quality park on a working farm with open vistas across the Vale of York. It enjoys a peaceful location with a lovely nature walk and on-site fishing, which is very popular. Young children will enjoy the play area. The toilet facilities are very good. A new amenity block, reception and 59 spacious fully serviced pitches are planned for 2020 and five wooden camping pods in a separate enclosed area are available for hire. The attractions of Northallerton and Thirsk are a few minutes' drive away

Open: March to October **Last arrival:** 20.00 **Last departure:** noon

Additional site information: 42 acre site.

LEISURE: ⌂ Indoor swimming pool ⌂ Outdoor swimming pool ⌂ Children's playground ⌂ Kids' club ⌂ Tennis court ⌂ Games room ⌂ Separate TV room ⌂ Golf course ⌂ Pitch n putt ⌂ Boats for hire ⌂ Bikes for hire ⌂ Cinema ⌂ Entertainment ⌂ Fishing ⌂ Mini golf ⌂ Watersports ⌂ Gym ⌂ Sports field ⌂ Stables
FACILITIES: ⌂ Baths/Shower ⊙ Electric shaver sockets ⌂ Hairdryer ❄ Ice Pack Facility ⌂ Baby facilities ⌂ Disabled facilities ⌂ Shop on site or within 200yds ⌂ BBQ area ⌂ Picnic area **WiFi** WiFi

NORTH STANLEY
Map 19 SE27

Places to visit

Norton Conyers, RIPON, HG4 5EQ, 01765 640333
www.nortonconyers.org.uk

Theakston Brewery & Visitor Centre, MASHAM, HG4 4YD, 01765 680000
www.theakstons.co.uk

Great for kids: Lightwater Valley Theme Park, NORTH STAINLEY, HG4 3HT
01765 635321, www.lightwatervalley.co.uk

Sleningford Watermill Caravan Camping Park
▶▶▶▶ 87%

tel: 01765 635201 **HG4 3HQ**
email: contact@sleningfordwatermill.co.uk **web:** www.sleningfordwatermill.co.uk
dir: Follow site sign on A6108 between North Stanley and West Tanfield.

The old watermill and the River Ure make an attractive setting for this touring park that is run by two enthusiastic managers. The site is laid out in two areas and the pitches are in meadowland close to mature woodland. Back-to-nature opportunities include a tree trail, bee garden, wild bird listings and river walks. Canoeing and fly fishing are also available.

Open: Easter and April to October **Last arrival:** 23.00 **Last departure:** 11.30

Pitches: * 🚐 from £23.50; 🚐 from £23.50; ▲ from £23.50; 8 hardstanding pitches; 49 seasonal pitches

Leisure: ✑

Facilities: 🏠 ☉ 🏳 ☀ ♿ ⑤ ℻

Services: 🔌 ⑤ 🛒 🪫 ⌀ Ⓣ

Within 3 miles: ⚓ ⛵

Additional site information: 14 acre site. 🐕 Dogs must be kept on lead at all times. Cars can be parked by caravans and tents. Awnings permitted. No fires, no noise after 23.00. Newspapers can be ordered, table tennis, tree trail, nature room, BBQs allowed on site, information room.

OSMOTHERLEY
Map 19 SE49

Places to visit

Mount Grace Priory, OSMOTHERLEY, DL6 3JG, 01609 883494
www.english-heritage.org.uk/visit/places/mount-grace-priory

Gisborough Priory, GUISBOROUGH, TS14 6HG
www.english-heritage.org.uk/visit/places/gisborough-priory

Great for kids: Thirsk Birds of Prey Centre, THIRSK, YO7 4EU, 01845 587522
www.falconrycentre.co.uk

OSMOTHERLEY
Map 19 SE49

Premier Park

Cote Ghyll Caravan & Camping Park
▶▶▶▶▶ 89%

tel: 01609 883425 **DL6 3AH**
email: hills@coteghyll.com **web:** www.coteghyll.com
dir: 7 mi A19 (awal carriageway) at 0481 (Northallerton jun tion). Follow signs to Osmotherley. Left in village centre. Site entrance 0.5 mile on right.

A quiet, peaceful site in a pleasant valley on the edge of moorland, close to the village. The park, which is served by two centrally located and well-equipped amenity blocks, is divided into terraces bordered by woodland, the only welcome distractions are the sounds of running water and birdsong. Mature trees, shrubs and an abundance of seasonal floral displays create a relaxing and peaceful atmosphere and the whole park is immaculately maintained. Under the same ownership, Cote Ghyll Mill opposite the park entrance serves a wide variety of cooked breakfasts and evening meals available as an eat in or takeaway facility. There are pubs and shops nearby and holiday statics for hire.

Open: March to October **Last arrival:** 20.00 **Last departure:** noon

Pitches: 🚐 🚐 ▲; 22 hardstanding pitches; 25 seasonal pitches

Leisure: ⚏

Facilities: 🏠 ☉ 🏳 ☀ ♿ ⑤ 🛒 🛒 WiFi

Services: 🔌 ⑤ 🍴 🪫 🛒 🪫 🪫 ⌀ Ⓣ

Within 3 miles: ⚓ ✑ ↻

Additional site information: 7 acre site. 🐕 Cars can be parked by caravans and tents. Awnings permitted. Quiet after 22.00, no camp fires. Freshly baked breakfast produce available. Nature trail, woodland walk to reservoir.

PICKERING
Map 19 SE78

Places to visit

Pickering Castle, PICKERING, YO18 7AX, 01751 474989
www.english-heritage.org.uk/visit/places/pickering-castle

Great for kids: North Yorkshire Moors Railway, PICKERING, YO18 7AJ,
01751 472508
www.nymr.co.uk

Wayside Holiday Park
▶▶▶▶ 84%

tel: 01751 472608 & 07940 938517 **Wrelton YO18 8PG**
email: wrelton@waysideholidaypark.co.uk **web:** www.waysideparks.co.uk
dir: 2.5 miles west of Pickering exit A170, follow signs at Wrelton.

Located in the village of Wrelton, this well-maintained seasonal touring and holiday home park is divided into small paddocks by mature hedging. The amenity block has smart, modern facilities. The village pub and restaurant are within a few minutes' walk of the park. Please note that this site has seasonal pitches only — caravans, motorhomes and tents are not accepted.

Open: March to October **Facilities:** 🏠 ☉ ♿ ℻ WiFi

Services: 🔌 ⑤ **Within 3 miles:** ⚓ ✑ ↻ 🎯 ⑤

Additional site information: 20 acre site. 🐕 🐾 Awnings permitted.

PITCHES: 🚐 Caravans 🚐 Motorhomes ▲ Tents 🏠 Glamping accommodation **SERVICES:** 🔌 Electric hook-up ⑤ Launderette 🍸 Licensed bar 🪫 Calor Gas ⌀ Campingaz Ⓣ Toilet fluid 🍴 Café/Restaurant 🛒 Fast Food/Takeaway 🪫 Battery charging ⚡ Motorhome service point * 2019 prices ⊘ No credit or debit cards 🐕 Dogs permitted ⊗ No dogs

POCKLINGTON   Map 17 SE84

Places to visit

Burnby Hall Gardens & Museum, POCKLINGTON, YO42 2QF, 01759 307125
www.burnbyhallgardens.com

South Lea Caravan Park
▶▶▶▶ 86%

tel: 01759 303467 & 07989 616095 **The Balk YO42 2NX**
email: south.lea@btinternet.com **web:** www.south-lea.co.uk
dir: *From A1079 (York to Hull road) between Barmby Moor and Hayton follow Pocklington
(B1247) and brown tourist signs. Site 400 yards on left.*

Located just off the main York road, South Lea Caravan Park is a tranquil, tidy and
level site – its entrance opens up onto 15 secluded acres. The five touring areas –
Sycamore, Birch, Ash, Oak and Willow – are serviced by a very well equipped and
spotlessly clean facilities block surrounded by colourful flower troughs; the
landscaping across the park is beautifully manicured. There's also a dog shower,
lush grass tent pitches, a football field and playground, good local walks, and a
bus service to local towns that stops at the front gate.

Open: March to October **Last arrival:** 20.00 **Last departure:** 16.00

Pitches: * 🚐 from £17.50; 🚏 from £17.50; ▲ from £17.50

Facilities: 🛁 ☉ 🌀 ⚹ 🛒 🎌 🎍

Services: 🛠 🔒 🐕

Within 3 miles: ⅃ ⌀ ∪ ◎ ⅊ ⅌ 🎬 🛒 🎲

Additional site information: 15 acre site. 🐕 Dog walk, dog shower. 🚗 Cars can be
parked by caravans and tents. Awnings permitted. Speed limit 5mph, no noise after
22.30, no kites or drones, children must be accompanied in toilet block. Water to most
plots.

RIPON   Map 19 SE37

See also North Stainley

Places to visit

Fountains Abbey & Studley Royal, RIPON, HG4 3DY, 01765 608888
www.nationaltrust.org.uk/fountains-abbey

Norton Conyers, RIPON, HG4 5EQ, 01765 640333
www.nortonconyers.org.uk

Great for kids: Thirsk Birds of Prey Centre, THIRSK, YO7 4EU, 01845 587522
www.falconrycentre.co.uk

Premier Park

Riverside Meadows Country Caravan Park
▶▶▶▶▶ 83%

tel: 01765 602964 **Ure Bank Top HG4 1JD**
email: info@flowerofmay.com **web:** www.flowerofmay.com
dir: *From A61 roundabout (north of bridge) in Ripon follow A6108 Leyburn and
Masham signs. At next roundabout, 2nd exit into Ure Bank. Road becomes Ure Bank
Top. Site at end of road.*

This pleasant, well-maintained site stands on high ground overlooking the River
Ure, one mile from the town centre. The site has an excellent club with a family
room and a quiet lounge. There are many walks to enjoy including those along
the river, and free WiFi is available through the park. Please note that prices for
caravans, motorhomes and tent pitches are for a maximum of 4 people and 1
car (electricity not included).

Open: Easter to October (restricted service: early and late season – bar open at
weekends only) **Last arrival:** dusk **Last departure:** noon

Pitches: * 🚐 from £26; 40 hardstanding pitches; 40 seasonal pitches

Leisure: 🎢 🎱 ▭ 🎵

Facilities: 🛁 ☉ 🌀 ⚹ ⅖ 🛒 🎌 🎍 📶

Services: 🛠 🗄 🍴 🏬 ⅃ 🔒 📞

Within 3 miles: ⅃ ⌀ ∪ ⅊ ⅌ 🎬

Additional site information: 28 acre site. 🐕 Dogs accepted by prior arrangement
only, dog walking track. Cars can be parked by caravans. Awnings permitted. No noise
after midnight. Multi-ball sports court.

ROBIN HOOD'S BAY

See also Whitby

Places to visit

Whitby Abbey, WHITBY, YO22 4JT, 01947 603568
www.english-heritage.org.uk/visit/places/whitby-abbey

Scarborough Castle, SCARBOROUGH, YO11 1HY, 01723 372451
www.english-heritage.org.uk/visit/places/scarborough-castle

Great for kids: Scarborough Sea Life Sanctuary, SCARBOROUGH, YO12 6RP,
www.sealife.co.uk/scarborough

LEISURE: 🏊 Indoor swimming pool 🏊 Outdoor swimming pool 🎢 Children's playground 🪁 Kids' club 🎾 Tennis court 🎱 Games room ▭ Separate TV room
⅃ Golf course ⛳ Pitch n putt 🚤 Boats for hire 🚲 Bikes for hire 🎬 Cinema 🎵 Entertainment 🎣 Fishing ◎ Mini golf 🏄 Watersports 🏋 Gym 🏅 Sports field ∪ Stables
FACILITIES: 🛁 Baths/Shower ☉ Electric shaver sockets 🌀 Hairdryer ⚹ Ice Pack Facility 👶 Baby facilities ⅖ Disabled facilities 🛒 Shop on site or within 200yds
🎌 BBQ area 🎍 Picnic area 📶 WiFi

ROBIN HOOD'S BAY
Map 19 NZ90

Grouse Hill Caravan Park
▶▶▶▶ 91%

tel: 01947 880543 & 881230 **Flask Bungalow Farm, Fylingdales YO22 4QH**
email: info@grousehill.co.uk **web:** www.grousehill.co.uk
dir: *From A171 (Whitby to Scarborough road), take loop road for Flask Inn (brown site sign).*

Grouse Hill Caravan Park

A spacious family park on a south-facing slope with attractive, mostly level, terraced pitches overlooking the North Yorkshire National Park. The site has quality, solar-heated toilet blocks, a treatment plant to ensure excellent drinking water, security barriers, play areas (including a woodland adventure play area), CCTV and WiFi. Heated wooden wigwams are available for hire. Please note that there are no hardstandings for tourers, only grass pitches, and this sloping site is not suitable for disabled visitors (there are no disabled facilities). This is an ideal base for walking and touring.

Open: March to October (restricted service: Easter to May – shop and reception reduced hours) **Last arrival:** 20.30 **Last departure:** noon

Pitches: ▣ ▣ Å ⋒; 30 hardstanding pitches; 20 seasonal pitches

Leisure: ◉

Facilities: ▣ ☺ ℱ ☀ ⅋ ⑤ [WiFi]

Services: ◘ ◎ ≛ ⫚ ♠ ⌀ [T]

Within 3 miles: ⌖ ↺

Additional site information: 14 acre site. ⚐ Cars can be parked by caravans and tents. Awnings permitted. No noise after 22.30. 8 family washrooms available.

Glamping available: Wooden wigwams.

Additional glamping information: All wigwams offer fridge, microwave, kettle, toaster, heater and picnic bench. Running Water wigwams also offer a toilet, TV, sink, table and four chairs. Cars can be parked by units

See advert below

ROBIN HOOD'S BAY *continued*

Middlewood Farm Holiday Park

▶▶▶▶ 90%

tel: 01947 880414 **Middlewood Lane, Fylingthorpe Y022 4UF**
email: info@middlewoodfarm.com **web:** www.middlewoodfarm.com
dir: *From A171 towards Robin Hood's Bay, into Fylingthorpe. Site signed from A171.*

A peaceful, friendly family park, enjoying panoramic views of Robin Hood's Bay, in a picturesque fishing village. The park has two toilet blocks with private facilities. The village pub is a five-minute walk away, and the beach can be reached via a path leading directly from the site, which is also accessible for wheelchair users. There are 14 wooden pods available for hire.

Open: 7 February to 7 January (restricted service: November to Easter – tents not accepted) **Last arrival:** 20.00 **Last departure:** 11.00
Pitches: * 🚐 from £19; 🚐 from £19; ▲ from £14; 🏠 see prices below; 21 hardstanding pitches
Leisure: 🛝 **Facilities:** 🛁 ☉ 🌣 ⚒ ⅙ 🛒 WiFi
Services: 🔌 🖱 🛒 ⬆ 🔒 🧺
Within 3 miles: ⚓ 🎣 🍴 $

Additional site information: 7 acre site. 🐕 Cars can be parked by caravans and tents. Awnings permitted. No radios or noise after 23.00. No dangerous dog breeds accepted.

Glamping available: Wooden pods from £42. **Changeover days:** Any day

Additional glamping information: Wooden pods offer microwave, fridge, kettle, heater, sockets, beds and lighting. Cars can be parked by units

See advert opposite

See advert opposite

Places to visit
Pickering Castle, PICKERING, YO18 7AX, 01751 474989
www.english-heritage.org.uk/visit/places/pickering-castle

North Yorkshire Moors Railway, PICKERING, YO18 7AJ, 01751 472508
www.nymr.co.uk

Great for kids: Flamingo Land Resort, KIRBY MISPERTON, YO17 6UX, 0800 408 8840, www.flamingoland.co.uk

Rosedale Abbey Caravan Park

▶▶▶▶ 89%

tel: 01751 417272 **YO18 8SA**
email: info@rosedaleabbeycaravanpark.co.uk **web:** www.rosedaleabbeycaravanpark.co.uk
dir: *From Pickering take A170 towards Sinnington for 2.25 miles. At Wrelton right onto unclassified road signed Cropton and Rosedale, 7 miles. Site on left in village.*

Set in a sheltered valley in the centre of the North Yorkshire Moors National Park, this popular park is close to the pretty village of Rosedale Abbey. It is divided into separate areas for tents, tourers and statics. It has well-tended grounds, and continues to be upgraded by the enthusiastic owners. Two toilet blocks offer private, combined facilities. There are six camping pods (with or without electricity) situated by the river. Please note that prices for caravans, motorhomes and tent pitches are for a maximum of 4 people and 1 car (electricity not included).

Open: March to October **Last arrival:** dusk **Last departure:** noon

Pitches: * 🚐 from £26; 🚐 from £26; ▲ from £26; 🏠 see prices below; 55 hardstanding pitches; 20 seasonal pitches
Leisure: 🛝
Facilities: 🛁 ☉ 🌣 ⅙ $ 🛒 🏠 🛒 WiFi
Services: 🔌 🖱 🛒 🔒 🧺 T
Within 3 miles: ⚓ 🎣 ↺

Additional site information: 10 acre site. 🐕 Dogs accepted by prior arrangement only. Cars can be parked by caravans and tents. Awnings permitted. No noise after 23.00. Freshly baked bread available.

Glamping available: Wooden pods from £40. **Changeover days:** Any day

Additional glamping information: Wooden pods; (sleep 5) maximum stay 2 nights (3 nights at bank holidays and in school holidays). Electricity, sockets, lighting, wooden decking included. 1 dog permitted per pod. Cars can be parked by units

---

See also Filey and Wykeham

Places to visit
Scarborough Castle, SCARBOROUGH, YO11 1HY, 01723 372451
www.english-heritage.org.uk/visit/places/scarborough-castle

Great for kids: Scarborough Sea Life Sanctuary, SCARBOROUGH, YO12 6RP, www.sealife.co.uk/scarborough

---

SCARBOROUGH
Map 17 TA08

Scalby Close Park
▶▶▶▶ 80%

tel: 01723 365908 **Burniston Road YO13 ODA**
email: info@scalbyclosepark.co.uk **web:** www.scalbyclosepark.co.uk
dir: *2 miles north of Scarborough on A615 (coast road), 1 mile from junction with A171.*

An attractive, well-landscaped park that is run by enthusiastic owners. The site has a shower block, laundry, fully serviced pitches and a motorhome service point. Just two miles from Scarborough, this makes an ideal base from which to explore both the coast and lovely countryside.

Open: March to October **Last arrival:** 22.00 **Last departure:** noon

Pitches: 🚐 🚍; 42 hardstanding pitches

Facilities: ⊙ 📡 ⚡ ☆ ♿ 🅂 WiFi

Services: 🔌 🔟 🔋 ⚡ 🗑 T

Within 3 miles: 🎣 ♪ ∪ ⚓ 🎍

Additional site information: 3 acre site. 🐕 🚫 Cars can be parked by caravans. Awnings permitted.

Killerby Old Hall
▶▶▶ 81%

tel: 01723 583799 **Killerby YO11 3TW**
email: killerbyhall@btconnect.com **web:** www.killerbyoldhall.co.uk
dir: *From A165 between Scarborough and Filey, at Cayton Bay roundabout into Mill Lane towards Cayton. At T-junction left onto B1261 signed Filey. Site on left.*

A small secluded park, well sheltered by mature trees and shrubs, located at the rear of the old hall. All pitches are handstandings with electric hook-ups. Use of the small indoor swimming pool is shared by visitors to the hall's holiday accommodation. A games room with billiard table, table tennis and amusement machines is an additional benefit and the children's playground also features a toddler facility.

Open: 14 February to 4 January **Last arrival:** 20.00 **Last departure:** noon

Pitches: * 🚐 from £18.50; 🚍 from £18.50; 30 hardstanding pitches

Leisure: 🏊 ⚲ 🎣 ✿

Facilities: 🏪 ⊙ ⚡ ⅁ WiFi

Services: 🔌 🔟 **Within 3 miles:** 🎣 ♪ ∪ ◎ ⚓ 🅂

Additional site information: 2 acre site. 🐕 Cars can be parked by caravans. Awnings permitted.

SCOTCH CORNER
Map 19 NZ20

Places to visit

The Green Howards Museum, RICHMOND, DL10 4QN, 01748 826561
www.greenhowards.org.uk

Easby Abbey, EASBY, DL10 7EU, 0370 333 1181
www.english-heritage.org.uk/visit/places/easby-abbey

Scotch Corner Caravan Park
▶▶▶ 80%

tel: 01748 822530 & 07977 647722 **DL10 6NS**
email: marshallleisure@aol.com
dir: *From Scotch Corner junction of A1 and A66 take A6108/A6055 towards Richmond. At roundabout take 3rd exit, A6108/A6055, approximately 350 metres to site entrance.*

A well-maintained and long-established all level site, ideal for a stopover or as a base to explore North Yorkshire. The Vintage Hotel, which serves food, can be accessed from the rear of the site.

Open: Easter or April to October **Last arrival:** 22.30 **Last departure:** noon

Pitches: * 🚐 from £24; 🚍 from £24; ▲ from £16; 4 hardstanding pitches

Facilities: 🏪 ⊙ ⚡ ☆ ♿ 🅂 🍺 🍴 🚻

Services: 🔌 🔟 🍺 🍴 🔋 ⚡ 🔋 🗑 T

Within 3 miles: 🎣 ♪ ∪ 🎍

Additional site information: 10 acre site. 🐕 Cars can be parked by caravans and tents. Awnings permitted. Recreation area for children, soft ball.

PITCHES: 🚐 Caravans 🚍 Motorhomes ▲ Tents ⌂ Glamping accommodation **SERVICES:** 🔌 Electric hook-up 🔟 Launderette 🍺 Licensed bar 🔥 Calor Gas ⊘ Campingaz T Toilet fluid 🍴 Café/Restaurant 🍔 Fast Food/Takeaway 🔋 Battery charging ⚡ Motorhome service point * 2019 prices ⊘ No credit or debit cards 🐕 Dogs permitted 🚫 No dogs

York Meadows Caravan Park
▶▶▶▶ 87%

tel: 01347 878508 & 01439 788269 **York Road YO60 6QP**
email: reception@yorkmeadowscaravanpark.com
web: www.yorkmeadowscaravanpark.com
dir: *From York take A64 towards Scarborough. Left signed Flaxton and Sheriff Hutton. At West Lilling left signed Strensall. Site opposite junction.*

Peacefully located in open countryside and surrounded by mature trees, shrubs and wildlife areas, this park provides all level pitches and a modern, well-equipped amenity block. Outdoor games such as draughts and snakes and ladders are available. A separate adjacent development of luxury lodges is planned.

York Meadows Caravan Park

Open: March to October **Last arrival:** 21.00 **Last departure:** noon

Pitches: * 🚐 from £19; 🚐 from £19; ▲ from £19; 45 hardstanding pitches; 20 seasonal pitches

Leisure: ⚠ ⚽

Facilities: 🛁 ⊙ 𝄐 ✳ ⚕ 🖫 WiFi

Services: 🔌 🗑 ⅄ 🛢 ⊘ T

Within 3 miles: ⚓ ⚲ 🎑

Additional site information: 12 acre site. 🐕 Cars can be parked by caravans and tents. Awnings permitted. No noise after 23.00, no skateboarding, hover boards, fires or Chinese lanterns. Fresh bread available. Outdoor table tennis.

LEISURE: 🏊 Indoor swimming pool 🏊 Outdoor swimming pool ⚠ Children's playground 🎣 Kids' club 🎾 Tennis court 🎱 Games room 📺 Separate TV room ⛳ Golf course 🏌 Pitch n putt 🚣 Boats for hire 🚲 Bikes for hire 🎬 Cinema 🎵 Entertainment 🎣 Fishing ⛳ Mini golf 🏄 Watersports 🏋 Gym ⚽ Sports field 🐎 Stables
FACILITIES: 🛁 Baths/Shower ⊙ Electric shaver sockets 𝄐 Hairdryer ✳ Ice Pack Facility 👶 Baby facilities ♿ Disabled facilities 🖫 Shop on site or within 200yds 🍖 BBQ area 🍴 Picnic area WiFi WiFi

Places to visit

Nunnington Hall, NUNNINGTON, YO62 5UY, 01439 748283
www.nationaltrust.org.uk/nunnington-hall

Castle Howard, MALTON, YO60 7DA, 01653 648333
www.castlehoward.co.uk

Robin Hood Caravan & Camping Park
▶▶▶▶ 88%

tel: 01653 628391 **Green Dyke Lane YO62 4AP**
email: info@robinhoodcaravanpark.co.uk **web:** www.robinhoodcaravanpark.co.uk
dir: *Access from B1257 (Malton to Helmsley road).*

A pleasant, well-maintained, grassy park in a good location for touring North Yorkshire. Situated on the edge of the village of Slingsby, the park has hardstandings and electricity for every pitch; 12 super pitches are available. The site has a centrally heated toilet block, and there is a treasure trail and play area for children.

Open: March to October **Last arrival:** 18.00 **Last departure:** noon
Pitches: * 🚐 from £24; 🚍 from £24; ▲ from £18; 12 hardstanding pitches
Leisure: 🅰 **Facilities:** 🖼 ⊙ 🥄 ✻ ♿ 🕃 🛒 🚮 WiFi
Services: 🔌 🕃 🛢 🛢 🗯 Ⓣ **Within 3 miles:** 🖉 ∪

Additional site information: 2 acre site. 🐕 Cars can be parked by caravans and tents. Awnings permitted. No noise after 23.00. Caravan hire, off licence, treasure trail.

See advert opposite

Places to visit

Scarborough Castle, SCARBOROUGH, YO11 1HY, 01723 372451
www.english-heritage.org.uk/visit/places/scarborough-castle

Pickering Castle, PICKERING, YO18 7AX, 01751 474989
www.english-heritage.org.uk/visit/places/pickering-castle

Great for kids: Scarborough Sea Life Sanctuary, SCARBOROUGH, YO12 6RP, www.scalife.co.uk/scarborough

Premier Park

Jasmine Caravan Park
▶▶▶▶▶ 88%

tel: 01723 859240 **Cross Lane YO13 9BE**
email: enquiries@jasminepark.co.uk **web:** www.jasminepark.co.uk
dir: *Take A170 from Pickering towards Scarborough. In Snainton, right into Barker's Lane (follow brown site sign). 0.5 mile, at crossroads left into Cross Lane. Site on left.*

A peaceful and beautifully-presented park on the edge of a pretty village, and sheltered by high hedges. This picturesque park lies midway between Pickering and Scarborough on the southern edge of the North Yorkshire Moors. The toilet block with individual wash cubicles is maintained to a very high standard, and there is a licensed shop, a children's playground, and it is possible for larger units can be accommodated on hardstandings (please check when booking). Please note, there is no motorhome service point but super pitches for motorhomes are available.

Open: March to October **Last arrival:** 20.00 **Last departure:** noon
Pitches: 🚐 🚍 ▲; 68 hardstanding pitches; 42 seasonal pitches
Leisure: 🅰 ☺
Facilities: 🖼 ⊙ 🥄 ✻ ♿ 🕃 🚮 WiFi
Services: 🔌 🕃 🛢 🗯 Ⓣ
Within 3 miles: 🖉 🖉 ∪ ◎

Additional site information: 5 acre site. 🐕 Cars can be parked by caravans and tents. Awnings permitted. No noise after 23.00. Baby changing unit.

STAINFORTH
Map 18 SD86

Places to visit

Malham National Park Centre, MALHAM, BD23 4DA, 01729 833200
www.yorkshiredales.org.uk/visit-the-dales/essential-information/tourist-infor-
mation/malham-national-park-centre

REGIONAL WINNER – NORTH EAST ENGLAND
AA CAMPSITE OF THE YEAR 2020

Knight Stainforth Hall Caravan & Campsite
▶ ▶ ▶ ▶   92%

tel: 01729 822200 **BD24 0DP**
email: info@knightstainforth.co.uk **web:** www.knightstainforth.co.uk
dir: *From west: A65 onto B6480 towards Settle, left before swimming pool signed Little
Stainforth. From east: through Settle on B6480, over bridge, 1st right.*

Located near Settle and the River Ribble in the Yorkshire Dales National Park, this
well-maintained family site is sheltered by mature woodland. It is an ideal base for
walking or touring the beautiful surrounding area. The toilet block is appointed to a
high standard and the lower part of the site benefits from the many trees that were
planted a few years ago. A superb local stone building houses a smart reception,
well-stocked shop, lounge and the Knights Table café and bistro, which features
locally-sourced produce on the menus. Fishing and WiFi are also available.

Open: March to October **Last arrival:** 22.00 **Last departure:** noon
Pitches: 🚐 🚌 ▲; 30 hardstanding pitches
Leisure: 🎠 🎱 🎣 ⚽
Facilities: 🛁 ⊙ 🗜 ❄ 🔔 🖪 🍽 🎌 📶
Services: 🔌 🗑 🛒 🍴 🏧 🚮 🛗 🔒 🥢 T
Within 3 miles: 🎿
Additional site information: 6 acre site. 🚗 Cars can be parked by caravans and tents.
Awnings permitted. No groups of unaccompanied minors.

STILLINGFLEET
Map 16 SE54

Places to visit

Merchant Adventurers' Hall, YORK, YO1 9XD, 01904 654818
www.theyorkcompany.co.uk

Mansion House, YORK, YO1 9QL, 01904 553663
www.mansionhouseyork.com

Great for kids: National Railway Museum, YORK, YO26 4XJ, 03330 161010
www.nrm.org.uk

Home Farm Caravan & Camping
▶ ▶   77%

tel: 01904 728263 **Moreby YO19 6HN**
email: home_farm@hotmail.co.uk **web:** www.homefarmyork.co.uk
dir: *6 miles from York on B1222, 1.5 miles north of Stillingfleet.*

A traditional meadowland site on a working farm bordered by parkland on one side
and the River Ouse on another. Facilities are in converted farm buildings, and the
family owners extend a friendly welcome to tourers. An excellent site for relaxing
and unwinding, yet only a short distance from the attractions of York. There are four
log cabins for holiday hire.

Open: February to December **Last arrival:** 22.00
Pitches: * 🚐 from £16; 🚌 from £16; ▲ from £16
Facilities: 🛁 ⊙ 🗜 ❄
Services: 🔌 🛒 🔒 🥢 T
Within 3 miles: 🎣 U 🎿
Additional site information: 5 acre site. 🚗 🐾 Cars can be parked by caravans and
tents. Awnings permitted. Family washroom.

SUTTON-ON-THE-FOREST
Map 19 SE56

Places to visit

Sutton Park, SUTTON-ON-THE-FOREST, YO61 1DP, 01347 810249
www.statelyhome.co.uk

Treasurer's House, YORK, YO1 7JL, 01904 624247
www.nationaltrust.org.uk/treasurers-house-york

Great for kids: Jorvik Viking Centre, YORK, YO1 9WT, 01904 615505
www.jorvik-viking-centre.com

Premier Park

Goosewood Holiday Park
▶ ▶ ▶ ▶ ▶   88%

tel: 01347 810829 **YO61 1ET**
email: nick@flowerofmay.com **web:** www.flowerofmay.com
dir: *From A1237 take B1363. In 5 miles turn right. Right again in 0.5 mile, site
on right.*

A relaxing and immaculately maintained park with its own lake and seasonal
fishing. It is set in attractive woodland just six miles north of York. Mature
shrubs and stunning seasonal floral displays at the entrance create an excellent
first impression and the well-located toilet facilities are kept spotlessly clean.
The generous patio pitches, providing optimum privacy, are randomly spaced
throughout the site, and in addition to an excellent outdoor children's play area,
you will find an indoor swimming pool and spacious clubhouse containing
games area, bar and bistro. There are holiday homes for hire. Please note that
prices shown are for a maximum of 4 people and 1 car (electricity not included).

Open: March to 2 January (restricted service: low season – shop, bar and pool reduced
hours) **Last arrival:** dusk **Last departure:** noon
Pitches: * 🚐 from £26; 🚌 from £26; 50 hardstanding pitches; 35 seasonal pitches
Leisure: 🏊 🎠 🎱 🎣
Facilities: 🛁 ⊙ 🗜 ❄ 🔔 🖪 🍽 🎌 🛒 📶
Services: 🔌 🗑 🛒 🍴 🛗 🔒 T
Within 3 miles: 🎿 🎒
Additional site information: 20 acre site. 🚗 Dogs accepted by prior arrangement
only. Multi-ball court. Cars can be parked by caravans. Awnings permitted. No noise
after midnight.

LEISURE: 🏊 Indoor swimming pool 🏊 Outdoor swimming pool 🎠 Children's playground 🧸 Kids' club 🎾 Tennis court 🎱 Games room 🖵 Separate TV room
🎿 Golf course 🏌 Pitch n putt 🚣 Boats for hire 🚲 Bikes for hire 🎬 Cinema 🎵 Entertainment 🎣 Fishing 🏌 Mini golf 🤽 Watersports 🏋 Gym 🏑 Sports field U Stables
FACILITIES: 🛁 Baths/Shower ⊙ Electric shaver sockets 🗜 Hairdryer ❄ Ice Pack Facility 🛒 Baby facilities 🦽 Disabled facilities 🖪 Shop on site or within 200yds
🍽 BBQ area 🎌 Picnic area 📶 WiFi

THIRSK
Map 19 SE48

Places to visit

Monk Park Farm Visitor Centre, THIRSK, YO7 2AG, 01845 597730
www.monkparkfarm.co.uk

Byland Abbey, COXWOLD, YO61 4BD, 01347 868614
www.english-heritage.org.uk/visit/places/byland-abbey

Great for kids: Thirsk Birds of Prey Centre, THIRSK, YO7 4EU, 01845 587522
www.falconrycentre.co.uk

Premier Park

Hillside Caravan Park
►►►►► 88%

tel: 01845 537349 & 07711 643652 **Canvas Farm, Moor Road YO7 4BR**
email: info@hillsidecaravanpark.co.uk web: www.hillsidecaravanpark.co.uk
dir: *From Thirsk take A19 north, exit at Knayton sign. In 0.25 mile right (cross bridge over A19), through village. Site on left in approximately 1.5 miles.*

A high quality, spacious park with first-class facilities, set in open countryside. The striking sandstone amenity block houses the airy reception, shop and office, plus there's a kitchen and laundry, two excellent family rooms, a disabled room, a recreation room, two self-contained flats and five luxury camping pods for hire, one of which is dog friendly. This is an excellent base for walkers and for those wishing to explore the Thirsk area. Please note, the park does not accept tents.

Open: 4 February to 4 January **Last arrival:** 21.00 **Last departure:** noon

Pitches: * ⊟ from £25; ⊟ from £25; ⋒ see prices below; 50 hardstanding pitches

Leisure: ⚲ ▢ ⊛

Facilities: ▤ ⊙ ⌗ ✳ ⛭ ⑤ ⊓ WiFi

Services: ⚡ ⑤ ⛟ ▪ T

Within 3 miles: ⚓ ↺

Additional site information: 9 acre site. ⊨ Cars can be parked by caravans. Awnings permitted. Self service coffee lounge.

Glamping available: Wooden pods ('mega pods') from £45. **Changeover days:** Any day

Additional glamping information: Mega pods equipped with toilet, shower, hand basin, kitchenette, TV, kettle, toaster, microwave and fridge. Cars can be parked by units.

WEST KNAPTON
Map 19 SE87

Places to visit

Pickering Castle, PICKERING, YO18 7AX, 01751 474989
www.english-heritage.org.uk/visit/places/pickering-castle

North Yorkshire Moors Railway, PICKERING, YO18 7AJ, 01751 472508
www.nymr.co.uk

Great for kids: Eden Camp Modern History Theme Museum, MALTON, YO17 6RT, 01653 697777, www.edencamp.co.uk

---

Wolds Way Caravan and Camping
►►►► 83%

tel: 01944 728463 **West Farm YO17 8JE**
email: info@ryedalesbest.co.uk web: www.ryedalesbest.co.uk
dir: *Signed between Rillington and West Heslerton on A64 (Malton to Scarborough road). Site in 1.5 miles.*

A park on a working farm in a peaceful, high position on the Yorkshire Wolds, with magnificent views over the Vale of Pickering. This is an excellent walking area, with the Wolds Way passing the entrance to the site. A pleasant one and a half mile path leads to a lavender farm, with its first-class coffee shop.

Open: March to October **Last arrival:** 22.30 **Last departure:** 19.00

Pitches: ⊟ ⊟ ⋏; 5 hardstanding pitches

Facilities: ⊙ ✳ ⛭ ⑤ ⊓ WiFi

Services: ⚡ ⑤ ⛟ ▪ T

Within 3 miles: ⚲

Additional site information: 7.5 acre site. ⊨ Cars can be parked by caravans and tents. Awnings permitted. Free use of microwave, toaster and TV. Drinks machine, fridge and freezer.

PITCHES: ⊟ Caravans ⊟ Motorhomes ⋏ Tents ⋒ Glamping accommodation **SERVICES:** ⚡ Electric hook-up ⑤ Launderette ⬛ Licensed bar
▪ Calor Gas ⊘ Campingaz T Toilet fluid ⧉ Café/Restaurant ⬛ Fast Food/Takeaway ⛟ Battery charging ⚡ Motorhome service point
* 2019 prices ⊗ No credit or debit cards ⊨ Dogs permitted ⊗ No dogs

WHITBY
Map 19 NZ81

See also Robin Hood's Bay

Places to visit

Whitby Abbey, WHITBY, YO22 4JT, 01947 603568
www.english-heritage.org.uk/visit/places/whitby-abbey

North Yorkshire Moors Railway, PICKERING, YO18 7AJ, 01751 472508
www.nymr.co.uk

Ladycross Plantation Caravan Park
▶▶▶▶ 95%

tel: 01947 895502 **Egton YO21 1UA**
email: enquiries@ladycrossplantation.co.uk **web:** www.ladycrossplantation.co.uk
dir: From A171 (Whitby to Teesside road) onto unclassified road (site signed).

The unique forest setting creates an away-from-it-all feeling at this peaceful touring park set in 30 acres of woodland and run by enthusiastic owners. The pitches are sited in small groups in clearings around two smartly appointed amenity blocks which offer excellent facilities – underfloor heating, no-touch infra-red showers, cubicles, kitchen prep areas and laundry facilities. Continuing investment in increasing numbers of fully serviced pitches and stylish oak lodges for hire or sale is matched by forest bramble clearing and planting of wild flowers. The site is well placed for visiting Whitby and exploring the North York Moors. Children will enjoy exploring the one-mile woodland and nature walks.

Open: March to November **Last arrival:** 20.00 **Last departure:** noon
Pitches: 🚐 🚃; 77 hardstanding pitches; 60 seasonal pitches

Facilities: ☺ 🕊 ✳ ⚒ 🖺 WiFi
Services: 🔌 🗑 🧺 ⬆ 🔒 🧴 T
Within 3 miles: 🎣 ⌖ ◎ ≋ ✈ 🎌

Additional site information: 30 acre site. 🐾 Dogs must be kept on leads in all areas of the park. Cars can be parked by caravans. Awnings permitted. No noise after 22.00.

WYKEHAM
Map 17 SE98

Places to visit

Scarborough Castle, SCARBOROUGH, YO11 1HY, 01723 372451
www.english-heritage.org.uk/visit/places/scarborough-castle

Pickering Castle, PICKERING, YO18 7AX, 01751 474989
www.english-heritage.org.uk/visit/places/pickering-castle

Great for kids: Scarborough Sea Life Sanctuary, SCARBOROUGH, YO12 6RP,
www.sealife.co.uk/scarborough

Premier Park

St Helens in the Park
▶▶▶▶▶ 90%

tel: 01723 862771 **YO13 9QD**
email: caravans@wykeham.co.uk **web:** www.sthelenscaravanpark.co.uk
dir: On A170 in village, 150 yards on left beyond Downe Arms Hotel towards Scarborough.

Set on the edge of the North York Moors National Park, this delightfully landscaped park is immaculately maintained and thoughtfully laid out; the stunning floral displays around the park are noteworthy. There are top quality facilities with smart family bathrooms planned for 2020 season, and a high level of customer care can be expected. The site is divided into terraces with tree-screening that creates smaller areas including an adults' zone. There are 10 camping pods for hire (eight have electricity). A cycle route leads through to the surrounding Wykeham Estate and there is a short pathway to the adjoining Downe Arms Country Inn. The licensed 'Squirrel's Nuts' dog-friendly café provides light refreshments, and a superb Aqua Park water activity area is nearby.

Open: 16 February to 15 January (restricted service: shop/café open from April to October only) **Last arrival:** 20.30 (arrivals from 13.30) **Last departure:** 11.00

Pitches: * 🚐 from £19; 🚐 from £19; ⛺ from £12.50; 🏠 see price below; 79 hardstanding pitches; 100 seasonal pitches

Leisure: 🎱 ⚽
Facilities: 🛁 ☺ 🕊 ✳ ⚒ 🖺 🍴 🚲 WiFi
Services: 🔌 🗑 🍴 🍺 🧺 ⬆ 🔒 🧴 T
Within 3 miles: 🎣 ⌖ ∪ ◎ ≋ ✈

Additional site information: 25 acre site. 🐾 Dogs must be kept on a lead at all times and never left unattended, and exercised in designated area or off site only. 3-acre dog exercise field. Cars can be parked by caravans and tents. Awnings permitted. No noise after 22.00, no open fires. Family and adult-only super pitches available, caravan storage.

Glamping available: Wooden pods from £30.

Additional glamping information: Wooden pods equipped with wall mounted heater, electric socket with USB ports, mirror, lights and blackout curtains. Beds and bed linen not provided. Cars can be parked by units.

LEISURE: 🏊 Indoor swimming pool 🏊 Outdoor swimming pool 🎱 Children's playground 🧒 Kids' club 🎾 Tennis court 🎱 Games room 📺 Separate TV room
🎣 Golf course ⛳ Pitch n putt ⛵ Boats for hire 🚲 Bikes for hire 🎬 Cinema 🎵 Entertainment 🎣 Fishing ◎ Mini golf 🏄 Watersports 🏉 Gym 🏏 Sports field ∪ Stables
FACILITIES: 🛁 Baths/Shower ☺ Electric shaver sockets 🕊 Hairdryer ✳ Ice Pack Facility 🚼 Baby facilities ♿ Disabled facilities 🖺 Shop on site or within 200yds
🍴 BBQ area 🍴 Picnic area WiFi WiFi

YORK
Map 16 SE65

See also Sheriff Hutton

Places to visit

The York Dungeon, YORK, YO1 9RD,
www.thedungeons.com/york

York Brewery, YORK, YO1 6JT, 01904 621162
www.york-brewery.co.uk

Rawcliffe Manor Caravan Park
►►►► 83%

tel: 01904 640845 **Manor Lane, Shipton Road YO30 5TZ**
email: christine@lysanderarms.co.uk **web:** www.lysanderarms.co.uk
dir: *From roundabout junction of A1237 and A19, take A19 signed York, Clifton and Rawcliffe. 1st left into Manor Lane, follow brown camping signs.*

A lovely little adults-only site tucked away behind the Lysander Arms and located only minutes from the centre of York. Each of the 13 generously-sized pitches is fully serviced with an individual chemical disposal point, and the central toilet block is very airy, modern and spotlessly clean. The grounds have been imaginatively landscaped. The pub offers good food and the York Park & Ride facility is a 10-minute walk away.

Open: All year **Last arrival:** 18.00 **Last departure:** 11.00

Pitches: 🚐 �16; 13 hardstanding pitches

Leisure: 🏊 🎣 🎵 🎯

Facilities: 🏠 ⊙ ⚙ 🕭 🚿 🚽 WiFi

Services: 🔌 🗑 🍺 🍴 🏪 🔋 🚽 🔒

Within 3 miles: 🚶 🎣 ⟳ ◎ 日 $

Additional site information: 4.5 acre site. Adults only. 🐕 Cars can be parked by caravans. Awnings permitted. No noise after 23.00. Chemical disposal points on each pitch.

SOUTH YORKSHIRE

WALES
Map 16 SK48

Places to visit

Bolsover Castle, BOLSOVER, S44 6PR, 01246 822844
www.english-heritage.org.uk/visit/places/bolsover-castle

Tropical Butterfly House, Wildlife & Falconry Centre, NORTH ANSTON, S25 4EQ,
01909 569416, www.butterflyhouse.co.uk

Premier Park

Waleswood Caravan and Camping Park
►►►►► 92%

tel: 07825 125328 **Delves Lane, Waleswood S26 5RN**
email: booking@waleswood.co.uk **web:** www.waleswood.co.uk
dir: *M1 junction 31 onto A57 towards Sheffield. At roundabout, left onto A618, at lights, right to Waleswood/Delves Lane. Caravan and Camping Park, 0.5 mile on Delves Lane on left.*

Located within the renowned Rother Valley Park, this superb caravan and camping park, which opened in 2019, is located in an elevated position commanding stunning rural views. All pitches, many of which are fully serviced, are generously spaced to maximise privacy and two amenity blocks are equipped with modern facilities and provide good privacy options for individuals and families. The combined reception, licensed café and small shop area operate generous opening hours and excellent walking and children's play facilities are also provided.

Open: All year **Last arrival:** 21.00 **Last departure:** noon

Pitches: * 🚐 from £25; �EV from £27; ▲ from £24; 125 hardstanding pitches

Leisure: 🎱 🎣 🎮 🎯

Facilities: 🏠 ⊙ 📶 🕭 $ 🚿 WiFi

Services: 🔌 🗑 🍺 🍴 🚽 🔒 T

Within 3 miles: ⟳ 🚴 🎣

Additional site information: 12.5 acre site. 🐕 Cars can be parked by caravans and tents. Awnings permitted. Dog walk, cycle wash area.

WORSBROUGH
Map 16 SE30

Places to visit

Monk Bretton Priory, BARNSLEY, S71 5QD, 0370 333 1181
www.english-heritage.org.uk/visit/places/monk-bretton-priory

Millennium Gallery, SHEFFIELD, S1 2PP, 0114 278 2600
www.museums-sheffield.org.uk

Great for kids: Magna Science Adventure Centre, ROTHERHAM, S60 1DX,
01709 720002, www.visitmagna.co.uk

Greensprings Touring Park
▶▶▶ 79%

tel: 01226 288298 **Rockley Abbey Farm, Rockley Lane S75 3DS**
email: greensprings_1@yahoo.co.uk
dir: *M1 junction 36, A61 to Barnsley. Left after 0.25 mile signed Pilley. Site in 1 mile at bottom of hill.*

A secluded and very peaceful farm site set amidst woods and farmland, with access to the river and several good local walks. There are two touring areas, one gently sloping. Although not far from the M1, there is almost no traffic noise, and this site is convenient for exploring the area's industrial heritage, as well as the Peak District.

Open: April to 30 October **Last arrival:** 21.00 **Last departure:** noon

Pitches: * 🚐 from £20; �"; from £20; ⛺ from £18; 30 hardstanding pitches;
22 seasonal pitches

Leisure: ⊕

Facilities: 🛁 ☉ ✳ ♿

Services: 🔌

Within 3 miles: ↧ ♪ ∪ ◎ ⊟ ⑤ 🛒

Additional site information: 4 acre site. 🐾 ⊛ Cars can be parked by caravans and tents. Awnings permitted.

WEST YORKSHIRE

BARDSEY
Map 16 SE34

Places to visit

Bramham Park, BRAMHAM, LS23 6ND, 01937 846000
www.bramhampark.co.uk

Thackray Medical Museum, LEEDS, LS9 7LN, 0113 244 4343
www.thackraymedicalmuseum.co.uk

Glenfield Caravan Park
▶▶▶▶ 89%

tel: 01937 574657 & 07761 710862 **Blackmoor Lane LS17 9DZ**
email: glenfieldcp@aol.com **web:** www.glenfieldcaravanpark.co.uk
dir: *3 miles from A1 junction 45. From A58 at Bardsey into Church Lane, past church, up hill. 0.5 mile, site on right.*

A very friendly and quiet rural site in a well-screened, tree-lined meadow. This site has an excellent toilet block and an increasing amount of hardstanding and fully serviced touring pitches. Discounted fees and food are both available at the local golf club. This is a convenient touring base for Leeds and the surrounding area.

Open: All year **Last arrival:** 20.00 **Last departure:** noon (late departures by prior arrangement)

Pitches: * 🚐 from £26; 🚐 from £26; 30 hardstanding pitches; 10 seasonal pitches

Facilities: 🛁 ☉ ℘ ✳ ♿ 🛏 ⊓ WiFi

Services: 🔌 ⑤ 🎱 🛒 ⚒ 🛢 ⊘

Within 3 miles: ↧ ♪ ∪ ◎ ⊟ ⑤

Additional site information: 4 acre site. 🐾 Adults only. Cars can be parked by caravans and tents. Awnings permitted. Walking maps available.

PITCHES: 🚐 Caravans 🚍 Motorhomes ⛺ Tents ⛺ Glamping accommodation **SERVICES:** ⚡ Electric hook-up 🔲 Launderette 🍷 Licensed bar
🔋 Calor Gas ⌀ Campingaz 🅣 Toilet fluid 🍽 Café/Restaurant 🏪 Fast Food/Takeaway 🔋 Battery charging ↯ Motorhome service point
* 2019 prices Ⓔ No credit or debit cards 🐕 Dogs permitted Ⓧ No dogs

Channel Islands

GUERNSEY

CASTEL   Map 24

Places to visit

Sausmarez Manor, ST MARTIN, GY4 6SG, 01481 235571
www.sausmarezmanor.co.uk

Fort Grey Shipwreck Museum, ROCQUAINE BAY, GY7 9BY, 01481 265036
www.museums.gov.gg/article/101090/Fort-Grey

Premier Park

Fauxquets Valley Campsite
►►►►► 88%

tel: 01481 255460 & 07781 413333 **GY5 7QL**
email: info@fauxquets.co.uk **web:** www.fauxquets.co.uk
dir: *From pier take 2nd exit at roundabout. At top of hill left into Queens Road. 2 miles. Right into Candie Road. Site opposite sign for German Occupation Museum.*

A beautiful, quiet farm site in a hidden valley close to the sea. The friendly and helpful owners, who understand campers' needs, offer good quality facilities and amenities, including spacious pitches and an outdoor swimming pool. There are sports areas, a nature trail, pigs, sheep and chickens for the children to visit, plus barbecue food and pizzas are available near the reception. There are fully serviced pitches and also four self-contained lodges for hire. Motorhomes up to 6.9 metres are allowed on Guernsey – contact the site for details and a permit.

Open: May to 1 September
Pitches: ⌖ Å ⌂
Leisure: �‒ ♨ ♦ ▢ ⚽
Facilities: ⌂ ☉ ℙ ☀ ♿ ⑤ ♨ ⊓ WiFi
Services: ⌂ ⑤ ⑩ ⊞ ⇥ ⋔ ⬛ ⊘ Ⓣ
Within 3 miles: ↓ ⌀ ∪ ◉ ⋙ ⋈ ⊟

Additional site information: 3 acre site. ⌁ Cars can be parked by tents. Awnings permitted. Birdwatching. Car hire can be arranged.

Glamping available: Log cabins; Safari tents.

Additional glamping information: Minimum stay 5 nights. Cars can be parked by units.

ST SAMPSON   Map 24

Places to visit

Sausmarez Manor, ST MARTIN, GY4 6SG, 01481 235571
www.sausmarezmanor.co.uk

Castle Cornet, ST PETER PORT, GY1 1AU, 01481 721657
www.museums.gov.gg/Castle-Cornet

Le Vaugrat Camp Site
►►► 90%

tel: 01481 257468 **Route de Vaugrat GY2 4TA**
email: enquiries@vaugratcampsite.com **web:** www.vaugratcampsite.com
dir: *From main coast road on northwest of island, site signed at Port Grat Bay into Route de Vaugrat, near Peninsula Hotel.*

Overlooking the sea and set within the grounds of a lovely 17th-century house, this level grassy park is backed by woodland, and is close to the lovely sandy beaches of Port Grat and Grand Havre. It is run by a welcoming family who pride themselves on creating magnificent floral displays. The facilities here are excellent and there are 18 electric hook-ups, plus several fully equipped tents for hire. A 'round the island' bus stops very close to the site. Motorhomes up to 6.9 metres are allowed on Guernsey – contact the site for details and a permit.

Open: May to mid September
Pitches: ⌖ from £27; ⌖ from £27; Å from £27; ⌂ see prices below
Leisure: ▢ ♨
Facilities: ⌂ ☉ ℙ ☀ ♿ ⑤ ♨ ⊓ WiFi
Services: ⌂ ⑤ ⇥ ⬛ ⊘
Within 3 miles: ↓ ⌀ ∪ ◉ ⋙ ⊟

Additional site information: 6 acre site. ⊗ Cars can be parked by caravans and tents. Awnings permitted. No pets.

Glamping available: Ready-erected tents from £53.

Additional glamping information: Ready-erected tents: beds, bedding (not towels) and cooking facilities are included. Electricity is not available. Cabanon Espace tents sleep 6. Bell tents sleep 3 (adults only). Cars can be parked by units.

VALE	Map 24

Places to visit

Guernsey Museum at Candie, ST PETER PORT, GY1 1UG, 01481 726518
www.museums.gov.gg/gmag

Great for kids: Castle Cornet, ST PETER PORT, GY1 1AU, 01481 721657
www.museums.gov.gg/Castle-Cornet

La Bailloterie Camping
►►►► 86%

tel: 01481 243636 & 07781 103420 **GY3 5HA**
email: info@campinginguernsey.com **web:** www.campinginguernsey.com
dir: *3 miles north of St Peter Port into Vale Road to Crossways, at crossroads right into Rue du Braye. Site 1st left at sign.*

A pretty rural site with one large touring field and a few small, well-screened paddocks. This delightful site has been privately run for over 50 years and offers good facilities in converted outbuildings, and a new woodland walk has been created. There are two, two-bedroom, well-equipped camping lodges, four top quality and very well-equipped safari tents (including a Cabanon tent) available for hire. The beaches and a supermarket are a short walk away. Motorhomes up to 6.9 metres are allowed on Guernsey – contact the site for detailed instructions.

Open: 15 May to 15 September **Last arrival:** 23.00 **Last departure:** 11.00

Pitches: * 🚐 from £20; ▲ from £20; 🏠 see prices below

Leisure: 🏕 ⚽ 🎯

Facilities: 🏠 ☉ ℗ ✳ ♿ 🔌 🍴 ☕ 🚿 WiFi

Services: 📞 🗑 🍴 🛒 🛁

Within 3 miles: ⛳ 🎣 ∪ ◎ 🚴 ✈ 日

Additional site information: 10 acre site. 🐕 Dogs by prior arrangement only, no dogs in safari tents or hired accommodation. Cars can be parked by tents. Awnings permitted. Volleyball net, boules pitch, mini golf. Car hire can be arranged.

Glamping available: Safari tents from £25; Pods from £20; Yurts from £18.
Changeover days: Any day

Additional glamping information: Minimum stay 2 nights. Safari tents: prices per adult; family packages available. Pods: prices per adult, maximum 2 people, fully equipped with bedding. Yurts: fully equipped, no bedding. Cars can be parked by units.

JERSEY	

ST MARTIN	Map 24

Places to visit

Mont Orgueil Castle, GOREY, JE3 6ET, 01534 853292
www.jerseyheritage.org/places-to-visit/mont-orgueil-castle

Maritime Museum, ST HELIER, JE2 3ND, 01534 811043
www.jerseyheritage.org/places-to-visit/maritime-museum

Great for kids: Elizabeth Castle, ST HELIER, JE2 3NU, 01534 723971
www.jerseyheritage.org/places-to-visit/elizabeth-castle

Premier Park	

Rozel Camping Park
►►►►► 89%

tel: 01534 855200 **Summerville Farm JE3 6AX**
email: enquiries@rozelcamping.com **web:** www.rozelcamping.com
dir: *Take A6 from St Helier through Five Oaks to St Martins Church, turn right onto A38 towards Rozel, site on right.*

Customers can be sure of a warm welcome at this delightful family-run park. Set in the northeast of the island, it offers large spacious pitches (many with electricity) for tents, caravans and motorhomes. The heated swimming pool has a separate children's paddling pool, and there is an on-site shop selling groceries, wine, beer and some camping supplies. Smart amenity blocks and a laundry room are provided. The lovely Rozel Bay is just a short distance away and spectacular views of the French coast can be seen from one of the four fields on the park. Motorhomes and caravans will be met at the ferry and escorted to the park if requested when booking. Fully equipped, ready-erected tents available for hire.

Open: May to mid September **Last arrival:** 20.30 **Last departure:** noon

Pitches: 🚐 🚐 ▲ 🏠

Leisure: ⚘ 🏕 🎱 ⬜ ⚽

Facilities: 🏠 ☉ ℗ ✳ ♿ 🔌 🚿 WiFi

Services: 📞 🗑 🛒 ⚓ ♨ 🗑 Ⓣ

Within 3 miles: ⛳ 🎣 ∪ ◎ 🚴 ✈

Additional site information: 4 acre site. 🐕 Cars can be parked by caravans and tents. Awnings permitted. No noise between 22.00–07.30. Free mini golf, table tennis. Freshly baked bread available.

Glamping available: Ready-erected tents.

Additional glamping information: Ready-erected tents are fully equipped. Cars can be parked by units.

TRINITY — Map 24

Places to visit

Hamptonne Country Life Museum, ST LAWRENCE, JE3 1HS, 01534 863955
www.jerseyheritage.org/places-to-visit/hamptonne-country-life-museum

Mont Orgueil Castle, GOREY, JE3 6ET, 01534 853292
www.jerseyheritage.org/places-to-visit/mont-orgueil-castle

Platinum Park

Durrell Wildlife Camp

▶▶▶▶▶ GLAMPING ONLY

tel: 01534 860097 & 07797 832534 **Les Augres Manor, La Profonde Rue
JE3 5BP**
email: ashley.mullins@durrell.org **web:** www.durrell.org/camp
dir: *From St Helier take A8 to Trinity. At T-junction right signed Rozel and Durrell
Wildlife. Site on right.*

Part of Jersey Zoo, the camp consists of 12 canvas geo domes set in a
beautifully landscaped area. Each dome, named after different Lemur species,
is sited in its own separate area offering good privacy. Inside is a king-size bed,
two singles, a wood-burning stove and clothing storage space. Set on wooden
decking, the domes have their own additional pod with high quality toilet, wash
basin and shower plus a spacious fully-equipped kitchen. Table and chairs on
the decking can be brought into the kitchen if the weather's not so good. Smaller
tipis are available for extra children or guests. Guests have free, unlimited
access to Jersey Zoo during its opening hours and can visit the excellent Café
Firefly, which serves breakfasts, lunches and early evening meals, plus takeaway
pizzas and Thai food. The whole holiday experience is quite magical.

Open: March to October **Last arrival:** 20.00 **Last departure:** 10.00

Facilities: 🛁 ⚒ ♿ 🚿 🌂 WiFi

Within 3 miles: 🎣 ∪ ⛵ 🗓 £ ⊙

Accommodation available: Geo domes from £140.

Changeover days: Any day

Additional site information: ⊗ No pets. No noise after 23.00. Free entry into Jersey
Zoo. Cars can be parked by units.

ISLE OF MAN

KIRK MICHAEL — Map 24 SC39

Places to visit

Peel Castle, PEEL, IM5 1TB, 01624 648000
manxnationalheritage.im/our-sites/peel-castle

House of Manannan, PEEL, IM5 1TA, 01624 648000
manxnationalheritage.im/our-sites/house-of-manannan

Great for kids: Curraghs Wildlife Park, BALLAUGH, IM7 5EA, 01624 897323
www.curraghswildlifepark.im

Glen Wyllin Campsite

▶▶▶ 80%

tel: 01624 878231 & 878836 **IM6 1AL**
email: tmdentith@manx.net **web:** www.glenwyllincampsite.co.uk
dir: *From Douglas take A1 to Ballacraine, right at lights onto A3 to Kirk Michael. Left onto
A4 signed Peel. Site 100 yards on right.*

This site is set in a peaceful wooded glen with bridges over a babbling brook that
divides the enclosed camping and touring areas, and where the only distractions
are the welcome ones of running water and birdsong. A long gentle sloping tarmac
road leads through the camping areas to a superb beach; a well-stocked shop and
hot food takeaway service are additional features. Ready-erected tents are
available and future plans include secluded lodges.

Open: mid April to mid September **Last departure:** noon

Pitches: 🚐 🚍 ⅄ 🏠

Leisure: ▭

Facilities: ⊙ ℗ ⚒ ♿ £ 🚿 🌂 WiFi

Services: 🔌 🗄 🍽 🛒 🔋

Within 3 miles: 🎣 ∪

Additional site information: 9 acre site. 🐕 Dogs must be kept under control. Cars can
be parked by caravans and tents. Awnings permitted. No excess noise after midnight.

Glamping available: Ready-erected tents.

PITCHES: 🚐 Caravans 🚍 Motorhomes ⅄ Tents 🏠 Glamping accommodation SERVICES: 🔌 Electric hook-up 🗄 Launderette 🍺 Licensed bar
🔒 Calor Gas ⊘ Campingaz T Toilet fluid 🍽 Café/Restaurant 🛒 Fast Food/Takeaway 🔋 Battery charging ⚡ Motorhome service point
* 2019 prices ⊗ No credit or debit cards 🐕 Dogs permitted ⊗ No dogs

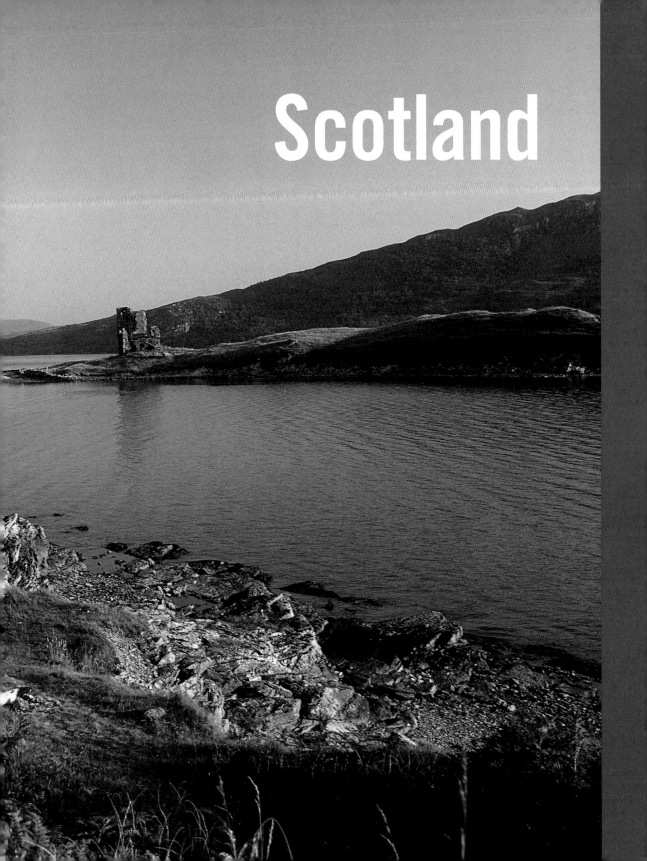

Scotland

Scotland

With its remarkable, timeless beauty, jagged coastline and long and eventful history, Scotland is a country with something very special to offer. Around half the size of England, but with barely one fifth of its population and nearly 800 islands, the statistics alone are enough make you want to pack a suitcase and head north without hesitation.

The Scottish Borders region acts as a perfect introduction and is an obvious place to begin a tour of the country. The novelist and poet Sir Walter Scott was so moved by its remoteness and grandeur that he wrote: 'To my eye, these grey hills and all this wild border country have beauties peculiar to themselves. I like the very nakedness of the land; it has something bold and stern and solitary about it. If I did not see the heather at least once a year I think I should die.' Abbotsford, Scott's turreted mansion on the banks of the River Tweed near Melrose, was re-opened to the public in the summer of 2013 following a £12 million programme of major improvements.

Consisting of 1,800 square miles of dense forest, rolling green hills and the broad sweeps of heather that lifted Scott's spirits, this region is characterised by some of the country's most majestic landscapes. Adjacent to this region is Dumfries & Galloway, where, at Gretna Green on the border with England, eloping couples have tied the knot since Lord Hardwicke's Marriage Act came into force in 1754; it still can boast around 1,500 weddings a year. Travel north and you discover mile upon mile of open moorland and swathes of seemingly endless forest that stretch to the Ayrshire coast. At a crucial time in the country's history, it is fascinating to reflect on another momentous event in the story of Scotland when, following the signing of the Declaration of Arbroath in 1320, it became independent and was ruled by Robert the Bruce. Dumfries & Galloway is littered with the relics of his battles.

Not far from Dumfries is the cottage where Robert Burns, the Bard of Scotland, was born in 1759. This tiny white-washed dwelling, constructed of thatch and clay, was built by the poet's father two years earlier. In a 2009 poll, TV viewers voted Burns the 'Greatest ever Scot' and his song *Is there for Honest Poverty*

opened the new Scottish Parliament in 1999. The cottage at Alloway is one of Scotland's most popular tourist attractions with a museum allowing the poet's collection of precious manuscripts, correspondence and artefacts to be housed in one building.

Scotland's two greatest cities, Glasgow and Edinburgh, include innumerable historic sites, popular landmarks and innovative visitor attractions. Edinburgh is home to the annual, internationally famous Military Tattoo; Glasgow, once the second city of the British Empire and yet synonymous with the dreadful slums and the grime of industry, has, in places, been transformed beyond recognition. The city hosted the Great Exhibitions of 1888 and 1901, was designated European City of Culture in 1990 and in 2014 became the setting for the highly successful Commonwealth Games.

To the north of Glasgow and Edinburgh lies a sublime landscape of tranquil lochs, fishing rivers, wooded glens and the fine cities of Perth and Dundee. There is also the superb scenery of The Trossachs, Loch Lomond and Stirling, which, with its handsome castle perched on a rocky crag, is Scotland's heritage capital. Sooner or later the might and majesty of the Cairngorms and the Grampians beckon, drawing you into a breathtakingly beautiful landscape of mountains and remote, rugged terrain. Scotland's isolated far north is further from many parts of England than a good many European destinations. Cape Wrath is Britain's most northerly outpost.

For many visitors, the Western Highlands is the place to go, evoking a truly unique and breathtaking sense of adventure. The list of island names seems endless – Skye, Mull, Iona, Jura, Islay – each with their own individual character and identity, and the reward of everlasting and treasured memories.

ABERDEENSHIRE

ABOYNE — Map 23 NO59

Places to visit

Crathes Castle Garden & Estate, CRATHES, AB31 5QJ, 01330 844525
www.nts.org.uk/visit/places/crathes-castle

Great for kids: Craigievar Castle, ALFORD, AB33 8JF, 01339 883635
www.nts.org.uk/visit/places/craigievar

Aboyne Loch Caravan Park

▶▶▶ 76%

tel: 01339 886244 **AB34 5BR**
email: info@aboynelochcaravanpark.co.uk **web:** www.aboynelochcaravanpark.co.uk
dir: *On A93, 1 mile east of Aboyne.*

Located on the outskirts of Aboyne on a small outcrop which is almost surrounded by Loch Aboyne, this is a mature site within scenic Royal Deeside. The facilities are well maintained, and pitches are set amongst mature trees with most having views over the loch. Boat hire is offered and fishing (coarse and pike) is available. There is a regular bus service from the site entrance.

Open: 31 March to October **Last arrival:** 20.00 **Last departure:** noon
Pitches: 🚐 🚍 ▲; 25 hardstanding pitches; 10 seasonal pitches
Leisure: 🎣 🖊
Facilities: 🛁 ☉ 🗜 ☀ 🚿 WiFi
Services: 🔌 🗓 ⚓ ♨ 📶 T
Within 3 miles: 🛴 ∪ ◎ 🛥 🚲 💲

Additional site information: 6 acre site. 🐾 Cars can be parked by caravans and tents. Awnings permitted. Fishing, boat hire, cycle trails. Car hire can be arranged.

ALFORD — Map 23 NJ51

Places to visit

Craigievar Castle, ALFORD, AB33 8JF, 01339 883635
www.nts.org.uk/visit/places/craigievar

Haughton House Holiday Park

▶▶▶ 79%

tel: 01975 562107 **Montgarrie Road AB33 8NA**
email: enquiries@haughtonhouse.co.uk **web:** www.haughtonhouse.co.uk
dir: *In Alford follow Haughton Country House signs.*

Located on the outskirts of Alford, this site is set within a large country park that has good countryside views. Now under the same ownership as Huntly Castle

Caravan Park (Huntly), this park receives the same attention to detail to ensure facilities are of a high standard; facilities are clean and well maintained. The pitches are set amid mature trees and the tenting area is in the old walled garden. There is plenty to do on site and within the country park which has various activities for children, including a narrow gauge railway that runs to the Grampian Transport Museum in nearby Alford.

Open: March to mid/end October **Last arrival:** 21.00 **Last departure:** noon
Pitches: 🚐 🚍 ▲; 71 hardstanding pitches; 20 seasonal pitches
Leisure: 🎠
Facilities: 🛁 ☉ 🗜 ☀ 🚿 🚿 🍴 WiFi
Services: 🔌 🗓 ⚓ ♨ 📶 T
Within 3 miles: 🛴 🖊 ◎ 💲

Additional site information: 22 acre site. 🐾 Cars can be parked by caravans and tents. Awnings permitted. No noise after 22.30. Putting green, fishing permits.

BANFF — Map 23 NJ66

Places to visit

Duff House, BANFF, AB45 3SX, 01261 818181
www.historicenvironment.scot/visit-a-place/places/duff-house/

Banff Links Caravan Park

▶▶▶▶ 86%

tel: 01261 812228 **Inverboyndie AB45 2JJ**
email: banfflinkscaravanpark@btconnect.com **web:** www.banfflinkscaravanpark.co.uk
dir: *From west: A98 onto B9038 signed Whitehills. 2nd right signed Inverboyndie. 4th left to site. From east (Banff): A98, right at brown 'Banff Links Beach' sign.*

This delightful small park, where the family owners are keen that their visitors enjoy their stay, is set beside the award-winning sandy beach at Banff Links with magnificent views over the Moray coast. Set at sea level, there is direct access to the beach and also a large grass esplanade and play area for children. A pleasant walk on good level paths by the sea will take you to either Banff or the small village of Whitehill, which has a leisure boat harbour. It is ideally located to explore this lovely coastline. Six static caravans are for hire.

Open: April to October **Last departure:** noon
Pitches: 🚐 🚍 ▲; 10 hardstanding pitches; 10 seasonal pitches
Facilities: 🗜 🚿 💲 🍴 WiFi
Services: 🔌 🗓 ⚓ ♨ 📶 T
Within 3 miles: 🛴 🖊 ∪ ◎ 🛥

Additional site information: 5.78 acre site. 🐾 Cars can be parked by caravans and tents. Awnings permitted.

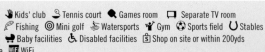

LEISURE: 🏊 Indoor swimming pool 🏊 Outdoor swimming pool 🎠 Children's playground 👶 Kids' club 🎾 Tennis court 🎱 Games room 📺 Separate TV room 🛴 Golf course 🏌 Pitch n putt 🚣 Boats for hire 🚲 Bikes for hire 🎬 Cinema 🎵 Entertainment 🎣 Fishing ◎ Mini golf 🏄 Watersports 🏋 Gym 🏟 Sports field ∪ Stables
FACILITIES: 🛁 Baths/Shower ☉ Electric shaver sockets 🗜 Hairdryer ☀ Ice Pack Facility 🚼 Baby facilities 🚿 Disabled facilities 💲 Shop on site or within 200yds 🍴 BBQ area 🍴 Picnic area WiFi WiFi

HUNTLY   Map 23 NJ53

Places to visit

Leith Hall, Garden & Estate, RHYNIE, AB54 4NQ, 01464 831216
www.nts.org.uk/visit/places/leith-hall

Glenfiddich Distillery, DUFFTOWN, AB55 4DH, 01340 820373
www.glenfiddich.com/uk/distillery/

AA CAMPSITE OF THE YEAR
FOR SCOTLAND 2020

Premier Park

Huntly Castle Caravan Park
▶▶▶▶▶   90%

tel: 01466 794999 **The Meadow AB54 4UJ**
email: enquiries@huntlycastle.co.uk **web:** www.huntlycastle.co.uk
dir: *From Aberdeen on A96 to Huntly. 0.75 mile after roundabout (on outskirts of Huntly) right towards town centre, left into Riverside Drive.*

A quality parkland site within striking distance of the Speyside Malt Whisky Trail, the beautiful Moray coast and the Cairngorm Mountains. The park provides exceptional toilet facilities, and there are some fully serviced pitches. The attractive town of Huntly is only a five-minute walk away, with its ruined castle plus a wide variety of restaurants and shops.

Open: April to October **Last arrival:** 20.00 **Last departure:** noon

Pitches: * 🚐 from £21.20; 🚐 from £21.20; 🅐 from £13.50;
51 hardstanding pitches; 10 seasonal pitches

Leisure: ⚲

Facilities: 🖼 ⊙ ℙ ⚒ ⅗ WiFi

Services: ⚡ ⑤ 🔧 ⚓ 🗝 Ⓣ

Within 3 miles: ⅃ ⌀ ⑤

Additional site information: 15 acre site. 🐕 Cars can be parked by caravans and tents. Awnings permitted. No noise after 23.00.

KINTORE   Map 23 NJ71

Places to visit

Pitmedden Garden, PITMEDDEN, AB41 7PD, 01651 842352
www.nts.org.uk/visit/places/pitmedden-garden

Tolquhon Castle, PITMEDDEN, AB41 7LP, 01651 851286
www.historicenvironment.scot/visit-a-place/places/tolquhon-castle/

Great for kids: Castle Fraser, KEMNAY, AB51 7LD, 01330 833463
www.nts.org.uk/visit/places/castle-fraser

Hillhead Caravan Park
▶▶▶▶   77%

tel: 01467 632809 **AB51 0YX**
email: enquiries@hillheadcaravan.com **web:** www.hillheadcaravan.com
dir: *From south: A96 at Broomhill Roundabout follow Kintore (and brown camping sign) onto B987. At mini-roundabout 1st left, immediately left signed Kemnay. Over A96, straight on at next roundabout, right signed Kintore. Site on right. From north: A96 at roundabout follow Kintore signs onto B987. 5th right into Forest Road. Over A96, 1st left to site on left.*

An attractive, nicely landscaped site, located on the outskirts of Kintore in the valley of the River Dee, with excellent access to forest walks and within easy reach of the many attractions in rural Aberdeenshire. The toilet facilities are of a high standard. There are good play facilities for smaller children plus a small café with TV and internet access.

Open: All year **Last arrival:** 21.00 **Last departure:** 13.00

Pitches: 🚐 🚐 🅐; 17 hardstanding pitches; 10 seasonal pitches

Leisure: ⚲

Facilities: 🖼 ⊙ ℙ ⚒ ⅗ ⑤ 🔧 🗝 WiFi

Services: ⚡ ⑤ 🍽 🛒 ⚓ ⌀ Ⓣ

Within 3 miles: ⅃ ⌀

Additional site information: 1.5 acre site. 🐕 Cars can be parked by caravans and tents. Awnings permitted. Caravan storage, accessories shop.

MACDUFF
Map 23 NJ76

Places to visit

Duff House, BANFF, AB45 3SX, 01261 818181
www.historicenvironment.scot/visit-a-place/places/duff-house/

Great for kids: Macduff Marine Aquarium, MACDUFF, AB44 1SL, 01261 833369
www.macduff-aquarium.org.uk

Wester Bonnyton Farm Site
▶▶ 68%

tel: 01261 832470 & 07813 443308 **Gamrie AB45 3EP**
email: clare@westerbonnyton.co.uk **web:** www.westerbonnyton.co.uk
dir: *From A98 (1 mile south of Macduff) take B9031 signed Rosehearty. Site 1.25 miles on right.*

A spacious farm site, with level touring pitches, overlooking the Moray Firth. The small, picturesque fishing villages of Gardenstown and Crovie and the larger town of Macduff, which has a marine aquarium, are all within easy reach. All the touring pitches have good views of the coastline. Families with children are welcome, and there is a play area and play barn.

Open: March to October

Pitches: 🚐 from £15; 🚐 from £15; ▲ from £15; 5 hardstanding pitches; 1 seasonal pitch

Leisure: 🄰 🔍

Facilities: 🛁 ☉ 🗗 ⑤ 🍴 📮 WiFi

Services: 🔌 🗑 🏪 🛒

Within 3 miles: ⅃ 🖋 ⛷ 🎿

Additional site information: 8 acre site. 🐾 Cars can be parked by caravans and tents. Awnings permitted.

MINTLAW
Map 23 NJ94

Places to visit

Aberdeenshire Farming Museum, MINTLAW, AB42 5FQ, 01771 624590
www.livelifeaberdeenshire.org.uk/museums/find-a-museum/aberdeenshire-farming-museum/

Deer Abbey, OLD DEER
www.historicenvironment.scot/visit-a-place/places/deer-abbey/

Aden Caravan and Camping Park
▶▶▶ 85%

tel: 01771 623460 **Station Road AB42 5FQ**
email: wardens@adencaravanandcamping.co.uk
web: www.adencaravanandcamping.co.uk
dir: *From Mintlaw take A950 signed New Pitsligo and Aden Country Park. Park on left.*

Situated adjacent to the 230-acre Aden Country Park, this is a small tranquil site offering excellent facilities. It is ideally located for visiting the many tourist attractions in this beautiful northeast coastal area. The site is only a short drive from the busy fishing towns of Fraserburgh and Peterhead, and as it is only an hour from Aberdeen's centre; this is an ideal spot for a short stay or a longer holiday, and there is one disabled-friendly static for hire. The adjacent country park plays host to numerous events throughout the year, including pipe band championships, horse events and various ranger-run activities.

Open: April to October **Last arrival:** 20.00 **Last departure:** noon

Pitches: * 🚐 from £24; 🚐 from £24; ▲ from £6.50; 🏠 see price below; 31 hardstanding pitches; 14 seasonal pitches

Leisure: 🄰 🔍

Facilities: 🛁 ☉ 🗗 ⅃ 📮 WiFi

Services: 🔌 🗑 🛒 🛒

Within 3 miles: ⅃ 🖋 ⑤

Additional site information: 11.1 acre site. 🐾 Cars can be parked by caravans and tents. Awnings permitted. See website for details.

Glamping available: 3 wooden pods from £50 per night.

Additional glamping information: Wooden pods sleep up to 4 people. Please see website for restrictions. Cars can be parked by units.

NORTH WATER BRIDGE
Map 23 NO66

Places to visit

Edzell Castle and Garden, EDZELL, DD9 7UE, 01356 648631
www.historicenvironment.scot/visit-a-place/places/edzell-castle-and-garden/

Dovecot Caravan Park
▶▶▶ 81%

tel: 01674 840630 **AB30 1QL**
email: adele@dovecotcaravanpark.co.uk **web:** www.dovecotcaravanpark.co.uk
dir: *From Laurencekirk on A90, 5 miles, at Edzell Woods sign turn left. Site 500 yards on left.*

A level grassy site in a country area close to the A90, with mature trees screening one side and the River North Esk on the other. The new and immaculate toilet facilities make this a handy overnight stop in a good touring area.

Open: April to October **Last arrival:** 20.00 **Last departure:** noon

Pitches: * 🚐 from £19.50; 🚐 from £19.50; ▲ from £16; 8 hardstanding pitches; 8 seasonal pitches

Leisure: 🔍

Facilities: 🛁 ☉ 🗗 ✳ ⅃ WiFi

Services: 🔌 🛒 🛒 Ⓣ

Additional site information: 6 acre site. 🐾 Cars can be parked by caravans and tents. Awnings permitted.

PETERHEAD
Map 23 NK14

Places to visit

Arbuthnot Museum, PETERHEAD, AB42 1QD, 01779 477778
www.livelifeaberdeenshire.org.uk/museums/find-a-museum/arbuthnot-museum/

Lido Caravan Park
▶▶▶ 81%

tel: 01779 480205 **South Road AB42 2XX**
email: phd.lido@gmail.com **web:** www.peterheadlidocaravanpark.co.uk
dir: *From A90 (Aberdeen to Peterhead road) at Invernetty roundabout take A982.*

This small site is located on The Lido with direct access to a small sandy beach with a nice play area and sand dunes. The management team maintain neat

LEISURE: 🏊 Indoor swimming pool   🏊 Outdoor swimming pool   🄰 Children's playground   🎿 Kids' club   🎾 Tennis court   🔍 Games room   📺 Separate TV room
⅃ Golf course   ⛳ Pitch n putt   🚣 Boats for hire   🚲 Bikes for hire   🎬 Cinema   🎵 Entertainment   🖋 Fishing   ◎ Mini golf   🏄 Watersports   💪 Gym   ⊕ Sports field   ♘ Stables
FACILITIES: 🛁 Baths/Shower   ☉ Electric shaver sockets   🗗 Hairdryer   ✳ Ice Pack Facility   🍼 Baby facilities   ⅃ Disabled facilities   ⑤ Shop on site or within 200yds
📮 BBQ area   🅿 Picnic area   WiFi WiFi

hardstanding pitches, and the static caravans and the older-style toilets are kept spotlessly clean. Each of the all-electric pitches has a view over Peterhead's busy harbour and there is always some boating activity taking place. The Maritime Heritage Centre, a few minutes' walk from the site, has an excellent café.

Open: March to October

Pitches: 🚐 🚌 ⛺; 15 hardstanding pitches; 16 seasonal pitches

Facilities: 🏪 ⊙ ℙ ⚙ ♿ ⑤ WiFi

Services: ⊕ 🔄 ↯ 🔒 🖉

Within 3 miles: ⤓ 🖉 ∪ ♨ ⟩ 🍴

Additional site information: 25 acre site. 🐕 Cars can be parked by caravans and tents. Awnings permitted.

PORTSOY   Map 23 NJ56

Places to visit

Duff House, BANFF, AB45 3SX, 01261 818181
www.historicenvironment.scot/visit-a-place/places/duff-house/

Portsoy Links Caravan Park
►►► 76%

tel: 01261 842695 & 842222 **Links Road, Portsoy AB45 2RQ**
email: contact@portsoylinks.org **web:** www.portsoylinks.org
dir: At Portsoy from A98 into Church Street. 2nd right into Institute Street (follow brown camping sign). At T-junction right, down slope to site.

Taken into community ownership under the auspices of the Scottish Traditional Boats Festival, this is a lovely links-type site with stunning views across the bay. There is a large, safe, fenced play area for smaller children and the toilet facilities are kept clean and well maintained. Portsoy is a typical small fishing port and has various eateries and shops; it is very convenient for visiting the other small fishing villages on north-east Scotland's coastal trail. There is a new bunk house in the old sail loft, which can be rented by individual rooms or whole use.

Open: All year **Last arrival:** 20.00 **Last departure:** noon

Pitches: * 🚐 from £15; 🚌 from £15; ⛺ from £10; 9 hardstanding pitches; 7 seasonal pitches

Leisure: 🛝

Facilities: 🏪 ⊙ ℙ ♿ 🎐 WiFi

Services: ⊕ 🔄 🔒

Within 3 miles: 🖉 ♨ ⟩ ⑤

Additional site information: 0.8 acre site. 🐕 Cars can be parked by caravans and tents. Awnings permitted. Coastal walks.

STRACHAN

Places to visit

Banchory Museum, BANCHORY, AB31 5SX, 01330 823367
www.livelifeaberdeenshire.org.uk/museums/find-a-museum/banchory-museum/

Crathes Castle Garden & Estate, CRATHES, AB31 5QJ, 01330 844525
www.nts.org.uk/visit/places/crathes-castle

Great for kids: Go Ape Crathes Castle, CRATHES, AB31 5QJ, 01603 895500
www.goape.co.uk/crathes-castle

STRACHAN   Map 23 NO69

Feughside Caravan Park
►►►► 85%

tel: 01330 850669 **AB31 6NT**
email: info@feughsidecaravanpark.co.uk **web:** www.feughsidecaravanpark.co.uk
dir: From Banchory take B974 to Strachan, 3 miles, take B976, 2 miles to Feughside B&B. Turn right after the B&B, caravan park on the right. Reception 100 yards past the entrance.

A small, well maintained family-run site, set amongst mature trees and hedges, located five miles from Banchory and with stunning views of Clachnaben hill. The site is ideally suited to those wishing for a peaceful location that is within easy reach of scenic Royal Deeside.

Open: April to October **Last arrival:** 20.00 **Last departure:** noon

Pitches: * 🚐 from £25; 🚌 from £25; ⛺ from £17; 10 hardstanding pitches; 12 seasonal pitches

Leisure: 🛝

Facilities: 🏪 ⊙ ℙ ⚙ ♿ 🎋 WiFi

Services: ⊕ 🔄 🔋 🔒 🖉

Within 3 miles: 🖉 ∪ ♨ ⑤

Additional site information: 5.5 acre site. 🐕 Pets to be on lead at all times and exercised off park. Cars can be parked by caravans and tents. Awnings permitted. Quiet after 22.00, no open fires.

TURRIFF   Map 23 NJ75

Places to visit

Fyvie Castle, TURRIFF, AB53 8JS, 01651 891266
www.nts.org.uk/visit/places/fyvie-castle

Turriff Caravan Park
►►►► 79%

tel: 01888 562205 & 562943 **Station Road AB53 4ER**
email: info@turriffcaravanpark.com **web:** www.turriffcaravanpark.com
dir: On A947, south of Turriff.

Located on the outskirts of Turriff on the site of an old railway station, this site is owned by the local community. The pitches are level and the attractive landscaping is well maintained. The site also has a rally field. There is a large public park close to the site which has a boating pond and a large games park where the annual agricultural show is held. The town is only five minutes' walk through the park and has a good variety of shops. This is an ideal base for touring rural Aberdeenshire and the nearby Moray coastline with its traditional fishing villages.

Open: late March to end October **Last arrival:** 18.00 **Last departure:** 11.00

Pitches: * 🚐 from £21.50; 🚌 from £21.50; ⛺ from £16; 10 hardstanding pitches; 9 seasonal pitches

Leisure: 🛝 ✪ **Facilities:** 🏪 ⊙ ℙ ♿ ⑤ 🎋 WiFi

Services: ⊕ 🔄 ↯ 🔒 🖉

Within 3 miles: ⤓ 🖉 ∪ ◎ ♨ ⟩

Additional site information: 5 acre site. 🐕 Cars can be parked by caravans and tents. Awnings permitted. No music or loud noise after 22.00. Reception open 09.00–13.00 and 16.00–18.00.

PITCHES: 🚐 Caravans 🚌 Motorhomes ⛺ Tents 🏕 Glamping accommodation **SERVICES:** ⊕ Electric hook-up 🔄 Launderette 🍺 Licensed bar
🔒 Calor Gas 🖉 Campingaz ⊤ Toilet fluid 🍽 Café/Restaurant 🎋 Fast Food/Takeaway 🔋 Battery charging ↯ Motorhome service point
* 2019 prices 🚫 No credit or debit cards 🐕 Dogs permitted ⊗ No dogs

ARGYLL & BUTE

CARRADALE
Map 20 NR83

Carradale Bay Caravan Park
▶▶▶ 90%

tel: 01583 431665 **PA28 6QG**
email: info@carradalebay.com web: www.carradalebay.com
dir: *A83 from Tarbert towards Campbeltown, left onto B842 (Carradale road), right onto B879. Site in 0.5 mile.*

A beautiful, natural site on the sea's edge with superb views over Kilbrannan Sound to the Isle of Arran. Pitches are landscaped into small bays broken up by shrubs and bushes, and backed by dunes close to the long sandy beach. The toilet facilities are appointed to a very high standard. An environmentally-aware site that requires the use of green toilet chemicals – available on the site. Lodges and static caravans for holiday hire.

Open: April to September **Last arrival:** 22.00 **Last departure:** noon
Pitches: 🚐 🚃 ▲
Facilities: ⊙ 𝄞 ✳ ⚓ ⓢ 🎋 WiFi
Services: 🔌 ⓟ Ⓣ
Within 3 miles: ⚓ ✐ ∪ ≋ ⚒
Additional site information: 8 acre site. 🚗 Cars can be parked by caravans and tents. Awnings permitted.

GLENDARUEL
Map 20 NR98

Places to visit
Benmore Botanic Garden, BENMORE, PA23 8QU, 01369 706261
www.rbge.org.uk/visit/benmore-botanic-garden/

Glendaruel Caravan Park
▶▶▶ 83%

tel: 01369 820267 **PA22 3AB**
email: mail@glendaruelcaravanpark.com web: www.glendaruelcaravanpark.com
dir: *A83 onto A815 to Strachur, 13 miles to site on A886. By ferry from Gourock to Dunoon take B836, then A886 for approximately 4 miles north. (Note: this route is not recommended for towing vehicles – 1:5 uphill gradient on B836).*

Glendaruel Gardens, with an arboretum, is the peaceful setting for this pleasant, well established wooded site in a valley surrounded by mountains. It is set back from the main road and screened by trees so that a peaceful stay is ensured. It has level grass and hardstanding pitches. A regular local bus service and a ferry at Portavadie (where there are retail outlets and eateries) make a day trip to the Mull of Kintyre a possibility. The Cowal Way, a long distance path, and a national cycle path pass the site. Static caravans and a 'little' camping lodge are available for hire.

Open: April to October **Last arrival:** 22.00 **Last departure:** noon
Pitches: 🚐 🚃 ▲; 15 hardstanding pitches; 12 seasonal pitches
Leisure: ⊕
Facilities: ⊙ 𝄞 ✳ ⓢ 🎋 WiFi
Services: 🔌 ⓟ 🚿 🔒 ⊘ Ⓣ
Within 3 miles: ✐

OBAN
Map 20 NM82

Places to visit
Dunstaffnage Castle and Chapel, OBAN, PA37 1PZ, 01631 562465
www.historicenvironment.scot/visit-a-place/places/dunstaffnage-castle-and-chapel/

Bonawe Historic Iron Furnace, TAYNUILT, PA35 1JQ, 01866 822432
www.historicenvironment.scot/visit-a-place/places/bonawe-historic-iron-furnace/

Great for kids: Dunollie Museum, Castle & Grounds, OBAN, PA34 5TT, 01631 570550, www.dunollie.org

Oban Caravan & Camping Park
▶▶▶ 85%

tel: 01631 562425 **Gallanachmore Farm, Gallanach Road PA34 4QH**
email: info@obancaravanpark.com web: www.obancaravanpark.com
dir: *From Oban centre follow signs for Mull Ferry. After terminal follow Gallanach signs. 2 miles to site.*

Situated two miles from Oban, this is a lovely site, with pleasant terraced areas that are separated by large swathes of well maintained grass and natural landscaping. Many pitches overlook the busy ferry route between Oban and the Isle of Colonsay. The site is convenient for the ferry terminal in Oban, and the train and bus stations provide easy access for public transport, making this an ideal site for both main holidays or for shorter stays. Well-equipped camping pods are located in an area that offers privacy.

Open: Easter, April to October (restricted service: Easter to end May and September to October – shop closed) **Last arrival:** 20.00 (later arrivals by prior arrangement) **Last departure:** noon
Pitches: * 🚐 from £21; 🚃 from £21; ▲ from £18; 🏠 see prices below; 40 hardstanding pitches; 10 seasonal pitches
Leisure: ⚠ ♠ ▭ ✐
Facilities: 🛁 ⊙ 𝄞 ✳ ⓢ 🎋 🎋 WiFi
Services: 🔌 ⓟ 🚿 ⚲ 🔒 ⊘ Ⓣ
Within 3 miles: ⚓ ∪ ≋ ⚒ 🎯 🏛
Additional site information: 15 acre site. 🚗 Cars can be parked by caravans and tents. Awnings permitted. No commercial vehicles, no noise after 23.00. Indoor kitchen for tent campers, fresh bread available each morning.

Glamping available: Wooden pods from £45. **Changeover days:** Any day

Additional glamping information: Wooden pods (sleep 4) offer electricity, heating, fridge, kettle, microwave, toaster and electric hob. Cars can be parked by units.

Additional site information: 6 acre site. 🚗 Cars can be parked by caravans and tents. Awnings permitted. Sea trout and salmon fishing, woodland walks, 24-hour emergency phone.

LEISURE: 🏊 Indoor swimming pool 🏊 Outdoor swimming pool ⚠ Children's playground 👦 Kids' club 🎾 Tennis court ♠ Games room ▭ Separate TV room
⚓ Golf course ⛳ Pitch n putt ⛵ Boats for hire 🚲 Bikes for hire 🎬 Cinema ♫ Entertainment ✐ Fishing ◎ Mini golf ◎ Watersports 💪 Gym ⊕ Sports field ∪ Stables
FACILITIES: 🛁 Baths/Shower ⊙ Electric shaver sockets 𝄞 Hairdryer ✳ Ice Pack Facility ⚓ Baby facilities ⚓ Disabled facilities ⓢ Shop on site or within 200yds
🎋 BBQ area 🎋 Picnic area WiFi WiFi

SOUTH AYRSHIRE

AYR
Map 20 NS32

Places to visit

Robert Burns Birthplace Museum, ALLOWAY, KA7 4PQ, 01292 443700
www.burnsmuseum.org.uk

Great for kids: Heads of Ayr Farm Park, ALLOWAY, KA7 4LD, 01292 441210
www.headsofayrfarmpark.co.uk

Premier Park

Craig Tara Holiday Park
▶▶▶▶▶ 87% HOLIDAY CENTRE

tel: 0800 975 7579 & 01292 265141 **KA7 4LB**
email: craigtara@haven.com **web:** www.haven.com/craigtara
dir: *A77 towards Stranraer, 2nd right after Bankfield roundabout. Follow signs for A719 and park.*

This lovely holiday centre on the outskirts of Ayr is set in a sheltered spot on the coast, with direct access to a small beach. The park has a great family atmosphere with welcoming staff and entertainment for all ages. The touring area is in a secluded area, with an amenity block and 40 fully serviced hardstanding pitches. At the heart of the holiday centre are various large complexes with show bars, restaurants, takeaways, computer games and slot machines. There are also good shops, a supermarket with a bakery, and a large soft play area. The pool complex facilities are excellent with flumes, slides, splash zones and overhead viewing walkways. There is a regular service bus to Ayr.

Open: mid March to end October (restricted service: mid March to May and September to end October – some facilities may be reduced) **Last arrival:** anytime (must be pre-booked) **Last departure:** 10.00

Pitches: ⛟ ⛴; 44 hardstanding pitches

Leisure: 🏊 ⛰ 🎣 ⛵ 🎵 ⚽

Facilities: 🛁 ☉ ⓰ 🛍 🚻 [WiFi]

Services: 🔌 🖲 🍽 🍴 ⊞ 🪧

Within 3 miles: 🎣 ∪ ◉ 🏌

Additional site information: 213 acre site. 🐾 Max 2 dogs per booking, certain dog breeds banned. Fresh produce from bakery. No commercial vehicles, no bookings by persons under 21 years unless a family booking. Nature walks (as part of Nature Rockz), table tennis, racket sports.

BARRHILL
Map 20 NX28

Places to visit

Bargany Gardens, OLD DAILLY, KA26 9QL, 01465 871249
www.bargany.com

Barrhill Holiday Park
▶▶▶▶ 83%

tel: 01465 821355 & 07718 389144 **KA26 0PZ**
email: relax@barrhillholidaypark.com **web:** www.barrhillholidaypark.com
dir: *On A714 (Newton Stewart to Girvan road). 1 mile north of Barrhill.*

A small, friendly park in a tranquil rural location, screened from the A714 by trees. The park is terraced and well landscaped, and a high quality amenity block includes disabled facilities. In addition to deluxe lodge pods with hot tubs, new luxury and much longer pods have been added and these have the bonus of a shower inside. The local bus to Girvan stops at the site entrance.

Open: March to January **Last arrival:** 22.00 **Last departure:** 10.00

Pitches: ⛟ from £20; ⛴ from £20; ⛺ from £13; 🏠 see prices below; 30 hardstanding pitches

Leisure: ⛰

Facilities: 🛁 ☉ ⓰ ✳ 🛍 🚻 [WiFi]

Services: 🔌 🖲 ⊞ [T]

Within 3 miles: 🎣 🛍

Additional site information: 6 acre site. 🐾 Cars can be parked by caravans and tents. Awnings permitted. No noise after 23.00.

Glamping available: 6 wooden pods from £90 with hot tub; £153 for a 2 night stay (including a stargazer pod with a hot tub).

Additional glamping information: Wooden pods: (sleeps 5). 6 have hot tubs, some have showers. Communal kitchen. Each pod has toilet, basin, microwave, TV, mini fridge, kettle, picnic table and fire pit. No glassware permitted in or around hot tubs. Hot tubs may not be used after 23.00. Minimum stay 2 nights. Cars can be parked by units.

DUMFRIES & GALLOWAY

ANNAN
Map 21 NY16

Places to visit
Ruthwell Cross, RUTHWELL, 0131 558 9326
www.historicenvironment.scot/visit-a-place/places/ruthwell-cross/

Great for kids: Caerlaverock Castle, CAERLAVEROCK, DG1 4RU, 01387 770244
www.historicenvironment.scot/visit-a-place/places/caerlaverock-castle/

Galabank Caravan & Camping Group
▶▶ 74%

tel: 01461 203539 & 07999 344520 **North Street DG12 5DQ**
email: margaret.ramage@hotmail.com
dir: *Site access via North Street.*

A tidy, well-maintained grassy little park with spotless facilities close to the centre of town but with pleasant rural views, and skirted by the River Annan.

Open: March to October **Last departure:** noon

Pitches: 🚐 from £15; 🚍 from £15; ▲ from £9

Facilities: 🛁 ⊙ ℉ ⊓

Services: 🖭

Within 3 miles: ⚲ ✐ ♨ ⊌ ⊟ ⑤

Additional site information: 1 acre site. 🐾 ⊕ Cars can be parked by caravans and tents. Awnings permitted. No commercial vehicles. Social club adjacent, washing machine and tumble dryer in ladies' block.

BRIGHOUSE BAY

Places to visit
MacLellan's Castle, KIRKCUDBRIGHT, DG6 4JD, 01557 331856
www.historicenvironment.scot/visit-a-place/places/maclellan-s-castle/

Broughton House & Garden, KIRKCUDBRIGHT, DG6 4JX, 01557 330437
www.nts.org.uk/visit/places/broughton-house

BRIGHOUSE BAY
Map 20 NX64

Premier Park

Brighouse Bay Holiday Park
▶▶▶▶▶ 90%

tel: 01557 870267 **DG6 4TS**
email: info@gillespie-leisure.co.uk **web:** www.gillespie-leisure.co.uk
dir: *From Gatehouse of Fleet take A755 towards Kirkcudbright, onto B727 (signed Borgue). Or from Kirkcudbright take A755 onto B727. Site signed in 3 miles.*

This top class park has a country club feel and enjoys a marvellous coastal setting adjacent to the beach with superb views. Pitches have been imaginatively sculpted into the meadowland, where stone walls and hedges blend in with the site's mature trees. These features, together with excellent, newly refurbished toilet facilities and the large range of leisure activities, make this an excellent park for families who enjoy an active holiday. The site has an 18-hole golf course with its own PGA professional. Many of the facilities are at an extra charge. Wooden pods and self-catering units are available for hire.

Open: All year (restricted service: 1 November to 31 December and 1 February to 31 March reduced hours at leisure club (closed throughout January)) **Last arrival:** 20.00
Last departure: 11.00

Pitches: * 🚐 from £23.50; 🚍 from £23.50; ▲ from £21.50; 🏠 see price below; 100 hardstanding pitches; 50 seasonal pitches

Leisure: 🏊 ⚗ 🎱 ⚲ 🎵 ✐ ⚲

Facilities: 🛁 ⊙ ℉ ✳ ♿ ⑤ ⊓ 🚿 📶

Services: 🖭 ⑤ 🚽 🍴 🛒 ⚓ 🔒 ⊘ Ⓣ

Within 3 miles: ⊌ ◎

Additional site information: 120 acre site. 🐾 Dogs must be kept on leads. Cars can be parked by caravans and tents. Awnings permitted. No noise after 22.30, no jet skis, 10mph speed limit on site. No open fires or fire pits. Mini golf, outdoor bowling green, jacuzzi, slipway, coarse fishing, sea angling, pony trekking (seasonal), mountain bike trails.

Glamping available: Wooden pods from £47.

Additional glamping information: Wooden pods: own camping equipment required but kettle, microwave, fridge, heating, lighting and exterior picnic seating provided. Minimum stay 2 nights. Cars can be parked by units.

DALBEATTIE
Map 21 NX86

Places to visit

Threave Garden & Estate, CASTLE DOUGLAS, DG7 1RX, 01556 502575
www.nts.org.uk/visit/places/threave-garden

Orchardton Tower, PALNACKIE, DG7 1QH
www.historicenvironment.scot/visit-a-place/places/orchardton-tower/

Glenearly Caravan Park
►►►► 86%

tel: 01556 611393 **DG5 4NE**
email: glenearlycaravan@btconnect.com **web:** www.glenearlycaravanpark.co.uk
dir: *From Dumfries take A711 towards Dalbeattie. Site entrance after Edingham Farm on right (200 yards before boundary sign).*

An excellent small park set in open countryside with good views of Long Fell, Maidenpap and Dalbeattie Forest. The park is located in 84 acres of farmland which has been carefully managed over the years to provide a peaceful and secluded location for a tranquil holiday. The attention to detail is excellent with neatly kept grass, well tended borders and an excellent amenity block. There's a fishing lochan and woodland plus a wildlife walk. Dalbeattie is a leisurely 10-minute walk away and the local bus passes the end of the farm road. The beautiful Solway coast is just five minutes away by car with Rockcliffe, Colvend and Kippford interesting places to explore. For the more adventurous, the mountain bike trails are numerous.

Open: All year **Last arrival:** 19.00 **Last departure:** noon

Pitches: * 🚐 from £20.50; 🚍 from £20.50; ▲ from £20.50; 33 hardstanding pitches; 10 seasonal pitches

Leisure: 🄰 🎣 ✐

Facilities: 🛖 ☉ ℙ ☼ ♿ WiFi

Services: 🔌 🔲 🍴 ⚡ 🔋

Within 3 miles: 🚲 ◎ 🚣 🎣 ⑤

Additional site information: 10 acre site. 🐕 Cars can be parked by caravans and tents. Awnings permitted. No commercial vehicles. Table tennis, pool table.

ECCLEFECHAN
Map 21 NY17

Places to visit

Robert Burns House, DUMFRIES, DG1 2PS, 01387 255297
www.dumgal.gov.uk/article/15733/Robert-Burns-House

Old Bridge House Museum, DUMFRIES, DG2 7BE, 01387 256904
www.dgculture.co.uk/venue/old-bridge-house-museum/

Great for kids: Dumfries Museum & Camera Obscura, DUMFRIES, DG2 7SW, 01387 253374
www.dumgal.gov.uk/article/15737/Dumfries-Museum-and-Camera-Obscura

---

Hoddom Castle Caravan Park

►►►►► 85%

tel: 01576 300251 **Hoddom DG11 1AS**
email: enquiries@hoddomcastle.co.uk **web:** www.hoddomcastle.co.uk
dir: *M74 junction 19, B725 signed Ecclefechan. At next roundabout left onto B7076. Right at crossroads in Ecclefechan, follow site signs. Left at T-junction onto B723. Right onto B725 to site. Or from Annan on B721 take B723 signed Lockerbie and follow site signs.*

A lovely, peaceful family park located close to Annan, with its large range of shops and eateries. There are three amenity blocks, one is adjacent to the reception in part of the old castle buildings. There are extensive grounds, with many walks including the Annan Way which borders the River Annan. The park is neatly divided into statics, seasonal tourers and touring pitches with a large area for tents, plus seven attractive wooden 'chill' pods and four Kelo huts for hire. Fishing, a 9-hole golf course and a large children's play area are available; the small restaurant and café are open daily.

Open: Easter or April to October **Last arrival:** 20.00 **Last departure:** 13.00

Pitches: 🚐 🚍 ▲ ⋔; 63 hardstanding pitches; 94 seasonal pitches

Leisure: 🄰 🎣 🚣 ♪ ✐

Facilities: 🛖 ☉ ℙ ☼ ♿ ⑤ 🍴 🪑

Services: 🔌 🔲 🍴 🍽 🍟 ⚡ 🔋 ⓣ

Within 3 miles: ◎

Additional site information: 28 acre site. 🐕 Cars can be parked by caravans and tents. Awnings permitted. No electric scooters, no gazebos, no fires, no noise after midnight.

Glamping available: Wooden pods; Kelo huts.

Additional glamping information: Dogs permitted in some pods and Kelo huts only. Cars can be parked by units.

GATEHOUSE OF FLEET   Map 20 NX55

Places to visit

MacLellan's Castle, KIRKCUDBRIGHT, DG6 4JD, 01557 331856
www.historicenvironment.scot/visit-a-place/places/maclellan-s-castle/

Cairnsmore of Fleet National Nature Reserve, GATEHOUSE OF FLEET, DG7 2BP,
01557 814435
www.nature.scot/enjoying-outdoors/scotlands-national-nature-reserves/
cairnsmore-fleet-national-nature-reserve

Premier Park

Auchenlarie Holiday Park

►►►►► 90% HOLIDAY CENTRE

tel: 01556 506200 DG7 2EX
email: enquiries@auchenlarie.co.uk web: www.swalwellholidaygroup.co.uk
dir: Direct access from A75, 5 miles west of Gatehouse of Fleet.

A well-organised family park set on cliffs overlooking Wigtown Bay, with its own
sandy beach. The tenting area, on sloping grassland surrounded by mature
trees, has its own sanitary facilities, while the marked caravan pitches are in
paddocks, with open views and the provision of high quality toilets. The leisure
centre includes a swimming pool, gym, solarium and sports hall; there's an
entertainment suite with live cabaret acts, and the Lavender Room offers beauty
treatments and massages. There are static caravans and lodges to rent — five
have hot tubs.

Open: mid February to October Last arrival: 20.00 Last departure: noon
Pitches: * 🚐 from £22; 🚐 from £22; ▲ from £22; 🏠 see prices below;
52 hardstanding pitches
Leisure: 🏊 🎠 🤾 🏐 🎵 🚴 ⚽
Facilities: 🛁 ⊙ 🗜 ✳ 🚿 🛍 🍴 🚲 ⊞ 🛒 WiFi
Services: 🔌 🔄 🍽 🍴 🛒 🛒 ⛽ 🛒 T
Within 3 miles: ⛳ ♘ ◎
Additional site information: 32 acre site. 🐾 Crazy golf, children's entertainment.
Glamping available: Swift S-pods from £45. Changeover days: Any day
Additional glamping information: Cars can be parked by units.

Anwoth Caravan Site
►►►► 86%

tel: 01557 814333 & 01556 506200 DG7 2JU
email: enquiries@auchenlarie.co.uk web: www.swalwellholidaygroup.co.uk
dir: From A75 into Gatehouse of Fleet, site on right towards Stranraer. Signed from town
centre.

A very high quality park in a peaceful sheltered setting within easy walking
distance of the village, ideally placed for exploring the scenic hills, valleys and
coastline. Grass, hardstanding and fully serviced pitches are available and guests
may use the leisure facilities at the sister site, Auchenlarie Holiday Park.

Open: March to October Last arrival: 20.00 Last departure: noon
Pitches: * 🚐 from £17; 🚐 from £17; ▲ from £17; 13 hardstanding pitches
Facilities: 🛁 ⊙ 🗜 ✳ 🛍 ⊞ WiFi
Services: 🔌 🔄 🛒 ⛽ 🛒 T
Within 3 miles: ⛳ 🚴 🛍
Additional site information: 2 acre site. 🐾 Cars can be parked by caravans and tents.
Awnings permitted.

GRETNA

Places to visit

Carlisle Cathedral, CARLISLE, CA3 8TZ, 01228 548151
www.carlislecathedral.org.uk

Tullie House Museum & Art Gallery Trust, CARLISLE, CA3 8TP, 01228 618718
www.tulliehouse.co.uk

Great for kids: Carlisle Castle, CARLISLE, CA3 8UR, 01228 591922
www.english-heritage.org.uk/visit/places/carlisle-castle

LEISURE: 🏊 Indoor swimming pool 🏊 Outdoor swimming pool 🎠 Children's playground 🪁 Kids' club 🎾 Tennis court 🎱 Games room 📺 Separate TV room
⛳ Golf course 🏌 Pitch n putt 🚣 Boats for hire 🚲 Bikes for hire 🎬 Cinema 🎵 Entertainment 🎣 Fishing ◎ Mini golf 🏄 Watersports 🏋 Gym 🏟 Sports field 🐴 Stables
FACILITIES: 🛁 Baths/Shower ⊙ Electric shaver sockets 🗜 Hairdryer ✳ Ice Pack Facility 🍼 Baby facilities 🦽 Disabled facilities 🛍 Shop on site or within 200yds
🍴 BBQ area ⊞ Picnic area WiFi WiFi

GRETNA
Map 21 NY36

King Robert the Bruce's Cave Caravan & Camping Park
▶▶▶▶ 79%

tel: 01461 800285 & 07779 138694 **Cove Estate, Kirkpatrick Fleming DG11 3AT**
email: enquiries@brucescave.co.uk **web:** www.brucescave.co.uk
dir: *Exit A74(M) junction 21, follow Kirkpatrick Fleming signs, north through village, pass Station Inn, left at Bruce's Court. Over rail crossing to site.*

The lovely wooded grounds of an old castle and mansion are the setting for this pleasant park. The mature woodland is a haven for wildlife; there is a riverside walk to Robert the Bruce's Cave and on-site coarse fishing is available. A toilet block with en suite facilities is especially useful to families. The site is convenient for the M74 and there is a good local bus service available nearby; the site is on a National Cycle Route.

Open: April to November (restricted service: November – shop closed, water restrictions)
Last arrival: 20.00 **Last departure:** 13.00

Pitches: 🚐 from £17; 🚍 from £17; ▲ from £13; 10 hardstanding pitches; 60 seasonal pitches

Leisure: /Λ 🔍 🎣 ⚽

Facilities: 🏠 ⊙ 🅿 ❄ ♿ 🖲 🚼 🎍 WiFi

Services: 🔌 🗑 🚼 ⚡ 🔋 🛢 🚙 ⊺

Additional site information: 80 acre site. 🐕 Dogs must be kept on leads at all times. Cars can be parked by caravans and tents. Awnings permitted. No noise after 23.00. First aid available.

Braids Caravan Park
▶▶▶▶ 78%

tel: 01461 337409 **Annan Road DG16 5DQ**
email: enquiries@thebraidscaravanpark.co.uk **web:** www.thebraidscaravanpark.co.uk
dir: *On B721, 0.5 mile from village on right, towards Annan.*

A very well-maintained park conveniently located on the outskirts of Gretna village. Within walking distance is Gretna Gateway Outlet Village, and nearby is Gretna Green with the World Famous Old Blacksmith's Shop. It proves a convenient stop-over for anyone travelling to and from the north of Scotland or Northern Ireland (via the ferry at Stranraer). The park has first-class toilet facilities and generously-sized all-weather pitches. Please note that tents are not accepted. A rally field and a meeting room are available.

Open: All year **Last arrival:** 20.00 (19.00 in winter) **Last departure:** noon

Pitches: 🚐 from £23; 🚍 from £23; 42 hardstanding pitches

Facilities: 🏠 ⊙ 🅿 ❄ ♿ WiFi
Services: 🔌 🗑 ⚡ 🛢 ⊺
Within 3 miles: 🛒

Additional site information: 5 acre site. 🐕 Cars can be parked by caravans. Awnings permitted.

KIRKCUDBRIGHT
Map 20 NX65

Places to visit

The Stewartry Museum, KIRKCUDBRIGHT, DG6 4AQ, 01557 331643
www.dgculture.co.uk/venue/the-stewartry-museum-kirkcudbright/

Tolbooth Art Centre, KIRKCUDBRIGHT, DG6 4JL, 01557 331556
www.dgculture.co.uk/venue/tolbooth-arts-centre-kirkcudbright/

Great for kids: Broughton House & Garden, KIRKCUDBRIGHT, DG6 4JX, 01557 330437
www.nts.org.uk/visit/places/broughton-house

Premier Park

Seaward Holiday Park
▶▶▶▶▶ 85%

tel: 01557 870267 **Dhoon Bay DG6 4TJ**
email: info@gillespie-leisure.co.uk **web:** www.gillespie-leisure.co.uk
dir: *A711 to Kirkcudbright. In Kirkcudbright right onto A755 signed Borgue and Gatehouse of Fleet. Left onto B727 signed Borgue. Through Borgue to The Dhoon, site on left.*

An attractive park with outstanding views over Kirkcudbright Bay which forms part of the Dee Estuary. Access to a sandy cove with rock pools is just across the road. Facilities are well organised and neatly kept, and the park offers a very peaceful atmosphere. The leisure facilities at the other Gillespie Parks are available to visitors at Seaward Caravan Park. There are five static homes and two mini lodges for hire.

Open: March to October (restricted service: March to Spring Bank Holiday and September to October – swimming pool closed) **Last arrival:** 20.00
Last departure: 11.00

Pitches: * 🚐 from £22; 🚍 from £22; ▲ from £18.50; 🏠 see prices below; 20 hardstanding pitches; 6 seasonal pitches

Leisure: 🏊 /Λ 🔍

Facilities: 🏠 ⊙ 🅿 ❄ ♿ 🖲 🎍 🛒 WiFi

Services: 🔌 🗑 ⚡ 🛢 🚙 ⊺

Within 3 miles: 🎿 🎣 ∪ ◎

Additional site information: 23 acre site. 🐕 Cars can be parked by caravans and tents. Awnings permitted. No noise after 22.30, 10mph speed limit on site. No open fires or fire pits. No children in play area after 22.30. Sea angling.

Glamping available: Mini lodges from £49.

Additional glamping information: Mini lodges: own camping equipment required. Minimum stay 2 nights. No pets allowed. Cars can be parked by units.

LANGHOLM
Map 21 NY38

Places to visit

Hermitage Castle, HERMITAGE, TD9 0LU, 01387 376222
www.historicenvironment.scot/visit-a-place/places/hermitage-castle/

Ewes Water Caravan & Camping Park
▶▶ 67%

tel: 013873 80386 **Milntown DG13 0BG**
dir: *Accessed directly from A7, approximately 0.5 mile north of Langholm. Site in Langholm Rugby Club.*

Situated in a very convenient location on the A7 and on the banks of the River Esk, this small, attractive park lies in a sheltered wooded valley close to an unspoilt Borders' town. There is a large playing area for games.

Open: April to September **Last departure:** noon
Pitches: ⊞ ⊟ ▲
Facilities: ⊙ ✳ ዿ ☷ ⊼
Services: ⊠ ⊟ ≟ ▯ ⊘
Within 3 miles: ⊥ ⊘ ⑤

Additional site information: 2 acre site. ⊮ ⊛ Cars can be parked by caravans and tents. Awnings permitted. Large playing area.

LOCKERBIE

See Ecclefechan

PALNACKIE
Map 21 NX85

Places to visit

Orchardton Tower, PALNACKIE, DG7 1QH
www.historicenvironment.scot/visit-a-place/places/orchardton-tower/

Threave Garden & Estate, CASTLE DOUGLAS, DG7 1RX, 01556 502575
www.nts.org.uk/visit/places/threave-garden

Barlochan Caravan Park
▶▶▶ 80%

tel: 01557 870267 **DG7 1PF**
email: info@gillespie-leisure.co.uk **web:** www.gillespie-leisure.co.uk
dir: *On A711 (Dalbeattie to Auchencairn road). Site signed before Palnackie.*

This is a lovely small caravan site situated within a short drive of the county town of Dalbeattie. It is ideally situated for exploring this particularly attractive area. The site has a number of static homes set on level terraces, with mature planting, whilst the caravan and camping pitches are located on the lower area, near the outdoor heated pool. There are hardstanding pitches, grass pitches with electricty for tents and two wooden pods. The site is part of the Gillespie Group and customers can use the facilities of their other sites.

Open: April to October (restricted service: April to Spring Bank Holiday and September to October – swimming pool closed) **Last arrival:** 20.00 **Last departure:** 11.30

Pitches: ⊞ ⊟ ▲ ⋔; 16 hardstanding pitches; 2 seasonal pitches
Leisure: ⊛ ⋀ ◣ ▢ ◢ ☺
Facilities: ⊡ ⌓ ✳ ዿ ⑤ ⊼ ⊟ ⒲
Services: ⊠ ⊟ ≟ ▯ ⊘ ⊤
Within 3 miles: ⊥ ◎

Additional site information: 9 acre site. ⊮ Cars can be parked by caravans and tents. Awnings permitted. No noise afrer 23.00. Family games and TV room.

Glamping available: 2 wooden pods.
Additional glamping information: Cars can be parked by units.

PARTON
Map 20 NX67

Places to visit

Threave Garden & Estate, CASTLE DOUGLAS, DG7 1RX, 01556 502575
www.nts.org.uk/visit/places/threave-garden

Threave Castle, CASTLE DOUGLAS, DG7 1TJ, 07711 223101
www.historicenvironment.scot/visit-a-place/places/threave-castle/

Loch Ken Holiday Park
▶▶▶▶ 87%

tel: 01644 470282 **DG7 3NE**
email: office@lochkenholidaypark.co.uk **web:** www.lochkenholidaypark.co.uk
dir: *On A713, north of Parton. Site on main road (Note: it is advisable not to use Sat Nav).*

Run with energy, enthusiasm and commitment by the Bryson family and team, this busy and popular park, with a natural emphasis on water activities, is set on the eastern shores of Loch Ken. With superb views, it is adjacent to the RSPB Ken-Dee Marshes reserve, with direct access to the loch for fishing and boat launching. It is also on the Galloway Red Kite Trail and on the edge of the glorious Galloway Forest Park. The park offers a unique base for you to explore and enjoy the outdoors in a peaceful and beautiful spot.

Open: February to mid November (restricted service: February to March (except Easter) and November – reduced shop hours) **Last departure:** noon

Pitches: ⊞ ⊟ ▲; 20 hardstanding pitches; 15 seasonal pitches
Leisure: ⬇ ⚲ ♫ ◢
Facilities: ⊙ ⌓ ✳ ዿ ⑤ ⊼ ⊟ ⒲
Services: ⊠ ⊟ ≟ ▯ ⊘ ⊤
Within 3 miles: ⊘ ⬇ ≟

Additional site information: 15 acre site. ⊮ Cars can be parked by caravans and tents. Awnings permitted. No noise after 22.00. Boat and canoe hire.

PORT WILLIAM
Map 20 NX34

Places to visit

Glenluce Abbey, GLENLUCE, DG8 0AF, 01581 300541
www.historicenvironment.scot/visit-a-place/places/glenluce-abbey/

Whithorn Priory and Museum, WHITHORN, DG8 8PY, 01988 500700
www.historicenvironment.scot/visit-a-place/places/whithorn-priory-and-museum/

Kings Green Caravan Site
►►► 81%

tel: 01988 700489 & 700738 **South Street DG8 9SG**
email: kingsgreencaravanpark@gmail.com **web:** www.kingsgreencaravanpark.com
dir: *Direct access from A747 at junction with B7085 towards Whithorn.*

Located on the edge of Port William, with beautiful views across Luce Bay as far as the Isle of Man, this is a community run site which offers good facilities and large grass pitches, with direct access to the pebble shore where otters have been seen. The road which runs along the coast is relatively traffic free so does not detract from the tranquillity of this small site. Two public boat launches are available. There are several good shops in the village and a local bus, with links to Whithorn, Garlieston and Newton Stewart, runs past the site.

Open: mid March to October **Last arrival:** 20.00 **Last departure:** noon

Pitches: 🚐 🚑 Å

Facilities: 🖴 ☉ ℙ ✳ ⅙ ⑤ 🚾 ☷ 🚻 WiFi

Services: 🕭 ⊙

Within 3 miles: ⌁ ℘ ≋

Additional site information: 3 acre site. 🐕 Cars can be parked by caravans and tents. Awnings permitted. No golf, no fireworks. Free book lending.

SANDHEAD
Map 20 NX04

Places to visit

Glenwhan Gardens, STRANRAER, DG9 8PH, 01581 400222
www.glenwhangardens.co.uk

Great for kids: Castle Kennedy Gardens, STRANRAER, DG9 8SL, 01776 702024
www.castlekennedygardens.com

Sands of Luce Holiday Park
►►►► 93%

tel: 01776 830456 **Sands of Luce DG9 9JN**
email: info@sandsofluce.com **web:** www.sandsofluce.com
dir: *From south and east: left from A75 onto B7084 signed Drummore. Site signed at junction with A716. From north: A77 through Stranraer towards Portpatrick, 2 miles, follow A716 signed Drummore, site signed in 5 miles.*

This is a large, well-managed holiday park overlooking Luce Bay. It has a private boat launch and direct access to a wide sandy beach, which proves popular with kite surfers. The Lighthouse is a truly upmarket restaurant and bar and the new Barn leisure complex was completed in 2019. Attached to the Lighthouse is the reception, and the staff at the bar can also handle arrivals and other enquiries; this arrangement significantly extends the checking in times. A wide range of entertainment, listed on daily planners, is on offer and includes kite flying, kite

surfing, foraging and cooking, and entertainers for both adults and children. There is a regular bus that passes the park entrance, and Stranraer, the Mull of Galloway or Port Logan Botanical Gardens are not far away by car.

Open: March to January (restricted service: November to January – toilet block and shower closed) **Last arrival:** 20.00 **Last departure:** noon

Pitches: 🚐 from £20; 🚑 from £20; Å from £15; 20 hardstanding pitches

Leisure: 🎢 🎣 🎵 ⊛

Facilities: 🖴 ☉ ℙ ✳ ⅙ ⑤ 🚾 ☷ 🚻 WiFi

Services: 🕭 ⊙ 🍴 🍽 ⊟ 🔋 ⌄

Within 3 miles: ⌁ ℘ ≋ ⚓

Additional site information: 75 acre site. 🐕 Owners must clear up after their dogs. Cars can be parked by caravans and tents. Awnings permitted. No quad bikes. Boat launching and storage. Indoor play area.

SANDYHILLS
Map 21 NX85

Places to visit

Threave Garden & Estate, CASTLE DOUGLAS, DG7 1RX, 01556 502575
www.nts.org.uk/visit/places/threave-garden

Orchardton Tower, PALNACKIE, DG7 1QH
www.historicenvironment.scot/visit-a-place/places/orchardton-tower/

Great for kids: Threave Castle, CASTLE DOUGLAS, DG7 1TJ, 07711 223101
www.historicenvironment.scot/visit-a-place/places/threave-castle/

Sandyhills Bay Holiday Park
►►►► 80%

tel: 01557 870267 **DG5 4NY**
email: info@gillespie-leisure.co.uk **web:** www.gillespie-leisure.co.uk
dir: *On A710, 7 miles from Dalbeattie, 6.5 miles from Kirkbean.*

A well maintained park in a superb location beside a beach, and close to many attractive villages. The level, grassy site is sheltered by woodland, and the south-facing Sandyhills Bay and beach, with their caves and rock pools provide endless entertainment for all the family. The leisure facilities at Brighouse Bay are available to visitors to Sandyhills Bay. Two wooden pods and two wooden wigwams are on offer.

Open: April to October **Last arrival:** 20.00 **Last departure:** 11.30

Pitches: * 🚐 from £21; 🚑 from £21; Å from £17.50; 🏠 see prices below; 9 hardstanding pitches

Leisure: 🎢

Facilities: 🖴 ☉ ℙ ✳ ⑤ ☷ 🚻 WiFi

Services: 🕭 ⊙ ⊟ 🔋 🛢 ⌀ T

Within 3 miles: ⌁ ℘

Additional site information: 15 acre site. 🐕 Cars can be parked by caravans and tents. Awnings permitted. No motorised scooters, jet skis or own quad bikes. No noise after midnight, no open fires.

Glamping available: Wooden pods from £47; wooden wigwams from £45.

Additional glamping information: Wooden pods and wooden wigwams offer kettle, microwave, fridge with freezer compartment, toaster. Wooden wigwams also offer TV and are dog friendly (£3 a night). Cars can be parked by units.

STRANRAER
Map 20 NX06

Places to visit

Glenwhan Gardens, STRANRAER, DG9 8PH, 01581 400222
www.glenwhangardens.co.uk

Great for kids: Castle Kennedy Gardens, STRANRAER, DG9 8SL, 01776 702024
www.castlekennedygardens.com

Aird Donald Caravan Park
►►►► 84%

tel: 01776 702025 **London Road DG9 8RN**
email: enquiries@aird-donald.co.uk **web:** www.aird-donald.co.uk
dir: From A75 left on entering Stranraer (signed). Opposite school, site 300 yards.

A spacious touring site set behind mature trees and within a five-minute walk of
Stranraer town centre at the head of Loch Ryan. It is an ideal base to tour the
'Rhins of Galloway', to visit Port Logan Botanic Gardens (half an hour's drive) or the
Mull of Galloway Lighthouse (a 45-minute drive). It provides a very convenient
stopover for the Cairnryan ferry to Ireland, but there's plenty to do in the area if
staying longer. A 25-pitch rally field is available.

Open: All year except 2 weeks at Christmas and New Year (restricted service: October to
March – tents not accepted) **Last arrival:** 22.00 **Last departure:** 11.00

Pitches: from £19; from £19; from £8; 24 hardstanding pitches

Leisure: ⋀ **Facilities:** 🚿 ⊙ 🦲 ⚷ 🍴 WiFi

Services: 🔌 🔯 🚮 ⛽ 🛢 ⊘

Within 3 miles: ↓ 🎣 ∪ 🌊 🌿 ⛳ 🛒

Additional site information: 12 acre site. 🐕 🐾 Cars can be parked by caravans and
tents. Awnings permitted. No commercial vehicles. Covered cooking area for tents.

Ryan Bay Caravan Park
►►► 81%

tel: 01776 889458 **Innermessan DG9 8QP**
email: ryanbay@hagansleisure.co.uk
dir: Innermessan on A77, 2 miles north of Stranraer.

Ryan Bay Holiday Park occupies an enviable position on the shores of Ryan Bay,
within easy reach of Stranraer and the ferry terminal at Cairnryan for a day trip to
Northern Ireland. It is also perfectly located for walking, fishing, water sports and
exploring the scenic Dumfries & Galloway coast. Some premium pitches and static
caravans are set beside the loch, making the most of the watery views, and this
well-established park is popular with families, offering good children's facilities
and the on-site Crofters Inn for adults. Investment and improvements are planned
by owners Hagans Leisure.

Open: March to October **Last arrival:** 22.00 **Last departure:** 10.00

Pitches: 🚐 🚍 ▲; 20 hardstanding pitches; 15 seasonal pitches

Leisure: ⋀ 🎵 🎣 ⚽

Facilities: 🚿 ✴ ⚷ 🍴 🏓 WiFi

Services: 🔌 🔯 🍴 ⛲ ⛽ 🛢 T

Within 3 miles: ↓ ∪ ◎ 🌊 🌿 ⛳ 🛒

Additional site information: 11 acre site. 🐕 Dogs must be kept on leads at all times.
Cars can be parked by caravans and tents. Awnings permitted. No noise after 22.00. No
football colours. Car hire can be arranged.

WIGTOWN
Map 20 NX45

Places to visit

Whithorn Priory and Museum, WHITHORN, DG8 8PY, 01988 500700
www.historicenvironment.scot/visit-a-place/places/whithorn-priory-and-
museum/

Drumroamin Farm Camping & Touring Site
►►► 91%

tel: 01988 840613 & 07752 471456 **1 South Balfern DG8 9DB**
email: enquiry@drumroamin.co.uk **web:** www.drumroamin.co.uk
dir: A75 towards Newton Stewart, onto A714 for Wigtown. Left on B7005 through
Bladnoch, A746 through Kirkinner. Take B7004 signed Garlieston, 2nd left opposite
Kilsture Forest, site 0.75 mile at end of lane.

Located near Wigtown and Newton Stewart, this is an easily accessible site for
those wishing to stay in a rural location; it is an open and spacious site overlooking
Wigtown Bay and the Galloway Hills. There is a large and separate tent field with a
well-equipped day room, while the touring pitches can easily accommodate rally
events. The toilet and other facilities are maintained in an exemplary manner. The
sheltered camp kitchen proves very popular, especially in adverse weather; a
drive-through motorhome service point is also available. The RSPB Crook of
Baldoon reserve is a 10-minute walk away. There is a good bus service at the top of
the road which goes to Newton Stewart, Wigtown and Whithorn. Two of the three
statics on site are for hire.

Open: All year **Last arrival:** 21.00 **Last departure:** noon

Pitches: 🚐 from £20; 🚍 from £20; ▲ from £17

Leisure: ⋀ 🔍

Facilities: 🚿 ⊙ 🦲 ✴ ⚷ 🍴 🏓 WiFi

Services: 🔌 🔯 🍴 ⛽

Within 3 miles: ↓ 🎣 🛒

Additional site information: 5 acre site. 🐕 Dogs on leads at all times. Cars can be
parked by caravans and tents. Awnings permitted. No fires, no noise after 22.00. Ball
games area.

WEST DUNBARTONSHIRE

BALLOCH   Map 20 NS38

Places to visit

Loch Lomond Bird of Prey Centre, BALLOCH, G83 8QL, 01389 729239
www.llbopc.co.uk

The Tall Ship at Riverside, GLASGOW, G3 8RS, 0141 357 3699
www.thetallship.com

Great for kids: Loch Lomond Sea Life Aquarium, BALLOCH, G83 8QL,
01389 721500, www.visitsealife.com/loch-lomond

Premier Park

Lomond Woods Holiday Park
▶▶▶▶▶   85%

tel: 01389 755000 **Old Luss Road G83 8QP**
email: lomondwoods@woodleisure.co.uk **web:** www.woodleisure.co.uk
dir: *From A82, 17 miles north of Glasgow, take A811 (Stirling to Balloch road). Left at 1st roundabout, follow holiday park signs, 150 yards on left.*

This site is ideally placed on the southern end of Loch Lomond, the UK's largest inland water and a designated National Park. This site has something to suit all tastes from the most energetic visitor to those who just wish to relax. Fully serviced pitches are available and there are three family rooms. There are loch cruises and boats to hire, plus retail outlets, superstores and eateries within easy walking distance. A drive or cycle ride along Loch Lomond reveals breathtaking views. There are two large boat storage areas. Please note that this site does not accept tents. Holiday caravans and lodges and three camping pods are available to let.

Open: All year **Last arrival:** 20.00 **Last departure:** noon

Pitches: 🚐 🚍 🏠; 115 hardstanding pitches; 55 seasonal pitches

Leisure: ⚓ 🎱 ☐

Facilities: 🛆 ☺ 🏳 ✳ ♿ 🅂 🏺 WiFi

Services: 🔌 🗑 ➕ ↯ 🔋 🅣

Within 3 miles: ⚲ 🖉 ∪ ◎ ≽ ≽

Additional site information: 13 acre site. 🐕 Cars can be parked by caravans. Awnings permitted. No jet skis, no commercial vehicles, no boats. Table tennis.

Glamping available: Wooden pods; en suite pods. **Changeover days:** Any day

Additional glamping information: Cars can be parked by units.

FIFE

ST ANDREWS   Map 21 NO51

Places to visit

St Andrews Castle, ST ANDREWS, KY16 9AR, 01334 477196
www.historicenvironment.scot/visit-a-place/places/st-andrews-castle

British Golf Museum, ST ANDREWS, KY16 9AB, 01334 460046
www.britishgolfmuseum.co.uk

Great for kids: St Andrews Aquarium, ST ANDREWS, KY16 9AS, 01334 474786
www.standrewsaquarium.co.uk

Platinum Park

Cairnsmill Holiday Park
▶▶▶▶▶

tel: 01334 473604 **Largo Road KY16 8NN**
email: cairnsmill@aol.com **web:** www.cairnsmill.co.uk
dir: *A915 from St Andrews towards Lathones. In approximately 2 miles site on right.*

Hidden behind mature trees and hedging in open countryside on the outskirts of the historic university town of St Andrews, this top quality holiday park is ideally placed for visiting the nearby town and to explore further afield in Fife or across the Tay Bridge to the city of Dundee and beyond. The facilities on offer at this park are simply excellent and include a swimming pool complex, bar and café, games room and a soft play area, in addition to the various play areas located throughout the park. There is a small fishing lochan with a walkway leading towards the town and the botanical gardens. The toilet facilities are first class with two blocks for the touring area and a separate block for the tent field. The six rooms in a bunkhouse means that extended family and friends can holiday together. The local bus service stops at the park entrance.

Open: All year (restricted service: winter – prior bookings only) **Last arrival:** flexible
Last departure: 11.00

Pitches: 🚐 🚍 ⛺ 🏠; 33 hardstanding pitches; 24 seasonal pitches

Leisure: 🏊 ⚓ 🎱 ☐ 🎵 🎣

Facilities: ☺ 🏳 ✳ ♿ 🅂 🏺 🍴 🐕 WiFi

Services: 🔌 🗑 🍺 🍽 ➕ ↯ 🔋 🛢 🅣

Within 3 miles: ⚲ ∪ ◎ ≽ ≽ ☷

Additional site information: 27 acre site. 🐕 Cars can be parked by caravans and tents. Awnings permitted. No noise after midnight. 1 car per pitch. Electric car hire (seasonal). Car hire can be arranged.

Glamping available: 2 wooden pods. **Changeover days:** Any day

Additional glamping information: Wooden pods (sleep 4) offer fridge, TV, microwave, toaster and kettle.

ST ANDREWS *continued*

Platinum Park

Craigtoun Meadows Holiday Park

▶▶▶▶▶

tel: 01334 475959 **Mount Melville KY16 8PQ**
email: info@craigtounmeadows.co.uk **web:** www.craigtounmeadows.co.uk
dir: *M90 junction 8, A91 to St Andrews. Just after Guardbridge right for Strathkinness. At 2nd crossroads left for Craigtoun.*

Craigtoun Meadows is only a short drive from the centre of St Andrews which has numerous tourist attractions, from historic buildings and harbour aquarium to the wide, sandy beach where the famous scene from *Chariots of Fire* was filmed. The site is set in part of the Craigtoun Estate and the holiday homes and touring area are separated by mature woodland and shrubs. The grounds are very well maintained and a large area of woodland has been set aside as a natural habitat for wildlife, and deer and red squirrels are seen regularly. The well maintained amenity block is centrally located and provides private facilities, including spacious showers and baths. The pitches are very large, fully serviced and are exceptionally well spaced. Two wooden pods, in a lovely setting, are available for hire. St Andrews is 'the home of golf' so the numerous courses in the area are a challenge for any golfer.

Craigtoun Meadows Holiday Park

Open: 15 March to October (restricted service: March to Easter and September to October – shop closed, reduced opening hours at restaurant) **Last arrival:** 21.00 **Last departure:** 11.00

Pitches: 🚐 🚍 ▲ 🏕; 56 hardstanding pitches; 12 seasonal pitches

Leisure: 🎡 🔍 ⚽

Facilities: 🚿 ☉ 🅿 ♿ 🪑 🌲 WiFi

Services: ⊖ 🔲 🍽 ⛽ 🛒 🚮

Within 3 miles: 🎣 🏌 ∪ ◎ 🚣 🛶 🎯 🏛

Additional site information: 32 acre site. 🚫 No pets. Cars can be parked by caravans and tents. Awnings permitted. No groups of unaccompanied minors. Putting green, zip wire, all-weather football pitch.

Glamping available: Wooden pods. **Changeover days:** Any day

Additional glamping information: Wooden pods: stays from 1 night to 2 weeks. Fridge, freezer, microwave, kettle, toaster and TV provided. Bring own bedding and cutlery. Amenity building within 50 metres. Cars can be parked by units

See advert below

LEISURE: 🏊 Indoor swimming pool 🏊 Outdoor swimming pool ⛰ Children's playground 🪁 Kids' club 🎾 Tennis court 🔍 Games room 📺 Separate TV room 🏌 Golf course ⛳ Pitch n putt 🚣 Boats for hire 🚲 Bikes for hire 🎬 Cinema 🎵 Entertainment 🎣 Fishing ◎ Mini golf 🏄 Watersports 💪 Gym ⚽ Sports field ∪ Stables
FACILITIES: 🚿 Baths/Shower ☉ Electric shaver sockets 🅿 Hairdryer ❄ Ice Pack Facility 🍼 Baby facilities ♿ Disabled facilities 🛒 Shop on site or within 200yds 🍖 BBQ area 🌲 Picnic area WiFi WiFi

HIGHLAND

ACHARACLE — Map 22 NM66

Places to visit

RSPB Glenborrodale, GLENBORRODALE, PH36 4JP, 01463 715000
www.rspb.org.uk/reserves-and-events/reserves-a-z/glenborrodale

Ariundle Oakwood National Nature Reserve, FORT WILLIAM, PH33 6SW,
01397 704716
www.nature.scot/enjoying-outdoors/scotlands-national-nature-reserves/
ariundle-oakwood-national-nature-reserve

Resipole Farm Holiday Park
▶▶▶▶ 84%

tel: 01967 431235 **Resipole Farm PH36 4HX**
email: accounts@resipole.co.uk **web:** www.resipole.co.uk
dir: *From A82 between North Ballachulish and Fort William take ferry from Corran to Ardgour. Left onto A861 signed Strontian. Through Strontian towards Salen. Site approximately 8 miles on right.*

Set within one of the most beautiful areas of Scotland, the views directly from the site over Loch Sunart to the remote West Highland mountains are truly stunning. The site is a perfect location for anyone who enjoys exploring mountains and lochs, seeing the amazing Scottish wildlife or just wants to relax and unwind in a truly tranquil place. The site has WiFi and a good mobile signal, a well-stocked shop and a slipway onto Loch Sunart. An art gallery adjoins the site.

Open: Easter to October **Last arrival:** 21.00 **Last departure:** noon
Pitches: 🚐 🚍 ▲; 🏠 see prices below; 20 hardstanding pitches; 20 seasonal pitches
Leisure: 🅰 🖊
Facilities: 🏠 ☉ 🗗 ☼ ⅙ 🖸 ☴ ☕ WiFi
Services: 🔌 🖸 🛒 ⅄ 🛢 🖋 ⊤
Within 3 miles: ⚓ 🎣
Additional site information: 8 acre site. 🐕 Cars can be parked by caravans and tents. Awnings permitted.
Glamping available: Wooden pods from £55.
Additional glamping information: Wooden pods offer 2 single beds (can convert to 3 beds), kettle, electric sockets, USB charge sockets, picnic bench and decking. Cars can be parked by units

---

AVIEMORE

Places to visit

The Strathspey Railway, AVIEMORE, PH22 1PY, 01479 810725
www.strathspeyrailway.co.uk

Great for kids: Landmark Forest Adventure Park, CARRBRIDGE, PH23 3AJ, 0800 7313446,www.landmarkpark.co.uk

---

AVIEMORE — Map 23 NH81

Aviemore Glamping
▶▶▶▶ 90% GLAMPING ONLY

tel: 01479 810717 & 07598 580327 **Eriskay, Craig Na Gower Avenue PH22 1RW**
email: enquiries@eriskay-aviemore.co.uk **web:** www.eriskay-aviemore.co.uk/
dir: *From south: exit A9 onto B9152 signed Aviemore. Take 2nd exit at roundabout signed town centre. 2nd exit at next roundabout. 5th left into Craig Na Gower Avenue (signed dental surgery). Site at end of lane.*

Aviemore is a well known outdoor enthusiasts' hotspot, attracting tourists throughout the year for hillwalking and climbing in the Cairngorms, watersports at Loch Morlich and Loch Insch and skiing in the winter. Aviemore Glamping is a bit of a hidden secret, located in the landscaped grounds of the owner's home just a short walk from the town centre. The four wooden eco-pods are beautifully built and luxuriously equipped with quality fittings and excellent en suite shower rooms; ideal for couples who are looking for something unique at a sensible price. The eco-pods are available all year and are heated to insulate against the chilly Scottish climate.

Open: All year **Last arrival:** 18.00 **Last departure:** 10.00
Facilities: 🏠 🗗 ☼ ☴ ☕ WiFi
Within 3 miles: ⚓ 🖊 ∪ 🗓 🖸 🖸
Accommodation available: Wooden pods.
Additional site information: 0.33 acre site. 🚫 Breakfasts available. Minimum stay 2 nights.

DUROR — Map 22 NM95

Places to visit

Glencoe Folk Museum, GLENCOE, PH49 4HS, 01855 811 664
www.glencoemuseum.com

Achindarroch Touring Park
▶▶▶ 80%

tel: 01631 740329 **PA38 4BS**
email: stay@achindarrochtp.co.uk **web:** www.achindarrochtp.co.uk
dir: *A82 onto A828 at Ballachulish Bridge then towards Oban for 5.2 miles. In Duror, site on left, signed.*

A long established, well-laid out park which continues to be maintained to a high standard by an enthusiastic and friendly family team. There is a well-appointed heated toilet block and spacious all-weather pitches and there are also 2- and 4-person wooden camping pods for hire. The park is well placed for visits to Oban, Fort William and Glencoe. A wide variety of outdoor sports is available in the area.

Open: 24 January to 16 January **Last departure:** 11.00
Pitches: * 🚐 from £16; 🚍 from £16; ▲ from £8; 🏠 see prices below; 21 hardstanding pitches; 10 seasonal pitches
Facilities: 🏠 ☉ 🗗 ☼ ⅙ ☴ WiFi
Services: 🔌 🛒 ⅄ 🛢
Within 3 miles: 🖊 ∪
Additional site information: 5 acre site. 🐕 Cars can be parked by caravans and tents. Awnings permitted. Groups by prior arrangement only. Campers' kitchen with freezer, kettle, microwave and boot dryer.
Glamping available: Wooden pods from £40.

EVANTON Map 23 NH66

Places to visit

Highland Museum of Childhood, STRATHPEFFER, IV14 9DH, 01997 421031
www.highlandmuseumofchildhood.org.uk

Black Rock Caravan Park

►►►► 80%

tel: 01349 830917 **Balconie Street IV16 9UN**
email: blackrocksholidays@gmail.com **web:** www.blackrocksscotland.com
dir: *Just off A9, 1 mile from the Cromarty Bridge.*

The River Glass flows along the side of this lovely park which is located in a small, almost secret valley near Black Rock Gorge, just a mile from the A9 and on the beautiful 'North Coast 500' route. There is a range of possibilities to suit all tastes including touring pitches, which include hardstandings and 34 fully serviced pitches, two wooden wigwams, an S-pod and a bunkhouse. It's an easy drive into Inverness, and the Black Isle provides a dolphin-watching experience at Channory Point; there's also great walking in nearby Glen Glass and Ben Wyvis. A regular bus service passes the site entrance and there's a railway station in nearby Alness.

Open: April to October **Last arrival:** 19.00 **Last departure:** noon
Pitches: 🚐 🚏 ▲ 🛖; 30 hardstanding pitches; 10 seasonal pitches
Leisure: ⚼
Facilities: 🛁 ☉ 🖤 ✳ ♿ 🛒 📶
Services: 🔌 🗑 �̄ ⬇ 🔒 🗑 Ⓣ
Within 3 miles: 🚶 🎣 🛒

Additional site information: 4.5 acre site. 🐾 Cars can be parked by caravans. Awnings permitted. No open fires, no noise after 23.00.

Glamping available: 2 wooden wigwams, 1 S-pod, 1 family luxury pod.

Additional glamping information: Cars can be parked by units.

FORT WILLIAM Map 22 NN17

Places to visit

West Highland Museum, FORT WILLIAM, PH33 6AJ, 01397 702169
www.westhighlandmuseum.org.uk

Ariundle Oakwood National Nature Reserve, FORT WILLIAM, PH33 6SW,
01397 704716
www.nature.scot/enjoying-outdoors/scotlands-national-nature-reserves/
ariundle-oakwood-national-nature-reserve

Glen Nevis Caravan & Camping Park

►►►►► 92%

tel: 01397 702191 **Glen Nevis PH33 6SX**
email: holidays@glen-nevis.co.uk **web:** www.glen-nevis.co.uk
dir: *From A82 (northern outskirts of Fort William) follow Glen Nevis signs at mini-roundabout. Site 2.5 miles on right.*

This is a large and very well maintained park, situated in Glen Nevis with easy access to the main footpath leading to Ben Nevis. Located a few miles from Fort William, the site is near Neptune's Staircase on the Caledonian Canal and the Great Glen. The site is divided into areas by beech hedges to give a sense of seclusion for caravan and motorhome users who have their own amenity blocks; tent campers have their own specific areas and large well-kept amenity blocks. To cater for those who are seeking a glamping experience, five luxury, wooden camping pods have been installed – all have unrivalled views towards Ben Nevis. The park has a restaurant and café.

Open: 15 March to October (restricted service: March and October – limited restaurant facilities) **Last arrival:** 22.00 **Last departure:** noon
Pitches: 🚐 🚏 ▲ 🛖 see prices below; 150 hardstanding pitches
Leisure: ⚼ 🍴 🎣 🎣
Facilities: 🛁 ☉ 🖤 ✳ ♿ 🛒 🍴 🛒 📶
Services: 🔌 🗑 🚽 🍴 🚲 �̄ ⬇ 🔒 🗑 Ⓣ
Within 3 miles: 🚶

Additional site information: 30 acre site. 🐾 Cars can be parked by caravans and tents. Awnings permitted. Quiet from 23.00–08.00.

Glamping available: Wooden pods from £60.

Additional glamping information: Wooden pods: dogs by prior arrangement only. Cars can be parked by units.

GAIRLOCH Map 22 NG87

Places to visit

Gairloch Heritage Museum, GAIRLOCH, IV21 2BH, 01445 712287
www.gairlochmuseum.org

Inverewe Garden, POOLEWE, IV22 2LG, 01445 781229
www.nts.org.uk/visit/places/inverewe

Gairloch Caravan Park

►►► 80%

tel: 01445 712373 **Strath IV21 2BX**
email: info@gairlochcaravanpark.com **web:** www.gairlochcaravanpark.com
dir: *From A832 take B8021 signed Melvaig towards Strath. In 0.5 mile turn right, just after Millcroft Hotel. Immediately right again.*

A clean, well-maintained site on flat coastal grassland close to Loch Gairloch. The owners and managers are hard working and well organised. The park offers hardstandings, good shrub and flower planting, new toilet and showers facilities, and a bunkhouse that provides accommodation for families.

Open: April to October **Last arrival:** 20.00 **Last departure:** noon
Pitches: 🚐 🚏 ▲; 13 hardstanding pitches; 8 seasonal pitches
Facilities: 🛁 ☉ 🖤 ✳ 🗑 📶
Services: 🔌 🗑 🚽 ⬇ 🔒 🗑 Ⓣ
Within 3 miles: 🚶 🎣 ◎ 🚣 🎣

Additional site information: 6 acre site. 🐾 Cars can be parked by caravans and tents. Awnings permitted. No noise after 23.00.

GLENCOE
Map 22 NN15

Places to visit

Glencoe Folk Museum, GLENCOE, PH49 4HS, 01855 811 664
www.glencoemuseum.com

Invercoe Caravan & Camping Park

►►►► 87%

tel: 01855 811210 **PH49 4HP**
email: holidays@invercoe.co.uk **web:** www.invercoe.co.uk
dir: *Exit A82 at Glencoe Hotel onto B863 for 0.25 mile.*

A level grass site set on the shore of Loch Leven, with excellent mountain views. The area is ideal for both walking and climbing, and also offers a choice of several freshwater and saltwater lochs. Convenient for the good shopping in Fort William. There are two 'micro lodge' wooden pods for hire.

Open: All year **Last departure:** noon

Pitches: 🚐 🚐 Å ⌂

Facilities: ☺ ℐ ⚬ ♿ 🖵 🌊 **WiFi**

Services: 🔌 🗑 🔋 ⚡ 🞉 **T**

Within 3 miles: ⚓ ℐ ⚓

Additional site information: 5 acre site. 🐕 Cars can be parked by caravans and tents. Awnings permitted. No large group bookings.

Glamping available: Wooden pods.

Additional glamping information: Cars can be parked by units.

JOHN O'GROATS
Map 23 ND37

Places to visit

The Castle & Gardens of Mey, THURSO, KW14 8XH, 01847 851473
www.castleofmey.org.uk

RSPB Dunnet Head, DUNNET, KW14 8XS, 01463 715000
www.rspb.org.uk/reserves-and-events/reserves-a-z/dunnet-head

John O'Groats Caravan Site

►►► 85%

tel: 01955 611329 & 07762 336359 **KW1 4YR**
email: info@johnogroatscampsite.co.uk **web:** www.johnogroatscampsite.co.uk
dir: *At end of A99.*

An attractive site in an open position above the seashore and looking out towards Orkney. Nearby is the passenger ferry that makes day trips to the Orkneys, and there are grey seals to watch, and sea angling can be organised by the site owners.

Open: April to September **Last arrival:** 20.00 **Last departure:** 11.00

Pitches: * 🚐 from £20; 🚐 from £20; Å from £19; 30 hardstanding pitches

Facilities: 🖼 ☺ ℐ ⚬ ♿ **WiFi**

Services: 🔌 🗑 🔋 ⚡ 🞉

Within 3 miles: ℐ ⚓

Additional site information: 4 acre site. 🐕 Cars can be parked by caravans and tents. Awnings permitted. No noise after 22.00.

LAIDE
Map 22 NG89

Places to visit

Inverewe Garden, POOLEWE, IV22 2LG, 01445 781229
www.nts.org.uk/visit/places/inverewe

Gruinard Bay Caravan Park

►►► 73%

tel: 01445 731556 **IV22 2ND**
email: stay@gruinardbay.co.uk **web:** www.gruinardbay.co.uk
dir: *From Inverness or Ullapool take A832 to Gairloch, follow signs to Laide. (NB on Inverness to Gairloch road – short stretch of single-track road with passing places just prior to Gairloch).*

With views across Gruinard Bay to the Summer Isles and the mountains, this is a lovely, small, beach-front park in a particularly peaceful location on the North Coast 500 route. There is direct access to a small sandy beach from where you can fish from the beach or rocks, and the site has free WiFi access. The small post office provides basic groceries, while larger shops can be found in Aultbea, Poolewe, Gairloch and Ullapool, where there are ferries to the Outer Hebrides. Being beside a beach, the site has no hardstandings but the grass pitches are on well-compacted shingle. The park and surrounding area abounds with wildlife – you may catch a glimpse of the occasional otter or seal.

Open: April to October **Last arrival:** 20.00 **Last departure:** 11.00

Pitches: 🚐 🚐 Å; 5 hardstanding pitches

Leisure: ℐ

Facilities: 🖼 ☺ ℐ **WiFi**

Services: 🔌 🗑 ⚡ 🔒

Within 3 miles: 🞉

Additional site information: 3.5 acre site. 🐕 Cars can be parked by caravans and tents. Awnings permitted. No noise after 22.00.

LAIRG
Map 23 NC50

Woodend Caravan & Camping Site

►►► 70%

tel: 01549 402248 **Achnairn IV27 4DN**
dir: *4 miles north of Lairg exit A836 onto A838, signed at Achnairn.*

A clean, simple site set in hilly moors and woodland with access to Loch Shin. The area is popular with fishing and boating enthusiasts, and there is a choice of golf courses within a 30-mile radius. A spacious campers' kitchen is a useful amenity. There's also a holiday cottage for hire.

Open: April to September **Last arrival:** 23.00

Pitches: 🚐 🚐 Å; 5 hardstanding pitches

Facilities: ☺ ℐ ⚬

Services: 🔌 🗑

Within 3 miles: ℐ ⚓

Additional site information: 4 acre site. 🐕 🐾 Cars can be parked by caravans and tents. Awnings permitted.

PITCHES: 🚐 Caravans 🚐 Motorhomes Å Tents ⌂ Glamping accommodation **SERVICES:** 🔌 Electric hook-up 🗑 Launderette 🍺 Licensed bar
🔋 Calor Gas ⚡ Campingaz **T** Toilet fluid 🍽 Café/Restaurant 🍟 Fast Food/Takeaway 🔋 Battery charging 🞉 Motorhome service point
* 2019 prices 🚫 No credit or debit cards 🐕 Dogs permitted ⊗ No dogs

ULLAPOOL
Map 22 NH19

Places to visit

Corrieshalloch Gorge National Nature Reserve, BRAEMORE, IV23 2PJ, 01445 781229
www.nts.org.uk/visit/places/corrieshalloch-gorge

Broomfield Holiday Park
►►► 81%

tel: 01854 612020 & 612664 **West Shore Street IV26 2UT**
email: sross@broomfieldhp.com **web:** www.broomfieldhp.com
dir: *Into Ullapool on A893, 2nd right after harbour.*

Set right on the water's edge of Loch Broom and the open sea, with lovely views of the Summer Isles. This clean, well maintained and managed park is close to the harbour and town centre with restaurants, bars and shops. The Ullapool ferry allows easy access to the Hebridian islands for day trips or longer visits.

Open: Easter or April to September **Last arrival:** 22.00 **Last departure:** noon

Pitches: * ⊞ from £21; ⊞ from £20; ▲ from £17; 104 hardstanding pitches

Leisure: ⟁ ✐

Facilities: ⊙ ✳ ᴕ ⑤ ♨ WiFi

Services: ☻ ⊡ ⬛ ⬛

Within 3 miles: ⚲

Additional site information: 12 acre site. ☝ Dogs must be on a lead at all times. Cars can be parked by caravans and tents. Awnings permitted. No noise at night.

SOUTH LANARKSHIRE

ABINGTON
Map 21 NS92

Places to visit

Museum of Lead Mining, WANLOCKHEAD, ML12 6UT, 01659 74387
www.leadminingmuseum.co.uk

Mount View Caravan Park
►►► 79%

tel: 01864 502808 **ML12 6RW**
email: info@mountviewcaravanpark.co.uk **web:** www.mountviewcaravanpark.co.uk
dir: *M74 junction 13, A702 south into Abington. Left into Station Road, over river and railway. Site on right.*

A delightfully maturing family park, surrounded by the Southern Uplands and handily located between Carlisle and Glasgow. It is an excellent stopover site for those travelling between Scotland and the south, and the West Coast Railway passes beside the park.

Open: March to October **Last arrival:** 20.45 **Last departure:** 11.30

Pitches: ⊞ ⊞ ▲; 42 hardstanding pitches; 18 seasonal pitches

Leisure: ⟁

Facilities: ⊡ ⊙ ᴕ ᴕ ⚲ ☰

Services: ☻ ⊡ ⬛

Within 3 miles: ⚲ ✐ ⑤

Additional site information: 5.5 acre site. ☝ Dogs must be exercised off site. Cars can be parked by caravans and tents. Awnings permitted. 5mph speed limit. Debit cards accepted (no credit cards). Emergency phone.

LEISURE: 🏊 Indoor swimming pool 🏊 Outdoor swimming pool ⟁ Children's playground 👶 Kids' club ⚲ Tennis court ♣ Games room ⬜ Separate TV room
⚲ Golf course ⛳ Pitch n putt ⛵ Boats for hire 🚲 Bikes for hire ⬛ Cinema ♫ Entertainment ✐ Fishing ◉ Mini golf 🏄 Watersports 🏋 Gym ⚽ Sports field ⛓ Stables
FACILITIES: ⬛ Baths/Shower ⊙ Electric shaver sockets ᴕ Hairdryer ✳ Ice Pack Facility 👶 Baby facilities ⚲ Disabled facilities ⑤ Shop on site or within 200yds
☰ BBQ area ☰ Picnic area WiFi WiFi

EAST LOTHIAN

DUNBAR
Map 21 NT67

Places to visit

Preston Mill & Phantassie Doocot, EAST LINTON, EH40 3DS, 01620 860426
www.nts.org.uk/visit/places/preston-mill

Great for kids: Tantallon Castle, NORTH BERWICK, EH39 5PN, 01620 892727
www.metconvironment.ana/visit-a-place/places/tantallon-castle/

Premier Park

Thurston Manor Leisure Park
▶▶▶▶▶ 88%

tel: 01368 840643 **Innerwick EH42 1SA**
email: holidays@verdantleisure.co.uk **web:** www.thurstonmanor.co.uk
dir: 4 miles south of Dunbar, follow site signs from A1.

A pleasant park set in 250 acres of unspoilt countryside. The touring (no tents) and static areas of this large park are in separate areas. The main touring area occupies an open, level position, and the toilet facilities are modern and exceptionally well maintained. The park boasts a well-stocked fishing loch, a heated indoor swimming pool, steam room, sauna, jacuzzi, mini-gym and fitness room plus seasonal entertainment. There is a superb family toilet block. Fly fishing is available.

Open: 15 February to January **Last arrival:** 23.00 **Last departure:** 10.00

Pitches: * ⌂ from £15; ⌂ from £15; 68 hardstanding pitches; 60 seasonal pitches

Leisure: 🏊 ⛰ 🚶 🎣 ⌂ 🎵 ✒ 🎯 ⚽

Facilities: 🚻 ☉ 🚿 ⚒ ♿ 🛉 🛒 🚽 WiFi

Services: 🔌 🗑 🍴 🍽 🍺 ⚡ 🛢 🐕 T

Additional site information: 175 acre site. 🐕 Cars can be parked by caravans. Awnings permitted. Quiet after 23.00.

Belhaven Bay Caravan & Camping Park
▶▶▶▶ 90%

tel: 01368 865956 **Belhaven Bay EH42 1TS**
email: belhaven@meadowhead.co.uk **web:** www.meadowhead.co.uk
dir: A1 onto A1087 towards Dunbar. 1 mile to site in John Muir Park.

Located on the outskirts of Dunbar, this is a sheltered park within walking distance of the beach. There is a regular bus service to Dunbar where there is an East Coast Main Line railway station. The site is also convenient for the A1 and well placed for visiting the area's many seaside towns and various visitor attractions. There is a large children's play area. Six static caravans and three wooden wigwam pods are available for hire.

Open: March to October **Last arrival:** 20.00 **Last departure:** noon

Pitches: ⌂ ⌂ 🏕 ⌂; 11 hardstanding pitches

Leisure: ⛰ **Facilities:** 🚻 ☉ 🚿 ⚒ ♿ 🛉 🚽 🛒 WiFi

Services: 🔌 🗑 ⚡ T

Within 3 miles: 🎣 ✒ ⛳ ◎ 🚣

Additional site information: 40 acre site. 🐕 Cars can be parked by caravans and tents. Awnings permitted. No rollerblades or skateboards, no open fires, no noise 23.00–07.00.

Glamping available: Wooden wigwams.

LONGNIDDRY
Map 21 NT47

Places to visit

Prestongrange Museum, PRESTONPANS, EH32 9RX, 0131 653 2904
www.prestongrange.org

Great for kids: Myreton Motor Museum, ABERLADY, EH32 0PZ, 07585 356931
www.myretonmotormuseum.co.uk

Premier Park

Seton Sands Holiday Village
▶▶▶▶▶ 87% HOLIDAY CENTRE

tel: 01875 813333 **EH32 0QF**
email: setonsands@haven.com **web:** www.haven.com/setonsands
dir: A1 to A198 exit, take B6371 to Cockenzie. Right onto B1348. Site 1 mile on right.

A well-equipped holiday centre facing onto the Firth of Forth with mature landscaping. A dedicated entertainment team offers plenty of organised activities for children and there are pleasant bars, a show bar and a modern restaurant. It offers good sports and leisure facilities, including a multi-sports court, swimming pool, 9-hole golf course and a variety of play areas, so there's always plenty to do without leaving the park. The touring area offers fully-serviced pitches set in lovely landscaping with a dedicated on-site warden. There is a regular bus from the site entrance, which makes day trips to Edinburgh easy. 150 holiday homes are available for hire. Please note, this site does not accept tents.

Open: mid March to end October (restricted service: mid March to May and September to end October – facilities may be reduced) **Last arrival:** 22.00 **Last departure:** 10.00

Pitches: ⌂ ⌂; 40 hardstanding pitches

Leisure: 🏊 ⛰ 🚶 🎣 🎵 ✒

Facilities: 🚻 🚿 ♿ 🛉 🚽 WiFi

Services: 🔌 🗑 🍴 🍽 🍺 🛢

Within 3 miles: ⛳

Additional site information: 1.75 acre site. 🐕 Maximum 2 dogs per booking, certain dog breeds banned. No commercial vehicles, no bookings by persons under 21 years unless a family booking.

WEST LOTHIAN

EAST CALDER
Map 21 NT06

Places to visit

Almond Valley Heritage Trust, LIVINGSTON, EH54 7AR, 01506 414957
www.almondvalley.co.uk

Malleny Garden, BALERNO, EH14 7AF, 0131 665 1546
www.nts.org.uk/visit/places/malleny-garden

Linwater Caravan Park

▶▶▶▶ 92%

tel: 0131 333 3326 **West Clifton EH53 OHT**
email: admin@linwater.co.uk **web:** www.linwater.co.uk
dir: *M9 junction 1, follow B7030 and Newbridge signs. Left after petrol station and Macdonalds onto B7030. 2 miles, turn right after Edinburgh International Climbing Arena (EICA), follow site signs.*

This is a farmland park in a peaceful rural area with access to good motorway and rail links enabling exploration of the heart of Scotland. The grounds are very pleasant and the toilets are kept in an exemplary manner. It is a particularly popular park, especially with those wishing to visit the Royal Highland Show, the Edinburgh Festival and Military Tattoo. There are four wooden wigwams (known as timber tents), three modern static rentals and a self-catering lodge in a half acre, for hire. A modern, good-sized and well-appointed campers kitchen was added in 2019.

Open: All year **Last arrival:** 21.00 **Last departure:** noon

Pitches: 🚐 🚍 ▲ 🏠; 22 hardstanding pitches

Leisure: ⚓ ✎

Facilities: 🛁 ⊙ 🦶 ☆ ⚁ ⑤ WiFi

Services: 🔌 🗄 ♨ 🛒 ⚒ 🗑 🐾 ⓣ

Additional site information: 5 acre site. 🐾 Maximum of 2 dogs per booking. Cars can be parked by caravans and tents. Awnings permitted. No noise after 23.00. No entry to main site after 9pm (late arrivals area). Takeaway food can be ordered for delivery, small shop sells basics only, woodland dog walk.

Glamping available: Wooden wigwams. **Changeover days:** Any day

Additional glamping information: Cars can be parked by units.

LINLITHGOW

Places to visit

Linlithgow Palace, LINLITHGOW, EH49 7AL, 01506 842896
www.historicenvironment.scot/visit-a-place/places/linlithgow-palace/

House of The Binns, LINLITHGOW, EH49 7NA
www.nts.org.uk/visit/places/house-of-binns

Great for kids: Blackness Castle, LINLITHGOW, EH49 7NH, 01506 834807
www.historicenvironment.scot/visit-a-place/places/blackness-castle/

LINLITHGOW
Map 21 NS97

Beecraigs Caravan & Camping Site

▶▶▶▶ 92%

tel: 01506 284516 & 284510 **Beecraigs Country Park, The Visitor Centre EH49 6PL**
email: mail@beecraigs.com **web:** www.beecraigs.com
dir: *M9 junction 3 (from east) or junction 4 (from west), A803 to Linlithgow. From A803 into Preston Road signed Beecraigs Country Park. Reception in visitor centre. (NB Preston Road route is steep and winding).*

Located on the hills above the town of Linlithgow with unrivalled views towards the Forth Bridges, Beecraigs Country Park has an excellent caravan and camping site, with two modern washrooms, large hardstanding pitches and a secluded tenting area, as well as two little lodges, sleeping 6 and 4 persons. There are extensive walks and cycle trails, an animal attraction and a very large play area for children. There is a lovely visitor centre, shop and café at the site entrance and there are good road and train links nearby, making trips into Edinburgh an easy affair; for those who wish something simpler, boat trips are available from the local canal centre.

Open: All year (restricted service: 25 to 26 December and 1 to 2 January – no new arrivals) **Last arrival:** 22.00 **Last departure:** noon

Pitches: * 🚐 from £21.40; 🚍 from £21.40; ▲ from £17.70; 🏠 see prices below; 23 hardstanding pitches

Leisure: 🛝

Facilities: 🛁 ⊙ 🦶 ☆ ⚁ 🍴 🛒 WiFi

Services: 🔌 🗄 🍴 ♨ ⚒ 🔒 ⓣ

Within 3 miles: ⚓ ∪ ♨ ⑤

Additional site information: 6 acre site. 🐾 Cars can be parked by caravans. Awnings permitted. Site standards apply. Country park facilities, WiFi only available in visitor centre.

Glamping available: Cabins (Little Lodges) from £42.20.

Additional glamping information: Little Lodges sleep 4 or 6. Maximum 1 dog per unit. Use of shower block on site. Cars can be parked by units.

LEISURE: 🏊 Indoor swimming pool 🏊 Outdoor swimming pool 🛝 Children's playground 👶 Kids' club 🎾 Tennis court 🎱 Games room 📺 Separate TV room ⛳ Golf course 🚩 Pitch n putt ⛵ Boats for hire 🚲 Bikes for hire 🎬 Cinema 🎵 Entertainment 🎣 Fishing ◎ Mini golf 🏄 Watersports 🏋 Gym 🏟 Sports field ∪ Stables
FACILITIES: 🛁 Baths/Shower ⊙ Electric shaver sockets 🦶 Hairdryer ☆ Ice Pack Facility 👶 Baby facilities ⚁ Disabled facilities ⑤ Shop on site or within 200yds 🍴 BBQ area 🛒 Picnic area WiFi WiFi

MORAY

LOSSIEMOUTH   Map 23 NJ27

Places to visit

Elgin Cathedral, ELGIN, IV30 1HU, 01343 547171
www.historicenvironment.scot/visit-a-place/places/elgin-cathedral/

Duffus Castle, DUFFUS, IV30 5RH
www.historicenvironment.scot/visit-a-place/places/duffus-castle/

Premier Park

Silver Sands Holiday Park
►►►►► 84%

tel: 01343 813262 **Covesea, West Beach IV31 6SP**
email: holidays@silver-sands.co.uk web: www.silver-sands.co.uk
dir: *Take B9040 from Lossiemouth, 2 miles to site.*

This is an ideal family park located on the Moray coast two miles from the busy
seaside town of Lossiemouth. There is direct access to a sandy beach and the
entertainment complex caters for both children and adults, with a pool, sauna,
steam room and a large gym. There is a well-stocked shop, takeaway food and a
small bistro-style café on site. With a golf course adjacent to the park and
several others within easy driving distance (including the world famous Nairn
Golf Course), this site makes a perfect base for golfers and those touring the
area. There are fully serviced hardstandings and 15 static caravans for hire.

Open: 24 March to end October **Last arrival:** 22.00 **Last departure:** noon

Pitches: 🚐 🚙 ▲; 94 hardstanding pitches; 17 seasonal pitches

Leisure: 🏊 ⛏ 🛝 🎣 🎵 ⛳

Facilities: 🛁 ☉ 🌐 ⚒ ⚙ 🏧 🛒 🎏 ♨ WiFi

Services: 🔌 🔋 🍴 🍽 🗑 🛒 🔋 ⚗ Ⓣ

Within 3 miles: ↓ ✎ ∪ ◎ 🎣 🎿

Additional site information: 60 acre site. 🐕 Cars can be parked by caravans and
tents. Awnings permitted. No noise after midnight. No commercial vehicles on touring
field. Crazy golf.

PERTH & KINROSS

BLAIR ATHOLL

Places to visit

Blair Castle, BLAIR ATHOLL, PH18 5TH, 01796 481207
www.blair-castle.co.uk

Killiecrankie Visitor Centre, KILLIECRANKIE, PH16 5LQ, 01796 473233
www.nts.org.uk/visit/places/killiecrankie

BLAIR ATHOLL   Map 23 NN86

Premier Park

Blair Castle Caravan Park
►►►►► 91%

Best of British

tel: 01796 481263 **PH18 5SR**
email: mail@blaircastlecaravanpark.co.uk web: www.blaircastlecaravanpark.co.uk
dir: *From A9 onto B8079 at Aldclune, follow to Blair Atholl. Site on right after crossing
bridge in village.*

An attractive site set in impressive seclusion within the Atholl Estate,
surrounded by mature woodland and the River Tilt. Although a large park, the
various groups of pitches are located throughout the extensive grounds, and
each has its own sanitary block with all-cubicled facilities of a very high
standard. There is a choice of grass pitches, hardstandings and fully serviced
pitches. This park is particularly suitable for the larger type of motorhome. There
are 8 wooden pods that each sleep two adults.

Open: March to November **Last arrival:** 21.30 **Last departure:** noon

Pitches: 🚐 from £21; 🚙 from £21; ▲ from £9.50; 🏠 see prices below;
155 hardstanding pitches; 68 seasonal pitches

Leisure: ⛏ 🎣 🎾 ⚽ **Facilities:** 🛁 ☉ 🌐 ⚒ ⚙ 🏧 🎏 WiFi

Services: 🔌 🔋 🔋 ⛽ 🔋 ⚗ Ⓣ **Within 3 miles:** ↓ ∪ ◎

Additional site information: 32 acre site. 🐕 Cars can be parked by caravans and
tents. Awnings permitted. Family park, no noise after 23.00.

Glamping available: Wooden pods from £35. **Changeover days:** Any day

See advert on page 343

PITCHES: 🚐 Caravans 🚙 Motorhomes ▲ Tents 🏠 Glamping accommodation **SERVICES:** 🔌 Electric hook-up 🔋 Launderette 🍴 Licensed bar
🔋 Calor Gas ⚗ Campingaz Ⓣ Toilet fluid 🍽 Café/Restaurant 🎏 Fast Food/Takeaway 🔋 Battery charging ⛽ Motorhome service point
* 2019 prices ◎ No credit or debit cards 🐕 Dogs permitted ⊗ No dogs

COMRIE
Map 21 NN72

Places to visit

Caithness Glass Visitor Centre, CRIEFF, PH7 4HQ, 01764 654014
www.caithnessglass.co.uk

Drummond Castle Gardens, MUTHILL, PH7 4HN, 01764 681433
www.drummondcastlegardens.co.uk

Twenty Shilling Wood Caravan Park
▶▶▶ 77%

tel: 01764 670411 **PH6 2JY**
email: alowe20@aol.com **web:** www.twentyshillingwoodcaravanpark.co.uk
dir: On A85, 0.5 mile west of Comrie towards St Fillans. Site opposite Tullybannocher café.

Situated on the outskirts of Comrie, this is a tranquil and mature site that offers terraced pitches in a well-maintained woodland setting which screens the site from the road. The site facilities are clean and well maintained and the family owners are very helpful. It is ideally located for exploring the Perthshire countryside – there are stunning drives to beautiful lochs and charming rural villages such as Comrie, which is a short walk away. There are various hiking and cycling trails, for all levels of ability, that can be accessed from the site. Please note, tents are not accepted.

Open: 18 March to 20 October **Last arrival:** 21.00 **Last departure:** 18.00
Pitches: ⊞ from £26; ⊞ from £26; 14 hardstanding pitches; 32 seasonal pitches
Leisure: ⚠ ⚫
Facilities: ⌂ ⊙ ⌱ ✳ ☰ WiFi
Services: ⊠ ⊠ ⛟ ⏁ ⬛ T
Within 3 miles: ⌁ ⌱ ⑤

Additional site information: 10.5 acre site. ⬚ Maximum of 2 dogs per pitch. Cars can be parked by caravans. Awnings permitted. Booking advisable at all times, no noise after 23.00. Woodland walk.

DUNKELD

Places to visit

The Ell Shop & Little Houses, DUNKELD, PH8 0AN, 01350 728641
www.nts.org.uk/visit/places/dunkeld

Loch of the Lowes Visitor Centre, DUNKELD, PH8 0HH, 01350 727337
scottishwildlifetrust.org.uk/reserve/loch-of-the-lowes/

DUNKELD
Map 21 NO04

Inver Mill Farm Caravan Park
▶▶▶▶ 80%

tel: 01350 727477 **Inver PH8 0JR**
email: invermill@talk21.com **web:** www.invermillfarm.com
dir: A9 onto A822 then immediately right to Inver.

A peaceful park on level former farmland, located on the banks of the River Braan and surrounded by mature trees and hills. The active resident owners keep the park in very good condition.

Open: mid March to October **Last arrival:** 22.00 **Last departure:** noon
Pitches: ⊞ from £22; ⊞ from £22; Å from £17; 3 hardstanding pitches
Facilities: ⌂ ⊙ ⌱ ✳ ⛄ WiFi
Services: ⊠ ⊠ ⛟ ⏁ ⬛ ⊘
Within 3 miles: ⌁ ⌱ ⑤

Additional site information: 5 acre site. ⬚ Cars can be parked by caravans and tents. Awnings permitted.

KINLOCH RANNOCH
Map 23 NN65

Places to visit

The Scottish Crannog Centre, KENMORE, PH15 2HY, 01887 830583
www.crannog.co.uk

Kilvrecht Campsite
▶ 76%

tel: 03000 0676380 **PH16 5QA**
email: enquiries.east@forestryandland.gov.scot
web: forestryandland.gov.scot/visit/forest-parks/tay-forest-park/kilvrecht-campsite
dir: From north shore: on B846 to Kinloch Rannoch. Follow South Loch Rannoch sign. Over river bridge, 1st right signed Kilvrecht. Approach via unclassified road along loch, with Forestry Commission signs.

Set within a large forest clearing, approximately half a mile from the road to Kinloch Rannoch which runs along the loch. This is a beautifully maintained site, with good clean facilities, for those who wish for a peaceful break. It also makes an ideal base for those who prefer the more active outdoor activities of hill walking (Schiehallion is within easy reach) or mountain biking; it is a great spot to observe the multitude of birds and wildlife in the area.

Open: April to October **Last arrival:** 22.00 **Last departure:** 10.00
Pitches: ⊞ ⊞ Å
Facilities: ⛄ ⊼
Services: T
Within 3 miles: ⌱ ⛏ ⑤

Additional site information: 17 acre site. ⬚ ⊜ Cars can be parked by caravans and tents. Awnings permitted. No fires.

LEISURE: 🏊 Indoor swimming pool 🏊 Outdoor swimming pool ⚠ Children's playground 👦 Kids' club 🎾 Tennis court 🎱 Games room 📺 Separate TV room ⌁ Golf course 🏌 Pitch n putt ⛵ Boats for hire 🚲 Bikes for hire 🎬 Cinema 🎵 Entertainment 🎣 Fishing ◎ Mini golf 🏄 Watersports 🏋 Gym ⚽ Sports field ♻ Stables
FACILITIES: ⌂ Baths/Shower ⊙ Electric shaver sockets ⌱ Hairdryer ✳ Ice Pack Facility 👶 Baby facilities ⛄ Disabled facilities ⑤ Shop on site or within 200yds ☰ BBQ area ⊼ Picnic area WiFi WiFi

Milton of Fonab Caravan Park

►►►► 90%

tel. 01796 472002 Bridge Road PH16 5NA
email: info@fonab.co.uk web: www.fonab.co.uk
dir: *From south: on A924, pass petrol station on left, next left opposite Bell's Distillery into Bridge Road. Cross river, site on left. From north (and Pitlochry centre): on A924, under rail bridge, turn right opposite Bell's Distillery into Bridge Road.*

This is a lovely, peaceful site set on the banks of the River Tummel on the outskirts of Pitlochry. Getting here is easy as the A9 is nearby and there is a good bus service and a mainline rail station in the town. The site is exceptionally well maintained, with large pitches, good washrooms and a well-stocked shop, and it is an ideal base for exploring this scenic part of Perthshire. The area is famous for the whisky industry, and Bells' distillery is a short walk from the site entrance, as is the Pitlochry Festival Theatre.

Open: 15 March to 3 November **Last arrival:** 21.00 **Last departure:** 13.00
Pitches: 🚐 🚍 ⛺; 74 hardstanding pitches
Leisure: ✐ **Facilities:** 🏪 ☉ ⌱ ☀ ☇ ⑤ WiFi
Services: 🔌 ⑤ ⛽ 🔋 ● ⊘ 🇹 **Within 3 miles:** ↕ ◎ ⪎ ⪤
Additional site information: 15 acre site. 🐕 Cars can be parked by caravans and tents. Awnings permitted. Couples and families only.

Faskally Caravan Park

►►►► 88%

tel: 01796 472007 PH16 5LA
email: info@faskally.co.uk web: www.faskally.co.uk
dir: *1.5 miles north of Pitlochry on B8019.*

A large park near Pitlochry, which is divided into smaller areas by mature trees and set within well-tended grounds. This family-owned site has two large amenity blocks and an entertainment complex with a heated swimming pool, bar, restaurant and indoor games area. There are numerous walks from the site and it is ideal for either a longer stay to explore the area or as a convenient stopover. A regular bus service is available at the site entrance.

Open: 15 March to October **Last arrival:** 23.00 **Last departure:** 11.00
Pitches: 🚐 🚍 ⛺; 45 hardstanding pitches
Leisure: ⪎ ⚫ ♫
Facilities: ☉ ⌱ ☀ ☇ ⑤ WiFi
Services: 🔌 ⑤ 🍺 🍽 ● ⊘ 🇹
Within 3 miles: ↕ ✐ ⛳ ⪤
Additional site information: 27 acre site. 🐕 Cars can be parked by caravans and tents. Awnings permitted.

PITCHES: 🚐 Caravans 🚍 Motorhomes ⛺ Tents 🛖 Glamping accommodation **SERVICES:** 🔌 Electric hook-up ⑤ Launderette 🍺 Licensed bar
● Calor Gas ⊘ Campingaz 🇹 Toilet fluid 🍽 Café/Restaurant 🍔 Fast Food/Takeaway 🔋 Battery charging ⚡ Motorhome service point
* 2019 prices 🚫 No credit or debit cards 🐕 Dogs permitted 🚫 No dogs

SCOTTISH BORDERS

LAUDER
Map 21 NT54

Thirlestane Castle Caravan & Camping Site
▶▶▶ 90%

tel: 01578 718884 & 07976 231032 **Thirlestane Castle TD2 6RU**
email: info@thirlestanecastlepark.co.uk **web:** www.thirlestanecastlepark.co.uk
dir: *Signed from A68 and A697, just south of Lauder.*

Located on the outskirts of Lauder, close to the A68 and within the grounds of Thirlestane Castle, this is an ideal site from which to explore the many attractions in the Scottish Borders. The amenity block is immaculately maintained and the pitches are behind the estate boundary wall that provides a secluded and peaceful location. There is a regular bus service from near the site entrance.

Open: April to October **Last arrival:** 20.00 **Last departure:** noon

Pitches: 🚐 🚉 ▲; 30 hardstanding pitches; 55 seasonal pitches

Leisure: 🄰 ✏

Facilities: 🛁 ⊙ 🕭 🍴 WiFi

Services: 🔌 🔄 ⊍

Within 3 miles: 🗻 💲

Additional site information: 5 acre site. 🚗 Cars can be parked by caravans and tents. Awnings permitted. Tourer storage facilities, discounted access to castle and grounds during opening hours.

PAXTON
Map 21 NT95

Paxton House Caravan Park
▶ 77%

tel: 01289 386291 & 07803 352706 **Paxton House TD15 1SZ**
email: info@paxtonhouse.com **web:** www. paxtonhouse.co.uk
dir: *From A1 (west of Berwick-upon-Tweed) take B6461 signed Paxton. In approximately 5 miles Paxton House entrance on left.*

This site is situated within the walled garden of the glorious 18th-century, John Adams designed Paxton House, just three miles from Berwick-upon-Tweed. Tourers who stay in the quaint caravan park are able to enjoy access to the extensive grounds of the house – with stunning herbaceous borders, wild woodlands, riverside walks and a fantastic playground, there is plenty to keep the whole family entertained. Guests can take advantage of a discount in the shop and tearoom, and take a tour of Paxton House for a small fee. There are plenty of interesting activities on the doorstep, including seaside and historic walks, theatres and sports centres.

Open: All year **Last arrival:** 18.00 **Last departure:** 10.30

Pitches: 🚐 🚉 🏠; 15 hardstanding pitches

Services: 🔌 🍽

Additional site information: 🚗 Cars can be parked by caravans. Awnings permitted.

Glamping available: 4 canvas cottages. **Changeover days:** Any day

Additional glamping information: Canvas cottages offer hardwood floor, wooden furniture, wood-burning stove, cooking facilities and en suite bathroom. Children and dogs welcome.

PEEBLES
Map 21 NT24

Places to visit
Kailzie Gardens, PEEBLES, EH45 9HT, 01721 720007
www.kailziegardens.com

Robert Smail's Printing Works, INNERLEITHEN, EH44 6HA, 01896 830206
www.nts.org.uk/visit/places/robert-smails

Great for kids: Go Ape Glentress Forest, PEEBLES, EH45 8NB, 01603 895500
www.goape.co.uk/peebles

Crossburn Caravan Park
▶▶▶▶ 88%

tel: 01721 720501 **Edinburgh Road EH45 8ED**
email: info@crossburncaravans.co.uk **web:** www.crossburn-caravans.com
dir: *0.5 mile north of Peebles on A703.*

A peaceful park, on the edge of Peebles and within easy driving distance for Edinburgh and the Scottish Borders. The park is divided by well-maintained landscaping and mature trees, and has good views over the countryside. There is a regular bus service at the site entrance and Peebles has a wide range of shops and attractions. The facilities are maintained to a high standard. Four-person wooden pods are available for hire. There is also a main caravan dealership on site, and a large stock of spares and accessories are available.

Open: March to November **Last arrival:** 21.00 **Last departure:** noon (later by arrangement)

Pitches: * 🚐 from £28; 🚉 from £28; ▲ from £12; 🏠 see prices below; 28 hardstanding pitches; 16 seasonal pitches

Leisure: 🄰

Facilities: 🛁 ⊙ 🕭 ✳ 🕭 💲 WiFi

Services: 🔌 🔄 🛒 ⊍ 🛢 ⊘ 🇹

Within 3 miles: 🗻 ✏ ∪

Additional site information: 6 acre site. 🚗 Cars can be parked by caravans and tents. Awnings permitted. No noise after 23.00.

Glamping available: Wooden pods from £48.

Additional glamping information: Wooden pods: last time of departure 11.00. Cars can be parked by units.

STIRLING

ABERFOYLE
Map 20 NN50

Places to visit
Inchmahome Priory, PORT OF MENTEITH, FK8 3RA, 01877 385294
www.historicenvironment.scot/visit-a-place/places/inchmahome-priory/

Great for kids: Go Ape Aberfoyle, ABERFOYLE, FK8 3SX, 0845 094 9032
www.goape.co.uk/aberfoyle

Premier Park

Trossachs Holiday Park
▶ ▶ ▶ ▶ ▶ 91%

tel: 01877 382614 **FK8 3SA**
email: info@trossachsholidays.co.uk **web:** www.trossachsholidays.co.uk
dir: *Access on east side of A81, 1 mile south of junction A821 and 3 miles south of Aberfoyle.*

An attractively landscaped and peaceful park with outstanding views towards the hills, including the munro of Ben Lomond. Set within the Loch Lomond National Park, boating, walking, cycling and beautiful drives over the Dukes Pass through the Trossachs are just some of the attractions within easy reach. Bikes can be hired from the reception and there is an internet café that sells home-baked items. There are lodges for hire.

Open: March to October **Last arrival:** 21.00 **Last departure:** noon
Pitches: * 🚐 from £24.50; 🚐 from £24.50; ▲ from £20; 46 hardstanding pitches;

24 seasonal pitches
Leisure: 🎱 🎣 🏓
Facilities: 🏪 ⊙ 🅿 ✳ ⑤ 🚻 WiFi
Services: 🔌 🗑 🛒 ↯ 🔋 🚽
Within 3 miles: ↧ ✎ ♻ 🛶 ⚓

Additional site information: 40 acre site. 🐕 Cars can be parked by caravans and tents. Awnings permitted. Groups by prior arrangement only. Woodland walk, cycling and trails.

BLAIRLOGIE
Map 21 NS89

Places to visit
Alloa Tower, ALLOA, FK10 1PL, 01259 211701
www.nts.org.uk/visit/places/alloa-tower

The National Wallace Monument, STIRLING, FK9 5LF, 01786 472140
www.nationalwallacemonument.com

Great for kids: Blair Drummond Safari & Adventure Park, BLAIR DRUMMOND, FK9 4UR, 01786 841456, www.blairdrummond.com

Witches Craig Caravan & Camping Park
▶ ▶ ▶ ▶ 90%

tel: 01786 474947 **FK9 5PX**
email: info@witchescraig.co.uk **web:** www.witchescraig.co.uk
dir: *3 miles northeast of Stirling on A91 (Hillfoots to St Andrews road).*

In an attractive setting with direct access to the lower slopes of the dramatic Ochil Hills, this is a well-maintained family-run park. It is in the centre of 'Braveheart' country, with easy access to historical sites and many popular attractions.

Open: April to October **Last arrival:** 20.00 **Last departure:** noon

Pitches: * 🚐 from £22.50; 🚐 from £22.50; ▲ from £17.50; 60 hardstanding pitches; 6 seasonal pitches

Leisure: 🎱
Facilities: 🏪 ⊙ 🅿 ✳ ⑤ 🚻 WiFi
Services: 🔌 🗑 🛒 ↯ 🔋 ⊘ 🚽
Within 3 miles: ↧ ✎ ♻ ◎ 🎡 ⑤

Additional site information: 5 acre site. 🐕 Cars can be parked by caravans and tents. Awnings permitted. Food preparation area, cooking shelters, baby bath and changing area.

LUIB
Map 20 NN42

Places to visit
Ben Lawers National Nature Reserve, KILLIN, FK21 8TY, 01567 820988
www.nts.org.uk/visit/places/ben-lawers

Glendochart Holiday Park
►►►► 74%

tel: 01567 820637 **FK20 8QT**
email: info@glendochart.co.uk **web:** www.glendochart-caravanpark.co.uk
dir: On A85 (Oban to Stirling road) midway between Killin and Crianlarich.

A small site located on the A85 some eight miles from Killin, with boating and fishing available on Loch Tay. It is also convenient for Oban, Fort William and Loch Lomond. Hill walkers have direct access to numerous walks to suit all levels of ability, including the nearby munro of Ben More. There is a regular bus service at the site entrance, and nearby Crianlarich provides access to the West Highland Railway, known as Britain's most scenic rail route, and also the West Highland Way. An ideal site as a stopover to the west coast or for a longer holiday.

Open: March to November **Last arrival:** 21.00 **Last departure:** noon

Pitches: * 🚐 from £18.50; 🚐 from £18.50; ⛺ from £15; 28 hardstanding pitches

Facilities: ⊙ ℙ ✳ ㅊ ⑤ 🍺

Services: ⊕ ⑤ ⚌ 🔒 ⌀

Within 3 miles: ℘

Additional site information: 15 acre site. 🐾 Cars can be parked by caravans and tents. Awnings permitted.

STIRLING

See Blairlogie

TYNDRUM
Map 20 NN33

Strathfillan Wigwam Village

►►►►► 80% GLAMPING ONLY

tel: 01838 400251 & 07817 483126 **Auchtertyre Farm FK20 8RU**
email: enquiries@wigwamholidays.com **web:** www.wigwamholidays.com
dir: From A82 (3 miles north of Crianlarich) site on right. Follow signs for Strathfillan Wigwams and farm shop.

The hand-crafted wooden wigwams provide good accommodation, especially for walkers as this site is on the West Highland Way. Available all year, each unit is well insulated, has electric panel heaters and an external wood-burner (wood is available at the Trading Post shop). They are spotlessly clean and well maintained. The wigwams have been grouped in small clusters, some have outstanding mountain views and others benefit from the seclusion of a woodland setting. The lodges, with kitchen, shower and toilet, cater for up to eight, and a small yurt is also available for hire. The surrounding area offers many walking and mountain bike opportunities (bike hire available), and various eateries can be found in Tyndrum, not far away. There is a local bus service at the end of the farm road. The site offers touring pitches as well.

Open: All year **Last arrival:** 20.00 (or by prior arrangement) **Last departure:** 10.30

Leisure: 🖵 🚲

Facilities: 🏠 ℙ ⑤ 🍺 🎋 WiFi

Within 3 miles: ℘

Accommodation available: Yurt; wooden wigwams.

Additional site information: 6 acre site. 🐾 No noise or music after 23.00. En suite wigwams have own kitchens. Cars can be parked by units.

SCOTTISH ISLANDS

ISLE OF ARRAN

KILDONAN — Map 20 NS02

Places to visit

Isle of Arran Heritage Museum, BRODICK, KA27 8DP, 01770 302636
www.arranmuseum.co.uk

Seal Shore Camping and Touring Site

►►►► 88%

tel: 01770 820320 **KA27 8SE**
email: enquiries@campingarran.com **web:** www.campingarran.com
dir: *From ferry terminal in Brodick turn left, 12 miles, through Lamlash and Whiting Bay. Left to Kildonan, site on left.*

On the south coast of Arran and only 12 miles from the ferry at Brodick, this is a peaceful, family-run site with direct access to a sandy beach. There are fabulous views across the water to Pladda Island and Ailsa Craig, and an abundance of wildlife. The site is suited for all types of touring vehicles but caters very well for non-motorised campers. The resident owner, also a registered fisherman, sells fresh lobsters and crabs, and on request will give fishing lessons on a small, privately owned lochan. There is an undercover barbecue, campers' kitchen and day room with TV. A bus, which stops on request, travels around the island. There are two wooden pods and one gypsy caravan for hire.

Open: March to October **Last arrival:** 21.00 **Last departure:** noon

Pitches: * 🚐 from £24; 🚐 from £24; ⚊ from £22; 🏕 see prices below; 16 hardstanding pitches

Leisure: 🎱 🎣 🎮

Facilities: 🏪 ☺ 🚰 ⚒ ♿ 🚿 🚽 🚻 WiFi

Services: 🔌 🔋 🛒 🔋 🚮 🛢 🅃

Within 3 miles: 🚶 🎣

Additional site information: 3 acre site. 🐕 Dog charge £1.00 per day. Cars can be parked by caravans. Awnings permitted. No fires, no gazebos, no noise after 22.00. Pods departure time 10am, car parking not available on all caravan pitches. Small shop selling basic essentials. Car hire can be arranged.

Glamping available: 2 wooden pods from £40. **Changeover days:** Any day

Additional glamping information: No cooking or smoking in pods.

KILMORY — Map 20 NR92

Premier Park

Runach Arainn

►►►►► 92% GLAMPING ONLY

tel: 01770 870515 **The Old Manse KA27 8PH**
email: runacharainn@gmail.com **web:** www.runacharainn.com
dir: *From ferry at Brodick, turn left onto A481 signed South and Lamlash. Through Lamlash and Whiting Bay. Approximately 9 miles to Kilmory. In Kilmory, 1st right, pass church to site.*

Runach Arainn, Gaelic for 'Secret Arran', lives up to its name – hidden away in a quiet and beautiful part of the Isle of Arran, just a 15-minute walk from a lovely

beach on the southern shore of the island. It offers superb 20ft-diameter yurts that were made in Scotland. The style of the interiors together with private bathrooms for each yurt (in an amenity building), create a charming camping experience that includes many creature comforts for a truly exceptional stay. Fire pits and outdoor cooking facilities are also available.

Open: February to November **Last arrival:** 22.00 **Last departure:** 10.00

Facilities: 🏪 ♿ 🚿 🚻 WiFi

Accommodation available: 3 yurts from £80 per night.

Changeover days: Any day

Additional site information: 2 acre site. 🚫 No pets, no stag or hen parties. Two yurts sleep 6; 1 yurt sleeps 4. Each has wood-burning stove (including oven and hob). Firewood. Dedicated private bathroom. Towels and bedding provided. Yurt field car-free with children's activities available. Yurts set around orchard and meadow.

ISLE OF MULL

CRAIGNURE — Map 20 NM73

Places to visit

Duart Castle, CRAIGNURE, PA64 6AP, 01680 812309
www.duartcastle.com

Shieling Holidays Mull

►►►► 88%

tel: 01680 812496 **PA65 6AY**
email: info@isleofmullcampsite.co.uk **web:** www.shielingholidays.co.uk
dir: *From ferry left onto A849 to Iona. 400 metres, left at church, follow site signs towards sea.*

A lovely site on the water's edge with spectacular views, and less than one mile from the ferry landing. Hardstandings and service points are provided for motorhomes, and there are astro-turf pitches for tents. The excellent toilet and shower facilities were fully refurbished for 2019. The park also offers cottages and unique, en suite Shieling cottage tents for hire and bunkhouse accommodation for families. There is also a wildlife trail on site.

Open: Early March to end October **Last arrival:** 19.30 **Last departure:** noon

Pitches: 🚐 from £27; 🚐 from £27; ⚊ from £20.50; 30 hardstanding pitches

Leisure: 🎣 🎮

Facilities: 🏪 ☺ 🚰 ⚒ ♿ 🚻 WiFi

Services: 🔌 🔋 🚮 🛢

Within 3 miles: 🚶 🎣 🛒

Additional site information: 7 acre site. 🐕 Cars can be parked by caravans and tents. Awnings permitted. No BBQs or open fires on any grassed areas – only permitted at designated campfire area or on shore. Wildlife trail and enchanting coastline. Car hire can be arranged.

ISLE OF SKYE

EDINBANE
Map 22 NG35

Places to visit

Dunvegan Castle and Gardens, DUNVEGAN, IV55 8WF, 01470 521206
www.dunvegancastle.com

Skye Camping & Caravanning Club Site

▶▶▶▶ 95%

tel: 01470 582230 & 024 7647 5426 **Loch Greshornish, Borve IV51 9PS**
email: skye.site@campingandcaravanningclub.co.uk
web: www.campingandcaravanningclub.co.uk/skye
dir: *Approximately 12 miles from Portree on A850 (Dunvegan road). Site by loch shore.*

This campsite is memorable for its stunning waterside location and glorious views, the generous pitch density, the overall range of its facilities, and the impressive ongoing improvements made by the enthusiastic franchisee owners. The layout maximises the beauty of the scenery, and genuine customer care is very evident – an excellent tourist information room and campers' shelter being just two examples. The amenity block has smart, modern fittings, including excellent showers, a generously proportioned disabled room and a family bathroom. This is a 'green' site that uses only eco-friendly toilet fluids, which are available on site. There is a shop, two yurts and two camping pods for hire. Non-club members are very welcome too.

Open: April to October **Last arrival:** 20.00 (earliest arrival 13.00) **Last departure:** noon

Pitches: 🚐 🚌 ▲; 🏠 see prices below; 44 hardstanding pitches

Leisure: ✐

Facilities: 🛁 ☉ ⊮ ✳ & ⑤ ☴ WiFi

Services: 🔌 ⑥ 🧺 ♨ ♿ ⌀ T

Within 3 miles: ↥ ↻

Additional site information: 7.5 acre site. 🐕 Cars can be parked by caravans and tents. Awnings permitted. Barrier locked 23.00–07.00. Car hire can be arranged.

Glamping available: 2 wooden pods from £43; 2 yurts from £80.
Changeover days: Any day

Additional glamping information: Wooden pods: 2 nights minimum stay. Yurts: 2 nights minimum stay. Cars can be parked by units.

STAFFIN
Map 22 NG46

Staffin Camping & Caravanning
▶▶▶ 82%

tel: 01470 562213 **IV51 9JX**
email: staffincampsite@btinternet.com **web:** www.staffincampsite.co.uk
dir: *On A855, 16 miles north of Portree. Turn right before 40mph signs.*

This site provides an ideal base to rest and appreciate the peace and tranquillity of the north of Skye. It is a large sloping grassy site with level hardstandings for motorhomes and caravans. The site has older but good amenities. Nearby Staffin has a village store and a number of cafés. Sea and loch fishing are available nearby and the Totternish Ridge and surrounding area offer ample hill walking opportunities. It is a relatively short drive over the Quirang to reach the ferry terminal at Uig.

Open: April to October **Last arrival:** 20.00 **Last departure:** 11.00

Pitches: 🚐 🚌 ▲; 18 hardstanding pitches

Leisure: ✐

Facilities: ☉ ⊮ ✳ & ☴ ☴ WiFi

Services: 🔌 ⑥ 🧺 ♨ ⌀

Within 3 miles: ✐ ↥ ⑤

Additional site information: 2.5 acre site. 🐕 ☻ Cars can be parked by caravans and tents. Awnings permitted. No music after 22.00. In wet weather may not be possible to park cars by accomodation. Picnic tables, kitchen area, campers' bothy.

Wales

Wales

Wales – a place of myth and legend, a country loved passionately by actors and poets and male voice choirs, a land of rugged mountain grandeur and craggy, meandering coastline. Crossing the Severn Bridge, you sense at once you are entering a completely different country. The culture is different, so are the traditions and so are the physical characteristics. With its lush hills and dramatic headlands, it has echoes of other Celtic lands – most notably, Ireland and Scotland.

Wales's legacy of famous names from the world of the arts is truly impressive. Richard Burton hailed from the valleys in South Wales, Anthony Hopkins originates from Port Talbot and Dylan Thomas was born over a century ago in a house on a hilltop street in Swansea. His birthplace in Cwmdonkin Drive can be hired for self-catering breaks and holidays and there is even the chance to sleep in the poet's tiny bedroom. Thomas described the house as 'a provincial villa…a small, not very well painted gateless house…very nice, very respective.'

Further west is the house where he lived in his final years. Thomas and his wife Caitlin moved to the Boat House at Laugharne, 40 miles from Swansea, in the spring of 1949. With its magnificent views across an expansive estuary, this was Dylan Thomas's perfect retreat and much of his creative writing was completed in the modest wooden shed on a bluff above the house. The Boat House is open to visitors and nearby Brown's Hotel, his favourite watering hole, offers the chance to relax and enjoy something to eat and drink.

On the Pembrokeshire coast, renowned for its beautiful beaches, is another, less familiar link with Dylan Thomas. The old fishing village of Lower Fishguard was home to a film unit of almost 100 people in the early months of 1971. Presided over by the film director Andrew Sinclair, filming of Thomas's classic play *Under Milk Wood* began, with Richard Burton and Peter O'Toole among the many film stars seen around the village. A young, virtually unknown David Jason, also appeared in the film. Sinclair and his team built false fronts on the dock cottages and created an undertaker's parlour – among other work. The National Eisteddfod in Llangollen is one of the most important events in the Welsh cultural calendar, celebrating the country's long heritage of storytelling, music and poetry.

Think of Wales and you often think of castles. The formidable Caernarfon Castle, the setting for the investure of the Prince of Wales in 1969, stands in the northwest corner of the country. Harlech Castle was built around 1283 by Edward I and from it are seen the peaks of Snowdonia. This glorious region of towering summits and crags, which has the highest range of mountains in England and Wales and is now a National Park, has long attracted walkers and climbers. Edmund Hillary and his team rehearsed here for the first successful assault on Everest in 1953. However, Snowdonia is not just about mountain peaks. There are plenty of gentler alternatives, including an extensive network of lowland routes, forest trails and waymarked walks. Below Snowdon lies the historic village of Llanberis, one of the region's most popular attractions and ideally placed for touring Snowdonia. Betws-y-Coed is another mountain resort with a range of delightful walks exploring picturesque river scenery and pretty, pastoral uplands.

For the buzz and vibrancy of the city, Swansea and Cardiff cannot be beaten, the latter boasting a lively café culture, docklands-style apartments, a science discovery centre that's fun for all the family, and the internationally renowned Wales Millennium Centre (Canolfan Mileniwm Cymru). However, in terms of Welsh scenery, there is so much waiting to be discovered and explored; the grand, immensely varied landscape of the Brecon Beacons, and the gentler, pastoral acres of the Welsh Borders – among a host of famed beauty spots throughout Wales.

◁ The Preseli Hills

ISLE OF ANGLESEY

BEAUMARIS
Map 14 SH67

Places to visit

Beaumaris Castle, BEAUMARIS, LL58 8AP, 01248 810361
cadw.gov.wales/daysout/beaumaris-castle

Kingsbridge Caravan Park
►►►► 84%

tel: 01248 490636 & 07774 842199 **Camp Road, Llanfaes LL58 8LR**
email: info@kingsbridgecaravanpark.co.uk **web:** www.kingsbridgecaravanpark.co.uk
dir: *From either Menai Bridge or Britannia Bridge follow signs for Beaumaris and A545. In Beaumaris (castle on left) take B5109 towards Llangoed, 2 miles to crossroads, turn left signed Kingsbridge.*

Peacefully located two miles from historic Beaumaris, this long-established park has been transformed by its caring owners into a must-stay destination for lovers of walking and wildlife. The generously sized pitches are located in two separate touring areas – one for families and one for adults only – each has its own modern, well-equipped amenity block that are smartly presented with quality decor and fittings. Fully serviced pitches with generous hardstandings were added in 2019.

Open: March to October **Last arrival:** 21.00 **Last departure:** noon

Pitches: 🚐 from £19; 🚏 from £19; ▲ from £19; 21 hardstanding pitches; 25 seasonal pitches

Leisure: ⚑ ⚽

Facilities: 🛁 ⊙ ⌁ ✳ ⑤ 📶

Services: 🔌 🗑 🛒 ⛟ 🛢 ⊘ Ⓣ

Within 3 miles: ⌁ ⌁ ∪ ≋

Additional site information: 14 acre site. 🐾 Cars can be parked by caravans and tents. Awnings permitted. No noise after 23.00, no camp fires.

DULAS
Map 14 SH48

Places to visit

Din Lligwy Hut Group, LLANALLGO, 0300 0256000
cadw.gov.wales/visit/places-to-visit/din-lligwy-hut-group

Premier Park

Tyddyn Isaf Caravan Park
►►►►► 93%

tel: 01248 410203 **Lligwy Bay LL70 9PQ**
email: mail@tyddynisaf.co.uk **web:** www.tyddynisaf.co.uk
dir: *Take A5025 through Benllech to Moelfre roundabout, left towards Amlwch to Brynrefail. Turn right to Lligwy at phone box. Site 0.5 mile down lane on right.*

A beautifully situated, and very spacious family park on rising ground adjacent to a sandy beach, with magnificent views overlooking Lligwy Bay. A private footpath leads directly to the beach and there is an excellent nature trail around the park. The site has very good toilet facilities, including a block with underfloor heating and excellent unisex privacy cubicles, a well-stocked shop, and bar/restaurant serving meals, which are best enjoyed on the terrace with its magnificent coast and sea views. A separate, quality amenity block with good privacy options is provided for campers, and a superb modern gym and business centre are additional benefits. Dogs are welcome in the two superb sea-view Mediterranean beach huts.

Open: March to October (restricted service: March to July and September to October – opening times in bar and shop reduced) **Last arrival:** 21.30 **Last departure:** 11.00

Pitches: 🚐 from £23; 🚏 from £23; ▲ from £18; 60 hardstanding pitches; 50 seasonal pitches

Leisure: ⚑ ▭ 🦯

Facilities: 🛁 ⊙ ⌁ ✳ ♿ ⑤ ⏢ 📶

Services: 🔌 🗑 🍽 🍴 ♨ 🛒 ⛟ 🛢 ⊘ Ⓣ

Within 3 miles: ⌁ ⌁ ≋ ≋

Additional site information: 16 acre site. 🐾 Cars can be parked by caravans and tents. Awnings permitted. No groups, loud music or open fires, maximum 3 units can be booked together. Baby changing unit. Woodland walk. Business centre.

DWYRAN
Map 14 SH46

Places to visit
Great for kids: Anglesey Sea Zoo, BRYNSIENCYN, LL61 6TQ, 01248 430411
www.angleseyseazoo.co.uk

AA GLAMPING SITE OF THE YEAR 2020

Premier Park

LLanfair Hall

91% GLAMPING ONLY

tel: 01248 440031 & 07946 388869 **LL61 6AX**
email: stay@llanfairhall.com **web:** www.llanfairhall.com
dir: *Cross Menai Strait on A55. Immediately left, then left onto A4080. After 8 miles right onto B4419, then 2nd left. Keep right at fork, 1st house on right.*

Located within a peaceful, small rural estate and convenient for Newborough Beach and many of Anglesey's attractions, this must-do holiday destination is perfect for that 'away from it all' experience, whether you're looking for an activity or relaxing break. Five large pods, created from seasoned wood and lined with sheep wool for extra insulation, are carefully equipped with specially designed furnishings, and all benefit from quality en suite wet rooms with shower, washbasin and toilet. In addition to some cooking and food storage facilities, a communal, well-equipped campers' kitchen, drying room and outdoor covered barbecue are also provided. The larger log cabin is ideal for families and a light-limiting policy ensures breathtaking views of the night sky. A large 18th-century barn has been converted to a base ideally suitable for large family groups or as a hub for team building exercises.

Open: All year **Last arrival:** anytime **Last departure:** 10.15

Facilities: 🛁 ☀ 🍴 🎾

Within 3 miles: 🎣 ∪ 🛒

Accommodation available: 5 wooden pods from £70; 1 log cabin from £50 per person per night (minimum stay 2 nights).

Changeover days: Any day

Additional site information: 5 acre site. 🐕 Table tennis, giant chess, outdoor pizza ovens, geodome.. Pods – personal BBQ/fire pit, fridge, bathroom, Freeview TV, double and sofa bed. Shared access to communal field kitchen, drying room, and covered BBQ building.

MARIAN-GLAS
Map 14 SH58

Places to visit
Din Lligwy Hut Group, LLANALLGO, 0300 0256000
cadw.gov.wales/visit/places-to-visit/din-lligwy-hut-group

Capel Lligwy, LLANALLGO, 03000 256000
cadw.gov.wales/visit/places-to-visit/capel-lligwy

Platinum Park

Home Farm Caravan Park
▶▶▶▶▶

tel: 01248 410614 **LL73 8PH**
email: enq@homefarm-anglesey.co.uk **web:** www.homefarm-anglesey.co.uk
dir: *On A5025, 2 miles north of Benllech. Site 300 metres beyond church.*

A first-class park run with passion and enthusiasm, set in an elevated and secluded position sheltered by trees, and with good planting and landscaping. The peaceful rural setting affords views of farmland, the sea and the mountains of Snowdonia. The modern toilet blocks are spotlessly clean and well maintained, and there are excellent play facilities for children both indoors and out. Facilities also include a visitors' parking area and a smart reception and shop. The area is blessed with sandy beaches, and the local pubs and shops cater for everyday needs.

Open: April to October **Last arrival:** 21.00 **Last departure:** noon

Pitches: * 🚐 from £25.50; 🚍 from £25.50; ⛺ from £21.50; 65 hardstanding pitches

Leisure: 🎱 🏊 🎣 ▢ ⚽

Facilities: 🛁 ⊙ ℙ ☀ ♿ 🛒 🍴 WIFI

Services: ⚡ 🗄 🔋 ↯ 🛢 ∅ Ⓣ

Within 3 miles: ⚓ 🎣 ∪ 🏊

Additional site information: 12 acre site. 🐕 Cars can be parked by caravans and tents. Awnings permitted. No roller blades, skateboards or scooters.

RHOS LLIGWY
Map 14 SH48

Places to visit

Din Lligwy Hut Group, LLANALLGO, 0300 0256000
cadw.gov.wales/visit/places-to-visit/din-lligwy-hut-group

Capel Lligwy, LLANALLGO, 03000 256000
cadw.gov.wales/visit/places-to-visit/capel-lligwy

Ty'n Rhos Caravan Park
▶▶▶ 80%

tel: 01248 852417 **Lligwy Bay, Moelfre LL72 8NL**
email: robert@bodafonpark.co.uk **web:** www.bodafonpark.co.uk
dir: Take A5025 from Benllech to Moelfre roundabout, right to T-junction in Moelfre. Left, approximately 2 miles, pass crossroads leading to beach, site 50 metres on right.

A family park close to the beautiful beach at Lligwy Bay, and cliff walks along the Heritage Coast. Historic Din Lligwy and the shops at picturesque Moelfre are nearby. All the touring pitches have water, electric hook-up and TV connection. Amenities, including toilets, showers and a laundry, are equipped with stylish fixtures and fittings. Please note that guests should register at Bodafon Caravan Park in Benllech where detailed directions will be given and pitches allocated.

Open: March to October **Last arrival:** 20.00 **Last departure:** 11.00
Pitches: 🚐 🚍 ▲; 4 hardstanding pitches; 48 seasonal pitches
Facilities: 🖼 ☉ ☀ ♿ 🛏 WiFi
Services: 🔌 🗑 🔒
Within 3 miles: ↓ 🔗 ∪ 🛶 🏧

Additional site information: 10 acre site. 🚗 Cars can be parked by caravans and tents. Awnings permitted. No campfires, no noise after 23.00. Boat park.

BRIDGEND

PORTHCAWL

Places to visit

Newcastle, BRIDGEND, 0300 0256000
cadw.gov.wales/visit/places-to-visit/newcastle-bridgend

Coity Castle, COITY, CF35 6BG, 03000 256000
cadw.gov.wales/visit/places-to-visit/coity-castle

Great for kids: Margam Country Park, PORT TALBOT, SA13 2TJ, 01639 881635
www.margamcountrypark.co.uk

PORTHCAWL
Map 9 SS87

Brodawel Camping & Caravan Park
▶▶▶▶ 84%

tel: 01656 783231 **Moor Lane, Nottage CF36 3EJ**
email: info@brodawelcamping.co.uk **web:** www.brodawelcamping.co.uk
dir: M4 junction 37, A4229 towards Porthcawl. After Grove Golf Club right into Moor Lane, follow site signs.

A constantly improving immaculately maintained family park close to the sea and other attractions, with a lush grassy touring field that provides generously sized pitches, all with electric hook-up and some hardstandings available. A smart amenity block with quality decor, modern efficient fixtures and fittings also provides

good privacy options and family wet rooms. A well stocked shop, caravan storage, indoor games room and WiFi are additional benefits.

Open: April to mid October **Last arrival:** 19.00 **Last departure:** 11.00
Pitches: * 🚐 from £21; 🚍 from £21; ▲ from £21; 4 hardstanding pitches; 40 seasonal pitches
Leisure: 🎠 🎯 **Facilities:** 🖼 ☉ 🔥 ☀ ♿ 🛏 🛒 WiFi
Services: 🔌 🗑 🔧 🔒 🔗 T
Within 3 miles: ↓ 🔗 ∪ ◎ 🛶 🎿 🏧

Additional site information: 4 acre site. 🚗 Cars can be parked by caravans and tents. Awnings permitted. No noise between 22.30–8.00. Free electrical sockets, undercover picnic area.

CARMARTHENSHIRE

LLANDDAROG
Map 8 SN51

Places to visit

The National Botanic Garden of Wales, LLANARTHNE, SA32 8HN, 01558 667149
www.botanicgarden.wales

Carmarthen Caravan Park
▶▶▶ 80%

tel: 01267 275666 & 07484 711340 **Coedhirion SA32 8BQ**
email: welshfarmhouse@hotmail.com **web:** www.welshfarm.co.uk
dir: M4 junction 49, A48 towards Carmarthen. Straight on at Cross Hands roundabout. Left at Fferm Coedhiriaon brown sign. Site entrance 1st right.

Ideally located between the end of the M4 and Carmarthen, this rural farm park provides a relaxing and peaceful environment for touring the many attractions in the area. All the gently sloping touring pitches have electric hook-ups and there are some hardstandings for larger units and motorhomes. The amenity block provides three unisex shower, washbasin and toilet rooms. The small lake adjacent to the park is a magnet for wildlife.

Open: All year **Last arrival:** 22.00 (later if pre-arranged) **Last departure:** 14.00
Pitches: 🚐 🚍 ▲ 🏠; 10 hardstanding pitches; 5 seasonal pitches
Leisure: ⚽ **Facilities:** 🖼 ☉ 🔥 ☀ 🛏 🛒
Services: 🔌 🗑 T
Within 3 miles: ↓ 🔗 🏧

Additional site information: 5 acre site. 🚗 ⊛ Cars can be parked by caravans and tents. Awnings permitted. No noise after midnight, no Chinese lanterns. Woodland walk. Car hire can be arranged.

Glamping available: Vintage caravan from £250 per week.

Additional glamping information: Cars can be parked by unit.

LLANDOVERY

Places to visit

Dolaucothi Gold Mines, PUMSAINT, SA19 8US, 01558 650177
www.nationaltrust.org.uk/dolaucothi-gold-mines

LLANDOVERY   Map 9 SN73

Llandovery Caravan Park
▶▶▶ 80%

tel: 01550 721065 **Church Bank SA20 0DT**
email: llandoverycaravanpark@gmail.com
web: www.llandovery-caravan-camping-park.co.uk
dir: *A40 from Carmarthen, over rail crossing, past junction with A483 (Builth Wells). Turn right for Llangadog, past church, 1st right signed Rugby Club and Camping.*

Within easy walking distance of the town centre and adjacent to the notable Llandovery Dragons Rugby Club, this constantly improving park is an ideal base for touring the Brecon Beacons and many local attractions. Most pitches have both water and a hardstanding, and guests are welcome to use the popular on-site rugby club lounge bar. Please note, a laundry is not provided, but there is one in the town.

Open: All year **Last arrival:** 20.00 **Last departure:** 20.00
Pitches: 🚐 🚌 🛆; 60 seasonal pitches
Leisure: 🏓 ⚽ **Facilities:** 🏢 ⊙ 🕭 WiFi
Services: 🔌 🍺 🆚 **Within 3 miles:** 🏃 🐾 ∪ 🎡 🛒 🏧

Additional site information: 8 acre site. 🐕 🚫 Cars can be parked by caravans and tents. Awnings permitted.

NEWCASTLE EMLYN   Map 8 SN34

Places to visit

Cilgerran Castle, CILGERRAN, SA43 2SF, 01239 621339
cadw.gov.wales/daysout/cilgerran-castle

Castell Henllys Iron Age Fort, CRYMYCH, SA41 3UT, 01239 891319
www.castellhenllys.com

Premier Park

Cenarth Falls Holiday Park
▶▶▶▶▶ 90%

tel: 01239 710345 **Cenarth SA38 9JS**
email: enquiries@cenarth-holipark.co.uk web: www.cenarth-holipark.co.uk
dir: *From Newcastle Emlyn on A484 towards Cardigan. Through Cenarth, site on right.*

Located close to the village of Cenarth where the River Teifi, famous for its salmon and trout fishing, cascades through the Cenarth Falls Gorge. With beautifully landscaped grounds and spotless amenities, the park also benefits from Coracles Health & Country Club with indoor swimming pool, well-equipped gym, sauna and steam room, a bar serving evening meals (with a dog friendly section), and a function room.

Open: March to November (restricted service: off-peak season – bar and meals available at weekends only) **Last arrival:** 20.00 **Last departure:** 11.00
Pitches: 🚐 from £23; 🚌 from £23; 🛆 from £23; 27 hardstanding pitches
Leisure: 🏊 🏊 🎢 🎱 🎵 🎯
Facilities: 🏢 ⊙ 🕭 ✳ ⅄ WiFi
Services: 🔌 🔋 🍺 🍽 🔋 ↯ 🔋 🅿
Within 3 miles: 🐾 🎡 🏧

Additional site information: 2 acre site. 🐕 Cars can be parked by caravans and tents. Awnings permitted. No skateboards or hover boards. Pool table.

Moelfryn Caravan & Camping Park
▶▶▶▶ 86%

tel: 01559 371231 **Ty-Cefn, Pant-y-Bwlch SA38 9JE**
email: info@moelfryncaravanpark.co.uk web: www.moelfryncaravanpark.co.uk
dir: *A484 from Carmarthen towards Cynwyl Elfed. Pass the shops on right, 200 yards take left fork onto B4333 towards Hermon. In 7 miles follow brown sign on left. Turn left, site on right.*

A small beautifully maintained park in an elevated position overlooking the valley of the River Tefi. Pitches are level and spacious, and well screened by hedging and mature trees. The centrally located amenity block has stylish decor, smart cladding, provision of good privacy options and excellent fixtures and fittings.

Open: March to 10 January **Last arrival:** 22.00 **Last departure:** noon
Pitches: * 🚐 from £14.50; 🚌 from £14.50; 🛆 from £13.50; 25 hardstanding pitches; 12 seasonal pitches
Facilities: 🏢 ⊙ 🕭 ✳ WiFi
Services: 🔌 🔋 🔋 🔒 🅿
Within 3 miles: 🏃 🐾 ∪ 🎡 🎢 🏧

Additional site information: 3 acre site. 🐕 Dogs must be kept on leads at all times and picked up after. Cars can be parked by caravans and tents. Awnings permitted. Games to be played in designated area only. Caravan storage, seasonal pitches.

Afon Teifi Caravan & Camping Park
▶▶▶▶ 84%

tel: 01559 370532 **Pentrecagal SA38 9HT**
email: afonteifi@btinternet.com web: www.afonteifi.co.uk
dir: *Signed from A484, 2 miles east of Newcastle Emlyn.*

Set on the banks of the River Teifi, a famous salmon and sea trout river, this secluded, family-owned and run park has good views. It is only two miles from the market town of Newcastle Emlyn. The large amenity block is equipped with modern fixtures and fittings, and free WiFi is available throughout the park. Dog owners will especially appreciate the 12 acres of land, including a river walk – here there are also benches to relax on and enjoy the sounds of the river and the birdsong.

Open: April to October **Last arrival:** 23.00
Pitches: 🚐 from £24; 🚌 from £24; 🛆 from £10; 22 hardstanding pitches; 25 seasonal pitches
Leisure: 🎢 🎱 🎯 🎯
Facilities: 🏢 ⊙ 🕭 ✳ ⅄ 🔋 🍽 🚹 WiFi
Services: 🔌 🔋 🔋 ↯ 🔒 🅿 Ⓣ
Within 3 miles: 🏃 ∪ 🏧

Additional site information: 6 acre site. 🐕 🚫 Cars can be parked by caravans and tents. Awnings permitted. No noise after midnight, no bikes or scooters to be ridden after dark. Riverside and woodland walks.

NEWCASTLE EMLYN *continued*

Argoed Meadow Caravan and Camping Site
▶▶▶▶ 83%

tel: 01239 710690 **Argoed Farm SA38 9JL**
email: argoedfarm@btinternet.com **web:** www.cenarthcampsite.co.uk
dir: *From Newcastle Emlyn on A484 towards Cenarth, take B4332. Site 300 yards on right.*

A warm welcome is assured at this attractive and immaculately maintained site, situated on the banks of the River Teifi and close to Cenarth Falls Gorge. The spotlessly clean amenity block provides very good privacy options for less mobile visitors.

Open: All year **Last arrival:** anytime **Last departure:** noon

Pitches: * 🚐 from £22; 🚐 from £22; 🛆 from £22; 5 hardstanding pitches; 10 seasonal pitches

Leisure: 🎣

Facilities: 🛁 ⊙ 🅿 ☀ 🕭 ⑤ 🧺

Services: 🔌 🗑 🍴 🏺 🛒

Within 3 miles: ∪ 目

Additional site information: 3 acre site. 🐾 🐕 Cars can be parked by caravans and tents. Awnings permitted. No bikes or skateboards.

ABERAERON
Map 8 SN46

Places to visit

Llanerchaeron, ABERAERON, SA48 8DG, 01545 570200
www.nationaltrust.org.uk/llanerchaeron

Cae Hir Gardens, CRIBYN, SA48 7NG, 01570 471116
www.caehirgardens.com

Aeron Coast Caravan Park
▶▶▶ 93%

tel: 01545 570349 **North Road SA46 0JF**
email: enquiries@aeroncoast.co.uk **web:** www.aeroncoast.co.uk
dir: *From Aberaeron on A487 (coast road) towards Aberystwyth. Filling station on left at entrance.*

A well-managed family holiday park on the edge of the attractive resort of Aberaeron, with direct access to the beach. All the spacious pitches are level. On-site facilities include an extensive outdoor pool complex, a multi-activity outdoor sports area, an indoor children's play area, a games room and an entertainment suite.

Open: March to October **Last arrival:** 23.00 **Last departure:** 11.00

Pitches: 🚐 🚐 🛆; 30 hardstanding pitches

Leisure: 🏊 🎢 🛝 🔍 🖵 🎵 🎾

Facilities: 🛁 ⊙ 🅿 ☀ 🕭 WiFi

Services: 🔌 🗑 🍴 🏺 🛒 🚽 🔒 🌀 ⊤

Within 3 miles: 🎣 ∪ 🏌 ⑤

Additional site information: 22 acre site. 🐾 Cars can be parked by caravans and tents. Awnings permitted. Families only. No motorcycles.

BORTH

Places to visit

Amgueddfa Ceredigion Museum, ABERYSTWYTH, SY23 2AQ, 01970 633088
www.ceredigionmuseum.wales/

Vale of Rheidol Railway, ABERYSTWYTH, SY23 1PG, 01970 625819
www.rheidolrailway.co.uk

LEISURE: 🏊 Indoor swimming pool 🏊 Outdoor swimming pool 🎢 Children's playground 🧒 Kids' club 🎾 Tennis court 🎱 Games room 🖵 Separate TV room 🏌 Golf course 🚩 Pitch n putt 🚣 Boats for hire 🚲 Bikes for hire 🎬 Cinema 🎵 Entertainment 🎣 Fishing ◎ Mini golf 🏄 Watersports 🏋 Gym 🏟 Sports field ∪ Stables
FACILITIES: 🛁 Baths/Shower ⊙ Electric shaver sockets 🅿 Hairdryer ☀ Ice Pack Facility 🍼 Baby facilities 🕭 Disabled facilities ⑤ Shop on site or within 200yds 🍴 BBQ area 🪑 Picnic area WiFi WiFi

BORTH
Map 14 SN69

Northfield Holiday Park
▶▶▶ 80% HOLIDAY HOME PARK

tel: 01970 871464 & 07798 915769 **Clarach Road SY24 5NR**
email: info@northfieldholidays.co.uk **web:** northfieldholidays.co.uk
dir: *Off A487, west towards B4353 at roundabout 1st exit onto B4572, bear left, holiday park on left.*

Celebrating 75 years as a holiday destination in 2020, this park provides 1980s and 1990s retro static caravans and two spacious timbered lodges for hire. Interiors of homes are very well maintained, equipped with lots of homely extras and generous spacing between units creates optimum privacy. The beautifully tended grounds create colour all year round due to the wide variety of indigenous and cultivated shrubs and hedging, which combine with some stunning coastal views to create an ambience of peace and relaxation.

Open: All year **Last arrival:** 23.00 **Last departure:** 10.00

Leisure: ⚽ ⛳

Facilities: 📷 ⊙ ℙ ⅋ 🚻 WiFi

Within 3 miles: ≥ 目

Additional site information: 2.5 acre site. 🐾 Dogs must be kept on leads, cleaned up after, not left unattended and restrictions apply. No ball games unless on play area. Children under 16 to be supervised at all times.

NEW QUAY
Map 8 SN35

Places to visit
Llanerchaeron, ABERAERON, SA48 8DG, 01545 570200
www.nationaltrust.org.uk/llanerchaeron

Premier Park

Quay West Holiday Park
▶▶▶▶▶ 88% HOLIDAY HOME PARK

tel: 01545 560477 **SA45 9SE**
email: quaywest@haven.com **web:** www.haven.com/quaywest
dir: *From Cardigan on A487 left onto A486 into New Quay. Or from Aberystwyth on A487 right onto B4342 into New Quay.*

This holiday park enjoys a stunning clifftop position overlooking picturesque New Quay and Cardigan Bay. It's an easy walk to a glorious sandy beach, and the all-action on-site activities include heated swimming pools, SplashZone, football, archery and fencing (with professional tuition), the Aqua Bar and terrace and a kiddies' Pic 'n' Paint room. There is a good range of holiday caravans.

Open: mid March to October

Holiday Homes: Sleep 8 Bedrooms 2 Bathrooms 1 Toilet 1 Microwave Freezer TV Sky/Freeview

Leisure: ≋ ≋ 🎢 👋 ♨

Facilities: 🛒 ⅋ 🚻 WiFi

Services: 🍽 🍴 🍔

Additional site information: The facilities provided in the holiday homes may differ depending on the grade. 🐾 Most dog breeds accepted (please check when booking). Dogs must be kept on leads at all times.

CONWY

BETWS-YN-RHOS
Map 14 SH97

Places to visit
Conwy Castle, CONWY, LL32 8AY, 01492 592358
cadw.gov.wales/visit/places-to-visit/conwy-castle

Bodnant Garden, TAL-Y-CAFN, LL28 5RE, 01492 650460
www.nationaltrust.org.uk/bodnantgarden

Plas Farm Caravan & Lodge Park
▶▶▶▶ 88%

tel: 01492 680254 & 07831 482176 **LL22 8AU**
email: info@plasfarmcaravanpark.co.uk **web:** www.plasfarmcaravanpark.co.uk
dir: *A55 junction 24, A547 through Abergele, straight on at 2 mini-roundabouts, follow Rhyd-Y-Foel signs, 3 miles. Left, follow signs.*

Ideally located for exploring the many attractions of the north Wales coast and within easy travelling distance of both Caernarfon and Chester, this constantly improving and beautifully landscaped park, set adjacent to a 16th-century farmhouse, is certainly a popular choice. There are superb pitches, many fully serviced and on a terraced area, serviced by a choice of amenity blocks, one with good privacy options. A new development of luxury lodges is located in the former camping area and a woodland walk guarantees peace and relaxation with only birdsong a welcome distraction. A quality laundry and campers' kitchen are additional benefits and a warm welcome is assured.

Open: March to October **Last arrival:** 19.00 **Last departure:** 11.00

Pitches: 🚐 🚍; 54 hardstanding pitches

Leisure: 🎣

Facilities: 📷 ⊙ ℙ ✳ ⅋ 🚻 WiFi

Services: 🔌 🍽 🍔 🔋 ⅂⅃ ⛽ Ⓣ

Within 3 miles: ⚽ 🎣 ♨ ≥ 目 ⓢ

Additional site information: 10 acre site. 🐾 Cars can be parked by caravans. Awnings permitted. No large groups, no campfires. Quiet after 23.00. Woodland walk, shopping service. Car hire can be arranged.

BETWS-YN-RHOS *continued*

Hunters Hamlet Caravan Park

►►►► 85%

tel: 01745 832237 & 07721 552105 **Sirior Goch Farm LL22 8PL**
email: huntershamlet@aol.com **web:** www.huntershamlet.co.uk
dir: *From A55 (westbound), A547 junction 24 into Abergele. At 2nd lights turn left by George and Dragon pub, onto A548. 2.75 miles, right at crossroads onto B5381. Site 0.5 mile on left.*

A warm welcome is assured at this long established, family-run working farm park adjacent to the owners' Georgian farmhouse. Well-spaced pitches, including 15 with water, electricity and TV hook-up, are within two attractive hedge-screened grassy paddocks. The well-maintained amenity block, includes unisex bathrooms. Please note, this site does not accept tents.

Open: March to October **Last arrival:** 22.00 **Last departure:** noon

Pitches: 🚐 from £18; 🚏 from £18; 30 hardstanding pitches

Leisure: 🛝

Facilities: 🛁 ☉ 𝔽 ✳ ♿ 🎴 📶

Services: 🔌 🔄 🚮 🚰

Within 3 miles: 🛒 ✎ 🖏

Additional site information: 2.5 acre site. 🐕 Dogs must not be left unattended. Cars can be parked by caravans. Awnings permitted. No football. Family bathroom.

LLANDDULAS   Map 14 SH97

Places to visit

Rhuddlan Castle, RHUDDLAN, LL18 5AD, 01745 590777
cadw.gov.wales/daysout/rhuddlancastle

Conwy Castle, CONWY, LL32 8AY, 01492 592358
cadw.gov.wales/visit/places-to-visit/conwy-castle

Premier Park

Bron-Y-Wendon Caravan Park

Best of British

►►►►► 88%

tel: 01492 512903 **Wern Road LL22 8HG**
email: stay@bronywendon.co.uk **web:** www.bronywendon.co.uk
dir: *From A55 towards Llandudno turn right at Llanddulas and A547 junction 23 sign, sharp right. 200 yards, under A55 bridge. Park on left.*

A top quality site in a stunning location, with panoramic sea views from every pitch and very good purpose-built toilet facilities including heated shower blocks. Pitch density is excellent, offering a high degree of privacy, and the grounds are beautifully landscaped and immaculately maintained. Super pitches are available. The staff are helpful and friendly, and everything from landscaping to maintenance has a stamp of excellence. An ideal seaside base for touring Snowdonia and visiting Colwyn Bay, Llandudno and Conwy.

Open: All year **Last arrival:** 19.00 summer/17.00 winter **Last departure:** 11.00

Pitches: * 🚐 from £23; 🚏 from £23; 110 hardstanding pitches

Leisure: 🛝

Facilities: 🛁 ☉ 𝔽 ✳ ♿ 📶

Services: 🔌 🔄 🚮 🛢 🧺 Ⓣ

Within 3 miles: 🛒 ✎ 🚴 ⚓ 🖏

Additional site information: 8 acre site. 🐕 Dogs must be kept on a lead at all times. Cars can be parked by caravans. Awnings permitted. No loose ball games, kites or frisbees. Late arrival bays, 4 holiday cottages, children's play area. Adjacent to Wales Coast path/cycle route.

LLANRWST

Places to visit

Gwydir Uchaf Chapel, LLANRWST, 0300 0256000
cadw.gov.wales/visit/places-to-visit/gwydir-uchaf-chapel

Trefriw Woollen MillsTREFRIW, LL27 0NQ, 01492 640462
www.t-w-m.co.uk

Great for kids: Conwy Valley Railway Museum, BETWS-Y-COED, LL24 0AL, 01690 710568, www.conwyrailwaymuseum.co.uk

---

LEISURE: 🏊 Indoor swimming pool 🏊 Outdoor swimming pool 🛝 Children's playground 🧒 Kids' club ⚏ Tennis court 🎱 Games room ⬚ Separate TV room 🛒 Golf course ⛳ Pitch n putt 🚣 Boats for hire 🚲 Bikes for hire 🎬 Cinema 🎵 Entertainment 🎣 Fishing ⚓ Mini golf 🤽 Watersports 🏋 Gym 🏉 Sports field ♘ Stables
FACILITIES: 🛁 Baths/Shower ☉ Electric shaver sockets 𝔽 Hairdryer ✳ Ice Pack Facility 🚼 Baby facilities ♿ Disabled facilities 🖏 Shop on site or within 200yds 🍖 BBQ area 🧺 Picnic area 📶 WiFi

LLANRWST
Map 14 SH86

Premier Park

Bron Derw Touring Caravan Park
▶▶▶▶▶ 88%

tel: 01492 640494 **LL26 0YT**
email: bronderw@aol.com **web:** www.bronderw-wales.co.uk
dir: A55 onto A470 for Betws-y-Coed and Llanrwst. In Llanrwst left into Parry Road signed Llanddoged. Left at T-junction, site signed at 1st farm entrance on right.

A previous AA campsite award winner, Bron Derw, once a dairy farm, is beautifully landscaped with stunning floral displays and surrounded by hills. The park has been built to a very high standard and is fully matured. All pitches are fully serviced, and there is a heated, stone-built toilet block with excellent and immaculately maintained facilities. The Parc Derwen adults-only field has 28 fully serviced pitches and its own designated amenity block. CCTV security cameras cover the whole park.

Open: March to October **Last arrival:** 21.00 **Last departure:** 11.00
Pitches: 🚐 from £25.50; 🚍 from £25.50; 48 hardstanding pitches; 17 seasonal pitches
Facilities: 🏠 ☺ ☞ ♿ 🛒 WiFi
Services: 🔌 🎲 🛒 ↯ T
Within 3 miles: ◞ 🏬

Additional site information: 4.5 acre site. 🐕 Cars can be parked by caravans. Awnings permitted. Children must be supervised, no bikes, scooters or skateboards, no noise after 23.00.

Bodnant Caravan Park
▶▶▶▶ 86%

tel: 01492 640248 **Nebo Road LL26 0SD**
email: ermin@bodnant-caravan-park.co.uk **web:** www.bodnant-caravan-park.co.uk
dir: From A470 in Llanrwst at lights take B5427 signed Nebo (opposite garage). Immediately right signed Nebo. Site 300 yards on right, opposite leisure centre.

This well maintained and stunningly attractive park is filled with flower beds, and the landscape includes shrubberies and trees. The statics are unobtrusively sited and the quality, spotlessly clean toilet blocks have fully serviced private cubicles.

All caravan pitches are multi-service, and the tent pitches serviced. There is a separate playing field and rally field, and there are some farm animals on the park to keep children entertained. Victorian farming implements are on display around the touring fields.

Open: March to end October **Last arrival:** 21.00 **Last departure:** 11.00
Pitches: 🚐 🚍 ▲; 20 hardstanding pitches
Facilities: 🏠 ☺ ☞ ♿ WiFi
Services: 🔌 🔋 ⊘
Within 3 miles: ◞ ◞ ≋ ⩲ ⩲ ⬇ 🍴

Additional site information: 5 acre site. 🐕 Cars can be parked by caravans and tents. Awnings permitted. No bikes, skateboards or camp fires, main gates locked 23.00–08.00, no noise after 23.00.

DENBIGHSHIRE

PRESTATYN
Map 15 SJ08

Places to visit

Basingwerk Abbey, HOLYWELL, CH8 7GH, 0300 0256000
cadw.gov.wales/visit/places-to-visit/basingwerk-abbey

Rhuddlan Castle, RHUDDLAN, LL18 5AD, 01745 590777
cadw.gov.wales/daysout/rhuddlancastle

Premier Park

Presthaven Beach Holiday Park
▶▶▶▶▶ 85% HOLIDAY CENTRE

tel: 01745 856471 **Gronant LL19 9TT**
email: presthavensands@haven.com **web:** www.haven.com/presthavensands
dir: A548 from Prestatyn towards Gronant. Site signed (Note: for sat nav use LL19 9ST).

Set beside two miles of superb sandy beaches and dunes (with donkeys on site at weekends), this constantly improving holiday park provides a wide range of both indoor and outdoor attractions. The small touring field at the park entrance offers all-electric pitches, a smart amenity block and a regular shuttle bus to main attractions. The centrally located entertainment area includes two indoor swimming pools, excellent children's activities and a choice of eating outlets.

Open: mid March to end October (restricted service: mid March to May and September to end October – facilities may be reduced) **Last arrival:** 20.00 **Last departure:** 10.00
Pitches: 🚐 🚍; 39 hardstanding pitches
Leisure: 🏊 ≋ 🎱 🎯 🎵
Facilities: 🏠 ☺ ♿ 🔋 🛒 WiFi
Services: 🔌 🎲 🍴 🍽 🍟 ↯
Within 3 miles: ◞ ◞ ∪ ◎ 🚌

Additional site information: 21 acre site. 🐕 Maximum 2 dogs per booking, certain dog breeds banned. No commercial vehicles, no bookings by persons under 21 years unless a family booking.

PITCHES: 🚐 Caravans 🚍 Motorhomes ▲ Tents 🏕 Glamping accommodation **SERVICES:** 🔌 Electric hook-up 🎲 Launderette 🍷 Licensed bar 🔋 Calor Gas ⊘ Campingaz T Toilet fluid 🍽 Café/Restaurant 🍟 Fast Food/Takeaway 🔋 Battery charging ↯ Motorhome service point
* 2019 prices 🚫 No credit or debit cards 🐕 Dogs permitted 🚫 No dogs

RHUALLT
Map 15 SJ07

Places to visit

Rhuddlan Castle, RHUDDLAN, LL18 5AD, 01745 590777
cadw.gov.wales/daysout/rhuddlancastle

Welsh Mountain Zoo, COLWYN BAY, LL28 5UY, 01492 532 938
welshmountainzoo.org

Penisar Mynydd Caravan Park
▶▶▶▶ 90%

tel: 01745 582227 & 07831 408017 **Caerwys Road LL17 0TY**
email: contact@penisarmynydd.co.uk **web:** www.penisarmynydd.co.uk
dir: *From A55 junction 29 follow Dyserth and brown caravan signs. Site 500 yards on right.*

A very tranquil, attractively laid-out park set in three grassy paddocks with a superb facilities block including a disabled room and dishwashing area. The majority of pitches are super pitches. Immaculately maintained throughout, the park is within easy reach of historic Chester and the seaside resort of Rhyl.

Open: 1 March to 15 January **Last arrival:** 20.00 **Last departure:** 20.00

Pitches: 🚐 from £16; 🚍 from £16; ▲ from £15; 71 hardstanding pitches; 30 seasonal pitches

Leisure: ⊛ **Facilities:** ☉ ✳ ⭑ ㅐ WiFi
Services: 🔌 🔯 🛒 🛁 🛢
Within 3 miles: ⌕ ⌔ ∪ ◉ 🎣 ☰ ⑤

Additional site information: 6.6 acre site. ⌁ Cars can be parked by caravans and tents. Awnings permitted. No cycling, no fires. Rally area.

FLINTSHIRE

HOLYWELL
Map 15 SJ17

Haulfryn Caravan Park
▶▶▶▶ 84%

tel: 07986 435564 **Babell Road, Babell CH8 8PW**
email: info@haulfryncaravanpark.co.uk **web:** www.haulfryncaravanpark.co.uk
dir: *A55 junction 31. 3rd exit to right, heading over flyover towards McDonalds. Follow A5026, take 1st exit on right. Turn right at Druids Inn and continue for 1.7 miles. Second property after chicken sheds on left.*

Located on a former garden centre and nursery and adjacent to a racecourse renowned in the late 1800s, this new family park opened for the 2019 season and is located between the historic city of Chester and the popular Victorian resort of Llandudno. All pitches are well spaced and are fully serviced and include hardstandings. A stylish amenity block provides a combined kitchen and laundry and excellent modern shower and toilet facilities.

Open: 1 March to 1 November **Last arrival:** 20.00 **Last departure:** 11.00

Pitches: * 🚐 from £20; 🚍 from £20; 29 hardstanding pitches

Facilities: 🛁 ⭑ ㅐ ㅐ
Services: 🔌 🔯 ⊞ ⊤
Within 3 miles: ⌕ ⌔ ∪

Additional site information: 1.8 acre site. ⌁ Dogs must be kept on leads at all times. Cars can be parked by caravans. Awnings permitted.

GWYNEDD

ABERSOCH
Map 14 SH32

Places to visit

Plas-yn-Rhiw, PLAS YN RHIW, LL53 8AB, 01758 780219
www.nationaltrust.org.uk/plas-yn-rhiw

Deucoch Touring & Camping Park
▶▶▶▶ 86%

tel: 01758 713293 & 07740 281770 **Sarn Bach LL53 7LD**
email: info@deucoch.com **web:** www.deucoch.com
dir: *From Abersoch take Sarn Bach road, at crossroads turn right, site on right in 800 yards.*

This is a colourful, sheltered site with stunning views of Cardigan Bay and the mountains that is situated just a mile from Abersoch and a long sandy beach. The friendly, enthusiastic, hands-on proprietors make year-on-year improvements to enhance their visitors' experience. Facilities include a superb chalet for dishwashing, outdoor hot showers for wetsuits, and a farmer's produce van delivers at weekends.

Open: March to October **Last arrival:** 18.00 **Last departure:** 11.00

Pitches: 🚐 🚍 ▲; 10 hardstanding pitches

Leisure: ⚞
Facilities: 🛁 ☉ ⌔ ✳ ⭑ ㅐ WiFi
Services: 🔌 🔯 🛁 🛢 ⊤
Within 3 miles: ⌕ ⌔ ∪ 🎣 🔥 ⑤

Additional site information: 5 acre site. ⌁ ⊛ Cars can be parked by caravans and tents. Awnings permitted. Families only.

Beach View Caravan Park
▶▶▶▶ 85%

tel: 01758 712956 **Bwlchtocyn LL53 7BT**
email: beachviewabersoch4@gmail.com **web:** www.beachviewabersoch.co.uk
dir: *A499 to Abersoch. Through Abersoch and Sarn Bach. Straight on at crossroads, next left signed Porth Tocyn Hotel. Pass chapel. Left at next Porth Tocyn Hotel sign. Site on left.*

A long established clifftop park with stunning views of both the sea and the countryside. The grounds are immaculately maintained, and pitches are mainly hardstanding with good electric hook-ups. Just a six-minute walk from the beach.

Open: mid March to mid October **Last arrival:** 21.00 **Last departure:** noon

Pitches: 🚐 from £25; 🚍 from £25; ▲ from £10; 47 hardstanding pitches; 40 seasonal pitches

Facilities: 🛁 ☉ ⌔ ✳
Services: 🔌 🔯 ⊞ 🛢 ⊘
Within 3 miles: ⌕ ⌔ ∪ 🎣 🔥 ⑤

Additional site information: 4 acre site. ⌁ Cars can be parked by caravans and tents. Awnings permitted. Families only.

Tyn-y-Mur Touring & Camping

▶▶▶▶ 84%

tel: 01758 712328 **Lon Garmon LL53 7UL**
email: info@tyn-y-mur.co.uk **web:** www.tyn-y-mur.co.uk
dir: *From Pwllheli into Abersoch on A499, sharp right at Land and Sea Garage. Site approximately 0.5 mile on left.*

A couples and family-only park in a glorious hill-top location overlooking a lush valley and with views extending across Abersoch to the mountains beyond Cardigan Bay. Good, clean, modern toilet facilities and spacious tent pitches on a level grassy field are on offer. A pretty shrub and flower display at the entrance surrounds a ship's anchor recovered from a Royal Navy frigate which was lost in the bay in 1948. There is a pathway from the site to private river fishing, and the beach at Abersoch is just a short walk away. Free WiFi is available throughout the park.

Open: April to October (opens mid March, weather permitting) **Last arrival:** 21.00 (earliest 13.00) **Last departure:** 11.00
Pitches: * 🚐 from £33; 🚌 from £33; ▲ from £21; 54 hardstanding pitches; 54 seasonal pitches
Leisure: ⚠ 🏌 ⚽
Facilities: 🏪 ⊙ ✳ ⏦ 🗠 WiFi
Services: 🔌 🔄 🍴 🔋 🔒 ⊘ Ⓣ
Within 3 miles: ↧ ∪ 🚲 ✦ 🅂

Additional site information: 22 acre site. 🐕 1 dog per unit. Cars can be parked by caravans and tents. Awnings permitted. Couples and families only. No open fires, no motorcycles, no noise after 23.00. Boat park.

Bryn Bach Caravan & Camping Site

▶▶▶▶ 80%

tel: 07391 561160 & 07899 061737 **Tyddyn Talgoch Uchaf, Bwlchtocyn LL53 7BT**
email: brynbach@abersochcaravanandcamping.co.uk **web:** www.abersochcamping.co.uk
dir: *From Abersoch take Sarn Bach road for approximately 1 mile, turn left at sign for Bwlchtocyn. Follow signs to site, approximately 1 mile on left.*

There are stunning views towards the beach and across the bay to the Snowdonia mountains, and a warm welcome is assured at this very well-maintained park on the outskirts of Abersoch. Pitch sizes are generous and a smart chalet houses the reception, a well-stocked shop and a cycle-hire facility. Quality family rooms are available in amenity blocks and two glamping bell tents on spacious decking with stunning views are also available for hire.

Open: March to October **Last arrival:** 19.00 **Last departure:** 11.00
Pitches: 🚐 🚌 ▲; 🏠 see prices below; 28 hardstanding pitches; 28 seasonal pitches
Leisure: 🏊
Facilities: 🏪 ⊙ 🏧 ✳ ⏦ 🅂 🗠 WiFi
Services: 🔌 🔄 🔋 ⇞ 🔒 Ⓣ
Within 3 miles: ↧ 🏌 ∪ 🚲 ✦

Additional site information: 3.5 acre site. 🐕 Cars can be parked by caravans and tents. Awnings permitted. No campfires, only breathable ground sheets permitted, children must return to pitch by 21.00. Boat/jet ski park.
Glamping available: Bell tents from £85.
Additional glamping information: Bell tents: Family and couples only, no dogs allowed in tents. Cars can be parked by units.

Rhydolion
▶▶▶ 73%

tel: 01758 712342 **Llangian LL53 7LR**
email: enquiries@rhydolion.co.uk **web:** www.rhydolion.co.uk/caravan_camping.htm
dir: *From A499 take unclassified road to Llangian for 1 mile, left, through Llangian. Site 1.5 miles after road forks towards Hell's Mouth and Porth Neigwl.*

A peaceful, small site with good views, on a working farm close to the long sandy surfers beach at Hell's Mouth. The simple toilet facilities are kept to a high standard by the friendly owners, and nearby Abersoch is a mecca for boat owners and water sports enthusiasts.

Open: March to October **Last arrival:** 22.00 **Last departure:** noon
Pitches: * 🚐 from £20; 🚌 from £20; ▲ from £20
Leisure: ⚽
Facilities: ⊙ ✳
Services: 🔌 🔄 🔋
Within 3 miles: ↧ 🏌 ∪ ◎ 🚲 ✦ 🅂

Additional site information: 1.5 acre site. 🐕 Dogs only accepted by prior arrangement. 🚗 Cars can be parked by caravans and tents. Awnings permitted. Families and couples only. Fridge freezers and microwave available.

BANGOR · Map 14 SH57

Places to visit
Penrhyn Castle, BANGOR, LL57 4HT, 01248 353084
www.nationaltrust.org.uk/penrhyncastle

Storiel, BANGOR, LL57 1DT, 01248 353368
www.storiel.cymru

Great for kids: GreenWood Forest Park, Y FELINHELI, LL56 4QN, 01248 671493
www.greenwoodforestpark.co.uk

Treborth Hall Farm Caravan Park
▶▶▶ 74%

tel: 01248 364399 **The Old Barn, Treborth Hall Farm LL57 2RX**
email: enquiries@treborthleisure.co.uk **web:** www.treborthleisure.co.uk
dir: *A55 junction 9, 1st left at roundabout, straight over at 2nd roundabout, site approximately 800 yards on left.*

Set in eight acres of parkland with its own trout fishing lake and golf driving range, this park offers serviced pitches in a sheltered, walled orchard. Tents have a separate grass area, and there is a good clean toilet block. A static holiday caravan, with access for the less mobile, is available for hire. This is a useful base for families, with easy access to the Menai Straits, Anglesey beaches, Snowdon and the Lleyn peninsula.

Open: Easter to end October **Last arrival:** 22.30 **Last departure:** 10.30
Pitches: * 🚐 from £27; 🚌 from £23; ▲ from £10; 34 hardstanding pitches
Leisure: ⚠
Facilities: 🏪 🗠 WiFi
Services: 🔌
Within 3 miles: ◎ 🚲 📅 🅂 🔄

Additional site information: 8 acre site. 🐕 Cars can be parked by caravans and tents. Awnings permitted.

PITCHES: 🚐 Caravans 🚌 Motorhomes ▲ Tents 🏠 Glamping accommodation **SERVICES:** 🔌 Electric hook-up 🔄 Launderette 🍴 Licensed bar 🔒 Calor Gas ⊘ Campingaz Ⓣ Toilet fluid 🍴 Café/Restaurant 🏧 Fast Food/Takeaway 🔋 Battery charging ⇞ Motorhome service point * 2019 prices 🚫 No credit or debit cards 🐕 Dogs permitted ⊗ No dogs

BARMOUTH

Map 14 SH61

Places to visit

Harlech Castle, HARLECH, LL46 2YH, 01766 780552
cadw.gov.wales/daysout/harlechcastle

Cymer Abbey, PENRHYNDEUDRAETH, LL40 2HE, 0300 0256000
cadw.gov.wales/visit/places-to-visit/cymer-abbey

Premier Park

Trawsdir Touring Caravans & Camping Park

 ►►►►► 93%

tel: 01341 280999 & 07798 520888 **Llanaber LL42 1RR**
email: enquiries@trawsdir.co.uk web: www.barmouthholidays.co.uk
dir: *3 miles north of Barmouth on A496, just past Nor Bar on right.*

Well run by the owners, this quality park enjoys spectacular views to the sea and hills, and is very accessible for motor traffic. The facilities are appointed to a very high standard, and include spacious cubicles containing showers and washbasins, individual showers, smart toilets with sensor-operated flush and underfloor heating. Tents and caravans have their own designated areas divided by dry-stone walls (both have spacious fully serviced pitches). The site is very suitable for large recreational vehicles, and there are camping pods for hire. There is an excellent children's play area and an illuminated concrete dog walk that leads directly to the nearby pub, which offers takeaway pizza and fish suppers, in addition to restaurant meals. Fast WiFi connection is available throughout the park.

Open: March to January **Last arrival:** 17.00 **Last departure:** 11.00

Pitches: * ⛟ from £20; ⛟ from £20; ▲ from £13; ⛺ see prices below; 70 hardstanding pitches; 30 seasonal pitches

Leisure: ⋔

Facilities: 🚿 ☺ ⌇ ❊ ⛖ 🖇 🍴 ⋔ 📶

Services: 🔌 🔲 🛒 ⬆ 🔒 ⊘ 🇹

Within 3 miles: ✐ ⛸

Additional site information: 15 acre site. 🐾 Cars can be parked by caravans and tents. Awnings permitted. Families and couples only. Milk, bread etc available from reception, camping equipment available.

Glamping available: Wooden pods from £38.

Additional glamping information: Minimum stay 2 nights. Pet-friendly and no-pets-allowed pods available. Pods offer balcony area, BBQ, sea views and TV. Cars can be parked by units.

Premier Park

Hendre Mynach Touring Caravan & Camping Park

►►►►► 88%

tel: 01341 280262 **Llanaber Road LL42 1YR**
email: info@hendremynach.co.uk web: www.hendremynach.co.uk
dir: *0.75 mile north of Barmouth on A496.*

A constantly improving site where the enthusiastic owners invest year on year to enhance the customer experience. Although there is a steep decent to the arrivals' area, staff are always on hand to assist. The beautifully maintained touring areas benefit from attractive hedge screening around the large well-spaced pitches that are equipped with water and TV hook-ups. Three camping pods, two static caravans with dog friendly options and a holiday home on site are also available to rent. A well-stocked shop provides a wide range of food, beverages and caravan spares. There is direct access to the seafront which leads to the town centre and its many attractions.

Open: 1 March to 9 January (restricted service: Winter months – shop closed) **Last arrival:** 20.30 **Last departure:** 10.30

Pitches: * ⛟ from £19; ⛟ from £19; ▲ from £17 ⛺; 85 hardstanding pitches; 10 seasonal pitches

Leisure: ⋔

Facilities: 🚿 ☺ ⌇ ❊ ⛖ 🖇 📶

Services: 🔌 🔲 🛒 ⬆ 🔒 ⊘ 🇹

Within 3 miles: ✐ ⛳ ⛸ 🎣 🏑

Additional site information: 10 acre site. 🐾 Cars can be parked by caravans and tents. Awnings permitted. No open fires, no hard ball games.

Glamping available: 3 wooden pods.

Additional glamping information: Maximum 4 people. Cars can be parked by units.

 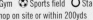

BETWS GARMON
Map 14 SH55

Places to visit
Snowdon Mountain Railway, LLANBERIS, LL55 4TT, 01286 870223
www.snowdonrailway.co.uk

Great for kids: Dolbadarn Castle, LLANBERIS, LL55 4UB, 0300 0256000
cadw.gov.wales/daysout/dolbadarncastle

Premier Park

Bryn Gloch Caravan & Camping Park
▶▶▶▶▶ 86%

tel: 01286 650216 **LL54 7YY**
email: eurig@bryngloch.co.uk **web:** www.campwales.co.uk
dir: On A4085, 5 miles southeast of Caernarfon.

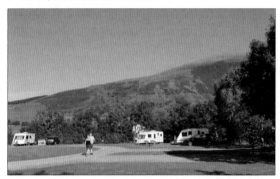

An excellent family-run site with immaculate modern facilities, and all level pitches in beautiful surroundings. The park offers the best of two worlds, with its bustling holiday atmosphere and the peaceful natural surroundings; there are plenty of walks in the area. The 28 acres of level fields are separated by mature hedges and trees, guaranteeing sufficient space for families wishing to spread themselves out. There are some excellent fully serviced camping pitches and static holiday caravans for hire.

Open: All year (restricted service: November to February – shop and games room closed) **Last arrival:** 21.00 **Last departure:** 17.00

Pitches: * 🚐 from £20; 🚐 from £20; 🛆 from £20; 80 hardstanding pitches; 80 seasonal pitches

Leisure: 🅰 🔍 ▢ ✐

Facilities: 🛖 ☺ 🅿 ✳ ♿ ⑤ 🚿 🎌 WiFi

Services: 🔌 ⑤ 🎂 🔋 ⚡ 🔧 ⊘ T

Within 3 miles: ⚲ ∪ ◎ 🌡

Additional site information: 28 acre site. 🐾 Cars can be parked by caravans and tents. Awnings permitted. No noise after 22.00. Heated family bathroom, mother and baby room, table tennis.

CAERNARFON
Map 14 SH46

See also Dinas Dinlle and Llandwrog

Places to visit
Welsh Highland Railway, CAERNARFON, LL55 2YD, 01766 516024
www.festrail.co.uk

Great for kids: Caernarfon Castle, CAERNARFON, LL55 2AY, 01286 677617
cadw.gov.wales/daysout/caernarfon-castle

Riverside Camping

▶▶▶▶ 89%

tel: 01286 678781 **Seiont Nurseries, Pont Rug LL55 2BB**
email: info@riversidecamping.co.uk **web:** www.riversidecamping.co.uk
dir: 2 miles from Caernarfon on right of A4086 towards Llanberis, follow signs at entrance.

Set in the grounds of a former garden centre and enjoying a superb location along the River Seiont, this park is approached by an impressive tree-lined drive. Immaculately maintained by the owners, there is a mixture of riverside grassy pitches and fully serviced pitches for caravans and motorhomes. Hardstanding pitches have electric hook-up, water, drainage and TV connection (particularly suitable for motorhomes). In addition to the smart amenity blocks, other facilities include an excellent café/restaurant, a volleyball court and boules pitch; river fishing permits are also available. The three superb chalets, each for six people, have wood-burning stoves, picnic gardens and Japanese hot tubs. This is a haven of peace close to Caernarfon, Snowdonia and offers some great walking opportunities.

Open: 14 March to October **Last arrival:** anytime **Last departure:** noon

Pitches: 🚐 🚐 🛆 🏠; 16 hardstanding pitches; 10 seasonal pitches

Leisure: 🅰 🔍 ✐ ⚽

Facilities: 🛖 ☺ 🅿 ✳ ♿ 🚿 🎌 WiFi

Services: 🔌 ⑤ 🔋 🔧 🎂 ⚡

Within 3 miles: ⚲ ∪ ◎ 🌡 🎣 🍴 ⑤

Additional site information: 5 acre site. 🐾 Awnings permitted. No fires, no loud music. Debit cards accepted (no credit cards). Family shower room, undercover picnic area, table tennis, volleyball. Woodland dog walk.

Glamping available: Tented lodges. **Changeover days:** Monday and Friday

Additional glamping information: Beds, linen and towels provided, fully equipped. Wood burner, no electricity. Dogs accepted in 2 units only. No stag or hen groups.

CAERNARFON *continued*

Llys Derwen Caravan & Camping Site
►►►► 86%

tel: 01286 673322 **Ffordd Bryngwyn, Llanrug LL55 4RD**
email: llysderwen@aol.com **web:** www.llysderwen.co.uk
dir: *A55 junction 11 (follow Bangor (A5) and Llanberis signs). At roundabout left signed Betws y Coed (A5) and Llanberis (A4244). At next roundabout right signed Llanberis. Right at T-junction signed Caernarfon onto A4086. Through Llanrug, left at Y Glyntwrog pub, site 500 metres on right.*

On the outskirts of the village of Llanrug, three miles from Caernarfon on the way to Llanberis and Snowdon. A beautifully maintained site with enthusiastic owners who are constantly investing to improve the facilities. The amenity block is appointed to a high standard and the immaculately maintained grounds are planted with an abundance of colourful shrubs and seasonal flowers.

Open: March to October **Last arrival:** 22.00 **Last departure:** noon
Pitches: * 🚐 from £27; 🚏 from £27; ▲ from £22
Facilities: 🛁 ⊙ ℙ ✳ ⚕
Services: 🚱 🗑 🛒 ⬇
Within 3 miles: ⅃ ℓ ∪ ⅝ ⅞ ⑤

Additional site information: 4 acre site. 🐕 🐾 Cars can be parked by caravans and tents. Awnings permitted. No open fires, no ball games, no noise after 22.00.

Plas Gwyn Caravan & Camping Park
►►►► 84%

tel: 01286 672619 **Llanrug LL55 2AQ**
email: info@plasgwyn.co.uk **web:** www.plasgwyn.co.uk
dir: *A4086, 3 miles east of Caernarfon, site on right. Between River Seiont and Llanrug.*

A secluded park in an ideal location for visiting the glorious nearby beaches, historic Caernarfon, the attractions of Snowdonia and for walking opportunities. The site is set within the grounds of Plas Gwyn House, a Georgian property with colonial additions; the friendly owners constantly improve the facilities. There is a 'breakfast butty' service and fresh tea and coffee is available for delivery to individual pitches. The pitches are all fully serviced with water, electricity and waste water disposal and most have hardstandings. Three 'timber tents' (wooden pods) and five static caravans are also available for hire.

Open: March to October **Last arrival:** 22.00 **Last departure:** 11.30
Pitches: * 🚐 from £24.50; 🚏 from £24.50; ▲ from £16 🏠; 10 hardstanding pitches; 8 seasonal pitches
Facilities: 🛁 ⊙ ℙ ✳ ⚕ ⑤ 🍺 📶
Services: 🚱 🗑 🛒 ⬇ 🛢 🚰 🚾
Within 3 miles: ⅃ ℓ ∪ ⅝ ⅞ 🎌

Additional site information: 3 acre site. 🐕 Cars can be parked by caravans and tents. Awnings permitted. Minimum noise 22.00 to midnight, complete quiet midnight to 08.00.

Glamping available: Wooden pods.

Additional glamping information: Wooden pods: maximum of 4 people per unit. Cars can be parked by units.

Eisteddfa
►►►► 91%

tel: 01766 522696 **Eisteddfa Lodge, Pentrefelin LL52 0PT**
email: info@eisteddfapark.co.uk **web:** www.eisteddfapark.co.uk
dir: *From Porthmadog take A497 towards Criccieth. Approximately 3.5 miles, through Pentrefelin, site signed 1st right after Plas Gwyn Nursing Home.*

A quiet, secluded park on elevated ground, sheltered by the Snowdonia Mountains and with lovely views of Cardigan Bay; Criccieth is nearby. The enthusiastic owners have carried out major investment in recent years to provide top-notch amenity blocks with good privacy options, especially for families. There's a field and play area, woodland walks, six superb slate-based hardstandings, a 'cocoon pod', and three static holiday caravans for hire, plus a three-acre coarse fishing lake adjacent to the park.

Open: March to October **Last arrival:** 22.30 **Last departure:** 11.00
Pitches: 🚐 from £18; 🚏 from £18; ▲ from £16; 🏠 see prices below; 17 hardstanding pitches; 20 seasonal pitches
Leisure: 🎱 ⚽
Facilities: ⊙ ℙ ✳ ⚕ 🍺 🎍
Services: 🚱 🗑 🛒 ⬇ 🛢 🚿
Within 3 miles: ⅃ ℓ ∪ ◎ ⅝ ⅞ 🎌 ⑤

Additional site information: 24 acre site. 🐕 Cars can be parked by caravans and tents. Awnings permitted. No noise after 22.30. Baby bath available.

Glamping available: 1 cabin (cocoon pod) from £22.50.

Additional glamping information: Cars can be parked by units.

Llwyn-Bugeilydd Caravan & Camping Site
►►► 85%

tel: 01766 522235 & 07752 784358 **LL52 0PN**
email: post@snowdoniacaravanpark.co.uk **web:** www.snowdoniacaravanpark.co.uk
dir: *From Porthmadog on A497, 1 mile north of Criccieth on B4411. Site 2nd on right. From A55 take A487 through Caernarfon. After Bryncir right onto B4411, site on left in 3.5 miles.*

This is a peaceful rural site, close to the coast and Snowdonia attractions, that has been greatly improved in recent years and offers well-spaced, mostly grass pitches and a stylish amenity block. Winter caravan storage and free WiFi are also available.

Open: March to October **Last arrival:** anytime **Last departure:** 11.00
Pitches: 🚐 🚏 ▲; 1 hardstanding pitches; 40 seasonal pitches
Leisure: 🅰 ⚽

LEISURE: 🏊 Indoor swimming pool 🏊 Outdoor swimming pool 🅰 Children's playground 👦 Kids' club 🎾 Tennis court 🎱 Games room 📺 Separate TV room
⅃ Golf course ⛳ Pitch n putt 🚣 Boats for hire 🚲 Bikes for hire 🎬 Cinema 🎭 Entertainment 🎣 Fishing ◎ Mini golf 🏄 Watersports 💪 Gym ⚽ Sports field ∪ Stables
FACILITIES: 🛁 Baths/Shower ⊙ Electric shaver sockets ℙ Hairdryer ✳ Ice Pack Facility 👶 Baby facilities ⚕ Disabled facilities ⑤ Shop on site or within 200yds
🍺 BBQ area 🎍 Picnic area 📶 WiFi

Facilities: 🏠 ⊙ 🅿 ☼ ☕ 🎪 WiFi
Services: 🔌 🗐 🔋
Within 3 miles: ⚓ 🎣 ∪ ◎ 🚣 ✈ 🏪

Additional site information: 6 acre site. 🐕 Cars can be parked by caravans and tents. Awnings permitted. No skateboards, no noise 22.30–08.00, caravan storage until evening of departure available if required (no charge).

DINAS DINLLE   Map 14 SH45

Places to visit

Inigo Jones Slateworks, GROESLON, LL54 7UE, 01286 830242
www.inigojones.co.uk

Caernarfon Castle, CAERNARFON, LL55 2AY, 01286 677617
cadw.gov.wales/daysout/caernarfon-castle

Great for kids: Welsh Highland Railway, CAERNARFON, LL55 2YD, 01766 516024
www.festrail.co.uk

Premier Park

Dinlle Caravan Park
►►►►► 87%

tel: 01286 830324 **LL54 5TW**
email: enquiries@dinllecaravanpark.co.uk **web:** www.thornleyleisure.co.uk
dir: *From A487 at roundabout take A499 signed Pwllheli. Right at Caernarfon Airport and brown camping signs.*

A very accessible, well-kept, grassy site adjacent to a sandy beach and with good views towards Snowdonia. The park, with a superb landscaped entrance, is situated on flat grassland that provides plenty of space for large groups. The man-made dunes offer campers additional protection from sea breezes. The lounge bar and family room are comfortable places in which to relax, and children will enjoy the exciting adventure playground. There are camping pods, with decking and barbecue areas, for hire. A golf club, a nature reserve and the Caernarfon Airworld Museum at the airport can all be accessed from the beach road.

Open: March to November **Last arrival:** 22.00 **Last departure:** noon
Pitches: 🚐 🚍 ⚠; 🏠 see prices below; 83 hardstanding pitches; 80 seasonal pitches
Leisure: ⚖ ⚠ 🎱 🎵
Facilities: 🏠 ⊙ 🅿 ☼ ⚕ 🏪 WiFi
Services: 🔌 🗐 🔟 ⚡ 🔋 ⚗
Within 3 miles: 🎣 ∪ 🚣

Additional site information: 20 acre site. 🐕 Cars can be parked by caravans and tents. Awnings permitted. No skateboards, scooters, hoverboards, boats or jetskis.
Glamping available: Wooden pods from £30. **Changeover days:** Any day
Additional glamping information: Wooden pods sleep 4. 1 double bed, 2 single beds. Minimum stay 2 nights. Cars can be parked by units.

DYFFRYN ARDUDWY   Map 14 SH52

Places to visit

Harlech Castle, HARLECH, LL46 2YH, 01766 780552
cadw.gov.wales/daysout/harlechcastle

Murmur-yr-Afon Touring Park
►►► 83%

tel: 01341 247353 **LL44 2BE**
email: murmuryrafon1@btinternet.com **web:** www.murmuryrafon.co.uk
dir: *On A496, north of Dyffryn Ardudwy.*

A long established park on the edge of the village with very good coastal views. A good base for touring the many attractions within the area and just a short distance from notable sandy beaches.

Open: March to October **Last arrival:** 22.00 **Last departure:** 11.00
Pitches: 🚐 🚍 ⚠; 37 hardstanding pitches; 30 seasonal pitches
Leisure: ⚠ **Facilities:** 🏠 ⊙ 🅿 ☼ ⚕ 🎪
Services: 🔌 🗐 🔋
Within 3 miles: ⚓ 🎣 🚣 🏪

Additional site information: 7.5 acre site. 🐕 Cars can be parked by caravans and tents. Awnings permitted.

LLANDWROG   Map 14 SH45

Places to visit

Welsh Highland Railway, CAERNARFON, LL55 2YD, 01766 516024
www.festrail.co.uk

Great for kids: Caernarfon Castle, CAERNARFON, LL55 2AY, 01286 677617
cadw.gov.wales/daysout/caernarfon-castle

White Tower Caravan Park
►►►► 91%

tel: 01286 830649 & 07802 562785 **LL54 5UH**
email: whitetower@supanet.com **web:** www.whitetowerpark.co.uk
dir: *From Caernarfon take A487 Porthmadog road. 1st right into Pant Road signed Llanfaglan and Saron. Site 3 miles on right.*

There are lovely views of Snowdonia from this park that is located just two miles from the beach at Dinas Dinlle. A very well maintained quality amenity block provides good privacy options and all pitches are fully serviced. Popular facilities include an outdoor heated swimming pool, a lounge bar with family room, and a games and TV room.

Open: March to 10 January (restricted service: March to mid May and September to November – bar closed weekdays) **Last arrival:** 23.00 **Last departure:** noon
Pitches: 🚐 from £20; 🚍 from £20; 50 hardstanding pitches; 50 seasonal pitches
Leisure: ⚖ ⚠ 🎱 ▭ 🎵
Facilities: 🏠 ⊙ 🅿 ⚕ WiFi
Services: 🔌 🗐 🔟 🔋 🔒
Within 3 miles: ⚓ 🎣 ∪ 🚣 ✈ 🏪

Additional site information: 6 acre site. 🐕 Cars can be parked by caravans. Awnings permitted.

PONT-RUG

See Caernarfon

PORTHMADOG — Map 14 SH53

Places to visit

Portmeirion, PORTMEIRION, LL48 6ER, 01766 770000
www.portmeirion-village.com

Great for kids: Ffestiniog Railway, PORTHMADOG, LL49 9NF, 01766 516024
www.festrail.co.uk

Premier Park

Greenacres Holiday Park
▶▶▶▶▶ 87% HOLIDAY CENTRE

tel: 01766 512781 **Black Rock Sands, Morfa Bychan LL49 9YF**
email: greenacres@haven.com **web:** www.haven.com/greenacres
dir: *From Porthmadog High Street follow Black Rock Sands signs between The Factory Shop and Post Office. Park 2 miles on left at end of Morfa Bychan.*

A quality holiday park on level ground just a short walk from Black Rock Sands, and set against a backdrop of Snowdonia National Park. All touring pitches are on hardstandings surrounded by closely-mown grass, and are near the entertainment complex. A full programme of entertainment, organised clubs, indoor and outdoor sports and leisure, pubs, shows and cabarets all add to a holiday experience here. The bowling alley and a large shop with a bakery are useful amenities. The superb touring field has excellent fully serviced Euro pitches, extensive, colourful planting and a smart, well-equipped amenity block.

Open: mid March to end October (restricted service: mid March to May and September to October – some facilities may be reduced) **Last arrival:** 22.00 **Last departure:** 10.00

Pitches: 🚐 🚃; 45 hardstanding pitches
Leisure: 🏊 🎠 🎣 🎵 ⚽
Facilities: 🛁 ☉ ♿ 🔋 🛒 📶
Services: 🔌 🔧 🍴 🍽 🛒 🔥 🧺
Within 3 miles: ⛳ 🎣 ⛴ ⛳ 🚤

Additional site information: 121 acre site. No commercial vehicles, no bookings by persons under 21 years unless a family booking, no open fires. 🐕 Maximum 2 dogs per booking, certain dog breeds banned.

PWLLHELI

Places to visit

Lloyd George Museum, LLANYSTUMDWY, LL52 0SH, 01766 522071
www.gwynedd.gov.uk/museums

Great for kids: Criccieth Castle, CRICCIETH, LL52 0DP, 01766 522227
cadw.gov.wales/daysout/criccieth-castle

PWLLHELI — Map 14 SH33

Premier Park

Hafan y Môr Holiday Park
▶▶▶▶▶ 92% HOLIDAY CENTRE

tel: 01758 612112 **LL53 6HJ**
email: hafanymor@haven.com **web:** www.haven.com/hafanymor
dir: *From Caernarfon take A499 to Pwllheli. A497 to Porthmadog. Park on right, approximately 3 miles from Pwllheli. Or from Telford, A5, A494 to Bala. Right for Porthmadog. Left at roundabout in Porthmadog signed Criccieth and Pwllheli. Park on left, 3 miles from Criccieth.*

Located between Pwllheli and Criccieth, and surrounded by mature trees that attract wildlife, this popular holiday centre provides a wide range of all-weather attractions. Activities include a sports hall, Dragon Lakes Outside Experiences, a large indoor swimming pool, a show bar and a high-ropes activity. There are also great eating options – the stylish Coast House bistro, Cakery ice cream and cake parlour, the Pizza Deck with wood-fired pizzas and the superb HMS Glendower bar over the bridge, and by The Splash Zone you'll find traditional fish and chips, Burger King, Papa John's and a Starbucks coffeehouse. The touring area includes 75 fully serviced all-weather pitches and a top notch, air-conditioned amenity block.

Open: mid March to end October (restricted service: mid March to May and September to end October – reduced facilities) **Last arrival:** 21.00 **Last departure:** 10.00

Pitches: 🚐 from £41; 🚃 from £41; 75 hardstanding pitches
Leisure: 🏊 🎠 🎣 🎵 🎾 🏋
Facilities: 🛁 🔋 ♿ 🔋 🛒 📶
Services: 🔌 🔧 🍴 🍽 🛒
Within 3 miles: ⛳ 🎣 ⛴ ⛳ 🚤 🎿

Additional site information: 500 acre site. 🐕 Maximum 2 dogs per booking, certain dog breeds banned. No commercial vehicles, no bookings by persons under 21 years unless a family booking.

Abererch Sands Holiday Centre
▶▶▶ 80%

tel: 01758 612327 **LL53 6PJ**
email: enquiries@abererch-sands.co.uk **web:** www.abererch-sands.co.uk
dir: *On A497 (Porthmadog to Pwllheli road), 1 mile from Pwllheli.*

Glorious views of Snowdonia and Cardigan Bay can be enjoyed from this very secure, family-run site adjacent to a railway station and a four-mile stretch of sandy beach. During the past two years, the amenity block has been completely refurbished to have stylish decor and modern, efficient fixtures and fittings. A large, heated indoor swimming pool, snooker room, pool room, fitness centre and children's play area make this an ideal holiday venue.

Open: March to October **Last arrival:** 21.00 **Last departure:** noon

Pitches: * 🚐 from £33; 🚃 from £32; ⛺ from £32; 70 hardstanding pitches
Leisure: 🏊 🎠 🎣 🏋
Facilities: 🛁 ☉ ❄ ♿ 🔋 📶
Services: 🔌 🔧 🛒 🔧 🔥 🧺 📶 📋
Within 3 miles: ⛳ 🎣 ⛴ 🚤 🎿 🎿 📅

Additional site information: 85 acre site. 🐕 Cars can be parked by caravans and tents. Awnings permitted.

LEISURE: 🏊 Indoor swimming pool 🏊 Outdoor swimming pool 🎠 Children's playground 🎣 Kids' club 🎾 Tennis court 🎮 Games room ▢ Separate TV room ⛳ Golf course 🏌 Pitch n putt 🚤 Boats for hire 🚲 Bikes for hire 🎬 Cinema 🎵 Entertainment 🎣 Fishing ◎ Mini golf 🏊 Watersports 🏋 Gym 🏉 Sports field ⛴ Stables
FACILITIES: 🛁 Baths/Shower ☉ Electric shaver sockets 🔋 Hairdryer ❄ Ice Pack Facility 🍼 Baby facilities ♿ Disabled facilities 🔋 Shop on site or within 200yds 🔥 BBQ area 🧺 Picnic area 📶 WiFi

TAL-Y-BONT · Map 14 SH52

Places to visit

Cymer Abbey, PENRHYNDEUDRAETH, LL40 2HE, 0300 0256000
cadw.gov.wales/visit/places-to-visit/cymer-abbey

Harlech Castle, HARLECH, LL46 2YH, 01766 780552
cadw.gov.wales/daysout/harlechcastle

Premier Park

Islawrffordd Caravan Park
▶ ▶ ▶ ▶ ▶ 93%

tel: 01341 247269 **LL43 2AQ**
email: info@islawrffordd.co.uk **web:** www.islawrffordd.co.uk
dir: From A496 into Ffordd Glan-Mor towards sea, follow brown campsite sign. Over rail line, site on left.

Situated on the coast between Barmouth and Harlech and within the Snowdonia National Park, this site has clear views of Cardigan Bay, the Lleyn Peninsula and the Snowdonia and Cader Idris mountain ranges. This is an excellent, family-run and family-friendly park that has seen considerable investment over recent years. Fully matured, the touring area boasts fully-serviced facilities; a superb toilet block with underfloor heating and top-quality fittings; there is private access to miles of sandy beach, adjacent to which is an excellent enclosed children's play area with imaginative quality equipment to satisfy small children, including a pirate ship. A superb restaurant and bar, 'Nineteen57', offers both formal and relaxed areas for enjoying locally-sourced food.

Open: 14 February to 3 January **Last arrival:** 20.00 **Last departure:** noon

Pitches: * 🚐 from £30; 🚐 from £30; 75 hardstanding pitches; 50 seasonal pitches

Leisure: 🏊 ⚑ 🎱 **Facilities:** 🖧 ☉ ⌔ ☼ 🏃 **WiFi**
Services: 🔌 🗑 🍺 🍴 🚮 🔋 ⚡ 🚽 🔋 ⚙ T
Within 3 miles: 🚴 🚣 💲

Additional site information: 25 acre site. 🐾 Cars can be parked by caravans and tents. Awnings permitted. Strictly families and couples only.

TYWYN · Map 14 SH50

Places to visit

Talyllyn Railway, TYWYN, LL36 9EY, 01654 710472
www.talyllyn.co.uk

Castell-y-Bere, LLANFIHANGEL-Y-PENNANT, 0300 0256000
cadw.gov.wales/visit/places-to-visit/castell-y-bere

Great for kids: King Arthur's Labyrinth, CORRIS, SY20 9RF, 01654 761584
www.kingarthurslabyrinth.co.uk

Ynysymaengwyn Caravan Park
▶ ▶ ▶ ▶ 85%

tel: 01654 710684 **LL36 9RY**
email: rita@ynysy.co.uk **web:** www.ynysy.co.uk
dir: On A493, 1 mile north of Tywyn, towards Dolgellau.

A lovely park set in the wooded grounds of a former manor house, with designated nature trails through 13 acres of wildlife-rich woodland, scenic river walks, fishing and a sandy beach nearby. The attractive stone amenity block is clean and well kept, and this smart municipal park is ideal for families. The attractive stone built amenity block is centrally heated, air conditioned and provides good privacy options; even dogs have their own external warm shower. The park is ideal for families and a fairy trail has been created within the woodland.

Open: March to November **Last arrival:** 23.00 **Last departure:** noon

Pitches: * 🚐 from £29; 🚐 from £26; ⛺ from £15; 10 hardstanding pitches; 5 seasonal pitches

Leisure: ⚑ 🎱
Facilities: 🖧 ☉ ⌔ ☼ 🏃 ⚑ **WiFi**
Services: 🔌 🗑 🔋 🚽 🔋 ⚙
Within 3 miles: 🚴 ∪ ◎ 🚣 🍴 💲

Additional site information: 4 acre site. 🐾 Cars can be parked by caravans and tents. Awnings permitted. Woodland walk.

MONMOUTHSHIRE

ABERGAVENNY · Map 9 SO21

Places to visit

Big Pit National Coal Museum, BLAENAVON, NP4 9XP, 0300 111 2333
museum.wales/bigpit/

Hen Gwrt, LLANTILIO CROSSENNY, 0300 0256000
cadw.gov.wales/visit/places-to-visit/hen-gwrt-moated-site

Great for kids: Raglan Castle, RAGLAN, NP15 2BT, 01291 690228
cadw.gov.wales/daysout/raglancastle

Wernddu Caravan Park
▶ ▶ ▶ ▶ 85%

tel: 01873 856223 **Old Ross Road NP7 8NG**
email: info@wernddu-golf-club.co.uk **web:** www.wernddu-golf-club.co.uk
dir: From A465, north of Abergavenny, take B4521 signed Skenfrith. Site on right in 0.25 mile.

Located north of the town centre, this former fruit farm, adjacent to a golf club and driving range, is managed by three generations of the same family, and has been transformed into an ideal base for those visiting the many nearby attractions. The well-spaced touring pitches have water, electricity and waste water disposal, and the smart modern amenity block provides very good privacy options. Site guests are welcome to use the golf club bar which also serves meals during the busy months; they are also eligible for half-price green fees. There is no shop on site but a daily newspaper service is provided, and a mini-market is less than a mile away.

Open: March to October **Last arrival:** 21.00 **Last departure:** noon

Pitches: 🚐 🚐 ⛺; 30 seasonal pitches
Leisure: 🚴 🎱
Facilities: 🖧 ☼ 🏃 🔋 ⚑ **WiFi**
Services: 🔌 🗑 🍺 🍴 🔋 🚽
Within 3 miles: ∪ ◎ 🍴 💲

Additional site information: 6 acre site. Adults only. 🐾 Cars can be parked by caravans and tents. Awnings permitted. No fires. No noise after 23.00. 20 touring grass pitches. Driving range, bar with sports TV.

PITCHES: 🚐 Caravans 🚐 Motorhomes ⛺ Tents 🏠 Glamping accommodation **SERVICES:** 🔌 Electric hook-up 🗑 Launderette 🍺 Licensed bar 🔋 Calor Gas ⚙ Campingaz T Toilet fluid 🍴 Café/Restaurant 🔋 Fast Food/Takeaway 🔋 Battery charging 🚽 Motorhome service point * 2019 prices ◎ No credit or debit cards 🐾 Dogs permitted ⊗ No dogs

ABERGAVENNY *continued*

Pyscodlyn Farm Caravan & Camping Site

▶▶▶▶ 82%

tel: 01873 853271 & 07816 447942 **Llanwenarth Citra NP7 7ER**
email: info@pyscodlyncaravanpark.com **web:** www.pyscodlyncaravanpark.com
dir: *From Abergavenny take A40 (Brecon road), site 1.5 miles from entrance of Nevill Hall Hospital, on left. From Brecon 4.5 miles past Crickhowell on right.*

With its outstanding views of the mountains, this quiet park in the Brecon Beacons National Park makes a pleasant holiday venue for country lovers. The Sugarloaf Mountain and the River Usk are within easy walking distance and, despite being a working farm, dogs are welcome but must be under strict control. The separate ladies' and gents' amenity blocks are appointed to a high standard. Please note that credit and debit cards are not accepted at this site.

Open: April to October
Pitches: * 🚐 from £15; 🚎 from £15; ▲ from £15
Leisure: 🏊
Facilities: 🛁 ⊙ 🧺 ✴ ♿
Services: 🔌 🗑 ♨ 🚽 🔒 🧷
Within 3 miles: 🎣 ∪ ◎ 🎪 ⑤

Additional site information: 4.5 acre site. 🐾 🐕 Cars can be parked by caravans and tents. Awnings permitted. No noise after 23.00, no open fires. Car hire can be arranged.

DINGESTOW   Map 9 SO41

Places to visit

Raglan Castle, RAGLAN, NP15 2BT, 01291 690228
cadw.gov.wales/daysout/raglancastle

Tintern Abbey, TINTERN PARVA, NP16 6SE, 01291 689251
cadw.gov.wales/daysout/tinternabbey

Bridge Caravan Park & Camping Site

▶▶▶ 86%

tel: 01600 740241 **Bridge Farm NP25 4DY**
email: info@bridgecaravanpark.co.uk
dir: *M4 junction 24, A449 towards Monmouth. Left onto A40 towards Abergavenny. Turn right (across dual carriageway) signed Dingestow (and brown caravan sign).*

The River Trothy runs along the edge of this quiet village park, which has been owned by the same family for many years. The touring pitches are both grass and hardstanding, and have a woodland backdrop. The quality facilities are enhanced by good laundry equipment. River fishing is available on site, and there is a dog walking area. The village shop is within 100 yards and a play field within 200 yards.

Open: Easter to October **Last arrival:** 22.00 **Last departure:** 16.00
Pitches: 🚐 🚎 ▲; 15 hardstanding pitches; 50 seasonal pitches
Leisure: 🏊
Facilities: 🛁 ⊙ 🧺 ✴ ♿ ⑤
Services: 🔌 🗑 🍴 🚽 🔒 🧷 Ⓣ
Within 3 miles: 🎣 ∪ 🚣 🎪

Additional site information: 4 acre site. 🐾 🐕 Cars can be parked by caravans and tents. Awnings permitted.

LLANVAIR DISCOED   Map 9 ST49

Places to visit

Chepstow Castle, CHEPSTOW, NP16 5EY, 01291 624065
cadw.gov.wales/daysout/chepstow-castle

Premier Park

Penhein Glamping

▶▶▶▶▶ 92% GLAMPING ONLY

tel: 01633 400581 **Penhein NP16 6RB**
email: enquiries@penhein.co.uk **web:** www.penhein.co.uk
dir: *M48 junction 2, A446 towards Chepstow. 1st exit at roundabout onto A48 signed Caerwent. Approximately 8 miles, through Caerwent, right signed Llanvair Discoed. 1st right at village sign, immediately left into private drive. Site 1.5 miles.*

Tucked away in secluded woodland surrounded by peaceful countryside, the six beautiful Alachigh tents are cosy and warm and kitted out with everything you need to feel at home. The sumptuous interiors have comfortable beds (a double, two truckle beds and a sofa bed for children), quality dining furniture, lanterns, a cold water sink, a large cool box and a wood-burning stove (wood provided), plus an en suite modern, low-level flushing toilet. Outside each tent there is a fire pit for BBQ and carved tree-trunk seating. There are level bark pathways between the tents, and a 'cheat's kitchen' in the centre of the site, with microwave, cooking hobs, a honesty bar, and a freezer as there is no electricity in the tents themselves. The separate shower block has a drying room, underfloor heating, monsoon showers and a Victorian style roll-top bath. In addition, there's a communal tent with a wood-burning stove and a wildflower meadow for games.

Open: March to November **Last arrival:** 19.00 **Last departure:** 11.00
Leisure: ⚽
Facilities: 🛁 ✴ 🍖 🏕
Within 3 miles: 🎣 ⑤ 🗑

Accommodation available: Alachigh.

Changeover days: Monday, Wednesday, Friday

Additional site information: 11 acre site. ⊗ No pets. 8-acre private wildflower and hay meadow, walks on 400-acre farm (woodlands and fields). Christmas and New Year bookings possible.

USK
Map 9 SO30

Places to visit
Caerleon Roman Fortress and Baths, CAERLEON, NP18 1AE, 01663 422518
cadw.gov.wales/daysout/Caerleon-roman-fortress-baths

Big Pit National Coal Museum, BLAENAVON, NP4 9XP, 0300 111 2333
museum.wales/bigpit/

Great for kids: Greenmeadow Community Farm, CWMBRAN, NP44 3XQ,
01633 647662
www.greenmeadowcommunityfarm.org.uk

Premier Park

Pont Kemys Caravan & Camping Park
▶▶▶▶▶ 87%

tel: 01873 880688 & 07976 960832 **Chainbridge NP7 9DS**
email: info@pontkemys.com **web:** www.pontkemys.com
dir: *From Usk take B4598 towards Abergavenny. Approximately 4 miles, over river bridge, bear right, 300 yards to site. For other routes contact site for detailed directions.*

A peaceful park next to the River Usk, offering an excellent standard of toilet facilities with family rooms. The adults-only field benefits from large fully serviced pitches with wide divisions for additional privacy, and a section of the park has fully serviced pitches. The park is in a rural area with mature trees and country views, and attracts quiet visitors who enjoy the many attractions of this area.

Open: March to October **Last arrival:** 21.00 **Last departure:** noon
Pitches: 🚐 from £20; 🚍 from £20; ▲ from £20; 29 hardstanding pitches; 25 seasonal pitches
Leisure: 🔲 ⚽
Facilities: 🏠 ⊙ 🌊 ☀ ♿ 🎛 WiFi
Services: 🔌 🌀 🔋 ⬆ 🔒 ⊘ 🔣
Within 3 miles: 🎣 🏌 🏪

Additional site information: 8 acre site. 🐕 Cars can be parked by caravans and tents. Awnings permitted. No music. Mother and baby room, kitchen facilities for groups.

PEMBROKESHIRE

BROAD HAVEN
Map 8 SM81

Places to visit
Llawhaden Castle, LLAWHADEN, 0300 0256000
cadw.gov.wales/visit/places-to-visit/llawhaden-castle

Great for kids: Scolton Manor Museum & Country Park, SCOLTON, SA62 5QL,
01437 731328
www.culture4pembrokeshire.co.uk/content.asp?nav=8

Creampots Touring Caravan & Camping Park
▶▶▶▶ 87%

tel: 01437 781776 **Broadway SA62 3TU**
email: creampots@btconnect.com **web:** www.creampots.co.uk
dir: *From Haverfordwest take B4341 to Broadway. Turn left, follow brown tourist signs to site.*

Set just outside the Pembrokeshire National Park, this quiet site is just one and a half miles from a safe sandy beach at Broad Haven, and the coastal footpath. Most of the well spaced pitches in the beautifully landscaped touring areas have hardstandings and the smart amenity block is equipped with quality fixtures and fittings.

Open: March to October **Last arrival:** 20.00 **Last departure:** 11.00
Pitches: 🚐 🚍 ▲; 47 hardstanding pitches
Facilities: 🏠 ⊙ 🌊 ☀ ♿ 🎛 WiFi
Services: 🔌 🌀 🔋 🔒 ⊘
Within 3 miles: 🎣 🏌 🏪

Additional site information: 8 acre site. 🐕 Cars can be parked by caravans and tents. Awnings permitted.

South Cockett Caravan & Camping Park
▶▶▶ 79%

tel: 07774 782572 & 01437 781296 **South Cockett SA62 3TU**
email: esmejames@hotmail.co.uk **web:** www.southcockett.co.uk
dir: *From Haverfordwest take B4341 to Broad Haven, at Broadway turn left, site 300 yards.*

A warm welcome is assured at this small site on a working farm. The touring areas are divided into neat paddocks by high, well-trimmed hedges, and there are good toilet facilities. The lovely beach at Broad Haven is only about two miles away.

Open: Easter to October **Last arrival:** 22.30
Pitches: 🚐 🚍 ▲; 25 seasonal pitches
Leisure: ⚽
Facilities: 🏠 ⊙ ☀ 🎛 WiFi
Services: 🔌 🌀 🔋 🔒 ⊘
Within 3 miles: 🏌 🏪

Additional site information: 6 acre site. 🐕 Cars can be parked by caravans and tents. Awnings permitted. No noise after dark.

FISHGUARD — Map 8 SM93

Places to visit

Pentre Ifan Burial Chamber, NEWPORT, SA41 3TZ, 0300 0256000
cadw.gov.wales/daysout/pentreifanburialchamber

Great for kids: OceanLab, FISHGUARD, SA64 0DE, 01348 874737
www.oceanlab.co.uk

Fishguard Bay Resort
▶▶▶▶ 90%

tel: 01348 811415 **Garn Gelli SA65 9ET**
email: enquiries@fishguardbay.com **web:** www.fishguardbay.com
dir: *Accessed from A487. Turn at park sign onto single track road. (Note: if approaching Fishguard from Cardigan on A487 ignore sat nav to turn right).*

Set high up on cliffs with outstanding views of Fishguard Bay, this site has the Pembrokeshire Coastal Path running right through its centre, so affording many opportunities for wonderful walks. The park is extremely well maintained, with a good toilet block, a common room with TV, a lounge with library, laundry and a well-stocked shop. There are three camping pods, one with en suite shower and hot tub, all with superb sea views and a 'pamper' pod is available for spa treatments.

Open: March to 9 January **Last arrival:** anytime **Last departure:** noon

Pitches: 🚐 🚎 ⛺; 🏠 see prices below; 10 hardstanding pitches

Leisure: ⑃ ◣ ⏹

Facilities: 🛁 ☉ 🗲 ✳ 💲 🍴 WiFi

Services: 🖴 🗓 🏧 🧳 🔒 ⊘ T

Within 3 miles: 🎣 ∪ ⛴ 🛥 🏕

Additional site information: 7 acre site. 🐕 Cars can be parked by caravans and tents. Awnings permitted. No commercial vehicles. Spa treatments. Freshly baked bread and pastries available.

Glamping available: 2 wooden pods from £55; 2 studio lodges from £85.
Changeover days: Any day

Additional glamping information: Wooden pods offer TV, fridge, BBQ, double sofa bed, 2 small bunk beds. Bedding is not included. Studio lodges offer TV, 2 double sofa beds, hot tub, BBQ area, decking, kitchen with fridge, microwave and shower and toilet. Cars can be parked by units.

HAVERFORDWEST — Map 8 SM91

Places to visit

Llawhaden Castle, LLAWHADEN, 0300 0256000
cadw.gov.wales/visit/places-to-visit/llawhaden-castle

Great for kids: Oakwood Theme Park, NARBERTH, SA67 8DE, 01834 815170
www.oakwoodthemepark.co.uk

Nolton Cross Caravan Park
▶▶▶ 81%

tel: 01437 710701 & 07814 779020 **Nolton SA62 3NP**
email: info@noltoncross-holidays.co.uk **web:** www.noltoncross-holidays.co.uk
dir: *1 mile from A487 (Haverfordwest to St Davids road) at Simpson Cross, towards Nolton and Broadhaven.*

High grassy banks surround the touring area of this park adjacent to the owners' working farm. It is located on open ground above the sea and St Bride's Bay (within one and a half miles), and there is a coarse fishing lake close by – equipment for hire and reduced permit rates for campers are available. There are shepherd's huts for hire and WiFi is available.

Open: March to December **Last arrival:** 22.00 **Last departure:** noon

Pitches: 🚐 from £13.20; 🚎 from £13.20; ⛺ from £13.20; 🏠 see prices below; 5 hardstanding pitches

Leisure: ⑃

Facilities: 🛁 ☉ ✳ 🍴 WiFi

Services: 🖴 🗓 🏧 🧳 ⊘ T

Within 3 miles: 🎣 ∪ ⛴ 💲

Additional site information: 4 acre site. 🐕 Pets must be kept on a lead. Cars can be parked by caravans and tents. Awnings permitted. No youth groups. Site shop open high season only.

Glamping available: 2 shepherd's huts from £40. **Changeover days:** Any day

Additional glamping information: Cars can be parked by units.

ST DAVIDS

Places to visit

St Davids Cathedral, ST DAVIDS, SA62 6RD, 01437 720202
www.stdavidscathedral.org.uk

St Davids Bishop's Palace, ST DAVIDS, SA62 6PE, 01437 720517
cadw.gov.wales/daysout/stdavidsbishopspalace

ST DAVIDS	Map 8 SM72

Premier Park

Caerfai Bay Caravan & Tent Park
▶ ▶ ▶ ▶ ▶ 93%

tel: 01437 720274 **Caerfai Bay SA62 6QT**
email: info@caerfaibay.co.uk **web:** www.caerfaibay.co.uk
dir: *From Haverfordwest on A487 towards St Davids, left at roundabout into Caerfai Road (Ffordd Caerfai) signed Caerfai Bay. Or from Fishguard take A487 to St Davids. At St Davids speed restriction sign turn left into Glasfryn Road. At roundabout, second exit into Caerfai Road (Ffordd Caerfai). Site on right at end of road, before beach car park.*

Magnificent coastal scenery and an outlook over St Bride's Bay can be enjoyed from this delightful site, located just 300 yards from a bathing beach. The park offers good roadways, modern water points, solar-heated wetsuit shower rooms and excellent toilet facilities, which include four family rooms. The lower field has been divided into separate dog free and dog friendly areas and low level lighting ensures a brilliant night sky on cloud-free days.

Open: March to early November **Last arrival:** 21.00 **Last departure:** 11.00
Pitches: * 🚐 from £22.50; 🚙 from £20; ▲ from £15; 33 hardstanding pitches
Facilities: 🛁 ☉ ℗ ❄ ♿ WiFi
Services: 🔌 🌀 🔋 ⚡ 🔋 ⊘ Ⓣ
Within 3 miles: ⬇ ℘ ≽ ⛷ Ⓢ

Additional site information: 10 acre site. 🐕 Cars can be parked by caravans and tents. Awnings permitted. Tent fields have dog friendly and non-dog areas, no skateboards or rollerblades, no audible devices after 22.00, Quiet from 23.00. Local farm shop nearby is open from end May to end August.

Tretio Caravan & Camping Park
▶ ▶ ▶ 83%

tel: 01437 781600 & 07814 588289 **SA62 6DE**
email: info@tretio.com **web:** www.tretio.com
dir: *From St Davids take A487 towards Fishguard, left at Rugby Football Club, straight on for 3 miles. Site signed, right to site.*

A warm welcome is assured at this long established family-orientated holiday destination in a rural location with superb country views and close to beautiful beaches. On-site facilities include an attractive well-equipped amenity block and a small shop selling essentials. The small cathedral city of St Davids is only three miles away.

Open: March to October **Last arrival:** 20.00 **Last departure:** 10.00
Pitches: 🚐 🚙 ▲; 1 hardstanding pitches; 8 seasonal pitches
Leisure: 🎱 ⬇ ⚽
Facilities: 🛁 ☉ ℗ ❄ ♿ 🍳 🎪 WiFi
Services: 🔌 🌀 🔋
Within 3 miles: ℘ 🏇 ≽ ⛷ 🎣

Additional site information: 6.5 acre site. 🐕 Cars can be parked by caravans and tents. Awnings permitted. Quiet after 22.00. Climbing wall, play area.

TENBY	Map 8 SN10

Places to visit

Tudor Merchant's House, TENBY, SA70 7BX, 01834 842279
www.nationaltrust.org.uk/tudormerchantshouse

Tenby Museum & Art Gallery, TENBY, SA70 7BP, 01834 842809
www.tenbymuseum.org.uk

Great for kids: Colby Woodland Garden, AMROTH, SA67 8PP, 01834 811885
www.nationaltrust.org.uk/colby-woodland-garden

Premier Park

Kiln Park Holiday Centre
▶ ▶ ▶ ▶ ▶ 86% HOLIDAY CENTRE

tel: 01834 844121 **Marsh Road SA70 8RB**
email: kilnpark@haven.com **web:** www.haven.com/kilnpark
dir: *Follow A477, A478 to Tenby for 6 miles. Then follow signs to Penally, site 0.5 mile on left.*

A large holiday complex complete with leisure and sports facilities and lots of entertainment for all the family. There are bars and cafés, including the stylish Harbwr Lights Bistro, and plenty of security. This touring, camping and static site is on the outskirts of town, and it's only a short walk through dunes to the sandy beach. The modern amenity block provides a stylish interior with underfloor heating and superb fixtures and fittings.

Open: mid March to end October (restricted service: mid March to May and September to end October – some facilities may be reduced) **Last arrival:** dusk **Last departure:** 10.00
Pitches: 🚐 🚙 ▲; 🏕 see price below; 60 hardstanding pitches
Leisure: 🏊 🏊 🎱 ⬇ 🎣 🎵 ⚽
Facilities: 🛁 ℗ ❄ ♿ Ⓢ 🍳 🎪 WiFi
Services: 🔌 🌀 🍽 🍴 ⬛ 🔋 ⊘
Within 3 miles: ⬇ ℘ ⛳ ◎ ≽ ⛷

Additional site information: 103 acre site. 🐕 Maximum 2 dogs per booking, certain dog breeds banned. No commercial vehicles, no bookings by persons under 21 years unless a family booking. Entertainment complex, bowling and putting green.

Glamping available: Safari tents from £129. **Changeover days:** Mondays and Fridays

Additional glamping information: Safari tents: minimum stay 3 nights. Cars can be parked by units.

TENBY *continued*

Trefalun Park
▶▶▶▶ 88%

tel: 01646 651514 **Devonshire Drive, St Florence SA70 8RD**
email: trefalun@aol.com **web:** www.trefalunpark.co.uk
dir: *1.5 miles northwest of St Florence and 0.5 mile north of B4318.*

Located within twelve acres of immaculately maintained grounds with a wide variety of indigenous and cultivated trees, shrubs and hedging, generously spaced pitches are all equipped with electric hook-up and most have level hardstandings with some designed for larger units. An excellent children's play park is located near entrance to the park and many activities are available at the nearby Heatherton Country Sports Park.

Open: Easter to October **Last arrival:** 19.00 **Last departure:** noon

Pitches: 🚐 🚏 ▲; 90 hardstanding pitches; 55 seasonal pitches

Leisure: ⋀

Facilities: 🛁 ⊙ ⌇ ✳ 🚽 WiFi

Services: 🔌 🔲 🔩 🖁 🚽 🔒 🚿 Ⓣ

Within 3 miles: ↓ ⁊ ◎ ⛷ 🎣 🔗

Additional site information: 12 acre site. 🚗 Cars can be parked by caravans and tents. Awnings permitted. No motorised scooters, no gazebos.

Well Park Caravan & Camping Site
▶▶▶▶ 83%

tel: 01834 842179 **SA70 8TL**
email: enquiries@wellparkcaravans.co.uk **web:** www.wellparkcaravans.co.uk
dir: *A478 towards Tenby. At roundabout at Kilgetty follow Tenby and A478 signs. 3 miles to next roundabout, take 2nd exit, site 2nd right.*

An attractive, well-maintained park with good landscaping from trees, ornamental shrubs and flower borders. The amenities include a launderette and indoor dishwashing, games room with table tennis, and an enclosed play area. The park is ideally situated between Tenby and Saundersfoot; Tenby just a 15-minute walk away, or the town can be reached via a traffic-free cycle track.

Open: March to October (restricted service: March to mid June and mid September to October – bar may be closed) **Last arrival:** 22.00 **Last departure:** 11.00

Pitches: * 🚐 from £20; 🚏 from £20; ▲ from £18; 16 hardstanding pitches

Leisure: ⋀ 🔊 ☐

Facilities: 🛁 ⊙ ⌇ ✳ 🚽 🪑 WiFi

Services: 🔌 🔲 🔩 🖁 🚽 🔒 🚿

Within 3 miles: ↓ ⁊ ◎ ⛷ 🎣 🔗

Additional site information: 10 acre site. 🚗 Cars can be parked by caravans and tents. Awnings permitted. Family groups only. TV hook-ups.

Wood Park Caravans
▶▶▶ 80%

tel: 01834 843414 **New Hedges SA70 8TL**
email: info@woodpark.co.uk **web:** www.woodpark.co.uk
dir: *A477 from Carmarthen to St Clears. At roundabout onto A477 signed Pembroke Dock. At Kilgetty roundabout left onto A478 signed Tenby. At next roundabout take 2nd exit signed Tenby (Note: ignore 1st exit signs for New Hedges and Saundersfoot). 2nd right to site (signed).*

Situated in beautiful countryside between the popular seaside resorts of Tenby and Saundersfoot, and with Waterwynch Bay just a 15-minute walk away, this peaceful site provides a spacious and relaxing atmosphere for holidays. The slightly sloping touring area is divided by shrubs and hedge-screened paddocks, and a licensed bar and games room are also available.

Open: Spring Bank Holiday to September (restricted service: September – bar may be closed) **Last arrival:** 22.00 **Last departure:** 10.00

Pitches: 🚐 🚏 ▲; 40 hardstanding pitches; 10 seasonal pitches

Leisure: ⋀ 🔊

Facilities: 🛁 ⊙ ⌇ ✳ WiFi

Services: 🔌 🔲 🔩 🖁 🔒 🚿

Within 3 miles: ↓ ⁊ ◎ ⛷ 🎣 🔗

Additional site information: 10 acre site. 🚫 🚫 Cars can be parked by caravans and tents. Awnings permitted. No groups, 1 car per unit permitted.

POWYS

BRECON
Map 9 SO02

Places to visit

Regimental Museum of The Royal Welsh, BRECON, LD3 7EB, 01874 613310
www.royalwelsh.org.uk

Tretower Court & Castle, TRETOWER, NP8 1RD, 01874 730279
cadw.gov.wales/daysout/tretowercourtandcastle

Premier Park

Pencelli Castle Caravan & Camping Park
▶▶▶▶▶ 92%

tel: 01874 665451 **Pencelli LD3 7LX**
email: pencelli@tiscali.co.uk **web:** www.pencelli-castle.com
dir: A40 onto B4588 (2 miles east of Brecon), follow signs to Pencelli.

Lying in the heart of the Brecon Beacons National Park, this charming park offers peace, beautiful scenery and high quality facilities. It is bordered by the Brecon and Monmouth Canal. The attention to detail is superb, and the well-equipped, heated toilets with en suite cubicles are matched by a drying room for clothes and boots, full laundry, and a shop. Super-fast WiFi is available throughout the park Regular buses stop just outside the gate and go to Brecon, Abergavenny and Swansea.

Open: 15 February to December (restricted service: mid February to Easter and 30 October to November – shop closed) **Last arrival:** 22.00 **Last departure:** noon
Pitches: * ⊞ from £28.80; ⊞ from £28.80; ▲ from £25; 40 hardstanding pitches
Leisure: ⚲ ⚑ ⚽
Facilities: ⊞ ☉ ℱ ✳ ⚅ ⑤ ☈ WiFi
Services: ⊞ ⑤ ⚖ ⚓ ⚑ ⌀ Ⓣ
Within 3 miles: ✐ ∪ ⚑ ☰

Additional site information: 10 acre site. ⊗ Only assistance dogs permitted. Cars can be parked by caravans and tents. Awnings permitted. No radios, music or camp fires.

BRONLLYS
Map 9 SO13

Places to visit

Regimental Museum of The Royal Welsh, BRECON, LD3 7EB, 01874 613310
www.royalwelsh.org.uk

Anchorage Caravan Park
▶▶▶▶ 84%

tel: 01874 711246 **LD3 0LD**
email: info@anchoragecp.co.uk **web:** www.anchoragecp.co.uk
dir: A40 to Brecon. At roundabout take A470 signed Hereford (this road becomes A438). Approximately 8 miles, at roundabout follow Bronllys signs. In Bronllys follow brown campsite signs.

A well-maintained site with a choice of south-facing, sloping grass pitches and superb views of the Black Mountains, or a more sheltered lower area with a number of excellent super pitches. The site is a short distance from the water sports centre at Llangors Lake.

Open: All year (restricted service: November to March – TV room closed)
Last arrival: 23.00 **Last departure:** 16.00

Pitches: * ⊞ from £14; ⊞ from £14; ▲ from £14; 8 hardstanding pitches; 60 seasonal pitches
Leisure: ⚲ ⚑
Facilities: ⊞ ☉ ℱ ✳ ⚅ ⑤ ☈ WiFi
Services: ⊞ ⑤ ⚖ ⚓ ⌀ Ⓣ
Within 3 miles: ✐ ∪

Additional site information: 8 acre site. ⚑ Cars can be parked by caravans and tents. Awnings permitted. Hairdresser.

BUILTH WELLS
Map 9 SO05

Places to visit
RSPB Carngafallt, RHAYADER, LD6 5HW, 01654 700222
www.rspb.org.uk/reserves-and-events/reserves-a-z/carngafallt

Premier Park

Fforest Fields Caravan & Camping Park
▶▶▶▶▶ 86%

tel: 01982 570406 **Hundred House LD1 5RT**
email: office@fforestfields.co.uk **web:** www.fforestfields.co.uk
dir: *From town centre follow New Radnor signs on A481. 4 miles to signed entrance on right, 0.5 mile before Hundred House village. (Note: if using sat nav, entrance is not centred on post code).*

This is a constantly improving, sheltered park surrounded by magnificent scenery and an abundance of wildlife. The spacious pitches are well laid out to create optimum privacy, and the superb eco-friendly amenity block is fuelled by a bio-mass boiler and solar panels. The glamping field with superb lake and country views, contains four yurts that have adjacent pod kitchens and a centrally located toilet; this all adds up to a genuine 'away from it all' experience, and the licensed Fforest café specialises in local produce. The historic town of Builth Wells and The Royal Welsh Showground are just four miles away.

Open: All year **Last arrival:** 21.00 **Last departure:** 18.00
Pitches: 🚐 🚙 ⛺ 🏠; 30 hardstanding pitches
Leisure: 🎡

Facilities: 🛁 ☉ 🎣 ❄ ♿ 🏪 🛒 WiFi
Services: 🔌 🔘 🍴 🛒 🔒 🗑 🅣
Within 3 miles: ⛳ 🎣 🚣 🚲 🎯

Additional site information: 15 acre site. 🐕 Dogs must be kept on leads at all times. Cars can be parked by caravans and tents. Awnings permitted. No loud music. Quiet after 22.30. Fridges, microwave, electric kettle and phone-charging available.

Glamping available: 4 yurts. **Changeover days:** Monday, Friday

Additional glamping information: Yurts sleep 4. Minimum stay 2 nights. Double bed (two single beds optional), wood-burning stove, wooden floors, decking area, fully-equipped kitchen pod. Off-grid – solar power only. 2 dogs permitted (additional deposit required).

CHURCHSTOKE
Map 15 SO29

Places to visit
Montgomery Castle, MONTGOMERY, SY15 6HN, 0300 0256000
cadw.gov.wales/daysout/montgomerycastle

Premier Park

Daisy Bank Caravan Park
▶▶▶▶▶ 85%

tel: 01588 620471 **Snead SY15 6EB**
email: enquiries@daisy-bank.co.uk **web:** www.daisy-bank.co.uk
dir: *On A489, 2 miles east of Churchstoke.*

Peacefully located between Craven Arms and Churchstoke and surrounded by rolling hills, this idyllic, adults-only park offers generously sized, fully serviced pitches; some with superb country views – all are situated in attractive hedged areas. The immaculately maintained amenity blocks provide smart, modern fittings and excellent privacy options. Camping pods, a pitch and putt course and free WiFi are also available.

Open: All year **Last arrival:** 20.00 **Last departure:** noon
Pitches: 🚐 from £21; 🚙 from £21; ⛺ from £21; 🏠 see price below; 45 hardstanding pitches; 40 seasonal pitches
Facilities: ☉ 🎣 ❄ ♿ 🏪 🛒 WiFi
Services: 🔌 🔘 🔒 🗑 🅣
Within 3 miles: ◎

Additional site information: 7 acre site. Adults only. 🐕 Cars can be parked by caravans and tents. Awnings permitted. Caravan storage.

Glamping available: Wooden pods from £35. **Changeover days:** Any day

Additional glamping information: Electric heater, electric light, BBQ, table and chairs provided. Guests must bring their own bed and bedding. Cars can be parked by units.

LEISURE: 🏊 Indoor swimming pool 🏊 Outdoor swimming pool ⛰ Children's playground 🧒 Kids' club 🎾 Tennis court 🎱 Games room 📺 Separate TV room ⛳ Golf course 🏌 Pitch n putt 🚣 Boats for hire 🚲 Bikes for hire 🎬 Cinema 🎵 Entertainment 🎣 Fishing ◎ Mini golf 🏄 Watersports 💪 Gym 🎯 Sports field ♘ Stables
FACILITIES: 🛁 Baths/Shower ☉ Electric shaver sockets 🎣 Hairdryer ❄ Ice Pack Facility 👶 Baby facilities ♿ Disabled facilities 🏪 Shop on site or within 200yds 🛒 BBQ area 🪑 Picnic area WiFi WiFi

CRICKHOWELL — Map 9 SO21

Places to visit

Tretower Court & Castle, TRETOWER, NP8 1RD, 01874 730279
cadw.gov.wales/daysout/tretowercourtandcastle

Big Pit National Coal Museum, BLAENAVON, NP4 9XP, 0300 111 2 333
museum.wales/bigpit/

Riverside Caravan & Camping Park
▶▶▶▶ 84%

tel: 01873 810397 **New Road NP8 1AY**
email: riversidecaravanpark@outlook.com **web:** www.riversidecaravanscrickhowell.co.uk
dir: On A4077, well signed from A40.

Within a few minutes' walk of the river and town centre with its excellent shopping and eating choices, is this all-level park. It is surrounded by mature hedges and trees to create privacy and has an excellent amenity block with stylish decor, modern fixtures and fittings and very good privacy options.

Open: March to October **Last arrival:** 21.00 **Last departure:** 11.00

Pitches: * 🚐 from £22; 🚍 from £22; ▲ from £22

Facilities: 🏠 ⊙ 🅿 ⚒ ♿ ⑤ WiFi

Services: ⚡ ⑤ 🍴 🛒 ⬇ 🔋

Within 3 miles: ↓ 🖉 ∪ ≒

Additional site information: 3.5 acre site. Adults only. 🐕 🔞 Cars can be parked by caravans and tents. Awnings permitted. No fires, no noise after 22.00. Large canopied area for cooking, drying clothes, etc.

LLANDRINDOD WELLS — Map 9 SO06

Places to visit

RSPB Carngafallt, RHAYADER, LD6 5HW, 01654 700222
www.rspb.org.uk/reserves-and-events/reserves-a-z/carngafallt

Disserth Caravan & Camping Park
▶▶▶▶ 84%

tel: 01597 860277 **Disserth, Howey LD1 6NL**
email: disserthcaravan@btconnect.com **web:** www.disserth.biz
dir: 1 mile from A483, between Newbridge-on-Wye and Howey, by church. Follow brown signs from A483 or A470.

By a 13th-century church, this is a delightfully secluded and predominantly adult park that sits in a beautiful valley on the banks of the River Ithon, a tributary of the River Wye. It has a small bar which is open at weekends and during busy periods. The amenity block and laundry are appointed to a high standard and provide good privacy options. The site offers a shepherd's hut and a wooden 'morphPod' for hire.

Open: March to October **Last arrival:** sunset **Last departure:** noon

Pitches: * 🚐 from £20; 🚍 from £20; ▲ from £16; 🏠 see prices below; 6 hardstanding pitches

Leisure: 🖉
Facilities: 🏠 ⊙ 🅿 ⚒ ♿ 🛒 WiFi
Services: ⚡ ⑤ 🍴 🛒 🔋 🔋 ⬇ T
Within 3 miles: ↓ ∪ 🗓 ⑤

Additional site information: 4 acre site. 🐕 Cars can be parked by caravans and tents. Awnings permitted. Quiet after 22.30, maximum 2 pets. No fires. Private trout fishing.

Glamping available: Wooden pod from £40; shepherd's hut from £30. **Changeover days:** Any day

Additional glamping information: Wooden pod offers twin beds; Shepherd's hut offers microwave, fridge, kettle, heating, pull-down double bed and private shower and toilet. Cars can be parked by units.

LLANGORS — Map 9 SO12

Places to visit

Regimental Museum of The Royal Welsh, BRECON, LD3 7EB, 01874 613310
www.royalwelsh.org.uk

Great for kids: Tretower Court & Castle, TRETOWER, NP8 1RD, 01874 730279
cadw.gov.wales/daysout/tretowercourtandcastle

Lakeside Caravan Park
▶▶▶ 83%

tel: 01874 658226 **LD3 7TR**
email: reception@llangorselake.co.uk **web:** www.llangorselake.co.uk
dir: Exit A40 at Bwlch onto B4560 towards Llangorse. Site signed towards lake in Llangorse village.

Surrounded by spectacular mountains and set close to Llangorse Lake, with mooring and launching facilities, this is a must-do holiday destination for lovers of outdoor pursuits, from walking to watersports, and even pike fishing for which the lake is renowned. The hedge- or tree-screened touring areas provide generously-sized pitches, and Elwyn's tree-surrounded, level and lush grass camping field is serviced by modern toilets and showers. There's a well-stocked shop, bar and café, with a takeaway, under the same ownership.

Open: Easter or April to October (restricted service: March to May and September to October – reduced opening hours in bar) **Last arrival:** 21.30 **Last departure:** 10.00

Pitches: * 🚐 from £18.25; 🚍 from £18.25; ▲ from £14; 16 hardstanding pitches

Leisure: 🎱 🎣 🖉
Facilities: 🏠 ⊙ 🅿 ⚒ ♿ ⑤ 🍴 ⊞ WiFi
Services: ⚡ ⑤ 🍴 🍽 🏪 🔋 ⬇ T
Within 3 miles: ∪ ≒ ⑤

Additional site information: 2 acre site. 🐕 No dogs permitted in hire caravans. Cars can be parked by caravans and tents. Awnings permitted. No open fires, noise to be kept to a minimum after 23.00. Boat hire in summer.

LLANIDLOES
Map 9 SN98

Places to visit

Bryntail Lead Mine Buildings, LLANIDLOES, 0300 0256000
cadw.gov.wales/visit/places-to-visit/bryntail-lead-mine-buildings

Gilfach Nature Reserve & Visitor Centre, RHAYADER, LD6 5LF, 01597 823298
www.rwtwales.org/node/3231

Premier Park

Red Kite Touring Park
►►►►► 87%

tel: 01686 412122 **Van Road SY18 6NG**
email: info@redkitetouringpark.co.uk **web:** www.redkitetouringpark.co.uk
dir: *From roundabout on A470 at Llanidloes take B4518 signed Pennffordd-las Staylittle. At next roundabout take 3rd exit signed Machynlleth. Over river. 1st left (B4518) signed Pennffordd-las Staylittle. Pass Clywedog Riverside Holiday Home Park on left, site in approximately 100 yards.*

Within a few minutes' walk of the historic town centre, this stunningly located park has been created on undulating hills and fields, which include two lakes, one being a habitat for newts. All pitches are fully serviced to include a green chemical disposal point and TV hook-up, and the superb amenity block with underfloor heating provides excellent fixtures and fittings coupled with privacy options for both men and women. Please note this is an adults-only park.

Open: March to January **Last arrival:** 19.00 **Last departure:** noon
Pitches: * 🚐 from £27; 🚐 from £27; 66 hardstanding pitches; 15 seasonal pitches
Leisure: 🖊
Facilities: 🏠 ⊙ 🖊 ⚹ ⛐ 🎋 WiFi
Services: 🔌 📋 ⬆ 🔒 🆃
Within 3 miles: 🎣 🛒

Additional site information: 20 acre site. Adults only. 🐕 Enclosed dog run, dog wash. Cars can be parked by caravans. Awnings permitted. Car hire can be arranged.

MIDDLETOWN
Map 15 SJ31

Places to visit

Powis Castle & Garden, WELSHPOOL, SY21 8RF, 01938 551944
www.nationaltrust.org.uk/powis-castle-and-garden

Bank Farm Caravan Park
►►► 81%

tel: 01938 570526 & 07753 685260 **SY21 8EJ**
email: bankfarmcaravans@yahoo.co.uk **web:** www.bankfarmcaravans.co.uk
dir: *13 miles west of Shrewsbury, 5 miles east of Welshpool on A458.*

This is an attractive park on a small farm that's maintained to a high standard. There are two touring areas located on both sides of the A458; each has its own amenity block and direct access to the hills, mountains and woodland. The site has an excellent display of topiary, trimmed hedges, trees and colourful shrubs. WiFi is available throughout the park, and both a pub serving good food and a large play area are nearby.

Open: March to October **Last arrival:** 20.00

Pitches: * 🚐 from £18; 🚐 from £18; ⛺ from £15
Leisure: 🅰 🎱 🖊
Facilities: 🏠 ⊙ ⚹ ⛐ 🎋 WiFi
Services: 🔌 📋 ⬆ 🔒

Additional site information: 2 acre site. 🐕 Cars can be parked by caravans and tents. Awnings permitted. Coarse fishing, jacuzzi, snooker room.

SWANSEA

PONTARDDULAIS
Map 8 SN50

Places to visit

RSPB Cwm Clydach, CLYDACH, SA6 5SU, 029 2035 3000
www.rspb.org.uk/reserves-and-events/reserves-a-z/cwm-clydach

Premier Park

River View Touring Park
►►►►► 86%

tel: 01269 844876 **The Dingle, Llanedi SA4 0FH**
email: info@riverviewtp.com
dir: *M4 junction 49, A483 signed Llandeilo and Ammanford. 1st left after layby. Site in 300 yards on left. (NB if approaching from north or west on A48 and using Sat Nav do not exit A48 before Port Abraham roundabout)*

Located in a peaceful valley surrounded by mature trees and with a river meandering through the lower touring areas, this long established holiday destination is constantly being improved by enthusiastic owners and wardens. A well-equipped amenity block is centrally located between upper and lower touring fields which are designated as 'family' and 'adults-only' respectively. Adjacent to the family field, a mini farm has been created – here there are chickens, lambs and a variety of small pig breeds. A barbecue house is available for hire.

Open: March to November **Last arrival:** 20.30 **Last departure:** noon
Pitches: 🚐 🚐 ⛺ 🏠; 46 hardstanding pitches; 16 seasonal pitches
Leisure: 🅰 🖊 ⚽ 🕹
Facilities: 🏠 ⊙ 🖊 ⚹ ⛐ 🛒 🍴 🎋 WiFi
Services: 🔌 📋 ⬆ 🔒 🚿 🆃
Within 3 miles: 🎣 ∪ ◎ ⛸

Additional site information: 6 acre site. 🐕 Cars can be parked by caravans and tents. Awnings permitted. No commercial vehicles.

Glamping available: Wooden pod.

Additional glamping information: Cars can be parked by units.

PORT EYNON
Map 8 SS48

Places to visit

Weobley Castle, LLANRHIDIAN, SA3 1HB
cadw.gov.wales/daysout/weobleycastle

Gower Heritage Centre, PARKMILL, SA3 2EH, 01792 371206
www.gowerheritagecentre.co.uk

Great for kids: Oxwich Castle, OXWICH, SA3 1ND, 01792 390359
cadw.gov.wales/daysout/oxwichcastle

Skysea Camping & Caravan Park
► ► ► ► 85%

tel: 01792 390795 **SA3 1NL**
email: booking@porteynon.com
dir: A4118 to Port Eynon, site adjacent to beach.

Set in an unrivalled location alongside the safe sandy beach of Port Eynon on the Gower Peninsula, this popular park is an ideal family holiday spot; it is also close to an attractive village with pubs and shops. The lush green sloping ground has been partially terraced to create excellent sea views and the luxurious amenity blocks provide superb fixtures and fittings combined with good privacy and family options.

Open: All year **Last arrival:** 22.00 **Last departure:** 15.00

Pitches: 🚐 🚙 🅰

Facilities: ☺ ♿ 🛒 WiFi

Services: 🔌 🗄 ⬆ 🔋 ∅ 🇹

Within 3 miles: 🎣 ∪ 🚣

Additional site information: 12 acre site. 🐕 Cars can be parked by caravans and tents. Awnings permitted.

RHOSSILI
Map 8 SS48

Places to visit

Weobley Castle, LLANRHIDIAN, SA3 1HB
cadw.gov.wales/daysout/weobleycastle

Gower Heritage Centre, PARKMILL, SA3 2EH, 01792 371206
www.gowerheritagecentre.co.uk

Great for kids: Oxwich Castle, OXWICH, SA3 1ND, 01792 390359
cadw.gov.wales/daysout/oxwichcastle

Pitton Cross Caravan & Camping Park
►► ►► ►► 91%

tel: 01792 390593 **SA3 1PT**
email: admin@pittoncross.co.uk **web:** www.pittoncross.co.uk
dir: 2 miles west of Scurlage on B4247, on the left.

Surrounded by farmland close to sandy Mewslade Bay, which is within walking distance across fields, this grassy park is divided by hedging into paddocks, with hardstandings for motorhomes available. Some areas are deliberately left uncultivated, resulting in colourful displays of wild flowers including roses and orchids. Rhossili Beach, which is popular with surfers, and the Welsh Coastal Path are nearby. WiFi is available in the touring caravan areas of the park. Both children's kites and power kites are sold on site, and instruction is available; Geocaching and paragliding are possible too.

Open: All year (restricted service: November to March – no bread, milk or newspapers)
Last arrival: 21.00 **Last departure:** 11.00

Pitches: * 🚐 from £27; 🚙 from £27; 🅰 from £20; 27 hardstanding pitches

Leisure: 🎱

Facilities: 🏪 ☺ 🅿 ❄ ♿ 🛒 🎣 WiFi

Services: 🔌 🗄 🔋 ∅ 🇹

Within 3 miles: 🎣 🚣

Additional site information: 6 acre site. 🐕 Dogs must be kept on leads at all times. Cars can be parked by caravans and tents. Awnings permitted. Quiet at all times. Charcoal BBQs must be off ground, no fire pits or log burning.

SWANSEA
Map 9 SS69

Places to visit
Swansea Museum, SWANSEA, SA1 1SN, 01792 653763
www.swanseamuseum.co.uk

Great for kids: Plantasia, SWANSEA, SA1 2AL, 01792 474555
www.swansea.gov.uk/plantasia

Riverside Caravan Park
▶▶▶▶ 80% HOLIDAY CENTRE

tel: 01792 775587 **Ynys Forgan Farm, Morriston SA6 6QL**
email: reception@riversidewansea.com **web:** www.riversidewansea.com
dir: *M4 junction 45 follow Swansea signs. Before joining A4067 turn left into private road signed to site.*

A large and busy park close to the M4 but in a quiet location beside the River Taw. This friendly, family orientated site has a licensed club and bar with a full high-season entertainment programme. There is a choice of eating outlets — the clubhouse restaurant, takeaway and chip shop. The park has a good indoor pool.

Open: All year (restricted service: in winter months — pool and club closed)
Last arrival: midnight **Last departure:** noon

Pitches: 🚐 🚑 Å

Leisure: 🏊 🎠 🔍 🔲 🎵 ✐

Facilities: 🛁 ☉ 🪒 ❄ 🖧 ⑤ 🍴 WiFi

Services: 🔌 🔄 🍽 🏧 🧳 🛒 🧺 🅃

Within 3 miles: 🏌 🖊 🎣 🎬

Additional site information: 5 acre site. 🐕 Dogs by prior arrangement only, no aggressive breeds permitted. Fishing on site by arrangement.

WREXHAM

BRONINGTON
Map 15 SJ43

Places to visit
Erddig, WREXHAM, LL13 0YT, 01978 355314
www.nationaltrust.org.uk/erddig

The Little Yurt Meadow
▶▶▶▶ 88% GLAMPING ONLY

tel: 01948 780136 & 07984 400134 **Bay Tree Barns, Mill Road SY13 3HJ**
email: sharon@thelittleyurtmeadow.co.uk **web:** www.thelittleyurtmeadow.co.uk
dir: *A525 from Whitchurch to Redbrook. In Redbrook left onto A495 (Oswestry). Right to Bronington. At staggered crossroads right into Mill Road.*

Located in a former meadow on the Shropshire–Welsh border, this site has become a luxury glamping destination for those wishing to escape from the pressures of everyday life. Three spacious yurts with stylishly furnished interiors are equipped with sumptuous beds, two settees (one converts to a sofa bed), a wood-burning stove, mini-cooker and lots of quality extras. Each yurt has its own allocated luxury shower room and there are areas for communal indoor and outdoor relaxation, including an excellent camping kitchen, honesty bar and outdoor Japanese hot tub.

Open: All year **Last arrival:** 23.00 **Last departure:** 11.00

Leisure: 🔍 🏏 ⚽

Facilities: 🛁 🪒 ❄ 🖧 ⑤ 🍴 🍴

Within 3 miles: 🏌 🖊 ◎ 🏇 ⛷ 🏇

Accommodation available: Yurts from £180 (up to 4 people). Dogs permitted if whole site rented together.

Additional site information: 3 acre site. 🚫 🚫 No noise after 23.00. Self-catering kitchen area, wet rooms, table tennis, darts, pool, hot tub. Yurts: minimum stay 2 nights from Thursday, Friday, Saturday, Sunday. Noise level to be kept to a minimum. Cars can be parked by units.

LEISURE: 🏊 Indoor swimming pool 🏊 Outdoor swimming pool 🎠 Children's playground 🖐 Kids' club 🎾 Tennis court 🔍 Games room 🔲 Separate TV room 🏌 Golf course 🏏 Pitch n putt 🚣 Boats for hire 🚲 Bikes for hire 🎬 Cinema 🎵 Entertainment ✐ Fishing ◎ Mini golf 🏄 Watersports 🏏 Gym 🏇 Sports field ⛷ Stables
FACILITIES: 🛁 Baths/Shower ☉ Electric shaver sockets 🪒 Hairdryer ❄ Ice Pack Facility 🍼 Baby facilities 🖧 Disabled facilities ⑤ Shop on site or within 200yds 🍴 BBQ area 🍴 Picnic area WiFi WiFi

EYTON
Map 15 SJ34

Places to visit

Erddig, WREXHAM, LL13 0YT, 01978 355314
www.nationaltrust.org.uk/erddig

Chirk Castle, CHIRK, LL14 5AF, 01691 777701
www.nationaltrust.org.uk/chirk-castle

WALES & OVERALL WINNER OF THE AA CAMPSITE OF THE YEAR 2020

Platinum Park

Plassey Holiday Park
▶▶▶▶▶

tel: 01978 780277 **The Plassey LL13 0SP**
email: enquiries@plassey.com **web:** www.plassey.com
dir: *From A483 at Bangor-on-Dee exit onto B5426 for 2.5 miles. Site entrance signed on left.*

A lovely park set in several hundred acres of quiet farm and meadowland in the Dee Valley. The superb toilet facilities include individual cubicles for total privacy and security, while the Edwardian farm buildings have been converted into a super restaurant, coffee shop, beauty studio and various craft outlets. There is plenty here to entertain the whole family, from scenic walks and a swimming pool to free fishing and use of the 9-hole golf course. For that memorable glamping experience there is a choice of large safari tents or stylish cabins complete with en suite facilities and private hot tubs.

Open: February to December **Last arrival:** 20.00 **Last departure:** noon

---

Pitches: 🚐 from £21.90; 🚍 from £21.90; ⛺ from £21.90; 🏠 see prices below; 85 hardstanding pitches; 60 seasonal pitches

Leisure: 🏊 ⚙ 🎣 🛝 🎿 ✨

Facilities: 🏪 ⊙ 🅿 ✳ 🔥 ♿ 🛒 🚿 WiFi

Services: 🔌 🗑 🍺 🍽 🎱 🛒 🔋 🚰 ⚗ T

Within 3 miles: ∪ ◎ 🎯

Additional site information: 10 acre site. 🐕 Cars can be parked by caravans and tents. Awnings permitted. No footballs or skateboards. No noise after 23.00. Sauna, badminton, table tennis, driving range.

Glamping available: 10 wooden pods (plodges) from £110 per night; 4 safari tents from £95 per night. **Changeover days:** Monday and Friday

Additional glamping information: Wooden pods (plodges) and safari tents: minimum stay 3 nights. Pods and safari tents fully furnished and equipped with hot tubs.

See advert opposite

OVERTON
Map 15 SJ34

Premier Park

The Trotting Mare Caravan Park
▶▶▶▶▶ 88%

tel: 01978 711963 **LL13 0LE**
email: info@thetrottingmare.co.uk **web:** www.thetrottingmare.co.uk
dir: *From Oswestry towards Whitchurch take A495. In Ellesmere take A528 towards Overton. Site on left. Or from Wrexham take A525 signed Whitchurch. In Marchwiel turn right onto A528 towards Overton. Through Overton to Ellesmere A528, site on right.*

Located between Overton-on-Dee and Ellesmere, this adults-only touring park is quietly located behind The Trotting Mare pub, which was totally refurbished for 2019. The majority of pitches are fully serviced, and creative landscaping and a free coarse-fishing lake are additional benefits. A superb amenity block is served by a bio-mass boiler and equipped with stylish decor and top-notch fixtures and fittings.

Open: All year **Last arrival:** 20.00 **Last departure:** noon

Pitches: 🚐 🚍 ⛺; 43 hardstanding pitches

Leisure: 🎣

Facilities: 🏪 ⊙ 🅿 ✳ ♿ WiFi

Services: 🔌 🗑 🍺 🍽 🚰 🔋

Within 3 miles: 🛝 ∪ ◎ 🅂

Additional site information: 4.2 acre site. Adults only. 🐕 Cars can be parked by caravans and tents. Awnings permitted. No commercial vehicles, no open fires, no gas bottles outside caravan or awning, no bikes, no ball games, no noise after 23.00. Car hire can be arranged.

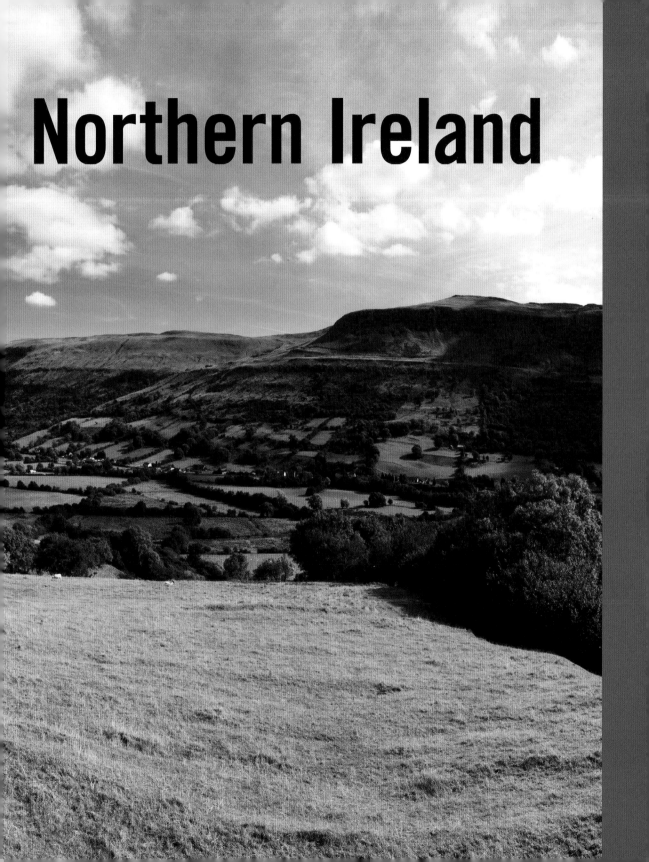

Northern Ireland

COUNTY ANTRIM

ANTRIM
Map 1 D5

Places to visit

Antrim Round Tower, ANTRIM, BT41 1BL, 028 9082 3207
discovernorthernireland.com/Antrim-Round-Tower-Antrim-P2813

Great for kids: Belfast Zoological Gardens, BELFAST, BT36 7PN, 028 9077 6277
www.belfastzoo.co.uk

Six Mile Water Caravan Park
▶▶▶▶ 83%

tel: 028 9034 0024 **Lough Road BT41 4DG**
email: sixmilewater@antrimandnewtownabbey.gov.uk
web: www.antrimandnewtownabbey.gov.uk/caravanpark
dir: *From A6 (Dublin road) into Lough Road signed Antrim Forum and Loughshore Park. Site at end of road on right.*

This is a peaceful touring site, surrounded by trees and mature hedges, that is part of a large municipal park with boating and outdoor sports opportunities; it is also adjacent to a golf club and within easy walking distance of Antrim and The Forum Leisure Complex. All the generously spaced pitches have hardstandings and electric hook-ups and in addition to a well-equipped amenity block, a lounge is also available. Plans for 2020 include a smart new restaurant at the New Gateway.

Open: March to October (restricted service: February and December – open at weekends only) **Last arrival:** 21.00 **Last departure:** noon

Pitches: 🚐 🚏 Δ; 37 hardstanding pitches

Leisure: 🔍 ⬜

Facilities: 🛁 ⊙ ℱ � & 🛒 🎋 WiFi

Services: 🔌 🗑 🍴 🛒 🖐

Within 3 miles: ⅃ ℘ ◎ 🛶 🗓 ⑤

Additional site information: 9.61 acre site. 🐾 Cars can be parked by caravans and tents. Awnings permitted. Maximum stay 7 nights. No noise between 22.00–08.00. Watersports, angling stands.

BALLYCASTLE

Places to visit

Carrick-a-Rede Rope Bridge and Larrybane Visitor Centre, CARRICK-A-REDE, BT54 6LS, 028 2073 3335
www.nationaltrust.org.uk/carrick-a-rede

Old Bushmills Distillery, BUSHMILLS, BT57 8XH, 028 2073 3218
www.bushmills.com

BALLYCASTLE
Map 1 D6

Causeway Coast Holiday Park
▶▶▶▶ 86% HOLIDAY CENTRE

tel: 028 2076 2550 & 07720 464465 **21 Clare Road BT54 5DB**
email: causewaycoast@hagansleisure.co.uk **web:** www.hagansleisure.co.uk
dir: *From A44 in Ballycastle follow Portrush sign (A2). 1st right into Moyle Road. At T-junction right into Clare Road.*

In an elevated location close to the seafront with views of Ballycastle Bay and Rathlin Island, this bustling holiday park is ideally located for visiting the many attractions along this unspoilt coastline including the Giant's Causeway just 15 minutes away. Facilities include a pub, a well-equipped indoor swimming pool with slide and an outdoor play area. Most of the grassed touring pitches have an electric supply. Please note that the site does not have hardstandings and tents are not accepted.

Open: March to October **Last arrival:** 23.00 **Last departure:** 10.00

Pitches: 🚐 🚏; 20 hardstanding pitches

Leisure: 🏊 ⚠ 🔍

Facilities: 🛁 ℱ & 🎋 WiFi

Services: 🔌 🗑 🍴 🛒 🖐 🔒 Ⓣ

Within 3 miles: ⅃ ℘ ∪ ◎ 🛶 🐟 🗓 ⑤

Additional site information: 28 acre site. 🐾 Quiet time 22.00–07.00, no children out after 23.00.

Watertop Farm
▶▶▶▶ 83%

tel: 028 2076 2576 **188 Cushendall Road BT54 6RN**
email: watertopfarm@aol.com **web:** www.watertopfarm.co.uk
dir: *From Ballycastle left at Margee bridge onto Cushendall Road (A2). Through Ballyvoy. Site on left just before Ballypatrick Forest. Or from Cushendall take A2, pass Ballypatrick forest, site on right.*

In an idyllic and peaceful location within easy reach of major attractions, this unique holiday destination provides very good standards for caravan, motorhome and camping customers. There are three strategically located areas that take full advantage of the surroundings – the lake, the farmland and woodlands. During holiday periods on-site attractions include lake boating, pony trekking, karting, and for indoor amusement there's a large multi-function games room and an animal barn with many domesticated breeds. There is also a superb two-bedroom chalet, with great views, that offers a wood-burner, fully-equipped kitchen and great outdoor furniture.

Open: Easter to October (restricted service: off-peak season – some activities restricted) **Last arrival:** anytime **Last departure:** 14.00

Pitches: 🚐 from £25; 🚏 from £25; Δ from £20; 8 hardstanding pitches

Leisure: ⚠ 🔍 ⬜

Facilities: 🛁 ⊙ ✳ & 🛒 🎋

Services: 🔌 🗑 🍴 🛒 🚰 🖐

Within 3 miles: ⅃ ℘ ∪ 🛶 ⑤

Additional site information: 1 acre site. 🐾 Cars can be parked by caravans and tents. Awnings permitted. No noise after 23.00, no camp fires.

LEISURE: 🏊 Indoor swimming pool 🏊 Outdoor swimming pool ⚠ Children's playground 👶 Kids' club 🎾 Tennis court 🔍 Games room ⬜ Separate TV room ⅃ Golf course 🏌 Pitch n putt 🚣 Boats for hire 🚲 Bikes for hire 🎬 Cinema 🎭 Entertainment 🎣 Fishing ◎ Mini golf 🏄 Watersports 🏋 Gym 🏑 Sports field ∪ Stables
FACILITIES: 🛁 Baths/Shower ⊙ Electric shaver sockets ℱ Hairdryer ✳ Ice Pack Facility 🍼 Baby facilities & Disabled facilities ⑤ Shop on site or within 200yds 🛒 BBQ area 🎋 Picnic area WiFi WiFi

BUSHMILLS
Map 1 D6

Places to visit
Old Bushmills Distillery, BUSHMILLS, BT57 8XH, 028 2073 3218
www.bushmills.com

DUNDONALD
Map 1 D5

Dundonald Touring Caravan Park
►►►► 81%

tel: 028 9080 9123 & 9080 9129 **111 Old Dundonald Road BT16 1XT**
email: dundonaldcaravanpark@lisburncastlereagh.gov.uk
web: www.dundonaldcaravanpark.com
dir: *From Belfast city centre follow M3 and A20 to City Airport. Then A20 to Newtownards, follow signs to Dundonald and Ulster Hospital. At hospital right at sign for Dundonald Ice Bowl. Follow to end, turn right, Ice Bowl on left, follow signs for caravan park.*

A purpose-built site in a quiet corner of Dundonald Leisure Park on the outskirts of Belfast. This peaceful park provides excellent, well-spaced, fully serviced pitches and is ideally located for touring County Down and exploring the capital. In the winter it offers an 'Aire de Service' for motorhomes and caravans with their own hygiene facilities.

Premier Park

Ballyness Caravan Park
►►►►► 93%

tel: 028 2073 2393 **40 Castlecatt Road BT57 8TN**
email: info@ballynesscaravanpark.com **web:** www.ballynesscaravanpark.com
dir: *0.5 mile south of Bushmills on B66, follow signs.*

A peacefully located, quality park with superb toilet and other facilities, on farmland beside St Columb's Rill, the stream that supplies the famous Bushmills Distillery which is close by. The friendly owners created this park with the discerning camper in mind and continue to invest year-on-year to enhance the customer experience. The site has fully serviced, hardstanding pitches and an indoor games barn, play park and football field, free WiFi, a centrally heated amenity building, an 8-acre dog walk and wildlife ponds. It is close to the Giant's Causeway, shops, pubs and restaurants; the Causeway Rambler bus stops at the site en route to the north coast attractions (April to September).

Open: 13 March to 31 October **Last arrival:** 21.00 **Last departure:** noon

Pitches: 🚐 from £26; 🚍 from £26; 49 hardstanding pitches

Leisure: 🏕 🎣 ▢ ⚽ 🏊 **Facilities:** 🏠 ☺ ℙ ☀ ♿ ⑤ WiFi

Services: 🔌 🔄 🍺 ⛽ 🔋 🚿 🚽 **Within 3 miles:** ✓ ✎

Additional site information: 23 acre site. 🐾 Cars can be parked by caravans. Awnings permitted. Library, accessories shop, dog walk and wildlife ponds.

BELFAST

DUNDONALD

Places to visit
Mount Stewart, NEWTOWNARDS, BT22 2AD, 028 4278 8387
www.nationaltrust.org.uk/mount-stewart

Giant's Ring, BELFAST, BT8 8LE, 028 9082 3207
discovernorthernireland.com/Giants-Ring-Belfast-P2791

Great for kids: Belfast Zoological Gardens, BELFAST, BT36 7PN, 028 9077 6277
www.belfastzoo.co.uk

Open: mid March to October (restricted service: November to March – Aire de Service restricted to motorhomes and caravans with their own bathroom facilities)
Last arrival: 23.00 **Last departure:** noon

Pitches: * 🚐 from £24; 🚍 from £24; ▲ from £16.50; 22 hardstanding pitches

Facilities: 🏠 ☺ ☀ ♿ ⑤ 🚿 ⧫ WiFi

Services: 🔌 🔄 🍺 🚽

Within 3 miles: ✓ ✎ ∪ ◎ 🎌

Additional site information: 1.5 acre site. 🐾 Cars can be parked by caravans and tents. Awnings permitted. No commercial vehicles or vans permitted (including any on tow). Dundonald International Ice Bowl, adjacent to the park, offers bowling, indoor play area, olympic-size ice rink (additional charges apply).

See advert on page 386

PITCHES: 🚐 Caravans 🚍 Motorhomes ▲ Tents 🏠 Glamping accommodation **SERVICES:** 🔌 Electric hook-up 🔄 Launderette 🍺 Licensed bar
🔥 Calor Gas 🔥 Campingaz ⊤ Toilet fluid 🍴 Café/Restaurant 🍟 Fast Food/Takeaway 🔋 Battery charging 🚽 Motorhome service point
* 2019 prices 🚫 No credit or debit cards 🐾 Dogs permitted 🚫 No dogs

COUNTY FERMANAGH

BELCOO   Map 1 C5

Places to visit

Florence Court, ENNISKILLEN, BT92 1DB, 028 6634 8249
www.nationaltrust.org.uk/florence-court

Premier Park

Rushin House Caravan Park

▶▶▶▶▶ 86%

tel: 028 6638 6519 **Holywell BT93 5DU**
email: enquiries@rushinhouse.com **web:** www.rushinhousecaravanpark.com
dir: *From Enniskillen take A4 west for 13 miles to Belcoo. Right onto B52 towards Garrison for 1 mile. Site signed.*

This park occupies a scenic location overlooking Lough MacNean, close to the picturesque village of Belcoo, and is the product of meticulous planning and execution. There are 24 very generous, fully serviced pitches standing on a terrace overlooking the lough, with additional tenting pitches below; all are accessed via well-kept, wide tarmac roads. Facilities include a lovely, well-equipped play area and a hard surface, fenced five-a-side football pitch. There is a slipway providing boat access to the lough and, of course, fishing; there is an access path to the lake that is suitable for less mobile visitors to use. The excellent toilet facilities are purpose-built and include family rooms.

Open: mid March to October (restricted service: November to March - Aire de Service facilities available) **Last arrival:** 21.00 **Last departure:** 13.00

Pitches: 🚐 🚏 Å; 38 hardstanding pitches

Leisure: 🏊 ▢ ⚽

Facilities: ☺ 🛇 ✳ ♿ 🎍 WiFi

Services: 🔌 🗑 🚽 🛒 🗑

Within 3 miles: ♨ 🚣 ⚓ 🛒

Additional site information: 5 acre site. 🐕 Cars can be parked by caravans. Awnings permitted. Lakeside walk.

IRVINESTOWN   Map 1 C5

Places to visit

Castle Coole, ENNISKILLEN, BT74 6JY, 028 6632 2690
www.nationaltrust.org.uk/castle-coole

Castle Balfour, LISNASKEA, BT92 0JE, 028 9082 3207
discovernorthernireland.com/Castle-Balfour-Lisnaskea-Enniskillen-P2901

Castle Archdale Caravan Park & Camping Site

▶▶▶▶ 83%

tel: 028 6862 1333 **Lisnarick BT94 1PP**
email: info@castlearchdale.com **web:** www.castlearchdale.com
dir: *From Irvinestown take B534 signed Lisnarick. Left onto B82 signed Enniskillen. In approximately 1 mile right by church, site signed.*

This park is located within the grounds of Castle Archdale Country Park on the shores of Lough Erne which boasts stunning scenery, forest walks and also war and wildlife museums. The site is ideal for watersport enthusiasts with its marina and launching facilities. Also on site there's a shop, licensed restaurant, takeaway and play park. There are fully serviced, hardstanding pitches.

LEISURE: 🏊 Indoor swimming pool 🏊 Outdoor swimming pool 🎢 Children's playground ✋ Kids' club 🎾 Tennis court 🎱 Games room ▢ Separate TV room
♨ Golf course ⛳ Pitch n putt 🚣 Boats for hire 🚲 Bikes for hire 🎬 Cinema 🎵 Entertainment 🎣 Fishing ◎ Mini golf 🏄 Watersports 🏋 Gym ⚽ Sports field ♘ Stables
FACILITIES: 🛁 Baths/Shower ☺ Electric shaver sockets 🛇 Hairdryer ✳ Ice Pack Facility 🍼 Baby facilities ♿ Disabled facilities 🛒 Shop on site or within 200yds
🍖 BBQ area 🎍 Picnic area WiFi WiFi

Open: April to October (restricted service: April to June and September to October – shop and bar closed on weekdays) **Last departure:** noon

Pitches: * 🚐 from £25; 🚌 from £25; ⛺ from £10; 150 hardstanding pitches

Leisure: 🎱 ⚽ 🎣

Facilities: 🛒 ☉ ❄ ♿ 🅂 🚿 🎪 WiFi

Services: 🔌 🅂 🍺 🍽 🚰 🔋 🔧 🔒 🍃 T

Within 3 miles: ♿ ⛵ 🎣

Additional site information: 11 acre site. 🐕 Cars can be parked by caravans and tents. Awnings permitted. No open fires, no noise after 23.00. Table tennis, woodland walk, cycling trail. Car hire can be arranged.

COUNTY TYRONE

DUNGANNON
Map 1 C5

Dungannon Park
►►►► 87%

tel: 028 8772 8690 & 03000 132132 **Moy Road BT71 6DY**
email: parks@midulstercouncil.org **web:** www.midulstercouncil.org
dir: M1 junction 15, A29 towards Dungannon, left at 2nd lights.

Set within the magnificent public Dungannon Park, with a fishing lake, cricket ground and regular concerts during the summer months, this family-friendly caravan park provides excellent fully serviced pitches and a stylish well-equipped amenity block. Another benefit is the attractive coffee shop.

Open: March to October **Last arrival:** 20.00 **Last departure:** noon

Pitches: 🚐 from £27.50; 🚌 from £27.50; ⛺ from £14.50; 24 hardstanding pitches

Leisure: 🎱 ⚽ 🎣 ⚽

Facilities: 🛒 ☉ 🎣 ❄ ♿ 🚿 🎪 WiFi

Services: 🔌 🅂 🍽

Within 3 miles: ♿ ⛳ 🎯 🅂

Additional site information: 4 acre site. 🐕 Dogs on leads. Cars can be parked by caravans and tents. Awnings permitted. No noise between 22.00–08.00, no generators, no commercial vehicles, speed limit 10mph, no dishwashing in toilet block.

COUNTY MAPS

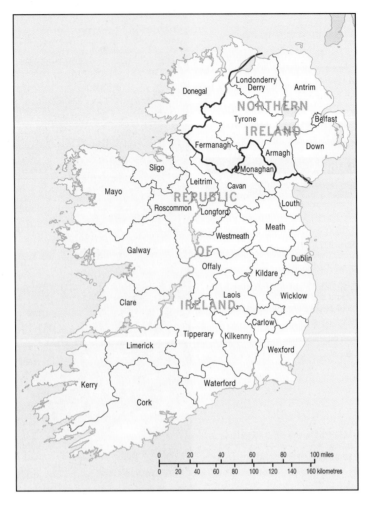

Londonderry
Derry
Donegal
Antrim
NORTHERN
Tyrone
Belfast
IRELAND
Fermanagh
Down
Armagh
Sligo
Monaghan
Leitrim
Cavan
Mayo
REPUBLIC
Louth
Roscommon
Longford
Meath
Westmeath
Galway
OF
Dublin
Offaly
Kildare
Laois
Wicklow
Clare
IRELAND
Carlow
Tipperary
Kilkenny
Limerick
Wexford
Kerry
Waterford
Cork

| 0 | 20 | 40 | 60 | 80 | 100 miles |
| 0 | 20 40 | 60 80 | 100 120 | 140 | 160 kilometres |

England

1 Bedfordshire
2 Berkshire
3 Bristol
4 Buckinghamshire
5 Cambridgeshire
6 Greater Manchester
7 Herefordshire
8 Hertfordshire
9 Leicestershire
10 Northamptonshire
11 Nottinghamshire
12 Rutland
13 Staffordshire
14 Warwickshire
15 West Midlands
16 Worcestershire

Scotland

17 City of Glasgow
18 Clackmannanshire
19 East Ayrshire
20 East Dunbartonshire
21 East Renfrewshire
22 Perth & Kinross
23 Renfrewshire
24 South Lanarkshire
25 West Dunbartonshire

Wales

26 Blaenau Gwent
27 Bridgend
28 Caerphilly
29 Denbighshire
30 Flintshire
31 Merthyr Tydfil
32 Monmouthshire
33 Neath Port Talbot
34 Newport
35 Rhondda Cynon Taf
36 Torfaen
37 Vale of Glamorgan
38 Wrexham

Orkney Islands

Shetland Islands

Na h-Eileanan
an Iar

Highland

Moray

SCOTLAND

Aberdeenshire

City of
Aberdeen

Angus

Perth &
Kinross

City of
Dundee

Argyll
& Bute

Stirling

Fife

East
Lothian

Argyll
& Bute

Stirling

18

22

Fife

Inverclyde

885

8820

Falkirk

City of
Edinburgh

North
Ayrshire

823

817

North
Lanarkshire

West
Lothian

Midlothian

North
Ayrshire

19

24

821

819

South Lanarkshire

Scottish
Borders

South
Ayrshire

Scottish
Borders

Dumfries &
Galloway

Northumberland

Tyne & Wear

Cumbria

Durham

Isle
of Man

North
Yorkshire

Lancashire

West
Yorkshire

East Riding
of Yorkshire

Isle of
Anglesey

Merseyside

6

South
Yorkshire

Conwy

30

Cheshire

Derbyshire

Lincolnshire

29

38

Gwynedd

ENGLAND

13

11

Shropshire

9

12

Norfolk

WALES

15

Ceredigion

Powys

16

14

10

5

Suffolk

Pembrokeshire

7

1

Carmarthenshire

Gloucestershire

4

8

Essex

Swansea

3

Oxfordshire

2

Greater
London

31

26

32

Wiltshire

Surrey

Kent

33

35

28

36

Cardiff

34

Somerset

Hampshire

West
Sussex

East
Sussex

27

37

Devon

Dorset

Isle of
Wight

Cornwall

Isles of
Scilly

Guernsey

Jersey

0   20   40   60   80   100 miles

0 20 40 60 80 100 120 140 160 kilometres

KEY TO ATLAS

Shetland Islands

24

Orkney Islands

22

Inverness

23

Aberdeen

Fort William

Perth

Edinburgh

Glasgow

20

21

Newcastle upon Tyne

Stranraer

Carlisle

Middlesbrough

Londonderry Derry

Larne

Belfast

Isle of Man

Kendal

18

19

24

1

Galway

Dublin

Leeds

York

Kingston upon Hull

Manchester

16

17

Holyhead

Liverpool

Sheffield

Limerick

Lincoln

Rosslare

14

15

Nottingham

Cork

Aberystwyth

Birmingham

Norwich

10

11

12

13

Cambridge

8

9

Carmarthen

Gloucester

Colchester

Cardiff

Oxford

LONDON

Guildford

6

7

Barnstaple

Bristol

4

5

Maidstone

Taunton

Southampton

Dover

2

3

Exeter

Bournemouth

Brighton

Plymouth

Penzance

Isles of Scilly

Channel Islands

24

Legend

M6	Motorway/toll motorway
® ®	Motorway junction full/restricted
A33	Primary route single/dual carriageway
◇ ◇ ◇	Service area/rest area
A34	Other A road single/dual carriageway
B3400	B road
	Unclassified road
⑨—⑥	Vehicle ferry/fast catamaran
● Linwood	Caravan and Camping
◉ Standlake	AA Campsite Award Winner
○ Malham	Town/Village name
	National boundary
ESSEX	English county name & boundary
CONWY	Welsh county name & boundary
MORAY	Scottish county name & boundary
	National Park

ISLES OF SCILLY

Old Grimsby
Bryher
New Grimsby
Higher Town
Tresco Town
St Martin's
St Mary's
Hugh Town
Old Town
Isles of Scilly (St Mary's)
Middle Town
St Agnes

SV

SW

Lundy

Hartland Point
Hartland

Morwenstow

Kilkhampton

Bude
Bude Bay
Strat
Widemouth Bay
Week St Mary
Crackington Haven

Boscastle
Tintagel
Delabole
Camelford

Port Isaac
St Teath
St Tudy
Bolventor
BODMIN MOOR
Blisland
Polzeath
Rock
Harlyn
St Merryn
Padstow
Porthcothan
Wadebridge
St Cleer
Rumford
Ruthernbridge
Bodmin
CORNWALL
Mawgan Porth
St Mawgan
St Columb Major
Lanivet
Dobwalls
Watergate Bay
Newquay
West Pentire
White Cross
Roche
Luxulyan
Lostwithiel
Liskeard
St Keyne
Holywell Bay
Cubert
Bugle
Pelynt
Rose
Summercourt
St Blazey Gate
St Blazey
Perranporth
Polperro
Zelah
St Stephen
Carlyon Bay
Fowey
St Agnes
Ladock
Polruan
Porthtowan
Grampound
Pentewan
Portreath
Blackwater
Chacewater
Truro
Tregony
Mevagissey
St Day
Gorran
Gorran Haven
St Ives Bay
Gwithian
Carnon Downs
Redruth
Portloe
Zennor
Camborne
Carnhell Green
Leedstown
St Just-in-Roseland
St Ives
Lelant
Hayle
Penryn
Portscatho
Falmouth
St Mawes
St Just
Penzance
Marazion
Ashton
Constantine
Mawnan Smith
Land's End
St Buryan
Newlyn
Rosudgeon
Praa Sands
Helston
Gweek
Sennen
Mousehole
Porthleven
Manaccan
Porthcurno
Treen
Mount's Bay
St Keverne
Mullion
Coverack
Kennack Sands
Cadgwith
Lizard
Lizard Point

For continuation pages refer to numbered arrows

CARDIGAN BAY

PEMBROKESHIRE

CARMARTHENSHIRE

SM

SN

SR

SS

CERE

PEMBROKESHIRE COAST NATIONAL PARK

MYNYDD PRESELI

PEMBROKESHIRE COAST NATIONAL PARK

St Brides Bay

Broad Sound

Carmarthen Bay

- Caravan and Camping
- AA Campsite Award Winner
○ Town/Village name

0   10 miles

0   10   20 kilometres

14

IRISH

SEA

Cemaes
Amlwch
Dulas
ISLE OF
Rhôs Lligwy
ANGLESEY
Marian-Glas
Llanerchymedd
Holyhead
Llanfachraeth
Benllech
Red Wharf
Bay
Trearddur Bay
Pentraeth
Llangoed
Holy
Island
Llangefni
Rhosneigr
Llanfairpwllgwyngyll
Menai
Bridge **Bangor**
Aberffraw
Y Felinheli
Newborough
Dwyran

Caernarfon
Bontnewydd
Llanrug
Dinas Dinlle
Llanwnda
Betws
Garmon
Llandwrog
Penygroes
Rhyd Ddu
Clynnog-fawr

Llanaelhaearn

Morfa Nefyn
Nefyn
LLEYN
Bodfuan
Llanystumdwy
PENINSULA
Tremadog
Prenteg
Maentwrog
Sarn
Criccieth
Porthmadog
Borth-y-Gest
Pwllheli
Llanbedrog
Harlech
Aberdaron
Y Rhiw
Abersoch
Llanbedr
Bardsey
Island
Dyffryn Ardudwy
Tal-y-bont
Barmouth
Fairbourne

Llwyngwril
Bryncrug
Tywyn
Pennal
Aberdyfi
Borth
Tal-y-bont
Llandre
Aberystwyth
Capel
Bangor

Llandudno
Deganwy
Rhôs-
on-Sea
Colwyn Bay
Penmaenmawr
Conwy
Llanddulas
Llansanffraid **Abergele**
Llanfairfechan
Glan Conwy
Betws-yn-Rhos
Llanllechid
Tal-y-Cafn
Llanfair
Bethesda
Talhaiarn
Llangernyw
Tal-y-Bont
Trefriw
Llanrwst
Bylchau
CONWY
Capel Curig
Betws-y-Coed
Dolwyddelan
Penmachno
Pentrefoelas
Beddgelert
Cerrigydrudion
Blaenau Ffestiniog
Mae
Ffestiniog
Penrhyndeudraeth
Bala
Talsarnau
Trawsfynydd
SNOWDONIA
GWYNEDD
NATIONAL
Ganllwyd
Llanuwchllyn
PARK
Dinas-Mawddwy
Dolgellau
Mallwyd
Llangadfa
Corris
Cemmaes
Road
Llanbrynmair
Machynlleth
Carno
Llanidloes
Ponterwyd

SH

SN

9

Llanfair
Llansanna
He

Beaumaris

● **Caravan and Camping**
◉ **AA Campsite Award Winner**
○ **Town/Village name**
0   10 miles
0   10   20 kilometres

For continuation pages refer to numbered arrows

20

| | | | | | | | | | | | | | | | |

Fort William

Acharacle

Kinlochleven

Kinloch Rannoch

Coll
Arinagour

Ballachulish
Glencoe
Duror

PERTH
KIN

Tobermory

Tiree
Scarinish

Lochaline
Craignure

ISLE
OF
MULL

A849

Lismore

Kerrera ● Oban

Tyndrum
Luib
Killin

NM

Dalmally
Crianlarich
Lochearnhead

Iona
Fionnphort

Luing

Scarba

ARGYLL AND
BUTE

STIRLING

LOCH LOMOND

NN

Inveraray

AND THE TROSSACHS
NATIONAL PARK

Aberfoyle

ST

Callande

Colonsay

Scalasaig

Oronsay

Lochgilphead

Glendaruel

Helensburgh

Balloch
W
DUNS
Dumbarton

E DUNS

Kils

JURA

Dunoon
Colintraive

GREENOCK

INVER

C GLAS

GLASGO

Port Askaig

Tarbert

Bute
Rothesay

Largs

RENS PAISLEY

M8

E RENS

EAST
KILBRIDE
Strathaven

ISLAY

Kennacraig

Claonaig

Great
Cumbrae
Island

NORTH AYRSHIRE

KILMARNOCK
Galston

S
LANA

Portnahaven

Gigha

Sound
of
Bute

Ardrossan
Kilwinning

Stewarton

NS

A846

Port
Ellen

NR

Carradale

ARRAN

Brodick
Lamlash

Irvine

Troon
Prestwick

A758

A719

Kilbirnie
Beith

Galston

EAST
AYRSHIRE

KINTYRE

Kilmory
Kildonan

Ayr

Cumnock

Campbeltown

Mull of Kintyre

Ailsa Craig

Maybole

SOUTH
AYRSHIRE

Girvan

NW

Belfast

Larne

Ballantrae

DUMF
GA

Barrhill

New
Galloway

Cairnryan

Newton Stewart

Parton

NX

Stranraer

Wigtown

Gatehouse
of Fleet

Portpatrick

Sandhead

Kirkcudbright

Luce Bay

Port William

Whithorn

Brighouse
Bay

Drummore

Burrow Head

Mull of
Galloway

C EDIN	City of Edinburgh
C GLAS	City of Glasgow
CLACKS	Clackmannanshire
C DUND	City of Dundee
E DUNS	East Dunbartonshire
E RENS	East Renfrewshire
INVER	Inverclyde
MDLOTH	Midlothian
N LANS	North Lanarkshire
RENS	Renfrewshire
W DUNS	West Dunbartonshire
W LOTH	West Lothian

NA

NB

Cape Wrath

Rudha Rhobhanais
(Butt of Lewis)
Port Nis
(Port of Ness)

Cellar
Head

Scourie

A894

Great
Bernera

A857

ISLE

LEWIS

Tiumpan
Head

Inchnadamph

A837

Carlabhagh
(Carloway)

A858

OF

A838

Lochinver

A858

Steornabhagh
(Stornoway)

A859

NA H–EILEANAN
AN IAR

A895

A858

A896

THE MINCH

A894

A837

A835

OUTER HEBRIDES

Scarp

Taransay

Scalpay

Gruinard
Bay

Laide

Ullapool

A832

A835

HARRIS

A859

Tairbeart
(Tarbert)

Gairloch

A832

Pabbay

Boreray

Berneray

Kinlochewe

Achnasheen

A832

Loch nam Madadh
(Lochmaddy)

A859

A865

NORTH UIST

A867

THE LITTLE MINCH

Uig

A855

A87

NG

Dunvegan

Edinbane

A850

A896

A890

HIGHLANDS

WEST

Cannich

NF

Benbecula

A865

Ronay

Wiay

ISLE

Portree

Raasay

Inner Sound

SOUTH
UIST

A863

OF

A87

Scalpay

Kyle of
Lochalsh

A890

A865

Drynoch

SKYE

A87

(Apr-Oct)

Loch Baghasdail
(Lochboisdale)

Eriskay

Cuillin Sound

Soay

A851

Sound of Sleat

A887

A87

Canna

Ardvasar

A82

Invergarry

BARRA

A888

Bàgh a' Chaisteil
(Castlebay)

Rùm

Mallaig

NORTH

Sandray

Eigg

A830

Arisaig

Kinlochleven

Mingulay

INNER HEBRIDES

Muck

A861

A830

Spean
Bridge

A82

Fort William

Point of
Ardnamurchan

NM

Acharacle

A861

A861

NL

Coll

Tobermory

A884

A861

Ballachulish

Glencoe

A82

A826

Duror

Arinagour

A848

Lochaline

A884

Tiree

Scarinish

20

ISLE

A849

Lismore

Craignure

A828

Ulva

OF

Kerrera

Oban

A85

Iona

Fionnphort

A849

MULL

Lorne

A816

Dalmally

Tyn

Crianlarich

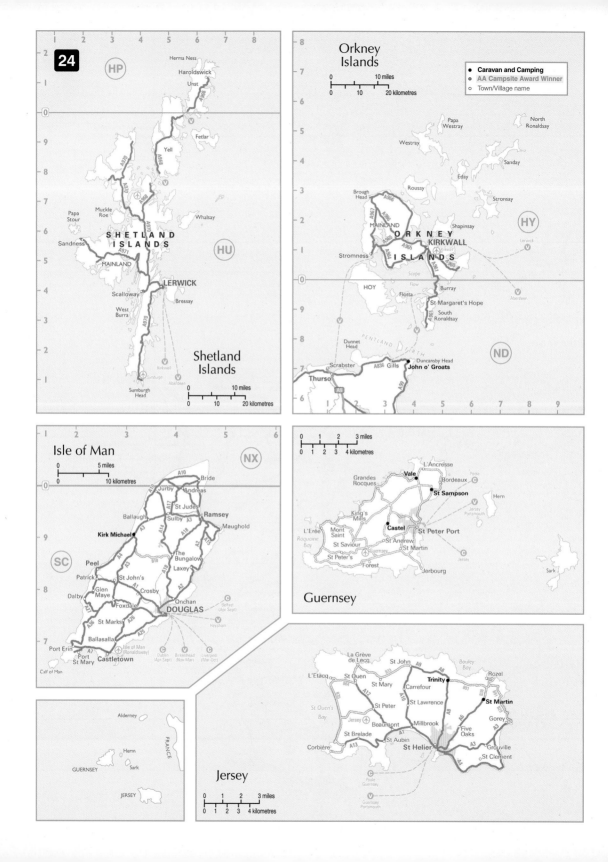

24

Shetland Islands

HP
HU

Herma Ness
Haroldswick
Unst
Fetlar
Yell
Muckle Roe
Papa Stour
Whalsay
Sandness
SHETLAND ISLANDS
MAINLAND
LERWICK
Scalloway
Bressay
West Burra
Sumburgh Head
Sumburgh
Kirkwall
Aberdeen

0   10 miles
0   10   20 kilometres

Orkney Islands

0   10 miles
0   10   20 kilometres

● **Caravan and Camping**
● **AA Campsite Award Winner**
○ Town/Village name

Papa Westray
North Ronaldsay
Westray
Sanday
Eday
Rousay
Stronsay
Brough Head
Shapinsay
MAINLAND
ORKNEY
KIRKWALL
Kirkwall
HY
Stromness
ISLANDS
Lerwick
Scapa Flow
HOY
Burray
Flotta
St Margaret's Hope
South Ronaldsay
Aberdeen
ND
Dunnet Head
PENTLAND FIRTH
Scrabster
Gills
Duncansby Head
John o' Groats
Thurso
A9

Isle of Man

NX

0   5 miles
0   10 kilometres

Bride
Jurby
Andreas
St Judes
Ballaugh
Sulby
Ramsey
Maughold
Kirk Michael
SC
The Bungalow
Laxey
Peel
Patrick
St John's
Crosby
Onchan
Glen Maye
Dalby
Foxdale
DOUGLAS
St Marks
Ballasalla
Belfast (Apr-Sept)
Heysham
Port Erin
Port St Mary
Castletown
Isle of Man (Ronaldsway)
Calf of Man
Dublin (Apr-Sept)
Birkenhead (Nov-Mar)
Liverpool (Mar-Oct)

Guernsey

0 1 2 3 miles
0 1 2 3 4 kilometres

L'Ancresse
Grandes Rocques
Vale
Bordeaux
Poole
St Sampson
Hern
King's Mills
Castel
St Peter Port
Jersey Portsmouth
L'Erée
Mont Saint
St Andrew
Roquaine Bay
St Saviour
St Martin
St Peter's
Guernsey
Forest
Jerbourg
Jersey
Sark

Jersey

0 1 2 3 miles
0 1 2 3 4 kilometres

La Grève de Lecq
St John
Bouley Bay
L'Etacq
St Ouen
Rozel
St Mary
Trinity
Carrefour
St Peter
St Lawrence
St Martin
St Ouen's Bay
Jersey
Beaumont
Millbrook
Gorey
St Brelade
Five Oaks
St Aubin
Grouville
Corbière
St Helier
St Clement
Poole Guernsey
Guernsey Portsmouth

Alderney
Herm
Sark
GUERNSEY
FRANCE
JERSEY

Index

C

I

ILFRACOMBE

IRVINESTOWN

J

JOHN O'GROATS

K

KENNACK SANDS

KENNFORD

KENTISBEARE

KESSINGLAND

KESWICK

KETTLEWELL

KILDONAN

KILKHAMPTON

KILMORY

KINGSBRIDGE

KINGSBURY

KING'S LYNN

KINLOCH RANNOCH

KINTORE

KIRKBY LONSDALE

KIRKCUDBRIGHT

KIRKLINGTON

KIRK MICHAEL

KNARESBOROUGH

L

LACOCK

LAIDE

LAIRG

LANCASTER

LANDFORD

LANGHOLM

LANGWORTH

LAUDER